IMMIGRANTS AND THE INDUSTRIES OF LONDON

To

Ba, Ma, Kim,

Quang, Tien, Chau, Han and Nam

Immigrants and the Industries of London, 1500–1700

Lien Bich Luu

Routledge
Taylor & Francis Group
LONDON AND NEW YORK

First published 2005 by Ashgate Publishing

2 Park Square, Milton Park, Abingdon, Oxfordshire OX14 4RN
52 Vanderbilt Avenue, New York, NY 10017

Routledge is an imprint of the Taylor & Francis Group, an informa business

First issued in paperback 2019

Copyright © Lien Bich Luu, 2005

Lien Bich Luu has asserted her moral right under the Copyright, Designs and Patents Act, 1988, to be identified as the author of this work.

All rights reserved. No part of this book may be reprinted or reproduced or utilised in any form or by any electronic, mechanical, or other means, now known or hereafter invented, including photocopying and recording, or in any information storage or retrieval system, without permission in writing from the publishers.

Notice:
Product or corporate names may be trademarks or registered trademarks, and are used only for identification and explanation without intent to infringe.

British Library Cataloguing in Publication Data
Luu, Lien Bich
　Immigrants and the Industries of London, 1500–1700.
　1. Alien labour – England – London – History – 16th century. 2. Alien labour – England – London – History – 17th century. 3. Immigrants – England – London – History – 16th century. 4. Immigrants – England – London – History – 17th century. 5. Industries – England – London – History – 16th century. 6. Industries – England – London – History – 17th century. 7. London (England) – Social conditions – 16th century. 8. London (England) – Social conditions – 17th century. 9. London (England) – Economic conditions – 16th century. 10. London (England) – Economic conditions – 17th century. I. Title
　331.6'2'09421'09031

US Library of Congress Cataloging in Publication Data
Luu, Lien Bich, 1967–
　Immigrants and the Industries of London, 1500–1700
　　p. cm.
　Includes bibliographical references and index.
　1. Alien labor – Great Britain – History. 2. Immigrants – England – London – History. 3. Industries – England – London – History. I. Title.
　HD8398.A2L88 2004
　331.6'2'0942109031–dc22

2004016093

ISBN 13: 978-0-7546-0330-6 (hbk)
ISBN 13: 978-0-367-26475-8 (pbk)

Contents

List of Figures — vii

List of Tables — ix

Acknowledgements — xi

List of Abbreviations — xiii

1 Introduction: Migration and the Diffusion of Skills — 1

2 Trade and Consumption — 27

3 Government and the Import of Foreign Skills — 53

4 Immigrants in Elizabethan London — 87

5 Reception and Treatment of Immigrants — 141

6 Silk Industry — 175

7 Silver Trade — 219

8 Beer Brewing — 259

9 Conclusion: Immigration in a Historical Perspective — 301

Appendix 1: Places of Origin Recorded in the Returns of Aliens, 1571 and 1593 — 309

Appendix 2: Occupations Recorded in Returns of Aliens, 1571 and 1593 — 313

Appendix 3: Numbers of Strangers Engaged in Luxury and New Trades in London, 1571 and 1593 — 316

Appendix 4: Processes of Silk Manufacture 317

Appendix 5: Processes of Beer Brewing 319

Appendix 6: Goldsmiths of Antwerp Origin in London, 1548–86 321

Bibliography 323

Index 359

List of Figures

1.1	Imports from France.	17
3.1	A street seller.	62
3.2	Edward VI's grant of Bridewell to the City of London.	77
4.1	Map of London.	89
6.1	Weavers' workshop.	185
7.1	Goldsmiths' workshop.	221
8.1	Ground plan of a brewhouse, 1561.	272
8.2	Rogers James, alien brewer.	283
8.3	Beer brewer, sixteenth century.	284

List of Tables

2.1	Populations of selected cities and towns in England, 1500–1700	36
2.2	Prices and wages in London, 1500–1600	45
3.1	A breakdown of expenses in silk manufacture	57
3.2	Patents granted 1561–1603	65
3.3	Types of patents granted to aliens 1560–1590	66
3.4	Project to introduce fustians in Bridewell, London 1596	79
4.1	Numbers of aliens in London, 1483–1621	92
4.2	Numbers of aliens in Middlesex, Surrey and Westminster, 1568–93	93
4.3	Linguistic groups of aliens in London: Proportional distribution, 1436–1593	100
4.4	Regions of origin and period of arrival of alien heads of households in London, 1571	102
4.5	Regions of origin and period of arrival of alien heads of households in London, 1593	103
4.6	Occupational groups of aliens in London, 1571 and 1593	116
4.7	Occupational groups of aliens and natives in London compared, 1540–1600	120
4.8	Residential distribution of aliens in the wards of the City of London, 1483–1593	122
4.9	Employment of English and alien servants in London, 1593	129
4.10	Economic and social structure of the alien community, 1483–1593	132
5.1	Patterns of church attendance, 1568–1593	151
5.2	Length of residence of aliens in London, 1571 and 1593	165
6.1	The international diffusion of the silk industry	177
6.2	Silk fabrics imported into London, 1559–1640	182
6.3	Raw silk imported into London, 1560–1620	183
6.4	Silk workers of Antwerp origin in London, 1568–1593	190
6.5	Silk weavers from Valenciennes and Walloon provinces in London, 1571	191
6.6	Residential distribution of alien silk workers in London, 1571	195
6.7	Admissions of alien silk-weavers, 1610–1694	197
6.8	Number of alien and English apprentices trained by aliens, 1662–94	203

6.9	Stages of silk manufacture in London, 1571 & 1593	214
6.10	Regions of origin and period of arrival of alien silk workers in London, 1571	215
6.11	Regions of origin and period of arrival of alien silk workers in London, 1593	216
6.12	Individual alien silk workers in London, 1594–5	217
7.1	Recorded numbers of alien goldsmiths working in London, 1468–1780	228
7.2	Numbers of alien goldsmiths admitted to the Goldsmiths' Company of London, 1546–1668	229
7.3	Employment categories of alien goldsmiths in London, 1546–98	237
7.4	Prominent English employers of aliens, 1549–73	238
7.5	Employment of servants by aliens in London, 1593	241
7.6	Huguenot apprentices and masters	246
7.7	Training of English and alien apprentices	247
8.1	Stages in the diffusion of beer brewing technology to London	261
8.2	Ale and beer production in London, 1574–1595	274
8.3	Estimates of costs of brewing a tun of beer in London, 1574–1636	277
8.4	Scale of production by alien and English beer brewers in London, 1574	279
8.5	Residential distribution of master and servant brewers in London, 1568 and 1571	280
8.6	Jacob Wittewrongle's inventory of a brewhouse, 1621	288
8.7	Partnerships among alien brewers, 1568–97	289
8.8	List of beer brewers in London in 1574	294

Acknowledgements

The intellectual inspiration for the research underpinning this book owes a great deal to the *Achievement Project* and the *Growth of a Skilled Workforce in London, 1500–1750*. Working under these interdisciplinary projects, I had the unique opportunity to work alongside eminent British, North American and European historians, and to participate in multi-disciplinary and international conferences on human creativity held in London, Oxford, Cambridge, Amsterdam, Antwerp and Paris during the course of my doctoral research. For this privilege I am deeply grateful to members of the Steering Committee of the *Achievement Project*, including Professor Martin Daunton, Dr Peter Earle, Professor Robert Fox, Dr Penny Gouk, Professor Derek Keene, the late Mr Gerry Martin, Professor Patrick O'Brien, Dr Alice Prochaska and Dr Simon Schaffer. The doctoral research was funded by the Renaissance Trust, and I would like to thank the Trustees, the late Mr Gerry Martin and Mrs Hilda Martin, for their extremely generous financial support. My gratitude also extends to the French Protestant Church of London for the award of the Huguenot Scholarship in 1993 to enable me to undertake archival research in Belgium. The doctoral thesis was submitted to the University of London in January 1997 and has been extensively revised for publication.

My own personal experiences as a refugee have helped me a great deal with the research and I very much hope that this book provides a useful historical dimension to contemporary immigration debates. The research would not have been possible without the immeasurable support and assistance from friends and colleagues over the years. My gratitude goes first of all to members of the Achievement Project and the Growth of the Skilled Workforce (Michael Berlin, Rob Iliffe and especially to David Mitchell) who have provided me with a stimulating environment to conduct research, and also to Olwen Myhill and the staff at the Centre for Metropolitan History.

On aspects of European history, I am extremely grateful to Dr Alastair Duke for his generous support and invaluable guidance which have vastly expedited the research, and to Professor Guido Marnef of Antwerp for allowing to benefit from his unrivalled knowledge of Antwerp history and sources. I am also grateful to the late Dr Marcel Backhouse, Dr Raingard Esser, Guillaume Delannoy, Dr Charles Littleton, and Dr Andrew Spicer for sharing with me their research and for many stimulating discussions, to Mrs G. van Donck for giving me access to her unpublished materials concerning Antwerp goldsmiths, and to Dr Clé Lesger for his constant encouragement and for supplying me with materials from continental libraries and archives.

Regarding English aspects of my research, I am grateful to Professor Caroline Barron and Dr Ian Archer for their support and for providing copies of manuscripts held in American libraries, to Professor Judith Bennett for many stimulating discussions on brewing and for sharing her research with me, and to Jim Bolton for his support and encouragement. I would also like to thank the thesis examiners – Dr Alastair Duke and Dr Vanessa Harding – for their invaluable suggestions of ways to improve the thesis for publication. Others have been supportive and encouraging in many ways, including Dr Graham Gibbs, Philippa Glanville, Professor Michael Hunter, Dr David Ormod, Professor Andrew Pettegree, Ms Natalie Rothstein, the late Professor Ralph Smith, and Randolph Vigne. Thanks are also due to Professor Nigel Goose, Dr Alastair Duke, Dr David Mitchell and Dr Owen Davies for sparing the time to give the book a final review, to Dr John Smedley for his editorial advice, support and encouragement, and to Dr Paul Newbury for help with final proof reading.

My greatest intellectual debt is owed to Professor Derek Keene, who supervised the development of my thesis. I have benefited enormously from his perceptive enquiries over the years, his careful intellectual nurturing and guidance, his masterly knowledge of London history, his constant support and encouragement, and his shared interest in interdisciplinary approaches and comparative history. Moreover, his outstanding works and his attention to historical accuracy have provided me with an admirable role model to follow.

Finally, this book has been a truly family affair. Without the unstinting support of my parents and their devotion to my children, I certainly would not have been able to complete this book. My husband has also been an enormous source of support, taking over the responsibilities of the children whenever possible to allow his wife to escape to the early modern world and indulge in academic affairs, and providing the critical platform to bounce ideas off. My sister is also my saviour, sparing weekends and evenings to help with babysitting. The children (Tien, Chau, Han and Nam) have brought so much joy and pleasure into my life and have given me additional reasons to succeed. This book is dedicated to them all.

L.B. Luu
Milton Keynes
25 July 2005

List of Abbreviations

AGR	Archives Generales du Royaume, Brussels
APC	*Acts of the Privy Council of England*, ed. J.R. Dasent, Vols I–XXXII (1890–1907)
BCCB	Brewers' Company Court Book
BL	British Library
CLRO	Corporation of London Records Office
Ellesmere	Ellesmere Manuscripts, Henry E. Huntington Library, San Marino, California
GCCB	Goldsmiths' Company Court Book
GL	Guildhall Library
GLRO	Greater London Records Office
HMC	*Historical Manuscripts Commission Reports*
Jour	CLRO, Journals of the Court of Common Council
Letter Book	*Calendar of Letter Books Preserved Among the Archives of the City of London at the Guildhall*, ed. R.R. Sharpe (11 vols, London, 1899–1912)
PCC	Public Record Office, Prerogative Court of Canterbury Wills
PRO	Public Record Office
Rep	CLRO, Repertories of the Court of Aldermen
RS	Royal Society, London

Chapter 1

Introduction: Migration and the Diffusion of Skills

Migration and Economic Development

There is a general consensus among historians that England experienced a profound economic change between the sixteenth and eighteenth centuries. At the beginning of this period, England was an economic backwater, standing on the edge of the economic heartland centred in Italy, the Mediterranean, the Low Countries and Germany. A good barometer of this relative economic underdevelopment was its overseas trade, characterized by the domination of a single export – cloth – which accounted for almost 80 per cent of England's total exports in 1565. The revenue from this single export was then expended on a long list of imports. Besides raw materials and luxury consumables such as wines and spices, many basic industrial items also came from abroad, from goods like crude iron, battery, nails, needles, pins, knives, paper, soap, glass, and mirrors to 'frivolities' such as tennis balls and children's dolls, and yards of sumptuous Italian luxury textiles such as velvets, silks, satins and taffetas.[1] Early modern England thus suffered from two economic problems: the love of foreign luxuries, and the lack of native skills to satisfy its own wants. Yet this very state of underdevelopment became the backbone of English economic progress, as it generated stimuli for individual creativity and fostered the national craving to transcend its existing limited international role, in other words, cultivating the *virtue* of adversity.[2] By the early seventeenth century notable industrial progress had been achieved. Reflecting on their industrial achievements in 1608, Londoners proudly proclaimed that while during Elizabeth's reign 'Englishmen were not so skilful in trades, to make all kind of wares ... but now ... the people [had] mightly increased both in number ... and in all good skill, and [were] skilful of all kind and manner of trades.'[3] At this date, John Stow also claimed that 'the best and finest knives in the world are made in London ... The Englishmen began to make all sorts of pins and at this day they excel all nations.[4] Many other goods were also now made in England, including those which had previously been imported from abroad such as silks, gloves and hops.[5]

Some historians trace the origins of industrial progress in England to the period of the Reformation, when it started to catch up with other European countries by establishing many new industries and by putting others on a commercially significant footing for the first time. Existing industrial sectors such as mining, metallurgy and textiles experienced considerable expansion, innovation and diversification, while new industries such as brass and copper, paper, alum, gunpowder and sugar refining were being developed. A whole range of consumer industries was also encouraged, such as soap, stockings, pins, needles, and pots and pans.[6] Prof. John Nef felt that the industrial achievement between 1540 and 1640 constituted 'an early industrial revolution'. In his celebrated study of the rise of the coal industry in 1932, he recognized that this 'early industrial revolution' was 'less important than that which began towards the end of the eighteenth century', but pointed out that these earlier developments were of great significance in laying the foundations for Britain's later industrialization.[7] Christopher Hill treated the 250 years between 1530 and 1780 as a unity, and believed the changes taking place in that period prepared England for the 'takeoff into the modern industrial world'.[8] Despite these changes, L.A. Clarkson believed that England by 1750 was still a long way from achieving the Industrial Revolution. Although industrial production was greater in volume and more diverse than had been the case in 1500, the quality was inferior to Continental standards, and the economy on the whole remained basically agricultural. However, it is perhaps fair to accept that by the early eighteenth century, as Prof. Donald Coleman noted, English industry was in a stronger position relative to the outside world than it had been two centuries earlier: it had caught up technically, it had a wider base from which to advance, and it had a bigger and wealthier home market.[9]

The causes of the British Industrial Revolution are complex and the explanations wide-ranging. Social mobility has been recognized as one of the key forces of change. In his article on 'The social causes of the British Industrial Revolution' published in 1967, Harold Perkin traced the social roots of industrial progress to the existence of a large 'middle rank', the dispersal of capital, the open social structure, and the roles of property and patronage as sources of mobility.[10] E.A. Wrigley, in a recent paper, has nicely summarized the chief agents of change, stating that the exceptional British economic success grew out 'of the corn sack, the cotton mill, and the coal mine', alluding thereby to the revolution in agriculture, textile and fuel. According to him, these changes were connected to the phenomenal growth of London. In his article on 'A Simple Model of London's Importance in Changing English Society and Economy 1650–1750', Wrigley mapped out how London's exponential demographic growth, riding on the back of massive internal migration, harnessed extensive changes in other parts of England – the creation of a national market, the change in agriculture and raw material supply, the improvement in commercial facilities and transport, and the introduction of higher real incomes, rationality, new forms of social mobility and consumption patterns.[11] In 1971, F.J. Fisher examined some of these links in greater depth. Describing London as 'the engine' of the English economy as well as engine of economic growth, Fisher investigated in particular the capital's role as a centre of consumption and centre of trade.[12]

But London above all was the centre of industry in England. A.L. Beier has in fact described London as the 'engine of manufacture'. With only some 180 trades in the Middle Ages, London by the 1690s could boast at least 721 different occupations within the City of London alone – the true figure was undoubtedly much higher, as many new industries were situated outside the city walls. These new industries were based on refining or finishing colonial produce, devoted to import substitution like glassmaking or metalworking, or catered to the new consumers of luxury commodities such as jointed furniture, coaches and clocks.[13] Particularly successful was London's effort to develop a native silk industry, which by the early eighteenth century employed 40 000 and 50 000 people in the capital.[14] Yet the question of how London expanded its pool of skills and built up its industrial base, laying the foundation of its economic might and its subsequent role as the workshop of the world, remains a neglected and nebulous subject. Such a need prompted the Centre of Metropolitan History to launch a three-year interdisciplinary project in 1992 to investigate the 'Growth of a Skilled Workforce in London' between 1500 and 1750. Set within the broader context of the project, the research upon which this book is based investigates the link between immigration and the expansion of the stock of human capital and skills in London in this period.

Massive internal immigration to London in the early modern period was recognized by Wrigley as the motor of demographic and economic change in the capital. However, he crucially omitted the role of Continental migrants, known as aliens and strangers, in the transformation of London. This is a serious omission, for two reasons. First, this was the principal conduit via which many skills and industries travelled from the more advanced parts of Europe to England, offering a faster route to industrial development. Second, England experienced an unprecedented scale of immigration in this period, enabling it to tap a rich source of human skill and technical expertise. Between 1550 and 1750, there were three principal waves of mass immigration from the Continent, constituting three of the four great west European migrations of the early modern period.[15] The first wave occurred in the spring and summer of 1567, once the government in Brussels regained control of the situation and news of Alva's imminent arrival spread. It has been estimated that between 60 000 and 100 000 people may have fled the southern Netherlands in this period, among whom were some of the wealthiest and most skilled.[16] The second wave of massive immigration occurred after 1585, when the southern Netherlands was recaptured by Spanish troops, typified by the fall of Antwerp in 1585. Perhaps as many as

100 000 to 150 000 people may have uprooted between 1585 and 1587 in search of a better life in the Dutch Republic, Germany and England.[17] In total, in the three-and-a-half decades between 1550 and 1585, 40–50 000 foreign refugees may have come to England,[18] or about a quarter of the total number of people leaving the southern Netherlands, with the majority gravitating towards the English capital. The third wave of refugees came in the late seventeenth century, when some 40–50 000 Huguenots may have fled France to England. Although the Huguenot immigration in the seventeenth century will be touched upon in some chapters, the primary focus is on the first two waves of immigrants who laid the industrial foundations in London.

Contemporaries on both sides of the Channel were acutely aware of the economic impact of the population movements outlined above. Fears of depopulation in Flanders were voiced before 1566; in 1566, many returned from exile, only to leave again in 1567. As the first mass exodus unfolded, Philip II was informed of the detrimental economic effects of the human plight precipitated by the troubles, with many people leaving the Netherlands with their families and tools to go to London and Sandwich, and how the establishment of the drapery in England destroyed local industry there.[19] Jacques Taffin, the Treasurer of Flushing (a rebel town in Zeeland), in an effort to press Elizabeth I for military support against Spain, plainly told her in 1573 of the need for reciprocity because: 'You receive many Strangers into the Realm ... so you find them good honest, and virtuous people, and the realm by them Receives many Commodities, as cunning in many sciences wherein before you were altogether ignorant.'[20] In England, the beneficial economic effects brought by immigrants were also acknowledged in elite circles. In his treatise on the cloth industry published in 1577, an English writer had observed that: 'by reason of the troubles grown in other Countries, the making of baies, friesadowes, Tuftmoccadowe [types of the New Draperies], and many other things made of wool, is mightly increased in England ... For this Cause we ought to favour the strangers from whom we learned so great benefits ... because we are not so good devisers as followers of others.'[21]

Historiography

The contribution of immigrants to the Tudor economy has received much attention from historians, and the current historiography has been approached from four perspectives: English economic history and industrialisation, the diffusion of innovations and technology, industrial case study and local community study.

English Economic History/Industrialization Perspective

Writing in the nineteenth century, when the Industrial Revolution was still in full swing, economic historians such as J.S. Burn, F.W. Cross, W. Cunningham and S. Smiles claimed that immigrants played a vital role in English industrial development.[22] The most influential work representing this school of thought is William Cunningham's *Alien Immigrants to England*, first published in 1897 (fifteen years after the appearance of his *Growth of English Industry*) and later reissued in 1969, testifying to its enduring appeal and relevance. In *Alien Immigrants*, Cunningham contended that the arrival of skilled artisans during the sixteenth and seventeenth centuries stimulated English economic development by precipitating a diffusion of advanced skills.[23] Although sharing Cunningham's broad argument, George Unwin felt that fifteenth-century immigrants were also significant. In his *Gilds and Companies*, published in 1908, he claimed that:

> the alien immigrants of the 15th and 16th centuries supplied the main factor in an industrial renaissance which had as much importance for the economic development of England as the literary and artistic renaissance had for its intellectual development. All branches of industry were affected by it; old handicrafts were revolutionized, new ones were created.[24]

In *The Economic History of England*, published in 1934, E. Lipson also accorded much significance to immigrants, declaring that the arrival of the Flemings in the fourteenth century constituted the first industrial landmark in the industrial history of England, and the influx of the Dutch and Walloons in the sixteenth century and Huguenots in the seventeenth century the second and third landmarks. Many branches of the national economy benefited from the arrival of aliens. In the sixteenth century, aliens introduced new industries such as new draperies, fine linen, copper and brass, glassmaking, paper, and cordage. They also revived the silk industry and improved the art of dyeing. In the seventeenth century, the Huguenots gave stimulus to a range of manufactures, including silk, linen, hats, soap and white paper. Like Cunningham, Lipson saw a clear link between overseas immigration and the subsequent rise of Britain to industrial supremacy, and he concluded that:

> the settlement of aliens must be assigned a prominent place among the factors which have helped to build up the industrial supremacy of England. The infusion of new blood enriched and strengthened the national life, while the technical skill and knowledge of the industrial arts, possessed by the strangers within her gates, enabled this country to wrest from her rivals the secrets of important industries and become the workshop of the world.[25]

Whatever their appeal, these general arguments are unsatisfactory, because they are largely narrative, telling us more about *what* industries aliens were involved in, rather than evaluative, explaining *why* and *how* they were involved.[26] If aliens did indeed make a significant contribution to the industries listed, then pertinent questions need to be examined. Why were they associated with particular industries? How were the skills transferred to these? How uniform was the process of diffusion? How important were local political, economic, and social developments in laying the necessary foundations for diffusion? Who were the immigrants? How homogeneous were their backgrounds and characteristics? And how did indigenous workers acquire the skills introduced by immigrants?

Diffusion of Innovations/Technology

From the 1950s, partly influenced by international policy of promoting technology transfer as a medium to alleviate world poverty, historians became more interested in analysing the significance of early modern migrations as the medium of diffusion of skills and technological innovations. However, due to the scant availability of early sources, the literature is extremely sparse, since most historical studies focus on later periods. In the 1980s, though, there was a proliferation of studies on technology transfer from Britain in the eighteenth and nineteenth centuries, including the excellent work of Kristine Bruland on technology transfer from Britain to Scandinavian countries, David Jeremy on technology transfer to America, as well as articles by Ian Inkster on the nature and process of technology transfer.[27] This reflects renewed interest in the subject subsequent to the recommendation by the Brandt Commission in 1981 of using technology transfer to alleviate inequality and poverty in the world.

Although there are only a few articles on the diffusion of innovations and technology in the early modern period, a review of this literature can delineate the fundamental issues for exploration in this study. A pioneering article on this subject was published by Warren Scoville in 1951 entitled 'Minority migrations and the diffusion of technology',[28] where he addressed several key issues. The first concerned the definition of 'diffusion'. Like other economic historians, Scoville saw that technical change involved three stages: invention (discovery of new techniques), innovation (using the method for the first time) and diffusion (the process of introducing new methods to another country without drastic modification). He argued that the diffusion of technology depended on the migration of artisans because it was closely bound up with skills and craftsmanship. In addition, skills were 'unarticulated' and not easily communicated by word of mouth or by the printed word. One writer has explained: 'the knowledge that underlines a skilful performance is in large measure tactic knowledge, in the sense that the performer is not fully aware of the details of the performance and finds it difficult or impossible to articulate a full account of those details'. In other words, knowledge embedded in skills cannot be readily codified or transmitted independently of the people who hold these skills.[29]

In a society where there was a heavy reliance on oral means of communication, skills were acquired principally through practice and 'learning-by-doing'.[30] One historian has described the process:

> In a period when only a small minority were able to read, and the opportunity to extend one's knowledge by help of books was minimal, the only way to learn a trade was through apprenticeship in a workshop. Here the apprentice was introduced to the trade by a master or journeyman, and ... after a learning period of four or five years, he was made a journeyman ... The journeyman was expected subsequently to seek to improve his education by moving from place to place, working for longer or shorter periods in workshops abroad.[31]

Scoville firmly believed that migration was an effective method of diffusion because of its selective nature. The hardships involved in uprooting from one's homeland meant that only the most resourceful, energetic and courageous would move.

According to Scoville, there were three types of migration in the early modern period: individual, group and minority. Individual migration was perhaps the most common method, involving the movement of a workman or entrepreneur who brought with him the skill, know-how or actual machines, or a traveller who acquired the skill and knowledge on travelling abroad. But the limitations of this method are obvious. As one person was acting as the carrier of new methods and knowledge, success or failure depended on his ability. Nor was this a very rapid method of diffusion, as the number of people a person could teach at any one time was limited. Group migration offered a second route for the dissemination of new methods and techniques with the migration of workers plying the same craft or in allied fields – such as Flemish weavers in the fourteenth century. Although this method was more effective in introducing new methods, it was more difficult to persuade a group of workers to migrate and settle in a foreign country (see Chapter 3 for a further discussion about the problems involved in plans to bring over Italian silk-weavers to England). The third method was minority migration, whereby a group of people who shared religious, cultural, social and political ties moved to a new country. This type of migration was often linked with persecution and forced migration, and regarded as the most effective means because it 'carried with it a whole set of institutions'. In addition, the limited possibility of return migration for those who had left for political or religious reasons also forced them to put down firm roots in the new homeland and make a new start.[32]

So what factors determined successful diffusion? These fall under two headings: the structural, and the behavioural. The structural factors are linked with conditions in the host environment and include those factors, as listed by Scoville, such as the level of economic and social development, general level of education, density of the population, presence of communication channels, geographical and occupational mobility, and the existence of vested interests. More critically, as Scoville pointed out, diffusion depended on the behaviour of three groups: the immigrants, the native population and the state. The fastest way for the indigenous population to acquire the skills was to learn from the immigrants, but the realization of this was determined by their relationship with the newcomers and by the willingness of the latter to teach them the requisite skills and to stay long enough to fulfil this aim. After all, life in a different culture, with perhaps a different official religion, language and diet, was not always congenial, leading some emigrants to feel dissatisfied and alienated, consequently prompting them to return home or emigrate elsewhere.[33] This means that factors affecting the quality of life of the immigrants were important, and the existence of an established immigrant community, the friendliness of the native population, and the ease of integration could all play a critical role. Positive government attitudes towards the immigrants and an encouraging immigration policy could also be vital in persuading them to stay long-term, as has been demonstrated in a recent study of technology transfer to Norway in the eighteenth century. Public funds were used to give immigrants their passage money, initial capital and resources to pay back loans. In addition, careful attention was paid to avoiding potential conflicts among the immigrant workers by putting together working teams according to nationality, and respect was accorded to the religious customs of workers.[34]

In 1972, Carlo Cipolla offered further insights into the 'Diffusion of Innovations in Early Modern Europe'. Having reiterated that 'before the Industrial Revolution, the propagations of innovations took place mostly through the migration of skilled craftsmen who decided to settle in a foreign country',[35] Cipolla first looked at the barriers to the diffusion of innovations, stressing that resistance to innovations was a major problem because not all innovations were desirable, and their immediate benefits not always obvious. Joel Mokyr gave us another interesting reason why resistance to new technologies is a natural and expected response. He explained that skills and experience are acquired over a lifetime, but the ability to learn new skills declines over the life cycle. Workers beyond the student or apprentice age can be expected to resist new techniques because innovation makes their skills obsolete and thus irreversibly reduces their expected lifetime earnings.[36] To promote their interests, craftsmen often organized themselves into guilds – the early modern equivalent of trade unions. These are regarded by some historians as technologically conservative and a powerful barrier to the diffusion of skills.[37]

Cipolla then moved on to outline the key factors that affected diffusion. The character of the immigrants was obviously an important determinant in the diffusion of skills, and the kind of economic contribution they made was influenced by their personal attributes such as age, skill, education, religion, social status, origins, experience and aspirations. Historians in particular have analysed the link between the Protestant religion and economic impact. After surveying the diaspora of the southern Netherlands and the establishment of immigrant communities, F.A. Norwood concluded that the refugees' Calvinistic zeal and their status as exiles may have been responsible for providing them with an additional motivation for work.[38] Heinz Schilling, however, suggested that the 'innovations and the economic modernization launched by the Flemish, Dutch and Walloon refugees were not the consequence of their Calvinistic beliefs, but of the fact that they emigrated from the most developed parts of sixteenth-century Europe'.[39] Hugh Trevor-Roper, on the other hand, stressed the connection between the minority status of the Protestants and their high achievement.[40]

The number of migrants also affected diffusion. In order to set up a new industry or introduce a new technique, a certain number of workers with the relevant skills was necessary to supply the skilled labour and to teach others. In the case of the New Draperies, D.C. Coleman concluded that:

> to bring effective transformation to so labour-intensive and widespread an industry as the rural textiles ... a considerable influx of workers with the new skills was necessary ... A handful of migrants, likely objects of xenophobic mistrust, would probably have made little impression on a native labour force which had long learnt a particular way of doing things.[41]

So what factors determined the mobility of labour? Cipolla believed that a satisfactory level of effective demand, political peace and/or religious tolerance, and government policies to attract skilled artisans, could 'pull' craftsmen into a given area. Thus, like Scoville, Cipolla recognized that the state could play an important role in the diffusion of innovations. On the push side, we can mention factors such as political conflicts, warfare and persecution. D.C. Coleman has called these 'non-economic factors' – the only ones capable of forcing a large number of people to uproot and move. But economic factors such as a lack of economic development, a lack of employment opportunities, and low wages could also be responsible for a continuous but small-scale outflow of people – as demonstrated by the examples of Ireland and Scotland.

Equally important to the process of diffusion was the responsiveness of the recipient society to the new innovations and technologies. Rosenberg believed this is critical: 'receptivity to new technologies, and the capacity to assimilate them whatever their origin has been as important as inventiveness itself'.[42] So what factors determined a country's receptiveness? Cipolla admitted it is difficult to determine what makes an environment responsive and what does not, and recognized that the diffusion of innovations is not a simple matter of introducing new methods of production but involves a certain *disposition*, a set of socio-cultural beliefs and attitudes. Priority to materialism and mechanical aptitude, for example, has been cited as a factor in economic and technological improvement.[43] There must be, in other words, a desire for material progress. Writing in the eighteenth century, Hume claimed that England's openness was one secret of its economic success,[44] and suggested that inter-state competition was a key force responsible for its constant search for improvement. This is because, as Mokyr has noted, competition led to emulation.[45]

In short, the articles by Scoville and Cipolla help us to delineate key themes to focus on in this study. These include conditions in the host country, resistance to innovations, and the role of native workers, government and immigrants. However, these articles neither elaborate on the processes of diffusion nor specify what roles migrants played. Here we have to turn again to the rich literature on technology transfer in the modern period for elucidation.

So what roles did migrants play in diffusion of innovations and technology? Writing on the diffusion of technological skills in the eighteenth century, Mathias reminded us that the process involved three stages. First, there had to be a domestic demand for a product. A second stage of diffusion involved the transfer of capital equipment for making products, and required the emigration of foreign craftsmen skilled in operating the new equipment and possessing the administrative and commercial expertise in running the business and the plant. Once foreign technology had been imported, it had to be adapted to local circumstances, and foreign workers with adaptive and creative skills were also required to modify foreign technologies.[46] In other words, migrants were required for the operation and adaptation of technologies in the new environment. Mathias distinguished between *formal* and *informal* knowledge, and argued that it was possible to transfer *formal* knowledge of technology through such media as extensive visits by foreigners to British workshops, and technical encyclopaedias and dictionaries giving details, engravings and descriptions of machines. However, he argued that these could not provide answers to the daily operational problems involved in applying the new technology, and the migration of workers was essential for the successful transfer of informal knowledge. 'The only way to transfer new technology,' concluded Mathias, 'was to attract the skilled artisans overseas. Virtually all recorded instances of transfer of new equipment, the invariable mechanism of diffusion, involved the emigration of skilled artisans and fitters. It was not just a question of erecting and adjusting the machine but staying to operate, maintain and repair it.'[47]

Successful technology transfer involved the mastering of requisite skills by native workers, so the second important role of emigrant skilled workers was their provision of training to native workers. David Landes has stressed that the emigration of British skilled workers was fundamental to the transfer of technology to Europe in the eighteenth century, partly because technology was still essentially empirical in this period and on-the-job training was the most effective method of communicating skills, and partly because formal training of native mechanics and engineers in technical schools, although significant in the long run, had less immediate importance. Foreign experts, therefore, were required to teach native workers the skills. He maintained that the greatest contribution of immigrant technicians and craftsmen from Britain was not what they did but what they taught. By training a generation of skilled workers, these immigrants enabled an indigenous industry to be developed.[48]

Foreign experts also fulfilled another function in technology transfer: a source of contacts and information. Morris-Suzuki, in a study of technology transfer to Japan, has shown that foreign experts (Chinese, German, Scottish, Swiss and Dutch), besides playing a crucial role in introducing a wide range of skills including pottery, mining and setting up a Western-style silk-reeling mill, also acted as links with the external world, supplying important sources of contacts and information. The presence of a significant number of Chinese residents in Nagasaki provided a small but important channel for the inflow of scientific and technological ideas in the late seventeenth century. She also pointed out that although some of the early advisers to Japan in the nineteenth century had no real technical expertise, they had that crucial ability to find out information: to read Western books, consult other Western specialists and, where necessary, to hire their own expert assistants. Furthermore, the presence of foreign workers provided opportunities for native workers to observe crafts and techniques from other parts of the world and gave them greater confidence to try out new methods for themselves.[49]

Many of these roles, particularly setting up equipment, providing the skilled labour, training native workers and acting as a source of contacts and information, are also relevant to the early modern period. Although most equipment in the early modern period was simple, the transfer of expertise was essential for the construction, improvement and operation of sophisticated industrial implements, such as draw-looms. The transfer of the dyeing industry also relied on migrant dyers who were familiar with the properties of raw materials and dyestuffs, and whose knowledge, derived from experience, was indispensable due to the absence of chemical analysis.[50] In addition, migrant craftsmen played an essential role in the acquisition of relevant raw materials. Recent studies show that many migrants settled in England in the sixteenth century frequently travelled back to the Continent to buy the necessary raw materials, indicating that knowledge of local markets was equally important in the transfer of industries.[51]

Industrial Case Study

The shortcomings of the traditional school of thought encouraged historians from the 1960s to undertake detailed case studies and examine the diffusion of industries long associated with immigrants from the Low Countries. In an article on the diffusion of the New Draperies published in 1969, D.C. Coleman offered us a revisionist view of the development of the New Draperies in England. Challenging the traditional view that immigrants from the Low Countries brought the industry to England, Coleman showed instead that their arrival merely speeded up the process of diffusion, and that without their immigration, the industry would still have been established, as the English textile industry was already undergoing structural changes as a result of shifts in fashions and consumer demands.[52] In other words, changes in the textile industry, rather than the influx of immigrants, provided the fertile soil for the establishment of the New Draperies in England. Immigration, according to the revisionist school of thought, was a secondary, not primary, factor in diffusion.

In another case study – glassmaking – Godfrey also dispelled myths surrounding its establishment in England. She agreed with traditionalists that the skills of the alien glass-makers were important in the foundation of the industry in England in the sixteenth century, but pointed out that this must be placed in a wider context. The rapid growth of the industry, she maintained, was only made possible by other factors such as the existence of an established glass industry in England, the availability of coal as a cheaper source of fuel, the strong desire to establish the industry, and the expansion of domestic demand. Prior to the arrival of Jean Carré, who is credited with the introduction of glassworks after 1567, there had been earlier attempts to establish glassmaking in 1549 and 1552. The shifting focus of production from luxury to ordinary usage in the 1560s ensured the existence of a mass market, while the grant of special concessions to aliens by the Crown also contributed.[53] Research by Coleman and Godfrey shows, then, that immigration was only one of the factors in the complex matrix of diffusion.[54]

In recent years, historians who advocate a model of endogenous technological change have expressed much scepticism over the role of immigrants in economic development. These believe in piecemeal technological change, resulting from *economies of practice*, from trial and error, from division of labour and specialization, commonly assumed to occur in sectors such as agriculture and mining.[55] Roger Burt, in his study of the role of German engineers in the mining industry, dismissed their importance because he contended that economic change in the early modern period was the product of a continuous process of diffusion and small-scale improvement rather than 'of revolutionary forces introduced by heroic inventors or visitors'. He therefore questioned the key role still accorded to minority immigration in revitalizing the Tudor and Stuart economy.[56] This conclusion may have been too sweeping, for the focus of his article was on the mining industry rather than on the role of German miners. Nowhere does he discuss who the German miners were, or their number, character and backgrounds, or consider the possible obstacles and constraints they experienced in their workings. Is it possible that they made little contribution because they were obstructed in their enterprises? The value of Burt's article lies more in alerting us to the varied nature of immigrants' influence – in some industries, they appear to have made a more significant, visible impact, in others their influence was negligible. Karel Davids, in his recent study of the contribution of immigrants to the Dutch Republic during 1580–1680, found that immigrants played a vital part in skill-intensive industries such as textiles and earthenware, but rather less in capital-intensive industries such as shipping and drainage technology.[57] This pattern is also vindicated by modern studies: immigrants, it is found, are unlikely to operate in an industry characterized by standardization, scale economies, high absolute costs, mass production and distribution.[58] Burt's finding, therefore, may not be applicable to other industries, and the call to dismiss the significance of immigrants may be premature. The urgent task is to develop an analytical framework to assess their contribution to the Tudor economy.

The basic problem with the three approaches outlined above is their occupational determinism, embodying an implicit assumption that new arrivals somehow had a trade/occupation lined up, and that life in a new, alien environment did not necessitate any fundamental adjustment. This may be true in cases where the workers had been specifically invited over to introduce a particular industry, or those who had come over as part of chain migration with some prior knowledge of local job opportunities and who were able to find employment with kinsmen. The case of mass migration is more problematic, as this was precipitated by political and religious factors, and motivated by the search for safety and freedom. The exodus normally comprised people from all social groups, and from heterogeneous occupational backgrounds. Some would be fortunate enough to find a livelihood in the new environment with great ease, but there would be plenty of others who struggled to stand on their feet, especially when the society they moved to was fundamentally different from that at home. For many, life in a new environment necessitated learning a new trade, a new skill to earn a living. Modern studies show that mismatch of skills has been a fundamental problem facing many migrants and refugees to the West in the twentieth century.[59] In Britain, the Chinese and the Italians who arrived in the 1950s are strongly associated with businesses such as restaurants, fish and chip shops and ice cream vans. Yet many of these 'entrepreneurs' came from a rural background and had not practised these trades in their homeland,[60] suggesting that economic opportunities in the host environment, rather than their origins, were more crucial in determining the occupational patterns of immigrants. However, this is not to deny that there were some immigrants who had the relevant skills and experience. Many Russian Jews who arrived in Britain at the turn of the century had the experience of making clothes, hats and furniture, enabling them to dominate the East End clothing trade. Many Turkish Cypriots who came to Britain in the 1950s also gravitated towards the clothing industry, partly because they possessed the skill in dressmaking, and partly because they were barred from more congenial and higher-status employment by their lack of English proficiency and formal qualifications.[61] Once immigrants had established themselves in a particular trade, they created opportunities for newcomers, who might or might not have the skill, to enter the business. Over a period of time, the informal process of labour recruitment reinforces the concentration of a particular ethnic group in a particular industry. Immigrant groups with strong informal networks thus transmit skills most effectively and rapidly.[62] A study of diffusion of industries, then, requires not only a bird's-eye, abstract examination of their long-term development, but also a personal, human focus on the migrants, the carriers of industrial technology and know-how, and the influences on their behaviour.

Local Studies of Immigrant Communities

The recent flood of studies concerning immigrants in English towns and cities, with a focus on prosopography, has provided a deep insight into the dynamics of the immigrant communities, and also thrown light on individual career paths. All the major sixteenth-century immigrant settlements have now been studied: recent publications include Nigel Goose on Colchester, Raingard Esser on Norwich, Marcel Backhouse on Sandwich, and Andrew Spicer on Southampton.[63] For London, in addition to the numerous publications by Irene Scouloudi, there are Andrew Pettegree's inspiring book on the *Foreign Protestant Communities in London*, and Charles Littleton's thesis on the French and Dutch Churches.[64] Three findings from this body of research are relevant to the theme of diffusion. First, they demonstrate the fluidity of immigrants' occupations, with dual occupations not uncommon.

Marcel Backhouse has shown that many of the immigrants who settled in Sandwich in the sixteenth century had to learn a new skill, and that those who had been farmers, smiths, shoemakers, millers and bookbinders had to learn skills as baize and say workers, talents which were desired by the town.[65] This raises the question how they learned their new vocations, possibly from a core group with the relevant skills and experience. Second, they illustrate the centrality of the Stranger Churches in the lives of the immigrants. In addition to their role as a disciplinary body and a 'pressure' group, the Stranger Churches also provided spiritual needs as well as poor relief in times of economic distress. As a focal point of contacts for their members, the Churches also satisfied social needs, allowing their members to forge, sustain or resuscitate informal networks, and maintain links with their homeland through the Churches' information networks. Many of the links were also economic in nature, with members providing employment and/or craft training to others. Third, local studies also dissipate the traditional image of homogeneous and static immigrant communities. Ridden with linguistic and cultural divisions, immigrant communities (principally Dutch and French-speaking communities) in sixteenth-century England formed separate and, sometimes, rival organizations. Furthermore, their members were highly mobile. Instead of putting down permanent roots in their first place of settlement in England, the immigrants moved from one community to another (sometimes as a result of government resettlement initiatives), and travelled back and forth to the Continent to buy wool and yarn for their trade, to arrange the sale of their goods and properties which their hasty departure had formerly prevented them from attending to, and to continue participation in political struggles there.[66] The inputs of these various historiographical approaches – economic history, diffusion, single-industry case study, and local immigrant studies – will be moulded into a framework for analysis in this study.

Approaches and Methodologies

This book examines the economic contribution of immigrants. London provides an obvious locale for such an investigation as it had the largest and most established immigrant community in England and is rich in sources. In addition, historians have long supposed that immigrants played a crucial role in the industrial expansion in London during the Elizabethan period, but this has not been researched and substantiated in a book-length study. It remains unclear how significant the alien factor was in the growth of London, and what the links between internal and external immigration, demographic and economic growth were. This book seeks to throw further light on the industrial development of London, but also to explore the nature and processes of diffusion in the early modern period, often portrayed as state-centric and monolithic in current literature. By focusing on three large and significant industries strongly associated with foreign immigrants such as beer brewing, silk weaving and silver-smithing, this book is able to compare and contrast the impact of immigrants upon various industries, as well as the nature and ingredients of successful diffusion.

The book uses two levels of analysis: structural and behavioural. The structural dimension examines the context in which new industries and skills become established, particularly London's enormous demographic growth, its opulence, its close links with dynamic European cities, and its pivotal role as the centre of trade, manufacturing and consumption in England. The behavioural focus explores the contribution of the government and the immigrants in industrial development. In Chapter 3, the government's initiatives to promote the establishment of foreign industries are analysed and their success is evaluated. But the principal focus of the book is on the immigrants' contribution, how their characteristics and the nature of their migration influenced the speed and types of skills diffused. In particular the book seeks to address three key issues. The first issue is to establish the different methods by which migrants moved to London, and to determine modes in which skills were transferred, as well as their nature and speed. There were several ways in which people migrated: chain, circular, and mass migration. Chain migration involved the migration of related individuals or households through a set of social arrangements by which people at the destination provided aid, information and encouragement to the newcomers.[67] This usually included a small number of people, so the diffusion of skills through this method might take a long time to complete. Circular migration encompassed the return of artisans or merchants to their place of origin after a few years of spending time abroad to acquire experiences and craft training, or to conduct business. Mass migration was less common and, like minority migration, was associated with persecution and political factors. Although the numbers affected tended to surpass other types of migration, the backgrounds of emigrants were also more likely to be heterogeneous and the contribution more varied. The second issue is to draw up the occupational profiles of the immigrants to establish any mismatch of skills or occupational changes, and explain occupational shifts as well as the means by which they acquired and learned new skills. This crucial question is often overlooked, and it is often assumed that the trades practised in the new host country were congruent with those in the homeland. Finally, the crucial subject of how skills were transmitted to the native population also merits further investigation. This third issue has been overlooked because historians often assume that the process was natural and automatic. However, this was far from the truth. Skill,

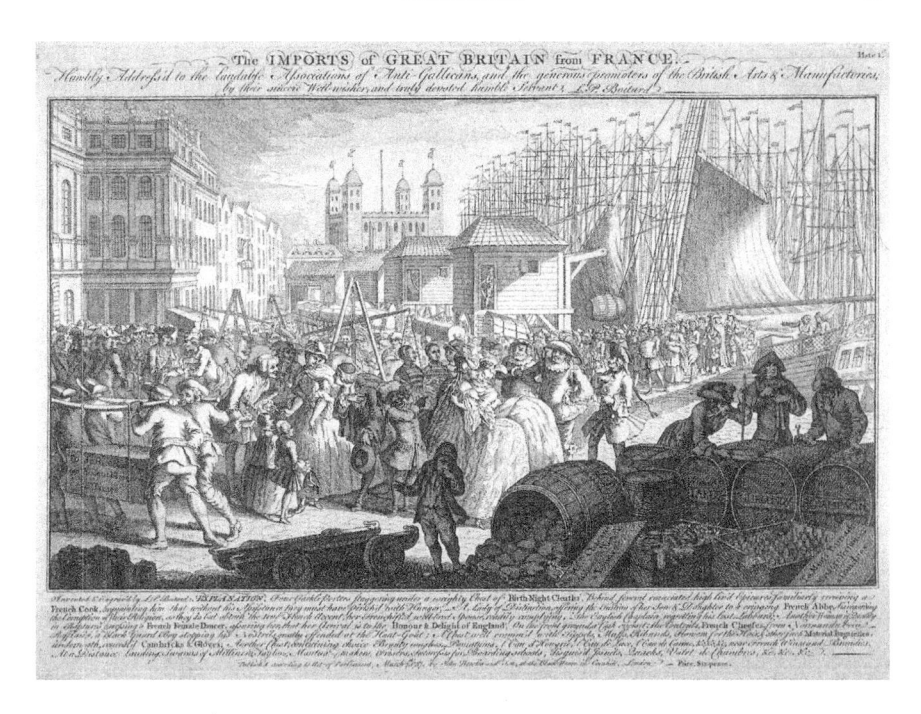

1.1 Imports from France
Source: **Guildhall Library**

as a form of property, was the underlying source of social status and a means of livelihood and, as such, it was not so readily imparted as often assumed. There were economic, social, cultural and legal barriers to diffusion which will be discussed, particularly in Chapter 5. In short, this book seeks to examine the nature and processes involved in diffusion, as well as the factors facilitating and impeding technological transfer in the early modern period.

Sources

This book uses a wide range of sources deposited in the archives held in London, Antwerp and Brussels. The most significant English sources are government census materials, known as the 'Certificates', or the 'Returns of Aliens', compiled to provide the central government with the essential information regarding the immigrant communities in England. For London, there are six major extant Returns of Aliens covering the period between 1568 and 1593.[68] Although varying in details and geographical coverage of the City, the Returns contain essential biographical information such as name, occupation, city of origin or previous abode, length and place of residence in London, church membership, number of children and number of servants. The Returns of November 1571 and 1593 contain other unique information: motives for emigration and the number of English servants employed, respectively. As the Returns for 1571 and 1593 are also the most detailed extant surveys,[69] they have been selected for detailed analysis in this study. Covering 4631 and 3930 individuals, these have been grouped into 1815 and 1079 households respectively for analytical purposes. Information contained in these two Returns was entered onto databases, making it possible to conduct relational analysis (relationship between particular skills and places of origin, and between particular skills and the time of arrival).

Although the Returns are undeniably a rich source of information for historical investigation, their use presents several problems.[70] The most serious is their questionable reliability, as the information recorded in the Returns was oral testimony given by the immigrants, making it difficult to verify its accuracy. The Lord Mayor recognized this problem and instructed the Aldermen in 1567 to put the immigrants 'upon their oaths if it shall seem needfull'.[71] The negative circumstances prompting the conduct of the Returns also compounded the problem of inconclusive accuracy. Often ordered in times of considerable economic and social tension between natives and immigrants, one of the principal aims of the Returns was to investigate whether the presence of aliens led to native unemployment. Under these circumstances, it is possible that aliens may have claimed to ply a trade not practised by natives, to reduce hostility and obtain governmental and local support for their settlement. Occupational information disclosed by immigrants in the Returns, therefore, should not be accepted at its face value.

Linguistic difficulties added to the problem, hindering direct communication between immigrants and officials undertaking the Returns. Having recently arrived, many aliens understandably had low proficiency in English, and in 1575 ministers of the Stranger churches had to be employed as interpreters as they were best 'acquainted with their language'. By the 1590s, when many aliens presumably had been in the capital for some time, it was still not clear to the authorities whether they could 'understand the English tongue'.[72] Most Returns were also conducted by word of mouth, and by English officials not familiar with foreign names. This often resulted in a great variety of name spellings, rendering it difficult to trace particular individuals in other records.

The Returns by their very nature give snapshots of the life of aliens in London, and an analysis based on one Return can only provide a partial insight into the immigrant community at a particular point in time. As the Returns only record the trades practised by immigrants at a particular juncture, an occupational analysis based on one Return can convey a very misleading picture, of a fixed and static occupational structure concealing changes and dynamism. Such an analysis only tells us what kinds of trades immigrants were involved in in a particular year, not what they did before or after the date of the survey, nor where and how they acquired a particular skill. Yet, these questions are crucial for us to understand the process of transfer as well as sources of change. Cross-checking occupational data contained in the Returns for 1571 and 1593 with others (both earlier and after) provides an indirect way of tracing career trajectories of the immigrants, and detecting any occupational changes.

Guild Records – Brewers, Goldsmiths and Weavers – have also been used to assess the contribution of aliens to trades in early modern London. All entries relating to aliens, as narrated in the company court minutes, were entered onto a database, making it possible to track the career of the individual immigrant in the relevant Company. Although rarely specifying the place of origin of the stranger (who was simply referred to as 'stranger', 'alien', or broadly as 'Dutch' and 'French'), the Court Minutes often give the name and nationality of his employer, and occasional references to place of residence in London. From these, it is possible to infer the circumstances of migration, the importance of chain migration among some groups, social networks among the strangers, relations between aliens and English craftsmen, the company's attitudes towards aliens, and the degree of reliance of a particular craft upon alien skills. It is also possible to use this information to draw up patterns of employment of alien servants by English masters in London, and to establish the degree of contact. The records of the City Livery Companies in many ways complement the information derived from the Returns of Aliens. However, one major drawback of these records is that they excluded many aliens who did not work within the jurisdiction of the livery companies, such as tailors. In times of economic distress, their members lodged copious complaints against aliens, forcing livery companies to turn to the city authorities for remedy. The records of the city, in particular the Repertories of the Court of Aldermen and the Journals of the Common Council at the Corporation of London Records Office, are invaluable in providing a broader view of the extent of the alien problem experienced by different crafts, the solutions sought and the resolutions adopted.

The various governmental and guild sources mentioned above provide biographical information of the immigrants and their interaction with the host society. However, they do not tell us about the attitudes of the immigrants towards their new homeland or relations within the immigrant communities. For such purposes, the records of the Stranger Churches are particularly useful. In addition to casting light on the dynamics of the immigrant communities and relations among their members, the records of the Dutch Church, deposited in Guildhall Library and published in J.H.

Hessels, *Ecclesiae Londino-Batavae Archivum, Epistulae et Tractatus* (3 vols, Cambridge, 1889–97), also demonstrate the valuable role played by the Church as guardian of the immigrants and as a pressure group for lobbying the Crown and various government ministers to confer protection. The account books of the French Church, which survive only for the period 1572–3, dealt with poor relief, and so have been utilized to establish the economic status of many French-speaking immigrants.

Although sources in London give an insight into the experience of strangers in their new life, they do not tell us about their past and their pre-migration characteristics. The Returns, for example, do not tell us the social status of the strangers in their native town, the particular circumstances that prompted their emigration, the reasons why some arrived in the Capital destitute, and whether they returned to their home city after a period spent in London. Therefore, sources in Belgium have been employed to throw light on these questions. Three types of source are useful. First, the archive of the *Conseil des Troubles* (Council of Troubles in Brussels), a tribunal set up in 1567 to deal with the disturbances, is particularly useful and contains much information about those who participated or were suspected to have participated in the political disturbances in the Low Countries between 1566 and 1568.[73] These suspected individuals were summoned (up to three times) to appear before a local court to explain their involvement. Many of the politically active, however, had fled the country before Spanish troops arrived in the summer of 1567. Sentences were therefore handed down in their absence – some were banished, others condemned to death. These various lists – summons lists (the *dagvaardingen door de Procureur-Generaal des Konings*), lists of names of those involved in the Troubles (*lijsten van personen in de troebelen gemengd*), and sentences (*vonnissen*) – are extremely useful for this study because they record the names of individuals and their occupations or status. These materials have made it possible to trace the occupations of immigrants in their country of origin, compare their occupations before and after migration, and characterize the occupational structure of cities in the Low Countries from which they originated.[74] The properties of those who were banished, executed or failed to appear were confiscated by the state, and the inventories of confiscated goods (*inventarissen van verbeurdverklaarde goederen*) make it possible to infer the levels of material wealth of immigrants in their homeland.[75]

These sources, however, present their own limitations. In the first place, occupational data sometimes refer to social status, denoted by terms such as 'bourgeois' or 'rich and wealthy', rather than to a trade or profession. In the second place, the number of people who could be traced is rather small, partly due to the nature of the source. The Council of Troubles was primarily concerned with identifying individuals involved in the political upheavals in the Low Countries in the summer of 1566, and dealt mainly with those who had lost a great deal of money or possessions. It is difficult, therefore, to trace many ordinary craftsmen who were not involved in the troubles or had few goods to lose. The sample which can be cross-checked may therefore be atypical of the population as a whole. The third issue is name spellings. The same person might be variously known by his patronymic, by his trade, or by his native town.[76] The task of tracing people through different manuscript sources is laborious and difficult, especially when the sources are in different languages (that is, checking names spelt by English clerks in English sources against sources in French and Dutch) and because sometimes names were translated.

As there were important groups of Antwerp artisans (particularly silk-weavers and goldsmiths) in London, the sources in the *Stadsarchief* there have also been searched. The voluminous legal documents or the *Certificatieboeken*, which often indicate the occupation and age of the individual concerned, are one possible useful source,[77] but the task of tracing individuals in these would be prodigious. It was therefore decided to look through the records of the relevant guilds. While the attempt to trace Antwerp silk-weavers in London in the Satijn-, Caffa- and Boratwerkers Guild was not successful, endeavours to track down Antwerp goldsmiths working in London in the Goud- en Zilversmeden Guild bore more fruit.[78] The accounts book for 1564–92 (A 4487), listing the names of new apprentices, new masters, payments and receipts, is the most useful source. Information gathered from this source has made it possible to establish whether Antwerp goldsmiths in London had completed their apprenticeship in Antwerp prior to their migration to London, their levels of experience, and whether they returned to their native city after a period in London. The employment of both London and Continental sources, then, enables us not only to determine pre- and post-migration characteristics of aliens, but also their motives for migration, the influence of their former economic and social status on their new life and, in the case of the goldsmiths, their occupational mobility after a period of time working abroad.

Notes

1. L. Stone, 'Elizabethan Overseas Trade', *Economic History Review*, 2nd Series, 1949, Vol. 2, No. 1, pp. 38–9; J. Boulton, 'London 1540–1700', in *The Cambridge Urban History of Britain, Volume II: 1540–1840*, ed. P. Clark (Cambridge, 2000), pp. 322, 326; J. Thirsk, *Economic Policy and Projects: The Development of a Consumer Society in Early Modern England* (Oxford, 1978), p. 2.
2. This concept was propounded by Arnold J. Toynbee and quoted in L.E. Eastman, *Family, Fields and Ancestors: Constancy and Change in China's Social and Economic History, 1550–1949* (Oxford, 1988), p. 258.
3. BL, Lansdowne MS 152/64/237.
4. Quoted in C.M. Cipolla, *Before the Industrial Revolution: European Society and Economy, 1000–1700* (London, 1993), p. 286.

5 Thirsk, *Economic Policy and Projects*, p. 2.
6 D.M. Palliser, *The Age of Elizabeth: England under the Later Tudors, 1547–1603* (London, 1992), pp. 277, 300–308; Thirsk, *Economic Policy and Projects*, p. 2; L.A. Clarkson, *The Pre-industrial Economy in England, 1500–1700* (London, 1971), pp. 105–16.
7 Quoted in A.E. Musson, *The Growth of British Industry* (London, 1978), p. 30.
8 C. Hill, *The Penguin Economic History of Britain: Reformation to Industrial Revolution* Vol. II (London, 1992), pp. 20, 22.
9 Clarkson, *The Pre-industrial Economy in England, 1500–1750*, p. 116; D.C. Coleman, *Industry in Tudor and Stuart England* (London, 1975), p. 15.
10 H. Perkin, 'The social causes of the British Industrial Revolution', *Transactions of the Royal Historical Society*, 5th Series, 1968, Vol. 18, pp. 123–43.
11 E.A. Wrigley, 'The divergence of England: The growth of the English economy in the seventeenth and eighteenth centuries', *Transactions of the Royal Historical Society*, 6th Series, Vol. X, 2000, p. 118; see also E.A. Wrigley, *People, Cities and Wealth: The Transformation of Traditional Society* (Oxford, 1988), D. Landes, *The Wealth and Poverty of Nations: Why Some are So Rich and Some so Poor* (London, 1998), and E.A. Wrigley, 'A Simple Model of London's Importance in Changing English Society and Economy 1650–1750', *Past and Present*, 1967, Vol. 37, pp. 44–70.
12 Printed in F.J. Fisher, 'London as an 'Engine of Economic Growth', in *London and the English Economy, 1500–1700*, ed. by P.J. Corfield and N.B. Harte (London, 1990), pp. 185–98.
13 A.L. Beier, 'Engine of Manufacture: The trades of London', in *London 1500–1700: The Making of the Metropolis*, ed. A.L. Beier and R. Finlay (London, 1986), p. 147; Boulton, 'London 1540–1700', p. 326.
14 Boulton, 'London 1540–1700', p. 326.
15 The other wave was the expulsion of the Jews in 1492: J.I. Israel, *The Dutch Republic: Its Rise, Greatness, and Fall, 1477–1806* (Oxford: 1995), p. 308.
16 The Duchess of Parma reported to Philip II that 100 000 people may have left the Netherlands when they heard the news that the Duke of Alva was coming with 10 000 soldiers to suppress the troubles, see J.S. Burn, *The History of the French, Walloon, Dutch and other Foreign Protestant Refugees settled in England, from the reign of Henry VIII to the Revocation of the Edict of Nantes* (London, 1846), p. 4; Geoffrey Parker believed that this estimate was too high, perhaps deliberately exaggerated to alarm Philip II. He calculated that perhaps 60 000 people left between 1567 and 1573, the period during which the Duke of Alva ruled the Southern Netherlands: see G. Parker, *The Dutch Revolt* (London, 1977), p. 119. The best estimates suggest a figure of 30–50 000 for the period 1567–73: see J. Briels, *De Zuidnederlandse immigratie, 1572–1630* (Haarlem, 1978), p.11. Briels believed about half of these went to England.
17 Israel, *The Dutch Republic*, p. 308.
18 A. Pettegree, *Foreign Protestant Communities in Sixteenth Century London* (Oxford, 1986), p. 299.
19 W.J.C. Moens, *The Walloons and their Church at Norwich* (Lymington, 1887/88), p. 6.
20 BL, Lansdowne 17/2.
21 R.H. Tawney and E. Power, eds, *Tudor Economic Documents* (London, 1924, 3 vols) Vol. 3, p. 212.
22 J.S. Burn, *The History of the French, Walloon, Dutch Refugees*; S. Smiles, *The Huguenots: Their Settlements, Churches, and Industries in England and Ireland* (London, 1867); F.W. Cross, *History of the Walloon and Huguenot Church at Canterbury* (Huguenot Society Publications, 15, 1898).
23 W. Cunningham, *Alien Immigrants to England* (London, 1897, reprint 1969).
24 G. Unwin, *The Gilds and Companies of London* (London, 1st edition 1908, 3rd edition 1938), p. 246.
25 E. Lipson, *The Economic History of England: The Age of Mercantilism*, Vol. 3 (London, 1934), pp. 56–7, 60–61.

26 For an excellent, concise evaluation, see N. Goose, 'Immigrants and English Economic Development in the Sixteenth and Early Seventeenth Centuries', in N. Goose and L. Luu, eds, *Immigrants in Tudor and Stuart England* (Brighton, 2005), pp. 136–160.
27 K. Bruland, ed., *Technology Transfer and Scandinavian Industrialisation* (Oxford, 1991); M. Berg and K. Bruland, eds, *Technological Revolutions in Europe: Historical Perspectives* (Cheltenham, 1998), D.J. Jeremy, *International Technology Transfer: Europe, Japan and the USA, 1700–1914* (Aldershot, 1991); D.J. Jeremy, 'Damming the Flood: British Government Efforts to Check the Outflow of Technicians and Machinery, 1780–1843', *Business History Review*, Spring 1977, Vol. 51, No. 1, pp. 1–34; I. Inkster, 'Mental Capital: Transfers of Knowledge and Technique in Eighteenth Century Europe', *Journal of European Economic History*, 1990, Vol. 19, pp. 403–41.
28 In 1952, Scoville published a two-part article surveying the role of the Huguenots in the diffusion of technology in early modern Europe. Unfortunately, these articles do not elaborate in depth the processes of diffusion nor offer an analytical framework that can be used for other similar studies.
29 R. Nelson and S. Winter, *An Evolutionary Theory of Economic Change* (Cambridge, MA, 1982), p. 73, quoted in K. Bruland, *British Technology and European Industrialization* (Cambridge, 1989), p. 108; see also J.R. Harris, 'Industrial Espionage in the Eighteenth Century', *Industrial Archaeology Review*, 1985, Vol. 7, pp. 127–38.
30 M. Berg and K. Bruland, 'Culture, Institutions and Technological Transitions', in Berg and Bruland, eds, *Technological Revolutions*, pp. 8–9; C.T. Smith, *An Historical Geography of Western Europe before 1800* (London, 1978), p. 548.
31 P. Stromstad, 'Artisan travel and technology transfer to Denmark, 1750–1900', in K. Bruland, ed, *Technology Transfer and Scandinavian Industrialisation* (Oxford, 1991), pp. 135–6.
32 See R. Gwynn, *The Huguenot Heritage: The History and Contribution of the Huguenots in Britain* (London, 1985), p. 169.
33 J.R. Harris, 'Movements of Technology between Britain and Europe in the Eighteenth Century,' in Jeremy, ed., *International Technology Transfer*, p. 24.
34 Rolv Petter Amdam, 'Industrial Espionage and the Transfer of Technology to the Early Norwegian Glass Industry', in Bruland, ed., *Technology Transfer and Scandinavian Industrialisation*, pp. 91–2.
35 C.M. Cipolla, 'The Diffusion of Innovations in Early Modern Europe', *Comparative Studies in Society and History*, 1972, Vol. 14, p. 48.
36 J. Mokyr, 'The Political Economy of Technological Change: Resistance and Innovation in Economic History', in M. Berg and K. Bruland, eds, *Technological Revolutions in Europe: Historical Perspectives* (Cheltenham, 1998), pp. 55–6.
37 Ibid., pp. 55–6; T. Morris-Suzuki, *The Technological Transformation of Japan: From the Seventeenth to the Twenty-first Century* (Cambridge, 1994), p. 20; see also S.R. Epstein, 'Craft Guilds, Apprenticeship, and Technological Change in Preindustrial Europe', *Journal of Economic History*, 1998, Vol. 58, No. 3, pp. 684–713.
38 F.A. Norwood, *The Reformation Refugees as an Economic Force* (Chicago, IL, 1942), pp. 145–77. Davis also argued that Protestants were preponderant in occupations with skills, novelty or prestige: see N.Z. Davis, 'Strikes and Salvation at Lyon', in idem, *Society and Culture in Early Modern France* (London, 1975), p. 7.
39 H. Schilling, 'Innovation through Migration: The Settlements of Calvinistic Netherlanders in Sixteenth- and Seventeenth-century Central and Western Europe', *Histoire Sociale/Social History*, 1983, Vol. 16, pp. 16, 31.
40 H.R. Trevor-Roper, 'Religion, the Reformation and Social Change', in *Religion, the Reformation and Social Change and Other Essays* (London, 1972), pp. 13–24. See also D.C. McClelland, *The Achieving Society* (Princeton, NJ, 1961), esp. pp. 145–9 for a discussion of the upbringing and the 'need for achievement' instilled in the children of minority groups.

41 D.C. Coleman, 'An Innovation and its Diffusion: The "New Draperies"', *Economic History Review*, 1969, Vol. 22, pp. 421, 426–7, 429.
42 Quoted in I. Inkster, 'Mental Capital: Transfers of Knowledge and Technique in Eighteenth Century Europe', p. 403; see also Goose, 'Immigrants and English Economic Development in the Sixteenth and Early Seventeenth Centuries', pp. 136–160.
43 Berg and Bruland, 'Culture, Institutions and Technological Transitions', in idem, eds, *Technological Revolutions in Europe*, p. 7.
44 Quoted in Inkster, 'Motivation and Achievement: Technological Change and Creative Response in Comparative Industrial History', *Journal of European Economic History*, 1998, Vol. 27, No. 1, pp. 39–40.
45 Mokyr, 'The Political Economy of Technological Change', in Bruland and Berg, eds, *Technological Revolutions*, p. 57.
46 P. Mathias, 'Skills and the diffusion of innovations from Britain in the eighteenth century', in idem, *The Transformation of England* (London, 1979), pp. 36–7.
47 Mathias, *The Transformation of England*, pp. 29, 35–6.
48 D.S. Landes, *The Unbound Prometheus: Technological Change and Industrial Development in Western Europe from 1750 to the Present* (Cambridge, 1969), pp. 147–51.
49 Morris-Suzuki, *Technological Transformation of Japan*, pp. 18, 64–5, 33.
50 D. Jacoby, 'The Migration of Merchants and Craftsmen: A Mediterranean Perspective (12th–15th Century)', in *Le Migrazioni in Europa secc. XIII–XVIII*, Instituto Internazionale di Storia Economica 'F. Datini' Prato, Serie II, Atti delle 'Settimane di Studi' e altri Convegni 25, S. Cavaciocchi, 1994, p. 553.
51 M.E. Backhouse, *The Flemish and Walloon Communities at Sandwich during the Reign of Elizabeth I (1561–1603)* (Brussels, 1995), pp. 135–62; C. Littleton, 'Social interaction of aliens in late Elizabethan London: Evidence from the 1593 Return and the French Church consistory "actes"', in R. Vigne and G. Gibbs, eds, *The Strangers' Progress: Integration and Disintegration of the Huguenot and Walloon Refugee Community, 1567–1889: Essays in Memory of Irene Scouloudi*, (Proceedings of the Huguenot Society, Vol. 26, 1995), pp. 147–59.
52 D.C. Coleman, 'An Innovation and its Diffusion: The "New Draperies"', pp. 421, 426–7, 429.
53 E.S. Godfrey, *The Development of English Glassmaking, 1560–1640* (Oxford, 1975), pp. 251–2, 256.
54 According to Karel Davids, other important factors included intellectual property rights, lack of restrictions on experimentation, specialization, and political decentralization. See his article on 'Technological change and the economic expansion of the Dutch Republic, 1580–1680', in *The Dutch Economy in the Golden Age* (Amsterdam, 1993), pp. 95–7.
55 K.G. Persson, *Pre-industrial Economic Growth: Social Organization and Technological Progress in Europe* (Oxford, 1988), pp. 7–13.
56 R. Burt, 'The international diffusion of technology in the early modern period: The case of the British non-ferrous mining industry', *Economic History Review*, 1991, Vol. 44, pp. 249–71.
57 Davids, 'Technological change and the economic expansion of the Dutch Republic', pp. 90, 93, 94.
58 R. Waldinger, *Through the Eye of the Needle: Immigrants and Enterprise in New York's Garment Trades* (New York, 1986), p. 21.
59 Ibid., pp. 1–2.
60 R. Palmer, 'The rise of the Britalian culture entrepreneur' in R. Ward and R. Jenkins, eds, *Ethnic Communities in Business: Strategies for Economic Survival* (Cambridge, 1984), pp. 89–104; J.L. Watson, 'The Chinese: Hong Kong villager in the British Catering Trade', in J.L. Watson, ed., *Between Two Cultures: Migrants and Minorities in Britain* (Oxford, 1984), pp. 181–213.
61 H. Pollins, 'The development of Jewish business in the United Kingdom', in Ward and

Introduction 25

Jenkins, eds, *Ethnic Communities in Business*, p. 83; S. Ladbury, 'Choice, chance or no alternative?', in Ward and Jenkins, *Ethnic Communities in Business*, p. 111.
62 Waldinger, *Through the Eye of the Needle*, pp. 25, 42.
63 N. Goose, 'The "Dutch" in Colchester: The Economic Influence of an Immigrant Community in the Sixteenth and Seventeenth Centuries', *Immigrants and Minorities*, 1982, Vol. 1, No. 3, pp. 261–80, and also N. Goose, 'The Dutch in Colchester in the 16th and 17th centuries: Opposition and integration', in R. Vigne and C. Littleton, eds, *From Strangers to Citizens: The Integration of Immigrant communities in Britain, Ireland and Colonial America, 1550–1750* (Brighton, 2001), pp. 88–98; Backhouse, *The Flemish and Walloon Communities at Sandwich during the Reign of Elizabeth I*; R. Esser, *Niederländische Exulanten im England des 16. und frühen 17. Jahrhunderts* (Berlin, 1996); A. Spicer, *The French-speaking Reformed Community and their Church in Southampton, 1567–c.1620* (Huguenot Society, new series, No. 3, London, 1997); L.H. Yungblut, *Strangers Settled Here Amongst Us: Policies, Perceptions and the Presence of Aliens in Elizabethan England* (London, 1996).
64 Pettegree, *Foreign Protestant Communities in Sixteenth-century London*; C.G.D. Littleton, 'Geneva on Threadneedle Street: The French Church of London and its Congregation, 1560–1625' (University of Michigan, unpublished PhD thesis, 1996).
65 Backhouse, *The Flemish and Walloon Communities at Sandwich*, pp. 71–108.
66 Ibid., Spicer, *The French-speaking Reformed Community and their Church in Southampton*; C. Littleton, 'Social interaction of aliens in late Elizabethan London'; D.J.B. Trim, 'Protestant refugees in Elizabethan England and confessional conflict in France and the Netherlands, 1562–c.1610', in R. Vigne and C. Littleton, eds, *From Strangers to Citizens: The Integration of Immigrant Communities in Britain, Ireland and Colonial America, 1550–1750* (Brighton, 2001), pp. 68–79.
67 C. Tilly, 'Transplanted Networks', in *Immigration Reconsidered: History, Sociology, and Politics*, ed. V. Yans-McLaughlin (Oxford, 1990), p. 88; Bolton, *Alien Communities*, pp. 30, 32.
68 These are 1568, May 1571, November 1571, 1581, 1583 and 1593. These Returns have been published by the Huguenot Society, see Kirk and Kirk, eds, *Returns of Aliens dwelling in the City and Suburbs of London*, Vol. 2, pp. 1–154; Scouloudi, ed., *Returns of Strangers in the Metropolis, 1593, 1627, 1635, 1639*.
69 See Kirk and Kirk, eds, *Returns of Aliens*, Vol. 10, No. 2, pp. 1–154; Scouloudi, ed., *Returns of Strangers*, pp. 145–221.
70 Pettegree mentions extreme mobility, inaccurate registration and progressive integration as the three main problems of using the Returns: see 'Protestant Migration during the Early Modern Period', in *Le Migrazioni in Europa Secc. XIII–XVIII*, Atti delle 'Settimane di Studi' e altri Convegni 25, Istituto Internazionale di Storia Economica 'F. Datini' Prato, pp. 446–7.
71 CLRO, JOR 19, f.31v (17 March 1567).
72 CLRO, JOR 20 (Part 1), f. 219v; JOR 23, f. 308v, 1594.
73 A. Jamees, *Inventaris van het archief van de Raad van Beroerten* (Brussels, 1980).
74 AGR, Conseil des Troubles, MS 18–21 (summons lists), MS 155 (lists of names of those executed and banished from Valenciennes), and MS 6 (sentences). Some of these materials have been published by A.L.E Verheyden in *Le Conseil des Troubles: Liste des condamnés, 1567–1573* (Brussels, 1961).
75 Inventories of confiscated goods, see Conseil des Troubles MS 163–6, MS 315A and 315bis (for Valenciennes), MS 328 (Tournai). Those who were suspected of participating in the Troubles were summoned three times to appear before the town magistrate. If they failed to appear after the third summon, steps were taken to confiscate their goods and property.
76 Backhouse, *The Flemish and Walloon Communities*, p. 17.
77 These cover the period from 1394 to 1797, and consist of 1325 volumes. They contain

information such as contracts of buying and selling merchandise, renting of buildings, donations, testaments, contracts or promises of marriage. These were registered by the city clerks and done on a voluntary basis.

78 See *Inventaris op het Archief van Gilden en Ambachten* (Stadsarchief Antwerpen, 1925).

Chapter 2

Trade and Consumption

London's importance in the early modern period stemmed from a unique blend of roles as Capital City, the seat of the Court, Parliament and judiciary, the hub of inland and overseas trade, the heart of pre-industrial manufacturing, the centre of service and social entertainment for the well-to-do and the central meeting point of the elite marriage market. Above all it was the concentration of trade and political power in the city which conferred greatness upon it. 'No other city in Europe,' concluded Ramsay, 'combined these two qualities of being at once the seat of a powerful and independent government and a maritime port of the first rank.'[1] London's multi-functional existence moulded its distinctive social structure and patterns of consumption. Like any other city, London's population contained multitudes of craftsmen, journeymen and apprentices, and below them an uncertain number of hawkers, vagrants and beggars,[2] but the capital also housed an unusually high number of merchants and members of the aristocracy and gentry, whose wealth and residence made it the centre of conspicuous consumption. As John Chartres has observed, consumption patterns in the Capital were radically different from those of the rest of England, as indicated by its high consumption of grain, meat, dairy and garden produce. In addition, Londoners also enjoyed a higher level of consumption of luxuries and exotic consumer goods[3] – byproduct of the higher wages and far superior levels of wealth found in the capital.

While London's roles as the centre of trade, consumption and manufacturing are well known, less familiar is its function as an 'information exchange',[4] drawing information (in a broad sense) from abroad, accumulating it, and disseminating it to other parts of the country, thereby serving as a nexus between Provincial England and Continental Europe. These two roles – absorption and dissemination – are implicitly recognized in the current historiography. John Styles has described the capital as 'a place where new products were imported, invented, endorsed, Anglicized, copied, adapted, reformulated and marketed'.[5] McKendrick, the staunch proponent of demand-led consumption, saw London as 'the shop window for the whole country, the centre of forms of conspicuous consumption which would be eagerly mimicked elsewhere, the place which set the style for the season and saw the hordes of provincial visitors and their retinues of servants carry back those styles to the rest of the country'.[6] London, then, was like a river from which provincial towns in England drew their source of information and inspiration, but this pool in turn was connected to Continental Europe. An examination of London's wider links is essential for an understanding of its emergence as the centre of consumption and production, as well as the massive demographic expansion of the City that underpinned such a development.

London's Commercial Links

Commercial ties formed a crucial link between England and the Continent. These links with the shores immediately opposite, particularly the Low Countries, had been established for centuries.[7] However, the establishment of a staple market in Bruges during the Middle Ages strengthened relations between England and the Low Countries, or more precisely, between England and Flanders. Bruges, the economic centre of Flanders, became the principal market for English wool, which was consumed by the clothmaking towns in the region.[8] In return for raw materials, the shops and warehouses of Flemish towns, especially Bruges, and the fairs of Brabant furnished many of the material goods desired by English consumers (textiles, metalwares, small manufactures, spices and luxury goods).[9] Commercial interdependence of the two areas resulted in a homogeneity in their culture and lifestyles, with 'many elements in the domestic setting, in dress and household furnishings, items of food and drink, and even objects of devotion' common to urban communities on both sides of the Channel.[10] Migration to England also bolstered the influence of the Low Countries.

In the sixteenth century, relations between England and the Low Countries became even closer, with the shift of the world economic centre from Bruges to Antwerp. For the English, the rise of the Antwerp entrepôt brought about significant changes. To start with, trade with Antwerp, centring on cloth, brought England greater wealth. Previously, in Bruges, English merchants could only sell wool, not cloth, because this was banned from sale to protect Flemish clothmaking towns. But wool exports declined as the English cloth industry expanded from the late fourteenth century, forcing English merchants to look elsewhere for outlets for their cloth. The fairs of Brabant, held at Antwerp and Bergen-op-Zoom, welcomed their products because these cities did not have a substantial cloth industry of their own. In addition, there were many buyers for English cloths, such as the West German merchants who visited these fairs.[11]

In the fifty years between 1500 and 1550, cloth exports from London grew in volume by 150 per cent.[12] Cloth sales peaked in 1550 at 132 767 pieces. A sharp increase in prices of cloth during the middle of the sixteenth century from £30 to £70 per piece (levelled off at £50 twelve years later) undoubtedly helped this buoyant export trade.[13] Lawrence Stone calculated that in 1565, 134 055 cloths worth £851 417, constituting 78 per cent of the total value of exports, were exported.[14] On average, the annual income from English exports *c.* 1560 was £750 000 or more.[15] Two-thirds of English overseas trade, carried by the 'swarm of hoys ferrying to and fro between the Thames and the Scheldt', concentrated on Antwerp, and the remaining third on France and the Iberian peninsula.[16] According to Fisher, during the third quarter of the sixteenth century, exports of cloths from London contracted by 25 per cent and experienced two slumps (1562–4 and 1571–3).[17]

The Antwerp market also offered all 'the conveniences of a hypermarket for international buying and selling'.[18] When the international 'clearing house' was located in Bruges, English merchants had to sell cloths at one market (Antwerp and Bergen-op-Zoom) and buy their necessities and luxuries at another (Bruges). With the rise of Antwerp as the great entrepôt and 'the warehouse of all Christendome',[19] English merchants could buy and sell in the same place, and obtain a high proportion of the commodities required. The range and diversity of goods traded at Antwerp was also amazing. In 1575, there were more than 150 different textile fabrics on sale.[20] Exotic products such as East Indian pepper and Barbary sugar, West German metallurgical goods, Low Countries fustians and worsteds, raw materials like madder and hops, Baltic timber, pitch, cordage, Italian silks and alum could all be obtained at Antwerp, which in turn absorbed almost the entire English cloth export.[21]

The rise of Antwerp promoted the massive expansion of London in the sixteenth century, because it offered the most convenient and easy access to Antwerp. The Scheldt, upon which Antwerp stood, was situated directly opposite to the mouth of the Thames estuary, rendering the journey relatively short. Although commercial relations between Antwerp and London were strengthened in the sixteenth century, their business partnership was formed in the previous century. In the fifteenth century, 195 Antwerp ships entered English ports, carrying £13 864 14*s.* 9*d.* worth of goods. Most of the ships headed for London: 114 vessels sailed into the capital, whose cargo was valued at £11 735 9*s.* 2*d.*, or nearly 85 per cent of the total. Antwerp ships were also involved in the export of wool in this period. In 1458, Antwerp ships carried 543^1/$_2$ sacks and 24 nails of wool, or 7 per cent of the total exported between 1448 and 1458 (7700 and 9300 sacks annually), most of which was bound for Italy.[22]

With the growing importance of the London–Antwerp trade axis an increasing number of merchants who had hitherto traded from provincial ports began to transfer their base of operations to London.[23] Consequently, London came to monopolize the cloth trade to the Continent. In the early years of the sixteenth century, London's cloth exports accounted for 43 per cent of the country's total woollen exports, but by the mid–1540s its share had doubled to 86 per cent. London thus 'owed its economic ebullience and its aldermen their wealth to virtually one thing only – the English woollen cloth traffic'.[24] The Merchant Adventurers, the Company monopolizing cloth export, contained the richest men in the City and supplied virtually all the lord mayors between 1550 and 1580. In other words, the merchants 'trafficking in cloths to Antwerp were in the mid-sixteenth century the effective masters of London'.[25] Wealth, however, was concentrated in few hands. In 1547–8, some forty merchants handled over half of London's cloth exports. One of the forty was Thomas Gresham, whose export of 1548 cloths was only exceeded by two other merchants.[26]

As English cloths were in great demand at Antwerp, English merchants were also brought to greater prominence, standing second in importance after the Italians.[27] There was a sizeable colony of English merchants at Antwerp, who from 1520 enjoyed extensive privileges, including payment of lower customs than even native Netherlanders, exemption from the excise on beer and wine, preferential treatment in the use of warehouses and the great crane on the Antwerp quay, and maintenance of a substantial house in the city as a permanent residence.[28] In the 1560s, the English mercantile community in Antwerp numbered some three or four hundred individuals.[29] During the Sinksen mart in May and early June, they were joined by hundreds of other men of the Merchant Adventurers, their servants and apprentices. Many had come only to sell their cloths, while others invested their proceeds in silks, spices and other goods.[30] But it is important to note that many of the factors and apprentices of the Merchant Adventurers belonged to the social elite: they were largely 'gentlemens sons, or mens children of good means or qualitie'.[31] Their aristocratic backgrounds and tastes were likely to affect what goods they purchased among the vast range on sale at the Antwerp market, while the simple act of purchasing new products for their own consumption could set off a new trend among their social equals. This was presumably how the 'Turkey carpet', which by the mid-sixteenth century had become a common feature in wealthier English households, penetrated the English market.[32] Increased trade may thus have resulted in the greater exposure of Englishmen to a life of luxury in Antwerp.

While Englishmen valued Antwerp as the main market for its cloths and as the principal source of its income, Antwerpers in turn also valued highly their English trade, which brought wealth and employment. During the period 1530–65, the Antwerp cloth-dyeing and finishing industry, whose skills added 30 per cent to the value of English cloths, flourished with the employment of more than 1600 people.[33] As the lords of Antwerp explained in 1563, the English were favoured and respected in their city more than any other nation because of the great number of townsfolk and artisans there whose livelihoods depended upon the finishing of English cloth.[34]

Equally significant was the power of English cloths in drawing three groups of merchants and their products to Antwerp, namely south German silver and copper, Portuguese spices, and Italian luxury textiles and exotic products. In total, more than 2040 foreign merchants are estimated to have been active in Antwerp in the twenty-six years between 1488 and 1514.[35] The number rose significantly in subsequent decades. In 1550 alone about 2000 merchants were active in international trade in Antwerp (400–500 from the Southern Low Countries).[36] Their presence boosted local employment and income, as they required basic facilities such as warehouses, lodging, food, entertainment as well as transport. In 1553, one Englishman claimed that English merchants spent annually £22 000 on warehouses, lodging and on travelling to and from Antwerp, while other foreign merchants spent £440 000.[37] While it is difficult to verify this, the visits of foreign merchants undoubtedly stimulated the local economy.

The south German merchants, absent from Bruges, came to Antwerp principally to buy English cloth with their copper and silver, of which they had plentiful supplies due to the flourishing of central European mining during the second half of the fifteenth and in the first half of the sixteenth century. It was probably through interaction with south German merchants in Antwerp that the English were able to gather the necessary industrial intelligence, and recruit the necessary staff for the development of the mining industry in sixteenth-century England.

The Portuguese, in need of copper and silver to finance their expanding colonial trade with Africa and Asia, in turn came to Antwerp because of the south Germans. Copper and silver were both needed by the Portuguese for their expanding colonial trade because copper was an essential medium of exchange in Africa, while silver was the chief means of payment for Asiatic spices.[38] Spices were the most sought-after commodity in Europe, with a wide range of uses: as cures for disorders such as plague, oedema and epilepsy, as aromatic substances for enhancing and preserving foods, as ingredients in perfumes, aphrodisiacs and love potions, and as a scarce and expensive way of making salted meat palatable and fresh meat interesting for the tables of the well-to-do.[39] In 1559, nearly £16 000 worth of cinnamon, cloves, nutmeg and pepper were imported into London – £12 000 was spent on pepper alone.[40]

The Italians were highly conspicuous in Antwerp. Italian merchants had been active in northern Europe for centuries but, according to Ramsay, there was a significant change in the way they operated in Antwerp. They were more numerous, predominant and more permanent, in contrast to previous centuries when they tended to operate individually or in small numbers or for limited periods of time, not mixing with the indigenous merchants.[41] This was due in part to the development of a safe and well-organized trans-Continental route across Germany and the Alps to Italy.[42] Italian merchants formed ten 'foreign nations' (for example, Milanese, Genoese, Florentine and Lucchese), and were recognized by the city government, each with its consuls and its privileges of jurisdiction. Besides Portuguese spices, Italians also came to buy English and Flemish textiles and German copperware for re-export to Istanbul and to the other Ottoman markets in the Levant, and brought their luxury textiles and raw materials (such as silk and gold thread) to sell.[43] More than 416 Italian merchants may have been active in Antwerp between 1550 and 1599: 200 merchants were recorded for the years between 1550 and 1554, but the number plummeted sharply to 60 between 1555 and 1564, fluctuating around 70–80 between 1565 and 1579, before dropping to 40 between 1580 and 1584, and thereafter levelling off at 20 from 1585.[44] As the Italians dominated Antwerp's business life (their speech was the language of the Bourse, their monopolized luxury textiles provided the largest item in the commodities market, and their advanced financial techniques set the pace for northern merchants), the rise and fall in their numbers signifies the peaks and troughs of the Antwerp trade during this period.[45]

The more intensified Antwerp–Italian connection brought about two effects. The first probable consequence was the greater influence of the more distant, vastly wealthier and materially more advanced civilizations of the Ottoman Empire, Persia and China,[46] channelled via Italy, on north-east Europe and London. Since the Middle Ages, Italy had been the centre of a dynamic re-export trade of Near and Far Eastern wares to the rest of the Europe.[47] They whetted the appetite of north European consumers with supplies of Byzantine, Persian and Chinese silk fabrics, Persian tapestries, fancy cotton fabrics from India, Chinese porcelain, various dyes, and all sorts of spices (pepper, ginger, cinnamon, saffron, cloves and many others).[48] In Italy, trade soon precipitated a process of import substitution. In textiles, for example, Lucca, Florence, Venice and other Italian towns began importing raw silk from the Levant for the production of silk fabrics to satisfy home demand. But overseas demand for their silk products, brought to trade by Italian merchants in London and Bruges, was so great that Italy became the main supplier of silk fabrics in the European market. In the case of cotton, the changes were also substantial. Milan, Cremona and other towns began to import cotton from the East in order to produce fustian, made with a mixture of cotton and wool. Their success was so great that Italian production could not satisfy both home and export demand. Italian merchants then introduced production in south Germany. Ulm, Ausburg and Nuremberg became leading export centres, selling fustians all over Europe. Import substitution, extending into export-led growth, was also experienced in other industries: the Venetian glass-, mirror- and crystal-making industries, the Venetian majolica industries, and the Venetian and other Italian jewelry crafts.[49]

In Antwerp, trade with Italy led to a similar process of import substitution. Around 1510, an artisan from Brescia, Pietro Franchi, established a new kind of dyeing using a deep red colour called *scarlotto*. In 1513, another Italian, Guido Andrea of Venice, introduced majolica pottery making, and in 1541, the Venetian Gian Michele Cornachini started to make glasses and crystals.[50] The Italians were also responsible for the introduction of other luxury industries such as silk-weaving and sugar refining.

Through Antwerp, many Italian-developed industries – silk, glass, sugar refining, tin-glazed ceramic – were later relayed to London during the great migration of the 1560s and 1570s.[51] As Keene has noted, the connection with Antwerp was crucial for industrial development in London because 'specialised crafts which had once been practised at a great distance from London were brought closer to the city and entered a commercial environment where trade and migration across the North Sea had been commonplace for centuries'.[52] In the Low Countries, one effect of the inflow of luxury goods was the establishment of local manufacture of similar items, particularly those lucrative trades monopolized by Italians, such as silks and glass. As Antwerp was a city frequently visited by Englishmen, it is possible that, as Keene argued, many of these new manufactures might have transferred to London of their own accord, perhaps through 'stimulus diffusion'. As Summerson noted, 'whereas the art of Italians and Frenchmen had to be fetched, the art of Antwerp flowed of its own accord'.[53] However, the process was accelerated by government policy and migration from the southern Netherlands.[54]

As Englishmen had most direct personal contacts with Antwerp, they naturally looked to it for models for emulation. Thus, when in 1566 Sir Thomas Gresham built the Royal Exchange, he copied the design of the Antwerp Bourse and brought nearly all the materials from Antwerp, and recruited skilled craftsmen there, such as a Flemish surveyor and Flemish masons and carpenters.[55] Having lived in Antwerp for many years, he was familiar with the city and had built up contacts and knew local sources of information. Architectural inspiration in London in the sixteenth and early seventeenth century, then, was 'derived from the city's closest trading partner, by direct observation, by imported or immigrant craftsmen, or by use of the abundant products of the Antwerp printing presses'. As the economic gravity in the Low Countries once again shifted in the late sixteenth century, from Antwerp to Amsterdam, the latter succeeded Antwerp as the dominant overseas influence on the style of building (and other aspects of material culture) in London.[56]

The Population of London

London's enormous size, making it the largest and the most important market for consumer goods, supplied a powerful stimulus for its industrial development. As the demographic history of London has been extensively discussed elsewhere,[57] it is sufficient here to identify some salient features relevant to the current discussion on industrial development. The first essential point to note about London's demographic development was the gigantic scale of its absolute growth. During the period between 1500 and 1700, historians agree that London grew from a peripheral city to a world metropolis, but they disagree on the extent of growth, owing in part to a lack of sources and varying definitions of London.[58] Estimates of the population of London vary greatly, but the most significant discrepancy in opinion concerns London's population levels after 1550. In 1500, estimates range between 40 000 and 60 000; but for 1550, between 75 000 and 120 000; for 1650, between 320 000 and 400 000, and for 1700, between 490 000 and 575 000. The most controversial figures are those produced by Finlay and Shearer, estimating 120 000 for 1550, 200 000 for 1600, 375 000 for 1650, and 490 000 for 1700.[59] Dismissing these estimates, Harding has shown that London's population was 'significantly lower at the start of the period and higher at the end', and that London experienced greater growth from the later sixteenth century than Finlay and Shearer's figures suggest.[60] The accepted benchmarks for London population, as recently quoted by Keene, are as follows: 50 000 inhabitants in 1500, 80 000 in 1550, 200 000 in 1600, and 500 000 in 1700.[61] If these figures are accepted, it means that between 1500 and 1700, the demand for basic goods and services in London probably grew by at least tenfold.

The 'explosive' growth of London in this period stimulated industrial development in several ways. Its gargantuan levels of consumption, for food, fuel and drink, rendered London the most important single market. In the 1690s, for example, Londoners were thought to have consumed 88 400 beeves and 600 000 sheep a year.[62] The metropolitan demand for food gave 'a definite stimulus to English agriculture' as cereals, dairy produce (cheese and butter) as well as garden produce had to be imported to meet burgeoning demand.[63] In the second half of the sixteenth century, London imported 20 000 quarters of corn in normal years, of which Kent alone supplied nearly 75 per cent. Milk and fresh butter also came from the neighbouring countryside, and in 1724 Defoe noted the 'general dependence of the whole country upon the city of London – for the consumption of its produce'.[64] In a period of high transport costs, the prodigious scale of the metropolitan demand for consumer goods made London the principal manufacturing centre in England, or in Corfield's words, London 'flourished as a manufacturing centre because it contained the largest single concentration of consumers in the country'.[65] Throughout the eigtheenth century, London remained the leading manufacturing centre in England, particularly in silk-weaving, brewing, shipbuilding, and many branches of metalworking and engineering.[66]

Demographic expansion also induced other innovations. The rapid pace of population growth exerted tremendous pressure on wood supplies, for cooking, domestic heating, brewing and a wide range of industrial activities such as metalworking, brickmaking, dyeing and glass-making. During the 1560s, this precipitated the search for ways to economize on fuel consumption. The new furnaces invented and introduced by immigrants were very successful in achieving this aim, reducing wood consumption by almost a third. However, this failed to solve the scarcity of wood, with prices rising by 780 per cent between 1540 and 1640, compared with 291 per cent general inflation for most of other commodities, including sea coal. By the 1570s, the cheaper sea coal from Newcastle had been adopted as an ubiqituous fuel in London.[67] Between 1580 and 1600, the quantity of coal transported to London trebled, from 50 000 to 150 000 tons, rising to 300 000 by the 1640s – a sixfold increase in a period when the population rose by nearly three-and-a-half times.[68] Changes in the city's fuel economy were essential for expansion in industries such as beer brewing and brick-making. 'The moment at which coal became London's general fuel,' according to Keene, 'opened up possibilities of vastly-increased energy consumption, and new prospects for building in brick, which after 1600 progressively became the dominant mode.'[69] Shipbuilding also received a further boost from the expansion of the coal trade.

The concentration of the workforce made greater division of labour and specialization possible, resulting in enhanced choice and higher quality. This occurred on two levels: clear division at each stage of production (cloth processes, for example, broke down into weaving, dressing,[70] dyeing and finishing), and specialization within a single manufacturing process – dyers might specialize in particular colours.[71] This led to a proliferation of crafts in London, from 180 trades and crafts in the late Middle Ages to more than 721 occupations by the 1690s.[72] The giant parish of St Giles Cripplegate alone, with a population of possibly 40 000 in 1700, added 260 new trades in the second half of the seventeenth century.[73] London's high population density may have facilitated the diffusion of new knowledge and crafts. Outside the city, in the border parishes, 15 houses occupied an acre, while within the walls the density might have been as high as 95 houses per acre. Furthermore, as London's population grew, buildings were subdivided into tenements.[74] In such a crowded and compact environment, Londoners were bound to have an intimate knowledge of the things going on in their neighbourhood.[75]

Another feature of London's growth was its intensity, particularly between

1580 and 1650. The growth of the English population was undoubtedly an important factor, but this rose only by 40 per cent,[76] not 333 per cent as experienced by London in the same period. The extraordinary growth of London, then, was also due to other factors. The temporary collapse of the English textile industry precipitated by the closure of the Antwerp Mart must have been a substantial factor bringing about a mass exodus to London in search of a better life.

Table 2.1 Populations of selected cities and towns in England, 1500–1700[77]

	1500	1550	1580	1600	1650	1700
London	50 000	80 000	100 000	200 000	400 000	575 000
Norwich	10 000	12 000	—	12 000	20 000	30 000
Birmingham	1 000			1 700	5 472	8–10 000
Bristol	9 500–10 000			12 000		20 000
Canterbury	—	—	—	—	6 000	
Colchester	<5 000	—	—	—	10 305	10 000
Dover	—	—	—	—	3 000	
Liverpool	—	700			c.2 500	5–7 000
Manchester						8–9 000
Maidstone	—	—	—	—	3 000	
Newcastle Upon Tyne	4 000					16 000
Plymouth	4 000		7 000			8 400
Southampton	—	—	—	4 200	—	3 000
York	7 000	8 000	—	12 000	12 000	11 000

Sources: P. Corfield, 'Urban Development in England and Wales in the Sixteenth and Seventeenth Centuries', in D.C. Coleman and A.H. John, eds, *Trade, Government and Economy in Pre-Industrial England: Essays presented to F.J. Fisher* (London, 1976), pp. 217, 222–3; Patten 'Urban Occupations in pre-industrial England', *Transactions of the Institute of British Geographers*, 1977, Vol. 2, pp. 100, 103, 106, 109, 110; J. de Vries, *European Urbanization 1500–1800* (London, 1984), pp. 270–71.

On a national level, London's pace of growth was also extraordinary. With a population of more than 575 000 people in 1700, London dwarfed other English towns and cities. It was 19 times the size of Norwich, and 25 times that of Bristol.[78] As Table 2.1 makes plain, it does not matter which point of comparison we take, London's population was larger than the total population of all the other English major cities and towns put together. This enormous discrepancy in size, and hence economic attractions, rendered London a magnet for inland migrants, who were probably aware of the opportunities to be found there. Internal migration seems to have flowed down the trade routes.[79]

Equally remarkable was the total proportion of the English population with exposure to London's life. In 1400, some 2 per cent of the English population lived in London, but by 1700, 10 per cent did so.[80] According to Wrigley, by 1750, one adult in six in England had direct experience of London life. Contacts with the remainder of the country were potentially considerable, and it is precisely for this reason that historians believe London may have acted as a powerful catalyst for changes in the customs, prejudices and actions of traditional England.[81]

Urbanization is believed to promote new values and new patterns of consumption. Modern studies show that there is a link between attitudes to innovation and size. In addition to the existence of a larger market and better communication links, it is found that what makes large cities prime sites for innovation is their social structure and prevailing psychological attitudes, which are more favourable to the adoption of new ideas, fashions and innovations.[82] Cities also act as nodes in a network in which new ideas flow from one part of the country to another.[83] It is also the case that city dwellers have a higher propensity to consume, and tend to be bigger spenders. Living in small, personal, stable, face-to-face societies, so the argument goes, people have less need for status and display.[84] This contrasts with cities where town dwellers, detached from families and local communities and traditional values, are more free to adopt new values and patterns of consumption and, living in a larger, more impersonal and anonymous urban environment, there is often a greater need to assert identities and status through 'material culture', in the form of dwellings, diet, dress, furnishings, decorations and ornaments.[85] In towns, information about the range of material goods available is also more accessible through advertising by merchants and shopkeepers in newspapers and windows, and through social mingling among and across classes, living as neighbours in confined urban spaces.[86] Demonstration effects enhance the propensity to consume. In addition, higher wages in cities also enable city dwellers to enjoy higher material living standards.

By 1750, London was not only the largest city in England, but also in Europe. Indeed, its development from a marginal city into one of Europe's most populous cities was remarkable. In mid-sixteenth century Europe, London ranked only sixth in terms of size, dwarfed by Naples, Venice, Paris and Antwerp. With a population of 212 000 in 1550, for example, Naples was three times as large as London, and Paris, with a population of 130 000, was nearly twice as large. By 1600, London had caught up with both of these cities, while its principal trading partner, Antwerp, had been eclipsed, its population halving in the same period. By 1650, London had moved up to second position, close behind Paris, while Naples lagged behind, now with only 176 000 people. By 1700, London had overtaken Paris to emerge as the biggest European city, and become three times as large as Naples.[87] With this demographic change, the magnetism of London, as a place of enormous opportunity for the young, ambitious and skilled European craftsmen to seek their fortunes, strengthened, and its role shifted from an absorber to a disseminator of new ideas, information, skills and innovations.

What lay behind the extraordinary expansion of London? Mass immigration was the motor of demographic change in early modern London, as it experienced more deaths than births due to the insanitary and increasingly crowded conditions found there. Yet calculating the total number of people moving into sixteenth-century London is notoriously difficult, as migrants were highly mobile and there were no registers recording their movements. This forces historians to rely on indirect measurements of immigration. Given that death rates were higher than birth rates, one way to establish the total number of immigrants is to calculate the difference between burial and baptismal rates, and from this extrapolate how many people were necessary for a given rate of growth. It has been projected that 5600 immigrants were needed annually to sustain the City's rate of growth between 1560 and 1625, and 8000 between 1650 and 1750.[88] But, as Peter Spufford has pointed out, these figures do not represent actual rates of immigration, but only the difference between immigration and emigration. Even taking 8000 immigrants as the benchmark, Spufford argued that this could mean 10 000 in and 2 000 out, or it could mean 28 000 in and 20 000 out, or any other combination of figures with the same difference between them.[89]

Beier believed that the rate of immigration to London was higher, at least 10 000 per annum. He calculated that for the period 1604–59, the mortality deficit in London was 3500 people. If London grew from 200 000 in 1600 to a minimum figure of 375 000 in 1650, the mortality deficit required at least 7000 persons per annum to come and settle. In reality, many more came to London, but were not recorded because they did not die in the capital. The floating population, he estimated, was 10 000 people.[90] The second way to calculate immigration into London, as Wrigley did for the later period, is to determine what proportion of the nation's surplus birth rate was absorbed by the capital. For the period between 1600 and 1650, the proportion was nearly half – 48 per cent – and if the total of births in the country outside London ran at about 22 000 a year, this means that some 10 500 people may have arrived in the capital annually.[91] If these figures are accurate, two million, rather than the one million immigrants suggested by Wareing, may have migrated to London between 1550 and 1750.[92]

Immigration into London fell broadly into two types – subsistence migration and betterment migration. Subsistence migration to London appeared to increase in the 1570s and 1580s, for during this period the number of vagrants dealt with by Bridewell Hospital, the chief institution dealing with vagrancy in London, rose greatly from 69 cases in 1560–61, to 209 in 1578–9, to 555 in 1600–1601, and 815 in 1624–5.[93] Royal proclamations issued in the 1580s prohibiting new building within a three-mile radius also confirm increased rates of subsistence migration: 'great multitudes of people [had been] brought to inhabit in small rooms whereof a great part are seen very poor, yea such as must live of begging or by worse means, and they heaped up together, and in a sort smothered with many families of children and servants in one house or small tenement'.[94] Many immigrants were drawn to the east of London which saw its population soar from 21 000 in 1600 to 91 000 by 1700.[95]

Why did immigrants come to London, especially from the 1580s onward? In addition to the growth of the English population and the decline of the textile industry, the attractions of London must be considered to explain its phenomenal growth. First, there was the seductive myth of the big city: 'bright lights, crowds, bustle, gaiety, opportunities for social and economic advancement; the big city is a magical place where all the streets are paved with gold, and all the maidens pretty'.[96] As the biggest city in England, London was naturally the magnet for provincial migrants. Perceived better employment opportunities also drew considerable numbers of migrants to London. From the 1580s, London may have experienced an increase due to the expansion in the shipping industry and the growth in demand for servants as a result of the prolonged stay in the capital by the upper classes. Prospective migrants probably learned of employment opportunities in London through an informal communications network centring upon the boarding houses in which they stayed or the taverns in which they drank.[97] In addition, given the high volume of migration to London, they probably knew someone – a kinsman, a relative, or a neighbour – who had already settled in the city, and this acquaintance made the decision to move less daunting. Another attraction of London was higher wages. Daily wage rates of skilled bricklayers, carpenters, plasterers and tilers in London were on average one-third higher than those in other parts of England. Even semi-skilled workers earned on average 26 per cent more per day in London than elsewhere in England. During the sixteenth century, when the price of food more than trebled, such a differential in wage rates may have encouraged many to seek work in London.[98] Even for the less fortunate, London offered much attraction because of its better provision of poor relief and the chance of finding a living by begging, or involvement in petty crime or prostitution.[99]

The growth of London was also fuelled by betterment migration, as many children from middling provincial backgrounds sought their fortunes in the growing metropolis.[100] Apprentices are believed to have formed 12 per cent of London's population in the mid-sixteenth century, and 15 per cent (or 30 000 apprentices) in 1600. Their number fell to 20 000 between 1640 and 1660, and by 1700 their share was just 4 or 5 per cent of the city population.[101] In other words, the number of apprentices failed to keep pace with London's population increase. However, their presence was significant in three ways. In the first place, it led to 'a thickening of the middle station in the city'.[102] With many originating from the upper echelons of society, some servants probably shared the consumption patterns of gentlemen. The mayoral proclamation in 1572 declared that 'of late time servants and apprentices within the city are by indulgence and lack of convenient severity grown to great disorder in excess of apparel and fashions thereof uncomely for their calling'.[103] In 1583, Philip Stubbs scornfully remarked that: 'It is very hard to know, who is noble, who is worshipful, who is a gentleman, who is not: for you shal haue those, which are neither of the nobilitie, gentilitie, nor yeomanrie ... go daiely in silkes, Veluetts, Satens, Damaskes, Taffeties and such like.'[104] This prompted much governmental concern because, as the sumptuary legislation in 1588 put it, it resulted in 'the confusion of degrees of all estates, amongst whom diversitie of apparell, hath bene alwayes a spetiall and laudable marke'.[105] Between 1450 and 1600, the government passed seven Acts and ten Proclamations to control 'excessive apparel'.[106] In the second place, their presence may have induced a significant transfer of wealth from the provinces to the Capital via apprenticeship premiums.[107] Lastly, return migration of apprentices to their place of origin helped diffuse skills and values of the metropolis to the provinces. Each year, more than 700 apprentices left London and headed for hamlets, villages, and towns throughout England, bringing valuable skills learned in the capital to the local economies.[108]

Servants formed a bigger social group than apprentices. It is estimated that by the 1690s there were some 120 000 servants in the capital, comprising one fifth of the total population.[109] The capital drew great numbers of both because of the presence of the Court, a high concentration of aristocratic, gentry, and middle-class households, as well as the attraction of the city companies. According to burial records, servants and apprentices made up a third to a half of the labour force in some parishes in London.[110] Their presence is regarded as conducive to industrial expansion because of emulative spending. Being close to the spending habits and lifestyle of the upper and middle classes, it is also believed that some servants may have imitated the spending habits of their social superiors, and therefore spurred demand of the lower classes.[111] Domestic service was the largest single source of employment for women, especially in the seventeenth century, and some historians believe that women possessed a higher propensity to consume.[112] This theory has been severely criticized by historians such as Ben Fine, because of its erroneous assumption that servants had the money and access to the market for desired consumer goods, and that social emulation in itself begat emulative spending.[113] According to Fine, servants were not paid in cash, but more commonly by goods in kind. Their exclusion from wage labour, he further explained, 'must have had an inhibiting effect on the development of both large-scale demand and mass markets'. In addition, their absorption into households held down demand for consumer goods depending on the growth of individual households as well as on cash wages. Limited evidence suggests that some apprentices (rather than servants) had the means to emulate their superiors and each other. In 1582, for example, the city of London had to issue an order forbidding apprentices from wearing any clothes of their 'owne nor [their] friends', but only those given by their masters.[114] In later articles, however, McKendrick, the prominent proponent of the demand approach, emphasized the key role played by the domestic servant as a carrier rather than an active consumer of fashion – transmitting changes in taste both from the upper classes to the working classes, and from London to the provinces.[115]

The presence of servants and apprentices gave London's population a distinctive youthfulness: roughly 40 per cent were below age 15.[116] The proportion under 15 may have been even higher, as in 1569, when a survey was undertaken to establish the number of men fit for military service in London, it was found that in a total population of 80 000 people, there were just over 18 000 men, or nearly 23 per cent, aged between 16 and 60.[117] There was also an extraordinary number of young males in the capital's population, perhaps as high as 70 per cent of the total population.[118] Although these provided a cheap source of labour, Beier has expressed doubts whether they would make good workers as they were new, young, less skilled, and probably less disciplined than adult workers.[119] As the young tend to be more experimental in tastes, however, they may have been more receptive to new products, and their openness may have been crucial for the success of germinating industries.[120] In sixteenth-century London, the high presence of men may have spurred the growth of the drink trade. Visiting London in the 1590s, the German Thomas Platter declared: 'I have never seen more taverns and alehouses in my whole life than in London.' In 1657, 924 alehouses were licensed in the city of London proper; within Westminster alone, there were 551 alehouses in 1631. By the 1730s, London, Middlesex and Surrey possessed a total of 6000 alehouses.[121]

Immigrants came from all over England, and what was remarkable was the distance they travelled. In an age when travel and communications over even ten miles could be slow and difficult, Rappaport found that as many as two-thirds of London's immigrant apprentices originated from towns at least eighty miles from the capital.[122] Indeed, in the early 1550s, most apprentices travelled an average of 115 miles to London to learn their crafts and trades, clearly signalling the importance of London as the centre of vocational training in England.[123] Apprentice immigrants, however, represented only a small minority, and it is uncertain where the others came from. It is possible that many also came from far afield. In fact, for the period before 1640, it has been suggested that those driven to towns by poverty tended to end up further from home than those going in a deliberate attempt to better themselves.[124] Evidence from the Bridewell records shows that this was true in the sixteenth and early seventeenth centuries, with many immigrants who ended up as vagrants in London originating from East Anglia, Yorkshire, the counties between London and Bristol, and from 1600, Ireland. However, the proportion of vagrants from the London area and the south-east increased significantly from 1600, suggesting the decline of long-distance migration after this date.[125]

The Consumers of London

The unique social structure of London, together with the wealth and higher incomes of its citizens, were responsible for shaping the distinctive consumption patterns in the capital. The presence of the royal household, based for the most part of the year at Whitehall or St James from the reign of Henry VIII, provided a powerful stimulus to luxury industries in London. The large size of the royal household meant that it possessed an enormous spending power of its own. In the 1630s, it numbered 2500 persons or more, including the private servants of the more senior officials. The total figure was likely to have been higher, as many of these had their own families. Indeed, the royal household may have been as large as a major provincial town, if the numerous would-be courtiers, petitioners and hangers-on, who were attracted by their presence, are also counted.[126] The Crown certainly was a big spender on luxuries. At the coronation of King James in 1603, Sir Baptist Hicks, a London mercer, supplied £5000 worth of silks and other stuffs. Between Michaelmas 1608 and 17 August 1609, he was paid £14 083 for 'wares etc.' sold to the Crown. On 16 June 1604, a warrant was issued to pay two jewellers £6423 for supplying pearls to the King.[127]

Besides its own spending power, the royal household also played a significant part in drawing to London the provincial gentry, aristocracy and their wealth. They came for various purposes: 'for a career, for business, for pleasure, most likely for all three'.[128] Some came to attend Parliament, and every session brought the entire peerage and more than 500 members of the gentry with their servants up from the country for weeks or months on end.[129] The extraordinary growth in litigation in the central courts brought the gentry to London on business, pushing up the demand for grain by 13 per cent during the legal terms as early as the 1570s.[130] Others came to escape the monotony of country life and the tedium of winter, to enjoy the social facilities in the capital, to find a marriage partner for a son or daughter, or even to keep better company with, 'men of more civilitie, wisdome and worth then your rude Country gentlemen or rusticall neighboures'.[131] From the 1580s, their visits became more frequent and for longer periods: many spent as long as nine months a year in the capital.[132]

The gentry and aristocracy concentrated particularly in the West End. Between 1591 and 1610, St Dunstan's in the west had 110 gentlemen and 15 knights and esquires buried there – the latter groups included many leading legal figures.[133] The main reason for the great numbers of gentlemen in this parish was the presence of two Inns of Court – Clifford's and Lincoln's.[134] The Inns provided an important centre of legal training, as many gentry, realizing the advantages of legal knowledge in a litigious age, sent their eldest son to receive training. By the 1610s, total attendance at any one time may have approached a thousand.[135] The influx of the elites contributed to the more permanent social polarization of London between East and West Ends.[136]

The presence of gentry and aristocracy provided a boost to conspicuous consumption in the capital. In the 1590s, individual courtiers were spending up to £1000 per annum on clothes.[137] As the visits by gentry and aristocracy to London were long and frequent, many also began to invest in property in the capital, contributing to a boom in demand for fashionable town houses. By the 1630s, as many as a hundred peers and several hundreds of the gentry owed or leased London houses, and if the number of landowners who stayed in temporary accommodation in inns and lodgings is included, the seasonal influx must have run into many hundreds of families, comprising several thousand individuals if wives, children and their servants are also included.[138] The influx of these social elites and the concurrent transfer of incomes derived from estates in the provinces bore important consequences for employment in London, reinforcing its role as a centre of production, consumption and emulation. As John Stow observed: 'with so many of England's gentlemen and their families for a good portion of the year out of the country and living in London, it is no wonder that retailers and artificers ... do leave the country towns where there is no vent and do fly to London where they are sure to find ready and quick market'.[139]

Besides the Court, the gentry, aristocracy and the professionals (lawyers and doctors), London also housed a significant number of merchants. It is difficult to establish their absolute number, but a subsidy in the 1590s provides some indication of their numerical significance. It listed some 486 London merchants as prosperous.[140] The total number is likely to be much greater. Using the burial data which show that merchants accounted for 11 per cent of London's adult male occupations during 1601–40, Nigel Goose has recently calculated that there were more than 5000 merchants in London in the early seventeenth century.[141] Many of these merchants made their fortunes from domestic rather than overseas trade – less than half of London's Jacobean aldermen were overseas merchants. Not only were London's merchants more numerous, but the fortunes of the richest London merchants dwarfed those in the provinces. Nearly two-fifths of those elected as aldermen in the first quarter of the seventeenth century were worth over £20 000, and the wealth of a few like Sir John Spencer, Sir William Craven and Sir Baptist Hicks was in six figures. In the provinces, on the other hand, fortunes of as much as £10 000 were extremely rare at any time before 1700.[142] As Archer has pointed out, London offered the most 'startling juxtapositions of wealth and poverty'.[143]

Social and Economic Conditions in London 1560–1600

Economic conditions in London, as in other parts of England, became less favourable for the poorer classes from the second half of the sixteenth century. Rapid population growth, combined with declining employment opportunities, rising inflation and falling wages, contributed to increasing social problems and poverty in the capital. Standards of living also declined throughout the sixteenth century, as inflation rose and real wages fell (Table 2.2).[144]

Prices had been steadily increasing since the beginning of the sixteenth century. Population growth is the key long-term explanation, but there are also other short-term factors. The first major price rise occurred in the 1550s, as a result of the enormous costs of war against France and Scotland during the 1540s, debasements, inflow of silver from abroad, and the increase in spending power resulting from the sale of monastic lands. The second dramatic rise occurred in the late 1580s and persisted into the 1590s. The enormous costs of warfare and bad weather also contributed to the severity of inflation in this period.[145]

Real wages also plummeted throughout the sixteenth century. In 1550, real wages fell to a low level, and again in 1590. However, they reached their lowest point in 1597. All in all, the 1590s were a difficult decade for Londoners and for the English people, characterized by high prices, failed harvests from 1594 to 1597, food shortages, increasing poverty and vagrancy, and war commitments in Ireland and against Spain.[146]

By increasing the pool of labour, enormous demographic expansion in London may have enforced the downward spiral of wages. Cheapness of labour in turn is believed to be a major barrier to change.[147] The vehement

Table 2.2 Prices and wages in London, 1500–1600

Year	Composite price series	Real wages
1500	94	107
1510	101	99
1520	122	82
1530	126	79
1540	116	87
1550	194	68
1560	235	75
1570	204	91
1580	234	85
1590	295	68
1595	332	65
1597	388	59
1600	334	69

Notes: The values above represent index values. The base period 1457–71 = 100.
Source: S. Rappaport, *Worlds Within Worlds: Structures of Life in Sixteenth-century London* (Cambridge, 1989), Chapter 5 and Appendix 3.

protest against the arrival of the labour-saving Dutch loom in the early seventeenth century seems to bear this out. As incomes fell as a result of declining wages, demand for industrial goods in London was also likely to fall. Yet some historians believe that falling wages could have had an opposite, beneficial, effect as labourers, driven by material desire for possession of an ever-widening range of goods, were willing to work harder and longer to maintain a certain level of consumption producing, in Jan de Vries' words, an 'industrious revolution'.[148] Joan Thirsk, on the other hand, cautioned against using wage rates of men as indicators of total earnings of families, as falling wages of men may have been offset by earnings of wives and children, and therefore a period of plummeting wages did not necessarily mean dwindling incomes and shrinking consumer demand.[149] Furthermore, there were also gainers. The landed gentry and merchants, for example, profited from the rising inflation of the sixteenth century, and their increased income may have spurred conspicuous consumption.[150]

Conclusion

The market for consumer goods in London in the sixteenth century, oiled by its prodigious population growth and rising income, was immense. London's interaction with northern European cities exerted a profound impact on its material culture and tastes. Londoners lusted after Italian luxury cloths and glasswares and Portuguese spices, and furnished their households with German metal wares and goods produced in the Low Countries. Their ability to pay enough to satisfy their insatiable appetite for foreign imports diminished, however, as the onset of the troubles in the Low Countries greatly affected the trade upon which their principal source of income was derived. Under these circumstances, concerted efforts were made to import foreign skills to develop the embryonic native consumer industries.

Notes

1. G. Ramsay, 'The Antwerp mart', in idem, *English Overseas Trade during the Centuries of Emergence* (London, 1957), p. 10.
2. Ibid., p. 2.
3. J. Chartres, 'Food consumption and internal trade', in A.L. Beier and R. Finlay, eds, *London 1500–1700: The Making of the Metropolis* (London, 1986) pp. 176–84.
4. A term used to describe the functions of Amsterdam: see W.D. Smith, 'The Function of Commercial Centers in the Modernization of European Capitalism: Amsterdam as an Information Exchange in the Seventeenth Century', *Journal of Economic History*, 1984, Vol. 44, No. 4, pp. 985–1005.
5. J. Styles, 'Product Innovation in Early Modern London', *Past and Present*, 2000, No. 168, p. 128.
6. N. McKendrick, J. Brewer and J.H. Plumb, *The Birth of a Consumer Society: The Commercialisation of Eighteenth-century England* (London, 1982), p. 21.
7. 'The Low Countries' is a convenient term used to describe the politically diverse, low-lying areas stretching from the river Somme in the south-west to the Zuider Zee in the north-east.
8. H. van der Wee, *The Low Countries in the Early Modern World* (Aldershot, 1993), p. 9.
9. V. Harding, 'Cross-Channel Trade and Cultural Contacts: London and the Low Countries in the Later Fourteenth Century', in C. Barron and N. Saul, eds, *England and the Low Countries in the Late Middle Age* (Stroud, 1995), p. 153.
10. Barron, 'Introduction', in Barron and Saul, eds, *England and the Low Countries*, p. 20; Harding, 'Cross-Channel Trade and Cultural Contacts', pp. 164–5.
11. W. Brulez, 'Bruges and Antwerp in the 15th and 16th Centuries: An Antithesis?', *Acta Historiae Neerlandicae*, 1973, Vol. 6, p. 3.
12. F.J. Fisher, 'Commercial Trends and Policy in Sixteenth-century England', in P.J. Corfield and N. Harte, eds, *London and the English Economy* (London, 1990), p. 83.
13. G.D. Ramsay, 'London, a satellite city', in idem, *The City of London in International Politics at the Accession of Elizabeth Tudor* (Manchester, 1975), p. 45.
14. L. Stone, 'Elizabethan Overseas Trade', *Economic History Review*, 2nd Series, 1949, Vol. 2, No. 1, p. 37.
15. Ramsay, 'London, a satellite city', p. 39.
16. Stone, 'Elizabethan Overseas Trade', pp. 40–41, 42; B. Dietz, 'Antwerp and London:

The Structure and Balance of Trade in the 1560s', in E.W. Ives and J. Knecht, eds, *Wealth and Power in Tudor England: Essays Presented to S.T. Bindoff* (London, 1978), p. 190.
17 Fisher, 'Commercial Trends and Policy', p. 83.
18 Dietz, 'Antwerp and London', p. 197.
19 Stone, 'Elizabethan Overseas Trade', p. 43.
20 E. Aerts and J.H. Munro, eds, *Textiles of the Low Countries in European Economic History: Proceedings of the Tenth International Economic History Congress, Leuven, August 1990* (Leuven University Press, 1990), p. 5; prices for these fabrics are printed in the contribution in this volume by A.K.L. Thijs, 'Les textiles au marche Anversois au XVIe siècle', pp. 76–86.
21 C.G.A. Clay, *Economic Expansion and Social Change: England 1500–1700*, Vol.1, (Cambridge, 1984), p. 197.
22 G. Asaert, 'Antwerp ships in English harbours in the fifteenth century', *The Low Countries History Yearbook*, 1979, Vol. XII, p. 33.
23 Clay, *Economic Expansion and Social Change*, Vol. 2 (Cambridge, 1984), p. 111.
24 Ramsay, 'London, a satellite city', p. 37, pp. 40–41.
25 Ibid.
26 P. Ramsey, 'Thomas Gresham a Sixteenth-century English entrepreneur?', in P. Klep and E. van Cauwenberghe, eds, *Entrepreneurship and the Transformation of the Economy (10th–20th Centuries): Essays in Honour of Herman van der Wee* (Leuven University Press, 1994), p. 488; see also Ramsay, 'London, a satellite city', for a discussion of links between political power and trade, pp. 33–80.
27 Bruges was dominated by Hanseatic, Italian and Catalan merchants: see Brulez, 'Bruges and Antwerp in the 15th and 16th Centuries', p. 13.
28 Ramsey, 'Thomas Gresham: A sixteenth-century English entrepreneur?', p. 488.
29 Ramsay, 'The Antwerp mart', pp. 17–18.
30 Ramsay, 'Antwerp: The metropolis at its zenith', in idem, *The City of London in International Politics*, p. 24.
31 Ramsay, 'The Antwerp mart', p. 18.
32 D.Keene, 'Material London in Time and Space', in L.C. Orlin, ed., *Material London, ca.1600* (Philadelphia, PA, 2000), p. 65.
33 A.K.L. Thijs, 'Structural changes in the Antwerp industry from the fifteenth to eighteenth century', in H. van der Wee, ed., *The Rise and Decline of Urban Industries in Italy and in the Low Countries* (Leuven University Press, 1988), p. 207; Keene, 'Material London', p. 63; M. Limberger, '"No town in the world provides more advantages": Economies of agglomeration and the golden age of Antwerp,' in P. O'Brien et al., ed., *Urban Achievement in Early Modern Europe: Golden Ages in Antwerp, Amsterdam and London* (Cambridge, 2001), p. 53.
34 G.D. Ramsay, 'Antwerp: The metropolis at its zenith', in idem, *The City of London in International Politics at the Accession of Elizabeth Tudor* (Manchester, 1975), p. 22.
35 Brulez, 'Bruges and Antwerp', pp. 9–10.
36 Limberger, '"No Town in the world provides more advantages"', p. 50.
37 R.H. Tawney and E. Power, eds, *Tudor Economic Documents* (1924), Vol. 3, p. 134.
38 Brulez, 'Bruges and Antwerp', p. 3; H. van der Wee, 'Structural changes in European long-distance trade, and particularly in the re-export trade from south to north, 1350–1750', in J.D. Tracy, ed., *The Rise of Merchant Empires: Long-distance Trade in the Early Modern World, 1350–1750* (Cambridge, 1990), p. 28.
39 F. Sherry, *Pacific Passions: The European Struggle for Power in the Great Ocean in the Age of Exploration* (New York, 1994), p. 15; J. Cummins, *Francis Drake* (London, 1995), p. 119.
40 J. Thirsk, *Economic Policy and Projects: The Development of a Consumer Society in Early Modern England* (Oxford, 1978), pp. 182–3.

41 Ramsay, 'Antwerp: The metropolis at its zenith', pp. 8–9.
42 Ibid., p. 9.
43 Van der Wee, 'Structural changes in European long-distance trade', p. 31.
44 P. Subacchi, 'Italians in Antwerp in the Second Half of the Sixteenth Century', in *Minorities in Western European Cities: Sixteenth–twentieth Centuries*, ed. H. Soly and A.K.L. Thijs (Brussels, 1995), p. 78.
45 Ibid., pp. 74, 78.
46 Keene, 'Material London', p. 65.
47 Van der Wee, 'Structural changes in European long-distance trade', p. 14.
48 Ibid., p. 24.
49 Ibid., pp. 24–5; for a discussion of the manufacture of fustians in England, see D. Mitchell and M. Sonday, 'Printed Fustians: 1490–1600', *CIETA Bulletin*, 2000, Vol. 77, pp. 99–117.
50 Subacchi, 'Italians in Antwerp', p. 83.
51 For a discussion of industries introduced, see Keene, 'Material London', pp. 66–7.
52 Ibid., p. 65.
53 Quoted in ibid., p. 64; Keene, 'Growth, Modernisation and Control: The Transformation of London's Landscape, *c*.1500–*c*.1760', in *Two Capitals: London and Dublin 1500–1840*, *Proceedings of the British Academy*, 2001, Vol. 107, p. 27.
54 Keene, 'Material London', p. 67.
55 Quoted in E. Lipson, *The Economic History of England: The Age of Mercantilism*, Vol. 3 (London, 1934), p. 56.
56 Keene, 'Growth, Modernisation and Control', p. 27.
57 R. Finlay, *Population and Metropolis: The Demography of London, 1580–1650* (Cambridge, 1981); R. Finlay and B. Shearer, 'Population growth and suburban expansion', in Beier and Finlay, eds, *London 1500–1700: The Making of the Metropolis*, pp. 37–59; V. Harding, 'The Population of London, 1550–1700: A review of the published evidence', *London Journal*, 1990, Vol. 15, No. 2, pp. 111–28.
58 See Harding, 'The Population of London 1550–1700', for a discussion of definitions of London.
59 Finlay and Shearer, 'Population growth and suburban expansion', p. 49.
60 Harding, 'The Population of London', p. 123.
61 Keene, 'Growth, Modernisation and Control', pp. 7–8.
62 J. Boulton, 'London 1540–1700', in P. Clark, ed., *The Cambridge Urban History of Britain, Volume 2: 1540–1840* (Cambridge, 2000), p. 324.
63 Fisher, 'The Development of the London Food Market, 1540–1640', in *London and the English Economy*, p. 66.
64 Ibid., pp. 65–6.
65 Beier, 'Engine of manufacture', p. 152.
66 Ibid., p. 151.
67 W.H. Te Brake, 'Air Pollution and Fuel Crises in Preindustrial London, 1250–1650', *Technology and Culture*, 1975, Vol. 16, pp. 357–8.
68 J. Hatcher, *The History of the British Coal Industry before 1700: Towards the Age of Coal*, Vol. 1 (Oxford, 1993), p. 41.
69 Keene, 'Growth, Modernisation and Control', p. 28.
70 This was carried out sometimes after weaving, sometimes after dyeing.
71 H. van der Wee, 'Structural changes and Specialization in the Industry of the Southern Netherlands', *Economic History Review*, 1975, Vol. 28, p. 204.
72 Beier, 'Engine of manufacture', p. 147; Boulton, 'London, 1540–1700', p. 326.
73 Beier, 'Engine of manufacture', pp. 147, 157.
74 L. Gowing, *Domestic Dangers: Women, Words, and Sex in Early Modern London* (Oxford, 1996), p. 21, quoting Finlay, *Population and Metropolis*, pp. 168–72.
75 See Gowing, *Domestic Dangers*, pp. 20–21.

76 A. Games, 'Clearinghouse and Countinghouse: London and Overseas Expansion', in *Migration and the Origins of the English Atlantic World* (Harvard University Press, 2001), p. 16.
77 I have only selected a few towns and cities which had a stranger population and/or which later rose to prominence for comparative purposes.
78 Clay, *Economic Expansion*, Vol. 1, p. 197.
79 J. Bolton, *The Alien Communities of London in the Fifteenth Century: The Subsidy Rolls of 1440 & 1483–4* (Stamford, 1998), p. 28.
80 Keene, 'Material London', p. 57.
81 Finlay, 'Population growth and suburban expansion', in idem, *London, 1500–1700*, p. 46; E.A. Wrigley, 'A simple model of London's importance in changing English society and economy, 1650–1750', in *People, Cities and Wealth: The Transformation of Traditional Society* (Oxford, 1987), p. 138.
82 H.W. Richardson, *The Economies of Urban Size* (Farnborough, 1973), pp. 39–42.
83 Morris-Suzuki, *Technological Transformation of Japan*, p. 33.
84 J. Brewer and R. Porter, eds, *Consumption and the World of Goods* (London, 1994), p. 5.
85 O'Brien, 'Reflections and mediations in Antwerp, Amsterdam and London in their golden ages', p. 19.
86 Ibid.
87 Boulton, 'London, 1540–1700', pp. 315–16
88 A.L. Beier, 'Social problems in Elizabethan London', *Journal of Interdisciplinary History*, 1978, Vol. 9, p. 205.
89 P. Spufford, 'Population Mobility in Pre-industrial England', *Geneologists' Magazine*, 1973, Vol. 17, p. 476.
90 Beier, 'Introduction: The significance of the metropolis', p. 9.
91 Ibid., pp. 9–10.
92 I.D. Whyte, *Migration and Society in Britain, 1550–1830* (Basingstoke, 2000), p. 71; J. Wareing, 'Migration to London and transatlantic emigration of indentured servants, 1683–1775', *Journal of Historical Geography*, 1981, Vol. 7, pp. 356–78.
93 Beier, 'Social problems in Elizabethan London', pp. 204, 209.
94 Quoted in Archer, 'Material Londoners?', in Orlin, ed, *Material London c.1600*, p. 183.
95 Games, 'Clearinghouse and countinghouse', p. 17.
96 P.J. Corfield, 'Urban Development in England and Wales in the Sixteenth and Seventeenth Centuries', in D.C. Coleman and A.H. John, eds, *Trade, Government and Economy in Pre-industrial England: Essays Presented to F.J. Fisher* (London, 1976), p. 214.
97 P. Benedict, 'French cities from the sixteenth century to the Revolution: An overview', in idem, ed., *Cities and Social Change in Early Modern France* (London, 1992), p. 16.
98 S. Rappaport, *Worlds Within Worlds: Structures of Life in Sixteenth-century London* (Cambridge, 1991), p. 83.
99 P. Clark and D. Souden, eds, *Migration and Society in Early Modern England* (London, 1987), p. 30.
100 Archer, 'Material Londoners?' p. 176.
101 Ibid., p. 184; Beier, 'Engine of manufacture', p. 158.
102 Archer, 'Material Londoners?' p. 184.
103 Ibid., p. 185.
104 P. Stubbes, *The Anatomie of Abuses* (1583), p. 10.
105 BL, Lansdowne MS 94/37.
106 J. Thirsk, 'The Fantastical Folly of Fashion: The English Stocking Knitting Industry, 1500–1700', in N. Harte and K.G. Ponting, eds, *Textile History and Economic History: Essays in Honour of Miss Julia de Lacy Mann* (Manchester, 1973), p. 51; for a discussion on the problems of enforcement, see F.E. Baldwin, *Sumptuary Legislation and Personal Regulation in England* (John Hopkins University Studies Series 44, No. 1, 1926); W. Hooper, 'The Tudor Sumptuary Laws', *English Historical Review*, 1915, Vol. 30, pp. 433–49.

107 Archer, 'Material Londoners?', p. 176; Boulton, 'London 1540–1700', p. 344.
108 Rappaport, *Worlds Within Worlds*, p. 314.
109 Beier, 'Social problems in Elizabethan London', p. 215.
110 Ibid., pp. 214–15.
111 H.J. Perkin, 'The social causes of the British Industrial Revolution', *Transactions of the Royal Historical Society*, 5th series, 1968, Vol. 18, p. 140; McKendrick et al., *The Birth of a Consumer Society*, pp. 21–2.
112 See Archer, 'Material Londoners?', p. 185; M. Finn, 'Women, consumption and coverture in England, c. 1760–1860', *Historical Journal*, 1996, Vol. 39, No. 3, pp. 703–22; M. Hilton, 'The female consumer and the politics of consumption in twentieth-century Britain', *Historical Journal*, 2002, Vol. 45, No. 1, pp. 103–4 for elaboration of the close relationship between women and consumption.
113 B. Fine and E. Leopold, 'Consumerism and the Industrial Revolution', *Social History*, 1990, Vol. 15, No. 2, pp. 166, 168.
114 CLRO, JOR 21, f.206v 21 May 1582.
115 Fine and Leopold, 'Consumerism and the Industrial Revolution', p. 169.
116 Beier, 'Social problems in Elizabethan London', p. 213.
117 Ramsay, 'London, satellite city', p. 33.
118 Beier, 'Social problems in Elizabethan London', p. 209.
119 Ibid., pp. 213–14.
120 O'Brien, 'Reflections and mediations', p. 35.
121 P. Clark, *The English Alehouse: A Social History, 1200–1830* (London, 1983), pp. 49, 44.
122 Rappaport, *Worlds Within Worlds*, p. 80.
123 Ibid., pp. 76–81.
124 Clay, *Economic Expansion and Social Change*, Vol. 1, p. 211.
125 Beier, 'Social problems in Elizabethan London', p. 206.
126 Clay, *Economic Expansion and Social Change*, Vol. 1, p. 203.
127 R.G. Lang, 'London's Aldermen in Business: 1600–1625', *Guildhall Miscellany*, 1971, Vol. 3, pp. 247, 254.
128 Quoted in M.G. Davies, 'Country Gentry and Payments to London, 1650–1714', *Economic History Review*, 1971, Vol. 24, p. 15.
129 Clay, *Economic Expansion and Social Change*, Vol. 1, p. 204.
130 Archer, 'Material Londoners?', p. 176; Clay, *Economic Expansion and Social Change*, Vol. 1, p. 203.
131 Ibid., p. 205; Archer, 'Material Londoners?', p. 177.
132 Rappaport, *Worlds Within Worlds*, p. 84.
133 Beier, 'Engines of manufacture', p. 155.
134 Ibid.
135 Clay, *Economic Expansion and Social Change*, Vol. 1, p. 204.
136 R.M. Smuts, 'The Court and its Neighborhood: Royal Policy and Urban Growth in the Early Stuart West End', *Journal of British Studies*, 1991, Vol. 30, No. 2, pp. 117–49, for discussions of attempts to curb expansion in West End.
137 Archer, 'Material Londoners?', p. 177.
138 Clay, *Economic Expansion and Social Change*, p. 205.
139 Rappaport, *Worlds Within Worlds*, p. 84.
140 R. Grassby, 'The Personal Wealth of the Business Community in Seventeenth-century England', *Economic History Review*, 1970, Vol. 23, p. 226.
141 Goose, 'Immigrants and English Economic Development in the Sixteenth and Early Seventeenth Centuries', pp. 136–160.
142 Clay, *Economic Expansion and Social Change*, Vol. 1, p. 201.
143 Archer, 'Material Londoners?', p. 182.
144 See also Y.S. Brenner, 'The Inflation of Prices in Early Sixteenth Century England', *Economic History Review*, 1961, Vol. 14, pp. 225–39; 'The Inflation of Prices in

England, 1551–1650', *Economic History Review*, 1962, Vol. 15, pp. 266–84; J. Thirsk, ed., *The Agrarian History of England and Wales, 1500–1640*, Vol. 4 (Cambridge, 1967), pp. 815–65; D. Woodward, 'Wage rates and living standards in pre-industrial England', *Past and Present*, 1981, Vol. 91, pp. 28–45.
145 See Rappaport, *Worlds Within Worlds*, especially Chapter 5.
146 See P. Clark, 'A Crisis Contained? The Condition of English Towns in the 1590s', in idem, ed., *The European Crisis of the 1590s: Essays in Comparative History* (London, 1985), pp. 44–66.
147 Morris-Suzuki, *Technological Transformation of Japan*, p. 44.
148 J. de Vries, 'Between purchasing power and the world of goods: Understanding the household economy in early modern Europe', in Brewer and Porter, eds, *Consumption and the World of Goods*, pp. 85–132.
149 Thirsk, *Economic Policy and Projects*, p. 173.
150 F.C. Lane, 'The Role of Governments in Economic Growth in Early Modern Times', *Journal of Economic History*, 1975, Vol. 35, p. 14.

Chapter 3

Government and the Import of Foreign Skills

The government's promotion of industrial development in England by encouraging skilled Continental artisans to settle there can be traced back at least to 1331, when Edward III issued his famous letters of protection to Flemish weavers, encouraging them to come and develop the cloth industry in England. What is harder to establish is the degree of involvement and the extent of its success, as there is little detailed research. But this very lack of evidence in itself may point to limited and haphazard intervention. The government's involvement during the sixteenth century is better known, thanks to Joan Thirsk's excellent study on *Economic Policy and Projects*. Still the best survey on the subject, Thirsk argued that the government's sustained efforts to set up new industries began around 1540, partly in response to the influence of humanism sweeping through Europe, and partly due to the desperate need to find alternative supplies to foreign imports. As a result, 14 projects were launched between 1540 and 1580, including iron founding, woad growing, oil production, madder growing, dyeing, canvas, fustians, and the making of small metalwares.[1] According to Thirsk, Elizabeth I's reign made the greatest contribution to industrial development, with a series of projects launched, in comparison with only one or two launched during Henry VIII's reign, three or four in Edward VI's reign, and none in Mary's reign.[2] Arguably, this more expansive involvement was made possible by her long reign but more particularly by the shift to the use of monopolistic patents, rather than letters of protection or financial grants and subsidies, as the principal means of industrial promotion. *Economic Policy and Projects* is excellent in charting the origins and success of projects, but we hear very little about the processes and procedures used to set them up. Although many of these projects relied on immigrants' skills, little attention has been paid to crucial questions such as how they were recruited, what problems were involved, or their precise contribution. The aim of this chapter is to offer an overview of government-initiated projects and a tentative evaluation of their success.

Projects Prior to Elizabeth I's Reign

Cloth Manufacture

The cloth industry formed the cornerstone of industrial development in the early modern period. As discussed in Chapter 2, in the fourteenth century England was a major exporter of wool to the Low Countries, and the Flemish cloth industry became reliant on English wool because it was both cheaper than native wool and of better quality.[3] Flemish cloth was then imported into England for consumption. Englishmen, in other words, were wearing Flemish cloth woven from their very own wool. In the long run, such a situation clearly could not be sustained. In the fourteenth century there was an acute awareness among English kings of the need to foster a cloth industry in order to reduce imports of foreign cloths and generate employment for the population. Edward III took action to promote the development of the cloth industry by encouraging Flemish weavers and allied workers to come and manufacture cloth in England. Secret emissaries were apparently sent to Flanders to tell Flemings of English prosperity in contrast to the wretched conditions there, of how their skills would be greatly welcomed in England, how they would live 'on fat beef and mutton', and how they could make a good living with their own labours.[4] At the same time, Edward III also issued letters of protection, taking the workers into his personal care. In 1331, for example, he granted letters of protection to John Kempe of Flanders. The letter reads:

> The king to all his bailiffs … to whom … greeting. Know you that since John Kempe of Flanders, weaver of woollen cloths, will come to stay within our realm of England to exercise his mystery here, and to instruct and teach those wishing to learn therein, and will bring with him certain men, servants and apprentices of that mystery, we have taken John and his aforesaid men, servants and apprentices, and their goods and chattels into our special protection and defence.[5]

In the next few years, two additional measures were taken: in August 1336, an embargo was laid on the export of English wool to Flanders; and in the following spring, letters of protection were offered in general terms to all foreign cloth workers wishing to settle in England.[6] Edward III thus pursued a policy of 'carrot and stick', which seemed to work, thanks to the poor conditions in Flanders.

In contrast to the relative stability and prosperity of England in the fourteenth century, Flanders was afflicted with a multitude of problems, including floods, endemic political strife, warfare, high taxation, hunger, violence and plague. Many Flemings were probably quite glad to leave their home town to come to England in search of a better life.[7] Moreover, the move would confer the additional advantage of a secure supply of wool necessary for the practice of their craft. English wools were regarded as the finest in Europe, and thought to be absolutely essential for producing the best luxury woollens for which there were no substitutes.[8] Not only was their livelihood affected by Edward III's periodic wool embargoes on Flanders, rising taxation also made English wool excessively expensive, putting their livelihoods at risk. John Munro calculated that between 1336 and the 1370s, the subsidy on wool export (first imposed in 1336) rose from 20 shillings to 50 shillings per sack, and by the 1390s, duties on wool represented almost 50 per cent of wholesale wool export price.[9] By moving to England, Flemish clothworkers enjoyed both a cheaper (25–35 per cent saving in costs) and a more secure supply of English wool.[10]

While it is unclear how many came as a result of this royal encouragement, there are reasons to believe that the number was quite substantial. The Flemish cloth towns were devastated by fifty years of strife with France, and many Flemish weavers accepted the King's offer. After the Flemish defeat at Cassel in 1328, 500 weavers and 500 fullers of Ypres were banished from Flanders, and in 1344, certain weavers of Poperinghe were condemned to exile in England.[11] By 1362, for example, the numbers of alien weavers in London had grown sufficiently great to prompt them to petition the Mayor and Aldermen of the City to grant them the powers to appoint three alien weavers to regulate the craft and activities of new arrivals.[12] What is also clear is that the royal favour perceived to be enjoyed by the Flemings provoked much jealousy among natives. During the Peasants' Revolt in 1381, some thirty or forty Flemings (who had taken refuge in the church of St Martin Vintry in London) were murdered.[13] The number of Flemish immigrants may have been lower in the following century as improved conditions reduced the need to emigrate. In 1484, there were in total only 30 alien weavers and their wives and servants recorded working in London.[14] Nevertheless, the English cloth industry, judging from exports, had made important headway. Cloth exports grew from 2500 – 3000 cloths per annum in the last years of Edward III (1327–1377) to 10–15,000 in the early years of Henry IV (1399–1413).[15] How much of this was due to the Flemish clothworkers remains to be investigated. According to Nigel Goose, the importance of foreign immigrants, notably John Kemp, to the establishment of cloth production from the fourteenth century has been exaggerated. He believes that the expansion of the industry in England at this time owed more to the low price of wool and availability of labour than it did to foreign innovation.[16] Nevertheless, what is clear is that the indigenous cloth industry was given a stimulus by a combination of favourable circumstances and by Edward III's policy.

Silk-weaving

The Crown's involvement in the promotion of silk-weaving to reduce expensive imports was less successful. This involvement may have started during the reign of Edward IV, when in 1461 we find him granting a house in Westminster to an Italian named George Domico. In return for this privilege, Domico promised to weave damasks, velvets, cloths of gold and silver, and to teach Englishmen the skills. However, Italian merchants apparently tried to prevent him from teaching his art in England, as they saw this as a threat to their own lucrative business.[17]

In the early sixteenth century, the Crown was involved in two proposals to encourage Italian silk-weavers to come to England. The first was made in 1537, when the Italian merchant Antony Guidotti sought to bring over Italian weavers to Southampton. In his letter to Cromwell, he wrote that during his visit to Messina, he saw how silk-weaving had made the city rich in the past fifteen years, and how the introduction of such a craft could bring jobs to declining port towns like Southampton. He spoke to several master silk-weavers in Messina, and persuaded a Florentine weaver to come to Southampton by making him a 'large offer'. He agreed to come over with 24 other workers on a ship. Guidotti stressed that the process of bringing over skilled workers involved great risks to his own life and great expenses, but he emphasized that 'if you encourage me, let me alone with the rest', implying that he wanted some advanced funds for the project. In addition, he wished to secure a monopoly of the trade for at least fifteen years.[18] It is unclear whether the workers actually left Messina. Millard claimed that 24 Sicilians did go to Southampton, and that Guidotti later proposed to bring a further six or seven of the 'cunningest' weavers from Florence. She further stated that he proposed to obtain all the raw silk needed from Antwerp, but apparently he spent the money given by the King for this purpose on Gascon wines, and nothing more was heard of the venture.[19] This raises the question of what happened to the Sicilian silk-weavers when the project failed in Southampton: did they move to London?

In 1559, a more detailed proposal to bring over Italian silk workers to London was sent to William Cecil, and this contained three separate documents: a brief proposal by Springham and Lok outlining their aims and objectives, a detailed breakdown of the costs involved, and Cecil's modification of the proposal – reflecting the sophistication of business plans at this date. In their proposal, Springham and Lok agreed to make all the necessary arrangements to set up the industry in London. In return, they wanted a monopoly of the trade during their lifetime, exemption from customs and duties, and the Queen's protection of their interests as merchants.[20]

Government and the Import of Foreign Skills 57

In a separate, detailed document, Springham and Lok outlined how the workers were to be brought over to England, and made some estimates of the costs involved (see Table 3.1). It appears that they had an agent in Italy, whom they referred to as a 'stranger', to make the necessary arrangements. The 'stranger' stated that he planned to bring over with him two chief weavers, one spinner, one dyer and one carpenter to set up the craft and to stay in England for five years. In other words, there was an awareness that a successful transfer required the migration of a group of workers with related skills, as well as a sufficient length of time for industrial know-how to germinate in foreign soil. He wanted someone to accompany him to Geneva and Venice to make arrangements with the workers. The English Crown was expected to provide all the necessary equipment, furniture and accommodation. It was estimated that the total cost would be 2000 crowns. In addition, a further 2000 crowns

Table 3.1   A breakdown of expenses in silk manufacture

Types of expenses	*Estimated costs (in crowns)*
1 Payment to the 'stranger' for making arrangements	100
2 Bringing over the relevant workers	
• 2 weavers	80
• 1 dyer	20
• 1 spinner	12
• 1 carpenter	12
3 Equipment and furniture – wheels, looms, vats	
4 Wages	260
• dyer	
• spinner	60 per year
• the 'stranger' and the men under him	40 per year
5 Raw silk	To be agreed
Summary	
Provision and furniture	2 000
Raw silk	2 000
Total	4 000

Sources: PRO SP12/8/33.

was requested for the purchase of raw silks (from Calabria and Sicily in Italy and Valencia in Spain) from time to time. In total, the project would cost at least 4000 crowns, or £1000.[21] Considering that in 1559 imported silk fabrics cost more than £32 000, this seemed a small price to pay.

Cecil endorsed the plan with a few modifications. First, instead of having a church after the Geneva model, Italian weavers were allowed a church 'according to the form of the Church of England'.[22] Second, they could have part of Bridewell and part of Winchester rents on the bank. Third, they could enjoy exemption from customs for seven years, instead of twenty. Fourth, they could have monopoly of the trade for ten years, instead of twenty. Fifth, they were given the freedom to buy and sell silks in London, but not other goods. In return for these privileges, it was required that some English people should be involved in the manufacturing process.[23]

There is no evidence to indicate that this plan was ever implemented. The success of all these plans depended largely on the agent to make the arrangements, and ultimately on the willingness of the workers to uproot and move to a foreign country. The fact that it did not materialize illustrates the great difficulty in persuading people to move, despite any financial incentives. It appears that the Italian weavers were unwilling to uproot themselves, deterred probably by linguistic, climatic and cultural differences, as well as the perceived unfriendliness of the English. The stories of the events of Evil May Day in 1517, when some 2000 London apprentices attacked Italian merchants, who were thought to enjoy excessive royal privileges, must have filtered back home to Italy, helping to forge a negative image of England. In addition, Bratchel argued that Italians would find it difficult to settle in the Anglo-Saxon environment of London, which was less cosmopolitan than Antwerp, to where many did emigrate. With the onset of the Reformation in England in the 1530s growing religious differences may have discouraged Catholic Italians even more from migrating.[24] Heavy punitive measures imposed by Italian states on prospective emigrants might also have acted as a significant deterrent.[25] Not only did they face the possible punishment of the death penalty on emigration, but the threat also effectively meant the complete cutting of ties with their homeland, for emigrants could never return. This was probably sufficient in itself to deter many from even contemplating the idea of emigration.

Besides difficulties of recruitment, a second problem with these proposals was their high and unrealistic expectations. Instead of focusing on developing a low-grade product for which there was a large local market, efforts concentrated on the manufacture of high-quality and expensive silk goods for the upper end of the market, intended to replace imports. Here planners may have overlooked the premium placed on 'brands', for surely aristocratic customers would not place the same kind of value on goods 'made in England' compared to those 'made in Italy'. The silk industry was eventually established in London, but in a manner very different from that initially envisaged.

Proposal to Set Up Dyeing and Finishing in London, 1553

In the mid-sixteenth century, when cloth exports to Antwerp peaked, William Cholmeley, a Londoner, petitioned Edward VI to support the setting up of a dyeing[26] and finishing industry in the city by taking two measures. The first was to confer on the industry formal recognition by appointing searchers to ensure that all cloths be 'truly and perfectly dyed' following the techniques of Antwerp. The second was to ban the sale of all foreign dressed cloths in London, to encourage a domestic industry. This could further be promoted by recruiting three or four workmen from Flanders (who would be glad to work for 20 marks [£5] or £20 at the most each) to teach Englishmen.[27] Cholmeley, in fact, had already set up a dyehouse in Southwark three years earlier in partnership with another Englishman, as he was not able to 'furnish a dye house with all things thereto belonging'. He employed an Antwerp dyer who was willing to work in England and had agreed to stay for the term of ten years. He claimed to make 100 marks a year in dressing kerseys, broadcloths and caps. In the pamphlet, he outlined clearly the reasons why he undertook such an enterprise. England annually exported some 150 000 cloths undyed and undressed. Such an export was wasteful because the dressing of these cloths in Flanders, Holland, Brabant, Zeeland, Eastland and Germany provided considerable employment there – 200 000 people earned their living from these. Clothworkers and dyers earned 20 shillings per cloth, so that the total annual income earned by the workers amounted to £150 000. In other words, other countries prospered and enriched themselves at the expense of England.

Yet in his enterprise, Cholmeley deplored that he faced considerable resistance from dyers, drapers and merchants. They raised seven objections, including the argument that Englishmen were not as good as the French and Flemish at dyeing, the Thames water was not as suitable as the water of the Scheldt or the Elbe for dyeing, that dyeing and finishing the cloths here rather than at Antwerp would lead to a decline in shipping, and that there was no woad necessary for dyeing. In his pamphlet, Cholmeley denounced such 'a foul slander upon the famous river of Thames', and asserted that with the technical help of an Antwerp dyer, he had dyed cloths as good as those on the Continent. However, a more insurmountable problem, as Cholmeley himself had recognized, was the general preference of customers for goods made overseas: 'no man,' Cholmeley stated, 'will meddle with any colours of cloth … unless it bear the name of French or Flanders dye; so that partly by that so many as be able to buy a cloth dyed in Flanders or France will not meddle with any cloth that is dyed within this realm'.[28] This necessitated him to request the King's intervention to ban the sale of foreign goods, thus forcing customers to buy cloths dyed at home.

Cholmeley's proposal was met with fierce resistance from the powerful Merchant Adventurers' Company which monopolized cloth export to the Low Countries. The question of whether cloths should be dyed and finished here or abroad also illustrates the wider conflict between the clothworkers and the Merchant Adventurers. In 1565, the complaints of the London clothworkers were brought before the Privy Council, and leading Merchant Adventurers were summoned to explain why they did not have more cloths finished in England. They contended that home finishing reduced the value of cloth at Antwerp because of lower native skills. Subsequently, the clothworkers were asked to prove their skills in a practical trial, and the result seemed to vindicate the Merchant Adventurers' claim.[29] But there were other reasons why the Merchant Adventurers preferred to ship unfinished cloth over the Channel. As Michael Limberger has explained, in this way the risks of loss or damage by seawater during shipping were considerably reduced. Furthermore, the location of the finishing industry in Antwerp, instead of England, made it possible for clients from Germany and central Europe to choose the colour and design of the final product, and even the artisan of their choice. At the same time, it gave the merchants the opportunity to control the process of finishing and dyeing, and the quality of the unfinished cloth, facilitating replacement on complaint.[30] Moreover, as Antwerp was also a big inter-regional market for dyeing materials, it made perfect sense to locate the dyeing industry there, to reduce the costs of importing these raw materials.[31] In 1566, a compromise was reached when the government passed legislation requiring the export of one dressed cloth to every nine exported undressed, to promote 'the better employment and relief of great multitudes of the Queen's Majesty subjects'.[32]

By 1600, there are signs that London was beginning to develop high-quality dyeing and finishing skills. In September 1606, for example, fustian dressers complained to the City about Stephen Smith, a Fishmonger, for 'inciting of men's apprentices to go beyond the seas, there to instruct and teach their trades, whereby sundry freemen are greatly prejudiced in their trades'. In June 1607, James Jacob, merchant tailor, was also found guilty of enticing 'sundry Fustiandyers and fustiandressers apprentices from their masters, and been a means that they have gone into France, to use those trades there to the damage of their masters and hurt of the commonwealth'.[33]

The detailed examination of these three examples is intended to elucidate the processes of procuring the necessary skills to set up domestic industries, as well as the obstacles involved. These obstacles included the existence of vested interests, the unyielding attitudes of customers, as well as the problems of recruiting workers. To some extent, the government could ameliorate the effects of the first two through its intervention, but with regard to workers' recruitment, it appears that non-economic factors were more forceful in encouraging workers to emigrate to England. The case of Flemish weavers demonstrates that, then as now, it was peace and stability that drew many Continental migrants, fleeing warfare and political conflict, to England.

Projects Launched During Elizabeth I's reign

Although some initiatives had already been undertaken prior to 1558, under Elizabeth I, as Joan Thirsk has emphasized, projects were launched on a new and much more expansive scale.[34] An analysis of the available import and export statistics for the beginning of the reign, extant for 1559 and 1565, makes it easier to understand why the government saw industrial development as an economic crusade. England was dangerously reliant on the export of a single product to sustain its livelihood. In 1565, besides cloths which accrued an income of £550 000, the only other notable but small items of export were corn (worth £14 600) and fish (worth £2300). And this was a good year! In a bad year, both fish and corn had to be imported. In 1559–60, for example, London alone imported £15 500 worth of corn and £15 400 worth of fish.[35] England was also heavily dependent on two Catholic powers, France and Spain, to supply her import needs. Given the tense political climate, there were real fears of embargoes, as well as resentment that England was enriching her enemies. While the Spanish products were more than paid for by exports, what infuriated Cecil was that French commodities (wine, salt, linen, canvas) had to be bought principally with bullion due to the heavy adverse balance of trade. In 1559, Cecil put the deficit at £100 000, and added bitterly: 'No country robbeth England so much as France.'[36] Fear of a potential political conflict created a sense of urgency in Cecil, who felt it was the duty of the state to remedy this situation, so that England could achieve economic independence and autarky, reverse the adverse trade balance and promote employment for the poor. This involved not only the pruning of imports, particularly those 'superfluities' such as playing cards, tennis balls and children's dolls, but also the domestic manufacture of goods previously imported from abroad, the largest items being fustians, worsteds (made from English wool), linen and canvas, and iron.[37] In 1562, an import prohibition was also introduced, forbidding the sale of a catalogue of metalware items, including girdles, knives, daggers, pins, gloves, points, and lockets.[38] But what was urgently needed was positive action.

The promotion of industrial development in Elizabeth's reign owed much to Cecil. He served as Secretary of State under Edward VI between 1550 and

3.1 A street seller
Source: Guildhall Library

1553, and for the first fourteen years of Elizabeth's reign. In 1572, he became Lord Treasurer.[39] Although Cecil's role as a statesman has received much attention from historians, his influence as an economic planner is less well known. On this issue, historians have mixed views. On the one hand, orthodox historians such as William Cunningham have maintained that Cecil had a 'carefully thought out and deliberate policy', portraying him as a meticulous planner, with an omnipotent hand in the economy.[40] Recent approaches, however, tend to be more critical. Michael Graves, in his recent biography of Cecil, concluded that 'in so far as the national economy was concerned Burghley had neither a master plan, a coherent theory, nor a grand co-ordinated strategy'. His economic management consisted largely of 'adhoc responses' to changing economic circumstances and limited resources, and Burghley was not an 'economist but, in sixteenth century terms, a patriot-politician'.[41] In terms of Cecil's priorities, Graves argued that economic development was subordinated to other considerations, such as the Crown's sustained financial viability, internal peace and stability and national defence, and it was these non-economic concerns which were the driving force behind Cecil's economic nationalism, seeking less dependence on imports by reviving old industries and developing new ones.[42] Lionel Williams reached a similar conclusion regarding Elizabethan economic policy, stating that Elizabethan:

> economic actions – often half-hearted, and compounded of a hotch-potch of inherited practices, paternalistic habits, and responses to the loudest and most persistent of various competing interests, pressure from the Commons, or immediate crises – display both consistency and its opposite. Economic considerations were surbordinate to the priorities of political survival amid dangers from within and without. Thus the only 'economic policy' safely attributable to the Elizabethan government is the pursuit of those priorities.[43]

Whatever its motives, there were some consistent strands in Elizabethan 'economic policy'. One was continued reliance on foreign expertise in industrial development. But the breed of foreign artisan working during Elizabeth's reign was quite different from their predecessors. As Williams has clearly explained, they fell into two broad categories. The first comprised those who usually came in response to a specific invitation to develop industries other than textiles by the grant of a monopolistic patent. The second category comprised those who came as a consequence of religious persecution, political upheaval and economic dislocation in their homelands. Their reception and treatment was determined by the character and causes of their migration, their number, and their skills in the manufacture of the new draperies.[44] The discussion here will focus first on the former group, leaving the second category to the next section.

Under the direction of Cecil, then, there was a change in the government's involvement in industrial development. Instead of undertaking direct risks by providing the necessary financial resources, the government began to rely on patents and monopolies to encourage aliens and native English entrepreneurs to take initiatives and shoulder the main responsibilities and risks involved. The patent system was a Continental practice. Patents were first issued in Berne as early as 1467 for the manufacture of paper, in Venice in 1469 for printing, and again in Venice in 1507 for the making of mirrors.[45] Patents were not used in England until 1552, however, when they were issued for glassmaking, and in 1554 to search for and work metals. After the 1560s, Cecil adopted this system wholeheartedly, and patents of monopoly 'flowed thick and fast'.[46] In seeking solutions to problems, Cecil often looked abroad for models and for guidance. He apparently had some special investigators in his employment, with foreign connections and perhaps of foreign birth, who regularly supplied him with ideas and information on economic projects in progress at home and abroad.[47] Cecil himself also had important personal overseas connections. Most significant was his personal link with the head of the expatriate community in Antwerp, John Fitzwilliam, who supplied him with confidential reports and information. He even ordered Cecil a copy of Guicciardini's *Description of the Netherlands*, first published in Italian in 1567,[48] suggesting, perhaps, the eagerness with which Cecil looked to the Netherlands as a model of development.

The aims of the patent system were several. It was generally designed to secure the benefits of inventions for the country. It was also intended to encourage the flow of superior Continental technology to England, and to reward the inventors for their labour and expense in order to encourage others, by giving them exclusive monopolies for between six and twenty years.[49] Rewards and protection against infringement were necessary because, as Daniel Höchstetter in his petition for the privilege of establishing water works clearly stated, 'skill and knowledge had not been procured or obtained without great charges, costs and travailes both to [patentee] and his friends'. If no rewards were given, Höchstetter argued that he would 'rather keep the means and skill in himself, till better time will serve, or else that he may find such consideration of the matter in some other place as may both maintain his credit and answer the charges and travels'.[50]

It is estimated that 200 patents were granted in the reigns of Elizabeth I and James I, but only 55 were granted between 1561 and 1603 (see Table 3.2).[51] Many of the early patents were granted to aliens, but after the 1580s, the patentees were largely native English. Why did the number of patents granted to aliens decline after the 1570s? A fundamental shift in the way in which patents were granted may have been a factor. As Joan Thirsk has shown, by the 1580s, some of the patentees were no longer inventors or skilled craftsmen, but rather courtiers, merchants and speculators who planned to

Table 3.2 Patents granted 1561–1603

Period	Alien grants	Native grants	Grants for regulating trade	Totals
1561–1570	15	8	0	23
1571–1580	4	7	1	12
1581–1590	2	11	1	14
1591–1600	0	4	2	6
1601–1603	0	0	0	0
Total	21	30	4	55

Sources: E.W. Hulme, 'The history of the patent system under the prerogative and at Common Law: A Sequel', *Law Quarterly Review*, 1900, Vol. 16, p. 52.

hire the services of such craftsmen while they carried the main financial risk.[52] The entrance of the well-to-do, she argued, greatly affected the diffusion of inventions, as these exploited the privileges much more vigorously. As previous patentees were men of limited resources, their knowledge spread easily because many of the jobs were labour-intensive, and once their servants had learned the skills, they could set up on their own. However, with the entrance of rich men, all was changed, since they could afford to hire agents and informers to suppress competitors. Although they were an 'irritant', Thirsk felt that the entrance of wealthy patentees did not have a pernicious effect on flourishing new industries.[53]

For What Kinds of Inventions were Aliens Granted Patents?

Table 3.3 lists the types of manufacture for which aliens received patents from the Crown between 1561 and 1589. Some were granted to promote the production of luxury consumer goods (white soap, window glass, drinking glasses and white paper), some to increase the supply of raw materials (alum and copperas, mining, madder, oil), and others to solve certain pressing problems (new ovens and furnaces to mitigate fuel shortage, and engines to raise water). This list is strikingly familiar, as many of the items already appeared in lists of foreign imports that were deplored, or in lists of skills that were positively desired.[54] The terms of the patents varied greatly between seven and twenty-one years, and it is unclear what factors determined the length of the patent. But, as Coleman has aptly pointed out, many of these patented

Table 3.3 Types of Patents granted to aliens 1560–1590

Date	Patents	Names	Terms (years)
1561	White soap	Stephen Groyett and Anthony Le Leuryer	10
1563	Making ovens and furnaces	George Gylpin and Peter Stoughberken	10
1563	Engines for draining waters	Burchsard Cranick	20
1564	Make alum and copperas	Cornelius de Vos	21
1564, 1565	Mining	Daniel Houghsetter and Thomas Thurland	Not indicated
1565	Spanish leather	Roger Heuxtenbury and Bartholomew Verberick	Not known
1565	White salt	Francis Berty	Not known
1567	Cut iron, save fuel and extract oil	Peter Anthony van Ghemen	21
1567	Window glass	Anthony Becku and John Carré	21
1568	Dyeing and dressing of cloth in the Flemish manner	Peter de la Croce	7
1565	Manufacture of machines for grinding	James Acontius	20
1568	Collecting madder and dyeing skins with it	Peter Backe	21
1569	Mining	Daniel Houghsetter (German)	21
1574	Method of sparing fuel	Jeremy Nenner and George Zolcher	7
1574	Sailcloths	John Collins	21
1574	Drinking glasses	James Verselyn	21
1578	Engines for raising water	Peter Morris (Dutch)	21
1586	Working oil out of woollen cloth	Francis Dal Arne (alien) and Robert Clarke	21
1589	Making white-paper from rags	John Spilman	10

Sources: J. Thirsk, *Economic Policy and Projects: The Development of a Consumer Society in Early Modern England* (Oxford, 1978), pp. 56–7; E.W. Hulme, 'The history of the patent system under the prerogative and at Common Law', *Law Quarterly Review*, 1896, Vol. 12, pp. 141–54; E.W. Hulme, 'The History of the patent system under the prerogative and at Common Law: A sequel', *Law Quarterly Review*, 1900, Vol. 16, pp. 44–56.

industries (alum, paper and glass) were not vital to the English economy. The most important economic activities of the time were concerned with the provision of food, clothing and shelter, yet they received the fewest patents.[55] The informal, spontaneous adaptation of new skills and innovations in these areas, perhaps by other types of migrants, made formal patents dispensable.

What Were the Conditions of a Patent?

The principle behind the adoption of the patent system during the reign of Elizabeth was to encourage inventions. There were two possible ways in which aliens acquired a patent: either by applying for a grant prior to arrival, or applying for one once in England. In 1563, for example, William Cecil wrote to Gaspar Seelar, a German, stating that he had obtained for him the Queen's licence to manufacture common salt in England, and advising him to come over directly.[56] It appears that Seelar wrote to Cecil and asked him to secure a patent on his behalf. Before granting patents, the Crown may have taken every necessary step to ensure that the alleged inventions were new and that their introduction would not affect existing trades. According to Cunningham, Cecil was extremely careful in granting patents, often taking much trouble to discover the merits of new inventions.[57] In 1567, for example, a group of French glassmakers petitioned the Crown for a twenty-one-year patent to produce Normandy window glass. The government consulted the Chiddingford glassmakers, enquiring whether they had made, or could make, that type of glass. Only when they replied they could not was a patent granted. The French glassmakers also had to agree to teach Englishmen their art.[58]

Teaching native workers the relevant skills was, in fact, a fundamental condition for granting patents, for this was the only way to ensure the continuation of the craft after the patent expired or the immigrants had left. In the first patent given to Henry Smyth in the reign of Edward VI, it was stated that it should also be 'a benefit to our subjects. And besides divers of them may be set on work and get their living and in time learn and be able to make the said glass themselves and so from time to time then to instruct others in that science and feat.'[59] Sometimes the patent mentioned the specified number of Englishmen that the patentee had to employ. The patent to Roger Heuxtenbury and Bartholomew Verberick for Spanish leather in April 1565, for example, insisted on the employment and instruction of one English apprentice for every foreigner employed.[60]

The patent also contained conditions regarding price and quality. It was occasionally required that the commodity made by the patentee should be subject to a periodical examination by some designated authority.[61] The patent issued to Roger Heuxtenbury and Bartholomew Verberick in 1565 required that the Spanish leather they made should be subject to inspection by the Wardens of the Company of the Leather Sellers to ensure that the skins were 'being well and sufficiently wrought'.[62] If the quality were found to be bad, the penalty was likely to be the revocation of the grant. A number of patents also stipulated that the commodities produced by the patentees should be of good quality and cheaper in price than imports. The patent to Gilpin and Stoughberken in 1563 for ovens and furnaces stated that their grant would be void if they were to 'prove extortionate in their charges'.[63]

What Were the Problems Involved in Using Patents to Attract Skilled Workers?

As a method of securing new inventions, the patent system presented its own problems. In cases where the patent was granted to aliens who were still overseas, there was the common problem of delays. Many took a long time to come after the issue of the patent, citing problems such as matrimonial restraints and the invasion of their homes by lodgers.[64] In his letter of April 1566, Daniel Höchstetter explained how his departure was delayed because 'our wives are very unwilling that we should depart from hence, for that our houses here are full of strangers' as a result of some festival in the town. He also stated that there was no rush for his departure to England because the houses and buildings required were not yet ready.[65] In July 1565, a patent was granted to Francis Berty for salt making. In April (presumably of 1566), writing from Bergen-op-Zoom (Barro), he explained how the ship carrying pans and other equipment for salt making had been suffering from adverse wind, and he was not certain whether it would arrive in England by the first of May. He requested the Crown not to cancel the grant owing to a short delay in coming to England to start the operations.[66] There is little evidence to suggest that Berty ever arrived, as the patent was subsequently surrendered to the Earl of Pembroke and others.[67] Due to these problems, Elizabethan patents normally contained a clause imposing a time limit. The patentee was expected to introduce his invention within a specified period, and delays could lead to annulment of the grant.[68] In a patent to George Gilpin and Peter Stoughberken to make ovens and furnaces, it was stated that the grant would be void in the case of patentees who failed to come over and put the grant into practice within two months.[69]

The second problem related to the disclosure of trade secrets. Some aliens were suspected of being very secretive and of wishing to keep their methods from being known to Englishmen.[70] In 1566, Thomas Thurland told Cecil that aliens were keeping secret the fact that there was gold and silver in the mines in Keswick.[71] This may have prompted the Crown to force prospective patentees to reveal manufacturing secrets in writing prior to the grant of patents, as illustrated by the patent for making saltpetre in 1561. Saltpetre was not made in England prior to this date, but imported via Antwerp. The Queen therefore bargained with Gerard Honricke, a German captain, to come over and teach her subjects 'the true and perfect art of making saltpetre as good as that made "beyond the seas"'. However, it was stipulated that the secrets of manufacture should be put in writing before the promised reward of £300 be paid. But when Honricke arrived in England, the Queen had already given the patent to two London tradesmen.[72]

The case of mining operations in Keswick also illustrates a host of other problems, ranging from the difficulties of teamwork, isolation and native hostility to problems of cultural adjustment. The desire to exploit mineral resources in England dated from the reign of Henry VIII, perhaps due to the influence of the importation of silver from the New World, which may have encouraged Europeans to search for precious metals nearer to home. At the beginning of the sixteenth century, France and especially Germany possessed advanced skills in engineering and chemical science. In 1528, Henry VIII appointed Joachim Höchstetter of Augsburg, a town famous for its mining technology, as principal surveyor and master of all mines in England and Ireland. He proposed to bring over six Germans to start work with 1000 Englishmen, and advised the building of a foundry at Combe-Martin under the supervision of another German.[73] It appears that little was achieved at the time. Later, his son, Daniel, succeeded him, and managed royal mines in England jointly with Thomas Thurland.[74] In May 1566, Thurland informed Cecil that gold and silver were found at Keswick, which according to him, was kept secret by the strangers.[75] Operations were ordered to begin immediately at Keswick and elsewhere in Cumberland. The government gave all the necessary assistance and support, as Höchstetter wrote: 'it is joyful news to us to understand that Master Secretary has shown himself so friendly and forward in this our work of our Minerall. And that his money has been so ready.' But he stressed that in the exploitation of mines there must be 'no want of money'.[76] From the beginning, however, the works at Keswick ran into difficulties, as there were few basic facilities for the German workers. Diet, for example, was an issue. German workers were used to drinking wine at mealtimes, but this was not available locally. Wine had to be brought, presumably to Keswick, from London, and was expensive. In July 1566, therefore, a licence was issued to Thomas Thurland and Daniel Höchstetter to open a tavern and sell wine near the mines.[77] In June 1568, Höchstetter informed Cecil that 'a preacher in their own language is much wanted amongst the workmen',[78] illustrating both the failure to attend to the spiritual needs of the workers as well as the presence of linguistic barriers experienced by German workers which prevented them from attending the local parish church. In any case, Cecil refused their request for a German-speaking pastor in 1568, and told them instead to attend their parish churches, presumably to discourage them from keeping to themselves and to encourage them to assimilate into the local community.[79]

More serious was the hostility towards the 400–500 German workers at Keswick. The existence of such a sizeable colony of foreign workers, in a remote and isolated area with no tradition of foreign immigration, was bound to provoke native attention and jealousy. In his letter to Johan Louver in October 1566, Daniel Höchstetter reported how one of his men, Leonarde Stoultz, was beaten up and later murdered by twenty Englishmen, while another key worker was beaten up by fifty English men. He also reported the problems involved in punishing the culprits. According to him, the Bishop of Carlyle wanted to execute the ringleaders, but this could not be implemented due to the intervention of Lady Ratcliffe. As a result the culprits could not be punished.[80] The actions of one of the managers, Thomas Thurland, did not help the situation. According to Daniel, Thurland did not act with firmness, believing that 'gentleness and friendliness' would do more good. Consequently, he failed to deter the workers from committing further troubles and as a result lost respect among the Germans.[81]

Höchstetter also recorded problems of working with English workers. Much money had been wasted because necessary things had not been finished on time, and he considered that the English workers were lazy.[82] In addition, he also experienced problems with his own German workforce. Some of them were not in 'good order' and obedient, and he planned to punish them according to the laws of his country. If that failed, he intended to send them back to Germany, but he stressed that he wished to avoid taking this measure, as they were too few in number already.[83]

Planting of Foreign Immigrant Communities in Provincial Towns

The other pillar of Cecil's economic policy was to maximize the opportunities presented by the mass immigration from the Low Countries by planting colonies in various provincial towns to promote their economic development. Provincial port towns such as Southampton and Sandwich suffered decline because of the increasing concentration of overseas trade in London, while changes in the textile industry spelt economic difficulties for the clothmaking towns of East Anglia.[84] It was hoped that the planting of foreign immigrant communities in these areas would help revive their flagging economies, through the diversification of their existing textile production (East Anglia) and introduction of industry to areas with an insignificant manufacturing base (Southampton, Sandwich).

The idea of provincial settlement was not new, and had already been the subject of experimentation during the reign of Edward VI. Apparently, Valérand Poullain, a pastor from Strasbourg who arrived in England with a considerable proportion of his Walloon congregation, first put forward the idea to the Duke of Somerset in 1548. The Duke of Somerset at the time was seeking ways to develop his ex-monastic estate at Glastonbury. The initial plan was to use a group of immigrants to establish hop-planting there, but this soon gave way to a clothmaking project.[85] It is not entirely clear whether the Glastonbury settlers were 'Flemish' or 'Walloons', but their number was quite sizeable; 46 households numbering a total of 230 people settled there, weaving worsteds and says, and dyeing them. After the Duke of Somerset's fall from power, the costs of maintaining these settlers fell on the Privy Council. In 1551, as the first families moved in, £500 was spent on equipment and on the conversion of the monastic brewhouse and bakehouse into dyehouses. However, when Mary came to power, these settlers left Glastonbury and moved to Frankfurt.[86] Although cut short by political changes, the Glastonbury project demonstrated the feasibility of planting colonies of foreign workers, and such experiments must have exerted a powerful influence on Somerset's Secretary, William Cecil.

Some fifteen settlements were established in provincial towns between 1561 and 1576, but only six of these were of substantial size. These were Sandwich (1561), Norwich (1565), Colchester (1565), Southampton (1567), Maidstone (1567) and Canterbury (1575).[87] How did these settlements establish, and how successful were they in achieving the objectives underpinning their foundation? The first of these official provincial settlements that established in Sandwich was in response to fears of overcrowding in London. A small number of Flemish emigrant families had already settled there, and in May 1561 they petitioned for official recognition of their community. The Sandwich Town Council then approached the Privy Council about the request, and there followed negotiations between these and the Dutch Church regarding the number and the types of artisans to move there. On 6 July 1561, two months after the request, Elizabeth I signed the letter patent, allowing 20–25 households, or 200–300 people, to settle there.[88] The patent cost the town £50, but £20 was contributed by the settlers.[89] Many recruits for Sandwich came from London: between 1561 and 1566 some 150 persons moved there from the capital.[90] To qualify for this resettlement, migrants had to possess the requisite skills demanded by the town of Sandwich, namely in the manufacture of baize, say and other cloths new to England. The selection process was carried out by ministers of the Dutch Church in London, and one of them, Peter Delenus, also made a brief trip to Sandwich to assist in the setting up of a church for the community in September.[91]

Why did they leave London for Sandwich? Available accommodation was probably one factor. In contrast to the overcrowding and relatively expensive accommodation in London (Stow reported that strangers living on waterfront wards were willing to pay £20 for a house previously let for 4 marks in 1560s),[92] it was rumoured in the capital that 200 homes were available for the foreign community in Sandwich.[93] Political reasons also motivated some to opt for Sandwich. Backhouse has shown that at least 32 of the 150 people who moved to Sandwich were Calvinist militants, and geographical proximity to Flanders was important because it meant they could cross the English Channel to fight the Spanish there when necessary.[94] Continued immigration from the Continent led to the rapid expansion of the Sandwich community, from some 406 persons (still well above the initial limit) in 1561 to some 2400 people by 1574, constituting a staggering 53 per cent of the total population.[95] Despite the resettlement of some Sandwich strangers in Colchester[96] and Norwich, and the expulsion of others, the continued influx into Sandwich exerted enormous strains on local resources, leading inevitably to grievances and tensions. And it was precisely this overwhelming size of the foreign immigrant community in Sandwich that led to its rapid collapse. Burghley's Sandwich experiment failed only 'after eight years of settlement, as a small minority of the natives turned against them, accusing them of taking away their livelihood. For a quarter of a century the Strangers played a vital role in the temporary revival of the economy of Sandwich, but in the 1580s the baize-making industry was in decay'.[97] Many Sandwich aliens headed to the Dutch Republic. Leiden with its thriving textile industry inevitably attracted the biggest number, where 281 families settled between 1576 and 1625, and a handful in other towns.[98] In 1582, there were only 1100 aliens left in Sandwich, falling further to 600 by 1585.[99]

The Norwich 'plantation', granted by the government in 1565 partly to alleviate pressures on Sandwich, achieved greater economic success. The whole process began when the Norwich authorities approached the Duke of Norfolk for assistance in establishing an alien community to arrest the 'decay' of the town precipitated by the decline of its worsted manufacture. It hoped to revive the economy by introducing the manufacture of 'Flanders commodities made of wool', and for this purpose requested to have thirty master workmen with up to ten servants each, or up to 300 people, to introduce the skills.[100] As the Duke already had contacts with a leading figure in the Dutch Church, Jan Utenhove, the process moved speedily, and in November 1565 Norwich obtained its letters patent at the Duke of Norfolk's expense.[101] Most newcomers to Norwich came from Sandwich, with the London churches assisting in the resettlement of 30 households.[102] As in Sandwich, the Norwich immigrant population soon expanded beyond its original quota. By 1582, there were more than 4600 immigrants (Dutch and

Walloons) in the city, forming a third of the whole population.[103] Their presence too attracted agitation, but the immigrants' contribution to the marked expansion of the New Draperies helped reduce tensions. Textile production after 1565 experienced rapid expansion: between 1567 and 1586 the number of cloths produced by aliens rose from 1200 to 38 700, a 3225 per cent increase in twenty years.[104] Renowned worldwide, the Norwich 'stuffs' were characterized by several distinct features. The first concerned their extraordinary variety. Before 1565, textile production focused on six products (worsteds, russels, lace, dornicks, linen and carded woollens), but by 1611 the Walloons were manufacturing 40 different types of cloths (including bays, says, ollyet, damasks, valures, carrells, grograins, and fustians) in Norwich.[105] The second distinguishing feature was the wide use of linen, silk and cotton, which increased choice as a greater variety could be made and gave the product an exotic quality. But another equally important feature of Norwich stuffs was their affordability. Cloths made by Norwich aliens were cheaper than those previously manufactured. The success of the New Draperies in Norwich lay precisely in the ability to provide a variety of cloths at different prices, 'cheap enough for the broad base of the population to buy, while other cloths were more upmarket, and could appeal to the more affluent of society'.[106] In concluding, Martin argued that the alien contribution was twofold: 'without the alien influence, the new draperies in Norwich would not have been so varied. Yet, the Norwich aliens brought not only their new cloths, but the good name associated with the quality of their products.'[107] However, the output of cloths by aliens declined from the 1580s as a result of a plummeting alien population. By 1624, there were fewer than 1000 Dutch and aliens in Norwich, dropping further to 678 by 1634.[108]

Like Norwich, the community in Colchester was established to achieve two aims: to revive the local textile industry, and to alleviate pressure on Sandwich. Late in 1561, Colchester approached the Privy Council for permission for the taking in of Dutch refugees. However, the Dutch settlers did not arrive until 1565, via Sandwich, numbering 55 people in 11 households. Their numbers grew slowly at first, producing an alien community of 185 by 1571, of whom 177 were Dutch.[109] The community gradually expanded, and by 1586 there were 1291 Dutch settlers present in the town, forming 20 per cent of the local population. Despite movements back and forth to the Continent, the Colchester community remained resilient, and by the early seventeenth century it had overtaken Norwich. In the mid-seventeenth century, the total Dutch population in Colchester was around 1500, making up 20 per cent of the town's population.[110]

The earliest settlers in Colchester followed a variety of trades. In the beginning, cordwainers were almost as numerous as clothworkers, and a handful of hop-planters were also included among their number. But from the

1570s, the number of cloth producers grew rapidly, mainly Flemish rather than Walloon, many of them originating in the bay-making centres of Flanders. As Nigel Goose has pointed out, the key Dutch contribution to Colchester was their introduction of lighter, cheaper cloths such as bays and says, known collectively as the 'new draperies', which appealed to a wider market. Rising on the back of the new draperies, the Colchester cloth industry experienced a remarkable revival. Until the early seventeenth century, the textile industry accounted for as much as 37 per cent of the occupied male population of the town, with baymaking as the leading occupation. Production continued to grow in the seventeenth century, reaching a peak in the 1680s. Overseas trade also expanded considerably as a result of the growing volume of new drapery exports to the Low Countries.[111]

The Southampton experiment was on the whole also successful, but its origins differed from the previous colonies. The economy of Southampton relied largely upon overseas trade, but this was in decline. Despite several attempts to establish textile production in the city in the late fifteenth and early sixteenth centuries, the city had not managed to develop a substantial manufacturing base.[112] However, alien communities of French and Italians had brought prosperity to the city in earlier periods, and it was against this background that the city hoped to revive a foreign community there. There is no evidence to suggest that Southampton directly petitioned for permission to establish a foreign community. In fact, the letter patent was probably granted as a result of refugees' initiatives. On 16 May 1567, refugees from the Low Countries sent a letter to Cecil and petitioned the Queen for permission to settle in England. The Queen directed these refugees to Southampton, presumably in response to its informal enquiries about establishing an alien community there. Two months after the request, a patent was granted, allowing 40 households, with up to 12 persons per household, or a total of 480 persons, to settle in Southampton. Thus the community in Southampton was potentially larger than that allowed in Sandwich and Norwich.[113] Unlike Sandwich and Norwich, however, Southampton never managed to fill its quota. In 1584, only 186 communicants were counted, and by 1596 there were only 296 aliens in the city.[114] Southampton's relative geographical remoteness from the Low Countries as well as re-migration by those who initially settled there to London provided two possible reasons why the community remained small. Besides the group of refugees who came direct from the Low Countries, some of the first settlers in Southampton came from London but soon returned to the capital after a short time, probably less than a year.[115] The smallness of the Southampton community, however, resulted in greater cohesion. The refugees were largely French-speaking, with a prominent group from Valenciennes who had established familial and business ties amongst themselves and with others from Tournai and Antwerp before moving to Southampton.[116] The refugees' principal economic contribution to Southampton concerned the production of the New Draperies and overseas trade. In 1573–4, Southampton exported 334 pieces of say and 140 bay. Although insignificant in comparison to Norwich, the manufacture of the new draperies, according to Spicer, did 'make a significant contribution to the town's economic life and overseas trade'.[117] The immigrant population in Southampton rapidly declined after 1604, as a result of assimilation, the devastating effects of plague epidemic, and the return of some exiles to the Continent. By 1635, the community had only some thirty-six members.[118]

Of the sixteenth-century planted communities, the Canterbury community, established in 1575, was probably most resilient, surviving into the eighteenth century. Its longer life span was in part due to the immigration of the Huguenots in the seventeenth century and in part to its success in developing a silk industry. Although the Mayor, Aldermen and Commonalty of Canterbury agreed to accept a group of strangers to settle in their city as early as 1567, there occurred long delays for reasons unknown, and it was not until 1575 that a major settlement of strangers began. This was the result of determined efforts made by Cobham, Lord Warden of the Cinque Ports, to reduce the number of immigrants at Sandwich.[119] Continued immigration, largely of French-speaking Walloons into Sandwich, led not only to the doubling of the immigrant population there, but also generated 'ethnic' tensions between the newly arrived Walloons and the more settled Dutch, with the Walloons forming a separate congregation. Another problem was piracy against Spanish ships, which caused diplomatic difficulties.[120] It was against this background that Cobham suggested to the Crown that the Walloons should move from Sandwich to Canterbury, where there were already 18 French refugees from Winchelsea, and to give them permission to manufacture new drapery.[121] Although Canterbury agreed to take 100 families, the number of settlers again exceeded the limit: in 1582 there were 1679, in 1591 2760, and in 1593 3013.[122] Thus the Canterbury alien population grew steadily in size during the 1580s and 1590s, during periods when some other communities experienced rapid decline. Its secret probably lay in its developing silk industry, providing employment for its residents as well as acting as a magnet for newcomers. Initially, the aliens in Canterbury also concentrated on the manufacture of the new draperies, making 'Florence serges, Orleans serges, Bays, Mauntes', but this gave way to silk-weaving by the 1590s, laying the foundations of an important industry after 1675.[123] It appears that Canterbury aliens were following in the footsteps of those in London, who from the 1570s had focused on silk-weaving. As many Canterbury aliens originated from the same French-speaking parts of the Low Countries as their London counterparts, predominantly from Armentieres,

Cambrai, Lille, Tournai, Valenciennes, and to a lesser extent French Flanders, Artois, Arras, Amiens and Picardy,[124] there is every reason to believe that personal, familial and kinship networks between the two communities were behind the parallel occupational shift. It is possible that, as silk manufacture expanded in London, a 'putting-out' system was developed, with some London alien entrepreneurs supplying Canterbury weavers with raw silk, and taking charge of the sale of silk fabrics in the capital. This will be discussed in more detail in Chapter 6. The Canterbury colony was, on the whole, successful, with the aliens bringing industry, employment and prosperity to the city.[125]

Promotion of Industrial Development by Local Governments in London

Governmental involvement in industrial development was twofold. On one level there were initiatives taken by the national government, intended to achieve economic independence and autarky, and maintain a favourable balance of trade. On another level were initiatives undertaken by the city government, prompted by the necessity of generating employment for the growing number of poor and idle people who thronged the streets of London. Their energy was directed at labour-intensive work-creation schemes, rather than capital-intensive projects.

Urban awareness of genuine unemployment and the theme of setting the poor to work was a commonplace in economic literature.[126] In 1535, William Marshall compiled a scheme of public works to provide jobs for the poor. In the 1540s, the 'Commonwealth men' also saw the setting up of new industries as a constructive solution to the problem of poverty. As Sir Thomas Smith demonstrated in his *Discourse of the Commonwealth* written in 1549, this was especially because the foreign goods that found a ready market in England and created much work used raw materials that cost very little.[127] These efforts to find work for the poor clearly demonstrated changing attitudes to the problem of poverty, the recognition that poverty was not an act of God but a human one, an awareness that different types of poverty should elicit different responses, and the growing acceptance that individual charity was no longer sufficient, but that an institutional approach was required.[128]

In London, this changing moral climate gave birth to various institutions to deal with the problem of the poor. St Bartholomew's Hospital was founded to take care of the aged and sick, Christ's Hospital the poor orphan children, while Bridewell was to provide vocational training for three classes of poor: the children of the poor who were only suitable for manual work, invalids able to undertake light employment, and sturdy rogues and 'loose women' convicted in the courts.¹²⁹ Originally a royal palace, Bridewell was given by Edward VI to the City of London in 1553, a few months before his death, for use as 'a workhouse for the poor and idle persons' (see Figure 3.2). Its founders envisaged that the poor could be set to work by introducing occupations such as the making of caps (then mostly imported from France), the making of ticking for feather beds, wool carding, wire-drawing and silk winding, while nail-making was reserved for the 'stubborn and fouler sort'. It was also conceived that wealthy London citizens would provide the necessary raw materials as well as purchase the finished goods at a fair price.¹³⁰ From about 1557, a number of working craftsmen were appointed as 'arts-masters' to whom the boys were apprenticed to be taught such trades as shoe-making, tailoring, silk-weaving, pin-making and flax-dressing. By the early eighteenth century, there were sometimes as many as 100 of these boys. When they left Bridewell, they were given £10 and the freedom of the city.¹³¹

With the tripling number of vagrants dealt with at Bridewell, from 69 vagrants in 1560–61 to 209 by 1578–9, these measures proved inadequate.¹³² In 1578, a meeting was called by the Aldermen to consider further 'means [by

3.2 Edward VI's grant of Bridewell to the City of London
Source: **Guildhall Library**

which] the vagrant and idle persons as well as men women and children wandering up and downe the severall streets of this city may be set on work'.[133] In August 1579, it was proposed that 'for the relief of the poor and for setting to work of vagrant people there are to set up in Bridewell certain arts, occupations, works and labors'.

The extensive list of occupations[134] to be promoted at Bridewell included the making of goods for the inmates' own use (making of shoes) but also the manufacture of many 'superfluities' figured prominently in the imports list in 1559 and 1565, the consumption of which was denounced by moralists. The desire for the domestic manufacture of these 'superfluities' to substitute foreign imports, then, also underpinned the work-creation projects in Bridewell. The Aldermen agreed to provide 'stocke and tools for those works ... [and] bedding, apparell and diet for those poor to be so set to work'.[135]

How did the governors of Bridewell seek to introduce manufacturing? Again, foreign expertise, recruited overseas, was sought to achieve this end. In 1575, Martyn Pynnotts, an immigrant weaver, was employed. However, he was ordered to leave to be replaced by an immigrant pin-maker, Nychas van Buescom, who promised to 'instruct and bring up children in that art'.[136] In 1593, several alien pin-makers were employed in Bridewell to provide work for the poor children and other idle persons there.[137] These pin-makers were to be provided with accommodation and rooms, and the necessary equipment and materials estimated to cost £100, though the governors were not sure how they could raise the money intended for such purposes.[138]

In 1594, the Puritan Alderman Sir Richard Martin contemplated a new scheme to set the poor to work in Bridewell, and again the employment of Continental skills figured prominently in his plans.[139] The scheme was to introduce the art of fustian manufacture in Bridewell, which cost a total of more than £300.

It appears that Martin appointed an agent, Edmond Gentill, to go abroad and make the necessary arrangements – bring over the artisans, tools and patterns and, more importantly, to 'inform himself in Arts and Sciences purposed to be undertaken'. This may explain why it took Gentill a year to fulfil these tasks. He first travelled abroad in March 1595, and it was not until March 1596 that the artisans were brought over. All the initial costs were borne by Richard Martin, who claimed the expenses once the artisans arrived. From the breakdown in Table 3.4, it is clear that a high proportion of the total costs involved paying agents, who made the necessary arrangements. Tools and patterns cost one-fifth of the total. It is unclear what the 'other charges' included – perhaps travel costs for the artisans and payment to Martin.[140]

So what were the attractions for the master artisans? In a detailed document dated June 1596, the governors of Bridewell outlined clearly how the idle and vagrants were to be set to work. Skilled artisans were to be employed to

Table 3.4   Project to introduce fustians in Bridewell, London 1596

Types of expenses	Cost
Wages of Edmond Gentill, March–June 1595	£28 18s.
Wages of Edmond Gentill, June 1595–March 1596	£40
Wages of Mr Newman (a governor of Bridewell who presumably accompanied Gentill)	£50
Tools and patterns	£60
Other charges	£123 2s. 5d.
Total	£302 8s. 5d.

Sources: CLRO Rep 24, ff. 46–5 (4 March 1596).

supervise 100 poor people in Bridewell. The poor would each receive £5 in the first year for food and drink. Masters would be given a loan of £200 to 'provide stuff to set the said poor to work' which they had to repay at the end of their time there. They were also granted a kind of monopoly from the Queen which forbade others (except their former apprentices) to use those 'instruments, tools and engines invented by them'.[141]

The City also utilized foreign expertise available in London to promote its aims. Conscious of the hostility to the rising numbers of aliens settled in the City and the hot debates surrounding their immigration, Aldermen agreed in 1573 that only artificers who 'teach their arts to Englishmen and set no strangers on work but their own children' should be allowed to remain.[142] The governors of Christ's Hospital sent their boys to be apprenticed with foreign masters to learn a trade[143] and accepted services of foreign artisans. In 1577, Peter Waller, a stranger, offered to teach and instruct 'certain of the poor children of the [Christ] Hospital in the art of making tapestry and arras'.[144]

The achievements of Bridewell, however, have been heavily criticised, partly because of its indiscriminate handling of vagrants, which contributed to the moral corruption of some inmates. Persons in need and out of work through no fault of their own, for example, were 'packte up and punnyshed alyke in Bridewell with roges, beggers, strompets and pylfering theves'. No distinction was made between the good and the bad, so the good were soon to be corrupted, and 'nothing is to be learned but lewdenes amongst that generation'.[145] In terms of training, it is said that only a handful of offenders benefited, because their number was overwhelming while resources were scarce. In the early seventeenth century, there may have been a thousand inmates in Bridewell.[146] In 1596, the fustian manufacture project in Bridewell employed only 100 people, so only some 10 per cent, or slightly more, received vocational training. The establishment of an industrial school in Bridewell was criticised in the later part of the eighteeenth century, as it was alleged that the 'arts-masters' were decayed masters, failures as craftsmen themselves and incapable of instructing or controlling the apprentices.[147] In the opinion of Beier, Bridewell was more a penal and judicial body rather than a training centre for the poor. Its failure to cope with the mounting problems in the seventeenth century, according to Beier, was also reflected in the measures to rid of the city and the country of vagrants by pressing them to foreign wars and by transporting them to the American colonies.[148] Although evidence is lacking, Beier calculated that a minimum of several hundred vagrants were sent to fight wars abroad, particularly from the late Elizabethan years.[149] There is more evidence concerning transportation. The first instance of large-scale transportation occurred between 1618 and 1619, when 99 children aged between 8 and 16 were sent to Virginia.[150] This was probably in response to the request by the Company of Virginia, desperate to find bodies to fill its newly claimed territory. The Company, for example, requested the City to give them '100 children for the better supply and increasing of their colony'. The City authorities complied with this request, as it offered a perfect solution to a range of needs. The Company offered the City £3 for every child. The children involved also benefited from the scheme: each child received an allowance of 40 shillings for clothes, apprenticeship until they reached 21 years of age (the girls until they got married), after that they were to be 'placed as tenants upon the public land houses with stock of corn and cattle ...'[151] Transportation thus bestowed financial rewards upon the city as well as opportunities for advancement for the children, and it continued on a large scale after 1622.

This survey of initiatives undertaken by national and local governments demonstrates the complex and non-linear process of diffusion in the early modern period and the operational problems involved. I shall now turn to an examination of the more informal, extensive and spontaneous development of skills, in response to perceived opportunities and constraints, by foreign immigrants living in the capital.

Notes

1 Thirsk, *Economic Policy and Projects*, pp. 24–49.
2 Ibid., p. 13.
3 See D.M. Nicholas, 'Town and countryside: Social and economic tensions in fourteenth-century Flanders', *Comparative Studies in Society and History*, 1967–8, Vol. 10, pp. 458–85.
4 M. McKisack, *The Fourteenth Century, 1307–1399* (Oxford, 1959), p. 367.
5 Printed in B.W. Clapp and H.E.S. Fisher, eds, *Documents in English Economic History* (London, 1977), p. 180, taken from PRO Patent Roll, 5 Edward III, pt 2, m. 25.

6 McKisack, *The Fourteenth Century*, p. 367.
7 C. Barron, 'Introduction: England and the Low Countries 1327–1477', in C. Barron and N. Saul, eds, *England and the Low Countries in the Late Middle Ages* (Stroud, 1995), pp. 10, 12.
8 J.H. Munro, 'Urban regulation and monopolistic competition in the textile industries of the late-medieval Low Countries', in E. Aerts and J.H. Munro, eds, *Textiles of the Low Countries in European Economic History, Session B-15: Proceedings of Tenth International Economic History Congress, Leuven, August 1990* (Leuven, 1990), p. 43, J.H. Munro, 'Industrial entrepreneurship in the late-medieval Low Countries: Urban draperies, fullers, and the art of survival', in P. Klep and E. van Cauwenberghe, eds, *Entrepreneurship and the Transformation of the Economy (10th–20th Centuries): Essays in Honour of Herman van der Wee* (Leuven, 1994), p. 378.
9 Munro, 'Urban regulation', p. 43; Munro, 'Industrial entrepreneurship', p. 378.
10 Munro, 'Industrial entrepreneurship', p. 378.
11 D. Jacoby, 'The Migration of Merchants and Craftsmen: a Mediterranean Perspective', *Le Migrazioni in Europa secc. XIII–XVIII*, Istituto Internazionale di Storia Economica 'F. Datini' Prato, Serie II – Atti delle 'Settimane di Studi' e altri Convegni 25, S. Cavaciocchi, 1994, p. 557; see also M. Carlin, *Medieval Southwark* (London, 1996), p. 150.
12 A.E. Bland and P.A. Brown, eds, *English Economic History: Select Documents* (London, 1914), [32] [Alien weavers in London 1362], p. 195.
13 Barron, 'Introduction: England and the Low Countries 1327–1477', p. 13.
14 J. Bolton, *The Alien Communities of London in the Fifteenth Century: The Subsidy Rolls of 1440 and 1483–4* (Stamford, 1998).
15 V. Harding, 'Cross-Channel Trade and Cultural Contacts', p. 154.
16 Goose, 'Immigrants and English Economic Development in the Sixteenth and Early Seventeenth Centuries', pp. 136–160.
17 M.K. Dale, 'The London Silkwomen of the Fifteenth Century', *Economic History Review*, 1933, Vol. 4, p. 332.
18 *Letters and Papers*, 29 Henry VIII, 560, pp. 206–7.
19 A.M. Millard, 'The Import Trade of London, 1600–1640' (unpublished University of London PhD thesis, 1956, 3 vols), Vol. 1, p. 50.
20 PRO SP12/8/32.
21 PRO SP12/8/33.
22 Pettegree, *Foreign Protestant Communities in Sixteenth Century London*, p. 143.
23 PRO SP12/8/35.
24 M.E. Bratchel, 'Regulation and Group-consciousness in the Later History of London's Italian Merchant Colonies', *Journal of European Economic History*, 1980, Vol. 9, No. 3, p. 604.
25 E. Ashtor, 'The Factors of Technological and Industrial Progress in the Later Middle Ages', *Journal of European Economic History*, 1989, Vol. 18, p. 20.
26 Some dyeing was carried out in London, with dyehouses situated along Thames Street. However, it appears that medium- and better-quality cloths were sent abroad to be dyed. The inventory of Austin Hynde (Alderman and clothworker who was elected Lord Mayor) in 1554 shows that he had a dyehouse at Holborne Bridge with equipment worth £27 5s. 6d. See PRO PCC Prob 2/257. I would like to thank Dr David Mitchell for drawing my attention to this example.
27 'William Cholmeley's project for dyeing cloth in England, 1553', printed in Tawney and Power, eds, *Tudor Economic Documents* (London, 1924), Vol. 3, pp. 130–48.
28 Tawney and Power, *Tudor Economic Documents*, Vol. 3, p. 138.
29 Ramsay, 'London, a satellite city', pp. 45–6.
30 Limberger, '"No town in the world provides more advantages"', p. 54.
31 Ibid.

32 Tawney and Power, eds, *Tudor Economic Documents*, 'An Act touching Cloth-workers and Cloths ready wrought to be shipped over the sea,' pp. 426–7.
33 Keene, 'Material London', p. 66; CLRO, Rep 27, Sept 1606 f. 262, Rep 28 June 1607, f. 52.
34 Thirsk, *Economic Policy and Projects*, p. 43.
35 Stone, 'Elizabethan Overseas Trade', p. 37.
36 Ibid., p. 39.
37 Ibid., pp. 43–4.
38 Tawney and Power, eds, *Tudor Economic Documents*, 'An Act avoiding divers foreign wares made by handicraftsmen beyond the seas', pp. 424–5.
39 M.A.R. Graves, *Burghley: William Cecil, Lord Burghley* (London, 1998), p. 50.
40 W. Cunningham, *The Growth of English Industry and Commerce in Modern Times*, Vol. 2 (Cambridge, 1907), pp. 75–84.
41 Graves, *Burghley: William Cecil, Lord Burghley*, pp. 159–60.
42 Ibid., p. 160.
43 L. Williams, 'The Crown and the Provincial Immigrant Communities in Elizabethan England', in *British Government and Administration: Studies Presented to S.B. Chrimes*, ed. H. Hearder and H.R. Loyn (Cardiff, 1974), p. 119.
44 Ibid., p. 117.
45 Thirsk, *Economic Policy and Projects*, p. 52.
46 Ibid.
47 Ibid., p. 53.
48 Ramsay, 'Antwerp: The metropolis at its zenith', p. 25.
49 S. Davies, 'The Early History of the Patent Specification', *Law Quarterly Review*, 1934, Vol. 50, p. 99; C. MacLeod, *Inventing the Industrial Revolution: The English Patent System, 1660–1800* (Cambridge, 1988), pp. 11–12; E.W. Hulme, 'The history of the patent system under the Prerogative and at Common Law', in two parts, *Law Quarterly Review*, Vol. 12 (1896), pp. 141–54, Vol. 16 (1900), pp. 44–56.
50 PRO SP 12/36/95. For a discussion of Germans, see also R. Esser, 'Germans in Early Modern Britain' in P. Panayi, ed., *Germans in Britain Since 1500* (London, 1995), pp. 17–27.
51 Davies, 'The Early History of the Patent Specification', p. 102, footnote 57; E.W. Hulme, 'The History of the Patent System under the Prerogative and at Common Law', *Law Quarterly Review*, 1900, Vol. 16, p. 52.
52 Thirsk, *Economic Policy and Projects*, pp. 56–7.
53 Ibid., pp. 59–60.
54 Ibid., p. 57.
55 Coleman, 'An Innovation and its Diffusion: The "New Draperies"', pp. 417–18.
56 Cunningham, *Growth of Industry*, Vol. 2, p. 77.
57 Davies, 'The Early History of the Patent Specification', p.106.
58 Cunningham, *Growth of Industry*, Vol. 2, p. 76; MacLeod, *Inventing the Industrial Revolution*, p. 12.
59 Davies, 'The Early History of the Patent Specification', p. 104.
60 Hulme, 'The history of the patent system' (1896), pp. 147–8.
61 Davies, 'The Early History of the Patent Specification', p. 105.
62 Hume, 'The history of the patent system' (1896), p. 148.
63 Ibid., p. 146.
64 Davies, 'The Early History of the Patent Specification', p. 100.
65 PRO SP12/39/57 23 April 1566.
66 PRO SP12/33/51 April; Davies, 'The Early History of the Patent Specification', p. 102.
67 Cunningham, *Growth of Industry*, Vol. 2, p. 77.
68 Davies, 'The Early History of the Patent Specification', p. 100.
69 Hulme, 'The history of the patent system' (1896), p. 146.

70 Davies, 'The Early History of the Patent Specification', p. 100.
71 *Calendar of State Papers Domestic Elizabeth 1547–80*, Vol. 39/80, p. 272.
72 Hulme, 'The history of the patent system' (1896), p. 145.
73 W. Cunningham, *Alien Immigrants in England* (London, 1897), pp. 121–2, Letters and Papers, Henry VIII, IV (ii), 5110, p. 2240.
74 Cunningham, *Alien Immigrants in England*, pp. 122–3.
75 SPD Eliz, 1547–80, Vol. 39/80, p. 272, 25 May 1566.
76 PRO SP12/39 23 April 1566.
77 *Calendar of Patent Rolls, 1563–66* C.66/1021, p. 393.
78 J.F. Crosthwaite, 'The Colony of German Miners at Keswick', *Transactions of the Cumberland and Westmoreland Antiquarian and Archaeological Society*, 1883, Vol. 6, p. 347.
79 Williams, 'The Crown and the Provincial Immigrant Communities in Elizabethan England', p. 124
80 PRO SP 12/40, ff. 2–3.
81 PRO SP 12/40, f. 3.
82 PRO SP 12/40, f. 1.
83 PRO SP12/40, ff. 3–4.
84 N. Goose, Pound
85 Williams, 'The Crown and the Provincial Immigrant Communities in Elizabethan England', p. 118.
86 Thirsk, *Economic Policy and Projects*, p. 36; L.H. Yungblut, *Strangers Settled Here Amongst Us: Policies, Perceptions and the Presence of Aliens in Elizabethan England* (London, 1996), p. 100.
87 A. Spicer has tabulated the varying size of these communities in his *The French-speaking Reformed Community and their Church in Southampton, 1567-c.1620* (Hugenot Society, new series, Vol. 3, 1997) on p. 161, but Maidstone is not included.
88 'Settlement of alien craftsmen in Sandwich, 1561', printed in Tawney and Power, eds, *Tudor Economic Documents*, p. 297.
89 Williams, 'The Crown and the Provincial Immigrant Communities in Elizabethan England', p. 122.
90 Backhouse, *The Flemish and Walloon Communities*, p. 20.
91 Pettegree, *Foreign Protestant Communities*, pp. 141–2.
92 For a discussion of overcrowding, see ibid., pp. 283–5.
93 Backhouse, *The Flemish and Walloon Communities*, p. 17.
94 Ibid., p. 20.
95 M. Backhouse, 'The Strangers at Work in Sandwich: Native Envy of an Industrious Minority, 1561–1603', *Immigrants and Minorities*, 1991, Vol. 10, No. 3, p. 78. Some historians such as Prof. Nigel Goose believe that Backhouse may have underestimated the size of the indigenous population. Backhouse, for example, calculated that there were 1800–1900 native inhabitants in the 1580s. Professor Goose, however, estimated that there were at least 3,810 native inhabitants, given that the annual average of native baptisms was 127. If this was accurate, the alien population did not outnumber the native population in 1573 and 1574, or at any other times. See Backhouse, *The Flemish and Walloon Communities*, pp. 21, 22, 31.
96 The first 50 settlers had come from Sandwich in 1568. See Backhouse, 'The Strangers at Work', p. 87.
97 Ibid., p. 94.
98 Ibid., p. 92.
99 Backhouse, *The Flemish and Walloon Communities*, p. 31.
100 Tawney and Power, eds, *Tudor Economic Documents*, 'Introduction of Strangers from the Low Countries to Norwich, 1564', pp. 298–9.
101 A. Spicer, *The French-speaking Reformed Community and their Church in Southampton*, p. 24; Williams, 'The Crown and the Provincial Immigrant Communities', p. 122.

102　Spicer, *The French-speaking Reformed Community and their Church in Southampton*, p. 24.
103　W.J.C. Moens, *The Walloons and their Church at Norwich*, Part 1 (Lymington, 1887/88), pp. 25–38.
104　L. Martin, 'The Rise of the New Draperies in Norwich, 1550–1622' in N.B. Harte, ed., *The New Draperies in the Low Countries and England, 1300–1800* (Oxford, 1997), p. 253.
105　Ibid., pp. 247, 254.
106　Ibid., pp. 248, 251, 267.
107　Ibid., p. 267.
108　Ibid., p. 255.
109　This discussion is based on N. Goose, 'The Dutch in Colchester in the 16th and 17th centuries: Opposition and integration', in R. Vigne and C. Littleton, eds, *From Strangers to Citizens: The Integration of Immigrant Communities in Britain, Ireland and Colonial America, 1550–1750* (Brighton, 2001), pp. 88–9.
110　Ibid., pp. 88–9.
111　Goose, 'The "Dutch" in Colchester: The Economic Influence of an Immigrant Community in the Sixteenth and Seventeenth Centuries', p. 266; Goose, 'The Dutch in Colchester in the 16th and 17th centuries', p. 90.
112　Spicer, *The French-speaking Reformed Community*, p. 71. In the fifteenth century, there were schemes to introduce cloth-finishers and dyers to Southampton, and in the sixteenth century silk-weaving: see Williams, 'The Crown and the Provincial Immigrant Communities in Elizabethan England', p. 118.
113　Spicer, *The French-speaking Reformed Community*, pp. 29–30.
114　Ibid., p. 161.
115　Ibid., p. 29.
116　Ibid., p. 159.
117　Ibid., p. 89.
118　Ibid., p. 164.
119　Williams, 'The Crown and the Provincial Immigrant Communities in Elizabethan England', p. 122.
120　A.M. Oakley, 'The Canterbury Walloon Congregation from Elizabeth I to Laud', in I. Scouloudi, ed., *Huguenots in Britain and their French Background, 1550–1800*, (London, 1987), p. 58.
121　Williams, 'The Crown and the Provincial Immigrant Communities in Elizabethan England', p. 122.
122　Spicer, *The French-speaking Reformed Community*, p. 161.
123　Williams, 'The Crown and the Provincial Immigrant Communities in Elizabethan England', p. 130; Oakley, 'The Canterbury Walloon Congregation', p. 59; F.W. Cross, *History of the Walloon and Huguenot Church at Canterbury* (Huguenot Society Publications, Vol. 15, 1898), pp. 184–5.
124　Oakley, 'The Canterbury Walloon Congregation', p. 58.
125　Ibid., p. 70.
126　Williams, 'The Crown and the Provincial Immigrant Communities in Elizabethan England', p. 119.
127　Thirsk, *Economic Policy and Projects*, p. 18.
128　G. Salgādo, *The Elizabethan Underworld* (London, 1977), p. 184.
129　Ibid., pp. 185–6.
130　Ibid., p. 186.
131　L.W. Cowie, 'Bridewell', *History Today*, 1973, Vol. 23, pp. 352–3.
132　A.L. Beier, 'Social Problems in Elizabethan London', *Journal of Interdisciplinary History* (1978), Vol. 9, p. 204.
133　CLRO, Letter Book Y, f. 271 (November 1578).

134 The list included working in the lighters and unlading of sand, and the carrying of sand, making of gloves, combs, inkle and tape, silk lace, pack-thread, pins, shoes, wool cards, nails, points, knives, bays, brushes, tennis balls, felts and picking of wool of felts, knitting hose, spinning woolen yarn, linen yard, and candlewick, drawing of wires, and thicking of caps by hand and foot. See CLRO, Letter Book Y 1575–9, 'Orders for Setting Rogues and Vagabonds on work in Bridewell', ff. 334v–339.
135 CLRO, Letter Book Y, ff. 334–9 August 1579.
136 CLRO Rep 18, f. 425 13 September 1575.
137 CLRO Rep 23, ff. 60–60v, f. 87, f. 94.
138 CLRO Rep 23, f. 125 22 Nov 1593.
139 Huntingdon Library, Ellesmere MS 2522, CLRO, Rep 24, f. 34 15 February 1597.
140 CLRO Rep 24, ff. 45–6.
141 Huntingdon Library, MS 2522 June 1596.
142 CLRO Rep 18, ff. 148v–149v.
143 Pettegree, *Foreign Protestant Communities*, p. 301.
144 CLRO Letter Book Y, f. 189.
145 Beier, 'Social Problems in Elizabethan London', p. 217.
146 Ibid., p. 219.
147 Cowie, 'Bridewell', p. 354.
148 Beier, 'Social Problems in Elizabethan London', p. 219.
149 Ibid.
150 Ibid.
151 CLRO JOR 31, ff.122–3, f.125v.

Chapter 4

Immigrants in Elizabethan London

Overview

In contrast to the more recent experience of overseas immigration in many English provincial towns, London, as the capital city and a trading centre located within the European circuits of commerce, was a highly cosmopolitan city with a deep-seated tradition of immigration, stretching as far back as the eighth century, with merchants regularly flocking to the City to conduct business. Particularly prominent among the foreign traders were the German merchants who had, by the 1170s, established a permanent base in Dowgate Ward in the capital. Popularly known to contemporaries as the 'merchants of the Steelyard', named after the building they occupied, these men included those from Hamburg, Lübeck, Cologne and its hinterland, and were members of the Hanseatic League, a loose confederation of German cities formed to promote trade by setting up a series of bases at strategic sites for their operation. By the mid-thirteenth century, merchants from France, Spain, Portugal and northern Italy had also established themselves in London.[1] As a result of their prominence, distinctive organization and the greater availability of evidence, the Hansards and the Italians, in particular, have attracted much historical interest. Recent studies, especially by Keene on the Hansards and Bratchel on the Italians, have thrown fascinating light upon the internal organization of the communities, their activities and relations with the host society. While drawing attention to the contrasting organizational structures of the Hansards and Italians, these studies also emphasize their strong collective identity and rotating migration, with young and unmarried men at the beginning of their careers being sent from the headquarters to spend a few years at each of the various European bases to gain professional training, before returning to the home city at a later stage in their lives. Residence in London thus formed a temporary, if not a necessary, phase in their professional career. In the early sixteenth century, the Italian and Hanseatic mercantile communities in London declined in significance, as trade could now be conducted at a more convenient location at Antwerp. There were probably only seventy Italian and eighty Hanse merchants resident in London at this date.[2] Although still a force to be reckoned with, the power of the Hanse and Italians may have waned by 1547.[3]

The foreign merchants were the most prominent and influential, but were greatly outnumbered by the humbler and poorer craftsmen who became more numerically significant from the fifteenth century. Pettegree has estimated that merchants and brokers perhaps formed only 10 per cent of some two thousand aliens in the capital in 1440.[4] Driven by the search for work and better economic opportunities, many moved in chain migration with their wives and children, and therefore found it easy to put down permanent roots in the new society. But like any other immigrant groups, their social behaviour also exhibited 'clannishness', preferring to marry women and employ servants from their own cultural backgrounds.[5]

These two parallel patterns of mercantile and artisan migration prevailed until 1550, when Edward VI's grant of a charter to religious refugees in London to set up their own churches fundamentally tranformed the character of immigration into the capital. With the foundation of Dutch and French Churches in that year, London became a haven for successive waves of religious and political refugees from conflict-ridden Europe in search of safety and religious freedom.[6] The Stranger Churches, as recent studies by Pettegree and Littleton have shown, occupied a highly significant position in the lives of these refugees, not only as expression of their collective identity, as sources of economic relief and charity and as pressure groups to the English government in times of economic friction, but also as centres for social gatherings, enabling immigrants to meet and keep in touch with events at home. However, there were some negative undesirable effects. Unlike earlier migrants, the greater identity and visibility of the refugees, fostered by the existence of their Churches, contributed to greater native hostility and debate about the desirability of their presence. While Londoners protested at the great numbers of 'bogus' refugees flocking to their city and the concomitant detrimental effects on living standards, supporters of the refugees (including members of the government and the Stranger Churches) sought to pacify this sentiment by pointing to the evidence contained in the Returns of Aliens of the benefits they brought, including the introduction of new and sought-after skills, the teaching of these skills to native servants and apprentices, and the creation of work. In the past, historians have relied uncritically on the evidence from the Returns which led them to overestimate the economic contribution of immigrants and to provide an undifferentiated characterization of the roles of different groups. But as the previous chapter has demonstrated, the Returns of Aliens as a historical source are flawed, and their use requires much greater care. Aware of these shortcomings, this chapter uses the Returns of Aliens as a starting point to establish the changing pattern of immigration into London and to assess its economic effects. Figure 4.1 shows the locations of the districts referred to in text.

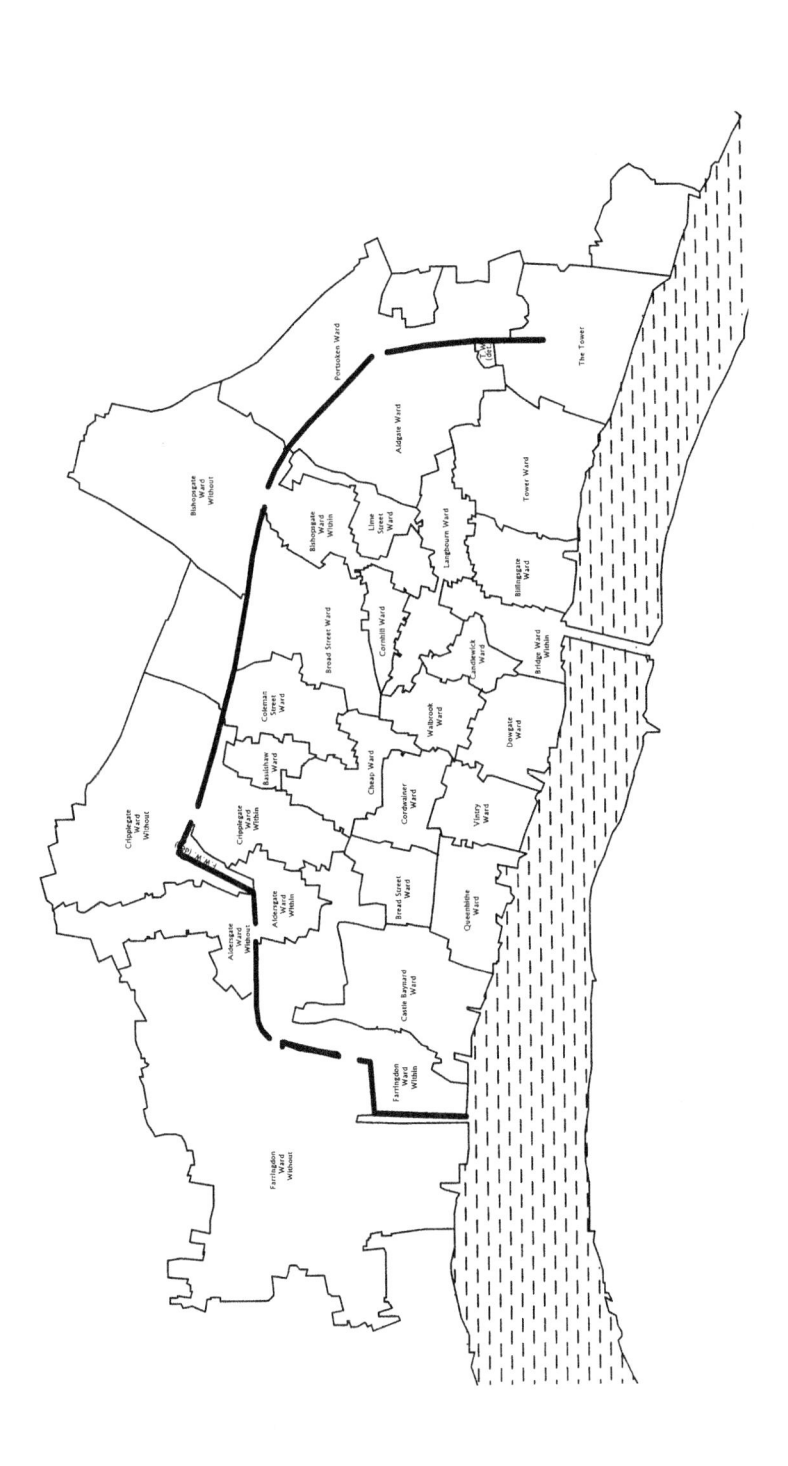

4.1 Map of London.
Source: Map drawn by Craig Spence for the ESRC-funded 'London in the 1690s' project based at the Centre for Metropolitan History, Institute of Historical Research, University of London.

The Size of the Foreign Community in England

The scale of immigration from the Continent into England increased dramatically between the fifteenth and sixteenth centuries. However, scant available evidence makes it extremely difficult to calculate its changing scale precisely. For the fifteenth century, the work of Sylvia Thrupp has made it possible to establish the size of the alien population in England and London. Using the subsidy returns, Thrupp has estimated that there were some 16 000 alien-born residents, including Irish and Scottish, in England in 1440. Of these, only a few thousands actually came from the Continent – approximately 3600 were of Dutch, French, Italian, Spanish and Portuguese backgrounds living in parts of England, and a further 2800 living in Middlesex, Surrey and London, bringing the total to some 6400 aliens in England.[7] By 1483–4, as Jim Bolton's recent invaluable study has shown, the alien population in London had increased to 3400, including men, women and children, forming at least 6 per cent of the London population, rather than the 2–4 per cent suggested by Thrupp.[8]

The total number of Continental immigrants in Elizabethan England rose dramatically. Tentative estimates put the immigration to England at 30 000 people in the six years between 1567 and 1573 alone – the period of repression associated with the reign of the Duke of Alva.[9] The total number who came during the Elizabethan period was likely to have been much higher, possibly 50 000 – though admittedly by no means all the 'Dutch' aliens stayed in England, as many went on to the Dutch Republic. From the Returns of Aliens, we know with some certainty that there were at least 16 000 Continental immigrants living in six English cities in the early 1570s – Canterbury, Colchester, London, Norwich, Sandwich and Southampton.[10] What is also clear is that the number who came to England formed only a small proportion of the total emigration from the southern Netherlands. Between 1567 and 1620, Briels has estimated that a total of some 210 000 refugees may have fled the southern Netherlands (60 000 are estimated to have fled between 1567 and 1573, and 150 000 between 1572 and 1620).[11] These figures have been criticized as too high, with some historians arguing for a lower figure of a maximum of 50 000 emigrants between 1567 and 1573, and 60-100 000 emigrants between 1572 and 1620, totalling 150 000 at the most for the period 1567 and 1620, rather than 210 000.[12] Of those leaving the southern Netherlands, then, 20–30 per cent chose to come to England.

The Size of the Alien Community in London

1550s

The alien community in London appears to have experienced three phases of development: rapid expansion from the fifteenth to the early sixteenth century, fluctuations between 1550 and 1585, and stabilization after 1585. As we have seen, London's alien population expanded steadily in the fifteenth century from roughly 2800 people in 1440 to 3400 in 1484, and its pace of growth quickened in the early sixteenth century, with the fastest expansion occurring during the reign of Edward VI, when the alien population doubled. Using membership lists of the Stranger Churches and tax subsidies, Pettegree has calculated that the number of strangers in London grew rapidly from 5000 to 6000 at the end of Henry VIII's reign to its peak in 1553 with 10 000 strangers (see Tables 4.1 and 4.2).[13]

There are two possible explanations for this massive expansion. The first concerns the religious developments on the Continent with the emergence of Calvinism as a major international religious force. Calvinism presented a greater threat than other brands of Protestantism because of its clear-cut beliefs, its missionary role and its firm organizational structure. The external planning of Calvinist missionary activity and the appeal of Calvinism to the elites also posed a new challenge for the state. While in earlier times groups in revolt tended to be composed of people of the same status, now rulers were faced with a frightening phenomenon of whole regions in rebellion, united in ideology and led by their ruling class.[14] To counter this new threat, the Catholic Church launched the Counter-Reformation in the 1540s, establishing more efficient and centralized agencies of persecution.[15] These developments stimulated significant migrations from France and the Netherlands. In the case of France, the first dynamic exodus abroad coincided with the emergence of Geneva as an important centre for French exiles in the mid-1540s. Other significant centres for French exiles were Metz, Neuchâtel, and Strasbourg. Events in the Netherlands followed a similar pattern. The beginnings of a significant exile movement followed the clamp-down on evangelical conventicles in the period 1544–6. During this time, increasing numbers of Protestants went into exile, to England, Strasbourg, Emden and Wesel. These years saw the establishment of the first organized exile congregation in Wesel, followed by the foundation of the French and Dutch-speaking churches in London in 1550, and the reorganization of the local church in Emden for the growing numbers of Dutch exiles now settled there in 1553.[16]

With the restoration of Catholicism in 1553, when Mary ascended the throne, many English and foreign Protestants left England to seek refuge on

Table 4.1   Numbers of aliens in London, 1483–1621

Year	Recorded nos of aliens				Estimated totals in London	% of London's total population
	(1) City (25 wards)	(2) City (26 wards)	(3) City and Middlesex	(4) City, Middlesex and Surrey	(5)	
1483	1 595	—	—	2 700	3 400	6.0
1547	—	—	—	—	5 000–6 000	—
1553	—	—	—	—	10 000	12.5
1559	—	—	—	—	c.6 000	—
1563	—	—	—	4 534	—	—
1568	3 689[a]	4 605[b]	6 532	6 704	—	—
1571 (May)	—	4 287	—	—	—	—
1571 (Nov.)	3 685[c]	4 631	—	—	—	—
1571 (Dec.)	—	—	6 603[d]	—	10 000	10.0
1573	—	—	—	7 143[e]	—	—
1581	—	2 445	4 047	—	—	—
1583	—	2 537	4 141	—	—	—
1593[1]	—	3 930[f]	—	—	—	—
1593[2]	4 857[g]	5 259	—	—	—	—
1593[3]	—	5 545	6 793	7 113	10 000	5.0
1621	—	—	—	10 000	—	—

Notes: The presentation of this table is based on the style adopted by Harding, 'The population of London, 1550–1700'. (1) The City, 25 Wards, excluding Bridge Without Ward. (2) The City, 26 Wards, including Bridge Without Ward and 'exempted places' within the City walls. (3) As in column 2, plus built-up parishes of Middlesex (identified in Table 4.2). (4) As in column 3, plus built-up parishes of Middlesex and Surrey (identified in Table 4.2). (5) Totals estimated by historians.
Figures in italics are totals stated in original MS.
[a]   I calculated this by deducting the number in Bridge Without Ward (916) from the total for 26 Wards (4605).
[b]   The number of aliens living in Blackfriars and St Marin-le-Grand was not included in the total for the City. To make the data comparable, I have added the number of aliens in Blackfriars (230) and St Martin-le-Grand (269) to the stated total of 4106 aliens in the 26 Wards.
[c]   I calculated this by deducting the number in Bridge Without Ward (946) from the total for 26 wards (4631).
[d]   A Return undertaken in December 1571 showed that there were 1972 aliens in Middlesex and adjoining areas. I have added this to the total for the City (4631).

e It is not clear what areas were surveyed, as the Return simply stated that this was the total number of aliens in 'the Citie of London, and the Subarbes adjoining'.
f This Return (in Dugdale MS) is imperfect, and the number of persons counted by Scouloudi is likely to be a low estimate, see Scouloudi, *Returns of Strangers*, pp. 73–5, 145.
g Calculate this by deducting the number in Bridge Without Ward (402) from the total for 26 wards (5259).

Sources: 1483: J.L. Bolton, *The Alien Communities of London in the Fifteenth Century*. 1547, 1553, 1559: Pettegree, *Foreign Protestant Communities*, pp. 77–8, 118–20. 1563: SP12/27/19 and 20 (printed in Kirk and Kirk, eds, *Returns of Aliens*, Vol. 10, No. 1, p. 293). 1568: Ibid., No. 3, pp. 330–439. 1571, May: Ibid., No. 1, pp. 402–79. 1571, November: Ibid., No. 2, pp. 1–139. 1571, December: Ibid., pp. 140–56. 1573: Ibid., p. 156. 1581: BL, Lansdowne MS 32/11 (also in Kirk and Kirk, eds, *Returns of Aliens*, Vol. 10, No. 2, pp. 215–19. 1583: PRO S12/160/27 (published in full in Kirk and Kirk, eds, *Returns of Aliens*, Vol. 10, No. 2, pp. 342–77). 1593[1]: (Dugdale MS), Scouloudi, *Returns of Strangers*, p. 74. 1593[2]: Lansdowne MS 74/31. 1593[3]: Ellesmere MS 2514. 1621: W.D. Cooper, *Lists of Foreign Protestants and Aliens Resident in England, 1618–1688* (Camden Society, old series, Vol. 82, 1862), p. iv.

Table 4.2 Numbers of aliens in Middlesex, Surrey and Westminster, 1568–93

	1568	1571	1581	1583	1593[1]	1593[2]
City	4106	4631[a]	4047	2537	4465	5545[a]
Exempted places within the City						
Blackfriars	230	—	247	275	508	—
Christ church, Aldgate	159	—	—	—	—	—
St Martin-le-Grand	269	—	—	—	286	—
Whitefriars	—	—	—	4	—	—
Sub-total	658	—	247	279	794	—
Middlesex and outlying areas north of the river						
Blackwall	—	15	—	—	—	—
Duchy of Lancaster	124	—	57	56	—	—
East Smithfield	358	284	426	445	—	—
Finsbury	94	86[b]	—	—	—	—
Fleet Yard, St. Brides parish	63	—	—	—	—	—
High Holborn	—	—	15	14	—	—
Halliwell St and Halliwell, Shoreditch	—	226	149	152	—	—
Hoxton	4	—	—	—	—	—
Limehouse	—	11	—	—	—	—
Minories	70	92	—	—	—	—

Norton Folgate and Clerkenwell	104	—	16	21	—	—
Poplar	—	18	—	—	—	—
Ratcliffe	—	19	—	—	—	—
St Giles in the Fields	16	7	—	—	—	—
St Johns Street and Charterhouse	36	—	—	21	—	—
St Katherine (by the Tower)	425	210	265	285	—	—
St Martins in the Fields	—	—	—	100	—	—
Shoreditch	66	32	—	44	—	—
Tower (Liberty)	—	16	—	—	—	—
Wapping	—	—	41	41	—	—
Whitechapel	92	169	143	146	—	—
Sub-total	1 398	1 165	1 209	1 325	—	1 248[c]

Surrey and Outlying areas south of the river

Bermondsey Street	98	—	—	—	—	—
Clink	49	—	—	—	—	—
Lord Montagues liberty	25	—	—	—	—	—
Sub-total	172	—	—	—	—	320[d]
Westminster	309	—	—	—	—	—
Total recorded	2 598	1 972	1 660	1 604	794	1 568
Numbers unaccounted for	11	807	204	—	—	—
Total	6 704	6 603	5 707	4 141	5 259	7 113

Notes: [a] Includes the number of aliens in Blackfriars and St Martin-le-Grand. [b] Covers Finsbury, Golding Lane, White Cross Street and Grub Street. [c] Includes Poplar, Ratcliffe, Whitechapel, St Katherine, East Smithfield, Stratford Bow, Mile End, Halliwell, Stoke Newington, Shoreditch, Norton Folgate, Golding Lane, White Cross Street, St Clements parish, St Martins in the Fields, Kinds Street. [d] Includes Redcliffe, Bermondsey, St Georges Parish, the Clink, Paris Garden, Newington, Lambeth.
Sources: 1568, 1571: *Returns of Aliens*. 1581: BL, Lansdowne MS 32/11. 1583: PRO SP12/160/27. 1593[1]: BL, Lansdowne MS 74/31. 1593[2]: Ellesmere, MS 2514.

the Continent. This exodus was magnified by the proclamation in February 1554 ordering all seditious and non-denizen aliens to depart.[17] Still, Pettegree has affirmed that this did not result in a general exodus of strangers from the capital. Despite a 40 per cent reduction in the number of strangers, there were still several thousands in London when Elizabeth I came to power in 1558.[18]

1560s and 1570s

The Returns of Aliens suggest that the reinstatement of Protestantism in England when Elizabeth I succeeded to the throne did not lead to a rush of foreign Protestants returning. A survey in January 1562/3 shows that of the 4534 aliens found living in London and the surrounding areas, only 371 arrived in the first year of her reign, 341 in the last 12 months, 2860 had come before her reign, and 962 came not for religious reasons. In other words, only 15 per cent had only recently arrived as religious refugees.[19] This conclusion appears to contradict other contemporary reports. As early as June 1559, Philip II's special envoy in London, Aquila, was reporting the movement of large numbers of people from the Low Countries to England.[20] The Returns may thus have underestimated the total number of aliens who came to London, partly because of the highly transient nature of the alien population in this period, with people constantly moving back and fro to the Continent as the political climate changed frequently from war to peace. Many French fled to England during the first religious war, only to return home after the Pacification of Amboise. The pattern was repeated with the renewal of hostilities in 1568 and the peace of 1570, and with the massacre of St Bartholomew's Day in 1572 the flow from France became a torrent. A similar pattern can be discerned for the Netherlands. As persecution intensified after 1558, many sought refuge in England, but some returned in 1563. The promise of religious toleration by the Moderation in 1566 led to the return of thousands of exiles, but with the collapse of the reform movement in 1567, many thousands of new refugees sought safety abroad.[21]

Judging from the total number of Returns ordered between 1566 and 1568 (ten altogether), it seems that immigration into London had peaked by this period. On 21 July 1568, William Cecil instructed the Lord Mayor to undertake another Return because 'the Queen being to understand that the number of strangers, coming over into the Realm out France, Flanders and other Countries' to escape persecution for the cause of rebellion, 'do daily abound and increase … that her realm shall be overcharged, with so great a multitude and especially of such as are reported to be lewd and evil disposed persons'.[22] The Return in 1568 found that the number of aliens in London and surrounding areas had increased to 6704, excluding 'the Spanish in Bridewell and many others in prisons'.[23]

The continued influx into London during the 1560s and 1570s produced genuine fears of subversion and espionage. The stationing of more than 10 000 Spanish soldiers in the Low Countries and the excommunication of Elizabeth by the Pope in 1570 greatly enhanced the threat of a Catholic invasion. On 13 October 1571, the Privy Council called the Mayor and Aldermen of London together and told them that the Pope and the King of

Spain were involved with the Duke of Norfolk in a plot to dethrone Elizabeth and put Mary Queen of Scots in her place. The Mayor passed the news on to the London companies, and presently it was common talk in the streets.[24] In 1572, Cecil prepared a list of the 'things requisite to be done for putting the coasts and the realm of England in readiness against invasion'.[25]

Concern with internal security was exacerbated by reports that spies and subversive elements may have infiltrated the incoming refugees. In October 1571, Cecil was warned by William Herlle (his intimate adviser)[26] that among the strangers there were 'papists, anabaptists, libertynes, drunkards, common women … murderers, thieves and conspirators …'.[27] To protect the security of the country, it was thought necessary to control the number of people arriving in England, especially London, particularly because some strangers were 'vehemently suspected or defamed of … evil living or … setters forward or favourers of … naughty religion'.[28] The first essential measure was to prevent further influxes of strangers to the Capital. On 25 October 1571, the Lord Mayor of London drew up a series of proposals to ensure greater security. A general search was to be made in all the port towns; the landing of all strangers, except merchants, was to be prevented; householders were not to admit into their houses or families any such strangers or set them to work; the gates of London should be watched, and six persons were to be appointed to guard the streets within the ward in the City, and a double number in some wards;[29] and all strangers' houses were to be secretly searched for armour and weapons. If any were to be found, they were to be put in safe custody.[30] In November 1571, the government also ordered a national survey of aliens in England. For London, this meant a second survey in the year, but this was different from all others in its unique task to find out the reasons why the immigrants had come to settle in the capital. The survey found 4631 aliens in the City, with a further 1972 in the Middlesex, making a grand total of 6603.

The number of aliens in London continued to expand in the 1570s, but at a modest rate. By 1573, there were 7143 aliens in the capital – an increase of only 540 immigrants since 1571. The influx following the St Bartholomew's Day Massacre in France in 1572 may have been responsible for this increase. The areas that suffered most severely were Paris, where some 2000 Protestants were slaughtered, and Orléans, Meaux, Rouen, Angers and Troyes.[31] Refugees from areas close to England escaped there by boat, while others in south-east France took the road to Geneva, where there had been a substantial French community. In 1561, the Venetian envoy to France claimed that Geneva was 'full of refugees, [numbering] as much as ten thousand'. This estimate is believed to have been accurate; from 1549 to 1587 Geneva probably received as many as twelve thousand French refugees, with the majority arriving in the aftermath of the massacre in 1572.[32]

The Returns of Aliens indicate that in the ten years between 1563 and

1573, the alien population in the City of London, Middlesex and Surrey only rose by 37 per cent, from 4534 to 7143 persons. This is a low estimate, and the actual number of aliens in London was likely to have been much higher for several reasons. First, local officials often had great difficulty in defining who was an alien.[33] Second, the variation in the geographical areas of the City covered by the Returns makes any direct comparison very difficult, and the Returns do not always state which areas of the city were included in the surveys. Third, there were problems of under-recording and even deliberate evasion. In October 1571, for example, William Herlle told William Cecil that the number of strangers had increased by 8000 to 10000 (without clarifying whether this referred to London or England). He complained that the surveys greatly underestimated the number of strangers because they only counted householders and omitted those such as children and servants because of 'negligence or bribery'. He also indicated that many stranger servants deliberately sought to 'absent themselves' until the search was over.[34] The fact that there were 1828 names on the membership lists of the Stranger Churches in 1571 who were not included in the surveys undertaken by English officials suggests that Herlle's complaint about under-recording may have been accurate.[35] Fourth, there was also the problem of tracing alien servants who lived and worked with English masters, many of whom were excluded from official surveys. There were at least 1000 alien journeymen working in the goldsmiths' trade, beer brewing and coopery.[36] If these various groups are taken into account, there may have been as many as 8000 to 10000 aliens in London in 1571.[37] If we use the higher estimate and assume that there were approximately 100000 native inhabitants, then the strangers formed approximately 10 per cent of London's total population during the early 1570s.[38]

Despite an estimated arrival of some 30000 aliens in England between 1567 and 1573, the foreign community in London experienced a relatively modest growth. Several factors explain this. There was some return migration to Holland and Zeeland after 1572, when an edict was issued ordering refugees from Holland to return home or face punishment. Following the publication of the edict on 7 March 1574, 3000 returned from Emden, presumably some also went back from London.[39] A more important explanation was the deliberate policy of containment and dispersal adopted to keep the alien population in London manageable. In response to popular discontent, the City of London in 1568 had promulgated a decree allowing only religious refugees to stay in the capital.[40] The Privy Council also sought to alleviate pressure on London by establishing five new provincial communities between 1566 and 1573. The Privy Council adopted a 'carrot-and-stick' policy to achieve this. For example, it prohibited aliens from trading with the Low Countries and from practising their handicrafts in London after

Christmas of 1571, intending thereby to force many strangers to depart for the provincial settlements. In 1574, the Privy Council also ordered the Stranger Churches to reject any new applicants for membership and dispatch them to other settlements in England. To assist recent arrivals to move on to other locations, the deacons of the French church disbursed part of the church's funds throughout the early 1570s. One positive effect of this dispersal policy may have been the dissemination of skills to a wider area in England. However, Cunningham argued that large areas of the country were unaffected by the influx of refugees. The method of their immigration and the necessity of distributing them in groups, he believed, had prevented them from being scattered generally, but 'at each centre the knowledge of the arts they practised was not kept entirely to themselves, but diffused itself ... rapidly among their English neighbours'.[42]

There were other reasons why a dispersal policy was necessary. In the first place, the Spanish Ambassador objected to the harbouring of refugees fleeing the Spanish Netherlands in England. It is possible that Elizabeth I, anxious to avoid offending Philip of Spain, insisted on dispersing the refugees to provincial towns where their increasing numbers would attract less notice from the Spanish Ambassador.[43] During the 1560s and 1570s, some Londoners also became increasingly hostile to strangers, as they believed that many social and economic problems were engendered by the increase in their numbers. In addition, the ecclesiastical situation in the capital caused much concern. By the early 1570s, the Dutch church in Austin Friars had become a model of reform for the Presbyterians who wanted to introduce similar practices used in the Stranger Churches into their own parish churches. Strong suspicion prevailed within the Privy Council that the Dutch church harboured English dissenters, and an order was issued in 1574 prohibiting the Dutch and Walloon churches from accepting new members.[44] For these reasons, it was considered pragmatic to keep the number of strangers in London within manageable limits.

1580s and 1590s

The Returns of Aliens indicate that the number of aliens in London declined by the early 1580s. In 1581, a Return recorded only 4 047 aliens in the City and Middlesex, or roughly a 40 per cent fall since 1571. It is possible that the Pacification of Ghent in 1578 and the brief period of peace in France may have caused the scale of immigration from the Low Countries and France to tail off at the end of the 1570s and the early 1580s. In addition, these events may have encouraged some refugees in London to return to their homeland.[45] But available evidence suggests that there was continuous immigration into London in this period. Littleton's study of the French church in London also confirms this. Of the 330 French-speaking households whose length of residence in London is recorded in 1593, 27 per cent had arrived in the period between 1567 and 1573, 17.5 per cent between 1574 and 1582, and 37 per cent between 1583 and 1589.[46] Although immigration appears to have slowed down in the early 1580s, the death toll from plagues may also have been a contributory factor to the apparent decline in the alien population. From the beginning of the 1560s, plague became 'the single most important cause of death in London', accounting for more than 15 per cent of all deaths from 1580 to 1650. According to Rappaport, there are 19 references to plague between 1563, the year of the first and most severe Elizabethan epidemic, and 1603. The only plague-free intervals were 1584–91 and 1595–1602.[47] Without continuous immigration, the effects of plagues and return migration would certainly have produced a declining alien population.

The scale of immigration into London soared again from the mid-1580s, as a result of the Spanish re-conquest of the southern Netherlands and the continuation of warfare and persecution in France. By 1593, the number of aliens in London appears to have regained its 1573 level. One Return taken between 12 and 15 May 1593 recorded 5 545 aliens in the City, 1 248 in Middlesex, and 320 in Surrey, making a total of 7 113 alien men, women, children and servants.[48] However, a third of these had been born in England. Although English by birth, these children were still regarded as aliens, and therefore were included in the total. Official surveys thus show that the number of aliens in 1593 was comparable to that in 1571. This figure again needs to be inflated, to 10 000 aliens, for the same reasons discussed above. However, by this date, the native population may have also increased dramatically to 180 000 inhabitants.[49] This means that in proportional terms, the number of aliens actually declined, from its peak of 12.5 per cent in 1553 to 10 per cent in 1571, and to 5 or 6 per cent by 1593 – a proportion similar to that in 1483.

The influx of religious refugees from the Low Countries and France appears to have altered the stranger community in London in important ways. One significant change was the balance between the French- and Dutch-speaking communities. In the fifteenth century, the Dutch-speaking immigrants formed an overwhelming majority of the strangers in London (90 per cent in 1436), but this proportion fell steadily. By 1593, they constituted only 55 per cent of aliens in the capital (see Table 4.3). The proportion of French-speaking immigrants, on the other hand, rose dramatically from 2 per cent in 1436 to 34 per cent in 1593. The decline in the proportion of Italians and Scots is also noticeable. In 1436, the Italians formed the second largest group of aliens, but by 1593 their numbers were dwarfed by the Dutch and French. In 1483, the Scots formed a significant proportion of the strangers in London, but only 37 were recorded in 1571.[50] Their decline may reflect the

Table 4.3 Linguistic groups of aliens in London: Their proportional distribution, 1436–1593

Groups		Percentages		
	1436	1483	1571	1593
Dutch/German	90.0	82.0	61.0	55.0
French	c.2.0	2.0	20.0	34.0
Italian	c.7.0	1.0	4.0	3.0
Scottish	—	10.0	1.0	0.5
Others	—	2.0	2.0	2.0
Origin not known/unidentified	1.0	3.0	12.0	5.5
Total %	100.0	100.0	100.0	100.0
Total No. of households	—	1 595	1 815	1 079

Notes: In the fifteenth century, personal names were often the only indicator of the place of origin of aliens. For this reason, they were often classified generally as 'Dutch', 'German' or 'French'. However, sixteenth-century sources such as Returns of Aliens enable us to establish their city/town/region of origin.

Sources: 1436: S. Thrupp, 'Aliens in and around London in the fifteenth century', in A.E.J. Hollaender and W. Kellaway, eds, *Studies in London History: Essays Presented to P.E. Jones* (London, 1969), pp. 251–72. 1483: J. Bolton, *The Alien Communities of London in the Fifteenth Century: The Subsidy Rolls of 1440 and 1483–4* (Stamford, 1998). 1571: R.E.G. Kirk and E.F. Kirk, eds, *Returns of Aliens Dwelling in the City and Suburbs of London*, Huguenot Society Publications, 1900–1908, Vol. 2, pp. 1–139; 1593: Scouloudi, *Returns of Strangers*, pp. 147–221.

inability of the Scots to compete with Continental immigrants in the London labour market. In the fifteenth century, there was a general need in London for migrants to fill the kind of labour shortages which the Scots could meet. However, in the sixteenth century there was a greater need for new skills and industries to diversify the economy, and perhaps Continental immigrants were better at meeting these.

Places of Origin

The origins of the aliens in London changed significantly between the fifteenth and sixteenth centuries. In the fifteenth century, the largest number of immigrants originated from Holland. Of a total of 1 547 Lowlanders mentioned in the Patent Rolls between 1435 and 1467, 34 per cent came from Holland, and then in descending order, Brabant (25 per cent), Zeeland

(9 per cent), Guelders (8 per cent), Flanders (6 per cent), Liège (5 per cent), Utrecht (4 per cent) and the remaining 9 per cent divided between Hainault, Artois/Picardy, Limburg, Friesia and Tournai.[51] The question of why aliens had come to England in the fifteenth century is problematic. Jim Bolton recently argued that they were filling a demand for labour and skills to serve the needs of a society in which the general standard of living was rising. However, he acknowledged that such a demand existed in equal, if not greater, measure in their homelands, as the aliens came from precisely the areas of Holland, Brabant and Zeeland where the economies were expanding. Political reasons, he explained, may have been decisive factors in persuading many to make the journey across the North Sea. In comparison with England, the northern Netherlands in the fifteenth century were racked by civil wars. It is noticeable that many of the migrants in 1436 came from the towns that were most affected by warfare, such as Gouda, Zevenbergen, Alkmaar and Zerikzee.[52] Such a movement was greatly facilitated by the existence of long-established interchange between England, the Low Countries and the Rhineland.

This raises the question as to why immigrants from the northern Netherlands did not move south in the fifteenth century to Bruges or Antwerp, where living standards and wages were much higher than those in London.[53] The mismatch of skills may have prevented the mobility of labour. Those who emigrated from Holland to London in the fifteenth century appear to have possessed largely traditional skills such as shoe-making, tailoring and brewing, and these were not the skills which were in demand by the expanding luxury crafts in the south. The move towards the production of high-quality textiles required skills in spinning, weaving and finishing, and suitable workers for this were available nearly exclusively in Flanders and Brabant.[54] The economic difference between the north and south Netherlands, then, was probably a key factor in preventing the mobility of labour. In any case, London was an attractive destination with good employment prospects.

In 1571, besides a sizeable group from the Rhineland, the other significant groups, in order of significance, were Dutch Flanders, Brabant and Walloon provinces, accounting for 35 per cent of the total householders. By 1593, the proportion from these three areas had risen to 47 per cent. In contrast to the process of chain migration in which only a handful of earlier migrants moved to London at a time, many had arrived *en masse*. Nearly half of the households surveyed in 1571 had arrived in the years between 1560 and 1571 (674 Dutch-speaking and 220 French-speaking households). By 1593, the relative importance of places of origin changed somewhat, with the highest number from Walloon provinces, then Brabant, Dutch Flanders, France and Rhineland (see Tables 4.4 and 4.5).

Table 4.4 Regions of origin and period of arrival of alien heads of households in London, 1571

Regions of origin	Period of arrival								Total for all, 1571	
	1500–40		1541–59		1560–71		Unknown			
	No.	%	No.	%	No.	%	No.	%	No.	%
Dutch/Flemish/German-speaking areas[a]										
N Netherlands	27		45		68		10		150	8.0
Brabant	13		35		150		8		206	11.0
Dutch Flanders	5		38		222		12		277	15.0
'Dutch'	10		54		146		33		243	13.0
Germany	1		3		16		—		20	1.0
Rhineland	31		87		72		16		206	11.0
Sub-total	87	5.0	262	14.0	674	37.0	79	4.0	1 102	61.0
French-speaking areas[b]										
'French'	13		32		36		7		88	5.0
Walloon provinces in the southern Netherlands[c]	1		15		148		7		171	9.0
France	28		38		36		6		108	6.0
Sub-total	42	2.0	85	5.0	220	12.0	20	1.0	367	20.0
Iberian and Italian										
Italy	3		24		27		9		63	3.8
Portugal	—		4		4		2		10	0.6
Spain	—		5		9		3		17	0.9
Sub-total	3	0.2	33	2.0	40	2.0	14	0.8	90	5.0
Others										
Denmark	—		—		1		1		2	0.1
Switzerland	1		—		4		1		6	0.3
Scotland	1		11		8		5		25	1.4
Turkey	1		—		—		—		1	0.1
English born	—		—		—		4		4	0.2
Travel back & forth	—		—		—		5		5	0.3
Sub-total	3	0.2	11	0.6	13	0.7	16	0.9	43	2.0
No data										
Unidentified places	—		10		11		2		23	1.0

Origin not given	14		26		100		50		190	11.0
Sub-total	14	0.8	36	2.0	111	6.0	52	3.0	213	12.0
Total	149	8.0	427	24.0	1058	58.0	181	10.0	1815	100.0

Notes: Sometimes a place of birth/origin is not given, and a stranger is recorded simply as 'Dutch' or 'French'.
[a] Henceforth will be referred to as 'Dutch/Flemish/German. [b] henceforth will be referred to as 'French'. [c] Henceforth will be referred to as 'Walloon provinces'. This method of classification is explained in Appendix 1.
Source: Kirk and Kirk, eds, *Returns of Aliens*, Vol. 10, No. 2, pp. 1–139. See also Table 3.4

Table 4.5 Regions of origin and period of arrival of alien heads of households in London, 1593

Regions of origin	\multicolumn{10}{c	}{Period of arrival}	Total for all present, 1593
	\multicolumn{2}{c	}{1520–59}	\multicolumn{2}{c	}{1560–71}	\multicolumn{2}{c	}{1572–83}	\multicolumn{2}{c	}{1584–93}	\multicolumn{2}{c	}{Unknown}		
	No.	%	No.	%	No.	%	No.	%	No.	%	No.	%
Dutch/Flemish/German												
N. Netherlands	6		13		16		13		6		54	5.0
Brabant	11		32		43		63		18		167	15.0
Dutch Flanders	4		34		36		58		17		149	14.0
'Dutch'	15		37		26		30		8		116	11.0
Germany	—		4		5		2		—		11	1.0
Rhineland	19		25		33		13		7		97	9.0
Sub-total	55	5.0	145	13.0	159	15.0	179	17.0	56	5.0	594	55.0
French												
'French'	6		10		7		10		—		33	3.0
Walloon provinces	1		42		61		55		30		189	18.0
France	14		22		39		53		15		143	13.0
Sub-total	21	2.0	74	7.0	107	10.0	118	11.0	45	4.0	365	34.0
Iberian and Italian												
Italy	10		5		4		12		1		32	3.0
Spain	—		1		—		2		—		3	0.3
Sub-total	10	1.0	6	0.6	4	0.4	14	1.3	1	0.1	35	3.0

Others

Denmark	—		—		1	—		—		1	0.1
Switzerland	—		1		8	—		—		9	0.8
Scotland	—		1		4	1		—		6	0.6
English born	—		1		1	1		6		9	0.8
Sub-total	—		3	0.3	14	1.3	2	0.2	6	0.6	2	2.0

No data

Unidentified places	1		1		8	9		5		24	2.2
Origin not given	4		4		11	7		10		36	3.3
Sub-total	5	0.5	5	0.5	19	1.8	16	1.5	15	1.4	60	6.0
Total	91	8.0	233	22.0	303	28.0	329	30.0	123	11.0	1 079	100.0

Note: Places of origin are listed in Appendix 1.
Source: Scouloudi, *Returns of Strangers*, pp. 147–221.

The Dutch Revolt and French Wars of Religion

The Dutch Revolt in the southern Netherlands and the civil wars in France were responsible for precipitating this mass emigration. The Dutch Revolt was sparked off by three main factors: political, economic and religious.[55] Political discontent against Spain had been brewing in the Netherlands since 1550, partly as a result of Philip's policies of political centralization. According to Geoffrey Parker, particularist feelings in the provinces of the Netherlands were strong, as a result of entrenched local institutions and traditions, different fiscal and legal systems, even separate languages.[56] Seventeen provinces were only welded into a political unit by Charles V to form a sort of 'United Netherlands' by 1550. All provinces owed obedience to Charles V, and on the whole, they obeyed the orders of the Brussels government. However, these provinces retained a significant degree of autonomy. Every province of the Netherlands had a representative assembly of its own, known as the States.[57] However, their local independence was progressively eroded by the introduction of far-reaching religious reforms in 1561 and the setting up of a special Inquisition by Philip II.[58] Political resentment was further aggravated by economic grievances resulting from rising taxation to pay for a war to defend Spanish Milan and Naples from the French. Although Spain sent large quantities of money to the Low Countries for the war, the Netherlanders were convinced that they were subsidizing Spain.[59] When they were asked again to provide more money in August 1557, the States-General agreed, but on one condition – Spanish troops must be removed from the Netherlands. In

January 1561, Spanish troops left, and this was the first major political victory for the Netherlands.

Political and economic grievances formed the seedbeds of the Dutch Revolt, but the final trigger probably lay in the unresolved issue of the Reformed religion. Calvinism made rapid progress in the Netherlands in the 1560s. The French-speaking communities at Tournai and Valenciennes were among the most active and well-organized in the Netherlands.[60] Their geographical proximity to France, linguistic bond with the French Protestants across the borders and industrial prosperity explain why these cities became Calvinist strongholds.[61] Commercial contacts were also important in the diffusion of Protestant ideas. Many French merchants travelled back and forth across an open border to trade in the Walloon towns and further north into Flanders, and they may have played a crucial role in the dissemination of books.[62] With the outbreak of the French Wars of Religion in 1562, many Huguenots took refuge in Walloon provinces, and were able to advise, teach and preach to their Netherlands co-religionists. Already in May 1561, Margaret of Parma expressed her concern that heresy 'grows here in proportion to the situation in our neighbours' countries'.[63] She may have exaggerated the contacts between the French and the Walloons, as there was quite a strong antipathy between these two groups dating back to wars in the late fifteenth century.

The government's response to the growth of the new religion was repression. Between 1521 and 1565, 2793 persons (almost 1 per cent of the total population) were accused of heresy in the province of Flanders.[64] This aroused much public resentment because the towns saw this as a serious threat to their public order, civic unity, economy, and to their privileges that safeguarded the process of justice and prevented total confiscation of property.[65] The public condemnation of persecution by the nobility led to the escalation of developments between 1564 and 1566. In 1564, William of Orange, a leading nobleman, gave a long speech in the Council of State, rejecting religious persecution and calling for freedom of conscience. The nobles sent the Count of Egmont on a special mission to Philip II to press for moderation of the religious persecution. The Count, upon his return to the Netherlands, believed that the King had agreed to the relaxation of heresy laws. However, the Segovia Woods letters of October 1565 made it clear that there was to be no change.[66] It is unclear whether this news prompted Protestants to escape to Germany or England. At this time, there was a growing willingness among a faction of nobles headed by Orange's brother, the Protestant Louis of Nassau, to consider the possibility of armed revolt. Orange persuaded this group that bloodshed could still be averted and that they should formally petition Margaret of Parma, Governess-General of the Netherlands (1559–67), for the redress of their grievances. On April 1566, three hundred noblemen presented Margaret of Parma with the *Request*. To avert an open revolt, Margaret of Parma published a Moderation that suspended the anti-heresy legislation temporarily and permitted Protestants to worship in areas where they were already established.[68]

The Moderation of 1566 had a far-reaching impact on subsequent events. It encouraged the Protestants to come out into the open, and persuaded many to return from exile. Open-air meetings were held, and in August 1566 the Iconoclastic Fury began to sweep over the Netherlands. Churches were attacked, and images, mass vestments and organs were destroyed.[69] The iconoclasm caused much panic, and in a desperate attempt to muster help, Margaret of Parma sent an alarming report to Philip II on 29 August 1566, claiming that half of the entire population was infected with heresy, and that over 200 000 people were up in arms against her authority.[70] Under much pressure, Philip II decided to resort to armed intervention, and sent the Duke of Alva to lead an army of 10 000 troops to the Netherlands to suppress the troubles.

The news of the impending arrival of the Duke sparked off a large exodus from the Low Countries. The Duke arrived in Brussels in August 1567 and set up a tribunal, the Conseil des Troubles, dubbed the 'Blood Council', to root out heresy. It is estimated that about 12 000 people were summoned to appear. Approximately 9000, including William of Orange, were sentenced by default and their possessions confiscated.[71] Among the 17 provinces in the Netherlands, Flanders suffered the highest number of condemnations (4077 people condemned), followed by Brabant (2028), Holland (1303), Tournai (1070) and Limburg (866).[72] Towns which were most affected included many prosperous and industrial towns, such as Tournai, Antwerp, Ypres and Valenciennes.[73] They also contained towns which formed part of a textile-producing group of cities in the southern Netherlands and northern France (for example, Ghent, Bruges, St Omer, Lille, Arras, Tournai, Valenciennes and Kortrijk), which had a reputation for their high-quality textiles.[74] The economic profiles of the towns suggest that textile workers were likely to be predominant among the emigrants.

The exodus from the Low Countries proceeded in two main waves – in the spring of 1567 and then again, following the first wave of arrests, in the winter of 1567–8. Those fleeing the Netherlands moved in three directions. From Amsterdam, the West Friesian towns of Friesland and Groningen, the flow was towards the north-western corner of Germany, especially Emden. From Flanders and Zeeland, emigrants took the sea route to England. From Brabant, southern Holland and Utrecht, the exiles gravitated mainly to Cleves and the Rhineland.[75] Perceived sympathy for their flight, the availability of economic opportunities, the ease of access, as well as the existence of an established exile community and Church were likely to have influenced these choices of destination.[76]

The military campaigns by the Spanish to recapture the southern Netherlands in the 1580s caused another major exodus. The former Calvinist strongholds in the south, Tournai and Valenciennes, were among the first to fall to Parma's political and military counter-offensive in the 1580s, and before long the Walloon churches of the south were suppressed. The closure of the churches sparked off a major exodus, partly to the traditional exile centres abroad but mostly to the free northern provinces. French-speaking churches were established in major towns in Holland to cater for the needs of the Walloon exiles, in Leiden in 1584, for example, and in Rotterdam in 1590.[77] Of the 159 households (out of 189) from Walloon provinces whose time of arrival is known in 1593, the largest cohort (61) arrived between 1572, and 1583, followed by a slightly smaller group (55) between 1584 and 1593 (see Table 4.5). This pattern diverged from that of Flanders and Brabant, whose exiles did not arrive in large numbers until the late 1580s. From 1582 onwards, Flanders became a theatre of military operations, and Bruges fell to Spanish hands in 1584. After Flanders was secure, Parma advanced to Brabant, and Spanish troops besieged Antwerp during the winter of 1584–5, causing starvation among its 80 000 inhabitants. In August 1585, Antwerp capitulated to Spanish troops. In the aftermath, Protestants who refused to re-convert to Catholicism were ordered to sell their homes and immovable possessions, and depart. Around half of Antwerp's population, some 38 000 people, is estimated to have emigrated largely to the north over the next four years.[78] The fall of Antwerp in 1585 did not precipitate large flows of refugees to London. According to the Return of 1593, only 63 households arrived from Brabant between 1584 and 1593. London appears to have been a less favoured destination than some of the booming towns in the Dutch Republic.

The growth of Calvinism also contributed to religious tensions in France. Mark Greengrass has estimated that in the decade 1560–70, there were roughly 1200 Protestant churches in France, with some 1 800 000 members. Although Protestants formed only about 10 per cent of the total population of France, they were unevenly distributed throughout the country.[79] Calvinism was particularly strong in Guyenne, Languedoc, Provence and Dauphiné – a region called Midi – but was largely absent in Burgundy, Champagne, Picardy (except Rouen) and Brittany. In Lyon, Calvinists formed some 33 per cent of the population.[80] Geographical proximity to Geneva partly explains the strength of Calvinism in these areas.

The social profile of the French Calvinist movement was increasingly skewed towards the social elites. While the earliest converts and even the bulk of the Protestants may have been made up of journeymen, artisans, master craftsmen, merchants and lawyers, Holt pointed out that during the period from 1555 until the outbreak of the Wars of Religion in 1562, a considerable number of the nobility began to convert to Calvinism. This development led to the politicization of French Calvinism, and religious issues increasingly became immersed in a political struggle at court between the Guises, the defenders of Catholicism, and the Bourbons and the Châtillons, the champions of Protestantism. In the hope of ending the violence between Protestants and Catholics, Catherine de Medici, who was ruling in the name of her young son, Charles IX (1560–74), issued the 'Edict of January' or 'Edict of Nantes' in 1562, giving Protestants the right to practise their religion without interference.[81] Calvinists were seen by Catholics as endangering local customs and traditional religion, and these signs of favour to Protestants provoked a violent reaction from Catholics, especially the noble House of Guise. The first civil war broke out in March 1562, when a Protestant congregation was massacred at Vassy by partisans of Francois, Duc de Guise.

In the period between 1562 and 1598 France was plunged into a series of eight civil wars. While the majority lasted only a year, foreign intervention prolonged the third civil war, which lasted two years, and the eighth, which lasted almost fourteen years. The outbreak of the first civil war led to the migration of refugees abroad, but the geographical concentration of Protestants in the south meant that many emigrated to Geneva rather than London.[82] However, the St Bartholomew's Day Massacre in 1572 stimulated a significant exodus to England. The areas which suffered most severely were Paris, where some 2000 Protestants were slaughtered, and Orléans, Meaux, Rouen, Angers and Troyes.[83] As these areas were close to England, many escaped there by water rather than to Geneva.

The exodus from France did not seem to occur on a large scale again until 1585. In July of that year, Henry III signed the Treaty of Nemours with the Catholic League. The treaty was a blow to Protestants. Not only did it revoke all the former edicts of pacification, but the practice of the 'so-called reformed religion' was forbidden everywhere in the kingdom. Pastors were to be banished, and Protestants were forced to abjure within six months or be exiled. The legal and military provisions for protection of Protestants were also revoked. This treaty led to the renewal of conflicts between Protestants and Catholics, and forced many Protestants to flee, as the only alternatives in France were arrest, confiscation of property or death.[84] It was not until the issue of Edict of Nantes in 1598 that the Protestants in exile were able to return to France.

Immigrants fleeing the Continent to England did not necessarily follow a linear path of migration, but moved step by step, in a process known as 'step migration'.[85] Those who escaped from west Flanders may have fled first to Brabant, in particular Antwerp, and later emigrated to London after the fall of Antwerp. The Return of 1593 recorded that Peter Rotinge was born in Flanders and his wife in Brabant, but that they had come from Brabant, and had lived in England for 14 years. It is unclear whether this meant that

Rotinge had initially fled from west Flanders to Brabant, and then moved to London in 1579, following the sack of Antwerp in 1578, or merely that he had lived in Brabant for many years before coming to London.[86] Other examples seem to indicate that some immigrants may have moved first to cities in the northern Netherlands, such as Amsterdam and Middelburg, and to Germany, before travelling to London. The Return of 1593 recorded that Davy Byyott was a Walloon born in Amsterdam, and that Jarmaine Saulyer was 'a Walloon of Middleburg'.[87] Danyell Taberkind was listed in the Return of 1593 as a Frenchman born in Frankfurt. He had lived in England for eighteen years, and was a member of the French church. His wife, on the other hand, was recorded as being born in Lille.[88] Again, it is uncertain whether these immigrants had fled to these areas during the disturbances in the 1560s or they simply belonged to families who had migrated to these places before the troubles. The absence of information on the last place of residence for all immigrants also makes it difficult to establish the general pattern of movement from the Low Countries and France. However, immigrants were more likely to be involved in step migration within the country of first settlement rather than between countries. In the previous chapter, it has already been noted that a group of refugees from Valenciennes moved to Southampton from London in 1567, and then later moved back to London, where economic opportunities were greater, while others were resettled from London to Sandwich, and from Sandwich to Norwich. Considerable movements were likely to occur in the initial first few years as immigrants sought to find a place which best met their needs.

Motives of Migration

In the face of persistent claims by natives and close government advisers that many aliens settling in London were not genuine refugees but economic migrants, and that some were criminals, anabaptists and sectaries, the Privy Council was compelled to act.[89] In November 1571 it instructed Aldermen undertaking the survey to include an extra search article: to find out the reasons why aliens had come to settle in the city. The response, however, was heavily coloured by the City's decree of 1568 allowing only religious refugees to stay in the City.[90] It should come as no surprise then that when the strangers were asked by officials for their reasons for moving to London, over 674 households, or 74 per cent of those who gave their reasons, told English officials that they had come because of 'religion' and the 'troubles' in the Low Countries, and only 138 householders (nearly 8 per cent) risked expulsion by confessing that they had come to look for work and seek a living.

The Privy Council recognized the questionable reliability of the survey, and accordingly took steps to check its accuracy. It appointed, for example, the Bishop of London to interview some of the strangers sent by the Lord Mayor (a total of six aliens, including one Scot).[91] Besides this, the Privy Council also instructed the Bishop to compare the 'presentments of the Wards' (that is, details found by local English officials) with certificates of the Elders of the Dutch, French and Italian church,[92] and membership lists of the English church. The report produced in December 1573 contained some alarming conclusions. Of the 7143 aliens living in the capital, the names of only 25 per cent (1763 aliens) could be found both in the Ward's presentments and in the certificates of the Stranger Churches; 12 per cent (889 aliens) claimed to be members of the English church had in fact lied as their names were not found on parish church membership lists; nearly 26 per cent (1828 aliens) were found on the Stranger Churches' registers but not on the 'presentments of the Wards', suggesting that they had escaped the notice of the English officials who conducted the surveys. Moreover, these had confessed to come 'to seek a living' rather than for religion. For the Privy Council, the most worrying aspect of the report was the finding that 37 per cent (2663 aliens) belonged to no church at all.[93] If this is added to the 889 aliens who had lied about their parish church membership, it means that nearly half of the aliens in London were not members of any church. This finding aroused suspicions in the Privy Council that many immigrants may have been Anabaptists, a movement known to have enjoyed a large following in the Netherlands. The English government saw the Anabaptists as a threat to the state, and in July 1575 ordered the burning of two Dutch Anabaptists in London.[94] The refugee churches sought to distance themselves from the Anabaptists. Thus, in the 1560s, when the minister Adriaen van Haemstede was suspected of Anabaptism, he was cut off from the church, together with a number of his followers including the famous merchant and historian Emanuel van Meteren.[95] As long as they could convince the Privy Council's expert examiners (among whom Edwin Sandys, the Bishop of London, was particularly prominent) that they were 'honest in conversation, … well-disposed to the good obedience of the queen's majesty and the realm' and that they were willing to join a church, aliens were permitted to stay. Those who refused to join any church were ordered to leave the city in February 1573.[96]

For opponents of aliens, the report confirmed their suspicions that many aliens had not come for religion, but for economic reasons. Yet neither church non-membership nor personal confessions are satisfactory yardsticks for determining economic motives, for several reasons. In the first place, non-membership of a church did not mean that aliens were not religious refugees, but that they were perhaps undecided or awaiting admission. When examined by the Bishop of London in February 1571, Hans Peniable plainly stated that he had not joined any church because he was not yet settled, and could not tell where he would obtain work.[97] That kind of explanation was probably accepted as fair, especially because application for admission was not a straightforward procedure. The easiest way to secure speedy acceptance into the church was to produce a letter of recommendation from another Reformed community from the Continent. But many arrived in London without such a letter, either because they had not been members of a community in their own country or because they had been constantly on the move. In this case, they had to undergo a rigorous process of examination to ensure that they understood the fundamental doctrines of the church.[98] Second, many aliens who were true political/religious refugees may not have wished to state their real reasons for moving to London, perhaps fearing that this would attract attention from the Spanish authorities in the capital, leading to possible arrests. Those involved in iconoclasm in the summer of 1566 in particular may have wanted to hide this from the authorities. This may explain why those such as Lievin Adraps from Tournai, Cornelis Bousin from Antwerp, Marcus de Palma from Antwerp and Julien Santere from Tournai, all settled in London in 1571, did not state their motives. They were among those who were condemned and banished by the Conseil des Troubles in 1567, and were clearly religious refugees, yet they did not state their fear of persecution or political motives for seeking refuge in London.[99]

The process of migration involved two interconnected decisions. The first concerned the question of whether to leave one's homeland or not, and the second related to the decision of where to go. It is difficult to deny that political and religious circumstances – the iconoclasm, the arrival of the Duke of Alva, and the hostilities consequent upon this – were compelling factors forcing many to leave the southern Netherlands. The real question is how many immigrants were directly affected. The time of departure would give some indication to this question: those who were most fearful of persecution, the hard core, were likely to have fled well before the arrival of the Duke in August 1567. On 11 April 1567, the day William of Orange left Antwerp, a chronicler, Godevaert van Haecht, reported that nearly 4000 had fled the city. Although this may be an exaggeration, a census of October 1568 stated that in the previous year more than three thousand had left the city because of the departure of the prince of Orange.[100] The unfolding of the brutalities of the Duke's regime, as reflected by the execution of some leading local noblemen including the Count of Egmont, might have sent some chilling vibes and persuaded those who perhaps initially did not fear for their lives to leave in the immediate years after the Duke's arrival. The third group might have left because their livelihoods were threatened by the decline of the textile industry in the southern Netherlands as a result of trading war between England and the Netherlands. In addition, there were also problems of food shortages due to the uncertain supply of Baltic corn as a result of war.[101]

The decision to come to England was influenced by two principal factors: religious freedom, and perceived economic opportunities. In 1569, Jan van der Noot, a native of Antwerp, indicated that he had chosen to take refuge in England because it was 'a most safe and sure harborough, where we live under your Majesties protection and safegarde in great libertie to serve God ...'.[102] Janssz Beverloo, on the other hand, having fled to Emden in December 1571, wrote to his wife of his intention to go from there to England, 'where business is good'.[103] Initially, some refugees harboured fears of not being able to find work in England, but were soon assured by letters sent home by friends and relatives. In 1568, many exiles from Norwich wrote to their families and friends in Ypres, telling them that life in England was cheaper than in Flanders, and that it was easy to make a living there. England was portrayed as a promised land: 'if you were here ... you would never think of returning to Flanders'.[104] These seem to confirm G.N. Clark's conclusion:

> The religious refugees fleeing the Low Countries during the 1560s had other countries open to them; they did not hurry over without looking where they were going. England offered them safety ... [and] better opportunities for profit than they had in the Netherlands or France. There was a market among the population which was growing in numbers and wealth; the chief raw material, wool, was near at hand, labour was cheaper; there were ... better conditions of law and order.[105]

Homeward-looking and the Sojourner Mentality

The involuntary nature of migration for many refugees, especially those from the southern Netherlands, affected their lives in London in several fundamental ways. For many aliens, life in England was far from settled, with constant travelling back and forth to the Continent. Some went to the Continent to conduct business, some were forced back to find work, while others went for personal needs (permission to marry, or death in a family).[106] For those who had been banished with no possibility of travelling back and forth, life in exile was particularly hard, as many had left families behind and were under constant pressure to return. The rare letters written to refugees in England between 1570 and 1571 provide an insight into the anxieties, agonies and sufferings facing many broken families, and how reunion of families was hampered by the impossibility of their husbands returning to fetch them, the dangers facing women and children travelling on their own, the need for passports to travel, the difficulty of finding someone trustworthy to take care of business, and the advice of remaining relatives not to leave.[107] In a letter to her husband, Isabeau Parent wrote: 'You ask me to come – wise people advise me not to go yet.'[108] Letters from wives or parents often expressed the hope that the exiles would return. In a letter written in February 1570, the wife of

Martin Plennart who had been banished from Valenciennes in 1568, confirmed that although the goods of those banished had been confiscated, his had not, and told him not to worry. She also reported that people were daily returning home, and wished that he could come back, as she could not go to England with the children because the roads were not safe. She also told him how his daughters were asking when he would return, and that one of them said that he could not, as his feet hurt too much.[109] In a letter to his son, a father urged him to come back for several reasons: business was improving (although local wool had to be used because of a shortage of English and Spanish wool), the police were not looking for him; it was safe to return as long as he kept a low profile concerning his religious beliefs; he could come back via Calais, and if he joined the people at the market there on Saturdays no one would notice him; and if he came back, he would be as safe as he was in England.[110] Other letters demonstrate the many agonies facing wives left behind with children. In a letter to her husband, Jacqueline Leurent wrote how she had been writing to him for two years but received no reply, and asked him what she should do about the properties, how to find money to feed the children, and what was the best way to get to him.[111]

Many also found it difficult to put roots down in their new homeland, as much of their wealth was still left abroad. Pettegree found that more than 25 per cent of strangers in London mentioned goods and property abroad in their wills. Besides merchants who had no reason to dispose of lands and goods abroad as they divided their time between London and the Continent, it is striking how many who fled as religious refugees did so as well. Many no doubt came to England without the intention of permanent settlement, and if they hoped to return, the laborious effort of selling-up was pointless. Perhaps they also kept property abroad as a form of insurance, if a similar order of expulsion like that under Mary's reign was ever to reoccur.[112] But an inescapable reason was that some, departing in haste and fearful for their lives, simply did not have the time to sell their property (though many managed to transfer their property over to another family member to avoid confiscation). In any case a short-notice property sale would not fetch the full market value. The retention of property abroad and the ability to transfer wealth had two possible consequences. It may have prevented family members from joining them in England. Justinne Ploiart wrote from Tournai to her brother Guillaume le Myeulx, who was living in London in February 1570, explaining how she would love to leave but could not, because of the difficulty of finding someone trustworthy to take care of his business, and that she was still waiting for her uncle to give her the money accrued from selling his goods.[113] In addition, material sacrifice and the loss of financial resources may have prevented refugees from taking the necessary steps to improve their status and conditions in London. Guillame Coppin, once a well-to-do merchant in

Valenciennes, had to make drastic revisions to his will in 1572 because 'by the trouble that passed in the lowe countries I lost a great deale of my goods which god had lent me'. His wife, who previously had been left with 2700 *livres tournois*, now had to be safisfied with the remains of his goods. His son, who was to have 1400 *livres*, would now get 300, with another 400 'when liberty shall be in the low countries and that profit and sale of my goods which are at Valenciennes may be made'.[114] Six years in exile in England, then, had not diminished Coppin's hopes of peace and eventual return to his homeland.

Hopes of return prompted many members of the French and Dutch Church to continue their struggle in the Netherlands against their Spanish masters from their secure base in exile, by supplying men, money and weapons. The London Stranger Churches, for example, provided William of Orange with financial assistance for his campaigns in 1568 and 1570, but the largest assistance came in April 1572 when over 500 troops were apparently recruited among the refugees and £500 raised to buy arms.[115] Many refugees saw their life in England as temporary, especially those from France. Most took advantage of a change in the war, a truce, or an edict of pacification, especially after 1598, to return home. For the refugees from the Netherlands, the situation was different. The promulgation of religious freedom in 1578 encouraged some to go back to their former homes in the southern cities, but the hopes raised by this soon proved illusory. The loss of Antwerp in 1585 had a great psychological impact, forcing Reformed exiles from Flanders and Brabant finally to face the painful prospect that they would never return to their homelands. Some opted instead to settle in Holland and Zeeland; those who remained in London increasingly attached greater permanency to their residence.[116] Although many exiles in Holland and London may have continued to regard 'Flanders' as their fatherland, they had to come to terms with the political reality. For the Dutch, the year 1585 marked a watershed, completing their transition from exiles to residents.

Occupations of Strangers

In the fifteenth century, the occupational structure of aliens and native English was comparable, with both groups catering for the basic needs of Londoners for food, clothing and shoes, and so on. In 1483, recent research by Bolton shows the largest occupational groups were 259 alien households (20 per cent) engaged in cloth/clothing industry, 168 (13 per cent) in leather/leather-working, 144 (11.1 per cent) in metal-working, and 119 in brewing (9.2 per cent).[117] By the early sixteenth century, Continental artisans in London still tended to pursue trades traditionally performed by English artisans. The Dutch church registers show that in 1550 the largest occupational groups among its members were 50 shoemakers and cobblers, 45 tailors and 37 assorted woodworkers (mainly joiners and chestmakers).[118] By 1561, Pettegree argued that there had been a marked shift away from these traditional occupations towards new and luxury crafts. There were now only 12 shoemakers in the Dutch list and 6 woodworkers, but 30 weavers, of which at least 9 were silk-weavers. The occupational structure of members of the French church also shows an overrepresentation of workers in certain trades: 28 of the 34 weavers in the French list were silk-weavers, along with 41 hatters, glovers, cappers, makers of 'superfluous goods' whose import was greatly resented.[119] In London and other parts of England, the refugees who arrived after the 1560s from the Continent came to be closely identified with the 'new' and luxury industries such as threadmaking, the New Draperies, linen weaving, lacemaking, sugar refining and glassmaking. These were products which had figured prominently in the imports list in 1559, and were types of industries the government was particularly keen to develop.[120]

The occupations of immigrants recorded in the Returns of Aliens of 1571 and 1593 are presented in Table 4.6.[121] From the table, it is clear that most aliens in Elizabethan London were artisans engaged in manufacturing activities rather than in trade or transport. The proportion of artisans increased by 10 per cent (from 59 to 69 per cent) between 1571 and 1593, in comparison with 3 per cent (from 17 to 20 per cent) of the proportion in non-manufacturing activities. It is significant to note the number of those of gentleman status, which although rising insignificantly from 12 to 14, does suggest that the emigration from France and the Netherlands in this period was of a different calibre.

The patterns of manufacturing activities of aliens in London show three striking facts. The first was a marked number working in the luxury trades, accounting for 14 per cent of all alien households in 1571 and 25.5 per cent in 1593. Expressed as a proportion of artisans, this concentration was even greater: 24 per cent of all artisans in 1571 were involved in the luxury trades, and 37 per cent in 1593.[122] The largest group within the luxury trades was the silk workers. In 1571, 183 households, or 72 per cent of all engaged in the luxury trades, were involved in silk-related activities, decreasing slightly to 71 per cent by 1593. The overall proportion engaged in the luxury trades, however, rose in 1593, with greater diversification as a result of the introduction of trades such as agate cutting, book selling, diamond cutting, sugar refining, and expansion of clockmaking, jewellery and silk dying. After the silk workers came the goldsmiths, with 39 noted in both 1571 and 1593. As many alien goldsmiths were journeymen, some working with English masters, the Returns underestimated their number. Between 1558 and 1598, there may have been as many as 500 alien goldsmiths working in London.[123]

Table 4.6 Occupational groups of aliens in London, 1571 and 1593

Types of activity	1571 No. of HH	%	1593 No. of HH	%
Non-manufacturing				
Professions	50	2.7	44	4.1
Miscellaneous services	42	2.3	20	1.8
Officials	1	0.1	0	0.0
Mercantile	184	10.1	126	11.7
Transport	25	1.4	8	0.7
Labouring	13	0.7	14	1.3
Sub-total	315	17.0	212	20.0
Manufacturing				
Luxury trades[a]	254	14.0	275	25.5
New trades[a]	26	1.4	22	2.0
Traditional trades	791	43.6	447	41.4
Sub-total	1 071	59.0	744	69.0
Others				
Gentleman	12	0.7	14	1.3
Live off alms/savings	10	0.6	3	0.3
No occupation	1	0.1	39	3.6
Miscellaneous	2	0.1	10	0.9
Sub-total	25	1.4	66	6.0
Occupation not given	404	22.0	57	5.0
Total	1 815	100.0	1 079	100.0

Notes: HH = heads of households. [a] These trades are listed in Appendix 2.
Sources: 1571: Kirk and Kirk, eds, *Returns of Aliens*, Vol. 2, pp. 1–139. 1593: Scouloudi, *Returns of Strangers*, pp. 147–221.

The proportion engaged in the new trades experienced a slight increase, from 1.4 per cent in 1571 to 2 per cent by 1593, with some important changes. The number of printers in London declined drastically, while the comfit makers, fustian weavers, orris workers, potmakers and weavers of crewel disappeared. It is unclear whether this reflected the shift of the manufacture of these products elsewhere, or the acquisition of these skills by native workers by the latter date. The number of perfumers of gloves, on the other hand, increased, and rash workers, starchers and stillers were recorded for the first time. It is believed that Mistress Dinghen van der Plasse, a refugee from Tienen in Brabant, may have introduced starching in the capital in 1564. She took in English girls as trainees, charging £4 and £5 to teach them how to starch, and 20 shillings for showing them how to prepare it. Ruffs soon became essential wear with men as well as with women who wanted to keep up with the fashion.[124]

This raises the question of why such a significant proportion now plied one of the luxury trades. Religion may provide a possible explanation, since many who arrived in London after the 1550s were Protestant refugees. Research into the socio-economic backgrounds of members of the Protestant movement suggests that certain occupations such as those in which skills were involved, those based on new technology, as in printing, new claims for prestige (jewellery or goldsmithing) or recent arrivals (silk manufacture) were over-represented.[125] Calvinism, in the words of Florimond de Raemond, attracted 'those whose trades contain a certain nobility of the spirit'.[126] However, this argument does not seem convincing, for it does not explain the differences of occupational activities of Protestant refugees settling in different cities in England. Another important explanation for the occupational shift relates to changes in places of origin of immigrants. The proportion from industrial, prosperous towns and cities in Brabant, Dutch Flanders and Walloon provinces increased from 36 to 47 per cent between 1571 and 1593. Again, this factor does not adequately explain the divergent occupational structure of aliens in different English towns and cities.

The overriding influence on the occupational patterns of immigrants was the nature of local demand and opportunities. As London was a centre of economic and political power, with a strong demand for skills to satisfy conspicuous consumption, it is to be expected that aliens with those skills would gravitate towards London. Even if they did not, the economic possibilities were compelling enough to encourage them to adapt their skills or learn those in high demand to earn a living. The importance of local opportunities in moulding occupational choices and patterns explains why strangers in London concentrated on silk and luxury trades, and those in the provincial towns on the New Draperies. In East Anglian towns, the demand for the 'New Draperies' meant that 'the great majority of the strangers had to learn weaving, wool combing and spinning … for the bay and say making were the most profitable occupations except those of the hosiers and the market gardeners'.[127] Similarly, in Sandwich, strangers who exercised different occupations in their country of origin, such as farmers, smiths, shoemakers, millers and bookbinders, became baize and say workers when they arrived in their new place of settlement.[128] Letters written by exiles to families back home also confirm considerable occupational mobility. Clement Baet, writing to his wife from Norwich in September 1567, told her that 'there is good trade in bays. Tell your sister that Lein [a proper name of Gelein] cannot come here to practice his craft [unspecified], because they only make bays here.' Gilles Navegeer, in a letter to his grandmother, told her how he had learnt bookbinding for the past eighteenth months, but 'that gave me too little profit, so that in 1569 I had taken to another trade, by which I hope to do better'.[129]

The Returns of Aliens may also have exaggerated the concentration of strangers in the new and luxury trades. Aware that one of their principal aims was to investigate whether they were competing with natives for jobs, some aliens may have lied about their occupation, as they did for church membership, and claimed to practise a 'new art', to avoid possible expulsion. This claim for the introduction of new 'arts' and trades became aliens' staunchest defence in periods of economic friction. In 1594, in response to the molestation of its members by informers, the Dutch church pointed out to the Lord Keeper of the Great Seal that its members introduced new skills and provided valuable employment to many English workers. Silk twisting, for example, was not 'used by Englishmen', and sixteen or eighteen alien silk twisters 'set on worke and maintaine under them a thowsand English poore people at the least'.[130] In other words, alien households were not rivals, but providers of jobs for many poor native English.

Despite this claim, the second striking fact about the occupational activities of aliens was the predominant proportion engaged in traditional crafts: 44 per cent in 1571, dropping slightly to 41 per cent by 1593. The number working in tailoring, botchering (mending old clothes), shoemaking, and shoe repairing experienced a sharper decline, from 23 per cent in 1571 to 15 per cent by 1593. Harassment and prosecution by the two Companies involved – the Merchant Tailors and the Cordwainers – were partly responsible for this decline.[131] Alien shoemakers were constantly harassed by native craftsmen and the Company of Cordwainders because shoemaking, as one informer claimed, was 'well exercised within this Realme, and wherein [there was] no nede of any Aliens …'.[132] Alien tailors faced even greater harassment. The fall in demand for clothing in London in the 1590s intensified competition for work between native and alien tailors. Native tailors accused aliens of expropriating work from them. In 1591, the Merchant Tailors' Company was pressed to take tougher action against aliens by the 'poorest sorte of the bretheren … [who] take discontentment and finde themselves agreed that forrinors and strangers which work inwardlie, and take the worke … out of freemens handes'.[133] The demand for clothing probably fell to its lowest point in 1598, as real wages entered a trough.[134] In March 1598, the poorer members demanded further 'ayde and assistance of [the] Company for the repressing and putting downe of forren Taylors'.[135] The Master and Wardens took up the matter with the Lord Mayor, who in turn appointed a committee to investigate the complaints by the tailors. The ensuing investigation apparently found 410 foreigner and stranger householders in the City, keeping 910 servants, making a total of 1320.[136] Following this report, the city prohibited foreigners and aliens from working in London, to alleviate pressure on the tailors,[137] but this failed to satisfy members of the Merchant Tailors, who wished to expel strangers and foreigners from London, a policy reluctantly adopted by the Company in the early seventeenth century. In September 1602, the Company was notified that, as a result of harassment by informers, 207 alien and foreign tailors had 'gonne', 68 were made free, and only 206 were 'nowe remayning'.[138] The Company also presented a bill in Parliament for the expulsion of foreigners.[139] However, the bill was rejected because it was regarded as 'unreasonable'. Having already spent over £100 on legal costs,[140] the Company decided not to go further but to examine 'the aucthorytie granted us by charter, which we find to be very large and liberal'.[141]

Guild harassment produced two possible effects, forcing aliens either to work clandestinely, or to move to occupations where there was no established guild. The second movement may have been responsible for the decline in the total number of trades practised by aliens, which plummeted sharply from 190 to 136 trades between 1571 and 1593.[142] The trades no longer practised by aliens included book printing and binding, locksmithing, sackcloth weaving and gun-related trades. This suggests that a process of consolidation had taken place in certain sectors, following an initial period of experimentation.

The employment of aliens in a narrower range of economic activities than the native population is also striking.[143] The strangers were concentrated overwhelmingly in the clothing industry (see Table 4.7), which absorbed more than 40 per cent of the alien artisan workforce in both 1571 and 1593, in comparison with over 20 per cent in a sample of native Londoners. Certain occupations were under-represented among the strangers. Most conspicuous was the absence of officials, though the relative under-representation of strangers in the professional, building, distribution and transport, and labouring categories in comparison with native Londoners is also striking.

The number of aliens engaged in mercantile activities was significant, but it was comparable to that of natives. The provenance of alien merchants in London had, however, now completely changed with the influx from the Netherlands. In the first half of the sixteenth century, the Italian and German mercantile communities, numbering 70 and 80 members respectively,[144] still dominated the alien London mercantile scene, but by the 1570s they were

Table 4.7 Occupational groups of aliens and natives in London compared, 1540–1600

Trades	% distribution of strangers City of London (26 wards) (1) 1571	City of London (2) 1593	City of London, Surrey, Middlesex (3) 1593	% distribution of natives Sample of London parishes (4) 1540–1600
Building	7.0	4.0	3.0	8.0
Clothing	42.0	47.0	44.0	22.0
Decorating/furnishing	1.0	2.0	1.5	1.0
Distribution/transport	2.0	1.0	0.5	6.0
Labouring	1.0	2.0	0.5	5.0
Leather	8.0	5.0	5.0	9.0
Merchants	13.0	13.0	11.0	13.0
Metalwork	8.0	8.0	11.0	9.0
Miscellaneous services	4.0	2.0	2.5	6.0
Miscellaneous production	5.0	5.0	7.0	2.0
Officials	0.1	—	—	4.0
Professions	4.0	5.0	3.0	6.0
Victualling	5.0	7.0	10.0	9.0
Total	100.0 (n) 1 386	100.0 (n) 956	100.0 (n) 1 735	100.0 (n) 2 388

Sources: Column 1, 1571: Kirk and Kirk, eds, *Returns of Aliens*, Vol. 2, pp. 1–139. Column 2, 1593: Scouloudi, *Returns of Strangers*, pp. 147–221. Column 3, 1593: Ellesmere MS 2514. Column 4;; Beir, 'Engine of manufacture: Trades of London' in L. Beier and R. Finlay, eds, *London 1500–1700: The Making of Metropolis* (London, 1986), pp. 141–67. The number of households in 1571 was 1815, in 1593 (col. 2) 1079 and in 1593 (col. 3) 1862. To make the data comparable with that of Beier, aliens whose occupations are unknown or classified as 'others' have been deducted from the totals.

outnumbered by those from the southern Netherlands. In 1571, the most significant group of merchants were 36 from Flanders (26 Flanders, 6 Ghent, 4 Bruges), 19 from Brabant (13 Antwerp and 6 Brabant), and 6 from Valenciennes. Only 9 were recorded from Italy (4 were stated to come from 'Italy' and 5 from Venice), and 2 from Cologne. Although the number of alien merchants was quite numerous, it is uncertain how many were able to conduct their business, especially as they were prohibited from trading with the Low Countries after Christmas 1571.[145] Apparently, many were able to travel back and forth to the Continent to conduct business, as in 1583 the French consistory instructed that elders and deacons, who in general were wealthy merchants and financiers, not to leave the country for business purposes without first informing their colleagues.[146]

Topographical Distribution of Strangers in London

Although aliens were dispersed throughout the City in the fifteenth and sixteenth centuries, there were also definite clusters (see Table 4.8). In 1483, the heaviest concentrations of aliens were along the riverside wards, with 34 per cent of aliens, especially Dowgate and Tower Wards. Next in importance were those in the eastern wards, where 24 per cent of aliens resided, principally in the ward of Portsoken and to a lesser degree Aldgate. There was also a significant concentration of aliens in northern and western wards, in Farringdon Within and Without, Cripplegate, and Aldersgate.[147] Data are not available for Southwark for 1483–4, but the number of aliens liable to pay subsidy in 1440 (445 aliens, wives included) suggests the presence of a significant community, largely of 'Doche' origins, south of the river.[148] In 1551, 281 alien households and 293 alien servants and apprentices were recorded in Southwark, with the greatest concentration in St Olave's Parish.[149]

In the sixteenth century, aliens continued to move into areas of traditional settlement, but there were significant changes in patterns. First, there was a marked decline in the proportion in riverside wards, from 34 to 21 per cent between 1483 and 1593. This decline was hastened by the City's policy of dispersal due to severe overcrowding in these areas, an inescapable problem resulting from the tendency of migrants to settle around their point of entry.[150] These Thames-side wards were generally the poorest, and there was a fear that overcrowding and subdivision of houses presented a health risk. In 1571, the City attempted to tackle the problems caused by strangers concentrating in riverside parishes by ordering that no leases falling vacant in Botolph's Wharf or Somer's Key should be let to aliens.[151]

The alien population in eastern wards, on the other hand, experienced overall expansion, especially from 1568 with the doubling of the population from 16 per cent to 32 per cent by 1593. Bishopsgate, situated outside the walls, saw the greatest increase in its alien population, from 2.7 per cent in 1483, 5 per cent in 1571, to 11 per cent by 1593, helped undoubtedly by its geographical proximity to the location of the French and Dutch churches in the more expensive inner ward of Broad Street. The concentration of the French-speaking immigrants in areas in close proximity to the Stranger Churches was much more pronounced than Dutch-speaking immigrants. In 1571, 16 per cent of all French-speaking immigrants settled in Bishopsgate,

Table 4.8 Residential distribution of aliens by the wards of the City of London, 1483–1593

Wards	1483[a] No.	%	1568 No.	%	1571 No.	%	1593 No.	%
Riverside wards								
Bridge	7	0.4	79	1.7	62	1.3	62	1.2
Billingsgate	77	4.8	247	5.4	271	5.9	245	4.7
Castle Baynard	21	1.3	111	2.4	53	1.1	71	1.4
Dowgate	191	12.0	166	3.6	123	2.7	189	3.6
Queenhithe	45	2.8	49	1.0	36	0.8	52	1.0
Tower	139	8.7	439	9.5	424	9.2	330	6.3
Vintry	61	3.8	69	1.5	88	1.9	49	0.9
Sub-total	541	34.0	1 160	25.0	1 057	23.0	998	19.0
Eastern wards								
Aldgate	80	5.0	259	5.6	328	7.0	504	9.6
Bishopsgate	43	2.7	233	5.0	376	8.1	577	11.0
Broad Street	41	2.6	145	3.1	179	3.9	265	5.0
Portsoken	216	13.5	76	1.7	139	3.0	323[c]	6.1
Sub-total	380	24.0	713	16.0	1 022	22.0	1 669	31.7
Northern and Western wards								
Aldersgate	60	3.8	320	7.0	296	6.4	369	7.0
Coleman Street	23	1.4	80	1.7	70	1.5	173	3.3
Cripplegate	86	5.4	277	6.0	178	3.8	187	3.6
Farringdon Without	104	6.5	176	3.8	248	5.4	177	3.4
Farringdon Within	46	2.9	311	6.7	192	4.1	508	9.7
Sub-total	319	20.0	1 164	25.0	984	21.0	1 414	27.0
Central wards								
Bassishaw	9	0.6	—	—	18	0.4	19	0.4
Bread Street	25	1.6	46	1.0	37	0.8	34	0.6
Candlewick Street	47	2.9	149	3.2	121	2.6	102	1.9
Cheap	33	2.1	50	1.1	31	0.7	24	0.5
Cordwainer	34	2.1	25	0.5	19	0.4	26	0.5
Cornhill	6	0.4	28	0.6	51	1.1	48	0.9
Langbourn	137	8.6	256	5.5	268	5.8	370	7.0
Lime Street	9	0.6	31	0.7	32	0.7	67	1.3
Walbrook	55	3.4	67	1.5	45	1.0	86	1.6

Sub-total	355	22.0	652	14.0	622	13.0	776	14.8
Total for 1483	1 595	100.0						
Southwark								
Bridge Without	No data	No data	916	20.0	946	21.0	402	76.6
Total			4 605[b]	100.0	4 631	100.0	5 259	100.0

Notes: [a] Based on alien subsidies. [b] The official figure for the wards was 4106, but this excluded the number living in St Martin-le-Grand (269) and Blackfriars (230). I have added the number living in these areas to make the data comparable with others. [c] This figure is illegible in the original MS.

Sources: 1483: Bolton, 'Aliens in fifteenth-century London: A Reappraisal'. 1568 and 1571: Kirk and Kirk, eds, *Returns of Aliens*, Vol. 2, pp. 1–139; Vol. 3, pp. 330–439. 1593: BL, Lansdowne 74/31.

in comparison to 4.5 per cent of Dutch-speaking immigrants. The absence of a well-established French community helps to explain this difference. For many French-speaking immigrants from Walloon provinces and France who had no kinsmen or relatives already in the city, or who were not familiar with the place, the Stranger Churches may have provided a point of orientation. There, the newcomers were likely to receive assistance in obtaining accommodation and work, either from the more established church members living in the city or from ministers, and could also enjoy the company of people who spoke their language and shared their culture. However, as Pettegree has pointed out, when strangers flocked to Austin Friars and to the French Church in Threadneedle Street, both situated in the Broad Street Ward in the prosperous heart of the City, Englishmen were made aware just how many strangers there were in the City. The effect was to stimulate a wave of hostile rumours about the vast numbers of strangers in the city, who made easy scapegoats for the high prices and food shortages.[152]

The overwhelming majority of strangers settled in areas north of the river. In 1568, for example, 84 per cent of the 6704 aliens surveyed settled in areas north of the river, and only 16 per cent south of the river. By 1593, the Returns suggest that the proportion north of the river had increased to 90–92 per cent, and the proportion south of the river declined to 8–10 per cent. It is worth highlighting two important points. First, nearly half (43 per cent) of those living in areas north of the river settled in 'exempted places' within the City's walls and in Middlesex. Second, the strangers concentrated largely on the edges of the city. In 1593, for example, the highest proportion of strangers settled in the eastern, northern and western edges of the city, in Aldersgate, Aldgate, Bishopsgate, and Farringdon Within. This distribution followed the general expansion of the city. The northern, eastern and southern (mainly Southwark) edges of the city witnessed the greatest growth. In 1560, they accounted for just 23 per cent of the metropolitan population; in 1600, they made up 40 per cent. With the rapid spread of the city, economic zoning became more marked, and three areas of specialization emerged: (1) the old city, largely within the old walls, which was mercantile in its economic orientation; (2) the new aristocratic West End, which was geared to big spending, the professions and Whitehall, and (3) the extra-mural areas, which were mainly focused on manufacturing. This suggests that production was expanding most rapidly on the northern, eastern and western edges of London.[153]

What factors determined these patterns of distribution of aliens in London? Why did the proportion in areas south of the river fall? The settlement of aliens in areas outside the City's walls was partly determined by the availability of space and housing. The supply of housing in intra-mural London was also contracting by 1600. On the other hand, rents were lower outside the walls and there was more space to work. Outside the City, 15 houses might occupy an acre of land, in comparison to the density of 95 houses an acre within the walls.[154] The cost and availability of 'plant' were not the only significant factors. Institutional constraints such as the City's exclusion or discouragement of certain trades from working within the walls also played a part. A number of manufacturing trades were affected – felt-making, tallow-chandlering, leatherworking, and the manufacture of alum, glass, oil, soap and starch. In 1623, when the City tried to force members of the Feltmakers' Company to move to areas outside the wall, 'their trade ... being noisome to their neighbours', they told the City that they would not want to work within the walls anyway, 'for they must have great deal of housing cheap and the use of much water in their trade and be near the fields for drying their wools'.[155]

Evasion of the city guilds' regulatory powers also exerted a powerful influence on residential patterns. In sixteenth-century London, there were more than a hundred guilds with extensive powers controlling and regulating manufacturing in the capital.[156] In order to have the right to engage independently in economic activity in London (the ability to set up a shop and to buy and sell goods), craftsmen must have served the mandatory seven-year apprenticeship. They also needed to possess the freedom of the City, which was indispensable for acquiring economic and other rights, and the guilds had virtual exclusive power to determine who obtained freedom and citizenship.[157] Some guilds, such as the Goldsmiths, had clear rules and policies for admitting foreigners and aliens; others, like the Merchant Tailors, did not. With the massive influx of aliens and provincial immigrants in the later sixteenth century, many London guilds struggled to deal with the increasing flow of unfree labour. However, by the end of the sixteenth century, their control over entry to London's crafts and industries had been seriously undermined by the rapid extension of the built-up area around the square mile of the old City, and by the growth of suburban production.[158] By the early seventeenth century, guilds had failed to curb the retail sale of goods by foreigners, or to restrict the practice of handicrafts to those who had secured an apprenticeship and were free of a Company.[159] The massive influx of immigrants into London and the sprawling spread of the metropolis indirectly undermined the City's guilds.

Even in their heyday, the guilds' control over crafts and industries in London was never complete, for two reasons. The existence of the privileged areas within the City walls and surrounding areas, known as the 'liberties' and 'exempt places', effectively undermined the power of the guilds. Many of these privileged areas were situated in the surroundings of monasteries, nunneries and other religious houses, and before the Reformation were controlled by ecclesiastical authorities rather than by the City or the Companies. During the Reformation, 23 religious houses in London were dissolved between 1536 and 1545. Some were consequently converted to aristocratic residences, others provided accommodation for large-scale governmental or industrial enterprises, such as workshops in the former Minoresses' precinct. In 1540, an Act of Parliament transferred the control of these houses to the Crown. The City attempted to purchase the rights to many of these precincts, but most were retained by the Crown or sold to individuals who enjoyed the same immunities as their former owners.[160] Some liberties were situated within the walls, such as Blackfriars in the south-west corners of the City and St Martin le Grand just north of St Paul's cathedral, but most lay outside the walls, including Whitefriars, Charterhouse and Clerkenwell (700 yards beyond Aldersgate), and St Katherine's next to the Tower.[161] Besides offering accommodation in central, prized districts of the city, these liberties and exempted places also provided extensive immunities, making them the favourite resort for both non-freemen and religious dissidents. In 1580, presumably in a dispute with the City and Companies, the residents of White and Black Friars reiterated their rights and immunities as follows. First, they claimed that the Mayor and his officers had no power to make arrests there; second, guilds had no freedom to conduct searches; third, craftsmen and artificers (even though they were not freemen of the City) were free to exercise their trades and mysteries; fourth, inhabitants were exempted from taxation, civic duties such as conducting watches of the city, serving on juries and holding offices. In other words, the inhabitants claimed exemption from all the City's laws and regulations.[162]

The alien population in exempted places rose. Blackfriars saw its alien population rising from 230 to 508 between 1568 and 1593;[163] in the case of

St Martin le Grand, where strangers made up half the population in 1550,[164] the alien population rose from 269 to 286 over the same period (see table 4.2). The possibility of working freely in the exempted places precluded the need to acquire a letter of denization, and this may explain why the number of denizens fell from 13 per cent in 1568 to 9 per cent in 1571 and 7 per cent in 1593. There was a close link between non-denizen status and settlement in exempted places. A survey of the alien population in exempted places in 1583 shows that of the 1604 aliens settled there, only 316 were denizens (19.7 per cent). Non-denizens, in other words, made up 80 per cent of the population in exempted places.[165]

Low rents, the need for space, access to water, and the desire to avoid institutional controls were some general factors shaping residential patterns of both strangers and non-free English craftsmen. There were also some unique factors affecting the spatial distribution of strangers in London. The movement of people through chain migration led to geographical concentration of immigrants from the same area/town. Over time, this process was cumulative, and areas with a long-established immigrant community would further attract newcomers, reinforcing their concentration in particular sites. With immigrant communities established in certain parts of London and Southwark, new arrivals could move straight from their places of origin.[166] This may explain why the Ward of Bridge Without (Southwark) continued to be an important place of settlement for aliens in the sixteenth century, particularly Dutch-speakers. In 1571, 21 per cent of alien households settled there, with the majority from the Rhineland and the northern Netherlands (25 per cent of Dutch-speaking immigrants lived there compared to 16 per cent of French-speaking). Within this ward, the 'Dutch' concentrated largely in the parish of St Olave, where they formed 81 per cent of the total 231 alien households settled there. The French-speaking immigrants, on the other hand, lived largely in the parishes of St Thomas Apostle and St George.[167] By 1593, the alien population in Southwark had halved in size, with only 7.6 per cent of alien households living there. This decline was partly related to the drying up of immigration from Dutch-speaking areas.

Provision of Skills and Employment to the Native Population

One of the most persistent complaints against aliens in London since the fifteenth century was their tendency to live together and work together. Evidence appears to support this. Carlin found that of the 293 alien servants and apprentices in Southwark in 1551, only 16 seem to have worked for Englishmen, while the remainder worked for other aliens, generally those of their own nationality,[168] which confirms the importance of chain migration. During the Elizabethan period, alien communities were no longer permitted to exist apart from the native inhabitants as economic 'enclaves'. Formal and informal pressure was exerted to force aliens to take on English servants and disseminate their skills. In 1573, this was made a prerequisite for their settlement in London. After much discussion of what kind of strangers should be allowed to stay in London, the Aldermen agreed that only alien artificers who 'teach their arts to Englishmen and set no strangers on worke but there own children' should be allowed to remain.[169] Governmental intervention was, in part, necessitated by the general perceived unwillingness of immigrants to teach their skills. A case brought before the French church on the 6 March 1560 illustrates this:

> Robert Laloé, Jean Pitéot and a young man, the brother of the said Pitéot, appeared in order to complain that the said young Pitéot, having learnt their trade of making moulds for buttons with his brother, did not want to work with his brother nor with those of his own nation, but was going off to work for an Englishman and teach them the trade, which, they say, will be the cause of great scandal and disorder.[170]

In other cases, strangers were reluctant to employ English servants because of concerns, they claimed, for the quality of workmanship. In 1567, in response to the pressure to employ English servants, aliens in Southampton stressed the need to employ their own servants to maintain standards in 'manufactures unknown in this country, as says, Spanish quilts … in which unskilful workmen would do damage; we do not object to teach Englishmen, and in time to take them'.[171] The fundamental reason for the apparent unwillingness of immigrants to teach their skills related to the *disincentive effects* – today their apprentices were their servants, but tomorrow they might become potential competitors.[172] This fear was exacerbated by the occupational mobility enjoyed by the freemen, allowing them to practise even trades which they had not been apprenticed in. This naturally aroused concerns among some aliens that once some native citizens had learnt the skills formerly taught by them, they could forbid non-denizen aliens from practising these, to reduce competition. These fears were clearly stated in a petition by strangers to Parliament in 1571:

> Those freemen that have been an apprentice by the space of seven years might after the attaining of their freedom, use any other trade or occupation although he had not bin an apprentice to the same by the space of seven years wherein the said poor Denizens and strangers do fear (that obtaining the same) the freemen of the said two cities of London and Norwich would not only intrude in any of their several occupations, whether they have lawful skill there of yea or no But also forbid them to work or use the same themselves for not having bin seven years an apprentice in

England thereunto. The like experience is before rehearsed although they well know, that a stranger by the Law may not be an Apprentice in England.[173]

In addition, the inability of alien children to learn a craft trade with English masters may also have strengthened economic ties among aliens, as some may have turned to their own fellow countrymen to provide work or training to their children, thus reinforcing the perceived economic separatism. It may also have promoted inter-generational transfer of skills, as aliens were forced to teach their own children their craft skills, thus perpetuating their domination in certain trades.

The strangers' continued unwillingness to impart their skills engendered much native indignation. In the face of this mounting hostility, the strangers were increasingly advised by those in government to employ English servants to pacify resentment and foster goodwill. In May 1586, a time when feelings against aliens were running high, Francis Walsingham advised the Dutch church to prepare 'a catalogue or register of all the names of born Englishmen, who are employed by strangers of your community or elsewhere'.[174] The Dutch church was grateful, and recorded that 'Her Majesty's Secretary, Sir Francis Walsingham, was always our good friend, who gave us excellent advice to shun the ill-will of the common people, and among other things, advised our people to employ the inhabitants of this country.'[175] This advice appears to have been taken seriously by the strangers. In 1593, in response to rising complaints against aliens as a result of deteriorating economic and social conditions, the Privy Council ordered a survey to find out the number of strangers who had violated the laws of the city by plying their craft, and how many employed poor English persons (see Table 4.9).[176] It was found that many families did not employ any servants. In 1593, for example, of the 1040 alien households recorded, 516 families had no servants or relied on their own labour, 212 households employed only an English workforce, and a further 149 households employed both English and strange workers.[177] The survey also found an impressive number of English employed by alien households: 1671 English compared to 686 stranger servants. Of these English servants, 950 English men and boys, and 457 English women and girls were kept in strangers' houses, while 264 were set to work.[178] The Dutch employed the majority of these servants, signifying perhaps an easier relationship between the Dutch and their English hosts, and the larger Dutch community. In January 1593, the ministers of the Dutch church compiled a report which showed that 570 members of the church set to work 830 English servants, and a further 460 servants were 'set to spin by certain yarn twisters', making a total of 1290 English servants.[179] A smaller number were employed by French church households. According to Littleton, the 336 French church households employed a total of 265 English people and 139 strangers in their workshops and homes.[180]

Table 4.9 Employment of English and alien servants in London, 1593

Categories of servants	No. of servants employed by alien householders			All alien heads of households
	Silk-weavers (120)	Goldsmiths (39)	Brewers (21)	(1815)
English				
Servants	12	7	7	53
Female servants	10	4	9	113
Journeyman	3	6	6	93
Apprentices	32	14	4	185
Kept	31	17	62	389
Set to work	31	7	58	263
Sub-total	119 66%	55 75%	146 80%	1 096 67%
Mean per master	1.0	1.4	7.0	0.6
Alien				
Servants	20	9	24	250
Female servants	9	8	4	176
Journeyman	29	1	8	96
Apprentices	3	—	—	22
Sub-total	61 34%	18 25%	36 20%	544 33%
Mean per master	0.5	0.4	1.7	0.3
Total	**180 100%**	**73 100%**	**182 100%**	**1 640 100%**
Mean per master	**1.5**	**1.9**	**8.7**	**0.9**

Source: Scouloudi, *Returns of Strangers*.

If these figures are accurate, they represented the success of the City authorities in promoting greater provision of employment for English servants, and may have provided the necessary weapon for the Privy Council to dampen popular unrest in the City against the strangers. The Privy Council was also concerned that English servants should learn skills from their stranger masters. This was reflected in the detailed breakdown in the survey of how the servants were actually employed. English servants were classified in six different categories: 'servants', 'female servants', 'journeymen', 'apprentices', 'kept' and 'set to work'. The significance of these various categories is unclear, particularly those classified as 'kept' and 'set to work'. The term 'kept' suggests that English servants were living in the household of the strangers and perhaps received food and accommodation as remuneration. Those who were 'set to work', on the other hand, may not have lived within the household, but it is unclear what their method of remuneration was. It is also striking that many aliens simply did not know the names of the overwhelming majority of their English servants, reflecting perhaps both the lack of direct contact, and language barriers.

It is also puzzling why only English servants were classified in these ways, and not the stranger servants. One possible explanation lies in the ages of the servants: those who were 'kept' and 'set to work' were possibly children rather than adults, suggesting that these were 'pauper apprentices'. During the Tudor period, apprenticeship was adopted by parish officials as a means of removing pauper children from the parish poor rates. Parish apprenticeship was regarded as fundamentally different from private apprenticeship because vocational training was less prominent, overridden by the need to support the child. Frequently, pauper apprenticeship was criticized for providing ratepayers with cheap labour. This may have been true in some cases, as parish apprentices were more prevalent in poorer trades, such as cordwaining and weaving, than in prosperous ones, which adds weight to the argument that they were providing cheap supplementary labour instead of receiving meaningful training.[181]

Another question that emerges is why strangers took on a large number of English servants in the 1590s. The availability of financial assistance may have been one factor. From the 1570s, the Aldermen of London agreed to make available 'stockes and tooles' and 'beddinge, apparrell and dyett' for the poor who were set to work in Bridewell. It is possible that a similar arrangement was made for any poor who were put to work with strangers. From the 1590s, strangers may have been more disposed to employ English servants, partly because they were advised to do so to pacify the growing resentment against them. Moreover, the growing labour needs in labour-intensive industries such as silk throwing and beer brewing probably encouraged strangers to turn to the local supply of cheap labour. The beer brewers employed the highest number of servants, a total of 182 servants, or 8.7 servants per master, followed by the silk-weavers with a total of 180 servants, or 1.5 servants per master. Most brewers' servants were kept and set to work, but the silk-weavers provided vocational training to over a quarter of their English servants. Pauper apprenticeship was less threatening to the strangers. By providing work rather than skills, the strangers were able to retain valuable craft secrets within their community. However, as long as pauper children were set to work, craft training remained a secondary concern to the City authorities.

A close examination of the social and economic structure of the alien households shows that even without governmental pressure they would have employed English servants on a greater scale after 1593 (see Table 4.10). In the fifteenth century, alien households were not disposed to employ English servants because there was an ample supply of servants of their own kind. In 1483, for example, the number of alien servants (730) in London outnumbered alien householders (357) nearly two to one. The supply of alien servants outweighed demand for them, prompting many to find work with English employers. In 1571, there was also a disinclination to employ English servants. Besides cultural and linguistic factors, the adequate supply of labour within the alien community obviated the need to turn to the native workforce. At this date, the number of alien servants almost equalled the number of householders. There was also a large pool of children – 1004 children in all in 1571 – some of whom were of an age to provide extra help with work. By 1593, the change in the balance between householders and servants necessitated the use of the native workforce. At a time of expanding production, the number of alien servants had actually declined as a result of reduced immigration from overseas. This might have forced alien masters to take on English apprentices. In 1593, alien householders outnumbered alien servants by two to one (1503 alien householders, in comparison with only 686 alien servants). The 3057 children could fill in some of the need, but some jobs, especially in brewing, where there was a great need, were not suitable for their employment. The examination of the social and economic structure of alien households also points to the different nature of migration into London during the fifteenth and sixteenth centuries. In the fifteenth century, the economic nature of migration can be seen in the preponderance of men and servants, with few women and children among the community, while the religious and political nature of migration in the sixteenth century produced a more balanced ratio between men and women and children, and between householders and servants.

Conclusion

Religious and political disturbances in the Low Countries and France during the 1560s–1580s precipitated a large influx of refugees into London, greatly enlarging the foreign community established there. As in any period, the arrival of Protestant refugees in early modern London stirred up a mixture of emotions, from fear over the pressure on economic resources, jobs, housing, and food, to humanitarian feelings of sympathy and admiration for their religious convictions. Their arrival attracted greater public attention due to their *visibility* deriving from their movements *en masse*, and greater identity and solidarity, as well as the international political tensions precipitated by their immigration. The following chapter examines the ensuing economic and political debates, and the integration of refugees into London society.

Table 4.10 Economic and social structure of the alien community, 1483–1593

Categories	1483	1571	1593
Households			
Male	357	964	1 503
Wives	183	[848][1]	1 142
Widows	—	—	162
Women	24	—	—
Women with English husbands	—	—	43
Non-householders			
Male	81	378 (sojourners)	293
Wives	21	—	61
Female	36	—	166
Children born abroad			
Sons	10	61	244
Daughters	10	72	245
Children	—	730	25
Children born in England			
Sons	—	—	1 393
Daughters	—	—	979
Children	—	102	171
Children in families with siblings born abroad & England	—	39	—
Servants			
Male	396	879	467
Female	49	—	219
Alien servants with Englishmen			
Male	269	—	—
Female	16	—	—
Others			
Chamberholders			
Male	53	—	—
Wives	19	—	—
Female	8	—	—
Merchants (male)	15	—	—

Parents	7	—	—
Wives of Englishmen	5	—	—
Miscellaneous	36	—	—
Denizens	—	604	—
Total	1 595	4 677[2]	7 113
English servants with alien masters			
Men and boys kept	—	—	950
Women and girls kept	—	—	457
English set to work	—	—	264
			1 671

Notes: [1] There is no separate figure for women. This is derived by deducting the number of children (1 004) recorded in the Return from the stated total, 1 852, of women and children.
[2] There might be an error here as the total number of aliens is stated to be 4 631.
Sources: Bolton, *Alien Communities of London in the Fifteenth Century*, pp. 16–17. 1571: Kirk and Kirk, *Returns of Aliens*, Vol. 10, No. 2, p. 139 (the summary of the 1571 Return published here does not contain separate figures for women and children; these figures are obtained from my database. 1593: Ellesmere MS 2514d (printed in Scouloudi, *Return of Strangers*, p. 90.)

Notes

1. D. Keene, 'The environment of Hanseatic commerce in London, A.D. 1100–1600', paper presented at Istituto Universitario di Architettura, Venice, June 1996, published in *Les étrangers dans la ville, xv–xviii siécles*, ed. J. Bottin and D. Calabi (Paris, 1998) (published in French).
2. M.E. Bratchel, 'Regulation and Group-consciousness in the Later History of London's Italian Merchant Colonies', *Journal of European Economic History*, 1980, Vol. 9, No. 3, p. 589; R. Esser, 'From the Hansa to the Present: Germans in Britain since the Middle Ages', in P. Panayi, ed., *Germans in Britain Since 1500* (London, 1996), p. 18; A. Pettegree, *Foreign Protestant Communities in Sixteenth Century London* (Oxford, 1986), p. 11.
3. Pettegree, *Foreign Protestant Communities*, p. 10.
4. Ibid., p. 11.
5. S. Thrupp, 'Aliens in and around London in the fifteenth century', in A.E. Hollaender and W. Kellaway, eds, *Studies in London History: Essays Presented to P.E. Jones*, (London, 1969), p. 265.
6. See Pettegree, *Foreign Protestant Communities*, Chapter 2, for a discussion of the foundation of the Stranger Churches, and Chapter 8 for discussion of the roles of the Churches in providing financial assistance, printed materials, training of ministers and a secure refuge for reformers.
7. S. Thrupp, 'A survey of the alien population of England in 1440', *Speculum*, 1957, Vol. 32, pp. 262–73.
8. J. Bolton, *The Alien Communities of London in the Fifteenth Century: The Subsidy Rolls of 1440 and 1483–4* (Stanford, CT, 1998), pp. 8–9.
9. G. Parker, *The Dutch Revolt* (London, 1977), p. 119; Pettegree, *Foreign Protestant Communities*, p. 299.

10   According to Williams, there were only 12 000 aliens in the 1570s: see L. Williams, 'The Crown and the Provincial Immigrant Communities in Elizabethan England', in *British Government and Administration: Studies Presented to S.B. Chrimes*, eds. H. Hearder and H.R. Loyn (Cardiff, 1974), p. 118.
11   J.G.C.A. Briels, 'De Zuidnederlandse immigratie 1572–1630', *Tijdschrift voor Geschiedenis*, 1987, Vol. 100, p. 336.
12   Briels gives various estimates. Between 1540 and 1630, he calculated that there were 175 000 emigrants from the southern Netherlands (direct émigré and first-generation descendants). He reckons 30 000 went to England, 30 000 to Germany, 150 000 to the Dutch Republic (of whom *c.*35 000 came to the Dutch Republic via England/Germany). See Briels, *Zuid-Nederlandse immigratie, 1572–1630* (Haarlem, 1978), p. 19. I am grateful to Dr Alastair Duke for bringing this point to my attention.
13   Henry Bullinger believed that there were as many as 15 000 foreign refugees in England in 1553. See Pettegree, *Foreign Protestant Communities*, pp. 78, 145.
14   A. Pettegree, 'Protestant Migration during the Early Modern Period', in *Le Migrazioni in Europa secc. XIII–XVIII*, Istituto Internazionale di Storia Economica 'F. Datini' Prato, Serie II – Atti delle 'Settimane di Studi' e altri Convegni 25, S. Cavaciocchi, 1994, pp. 441–58; R.D. Gwynn, *Huguenot Heritage: The History and Contribution of the Huguenots in Britain* (London, 1985), pp. 10–12.
15   Pettegree, 'Protestant Migration', pp. 442–3.
16   Ibid., pp. 443–444.
17   Ibid., p. 117; see also Pettegree, 'The Foreign Population of London in 1549', *Proceedings of the Huguenot Society*, 1984, Vol. 24, pp. 141–6; A. Pettegree, 'The Stranger Community in Marian London', *Proceedings of the Huguenot Society*, 1987, Vol. 24, pp. 390–402.
18   Pettegree, *Foreign Protestant Communities*, pp. 119–20.
19   PRO SP12/27/19 & 20, 20 January 1562/3, printed in R.E.G. Kirk and E.F. Kirk, eds, *Returns of Aliens Dwelling in the City and Suburbs of London*, Huguenot Society Publications, 1900–1908, Vol. 10, No. 1, p. 293.
20   Pettegree, *Foreign Protestant Communities*, p. 236.
21   Ibid., p. 217.
22   PRO SP12/47/19 21 July 1568.
23   Printed in Kirk and Kirk eds, *Returns of Aliens*, Vol. 10, No. 1, p. 439.
24   C. Read, *Lord Burghley and Queen Elizabeth* (London, 1960), p. 42.
25   PRO SP12/89/15 29 September 1572.
26   See R. Pollitt, '"Refuge of the Distressed Nations": Perceptions of Aliens in Elizabethan England', *Journal of Modern History*, 1980, Vol. 52, No. 1, pp. D1001–D1019, for an interesting discussion of Herlle's various proposals to Cecil to control the alien populations.
27   PRO SP12/81/34 & 35.
28   CLRO JOR.19, 22 November 1567, ff. 81–81v.
29   Twelve men should be appointed in each of these wards: Farringdon without, Cripplegate, Tower and Billingsgate.
30   PRO SP12/81/53I (Lord Mayor of London to Privy Council); also in CLRO, Letter Book X, 1570–73, f. 68v.
31   M.P. Holt, *The French Wars of Religion, 1562–1629* (Cambridge, 1995), pp. 91, 94.
32   W. Naphy, *Calvin and the Consolidation of the Genevan Reformation* (Manchester, 1994), p. 123; H. Kamen, *The Iron Century: Social Change in Europe, 1550–1660* (London, 1971), p. 420.
33   L.H. Yungblut, *Strangers Settled Here Amongst Us: Policies, Perceptions and the Presence of Aliens in Elizabethan England* (London, 1996), p. 14.
34   PRO SP12/84/34
35   See below.

36 See Chapters 6–8.
37 See also Pettegree, *Foreign Protestant Communities*, p. 299.
38 V. Harding, 'The Population of London, 1550–1700: A Review of the Published Evidence', *London Journal*, (1990), Vol. 15, p. 112.
39 I am grateful to Dr Alastair Duke for this information.
40 CLRO JOR 19, f. 132v 19 October 1568. Strangers who did not come for religious reasons were ordered to leave the Capital after one day and one night.
41 C.G.D. Littleton, 'Geneva on Threadneedle Street: The French Church of London and its Congregation, 1560–1625' (University of Michigan unpublished PhD thesis, 1996), pp. 231, 235.
42 W. Cunningham, *Alien Immigrants in England* (London, 1897), pp. 181–2.
43 Ibid., pp. 154–5.
44 O.P. Grell, *Dutch Calvinists in Early Stuart London: The Dutch Church in Austin Friars, 1603–1612* (Leiden, 1989), pp. 12–14.
45 The high mobility of the alien population also accounts for the fluctuation in their numbers. For a discussion of this, see C. Littleton, 'Social interactions of aliens in late Elizabethan London: Evidence from the 1593 Return and the French Church consistory "actes"', in R. Vigne and G. Gibbs, eds, *The Strangers' Progress: Integration and Disintegration of the Huguenot and Walloon Refugee Community, 1567–1889* (Proceedings of the Huguenot Society, Vol. 26, 1995), pp. 149–51.
46 Littleton, 'Social interactions', p. 149.
47 S. Rappaport, *Worlds Within Worlds: Structures of Life in Sixteenth-century London* (Cambridge, 1989), p. 72.
48 Ellesmere MS 2514.
49 Harding, 'The Population of London', p. 112.
50 See J.A. Galloway and I. Murray, 'Scottish Migration to England, 1400–1560', *Scottish Geographical Magazine*, 1996, Vol. 112, pp. 29–38.
51 C. Barron, 'Introduction: England and the Low Countries 1327–1477', in *England and the Low Countries in the Late Middle Ages*, p. 13; also Bolton, *Aliens in the Fifteenth Century*, p. 30.
52 Bolton, *Aliens in the Fifteenth Century*, p. 34.
53 For a comparison of wages, see J.H. Munro, 'Urban Wage Structures in Late-medieval England and the Low Countries: Work Time and Seasonable Wages', in I. Blanchard, ed., *Labour and Leisure in Historical Perspective, Thirteenth to Twentieth Centuries: Papers presented at Session B-3a of the Eleventh International Economic History Congress, Milan 12th–17th September 1994* (Stuttgart, 1994), pp. 65–78.
54 H. van der Wee, *The Low Countries in the Early Modern World* (Aldershot, 1993), p. 212.
55 See H. van der Wee, 'The economy as a factor in the start of the revolt in the southern Netherlands', *Acta Historiae Neerlandicae*, 1971, Vol. 5, pp. 55–6.
56 Parker, *The Dutch Revolt*, pp. 22, 34–5; H.G. Koenigsberger, 'Dominium Regale or Dominium Politicum et Regale: Monarchies and Parliaments in Early Modern Europe', in idem, *Politicians and Virtuosi: Essays in Early Modern History* (London, 1986), p. 15.
57 See Koenigsberger, 'Why did the States General of the Netherlands become revolutionary in the Sixteenth Century?', *Parliaments, Estates and Representation*, 1982, Vol. 2, pp. 103–11; idem, 'The States-General of the Netherlands before the Revolt', in *Estates and Revolutions: Essays in Early Modern European History* (London, 1970), pp. 125–43; some historians regard political fragmentation and the inherent instability of this political structure as one prime precondition of the Revolt; see J.W. Smit, 'The Netherlands Revolution', in R. Forster and J.P. Greene, eds, *Preconditions of Revolution in Early Modern Europe* (London, 1970), pp. 27–36.
58 See Parker, *The Dutch Revolt*, pp. 60–61.
59 Ibid., pp. 37–8.

60 A. Pettegree, *Emden and the Dutch Revolt: Exiles and the Development of Reformed Protestantism* (Oxford, 1992), p. 241.
61 Kossmann argued that the social and economic conditions in the more industrialized southern provinces contributed to the rapid spread of Calvinism among the lower middle classes and the workmen in urban centres like Tournai, Valenciennes and Antwerp. Kossmann also believed that the poor relief organized by the reformed congregations may have won the support of a number of destitute people. See E.H. Kossmann and A.F. Mellink, eds, *Texts Concerning the Revolt of the Netherlands* (Cambridge, 1974), p. 8.
62 Parker, *The Dutch Revolt*, pp. 58–9.
63 Ibid., p. 58. Between 1523 and 1566, a minimum of 1300 persons were executed for heresy and related offences in the Low Countries – that is, two-fifths of all Protestants put to death in western Europe before the outbreak of the religious wars. Overall, perhaps 7–8000 persons might have been affected by the anti-heresy legislation. This would give a figure of 0.23 per cent of the total population of around 3 million. I thank Alastair Duke for this information.
64 Parker, *The Dutch Revolt*, pp. 60–61.
65 For a discussion on the extent of opposition to religious persecution, see M. van Gelderen, *The Political Thought of the Dutch Revolt, 1555–1590* (Cambridge, 1992), pp. 36–7.
66 Parker, *The Dutch Revolt*, pp. 66–7.
67 W.S. Maltby, *Alba: A Biography of Fernando Alvarez de Toledo, Third Duke of Alba, 1507–1582* (London, 1983), pp. 129–30.
68 Ibid., pp. 130–31.
69 See Kossman and Mellink, eds, *Texts Concerning the Revolt of the Netherlands*, p. 10; P. Mack, 'The Wanderyear: Reformed Preaching and Iconoclasm in the Netherlands', in J. Obelkevich, ed, *Religion and the People, 800–1700* (Chapel Hill, NC, 1979), pp. 191–220.
70 Parker, *The Dutch Revolt*, p. 82.
71 These estimates are made by A.L.E. Verheyden, *Le conseil des troubles: liste des condamnés, 1567–1573* (Brussels, 1961). Verheyden's estimates are not completely reliable, as there is evidence of double-counting.
72 The number of condemnations in other provinces is as follows: Hainaut (826), Gelderland (504), Friesland (412), Utrecht (313), Groningen (221), Overijssel (93), Luxemburg (43), Namur (43), Artois (42), Drenthe (3), places not certain (16); see A.L.E. Verheyden, *Le Conseil des Troubles* (Brussels, 1981), p. 133.
73 R.S. DuPlessis, *Lille and the Dutch Revolt: Urban Stability in an Era of Revolution, 1500–1582* (Cambridge, 1991), pp. 233, 235; see also Verheyden, *Le Conseil des Troubles*, pp. 133, 136–7.
74 G. Clark, 'An Urban Study During the Revolt of the Netherlands: Valenciennes 1540–1570' (University of Columbia unpublished PhD thesis, 1972), pp. 29, 32.
75 J.I. Israel, *The Dutch Republic: Its Rise, Greatness, and Fall, 1477–1806* (Oxford, 1995), p. 160.
76 R. Gwynn, *The Huguenot Heritage: The History and Contribution of the Huguenots in Britain* (London, 1985), pp. 40–41.
77 A. Pettegree, 'The French and Walloon Communities in London, 1550–1688', in O.L.P. Grell, J.I. Israel and N. Tyacke, eds, *From Persecution to Toleration: The Glorious Revolution and Religion in England* (Oxford, 1991), pp. 85–6.
78 Israel, *The Dutch Republic*, p. 219; Parker, *The Dutch Revolt*, pp. 208–16.
79 Holt, *The French Wars of Religion*, p. 30.
80 M. Prestwich, 'Calvinism in France, 1555–1629', in M. Prestwich, ed, *International Calvinism* (Oxford, 1985), pp. 73, 90, 91.
81 Holt, *The French Wars of Religion*, pp. 44–7.

Immigrants in Elizabethan London

82 For a discussion of the French community in Geneva, see Naphy, *Calvin and the Consolidation of the Genevan Reformation*, pp. 124–43.
83 Holt, *The French Wars of Religion*, pp. 91, 94.
84 Ibid., pp. 124–5.
85 This involves the migration of people in stages: see P. White and R. Woods, eds, *The Geographical Impact of Migration* (London, 1980), p. 36.
86 Scouloudi, *Returns of Strangers* (1593), entry 911.
87 Ibid., entries 157, 927.
88 Ibid., entry 994.
89 Pettegree, *Foreign Protestant Communities*, p. 218.
90 CLRO JOR 19, f. 132v 19 October 1568. Strangers who did not come for religious reasons were ordered to leave the Capital after one day and one night.
91 Kirk and Kirk, eds, *Returns of Aliens*, Vol. 10, No. 2, pp. 155–6.
92 For an excellent discussion of the origins of the Italian church, see O. Boersma and A.J. Jelsma, eds, *Unity in Multiformity: The Minutes of the Coetus of London, 1575 and the Consistory Minutes of the Italian Church of London, 1570–1591* (Huguenot Society Publications, Vol. 56, 1997), pp. 3–51; the appendix lists details for the 207 members of the Italian church in London in the period 1567–1593, see pp. 209–59.
93 PRO SP12/84/1, f. 433; printed in Kirk and Kirk, eds, *Returns of Aliens*, Vol. 10, No. 2, p. 156.
94 A congregation of 27 Flemish Anabaptists were arrested at Whitechapel Without Aldgate on Easter Day 1575.
95 M. Evers, 'Religiones et Libertatis Ergo: Dutch Refugees in England and English Exiles in the Netherlands', in *Refugees and Emigrants in the Dutch Republic and England: Papers of the Annual Symposium held on 22 November 1985* (Leiden, 1986), p. 11.
96 M.B. Pulman, *The Elizabethan Privy Council in the Fifteen-seventies* (London, 1979), pp. 125–7; CLRO JOR 20 (1), f. 119v 26 February 1573.
97 Kirk and Kirk, eds, *Returns of Aliens*, Vol. 10, No. 2, pp. 155–6.
98 Pettegree, *Foreign Protestant Communities*, p. 219.
99 See Verheyden, *Le Conseil des Troubles: Liste des condamnés, 1567–1573*.
100 G. Marnef, *Antwerp in the Age of Reformation: Underground Protestantism in a Commercial Metropolis, 1550–1577* (London, 1996), p. 109.
101 Evers, 'Religiones et Libertatis Ergo', p. 8.
102 P. Collinson, 'England and International Calvinism, 1558–1640', in M. Prestwich, ed., *International Calvinism, 1541–1715* (Oxford, 1985), p. 197.
103 J. van Vloten, *Nederlands Opstand tegen Spanje, Volume 1: 1567–1572* (1856), p. 269; see also letters reproduced by H.Q. Janssen, 'De hervormde vlugtelingen van Yperen in Engeland', *Bijdragen tot de oudheidkunde en geschiedenis, inzonderheid van Zeeuwsch-Vlaanderen*, 1857, Vol. 2, pp. 211–304.
104 Evers, 'Religiones et Libertatis Ergo', p. 9.
105 G. Clark, *Wealth of England*, pp. 50–51.
106 C. Littleton, 'Social interaction of aliens in late Elizabethan London: Evidence from the 1593 Return and the French Church consistory "actes"', in R. Vigne and G. Gibbs, eds, *The Strangers' Progress: Integration and Disintegration of the Huguenot and Walloon Refugee Community, 1567–1889: Essays in memory of Irene Scouloudi*, (Proceedings of the Huguenot Society, Vol. 26, 1995), p. 150.
107 A.L.E. Verheyden, 'Une correspondance inédite adressée par des familles protestantes des Pays-Bas à leurs coreligionnaires d'Angleterre (11 novembre 1569–25 février 1570)', *Bulletin de la commission Royale D'historie*, Académie Royale de Belgique, 1955, Vol. 120, see letters 12, 26, 27, 28, 29. I am extremely grateful to Guillaume Delanoy (Lausanne, Switzerland) for his assistance with the translation of these letters, which are currently being prepared for publication.
108 Ibid., Letter 28, pp. 148–9.

109 Ibid., Letter 12, p. 128–9.
110 Ibid., Letter 40, p. 166.
111 Ibid., Letter 31, pp. 152–3.
112 Pettegree, *Foreign Protestant Communities*, pp. 229–31.
113 Verheyden, 'Une correspondance', Letter 27, pp. 146–8.
114 PRO PCC 1573 (26 Peter), ff. 195v–196, also discussed in Pettegree, *Foreign Protestant Communities*, pp. 227–8.
115 Pettegree, *Foreign Protestant Communities*, p. 253.
116 Ibid., p. 259; see also A. Pettegree, 'The French and Walloon Communities in London, 1550–1688', pp. 77–96.
117 See Bolton, *The Alien Communities of London in the Fifteenth Century*, pp. 20, 23; for occupations of aliens in fifteenth-century Southwark, see also Carlin, *Medieval Southwark*, pp. 150–54.
118 Pettegree, *Foreign Protestant Communities*, pp. 146–7. This source only includes those who were members of the church, and excludes numerous aliens involved in trades such as tanning and working of leather, beer brewing and the auxiliary art of making barrels who were not members of the Dutch church.
119 Ibid., pp. 146–7.
120 L. Williams, 'The Crown and the Provincial Immigrant Communities in Elizabethan England', pp. 117–31; Cunningham, *Alien Immigrants*, pp. 177–80.
121 There are methodological problems involved in using occupational labels. For a discussion of these problems, see P.J. Corfield, 'Defining urban work', in D. Keene and P.J. Corfield, eds, *Work in Towns*, pp. 213–20; D. Keene, 'Continuity and development in urban trades: Problems of concepts and the evidence', in *Work in Towns*, p. 10; J. Patten, 'Urban occupations in pre-industrial England', *Transactions of the Institute of British Geographers*, 1977, Vol. 2, pp. 301–2; J. Boulton, *Neighbourhood and Society: A London Suburb in the Seventeenth Century* (Cambridge, 1987), pp. 65–73.
122 Another Return of 1593 shows that 37 per cent of strangers surveyed were employed in the luxury trades: see Ellesmere MS 2514.
123 See, L.B. Luu, 'Aliens and their impact on the goldsmiths' craft in London in the sixteenth century', in D. Mitchell, ed, *Goldsmiths, Silversmiths and Bankers: Innovation and the Transfer of Skill, 1550 to 1750* (London, 1995), pp. 43–52; see also Chapter 6.
124 For a fuller discussion of this occupation, see Thirsk, *Economic Policy and Projects*, pp. 85–6.
125 N. Davis, 'Strikes and Salvation at Lyon', in idem, *Society and Culture in Early Modern France* (London, 1975), p. 7.
126 Quoted in P. Benedict, *Rouen During the Wars of Religion* (Cambridge, 1981), pp. 80–81. For a discussion of the connection between Calvinist doctrine and wealth, see P. Benedict, 'Faith, Fortune and Social Structure in Seventeenth-century Montpellier', *Past and Present*, 1996, Vol. 152, pp. 46–78. For the Low Countries, initially (1520s and 1530s) the new doctrines attracted support from the intelligentsia – clergy, schoolmasters, printers – and then it spread to skilled artisans. See A. Duke, 'The Face of Popular Religious Dissent, 1520–1530', in *Reformation and Revolt in the Low Countries* (London, 1990), pp. 14–15, 33–9, and p. 37, footnote 60.
127 W.J.C. Moens, *The Walloons and their Church at Norwich: Their History and Registers 1565–1832* (Huguenot Society Publications, Vol. 1, 1887–8), p. 71.
128 M. Backhouse, 'The Flemish Refugees in Sandwich, 1561–1603', in *Revolt and Emigration* (Dikkebus, 1988), p. 98.
129 Printed in Moens, *The Walloons and their Church at Norwich*, pp. 220–23. I thank Alastair Duke for translating from the original for me; see H.Q. Janssen, 'De hervormde vlugtelingen van Ypren in Engeland', *Bijdragen tot de oudheidskunde en Geschiedenis, inzonderheid van Zeeuwsch-Vlaanderen*, Vol. 2 (1857), pp. 231, 273.
130 Hessels, *Ecclesiae Londino-Batavae Archivum*, Vol. 3, No. 1, [1287], pp. 963–4.

131 In 1593, a bill was proposed to bar strangers from practising trades such as shoemaking. See Scouloudi, *Returns of Strangers*, p. 65.
132 PRO SP46/24/159d, 160.
133 GL, MF 326, Court Minutes, Vol. 3, 1575–1601, f. 241v.
134 In 1597, the index of real wages stood at 59: see Rappaport, *Worlds Within Worlds*, p. 407.
135 GL, MF 326, Court Minutes, Vol. 3, 1575–1601, f. 367.
136 CLRO JOR 24 23 March 1598, ff. 382v–384.
137 Ibid.
138 Merchant Tailors' Hall, Ancient Manuscript Books, Vol. 54 T3, ff. 113.
139 GL, MF 326, Court Minutes, Vol. 3, 1575–1601, f. 440v.
140 N.V., Sleigh-Johnson, 'The Merchant Taylors Company of London, 1580–1645: With Special Reference to Politics and Government' (University of London unpublished PhD thesis, 1989), p. 338.
141 GL, MF 327, Court Minutes, Vol. 5, 1601–11, ff. 1–4.
142 The number of trades in London trebled from 154 in the 1520s to 490 in the 1690s, reflecting increased specialization. See D. Keene, 'Continuity and development in urban trades: Problems of concepts and the evidence', in D. Keene and P.J. Corfield, eds, *Work in Towns* (Leicester, 1991), p. 7.
143 H. Pollins, 'Immigrants and Minorities – The Outsiders in Business', *Immigrants and Minorities*, 1989, Vol. 8, p. 256.
144 Bratchel, 'Regulation and Group-consciousness', p. 589, Raingard, 'From the Hansa to the Present: Germans in Britain since the Middle Ages', p. 18.
145 Littleton, 'Geneva on Threadneedle Street', pp. 231, 235.
146 Littleton, 'Social interaction of aliens', p. 150.
147 See Bolton, *Alien Communities in London in the Fifteenth Century*, p. 13.
148 Carlin, *Medieval Southwark*, Chapter 6; Bolton, *Alien Communities in London in the Fifteenth Century*, p. 5.
149 Carlin, *Medieval Southwark*, p. 155.
150 Bolton, *Alien Communities in London in the Fifteenth Century*, p. 15.
151 Pettegree, *Foreign Protestant Communities*, p. 284.
152 Ibid., p. 83.
153 A.L. Beier, 'Engine of manufacture: The trades of London', in A.L. Beier and R. Finlay, eds, *London 1500–1700: The Making of the Metropolis* (London, 1986), pp. 155–6.
154 L. Gowing, *Domestic Dangers: Women, Words and Sex in Early Modern London* (Oxford, 1996).
155 Quoted in Littleton, 'Geneva on Threadneedle Street', p. 67.
156 Beier, 'Engines of manufacture', p.157. There were 111 trades in London during reign of Henry V (1413–22); W. Kahl, *The Development of London Livery Companies: An Historical Essay and a Select Bibliography* (Boston, MA, 1960), p. 2.
157 Rappaport, *Worlds Within Worlds*, pp. 29, 31.
158 J.R. Kellett, 'The Breakdown of Gild and Corporation Control over the Handicraft and Retail Trade in London', *Economic History Review*, Series 2, 1957–8, Vol. 10, pp. 381–2.
159 Ibid., p. 382.
160 Rappaport, *Worlds Within Worlds*, pp. 34–5; Keene, 'Growth, Modernisation and Control', p. 25.
161 Rappaport, *Worlds Within Worlds*, pp. 34–5.
162 PRO SP12/137/74 April 1580.
163 Kirk and Kirk, eds, *Returns of Aliens*, Vol. 10, Vol. 3, p. 411; Vol. 2, p. 443.
164 Pettegree, *Foreign Protestant Communities*, p. 18.
165 Kirk and Kirk, eds, *Returns of Aliens*, Vol. 2, 1583, pp. 376–7.
166 Bolton, *Alien Communities in London in the Fifteenth Century*, pp. 30–32.
167 Based on a computer analysis of the Return of Aliens of 1571.

168 Carlin, *Medieval Southwark*, p. 154.
169 CLRO, Rep 18, ff. 148v–49v.
170 Quoted in B. Cottret, *The Huguenots in England: Immigration and Settlement c.1550–1700* (Cambridge, 1991), pp. 245–6.
171 *Calendar of Domestic Papers, Elizabeth, Addenda, 1566–79*, p. 32.
172 K.G. Persson, *Pre-industrial Economic Growth: Social Organization and Technological Progress in Europe* (Oxford, 1988), p. 9.
173 Hessels, *Ecclesiae Londino-Batavae Archivum*, Vol. 3, No. 1, [157], pp. 126–8.
174 Ibid., Vol. 2, [220], pp. 794–5.
175 Ibid.
176 *Acts of Privy Council, 1591–92*, pp. 507–8.
177 Scouloudi, *Returns of Strangers*, p. 82.
178 Ellesmere MS 2514; see also I. Scouloudi, 'The Stranger Community in the Metropolis, 1558–1640', in idem, ed, *Huguenots in Britain and Their French Background, 1550–1800*, (London, 1987) pp. 47–8.
179 Washington, Folger Shakespeare Library, MS v.b 142, f. 87. I am extremely grateful to Prof Derek Keene for finding and transcribing this document.
180 Littleton, 'Social interaction of aliens in late Elizabethan London', p. 152.
181 This discussion is based on D. Simonton, 'Apprenticeship: Training and Gender in Eighteenth-century England', in M. Berg, ed., *Markets and Manufactures in Early Industrial Europe* (London, 1991), pp. 227–34; see also C. More, *Skill and the English Working Class, 1870–1914* (London, 1980), pp. 41–52, for a discussion of different types of apprenticeship.

Chapter 5

Reception and Treatment of Immigrants

The successful diffusion of industries in London depended on the acquisition of requisite skills by native artisans. The quickest method to achieve this end was to learn the skills from experienced practitioners – the immigrants – but this required the fulfilment of two preconditions. In the first place, immigrants had to be willing to settle in the host country for long enough to take on apprentices and impart their skills. In addition, they had to be willing to teach their knowledge and expertise. Both of these requirements were determined by the satisfaction of immigrants with their life, which in turn was contingent upon the existence of economic security guaranteed by the law, the prospects for social improvement, the positive policies of the host government, and reception by the indigenous population.

Fulfilment of these conditions was hindered in certain respects by the ambivalent reception given to the immigrants. Their arrival provoked very different reactions from different sections of society, depending in part on the general economic and social climate and the socio-economic status of the host population. In general, compassion displayed by some wealthier members of society was mingled with resentment felt by some poorer members of society. Public reaction was also shaped by the character of the incoming aliens, depending on who they were, and why and how they arrived in the capital. Broadly speaking, aliens fell into three groups. The first type can be conveniently labelled *economic migrants*, such as the beer brewers, whose integration into London society presented no problems. Next came the *wanderjahre craftsmen*, such as the goldsmiths, whose primary aim was to broaden their craft training. Until the late sixteenth century, these tended to return to their home city after spending a few years abroad, and again caused no concerns. The arrival of the third group, the *refugees*, received a more mixed reception. On the one hand, they were greeted with compassion and charity, and the Puritans were 'foremost among those charitably minded Englishmen who collected and gave money for the support of the poor among the strangers'.[1] On the other hand, they were met with resentment. As Pettegree has observed: 'the skills the newcomers brought with them were widely feared and their privileges deeply resented'. If the municipal authorities would not act to curb competition, the native craftsmen were prepared 'to take matters into their own hands'. Serious riots against immigrants were only narrowly averted in London in 1563 and in Norwich in 1571, and English artisans kept up a steady battery of complaints and petitions for much of Elizabeth's reign.[2]

It is difficult to ascertain the degree of satisfaction of aliens with their lives in London. On the one hand, evidence such as wills suggests that aliens were progressively integrated into English society. After examining one hundred extant wills, Andrew Pettegree concluded that 'by the end of the century, London's foreign community had an increasingly settled and prosperous air about it. A high proportion of its more affluent members had developed fruitful contacts with their English neighbours, and even among the less well-off the growing number of children born in England suggested that the process of peaceful assimilation would quicken as time went on.'[3] Yet other evidence paints a less rosy picture, pointing to the difficulties facing the alien community during the 1590s, as indicated by the departure of some members for the Dutch Republic. It is unclear how many emigrated, but the freemen registers of Amsterdam and Leiden indicate that emigration from England escalated during the 1590s and thereafter,[4] with higher emigration from provincial towns. While 127 stranger families emigrated from London to Leiden between 1576 and 1640, the number from Colchester was 245, Sandwich 419 and Norwich 597.[5] The apparent higher rates of emigration from provincial towns could reflect both the less favourable economic and social conditions there, and the greater suitability of the skills of the emigrants to the new environment. Their decision to leave England, then, suggests that they had found somewhere with better opportunities. To understand why some aliens were able to assimilate into London society while others experienced profound difficulties, it is necessary first to examine their legal position in English society and their opportunities for social advancement.

Legal Status

The existence of prospects for social improvement is probably one of the most potent determinants of immigrants' satisfaction with life in a new homeland. Yet the legal division of people into different categories with their varying rights in this period presented considerable obstacles to integration. Overseas immigrants in England faced two types of legal barriers: (1) the common law, and (2) civic laws and customs. Bacon identified four types of persons known to the law of England: (1) alien enemy; (2) alien friend; (3) denizen, and (4) natural-born subject.[6] Allegiance was the key criterion to distinguish a subject from an alien.[7] Those born in England or in countries under the allegiance of the dominion of the King were subjects; those born in territory outside the dominion of the King were aliens.[8] Citizenship, then, had a territorial dimension, as the place of birth and political allegiance were essential in determining status. The concept of a genuine English subject, as opposed to a stranger, may have evolved under the pressures of the movements of population during the Hundred Years War.[9]

Aliens fell into two types, and their rights and privileges were determined by which category they fell into. Alien enemies were those who owed allegiance to a sovereign hostile to the King of England. The Crown possessed absolute rights and powers over alien enemies, including the power to expel. Alien friends had most of the rights of subjects, and were protected by the law, owed temporary allegiance to the King, and were obliged to take the oaths required of subjects.[10] In general, aliens faced several restrictions, most of which were introduced during the reign of Richard III (1452–85) and were reinstated in the early sixteenth century by Henry VIII. With regard to property rights, aliens were prohibited from leasing property, opening or keeping a shop, and purchasing property. With regard to their tax status, aliens were required to pay a double rate of taxation. They were not allowed to engage in retail or 'foreign bought and sold', designed to prevent non-freemen conducting business among themselves.[11] They could work and employ up to two alien journeymen, but were forbidden from taking on alien apprentices and from working as householders as they could not have a shop of their own. Aliens, particularly those born under the allegiance of a political enemy, also faced the possible danger of expulsion in times of war and political conflict. In February 1554, for example, Mary gave all seditious and non-denizen aliens twenty days to depart from the realm. In early 1558, when Francophobia spread as a result of war between England and France, a proclamation was issued authorizing any citizen to arrest non-denizen Frenchmen.[12] In theory, then, aliens had few rights, but in practice their economic freedom was probably greater, depending on the extent to which the statutes were rigidly enforced.

To overcome many of the impediments to social improvement, aliens could become adopted subjects, or *denizens*, with the acquisition of a letter patent. This would give them permanent residency and superior economic rights. The power to create such subjects lay with the Crown, and the rights they conferred depended upon the wording of the particular letter. The status of denizen cannot therefore be precisely defined. A denizen, it appears, had some but not all of the privileges of a British subject. The status of denizen took effect from the date of the grant, and not earlier.[13] However, the letter was quite easy to obtain as there were no prerequisites for the grant of denization. But the letter of denization had a fundamental drawback: denizens could not inherit real property, and the transmission of this status of being a denizen to his descendants depended on the terms of the grant, which might be in the form of a limitation such as to 'X and his heirs' to 'X and his heirs male', or in some similar form.[14] According to Cottret, the stranger was envisaged essentially in relation to the *law of property* rather than *employment*, indicating an obsession with transfer through inheritance.[15]

Denizens could work as masters because they could keep a shop, employ up to four alien journeymen, purchase land, and allow their children to be apprenticed with English masters. Those who wished to improve their life in London found it expedient to acquire such a letter, and until the 1560s the cost was still reasonable, between 6s. 8d. and £1 13s. 4d., with many paying at the lower end of the scale.[16] Evidence shows that only a minority of aliens acquired the letter of denization. The Returns of Aliens show that in 1568, 13 per cent of aliens were denizens, falling steeply to 9 per cent in 1573, and to 7 per cent by 1593. Yet the number of householders (those who kept shop) showed a steady increase: nearly 21 per cent were classified as householders in 1571, and 24 per cent in 1593 (see Chapter 4, Table 4.10). These figures suggest that the authorities probably turned a blind eye to the regulations.

There are a number of reasons why the number of denizens declined. The cumbersome process involved may be partly responsible. To obtain a letter, a stranger had to present a petition, which meant hiring a scrivener to write it, and if favourably received, a patent would be granted. The length of time taken between the initial entry of the grant and the final registration of the patent varied between a few days and several months.[17] The rising cost of purchasing a letter of denization could also have been a key factor. By 1582, the fee had risen dramatically to approximately £2 12s. 4d.[18] This amount of investment was simply beyond the means of many aliens, especially recent arrivals. The 1582 subsidy shows that of the 1840 aliens assessed for subsidy in that year, nearly 74 per cent paid just the basic poll tax of 8d. per head as they neither had goods worth £3 or more, nor land over the value of £1.[19] For those who could afford it, the letter was not worth the trouble, as its fundamental benefit had disappeared with the passage of an Act of Common Council in 1574, forbidding London citizens to take as apprentice any person whose father was not the son of an English man, or born 'within the Queens dominion'. This meant that children of denizens could no longer serve apprenticeship, hence one crucial difference between an alien and a denizen had been obliterated.[20] During the period 1558–1603, there were 1962 patents granted, and of these, 1669 were secured during the first twenty years of Elizabeth's reign, and only 293 were obtained after 1578. During the latter part of the reign, it appears that many strangers did not feel the patents were worth the trouble.[21]

Aliens could also become naturalized subjects by a special Act of Parliament 'with the assent of the whole nation', but this was prohibitively expensive. The key distinction between a denizen and a naturalized subject related to inheritance rights: a naturalized subject could inherit and bequeath his property to his children, and enjoy the full economic freedom and tax status of a natural-born subject. Yet few aliens ever acquired this status, as cost was a major obstacle. In 1551, it was reported that the letter of naturalization cost only £4, yet other estimates put it at between £65 and £100.[22] During Elizabeth's reign, only 12 Acts were granted, compared with 71 granted between 1603 and 1640.[23]

Besides the stranger's relationship to the sovereign, there was also his place within a town. Towns had extensive privileges bestowed by ancient charters. The key differentiation among townsmen was the *freedom* of the city. As John Evans has explained:

> The all-important dividing line among townsmen was between freemen and non-freemen. Freedom of the city involved both privileges and obligations set down in local ordinances and enforced in the Lord Mayor's Court. The effect of these ordinances was to provide the freemen, or citizenry, with a virtual monopoly over both political and economic affairs. Only freemen could hold civic office and only freemen could vote in municipal and parliamentary elections. Non-freemen and 'foreigners' were prohibited from taking on apprentices.[24]

Commonly acquired through servitude of a seven-year apprenticeship, freedom could also be attained through patrimony (descent) or marriage, or redemption. Freemen of a given city were its citizens, with full economic rights, the most important of which was the ability to engage independently in economic activity, such as the freedom to sell and buy goods between them, retail, and open a shop. Non-freemen were known as *foreigners*, a term used to describe a newcomer to the town, and possessed limited rights.

Few aliens or strangers acquired the freedom, as they were barred from serving apprenticeship. The only real possibility was through redemption or purchase, but this required 'extraordinary means' or 'talents'. The request for admission usually came from the Crown or prominent members of government. In 1581, probably at the instigation of Sir Francis Walsingham, nine alien brewers were granted freedom by redemption at a fee of £50 each.[25] In 1609, the King made a special plea on behalf of Robert Thiery that he be admitted into the freedom of the City because of his extraordinary skills and inventions, being the first in England to weave material from the silk of silkworms nourished in England. In this instance, it was agreed that he should be admitted to the Weavers' Company on payment of 6s. 8d.[26] The City of London received frequent requests to grant freedom by redemption from 'such honorable persons and good lords and friends', placing the City's governors in an awkward dilemma. Writing to the Earl of Warwick in November 1579, the Lord Mayor explained his predicament:

> It may be that your Lordship is informed that the matter of freedom is of no great importance, howbeit the populousness of this city and specially of the poor and

artificers and other is such, and the increase of strangers of that sort so great, and our granting of such freedoms has been so frequent by mean of our readiness to satisfy the requests ... that our citizens be in very hard case and do much grudge against us.[27]

In response to the Earl's several letters for the admission of John Leonard and Henry Rodes, both strangers, the Lord Mayor felt the need to state his reasons even more bluntly in a separate letter:

Our number of poor artificers and citizens is so great, and eaten out of their trades and livings by strangers and foreigners, that they doe greatly grudge against us for overready granting of freedoms whereby we are constrained in duty and conscience and for avoiding of great misliking of our governance to stay such grants.[28]

He also explained other reasons for his refusal, including the fear of native impoverishment and the burden on poor relief, the economic malaise of the country, and the right of natives to find work:

Her majesty subjects ... are eaten out by strangers artificers, to their undoing and our burden and the unnatural hardness to our own country, whereas none of her majesties subjects can be suffered (be they never so excellent in any art) in their country too live by their work.

The request by Lady Anne Wraye for the admission of her servant, Thomas Hudd, was also refused. However, the Lord Mayor granted Wilson's request to give Henry Rodes the freedom of the City.[29] In total, only a small percentage of aliens received the freedom of the City. In 1593, 70 aliens, or 1 per cent, were recorded as free denizens (those with the letter of denization and the freedom of the City).[30] Only a small percentage of aliens thus achieved upward mobility and had the opportunity to socialize and mix with English freemen at social occasions organized by the City's companies.

Relations with Native Citizens

From the foregoing discussion, it is clear that relations between aliens and native citizens varied widely, depending on the groups involved. John Strype, for example, had noted that:

the English Nature being somewhat inhospitable to Strangers, jealous of their Industry, and suspecting them to get their Trade away from them, the wiser and better sort were rather for cherishing these Strangers, as well as perceiving what Advantages they brought to the Nation, both for their Callings and Examples of Thrift and Diligence, as also by rendring the Queen's Enemy weaker by the dispeopling of his Countries, and abating of his Trade and Traffic. They had also a religious Compassion for such as left their own Country and Friends, and plentiful Living, (as most of them did) for the sake of God and Truth.[31]

During Elizabeth's reign, hostility and resentment against aliens seemed to increase, as indicated by the threats of violence in 1567, 1586, 1587, 1593 and June 1595. The most serious threat was a slanderous pamphlet published in April 1593, when apprentices demanded the departure of all Flemings and French, declaring that:

> It is best for them to depart out of the realm of England between this and the 9th of July next. If not, then to take that which follows ... Apprentices will rise to the number of 2336. And all the apprentices and journeymen will down with the Flemings and strangers.[32]

How serious were these threats? In evaluating these, some historians have suggested that the Privy Council's reactions may have made the threats more serious than they were. Roger Manning has pointed out that the plot against aliens in September 1586, for example, may have been nothing more than loose talk, but when the Crown demanded a response from the City magistrates, this may have made the conspiracy appear more serious than it probably was.[33] Ian Archer, on the other hand, stressed the need to see the threat of popular action as a negotiating strategy, designed to remind the magistrates of their obligations to redress apprentice grievances. He emphasized that there never was an actual anti-alien riot in Elizabethan London, but there were plenty of libels threatening action. The absence of riots, he concluded, may reflect the particular diligence of magistrates, the difficulties of conspiracy among apprentices in a world ruled by householders, and the success of libels in encouraging governors of companies, supported by the aldermanic elite, to take action against strangers.[34]

The question of whether Londoners were xenophobic has also provoked serious debate among historians. In a recent paper, Joe Ward contended that the term 'xenophobia' is perhaps too strong, preferring to use 'antipathy', and reminded us how *antipathy* existed side by side with *sympathy*. He urged historians to 'avoid leaping to the conclusion that xenophobia was an essential characteristic of life in early modern London. There surely was, at times, considerable antipathy towards aliens among some Londoners, but even in the highly competitive economic environment of the late 16th century there was also sympathy among the non-elite for their plight as religious refugees.'[35] Nigel Goose also dismissed xenophobia, and pointed to the tendency by contemporary writers to 'plagiarize' each other's comments about xenophobia.[36] Laura Yungblut, on the other hand, stressed a 'dichotomy' of attitudes, underlying how Londoners were often torn by the need to offer religious sanctuary to immigrants and the perception of economic benefits brought by these, and by the view that these represented a possible threat. She also made clear that hostility towards aliens was by no means confined to the lower classes.[37] For Ian Archer, the notion of power helps explain different attitudes towards aliens, and why large producers welcomed aliens who represented new skills and lower costs, and why smaller producers and journeymen resented aliens who posed increased competition.[38] Thus, in the case of weaving, Alfred Plummer found master weavers more hospitable than journeymen to strangers, and welcomed the addition of skills, especially in the more expensive branches such as the weaving of figured silk damasks and velvets. Journeymen, on the other hand, resented any claims to superiority of craftsmanship and feared increasing competition for work and scarce living accommodation. They were especially hostile to unqualified alien weavers.[39]

While 'xenophobia' may be too strong a term to describe the feelings of some English against aliens, it is difficult to deny that there was a growing feeling of resentment and hostility in the last decades of Elizabeth's reign. During this period, there were occasional outbursts of hostility towards aliens, and these followed a basic pattern: economic and social stress precipitated attacks on aliens, harassment and molestation by informers; these were then followed by written complaints to the City's governors, ministers of the Dutch and French churches, and the Queen. Hostility, however, tended to be localized, directed at a particular group or at those living in a particular area. What needs explaining, therefore, is not so much whether Londoners were xenophobic and to what degree, but rather the important questions of why Londoners were seemingly more hostile after the 1580s, what were the responses of aliens and of national and city governments, and what were the consequences.

Hostility towards aliens in early modern London was complex, rooted in a multiplicity of social and economic factors. Contemporary complaints often pointed to social exclusiveness of aliens, their unwillingness to impart skills, their unfair trading practices and their transport of profits abroad as the primary reasons.[40] John Strype, the great antiquarian of London, of Dutch descent, writing in 1720, pointed to economic jealousy and fears of effects on their livelihood due to competition.[41] Historians also attribute many economic factors to native dislike of aliens, including 'encroachment on privileges, jealousy of aliens' prosperity, objection to their engaging in retail trade, their great numbers, and perhaps the most important of all, the general economic strains and conflicts, in England during that period, for which the aliens made an excellent scape-goat'.[42] This question of scapegoating raises a very important issue of identification and visibility. Aliens were easy targets because legislation and laws made them highly visible and identifiable, through distinction, categorization, discrimination and exclusion. Immigrants born overseas under the political allegiance of a foreign king were labelled 'aliens' or 'strangers', and were distinguished from 'native-born' English, whose rights, it was felt, should be protected. This distinction formed the basis of economic discrimination and lay at the heart of hostility.

Most historical explanations of hostility focus on general factors rather than specific causes of its increase after the 1580s. To understand this, it is essential to examine the demographic development of the City during this period. The English population expanded from 2.5–3 million in 1500 to 4 million in 1600,[43] and although modest by modern standards, at the time many Englishmen thought that the country was overpopulated, partly because of frequent occurrences of bad harvests and plague, and widespread unemployment. Most of this demographic increase was absorbed by London, and between 1580 and 1600 London's population nearly doubled, undoubtedly causing a lot of social and economic strains. In addition, as Beier has noted, the preponderance of young, single men among London's population increased the propensity to turn to violence as a means of conflict resolution. The City was full of restless, predominantly young and single men, separated from their families and local communities, and employed in low-paid and transient jobs.[44] The various elements of the London 'crowd' (including servants, apprentices, masterless men, soldiers, vagrants) may have totalled 100 000, or nearly 50 per cent of London's population in the 1590s.[45] Manning asserted that on only four occasions – in 1584, twice in 1595, and in 1618 – did crowds of more than 1000 persons participate in riots. Yet he admitted that London crowds were more difficult to control because, in contrast to rural protests, the size of the crowd could grow very quickly if participants called upon sympathetic bystanders for assistance.[46]

Some historians believe that the population turnover and the sheer size of London produced 'anomie' similar to that described in sociological studies of nineteenth- and twentieth-century cities. Peter Clark and Slack have suggested recently that:

> The rapid growth of London and its high turnover of population may have led to that impersonality which is said to have occurred in some great continental cities in the sixteenth and seventeenth centuries and which are usually associated with the modern metropolis.[47]

It is believed that such an impersonal and anonymous environment may have contributed to xenophobia because it increased the individual's need for belonging, and encouraged them to make what psychologists call the 'in-group/out-group distinction'. To relate self to group, the individual uses categorization, identity, comparison and psychological distinctiveness. Psychological research shows that mere categorization is sufficient to produce inter-group discrimination, even when there is no conflict of interest and there is no past history of inter-group hostility.[48]

Other historians disagree with this view. Roger Finlay has recently concluded that, due to the very small size of many city parishes, 'it is difficult to argue that ... people were less likely to know each other than in rural parishes', except mobile individuals such as servants and apprentices. Clark and Slack noted that 'face-to-face relationships may have been preserved ... in separate streets and quarters of towns which were dominated by a single occupational group'.[49] The argument that London life was essentially anonymous, with individuals having fewer family and community ties, and their social contacts being more casual and transitory, has also been dismissed by Robert Shoemaker. He has criticized this view because he believes it is based on weak theoretical models and insufficient research. This argument, he maintained, is closely linked to the idealization of rural society as close-knit and unchanging, in contrast to urban anonymity and mobility, popular in nineteenth-century sociological models. To contemporaries, he stressed, the virtues of urban life may outweigh the vices.[50] Boulton's study of the persistence of households after ten years in the Boroughside District of St Saviour's, Southwark confirms Finlay's conclusion that the 'stability of London's population has been underestimated'. The study found that a significant number of households in the Boroughside district (43 per cent) spent a substantial proportion of their lives within a relatively small urban area. There was mobility, but most of it was short-range, suggesting perhaps that there was a strong sense of attachment to the local area.[51]

The most convincing explanation for growing hostility was related to increasingly overcrowded conditions in the capital. As more and more people were packed into a small area, the opportunity for conflict was likely to increase. Ian Archer has argued that life in early modern London was far from anonymous and impersonal, and that the obligations of neighbourhood were taken seriously. Neighbours, for example, visited each other when sick and were well-informed about each other's behaviour because much popular sociability took place within the street. But he also pointed out that the same conditions which 'made neighbours so aware of each other's shortcomings multiplied the occasions of conflict. This was because many disputes originated in the cramped conditions of the urban environment.'[52] With tens of thousands of people living and working within the walls of a city covering not much more than a square mile,[53] it would be difficult to avoid conflicts with neighbours living at close quarters.

While living in close proximity with their English neighbours, aliens also seemed to lead a separate life, attended their own church, married their own kind, and employed their fellow countrymen. As a complaint of 1571 put it: 'though they be denized or born here amongst us, yet they keep themselves severed from us in church, in government, in trade, in language and marriage'.[54] It was precisely this seeming cultural separatism which probably provoked much resentment.

Attendance at the local English parish churches would provide an ideal opportunity for aliens to socialize with their English neighbours. Yet many aliens preferred to attend their own church. In 1568, 58 per cent of aliens attended the Stranger Churches, and only a third the English church. Those living in the suburbs such as St Katherine's, Whitechapel and East Smithfield were more likely to attend their local parish church than those living in the City. Of those 1972 aliens surveyed living in these areas in December 1572, over 61 per cent attended the English church, 11 per cent the Dutch church, and 21 per cent of the French church.[55] There were practical reasons why people went to the English church in their parish: it was nearby.[56] In addition, many aliens who lived in the suburbs had arrived in London before the Stranger Churches were founded in 1550.

By 1593, however, the proportion of aliens attending English churches had declined to 14 per cent, while the total attending the Stranger Churches increased to 70 per cent (see Table 5.1). The preponderance of refugees among the recent arrivals may partly account for this change. For these, there were good reasons why membership of a Stranger Church was highly valued and preferred. Stranger Churches offered them the means to worship in their native language, and gave them a measure of social identity and representation. They were also a meeting place for many strangers uprooted from their homelands needing social and emotional support from fellow

Table 5.1   Patterns of church attendance, 1568–1593

Church membership	1568 No.	1568 %	1571 No.	1571 %	1593 No.	1593 %
English church	1 815	27.0	939	20.3	549	14.0
Dutch church	1 910	28.5	1 450	31.3	1 376	35.0
French church	1 810	27.0	1 284	27.7	1 344	34.0
Italian	161	2.4	92	1.9	29	0.7
No church	1 008	15.0	866	18.7	131	3.3
Denizens	—	—	—	—	519	13.0
Total	6 704	100	4 631	100	3 948	100

Sources: Kirk and Kirk, eds, *Returns of Aliens*, vol. 10, No. 1, p. 439; Vol. 10, No. 2, p. 139; Scouloudi, *Returns of Strangers*, p. 90

countrymen, and a place of information exchange whereby strangers could be kept informed about developments back home. Equally important was the economic benefit provided by membership of the Stranger Churches. They were the sources of alms and relief in times of economic hardship. Aliens could also rely on the ministers and elders of their church to lobby the government on their behalf.[57] Thus economic and social necessity encouraged aliens to rely on their own community.

With few opportunities for social contact, it therefore comes as no surprise that the scale of inter-marriage between aliens and English was also insignificant. In 1571, there were 43 cases of intermarriage (or 2 per cent of strangers who were married). Most of these were between an alien man and an English woman; only six cases involved an alien woman and an Englishman. It is striking that three-quarters of those who intermarried in 1571 were members of the English church rather than of the Stranger Churches and had been resident in England for ten years or more. This suggests that the length of residence was critical in determining the choice of partner. By the 1590s, marital assimilation among the aliens remained relatively insignificant, and only 7 per cent of aliens in the City (or 75 cases) had an English spouse.[58]

In the area of employment, some good progress was made. In 1571, only 13 per cent of a total of 964 alien servants listed in the Return of Aliens had contact with English masters. By 1593, over half of the 1079 alien households had some contact with English servants and employed them in their workshops.[59] This greater contact resulted in part from the government's pressure on aliens to employ English servants.

Social contacts between aliens and their English hosts in general were partly restricted by linguistic barriers. Many new arrivals could not speak English, and this is made amply clear by the fact that ministers of the Stranger Churches frequently had to accompany English officials when they went to conduct their surveys during the 1570s because they were 'best acquainted with the language'. By the 1590s, it was still not clear to the authorities whether the aliens could 'understand the English tongue' or not.[60] Language barriers thus promoted social segregation, encouraging aliens to work, live, worship and marry among themselves.

In reality, there was more social mixing than this evidence suggests. There were Englishmen who attended one of the Stranger Churches and spoke foreign languages. The Italian church in London, for example, attracted an insignificant number of English people. Many members of the upper strata of English society were attracted by Italian culture and language, which often formed part of their education. The taste of the English elite for Italian culture invited sarcastic comments from contemporaries, who complained about English noblemen preferring to attend the Italian church, attracted not by religious motives, but by the desire to practise their knowledge of Italian. The lack of sources makes it difficult to establish the number of Englishmen attending the London Italian church, but the presence of three English elders in its consistory of 1570 – in a total of six – indicates that the number was significant.[61] The relationship of the elite with aliens, then, may have been very different from that of the lower strata of society.

Issues of Conflict, 1550s–1570s

In London, conflict between aliens and English also developed partly because there was an absence of a framework clearly defining the economic rights of aliens. Unlike other provincial immigrant communities, there was no prior agreement with the civic authorities as to how many aliens should settle in the capital and what rights they should expect to enjoy. The Royal Charter granted to the stranger community in London in 1550 dealt mainly with religious privileges, and there was no stipulation with regard to the economic freedom which they might expect to enjoy. In this respect, the letters patent to the London stranger community differed from almost all the later charters.[62] This meant that their only form of protection was the goodwill of the Queen, the Privy Council, the rulers of London and the ministers of their churches.

Tensions arose as a result of conflict over a few common issues. A common source of conflict, especially between the 1550s and 1570s, was the perceived sizeable number of aliens in the capital, which at times was wildly exaggerated. In 1551, a rumour spread that 40 000 or 50 000 strangers had come to England, and that most of them were living in London. The source of this rumour, according to the Spanish observer, 'was the German Church, where 1,000 and more persons have been seen together at one time, and the enrollment of foreigners ... though in truth their number hardly exceeds 4,000 or 5,000 heads in all'.[63] In other words, such gatherings in the heart of the City in Austin Friars made aliens more visible. This rumour prompted five or six hundred men to complain to the Mayor and Aldermen of London that 'by reason of the great dearth they cannot live for these strangers, whom they were determined to kill up through the realm if they found no remedy'.[64]

In order to obtain accurate information to dispel these kinds of rumours and to establish the background of aliens, the Elizabethan government after 1559 began to order regular certificates of aliens. The Privy Council would send a 'precept' to the Lord Mayor of London, who then instructed the 26 Aldermen to count the number of aliens living in their wards. Certificates of aliens were then sent to the Privy Council, normally with details of names, occupations, total number of people in a household, length of residence, and church membership. Between 1561 and 1593, there are 24 extant certificates, but only a few of these are complete and detailed. Nine of these were ordered in two years between 1567 and 1568, and this is indicative of the scale of immigration as well as the degree of popular discontent against aliens in this period. In 1567, apprentices and servants, organized an insurrection against aliens, particularly against the Flemings, because they thought their number had increased greatly. The government's response was to order three certificates of strangers, and the results were dispatched to Livery Companies to be read out to their members to show that there were only 3562 aliens in the city and 'no more'.[65] Popular unrest against aliens increased in 1568, when a large number of refugees arrived from the Spanish Netherlands and France, and this is indicated by the six certificates ordered. In response to public opinion and constant rumours of spies among the incoming refugees, the City of London imposed a rigorous screening process to sort religious refugees from economic migrants. On 19 October 1568, the City issued an order allowing only religious refugees to remain in the capital.[66]

The question of whether immigrants were genuine refugees or economic migrants also dominated discussions during the 1570s. This was hotly debated because it related to the question of whether London could afford to be charitable to aliens at a time when its own native citizens were experiencing economic difficulties and widespread unemployment. On the one hand, there was a display of compassion and charity. The lists of receipts in the earliest extant account book of the French church which runs from November 1572 to December 1573 show donations were made by Puritans, including the Mayor and Aldermen of Leicester, the Dean of Durham (William Whittingham), a group of young men from Grays Inn and the Alderman Richard Martin, Master of the Mint. Following the influx of French refugees in the aftermath of the St Bartholomew Massacre in 1573, the Archdeaconry of York donated £50 for the poor refugees of the French church.[67] Such compassion existed alongside indifference and resentment felt by those lower down the social scale. They, like the minister who preached to his congregation in London in 1570, probably believed that immigrants were 'not here for religion: but rather are here to take away the livings of our own Citizens and countrymen, and to eat by trade the bread out of their mouths'.[68]

The deteriorating economic and social conditions from the late 1560s undoubtedly hardened native attitudes towards aliens. In times of unemployment and economic distress, they felt less benevolent and charitable. During the 1560s, employment opportunities in London may have contracted as the boom in the cloth trade ceased. The same forces that engendered a large influx of refugees to the capital also served to disrupt English foreign trade, especially the embargoes in 1563–4 and 1568–73, as well as the sack of Antwerp in 1576. During 1560–72, an average of 92 600 cloths were exported annually from London, down by one-fifth from the average of 115 200 cloths in the 1550s.[69] After the fall of Antwerp, English merchants were forced to re-orientate and look for new markets, which were eventually developed in the Baltic and the Mediterranean.

Those working in the cloth-related sectors were the first to feel the impact of this. From the mid-1560s, impoverished householders began to complain about unemployment, and called for an end to the export of unfinished cloths, as the finishing and dressing of these in England rather than in the Low Countries would provide additional employment. By the early 1570s, complaints about unemployment in London were voiced by those in other crafts. Petitioners attributed the problem to three factors: (1) competition from foreigners and strangers for work; (2) the increase in the use of apprentices instead of journeymen, and (3) the growing numbers of freemen pursuing occupations other than those formally associated with their companies.[70] While employment opportunities in London shrank, its population multiplied rapidly, and consequently exacerbated the problem. The expanding shipbuilding industry, enjoying unprecedented growth in the 1570s,[71] partly helped to absorb some of the City's male population. Ironically, this growth was spurred by events in Antwerp. Before the 'Troubles' disrupted the Low Countries, London's proximity to the emporium of Antwerp discouraged 'any initiative to speculative exploration'. With the closure of the Antwerp market, English merchants had to find alternative markets for their cloth exports, and were compelled to 'seek for themselves at source those multifarious commodities that they had previously purchased at second hand on the Antwerp market'.[72] To reach these more distant places, it was imperative to construct a large ocean-going merchant fleet. According to Stone, the dependence of shipping expansion upon the disruption of Antwerp by the 'Troubles' is illustrated by the fact that 51 ships of over 100 tons were built between 1571 and 1576, the period leading up to the sack of the city by Spanish forces. In the ten years to 1582, England's merchant fleet doubled in size.[73] At a time when the cloth industry was in decline, expanding employment opportunities in shipbuilding may have been an essential factor in attracting male migrants to London from the 1570s.

Influenced by the belief that many aliens had come for economic rather than religious reasons, Londoners blamed them for causing rising prices, shortages of necessities and unemployment. Thus, years of price rises – 1567/8, 1571, 1573, 1586, 1595/6 – precipitated attacks on strangers by servants. In 1573, a year when the average index of the price of grains jumped from 368 in 1572 to 478,[74] the abusive behaviour of the apprentices and servants towards strangers necessitated intervention by the City authorities. It appears that strangers living in London complained to the City authorities that they 'have been of late molested and evil entreated going into the street about their business, by servants and apprentices undiscreetly and without order whereof hurt may ensue'. An order was therefore sent to the City's Livery Companies, commanding them to call a meeting of their members and instruct them not to 'misuse molest or evil entreat any strangers ... but shall gently suffer them to pass without let or vexation'.[75] The Lord Mayor also wrote to the Stranger Churches, instructing them to advise their members to stay indoors between 9 p.m. and 5 a.m., for their own protection.[76]

Various complaints were also sent to the City. In 1573, even Cornhill, a wealthy ward with a small number of aliens, felt the effects and complained of the 'continual and daily resort of strangers of divers nations unto this city ... [which] is the cause of great scarcity of victuals raising rents and continual increasing of beggar Idle vagabonds and thieves of our own countrymen and nation'.[77] The root of the problem, in fact, lay in London's over-rapid demographic expansion, growing unemployment as a result of a decline in the cloth trade, the severe inflation (price indices rose from 220 to 272 between 1572 and 1573) and the decline in wages (wage indices fell from 84 in 1572 to 69 in 1573).[78] The events of 1573 appear to have swung public opinion against aliens, as indicated by the passing of the Act of Common Council in 1574, henceforth forbidding the children of denizens from serving apprenticeship.

Another persistent source of complaint against aliens concerns the question of the seven-year apprenticeship. The Statute of Artificers of 1563 stipulated that artisans must serve a seven-year apprenticeship before they could ply their craft, but it is unclear whether Continental immigrants were likewise required to serve an English apprenticeship. The Goldsmiths' and Weavers' Companies accepted Continental immigrants with shorter training (silversmiths from Antwerp served a customary six-year apprenticeship, while silk-weavers from France five years), so it appears that overseas immigrants were not required to serve an English seven-year apprenticeship, and only had to produce proof of their Continental training. This presented problems for some immigrants, especially those who had fled in fear for political or religious reasons. Their secretive or hasty departure prevented them from making the necessary arrangements to obtain a letter from the relevant guild or city authority to certify their training. Once in England, their desire to conceal their place of refuge may have prevented them from writing home for a letter. Some immigrants may also have changed their vocation in London, therefore a letter from home certifying their previous trade would in any case be irrelevant. A common complaint was that, as expressed in 1571, 'although none or very few of [aliens] had served a seven-year apprenticeship, they used all the several crafts and occupations that any man of this kingdom doth use'.[79] The admission of aliens into relevant guilds could alleviate concerns that the capital was inundated with unqualified and untrained artisans from the

Continent. Unfortunately, many London guilds (such as the Merchant Tailors) had no policy of admitting aliens, forcing them to work illegally, either in the suburbs or in privileged places such as St Martins le Grand, Black Friars, Clerkenwell, the Duchy of Lancaster, St Katherines, White-chapel or Southwark.[80] The problem with these areas was that they also attracted other English non-freemen, and poor provincial immigrants. Thus, hostility was accentuated by the congregation of aliens among the disadvantaged and marginal groups in areas where poverty was an enduring aspect of life. Economic hardship therefore encouraged xenophobia.

The national government could perhaps have helped ease the situation by issuing letters of denization or naturalization free of charge, similar to the General Act of Naturalization in 1709, which allowed the wholesale naturalizing of alien subjects.[81] Yet the introduction of such a policy would have aroused strong opposition from the City. In May 1587, the Privy Council proposed that foreigners, strangers and freemen should have equal rights and liberties in the cloth market in London. The Lord Mayor opposed such a move, pointing out that:

> It is not unknown to your Honorable what griefs have been conceived and libelled of late against the strangers inhabiting among us ... Now this farther liberty granted to Strangers what effect it may work in the minds of these stirring and discontented persons wee leave to your Honorable to be considered of ....[82]

The experience of Evil May Day, in addition to the belief that the grant of privileges to aliens would disadvantage native-born English, probably deterred the City of London from adopting a more open policy. It was also feared that, as the Lord Mayor's letter to the Earl of Warwick in 1579 made clear, impoverished English would impose a financial burden on the City by requiring poor relief, and would riot against the City's authority.[83] The belief that strangers transported their wealth abroad also made it undesirable to provide them with opportunities to get rich.

In the 1590s, the requirement of a seven-year apprenticeship was extended to merchants, reflecting a desire to curtail their power. Resentment against alien merchants stemmed partly from their domination of the lucrative overseas trade, and partly from the extensive commercial privileges they were perceived to enjoy. English overseas trade was handled largely by foreign merchants and carried in foreign shipping. At the beginning of the sixteenth century, the Hanseatics, the Italians and a small number of other foreign merchants between them took more than half of London's exports of cloth and provided more than half of its imports.[84] Brian Manning has also suggested that Lord Burghley disliked alien merchants because he thought they exported their profits in the form of plate and bullion instead of reinvesting them in the English economy.[85]

During Elizabeth's reign, native merchants and retailers sought to reduce the aliens' domination and privileged position in England's overseas trade. They were probably responsible for the anonymous 'Complaint of the Citizens of London against the great number of strangers in and about this city' addressed to the Queen in September 1571. Finding themselves 'aggrieved at two sorts of strangers settled here amongst us – merchants and handicraftsmen', 'the Subjects of England and Citizens of London' penned seven complaints, six of which were directed at alien merchants.[86] In the following year, native merchants and retailers proposed an Act in Parliament to prevent strangers who had not served a seven-year apprenticeship from retailing foreign goods in England.[87] The bill was not passed, as another Act had already prevented aliens and denizens from retailing imports in London. In 1592, the question of whether aliens and denizens should be allowed to engage in retailing imports was again debated in the House of Commons, indicating that the previous Act had not been effective. The discussion broadened out to include a consideration of whether a more liberal policy towards aliens should be adopted. Sir John Wolley advocated the adoption of a liberal policy because he felt that 'the Riches and Renown of [London] comes by entertaining of Strangers and giving liberty unto them. Antwerp and Venice could never have been so rich and famous but by entertaining of Strangers, and by that means have gained all the intercourse of the World'. Other councillors urged charity to the strangers because these were godly people:

> We ought not to be uncharitable ... [Strangers'] riches ... growth chiefly by Parsimony... Though they be a Church by themselves, their Example is profitable amongst us, for their Children are no sooner able to go, but they are taught to serve God and to flee idleness; for the least of them earns his meat by his labour. Our Nation is sure more blessed for their sakes.[88]

Sir Walter Raleigh, however, raised strong objections, declaring that: 'Whereas it is pretended that for strangers it is against Charity, Honour, against profit to expel them; in my opinion it is no matter of charity to relieve them ... The Dutchman is to fly to no man but for his profit, and they will obey no man long ... They are the people that maintain the King of Spain in his greatness.' The Bill was ratified and an Act for the maintenance of English artificers and handicraftsmen was passed, allowing only those, including merchants and retailers, who had completed a seven-year apprenticeship to practise their trade in London.[89] The House of Lords, however, threw out this bill when it was presented before it.[90]

Issues of Conflict in the 1590s

Complaints of unemployment and impoverishment of native artisans were relentless in the 1590s. Native artisans complained they could not find work because, as the tailors put it, 'foreigners and strangers which work inwardly … privately within their houses or shops latessed or glassed from the open show to the streetward … and take the work … out of freemens hands'.[91] The ability of aliens to obtain work in these difficult times was attributed to the belief that they offered more competitive prices, made possible by living in cheap and overcrowded conditions, by their use of untrained labour, and by their evasion of charges. The Weavers claimed that:

> The most part of the strangers and foreigners dwellings are in chambers and odd corners, being divers families in one house, having their work wrought by the youths aforesaid, do and may live at far smaller expense, and work for lesser gains, and sell for less profit, then your petitioners can or may do to live by. And thereby have almost got all the work and employment of the said Trade of weaving from your petitioners being freemen, dwelling within this city, taking and keeping Apprentices as the laws and customs of the same enjointh them and contributors to all public charges.[92]

In reality, these conditions were partly imposed on aliens. Because they could not be admitted to guilds and the freedom of the City, they did not have to pay many charges such as quarterage (quarterly fee to the guild), and ironically, discrimination became the main source of competitiveness in hard times.

Resentment against aliens in the 1590s was spurred by two factors. First, worsening economic and social circumstances were once again responsible for the apparently increased hostility, and unleashed a renewed wave of xenophobic attacks on aliens. Shrinking employment opportunities and falling standards of living contributed to mounting social problems such as unemployment, poverty and vagrancy in London. In 1596, when bread prices rocketed, the number of householders requiring relief jumped to 4132. These figures underestimate the levels of poverty in London, as they cover mainly the well-off intra-mural parishes.[93] Poverty was also geographically concentrated. Of the 4015 poor householders identified by aldermen as deserving to share the Royal Donation of £200 in January 1596, over half lived in the five outer wards: Farringdon Without, Aldersgate, Cripplegate, Bishopsgate and Portsoken.[94] These large wards contained a high proportion of non-freemen such as aliens and foreigners.

Second, there was growing dislike of foreigners by the ruling class. During this period, William Webbe, Lord Mayor in 1591–2, and the Common Council spoke out against the employment of alien artisans when qualified native craftsmen were without work.[95] In April 1593, apprentices threatened to kill Flemings and Frenchmen in the City if they did not leave within three months.[96] Before this investigation was completed, the following rhyme was written upon the wall of the Dutch churchyard on 5 May 1593:

> You, strangers, that inhabit in this land,
> Note this same writing, do it understand.
> Conceive it well, for safeguard of your lives,
> Your goods, your children, and you dearest wives.[97]

Of all libels, the Privy Council regarded this as exceeding 'the rest in lewdness', and took prompt steps to find the culprits. On the 10th May 1593, the Lord Mayor offered a large reward of 100 crowns in gold to 'whosoever shall discover and bring perfect knowledge unto the Lord Mayor ... what person or persons has written, dispersed or set up the said libels'.[98]

The perceived unwillingness of aliens to impart their craft skills also added to much resentment, particularly when in 1573 the City's aldermen had made this a precondition for allowing them to settle in the city. Despite various governmental attempts, Londoners still lamented in 1616 that the immigrants':

> Cheifest cause of [entertainment] here of late was in charity to shroud themselves from persecution for religion. And being here, their necessity become the Mother of their Ingenuitie in devising many trades, before to us unknowne. The state notinge their diligence, and yet preventinge the future inconvenience enacted that they should enterteine Englishe apprentices and servants to learne these trades, the neglect whereof giveth them advantage to keepe their misteries to themselves.[99]

Redress of Grievances

The steps adopted by native artisans to seek answers for their grievances varied. In 1595, the yeomen weavers apparently printed 40 copies of a pamphlet listing various complaints, which was addressed to the ministers of the alien churches urging them to 'exhort their countrymen to charitable dispositions and conformity of orders'. The pamphlet caused great offence because of the way it was written. The weavers were forced to re-submit their petition and succeeded in forcing the Company to amend its ordinances, reiterating the greater rights to which English freemen were entitled.[100]

Other less pleasant methods, such as the employment of informers, were also used to harass aliens, presumably with the intention of stopping them working or persuading them to leave. In a petition addressed to the Queen in 1599, members of the Dutch and French churches explained how informers 'live by the sweat of poor strangers brows, And when they vex them to make of some, [10 shillings, 14, 18], and of some 20 shillings more or less ... and the poor strangers for fear of them, glad to be quiet so'. They begged the Queen to take action to stop informers molesting and daily vexing strangers, so that they could practise their trades to 'maintain themselves, their wives, children and families'.[101] In another petition dated 22 January 1600, the Dutch and French churches reported how their members were afraid to go out because of the actions of informers, while others were arrested.[102] However, none of these measures were as extreme as that proposed by the Merchant Tailors' Company. With no policy of admitting aliens the Company, dominated by merchants, did not appreciate the problem facing artisan members until the 1590s, when the economic hardship hit them hard. As the Company did not have regulatory powers over aliens who were working secretly and illegally, it had to turn to the City to deal with the problem. Poorer members of the Merchant Tailors' Company, however, pressed for the expulsion of foreigners and aliens. Such a move was strongly opposed by the City and Privy Council on humanitarian and political grounds.[103] The Company initially also resisted such a move, but after many complaints, decided to endorse it after 1601. The Company adopted two measures to achieve this aim. It employed informers to harass foreigners and aliens. The Company also presented a bill in Parliament for the expulsion of foreigners,[104] but was rejected because it was regarded as 'unreasonable'. The Company therefore, having already spent over £100 on legal costs,[105] and uncertain of the outcome, decided 'not to proceed any further in parliament'.[106]

The escalating tension between native and alien tailors in the 1590s ensued in part from the Company's failure to recognize, define and regulate the activities of aliens. In Norwich, attempts were made from the beginning to restrict competition between native and aliens in popular trades, by permitting alien tailors, botchers 'menders of old clothes', shoemakers and cobblers to 'sell such things as they do work, to their own country men, and to none of [our] english nation'.[107] In London, such a regulation was absent. It was not until the Company's failure to expel aliens and foreigners, and after much lobbying by the stranger communities, that such a measure was reluctantly adopted. In October 1608, the French and Dutch churches appealed to the Company on humanitarian grounds to allow Dutch and French tailors to remain in London,[108] and promised that their members would be obedient. In 1608, the Company therefore agreed to allow 24 masters, who were not to be replaced when they died, and 34 servants to work in London,[109] providing they worked only for stranger customers, employed English servants, allowed the wardens to search their premises, and provided a bond of £20 each to the Lord Mayor. This new working arrangement sought to bring aliens under greater control by the Company, and prevent them being serious competitors. However, the strangers, in their reply, stated their inability to employ English servants because of a lack of work, and to pay a large bond because 'they are very unable and some of them not worth so much as is required at their hands'.[110]

Aliens' Responses

Faced with increasing discrimination, harassment from informers and threats of violence from servants, some aliens became increasingly disillusioned with their lives in London. This may have provoked Peter Coale, an immigrant 'painter-drawer' who lived in Aldersgate Street, to threaten to set the City on fire.[111] Others began to emigrate. In a report to the Privy Council in January 1593, ministers of the Dutch church recorded that 'many members of the said church do daily depart'.[112] They emigrated largely to the Dutch Republic, which actively encouraged them. In August 1593, the Amsterdam preacher Peter Plancius spread the news that several towns in Holland 'desire to encourage persons from England who wish to settle there'. Plancius assured them that these areas were far from their enemies, living was cheap there, and the Church enjoyed peace. He also enclosed a resolution of Harderwijk, a small fishing town on the Zuiderzee in Gelderland with a population of less than 3000, which guaranteed full rights to those who came over. Those who had craft skills or were drapers were particularly encouraged and were promised 'immunities ... over and above those of the ordinary citizens'.[113] In the 1590s, towns, especially in Holland, were competing to attract immigrants from the southern Netherlands[114] by offering specific advantages, such as tax privileges, free housing and free burghership (citizenship), and even working capital bearing no rent. Often, the new settlers were allowed to practise their trade outside the guilds. At times, premiums were paid. For example, in 1577 the city of Haarlem contracted Jan Hendrixsz from Brabant, who promised to work for six years in return for 72 guilders. In 1598, 34 immigrants obtained sums ranging from 300 to 700 pounds for operating a loom in Haarlem. Gouda converted six disused monasteries into workshops for weaving and dyeing premises, manned by Flemish refugees.[115]

Harderwijk hoped to reap the economic benefits from an influx of immigrants. This willingness to offer privileges to immigrants to attract skills was in direct contrast to the attitude in London, where the concern was that aliens should not enjoy more rights and privileges than the native-born. Then again, Harderwijk was nothing in size in comparison to London, and also had no history of riots against aliens. Admissions into citizenship of Harderwijk, although they do not necessarily reflect the actual number settling in the town, suggest that few took up this offer, as this small town presented few opportunities for aspiring artisans. Between 1581 and 1600, only one person from Scotland became a citizen, and between 1636 and 1655, one person from England.[116] Larger towns were more successful, particularly Amsterdam and Leiden where freemen registers suggest that emigration from England escalated during the 1590s and thereafter.[117]

Rising wages in the Dutch Republic, an indicator of the robustness of the economy at times of falling wages in London, were the second attraction for prospective emigrants. Wages for masters and journeymen in west Netherlands grew consistently from 1575. Wages for masters doubled between 1575 and 1595, from 9.57 stuivers to 18.59 stuivers per day (summer wages). Over the same period, wages for journeymen also doubled, from 8 to 16.70 stuivers per day. Wages for the unskilled increased less, from 5.75 to 11.75 stuivers.[118] In other words, those with skills received healthy financial rewards. Religious freedom and the ease of upward mobility also proved equally enticing. In an age when many communities suppressed religious nonconformity and discriminated against aliens, Amsterdam welcomed people from all religions and nationalities. There was also no obstruction to upward mobility, as the status of *poorter* (citizen) could be acquired at a small cost (8 florins until 1622, and 14 florins thereafter). The city of Amsterdam also assisted newcomers, finding housing for them and offering inducements to masters deemed capable of starting new industries or improving techniques in those already established.[119]

What kinds of craftsmen from England were most likely to move to the Dutch Republic? The occupational backgrounds of those who emigrated to Amsterdam between 1531 and 1606 offer a clue. The largest groups, in descending order, were those involved in clothing, taverns and public houses, trade and transport (merchants), and metalworking.[120] The exodus of these immigrants from England not only represented a considerable loss of valuable skills and capital, but also the news spread by these about the conditions in England may have discouraged others from coming.

Alien Community: The Assimilation Model

The previous discussions stress how growing mobility within the alien community resulted in part from the economic and social conflicts with the native population from the late 1580s. This may have affected only a small number of aliens. Others, as some historians have shown, lived in harmony and prosperity with their English neighbours. Martha Carlin argued that: 'aliens in Southwark, as in Westminster, generally lived in social and commercial amity with their English neighbours. The aliens attended the existing churches, held parish offices, joined parish guilds and contributed to local charities.'[121] But Carlin is referring to the fifteenth- and early sixteenth-century Southwark; during the late sixteenth century, where the situation was rather different. Some of the troubles of the 1590s originated there. In 1592, the feltmakers rioted in Southwark, and in 1593 'some lewd and ill affected persons had set up gates and posts in Southwark, and let fall in the streets divers libels threatening hurt and destruction to the strangers'. The City authorities were so anxious to quell the troubles that it offered a reward of 100 crowns to anyone revealing the culprits to the Lord Mayor and Aldermen.[122] In June 1595, there were further arrests in Southwark of 'lewde and insolent apprentices … for their lewde offences'. The Lord Mayor also instructed the Alderman to appoint honest householders to 'double watch' the ward from five in the morning to nine o'clock at night, and ordered that masters should during the day 'keep [their] servants and apprentices within their houses, and their weapons in such sorte, as that no violence or outrage be attempted or committed by any of them. …'.[123] Manning has underlined that the disproportionate concentration of vagrants, runaway apprentices, discharged soldiers and sailors, unemployed or under-employed artisans (or, as a report of the disorder in Southwark in 1592 put it, 'lo[o]se and master less men') and the inability of the magistrates to keep the peace there made areas like Southwark prone to such disorders.[124]

Nevertheless, the argument of stability is a valid one, and it should not be forgotten that within the alien community there was a core, stable element. Table 5.2 can be used to support this: while in 1571 nearly 57 per cent had been in London 10 years or less, by 1593 this had precipitously fallen to 34 per cent, and the number living here between 11 and 30 years had risen to nearly 44 per cent. In 1571, only one alien had been here between 61 and 70 years; by 1593 the number had risen to five. Despite the apparent rising discrimination, the threats of violence and the persistent native complaints, many aliens did put down firm roots in the capital and some aliens, particularly the brewers, did prosper. They also developed a bond with their local community, as indicated by charitable bequests to the local poor.

In his will in 1568, Nichas Webling, a Southwark brewer, gave a total of £9 to the poor, including 20 shillings to the poor of St Thomas Hospital in Southwark, 20 shillings each to the poor of four different London prisons, and £4 to the parish church of St Olave towards the maintenance of the free school. Another brewer, Roger James, also remembered the poor of All Saints Barking, London, giving them £5 per annum for the next ten years, £5 to the poor children of Christ Hospital, and £10 to the poor of the Dutch church.[125] This suggests that the troubles and riots discussed above may have been localized, affecting only a proportion of aliens living in the capital.

Table 5.2 Length of residence of aliens in London, 1571 and 1593

Length	1571	%	1593	%
0–10 years	1 028	56.6	370	34.3
11–20 years	275	15.0	235	21.8
21–30 years	180	10.0	235	21.8
31–40 years	88	4.8	75	7.0
41–50 years	48	2.6	27	2.5
51–60 years	13	0.7	6	0.6
61–70 years	1	0.06	5	0.5
Unknown	173	9.5	120	6.6
Travelling back and forth	5	0.3	—	—
Born here	4	0.2	1	0.09
Others			5	0.5
Total	**1 815**	**100.0**	**1 079**	**100.0**

Sources: Kirk and Kirk, eds, *Returns of Aliens* (1571); Scouloudi, *Returns of Strangers* (1593).

Government Policies

The nature of the government's policies towards the immigrants remains a source of contention. Joe Ward is convinced that the 'Elizabethan government encouraged the immigration of skilled artisans from the Continent in order to bolster English industry … [It therefore] adopted measures to encourage Dutch and French religious refugees to settle in England.'[126] Yet the term 'encouraged' is highly ambiguous and misleading, suggesting that immigrants were actively urged to come over. This was only true for a very small number of skilled artisans who were recruited to establish particular industries. For the majority of others, they were 'encouraged' only in the sense that they were given certain privileges such as their own churches and protection. According to Boersma and Jelsma, this was done for two reasons: compassion and calculation. They concluded that 'there was support of Protestant fugitives, as long as this did not harm English interests and up to the point where it might cause national unrest. Helping Protestant minorities in Holland and France and granting Protestant refugees a safe and hospitable refuge offered political advantages, notably the weakening of England's most powerful rivals in Europe … It also procured economic advantages, because of the expertise which the immigrants possessed in certain trades such as printing and brewing.'[127]

For London, it is also necessary to differentiate the policies of the national government (the Privy Council) from those of the City of London. At times, these policies were synonymous, but at times they diverged. In both circles, there was an awareness of a need to offer these Protestant refugees a home, and some appreciation of the potential economic benefits offered by them. There was also some sympathy for the refugees.[128] But the Elizabethan government during this period was preoccupied with the preservation of order and defence of the country against foreign invasion. The Privy Council and the City of London policies both showed concern over security issues, and both unanimously agreed that only religious refugees were to be allowed to stay in London.[129] Both the Privy Council and the City of London promoted the employment of English servants by aliens, but perhaps for different reasons: the need to pacify natives on the one hand, and the need to create jobs for the poor on the other.

On occasion, the City of London adopted tougher policies towards aliens, as in 1568, when it permitted non-religious refugees to stay in the City only one day and one night. In 1587, it rejected the proposal by the Privy Council to grant equal rights to aliens and foreigners in the cloth market.[130] Its policies towards strangers were dictated by two considerations: the preservation of the City's laws and customs, such as those concerning retail and apprenticeship, and the maintenance of law and order by being responsive to public opinion. In times of economic prosperity, the enforcement of the City's laws and policies was lax. However, in times of economic difficulty, enforcement became tougher, partly due to public pressure. In 1565 and 1587, for example, both years of high prices, strangers were ordered not to keep open shops.[131] In 1582, Christopher Barker, a stationer, was fined for taking the son of an alien as apprentice. For his punishment, he was ordered to pay 20 shillings, and 'at his charges' to print 200 copies of the Act 'for the service of the City'.[132]

In addition, the City of London also passed controversial new Acts limiting the rights of the children of aliens and denizens born in England. After 1574, as has been indicated, children of alien-born parents could no longer be bound apprentice with English masters. In September 1582, Bryan Savell, a clothworker, was ordered to discharge Bryan Marrowe, the son of Peter Marrowe, stranger. As this 'was done in ignorance', Bryan Savell was ordered only to pay a fine of 20 shillings, while William Tyrone was ordered to pay 40 shillings for taking on William Marrowe, also son of a stranger.[133] Free denizens sought to make the Act 'frustrate and void', arguing that it was 'contrary to all humanitie and reason', and that their children were deprived of the 'freedom liberty and benefit of their native country ... naturally due unto them'.[134] Their petition was not successful, as in 1583 John Vere, a Frenchman 'being a free denizen', had to request John Hertford to petition the

Lord Mayor on behalf of his son, already serving three years of his nine-year apprenticeship with John Yeoman, a merchant tailor, to continue his apprenticeship and receive his freedom at the end of his service.[135]

There was also much debate about the question of whether children born in England of alien-born parents should be regarded as English. Two arguments against this were put forward. First, it was reported in 1576 that: 'sundry persons being strangers … have of purpose brought over their wives from the parts beyond the seas, to be delivered with child within this city, and in other places within this realme of England, and thereof do take speciall testimonials thereby to win to those children the liberty that other Englishmen do enjoy.'[136] Second, it was argued that a child of alien parents should not be regarded as English because 'he cannot be a perfect loyal subject for that he hath no genealogie of native english but all foreign and strangers unto whom (as to his kindred) nature bindeth him'.[137] It was therefore considered unfair to grant such privileges to those children of strangers who 'retaine an inclination and kinde affection to the countreyes of their parents'.[138] After much debate, it was finally decided in 1604 to 'place the children, born within this Realme, of foreign parents as aliens made denizens'.[139]

Repeated offences suggest that restrictive alien legislation may not have been strictly enforced, and that, in reality, aliens probably enjoyed more freedom. Take, for instance, the law regarding opening a shop. Aliens were allowed to keep 'closed' shops, and thus were prohibited from openly displaying their wares to the public. The underlying aim was to prevent passers-by being tempted to go and place orders, and to alleviate the fear that competition posed by strangers would reduce the market for English goods. In 1556, the Chamberlain of the City was instructed to shut discreetly the shop windows opening onto the streets and lanes of all strangers born and foreigners, placing lattices before them. In 1566, the Chamberlain was again ordered in 'quiet manner' to cause all foreigners and strangers born to shut their shop windows.[140] The trouble persisted, and in 1568 an alien was ordered to 'shut up' a cordwainer shop in Cornhill 'in the heart of the city'.[141] The persistence of this offence can be explained by the need for natural light in order to work. This was finally recognized, and in 1587 aliens were ordered to have their shop windows and doors 'made in such sort as people passing by may not see them at work, and so as their wares and merchandises remaining and being within the same their shops or places give no open show to any people passing by', and at the same time 'leave convenient light for them to work'.[142]

Conclusion

Attitudes towards strangers were complex, and appear to have been intricately linked to political, economic and social conditions. Tension was particularly acute in the late 1580s and 1590s, when the aliens provided a convenient scapegoat for economic difficulties, engendered largely by rapid demographic growth, decline in employment opportunities and living standards, failed harvests, and financial drain resulting from warfare. Anti-alien riots did not actually materialize, and it is possible that they were mere threats, designed to bring pressure upon the City's governors to take ameliorative action. However, deteriorating economic conditions and the concomitant xenophobia inflicted particular hardship on the strangers, and these may have persuaded some to emigrate to the northern Netherlands, where economic prospects appeared brighter.

Unlike provincial communities, economic considerations appear to have been secondary to security and political issues in influencing government policies towards the refugees in London during the 1560s and 1570s. Those who were permitted to remain in London had to prove first of all that they had come for religious reasons and that they were Protestant refugees. In his most recent work, Professor Pettegree concedes that the exiles in England may have been accepted for purely spiritual reasons.[143] Many ordinary Londoners, on the other hand, were probably indifferent to the question of whether the strangers were religious refugees or not. The awareness of this issue probably prompted the government to disperse aliens to provincial towns, and to encourage those remaining in London to employ English servants and teach them their skills.

Notes

1. P. Collinson, 'The Elizabethan Puritans and the Foreign Reformed Churches in London', in *Godly People: Essays on English Protestantism and Puritanism* (London, 1983), p. 269.
2. A. Pettegree, '"Thirty Years On": Progress towards integration amongst the immigrant population of Elizabethan London', in J. Chartres and D. Hey, eds, *English Rural Society, 1500–1800: Essays in Honour of Joan Thirsk* (Cambridge, 1990), p. 298.
3. Ibid., p. 309.
4. For emigration to Amsterdam, see J.G. van Dillen, *Bronnen tot de geschiedenis van het bedrijfsleven en het gildewezen van Amsterdam*, eerste deel, 1512–1611 (Rijks geschiedkundige publicatien, Vol. 69, 1929), p. xxxiv.
5. See J.W. Tammel, *The Pilgrims and Other People from the British Isles in Leiden, 1576–1640* (Isle of Man, 1989), pp. 320–35.
6. M.J. Jones, *British Nationality Law and Practice* (Oxford, 1947), p. 31.
7. Allegiance, according to Coke, was the 'mutual bond and obligation between the king and his subjects, whereby the subjects are called his liege subjects, because they are bound to obey and serve him, and he is called their liege lord because he should

maintain and defend them'. Two elements, then, were involved in the concept of allegiance: protection by the King, and obedience by the subject. See Jones, *British Nationality Law and Practice*, p. 32.

8   D. Statt, 'The birthright of an Englishman: The practice of naturalization and denization of immigrants under the later Stuarts and early Hanoverians', *Proceedings of the Huguenot Society*, 1989, Vol. 25, No. 1, p. 62.
9   B. Cottret, *The Huguenots in England: Immigration and Settlement c.1550–1700* (Cambridge, 1991), p. 51.
10 Statt, 'The birthright of an Englishman', p. 62.
11 See Scouloudi, *Returns of Strangers*, p. 41.
12 Ibid., p. 6.
13 Jones, *British Nationality Law and Practice*, p. 39.
14 Ibid.
15 Cottret, *The Huguenots in England*, p. 54.
16 Scouloudi, *Returns of Strangers*, p. 4.
17 Ibid., pp. 3–4.
18 BL, Egerton MS 2599, f. 234 ('The charges of a Denison 1582')
19 Scouloudi, *Returns of Strangers*, pp. 18–23.
20 J.H. Hessels, ed., *Ecclesiae Londino-Batavae Archivum, Epistulae et Tractatus* (3 vols, Cambridge, 1889–97), Vol. 3, Part 1, pp. 272–3.
21 Scouloudi, *Returns of Strangers*, p. 5.
22 Calendar of State Papers, Spanish, 1550–1552, Vol. 10, p. 265; Scouloudi, *Returns of Strangers*, p. 4; R.Vigne and C. Littleton, *From Strangers to Citizens: Integration of Immigrant Communities in Great Britain, Ireland and the Colonies, 1550–1750* (Brighton, 2001), p. 512.
23 Scouloudi, *Returns of Strangers*, p. 5.
24 Quoted in Cottret, *The Huguenots*, pp. 54–5.
25 GL, Brewers MS 5445/6 12 October 1581
26 Scouloudi, *Returns of Strangers*, p. 11.
27 CLRO, Remembrancia, Vol. 1 [69].
28 Ibid. [30–31], [63], [69].
29 Ibid. [53], [69].
30 Scouloudi, *Returns of Strangers*, p. 13.
31 J. Strype, *A Survey of the Cities of London and Westminster …* (London, 1720), Book 5, pp. 300, 303.
32 J. Strype, *Annals of the Reformation* (Oxford, 1824, 4 vols), Vol. 4, pp. 234–5.
33 R.B. Manning, *Village Revolts: Social Protest and Popular Disturbances in England, 1509–1640* (Oxford, 1988), pp. 203–4.
34 I. Archer, *The Pursuit of Stability: Social Relations in Elizabethan London* (Cambridge, 1991), pp. 4–5, 7.
35 J.P. Ward, 'Fictitious shoemakers, agitated weavers and the limits of popular xenophobia in Elizabethan London', in Vigne and Littleton, eds, *From Strangers to Citizens*, pp. 80–87.
36 N. Goose, 'Xenophobia in Elizabethan and early Stuart England: An epithet too far?', in N. Goose and L. Luu, eds, *Immigrants in Tudor and Early Stuart England* (Brighton, 2005), pp. 110–135.
37 L.H. Yungblut, *Strangers Settled Here Amongst Us: Policies, perceptions and the Presence of Aliens in Elizabethan England* (London, 1996), pp. 44–5.
38 Archer, *The Pursuit of Stability*, p. 133; see also Ward, *Metropolitan Communities*, p. 142
39 A. Plummer, *The London Weavers' Company, 1600–1970* (London, 1972), p. 147.
40 See complaint in 1571, PRO SP12/81/29 'A complaynt of the Cytizens of London against the great number of strangers in and about this cytty', printed in T.H. Tawney and E. Power, eds, *Tudor Economic Documents* (London, 1924, 3 vols), Vol. 1, pp. 308–9.

41 Strype, *A Survey of the Cities of London and Westminster*, Book 5, pp. 300, 303.
42 Quoted in Yungblut, *Strangers Settled Here Amongst Us*, p. 45.
43 L.A. Clarkson, *The Pre-industrial Economy in England, 1500–1750* (London, 1971), p. 26.
44 L. Beier, 'Social Problems in Elizabethan London', *Journal of Interdisciplinary History*, 1978, Vol. 9, p. 221.
45 Manning, *Village Revolts*, pp. 193–4.
46 Ibid., p. 194.
47 Quoted in J. Boulton, 'Residential mobility in seventeenth-century Southwark', *Urban History Yearbook*, 1986, pp. 1–2
48 V. Reynolds and I. Vine, eds., *The Sociobiology of Ethnocentrism: Evolutionary Dimensions of Xenophobia, Discrimination, Racism and Nationalism* (London, 1987), pp. 17–19, 30.
49 Quoted in Boulton, 'Residential mobility in seventeenth-century Southwark', p. 2.
50 R. Shoemaker, *Prosecution and Punishment: Petty Crime and the Law in London and Rural Middlesex, c.1660–1725* (Cambridge, 1991), p. 10.
51 Boulton, 'Residential mobility', p. 11.
52 Archer, *The Pursuit of Stability*, p. 76, pp. 78–9.
53 Rappaport, *Worlds Within Worlds*, p. 71.
54 PRO SP12 /81/29 'A complaint of the citizens of London against the great number of strangers in and about this city'.
55 PRO SP12/84/1
56 Evers, 'Religionis et libertatis ergo', p. 11. In Norwich, some of the Dutch preferred to go to the parish churches to avoid paying both the obligatory poor relief as well as contributing to their own poor. The Stranger and English churches were different because, whereas the Stranger Churches had autonomous powers of discipline, there was no discipline in the parishes. The foreign churches were free to adopt orders of sermons and other services which were 'most pure', whereas Englishmen were bound to the use of a Prayer Book: see Collinson, 'The Elizabethan Puritans and the Foreign Reformed Churches in London', p. 256.
57 Many issues relating to assimilation are discussed in L.B. Luu, 'Assimilation or Segregation', in R. Vigne and G. Gibbs, eds, *The Strangers' Progress: Integration and Disintegration of the Huguenot and Walloon Refugee Community, 1567–1889: Essays in Memory of Irene Scouloudi* (Proceedings of the Huguenot Society, Vol. 26, 1995), pp. 167–8.
58 Ibid., pp. 168–9.
59 Ibid., pp. 164–6.
60 CLRO JOR 20 Part 1, f. 219v (1575), JOR 23, f. 308v (1594). Dutch ministers also acted as interpreters when the Flemish Anabaptists were interrogated in 1575.
61 O. Boersma and A.J. Jelsma, eds, *Unity in Multiformity: The Minutes of the Coetus of London, 1575 and the Consistory Minutes of the Italian Church of London, 1570–1591* (Huguenot Society Publications, Vol. 56, 1997), pp. 25, 28. Of the 161 members of the Italian church, 63 of them were Dutch, mostly from cities in the southern Netherlands. Many joined the Italian church because of divisions within the Dutch church on the question of armed resistance: see p. 26.
62 F.A. Norwood, *The Reformation Refugees as an Economic Force* (Chicago, IL, 1942), pp. 33–4.
63 Calendar of State Papers, Spanish, 1550–52, Vol. 10, pp. 278–9.
64 Calendar of State Papers, Foreign, 1547–53, pp. 119–20.
65 London, Goldsmiths' Hall, Court Minutes Book, Vol. 9, f. 352.
66 CLRO JOR 19, f. 132v 19 October 1568.
67 French Protestant Church, Soho MS 194, f. 84v. See Collinson, 'The Elizabethan Puritans and the Foreign Reformed Churches in London', pp. 268–271, for more details of the collections made to the Stranger Churches.

68 R. Porder, *A Sermon of gods fearefull threatnings for Idolatrye ... with a Treatise against Usurie ... Preached in Paules Churche Maye 1570* (London, 1570), ff. 103–103v.
69 Rappaport, *Worlds Within Worlds*, p. 98.
70 Ibid., pp. 87–122.
71 Shipping owned in London rose from 12 300 tons in 1582 to 35 300 tons in 1629, and to about 150 000 tons by 1686. Tens of thousands of people were involved in repairing, maintaining and supplying these ships, and in providing lighterage, quayside, warehouse, as well as the provision of port services such as loading and unloading. See Clay, *Economic Expansion and Social Change*, Vol. 1, p. 202.
72 L. Stone, 'Elizabethan Overseas Trade', *Economic History Review*, 2nd Series, 1949, Vol. 2, pp. 41, 43.
73 Ibid., p. 52.
74 J. Thirsk, ed., *The Agrarian History of England and Wales, Volume 4: 1500–1640* (Cambridge, 1967), p. 819.
75 CLRO JOR 21, f. 119v.
76 CLRO Rep 17, f. 372.
77 Guildhall Library (GL), MS 4069/1, ff. 11v–12, Cornhill Ward, Wardmote Inquest.
78 Rappaport, *Worlds Within Worlds*, pp. 406–7. All indices begin with a value of 100 in 1457–71: see p. 124.
79 PRO S12/81/29.
80 J. Strype, *Stow's Survey of London* (London, 1720), Book 5, p. 299.
81 D. Statt, *Foreigners and Englishmen: The Controversy over Immigration and Population, 1660–1760* (London, 1995), see especially Chapter 4, pp. 99–120.
82 PRO SP12/201/31 17 May 1587.
83 CLRO, Remembrancia, Vol. 1 [53].
84 C.G.A. Clay, *Economic Expansion and Social Change: England 1500–1700* (Cambridge, 1984, 2 vols), Vol. 2, pp. 105–6.; B. Dietz, 'Antwerp and London: the Structure and Balance of Trade in the 1560s', in E.W. Ives and J. Knecht, eds, *Wealth and Power in Tudor England: Essays Presented to S.T. Bindoff* (London, 1978), pp. 192–3.
85 Manning, *Village Revolts*, p. 195.
86 According to this, alien merchants committed six offences because they: (1) took lodgings and houses within the city; (2) kept their merchandises as long as they liked; (3) sold their merchandise by retail; (4) did not keep their money within England; (5) sold merchandises one to another, and (6) formed a commonwealth within themselves. PRO SP12/81/29. This complaint is discussed in great detail by Littleton, 'Geneva on Threadneedle Street', pp. 171–4.
87 PRO SP12/88/36.
88 S. D'Ewes, *The Journals of all the Parliaments during the Reign of Queen Elizabeth* (London, 1682), p. 505.
89 Hist. Mss. Com. III, Appendix 6, 1592.
90 Yungblut, *Strangers Settled Here Amongst Us*, p. 41.
91 GL, Merchant Tailors' Court Minutes, Vol. 3, f. 241v.
92 GL, MS 4647, f. 257–8.
93 Beier, 'The significance of the metropolis', p. 18.
94 M.J. Power, 'London and the control of the "Crisis" of the 1590s', *History*, 1985, Vol. 70, p. 375.
95 Manning, *Village Revolts*, p. 204.
96 Strype, *Annals of the Reformation*, Vol. 4, pp. 234–5.
97 Ibid., pp. 234–5.
98 CLRO JOR 23, f. 191.
99 PRO SP14/88/112 (October 1616).
100 For further details, see F. Consitt, *The London Weavers' Company* (Oxford, 1933), pp.

147-8; this pamphlet is discussed in more detail in Chapter 6.
101 Hessels, ed., *Ecclesiae Londino-Batavae Archivum*, Vol. 3, No. 1, [1441], pp. 1037-8.
102 Ibid., [1489], pp. 1056-7.
103 GL Merchant Tailors' Minutes Book, Vol. 3, f. 388v.
104 Ibid., f. 440v.
105 N.V. Sleigh-Johnson, 'The Merchant Taylor's Company of London, 1580-1645: With Special Reference to Politics and Government' (University of London unpublished PhD thesis, 1989), p. 338.
106 GL, Merchant Tailors' Company, CM Vol. 5 1601-11, ff. 1-4.
107 PRO SP12/77/58 'Norwiche booke of orders for the straungers', Article 16.
108 GL, MTC CM Vol. 5 1601-1611, f. 330 An agreement concerning French and Dutch tailors.
109 Scouloudi, *Returns of Strangers*, p. 96.
110 Hessels, *Ecclesiae Londino-Batavae Archivum*, Vol. 3, No. 1, pp. 1688, 1689.
111 Manning, *Village Revolts*, p. 204.
112 Washington, Folger Library, MS V.b. 142, f. 87.
113 J. Lindeboom, *Austin Friars: History of the Dutch Reformed Church in London, 1550-1950* (The Hague, 1950), p. 120; Hessels, ed., *Ecclesiae Londino-Batavae Archivum*, Vol. 3, No. 1, pp. 956-8; ibid., Vol. 2, pp. 867-9.
114 M. Hart, 'Freedom and restrictions: State and economy in the Dutch Republic, 1570-1670', in K. Davids and L. Noordegraaf, eds, *The Dutch Economy in the Golden Age*, Vol. 4 (Amsterdam, 1993), pp. 105-30.
115 Ibid., p.118.
116 I would like to thank Dr Clé Lesger for this information.
117 J.G. van Dillen, *Bronnen tot de geschiedenis van het bedrijfsleven en het gildewezen van Amsterdam*, eerste deel, 1512-1611 (Rijks geschiedkundige publicatien, Vol. 69, 1929), p. xxxiv.
118 J. de Vries, 'The labour market', in Davids and Noordegraaf, eds, *The Dutch Economy in the Golden Age*, Vol. 4, p. 73.
119 V. Barbour, *Capitalism in Amsterdam in the 17th Century* (Ann Arbor, MI, 1963), p. 16.
120 Van Dillen, *Bronnen tot de Geschiedenis van het Bedrijfsleven en het Gildewezen van Amsterdam*, pp. xxxviii, xxxix, xliii.
121 Carlin, *Medieval Southwark*, p. 156.
122 See Scouloudi, *Returns of Strangers*, p. 58.
123 CLRO JOR 24, f. 22v.
124 Manning, *Village Revolts*, p. 188; CLRO Remembrancia, Vol. 1 [662] 'Disorder in Southwark' 30 May 1592.
125 PRO Prob 11/50 ff.178 (Nicha Webling), Prob 11/79 ff. 147-51 (Roger James).
126 Ward, 'The Limits of popular xenophobia in Elizabethan London', in Vigne and Littleton, eds, *From Strangers to Citizens*, p. 83.
127 Boersma and Jelsma, eds, *Unity in Multiformity*, p. 3.
128 In November 1573, Richard Martin, Alderman of Farringdon Ward Within, personally donated £6 13s. 4d. to the poor of the French Protestant Church, Soho Square, MS 194, f. 145.
129 CLRO JOR 19, f. 132v 19 October 1568.
130 For details of the proposal to grant equal rights to aliens and foreigners in the cloth market, see PRO SP12/201/31 17 May 1587.
131 CLRO, Letter Book V, f. 35v; Rep 21, f. 430v (May 1587).
132 CLRO, Letter Book Z, f. 241v, 266.
133 CLRO, Letter Book Z, 1579-1584, f. 241v
134 PRO SP15/24/67 1580.
135 CLRO, Remembrancia, Vol. 1 [543].
136 CLRO Rep 19, f. 38v.

137 PRO SP12/157/2 A note of an act touching the custome of strangers borne in this realme ought to pay, 1582.
138 Hessels, ed., *Ecclesiae Londino-Batavae Archivum*, Vol. 3, No. 1, [307], pp. 270–2; CLRO JOR 20, Part 1, ff. 176v–177v.
139 Journals of the House of Commons, Vol. 1 1604 21/4.
140 Scouloudi, *Returns of Strangers*, p. 42.
141 CLRO Rep 16/f. 385v 29 July 10 Reign.
142 CLRO Rep 21, f. 430v May 1587.
143 A. Pettegree, *Emden and the Dutch Revolt: Exiles and the Development of Reformed Protestantism* (Oxford, 1992), p. 227.

Chapter 6

Silk Industry

Historiography

Silk, a textile product beautiful and lustrous to the eye, soft to touch, and elegant to wear, had long been regarded as an exotic luxury by European consumers. Adornment with such a material represented wealth, power and status, and the secrets of its manufacture were eagerly sought after. Yet the process of diffusion was painfully slow and arduous. Silk manufacture originated in China in 2700 BC and its diffusion to Europe, via Byzantium and the Near East, took more than ten centuries.[1] The Europeanization of silk manufacture began in the eleventh or twelfth century, when Italy established an industry. For the next four or five centuries, Italy retained its monopoly of this highly lucrative and prized industry, partly as a result of its imposition of stringent regulations to inhibit the transfer of textile workers from one locality to another.[2] The efforts to establish manufacture in England began in the fifteenth century, but took almost three centuries to bear fruit. Silk fabrics were probably first woven in England in the second half of the sixteenth century, but the nascent industry was unable to satisfy aristocratic demand, and large quantities of high quality and expensive silks continued to be imported from Italy. It was not until the late seventeenth century that the English silk industry acquired an international reputation. By the early eighteenth century, England had become a significant centre of silk production. Based in Spitalfields (London), Canterbury and Norwich, the industry employed more than 300 000 persons in 1713, and had more than 8000 looms in operation in London alone.[3]

The foundation and sustained expansion of the English silk industry owed much to the immigration of workers from the southern Netherlands, France and Holland during the sixteenth and seventeenth centuries. Yet the point of take-off, as well as the exact origins of the industry in England,[4] remain nebulous, with some historians emphasizing the role of the Huguenots in the seventeenth century, and others the vital contribution of earlier immigrants. Ralph Davis asserted that the English silk industry took off in the 1680s, as a consequence of increased Anglo-French commercial rivalry and the immigration of Huguenot refugees from France. Prior to this, England had only a small silk industry, almost wholly confined to making ribbons for most of the seventeenth century.[5] Christopher Clay, on the other hand, contended that the silk industry owed its origin 'entirely to the immigration of Protestant refugees from France towards the end of the sixteenth century, and received a considerable shot in the arm from a further wave of Huguenot immigration in the 1680s'.[6] G. Unwin and E. Kerridge insisted that the silk industry was established in England in the second half of the sixteenth century by refugees from the Low Countries and France.[7] These views, in fact, are not exclusive of each other. A successful transfer of a new industry often depended not on a single, but a *continuous* injection of skills stretching over a long period. The rise of the silk industry in England, therefore, was due not to a single group, but to the *cumulative* contribution of immigrants who came in the sixteenth and seventeenth centuries.

Besides presenting a panoramic view of the international diffusion of silk manufacture, this chapter is primarily concerned with the processes by which it was established in London. This necessitates the examination of four principal issues. The motor of any industrial transfer is consumer demand, so the first task is to determine the extent of demand for silks in London particularly in the sixteenth and seventeenth centuries. As immigrants monopolized the London silk industry, the next task is to establish their scale of immigration, not only to give an idea of the prerequisite number of workers involved in a successful transfer, but also to help ascertain the extent of their contribution. The third issue relates to the crucial question of why and how silk manufacture in England came to be so *closely identified* with French-speaking immigrants from the Low Countries and France. To answer this question fully, it is necessary to examine their occupational backgrounds, economic opportunities, the constraints that confronted them, and the nature of their informal social networks. Did London immigrants face the problem of *mismatch* of skills? What did silk-weaving offer in terms of opportunities? How close were their social networks? The last issue to investigate is the question of how and when the London silk industry became Anglicized. Did native weavers learn the requisite skills from immigrants? How were these disseminated? What were the problems involved? How long did this process of local diffusion take?

Europeanization of Silk Manufacture

Italy was the first European country to establish a silk industry, but the process by which it acquired the skills is not clear. Some historians believe that trade with the Near East stimulated production there through the process of import substitution. In the eleventh century, Italians exported woollen cloth and some linen to Syria and Palestine, and imported silk fabrics of Syrian manufacture. Italian manufacturers then imitated and improved the Oriental patterns, perhaps with the assistance of Jewish, Greek and Arab immigrants who brought their expertise from Greece and the Near East. Italy gradually became the main supplier to northern European consumers.[8] Mazzaoui, however, has stressed that there were two separate developments. First, direct contacts with the Levant led to the introduction of techniques of silk manufacturing, most likely by Greek and Muslim slaves, in Venice, Genoa and Milan by the early 1200s. A second, older tradition of silk working took root in Tuscany, notably in Lucca, Florence, Pisa and Arezzo. Lucca achieved international fame for its workmanship of the more elaborate and costly fabrics, thanks to its technological edge in weaving and dyeing, and its closely guarded monopoly over advanced implements such as looms and combs for brocades and velvets and the silk twisting mill.[9] The exodus between 1307 and 1370 of thousands of skilled craftsmen from Lucca to Florence, Bologna,

Table 6.1 The international diffusion of the silk industry

Stage 1: 2700 BC	Sericulture and silk-weaving established in China
Stage 2: Second and third centuries	Diffusion to East Asia: Chinese immigrants introduced sericulture and silk-weaving to Japan and Korea
Stage 3: Fourth and sixth centuies	Silk-weaving established in Persia (fourth century) and Byzantium. Monks or merchants introduced sericulture to Byzantium in sixth century
Stage 4: Eighth century	Moors introduced silk-weaving to Spain
Stage 5: Tenth–thirteenth centuries	Establishment of silk industry in Italy, Lucca, Florence and Venice
Stage 6: Fifteenth century	Spread of silk industry within Italy; diffusion to France and northern Europe: Paris, Tours, Cologne and Bruges
Stage 7: Sixteenth century	Diffusion to Antwerp
Stage 8: Mid-sixteenth century	Diffusion to London and Amsterdam
Stage 9: Seventeenth century	Consolidation of English silk industry with arrival of Huguenots

Sources: D. Kuhn, *Textile Technology: Spinning and Reeling* (Vol. 5, Part 9, Cambridge, 1988), pp. 418–33; A. Wittlin, 'The development of silk weaving in Spain', *Ciba Review*, 1939, Vol. 2, No. 20, pp. 707–721; M.F. Mazzaoui, 'Artisan migration and technology in the Italian textile industry in the late Middle Ages (1100–1500)', in R. Comba, G. Piccinni and G. Pinto, eds, *Strutture familiari epidemie migrazioni nell'Italia medievale* (Edizioni Scientifiche Italiane, 1984), pp. 519–34.

Genoa, Milan, Venice and beyond the Alps to France and Germany, where there were sizeable colonies of Lucchese silk merchants, further promoted the dominance of Lucchese modes of production. With the decline of Lucca's silk industry, Florence assumed the lead in silk manufacture in central Italy in the fifteenth century.[10]

At the beginning, the Italian silk industry depended largely on imported raw silk. Between 1337 and 1340, Lucca imported annually some 165 000 pounds of silk (chiefly of Turkestanian and Chinese origin). Later, thanks to a suitable climate, sericulture developed in Sicily and Calabria.[11]

The process of diffusion of silk manufacture from Italy to northern Europe accelerated in the fifteenth century, thanks to the functional role of Italian merchants. Domenico Sella, for example, has explained how merchants occupied a nexus between demand and migration: 'by bringing to a country manufactured goods produced in another, [merchants] created, when successful, a demand for them; and once a sufficiently large demand had been created, it became possible and indeed attractive for artisans to come and set up shop in that area'. Although largely speculative, Sella further pointed out that: 'it is no mere coincidence that long before it harboured refugee silk-makers from Italy and long before it emerged as a major centre of the silk industry, a city like Lyons had served as the headquarters of Italian merchants and as the distributing centre of Italian silk goods in France'.[12]

This model was applicable to Bruges, one of the first northern European cities to successfully establish a silk industry in the fifteenth century. Venetian and Genoese merchants brought silk to Bruges to trade, and it appears that local weavers, partly necessitated by a declining traditional cloth industry in Flanders,[13] and partly encouraged by the presence of a large number of wealthy consumers in Bruges, developed a native silk industry by copying. But rather than imitating high-quality and expensive Italian silks to substitute imports, native weavers wisely developed a different and cheaper product – satin – woven with a mixture of wool and silk. This pragmatic move by Bruges weavers to develop a differentiated product aimed at non-aristocratic consumers reflected the recognition of their inability to compete with Italian goods at this stage. It is uncertain when the process of imitation began, but it was not until 1496 that the satin-weavers were sufficiently numerous and powerful to organize themselves into a guild in Bruges. After the satin industry had been consolidated, efforts were then made to develop the manufacture of costly, pure silk goods, and it was only at this stage that Italian silk-weavers were employed, indicating the inability to imitate the higher level of skills involved. In 1538, the local council granted a Milanese resident in Bruges, Francesco de Prato, a loan of 500 Flemish pounds, with the prospect of a further 2000 pounds provided that 100 looms were in operation manufacturing velvet and satin within a year and a half. However, Prato went bankrupt, unable to set up even 25 looms.[14] In the second half of the sixteenth century, Bruges still manufactured a great quantity of fustians, says, satins and silks, but the industry appears to have declined steadily. In 1500, there were some 200 people engaged in the industry.[15] By 1566, the industry had experienced decline. Although Guicciardini reported that 'large quantities of fustians, says, satins, cloth and tapestries were made here [and that] very large quantities of silk were prepared for all purposes, so that those skills (crafts, mysteries) are included among the 68 crafts (guilds)', he also stressed that 'the butchers, fishmongers, brokers and shippers are the most important [trades]'.[16]

The relative decline of silk manufacture in Bruges was in part due to the migration of the industry to Antwerp, which by the mid-sixteenth century had eclipsed Bruges as the international centre of commerce. In 1500, a first satin worker, Denijs van Hulshout, probably from Bruges, became a citizen in Antwerp. As in Bruges, the silk industry in Antwerp was initially confined to the manufacture of satin. Once satin-weaving was firmly established, attempts were then made to produce more expensive silk products, and these endeavours at product differentiation became more apparent in the 1530s and 1540s. It is uncertain whether these preceded attempts in Bruges, but in 1536 the Antwerp magistrate agreed to give financial support to a damask-weaver from Beauvais, Niclaus Davidt. In 1546 the merchant-entrepreneur Jan Nuyts also received a state subsidy to manufacture expensive silk stuffs.[17] In 1555, a Genoese Étienne de la Torre, was employed by the city to promote the manufacture of silk.[18] The silk industry in Antwerp was greatly stimulated by a substantial influx of immigrants from Walloon provinces in the 1570s and 1580s. In 1582, of the 800 masters recorded in Antwerp, nearly a quarter had fled from Flanders and the area around Tournai between 1579 and 1582.[19] In 1584, the silk industry in Antwerp employed some 4000 people, producing satins, damasks, bourats, grosgain, velvets and armoisin.[20] After the fall of Antwerp in 1585, many silk-weavers fled the city and settled in the Dutch Republic, particularly Amsterdam, while some left for London.[21]

Silk Consumption and Production in London in the Fourteenth and Fifteenth Centuries

As the home of the Court, the nobility and the well-to-do, there was an insatiable demand for silks in London, enhanced by several developments in the fourteenth and fifteenth centuries. There was an increase in the number of wealthy consumers as a result of increasing profusion of opportunities at the Court, in the professions and in a range of urban occupations.[22] In addition, the general rise in living standards after the Black Death increased fashion-consciousness among the wealthy. In a period of widespread belief that social differentiation and status should be reflected in a person's clothing, increases in disposable income naturally led to rising tendencies for sumptuous display. Already at the end of the fourteenth century complaints were vehemently voiced that 'the fashions were continually changing and everyone was endeavouring to outshine his neighbour in the richness of his habit and the novelty of its form'.[23] This prompted much governmental concern because, as a sumptuary legislation in 1588 put it, it resulted in 'the confusion of degrees of all estates, amongst whom diversity of apparel, has been always a special and laudable mark'.[24] A gradual shift in fashions away from costly traditional woollen fabrics, prized for their fine quality and durability, towards lighter, cheaper, more attractive, although flimsier fabrics, also presented new market opportunities.[25] Heavy woollens gave way to the New Draperies and silks, with silk garments finding their way into the wardrobes of 'ordinary people'.[26] In 1583, Philip Stubbs observed that: 'It is very hard to know, who is noble, who is worshipful, who is a gentleman, who is not: for you shall have those, which are neither of the nobility, gentility, nor yeomanry, go daily in silks, velvets, satins, damasks, taffetas and such like, nothwithstanding that they be both base by birth, mean by estate and servile by calling'.[27]

In the fourteenth century silk fabrics were imported into London almost exclusively by Italians. But the Venetian galleys were sailing to Flanders rather than to England in the fourteenth century, so the silks arrived in London in Flemish ships with a variety of goods of north European origin.[28] From the later 1390s, the Venetian and subsequently the Florentine galleys, the main carriers of these luxury cloths, went directly to London or Southampton. There was an important Italian colony in London, mostly of Florentines and Lucchese, dealing in silk and silk fabrics. The principal kinds of cloths recorded in London custom accounts for the late fourteenth century were baldekins of silk and damask, rakemas and satin, and expensive fabrics with costly dyes or gold or silver thread or a complex weave, such as brocades and velvets, were also imported. In the fifteenth century, when the Venetian galleys tended to call at Southampton, the silks were sent by road or coast to London, rather than retailed in the town for local consumption. Paul Morelli, the principal Florentine agent in the port of Southampton in the 1440s, imported tartarin, damask, velvet and raw silk in a Venetian galley, and sent bales and bundles of silks by various carriers to London.[29] The quantity of silk fabrics imported into London in this period is unknown, but the number of Italian merchants and English mercers dealing with luxury fabrics in London provides some indication of the extent of the trade. Between 1436 and 1439, some 150 London mercers may have been involved in the dealing of luxury fabrics.[30] The import of luxury fabrics aroused much governmental concern, and a host of sumptuary legislation was introduced to restrict their consumption to the top echelons of society. The first attempt was made in 1337, when a statute was passed prohibiting people from wearing 'anything but English cloth, except the king and Royal family' and no man was to wear 'any facings of silk or furs but such as could expend an hundred pounds a year'. Between 1337 and 1604, when sumptuary legislation was repealed, ten major Acts of Apparel and minor ones were passed to control dress. These Acts were passed with several motives: to protect the embryonic native cloth industry, to reduce import bills, but also to prevent the confusion of social order. The royal household, however, employed its own silk-weaver. On 7 September 1385, Richard II retained Bendenell de Beek to manufacture cloth of gold and silk especially for him. However, after Bendenell's departure, Italian merchants supplied silk fabrics to the Wardrobe. During 1392–4, the Lucchese Lowys Angvill and the Florentine James Dyne sold cloth of gold, tartarin, taffata and Cyprus gold thread to the Wardrobe.[31]

There was some silk manufacture in London in the Middle Ages, but this was confined to the production of narrow silk wares, such as silk thread, laces, fringe, ribbons, purses and girdles.[32] 'Gentlewomen' dominated this trade, because they could afford the expensive raw materials, and had access to long-distance markets and to customers.[33] It is estimated that there were 123 silkwomen working in London between 1300 and 1500.[34] In 1384, some 400 lb of raw silk was imported to meet their needs.[35] By the fifteenth century, the trade may have expanded, as in 1455, the silkwomen saw imports of narrow silk goods from Cologne as a threat to their trade and successfully obtained a ban on imports, indicating their power and influence.[36] The statute forbade the import of ribbons, laces, girdles, corses or points, but did not refer to 'stuffs of the whole piece', because, as Francis Bacon later observed in 1632, 'the realm had of them no manufacture in use at that time'.[37] By the mid-sixteenth century, the trade had become sufficiently important for the Weavers' Company to fix wages, and it was men, not women, who came to dominate silk production. At this date, English silk production still concentrated on narrow silk wares, as detailed instructions of the Weavers' Company for the proper manufacture of silk only referred to narrow silk products such as laces, ribbons and bands. Despite three Crown-sponsored attempts to establish broad silk manufacture in England in the fifteenth and sixteenth centuries – in 1461, 1537 and 1559 – there was little, if any, broad silk-weaving in London by the mid-sixteenth century.

Consumption and Production During Elizabeth's Reign

The demand for silk goods expanded enormously during Elizabeth's reign (see

Table 6.2). Those who could afford it insisted on wearing clothes that were 'far fetched and dear bought'.[38] The result was a dramatic rise in imports. The value of imported silk fabrics rose by 265 per cent, from an estimated value of £32 000 in 1559, the sixth largest item imported, to £117 000 in 1634.[39]

In 1600, over 210 000 yards of velvets, satins, taffetas, sarcenets, lawns and cambrics were imported in London.[40] The level of consumption was likely to have been even higher, as there was an immense smuggling trade in luxury cloths to avoid high customs and duties.[41] In 1597, for example, it was claimed that 250 chests containing no less than 97 500 yards of velvets were imported illegally from Stade.[42] Some of these imported silks were later re-exported, but this proportion was small, and a large part was destined for domestic consumption.[43] The number of mercers in London was estimated in 1600 to have multiplied from 30 in Queen Mary's reign to 300.[44] However, many of these did not trade exclusively in silk goods.

The excessive level of silk consumption continued to plague the government during the Elizabethan period. In 1574, a 'Proclamation for apparel' spelt out two particular concerns. The first was that 'the excesse of apparel and the superfluitie of unnecessary foreign wares' would lead to a 'manifest decay of a great part of the wealth of the realm ... by bringing into the realm such superfluities of silks, cloths of gold, silver and other most vain devises'. The other was with the 'wasting and undoing of a great number of young gentlemen ... seeking by show of apparel to be esteemed as gentlemen'. Such ostentation, it was said, consumed their goods and the lands their parents left behind, and caused them to run into debts in pursuit of the display of these costly dress materials.[45] The ruining effects on other trades also necessitated the restraining of consumption of silks. The Skinners of London, for example, complained to the Queen in 1590 that their trade was greatly decayed, and that they could hardly earn a living to maintain their families

Table 6.2 Silk fabrics imported into London, 1559–1640

Year	Value (nearest £1000)
1559	32 000
1565	44 000
1622	80 000
1634	117 000
1640	65 000

Sources: PRO SP12/8/31; BL, Lansdowne MS 8/17; A.M. Millard, 'The Import Trade of London, 1600–1640' (University of London PhD thesis, 1956), Appendix 2, Tables 3 and 4.

because 'the usual wearing of furs is utterly neglected and eaten out by the too ordinary lavish and unnecessary use of velvets and silks, drinking up the wealth of this realm'.[46] Attempts to restrict silk consumption met with little success, so in 1597 the government acknowledged this failure with yet another 'Proclamation of Apparel'.[47] This inability to control consumption made the need to establish a domestic industry all the more urgent, both to prevent a drain on national wealth and to create employment.

Parallel with increased imports of silk fabrics was a substantial increase in the quantity of raw silk imported between 1560 and 1640, reflecting the growth in domestic silk manufacture. Table 6.3 demonstrates that the manufacture of silk in England expanded enormously between 1565 and 1592–3. This was at a time when the quantity of imported raw silk rose fivefold, and in the early decades of the seventeenth century, doubled.

The other indirect evidence of increased production is reflected in Cecil's concerns about falling revenue from customs and duties of imported silks. It was suggested to Cecil that the government should impose customs on those goods made at home. Initially, Cecil was reluctant to adopt such a measure because of the fear that this would drive away the strangers whom he had welcomed to settle in England in the first place. He was, however, assured that 'there is no reason to fear that it would drive the makers out of the realm, for if they live anything near so well at home … they would not have stayed so long from their native country'.[48] In 1594, it was decided to 'search and seal,

Table 6.3 Raw silk imported into London, 1560–1620

Year	Value (£)	Quantity (lbs)
1559–60	9 920	[12 000]
1560	7 130	[9 500]
1565	8 004	[11 000]
1592–3	40 000	52 000
1600	62 648	[84 000]
1601	[78 000]	104 000
1620–21	[126 000]	168 611

Note: Figures in square brackets are calculated from known data. It is assumed that 1lb of silk cost 15*s*.
Sources: BL, Harleian MS 1878/82; PRO SP12/275/142I; S.M. Jack, *Trade and Industry in Tudor and Stuart England* (London, 1977), pp. 106–7; A.M. Millard, 'The Import Trade of London, 1600–1640', Vol. 1, p. 45; L. Stone, 'Elizabethan Overseas Trade', *Economic History Review*, Vol. 2, 1949, p. 49; Thirsk, *Economic Policies and Projects*, p. 184.

and exact duties on all the new draperies, as French serges, worsteds, fustians, blankets, and [etc.], made in England, chiefly by strangers, which have hitherto been exported free'.[49] This may not have affected the silk industry as it only catered for the domestic market in this period.

The growth of silk manufacture in London was stimulated by the large-scale immigration from the Continent. There is evidence in various contemporary sources to support this. The Book of Fines, which records goods seized from those who illegally retailed in the City of London, makes frequent references to strangers hawking silk products in the streets of London in the 1590s.[50] In 1600, it was reported that 'the strangers make tuff taffetas, wrought velvets, figured satins and other sorts of silk mingled with thread and wool … in abundance'.[51] The Returns of Aliens also point to a similar conclusion. They show that between 1571 and 1593, the proportion of stranger households engaged in silk-weaving rose from 10 to 20 per cent. The total number involved multiplied dramatically. In 1571, 183 stranger heads of households and their 54 servants were recorded as working in silk manufacture, by 1593 the number had risen to 376 masters.[52] Assuming an average household size of 4.8 people, the total number of people involved in silk manufacture in London probably rose from 932 to 1800 people between 1571 and 1593.[53] This sizeable number was undoubtedly one of the key factors ensuring the success of the industry. But where did these strangers come from? How skilled were they? What kinds of silk goods were they producing?

Alien Silk Workers in London

Specialization

The majority of alien silk workers were involved in weaving. Of the 183 silk workers recorded in 1571, 81 per cent were described as 'silkweaver', 10 per cent were involved in preparing silk yarn (throwing, spinning, twisting), and less than 3 per cent were dyers. It is difficult to determine what types of silk goods were produced in London by aliens in this period. Probably aliens were involved in weaving silk goods similar to the kinds developed in the Low Countries. Although by 1600 it was noted that strangers were producing great quantities of tuftaffetas, wrought velvets, figured satins and other sorts of silk mingled with thread and wool,[54] these were not being made in large quantities in 1571 as no weavers specializing in them were recorded at this date. Only one lustringmaker was recorded.[55] The majority of silk-weavers were likely to have been producing cheap and mixed silks. Silk was an expensive raw material, and as has been noted, an innovation developed in the Low

6.1 Weavers' workshop
Source: Rijksmuseum, Amsterdam

Countries was to mix it with other fibres such as linen and wool to reduce the costs. Considered unsuitable for clothing by the elite, these cheaper and mixed silks were probably used by them for linings of expensive garments and fine bed curtains, and other purposes, such as making silk handkerchiefs. Natalie Rothstein found in an occasional inventory in the seventeenth century a good worsted garment lined with a cheaper silk. Silks made in England, then, were designed to complement rather than substitute for imports of high-quality silks, and this product differentiation was undoubtedly a crucial factor in the expansion of the industry. While the wealthy classes may have been willing to buy local-made silks for linings and other purposes, they were less likely to switch from wearing Italian silks to those home-made. This may explain why, despite increased silk manufacture in England at the end of the sixteenth century, high-quality silks continued to be imported in large quantities. However, over time, as the skills built up and the reputation of the English silk industry increased, imports were likely to decrease.

By the early 1590s, there was already a greater diversification in the silk industry in London. A Return in 1593 not only recorded 120 silk-weavers in the City, but also 22 taffeta-weavers, 4 tufted taffeta-weavers, and 7 velvet-weavers. Taffeta, which formed the ground for tuftaffeta, was a thin, plain weave and was the easiest weave of all. Tufted taffeta- and velvet-weavers were highly skilled. Tufted taffeta, which could be either all silk or half linen, had long been imported into England. It is believed that all-silk tufted taffeta manufacture in London probably began in about 1590.[56] Silk-weaving was highly labour-intensive, and production per day of even plain silks was very small. It is estimated that it would take the most industrious weaver (together with his assistants) three-and-a-half days to weave a dress length of 14 yards of plain material.[57] Strangers also made other goods. According to the Book of Fines,[58] goods which were sold in the streets of London in the 1590s included fustians, hatbands, cushions, callacow, laces, silk buttons, silk and velvet girdles (for children), black silk lace without purle, and Dutch grograin.[59]

By the early seventeenth century, a greater variety of silk products were made in London. Sipers, a transparent silk cloth formerly imported from Cyprus, was being produced in Canterbury as early as 1595, and by 1618 it was also produced in Bishopsgate in London. Figured silk satin too was made in the capital from 1615, and tissues of gold-and-silver thread, commonly called cloths of gold, from about 1611.[60] By 1618, some of the London strangers had introduced the manufacture of silk cobweb lawn, suitable for ruffs, veils and kerchiefs. On 15 January 1610, John Mallio, a cobweb lawn-weaver, was admitted as a foreign master, paying £5.[61] By 1635, alien weavers produced plushes (mainly used for rugs, curtains and upholstery), wrought grograins (used for ribbons, facings, vestments and costumes), figured satins and divers other broad silk wares.[62] Complaints by native weavers also offer an indirect, fascinating insight into how the trade operated. London weavers in 1635 complained that it was hard for them to make a living, as alien weavers and brokers living in the capital sold goods for others from Canterbury, Norwich and other places within England, and how they went 'from shop to shop, in London and Westminster and other places, furnishing the mercers and haberdashers therewith, and often retailing such silk wares at the houses of the Nobility and Gentry'.[63]

Origins

The evidence from the Returns of Aliens shows that stranger silk workers in London in the sixteenth century came predominantly from the southern Netherlands, and only a handful from France itself – a conclusion which differs markedly from that presented by Christopher Clay. In 1571, the largest groups, in descending order, originated from Walloon provinces, Flanders, and Brabant. Immigrant silk-weavers from France and Italy were also recorded, but these were small in comparison to those from the Netherlands.

Particularly striking was the number of silk-weavers from Walloon provinces, which increased dramatically at the end of the sixteenth century as a result of continued political and religious upheavals. While there were only 54 silk-weavers recorded to have come from Walloon provinces in 1571, by 1593, 99 aliens, or nearly half of all silk-weavers in London, originated from there. However, there were significant changes in the city of origin. In 1571, the largest group of silk workers came from Valenciennes, which accounted for 10 per cent of the total, whereas in 1593 the dominant group came from Tournai, amounting to 20 per cent.

A significant proportion of silk-weavers also came from Flanders. As has been noted earlier, Bruges was once an important centre of silk manufacture, but this industry had declined by 1560s. In 1571, 19 per cent of silk-weavers originated from Flanders, but this proportion fell to 11 per cent by 1593. Over the same period, the share from Brabant increased from 5 to 11 per cent, largely as a result of the immigration after the fall of Antwerp in 1585. The number from Brabant rose from 9 to 18 between 1571 and 1593, with two-thirds arriving in the period between 1584 and 1593. This insignificant scale of immigration after 1585 reflects the relative unattractiveness of London to many potential emigrants leaving Antwerp. Indeed, many Antwerp silk-weavers, along with others, chose to move to Amsterdam instead, laying the foundations of the silk industry there.

Many stranger silk workers in London in 1571 appear to have come for religious reasons, as is reflected in their period of arrival. More than 80 per cent of all the silk workers in London in 1571 had arrived between 1560 and 1571, and only 13 per cent between 1540 and 1559. The silk-weavers were particularly affected by the religious and political disturbances in the Low Countries, as 63 per cent arrived in the five years between 1566 and 1571 alone. Several of the silk workers from Walloon provinces escaped to London to avoid persecution. Guillame Coppin, Wolfgang de Faloize, Pierre Gruel and Bon Raparlier, who indicated in the Return of 1571 that they were silk weavers from Valenciennes, had all been banished from that city, and their goods confiscated by the Conseil des Troubles.[64] The pre-eminence of religious motives in the immigration of the silk workers is also supported by the patterns of their church membership. Of the 183 silk workers in London in 1571, 88 per cent were members of the Stranger Churches, but 65 per cent of these were members of the French church, reflecting the predominance of French-speaking immigrants among the silk-weavers. The events of the 1570s, 1580s and 1590s also had a considerable effect on the immigration of silk workers. More than a third of the silk workers surveyed in 1593 had arrived in London between 1572 and 1583, and a further 35 per cent between 1584 and 1593. This development fitted in with the overall pattern of immigration to London. However, the events of these decades had a less dramatic effect than those between 1566 and 1571.

Silk manufacture had recently been established in the southern Netherlands at the beginning of the sixteenth century, and the types of silks made there were different from those of Italy, focusing more on cheaper and lower-quality silks. Yet it is striking that such a high proportion of silk workers in London came from Walloon towns, which generally had a reputation for high-quality light textiles rather than for silk manufacture.[65] Valenciennes, for example, excelled in the manufacture of light cloths such as says, linen muslins and laces, but there is little evidence to suggest that there was a significant silk industry.[66] Indeed, occupational evidence collected by Alastair Duke for 346 Protestants who were persecuted for heresy in Valenciennes in the sixteenth century (some of whom escaped to London) shows that none of these practised silk-weaving in their native town. Of these 346 people, over half were engaged in linen and say weaving.[67] The occupations of refugees from Valenciennes recorded in the Return of 1571, on the other hand, show that 64 per cent of these was engaged in silk-weaving in London, an occupation which apparently was not practised in Valenciennes. Tournai, too, was also renowned for its light woollens. With some 25 000 people, Tournai was one of the ten largest towns in the Low Countries in the sixteenth century, and was among the most important export centres of cloth. As early as the twelfth and thirteenth centuries, it had produced light woollens for foreign markets. In the late sixteenth and early seventeenth centuries, it produced woollen damasks, mixed cloths and women's stockings for export.[68] By the mid-sixteenth century, Tournai had also moved into silk manufacture, producing satins, gold cloths and silk damasks, as well as mixed silks.[69] However, it is unclear how significant the industry was in Tournai.

This apparent lack of correlation points to the strong possibility that some immigrants may have changed their occupations upon arrival and during their stay in London. There is some direct evidence to support this. Pieter Seghers, a merchant, arrived from Ghent on 30 July 1567, and during his two-year stay in the capital, recounted that he had no money and subsequently had to work as a button-maker and a silk worker, both professions he had learned there.[70] In the eighteenth century, Natalie Rothstein also has found that many Huguenots changed to silk-weaving from related trades, and concluded that 'there is not much evidence to prove that the professions of the majority in France had been *silk* weaving ... Refugees were weavers, but they *became* silk weavers. In their country of origins they made certain coarse types of woollen cloth.'[71]

The hypothesis that the skills in silk-weaving may have been learned in London can also be tested positively in two ways. In the first place, we can compare the occupations of silk-weavers in the Returns of 1571 and 1593 against each other, and with Returns from other dates. Only five silk-weavers recorded in the 1593 Return (or 4 per cent) could be traced in the 1571

Return, and none of these had changed their occupation to silk-weaving between these dates. Occupational change, however, was likely to take place in the immediate years after arrival, and as many silk workers arrived in London in the late 1560s, a more fruitful line of enquiry would be to focus on the silk-weavers recorded in the 1571 Return. The sources for the 1570s are also better than for the 1590s. In the first place, there are three detailed Returns of Aliens for the period between 1568 and 1571, and these can be used to trace the occupations of strangers in their early years of settlement in London. Second, the availability of valuable documents in the Conseil des Troubles Archive also renders it possible to trace former occupations of aliens in their hometown. This exercise focuses on the silk workers from Antwerp and Valenciennes, cities where a sizeable group of alleged silk-weavers originated, and where there are good documents available.

Did silk workers from Antwerp experience occupational change during their stay in London? The findings are summarized in Table 6.4, and two broad occupational changes seem to have occurred. In the first place, some immigrants from Antwerp may have adapted their skills from trades related to silk-weaving. Claude Dottegnie, for example, was recorded in 1571 as a silk-weaver from Italy. He had, in fact, lived in Antwerp for several years before moving to London some time after 1559. In Antwerp, he is known to have been a wool comber, and when he moved to London he became a schoolmaster in 1561, a buttonmaker in 1568 and a silk-weaver by 1571. It is possible that he learnt the skill of silk-weaving in Antwerp,[72] but if so, he was unable, or chose not, to practise it on his first arrival in London. The second occupational adjustment concerns the shift from silk-weaving to other, sometimes unrelated, trades. Dennis Bonange, described as a silk-weaver in 1568, appeared to have found lace-making a much more profitable trade, as by 1571 he was recorded as 'weaver of onell lace'. Francois Marquin, on the other hand, gave up weaving altogether, and by 1583 had become a schoolmaster.[73] The previous occupations of immigrants from Valenciennes are summarized in Table 6.5. These indicate that many who had stated that they were silk- weavers in London in 1571 had in fact been well-to-do merchants in Valenciennes,[74] and had changed their occupation to silk-weaving during their stay in London. Two of these – Guillaume Coppin and Bon Raparlier – had previously lived in Southampton, probably only for a short time.[75]

So what are the possible explanations for this occupational mobility? One probable factor relates to the constraints operating in London, as many former merchants could not resume mercantile activities, due in part to the disruptions to trade caused by the troubles in Valenciennes, and in part to the prohibition by the Privy Council of trading with the Low Countries. The Port Book for 1571 indicates that few merchants from Valenciennes were able to resume trading in London. Only two from Valenciennes who were described

Table 6.4 Silk workers of Antwerp origin in London, 1568–1593

Name	Occupation in 1568	Occupation in Nov. 1571	Occupation in 1593
Dennis Bonange	Silk-weaver	Weaver of onell lace	
Louis Capel	Servant to silk dresser	Silk twister	
Anthony Capelle	Silk-weaver		
Philip Carden		Silk-weaver	
Jean Carlishewe			Silk weaver (1583)
Pierre Castelain	Lanifex (1562)		
Claude Dottegnie	Button maker		Silk-weaver
Ferdinand Dottegnie			Silk-weaver
Jan Elste			Silk spinner
Jan James			Silk twister
Elizabeth Malliard (husband's occ)	Linen-weaver	Silk-weaver	
Francois Marquin		Silk-worker	Schoolmaster (1583)
Peter & Gielis Martyn		Servant to silk-weaver	Servant to silk-weaver
Jan Millehomme	Silk worker	Silk-weaver	
Jane Mownttadewe	Silk-weaver		
Abel Mynor	Servant to silk-weaver		
Mozes Petefryer		Servant to silk-weaver	Servant to silk-weaver
Galetta Torr		Silk worker	

Sources: Kirk and Kirk, eds, *Returns of Aliens* (1568, November 1571, 1583 – for further details, see p. 79); Scouloudi, *Returns of Strangers* (1593).

as merchants in both the Return of 1571 and Conseil des Troubles documents can be traced in the Port Book – Peter Sohier who imported brushes and Francois Voizin who imported mockadoes.[76] The second probable explanation lies in their destitute economic condition, which may have forced them to find a handicraft occupation to earn a living. Many of the refugees from Valenciennes had been banished from the city, and their goods and properties had been confiscated by the Conseil des Troubles. Some arrived with very little money. Guillame Coppin, once a well-to-do merchant from Valenciennes, lost a great deal of his possessions when he was banished from his home city, and this may have forced him to take up silk-weaving in London. In his will in 1572, some six years after his arrival in England, Guillame Coppin still hoped to recover his goods in Valenciennes 'when liberty shall be in the low countries and that profit and sale of my goods which

Table 6.5 Silk-weavers from Valenciennes and Walloon provinces in London, 1571

Name in CT sources	Name in London	Occupation in London in 1571	Occupation in London 1568–1571	Occupation in Valenciennes
Guillame Coppin	William	Silk-weaver		*Marchant*
Wolfgang De Faloize	Offulgan Falowis	Silk-weaver		*Marchant*
Pierre Gruel	Peter Grevyll	Caulmaker/ Silk-weaver		*Marchant*
Roland de Hetreu	Roland Hetrewe	Silk-weaver		*Marchant*
	Jacob Hugobert	Marchant	Hatband Maker	
	Peter Locar	Silk-weaver	Thread winder	
Bon Raparlier	Browne Aperlie	Silk-weaver		*Merchier*
	Nicholas Remy	Silk-weaver	Buttonmaker	
Pierre Sohier	Peter Sawier	Merchant		*Marchant*
Pierre Thiefrize	Peter Tyfry	Silk-weaver		Bourgeois/ Merchant
Francois Voizin	Fraunces Voisin	Merchant		Notable and rich

Notes: CT Conseil des Troubles.
Sources: AGR, Conseil des Troubles, MS 155; MS 315A, MS 315 bis; Kirk and Kirk, eds, *Returns of Aliens* (1568, 1571); G.W. Clark, 'An Urban Study During the Revolt of the Netherlands: Valenciennes 1540–1570', (University of Columbia PhD thesis, 1972); A.L.E. Verheyden, 'Une correspondence inédite addressée par des families protestantes des Pays-Bas à leurs coreligionnaires d'Angleterre (11 novembre 1569–25 février 1570)', Académie Royale de Belgique, *Bulletin de la commission Royale D'histoire*, 1955, Vol. 120, p. 137.

are at Valenciennes may be made'[77] – a hope never materialized. When he fell ill, he had to rely on poor relief from the French church, and in December 1572 the London deacons also gave his wife two shillings to buy a blanket.[78] But why did these refugee merchants change to silk-weaving? Silk-weaving was a lucrative trade, and offered plenty of opportunities to make a living. Furthermore, some of these merchants may have been involved in trading high-quality textiles in their home town, and were probably familiar with some aspects of silk manufacture. Merchants-turned-silk-weavers had an additional advantage: the knowledge of where to obtain raw silks. In the Return of 1593, the wife of Danyell Gislinge, a merchant, was recorded as a silk-weaver. Her husband may have supplied her with raw materials as well as acting as an agent for her products.[79]

If occupational change did occur, it raises the crucial question of how skills were acquired by immigrants. The Stranger Churches may occupy a nodal point in the process of inter-group diffusion. As has been pointed earlier, an overwhelming majority of alien workers (88 per cent) were members of the Stranger Churches, with the majority belonging to the French church (65 per cent), and a smaller proportion (23 per cent) to the Dutch church. The proportion of all French-churchgoers who were silk-weavers was also greater: 24 per cent in 1571 and a third in 1593, in comparison with only 8 and 11 per cent of Dutch church members, respectively. This evidence helps us to understand why silk-weaving became closely identified with the French-speaking community.

There are two additional reasons for this development. Prior to the substantial influx of silk workers after the 1560s, there was already a small but significant number of silk workers in London who also originated from Walloon-speaking parts of the Netherlands. Of the 183 silk workers in London in 1571, more than 14 per cent were already living in the City by 1559, and a third of these had also originated from Walloon towns. It is unclear whether these had been trained in silk-weaving, or developed the skill in London. However, their longer residence meant that they were better acquainted with the opportunities in London, and they probably established the London silk industry, providing opportunities for the later refugees, who may not themselves have been silk workers by training. As the industry grew, more were able to move into it, and this may account for some of the refugees switching to silk after they had practised another trade in London. In addition, the smaller size of the French church allowed greater cohesion and group solidarity among its members. In November 1571, the Dutch church had 3643 members, in comparison with French church membership of 657, which was dominated by Walloons.[80] The Walloons possessed strong group solidarity and the characteristics of what modern sociologists call the 'middleman minorities'. Many expected their stay in England to be temporary, which was reflected in their maintenance of close ties with their homeland and involvement in the political events there.[81] As Andrew Spicer has shown, the refugees from Valenciennes formed a close-knit group, buttressed by family ties. Guillame Coppin, for example, married into the Sohiers, a powerful family from Valenciennes, and he and Bon Raparlier had settled in Southampton before being involved in step-migration to London.[82] These strong ties may have limited their contacts with other immigrant groups and the native population, but in turn acted to strengthen the solidarity of the group and their economic ties.[83] This group solidarity meant that once some immigrants had taken up a trade, others belonging to the group were likely to have been encouraged to do the same. Skills were likely to have been developed collectively and shared among the immigrants. Native weavers greatly resented this, and bitterly complained in 1595 against alien weavers who did not share with them the skill, and yet 'do not refuse to teach their countrymen, which new come over, the art of silk weaving, though *before* they were a tailor, a cobbler, or a joiner'.[84]

Geographical Concentration

Once the strangers had learnt the skill, it might have taken years of practice before they could make a lucrative living. In the intervening years, sparse evidence suggests that some strangers struggled to make a living from their new trade. In 1572, soon after Guillame Coppin had taken up silk-weaving, he was receiving relief from the French church on account of his 'nescesites'. Pierre Locart (Peter Locar), who had changed from thread winding to silk weaving some time between 1568 and 1571, received 2 shillings from the French church on 10 September 1573 due to his 'mallade'.[85]

Many of the successful stranger silk-weavers in London in the 1590s had been practising the trade for many years. Nicholas Remy, a relatively successful silk-weaver at the time of his death in 1595, may have been practising the trade for over twenty-four years. Remy, who arrived as early as 1559, was a buttonmaker (of course, he could be making silk buttons) in 1568, and became a silk-weaver some time between 1568 and 1571. He was a denizen, and belonged to the French church. He resided in St Stephen's Parish, in Colman Street Ward, and kept three English servants and set two English servants to work. The total value of his bequests is some measure of his wealth: he bequeathed to his eldest daughter two beakers of silver; £3 to the poor of the French church, 5 shillings to the sexton of the parish church of St Stephens, and £50 to his wife Mary.[86]

Stranger silk-weavers who possessed a considerable number of looms in 1594 had also been in London for a number of years. Many of these had originated from Walloon provinces, and arrived after the 1560s. Jacques Cembronc, from the Walloon provinces, had been in London since 1584, and it is unclear when he took up silk-weaving, but by 1594 he was a successful silk-weaver, possessing seven looms. Michael Fever, who possessed nine looms, had been in London since 1560. However, Fever did not take up silk-weaving as soon as he arrived in London, as he was recorded as a minister in 1568, and it is unclear when he took up the trade.[87]

The spatial concentration of strangers in particular areas further encouraged the consolidation of skills and their rapid spread among the immigrants. The main concentrations of stranger silk-weavers were in the wards of Bishopsgate and Cripplegate, and in Southwark (see Table 6.6). In 1571, out of a total of 128 stranger families in the Ward of Bishopsgate, more than a third were classified as silk workers. In 1571, 8 per cent of the 366 households in the Bridge Without Ward were engaged in silk-weaving, a much smaller proportion than in Bishopsgate. In Cripplegate Ward, of a total of 82 stranger families, 23 per cent were engaged in silk-weaving.[88] Before the large influx during the 1560s, there were already stranger silk workers in the wards of Bishopsgate and Cripplegate who had lived there for a number of years. In Bishopsgate Ward, for example, there were Domynick Bewxer, a silk-weaver from France, who may have living there since 1546, and Peter Foye, a silk-weaver from Tournai, who had been there since 1560. The skill in silk-weaving may have been originally developed and perfected by these established residents, who later passed it on to their fellow countrymen.

The clustering of stranger silk workers followed ethnic lines. The majority of the stranger silk workers in St Botolph Parish in Bishopsgate came from Walloon provinces. In 1571, of the 31 stranger silk worker households in the parish of St Botolph Bishopsgate, nearly 65 per cent were of Walloon origin. The silk-weavers in St Olave in Southwark, on the other hand, were largely Dutch-speaking. In 1571, of the 15 stranger silk-weavers living there, 80 per cent were from Flanders, Brabant or Holland. The silk workers in St Giles Cripplegate were also largely Dutch-speaking. Of the 15 stranger silk workers there, 80 per cent were classified as from 'Burgundy', 'Under the Emperor' or Flanders, terms which usually denoted their origins in the Dutch-speaking parts of the Low Countries. These patterns of ethnic distribution played a critical role in the development of the silk industry in these areas. As Bishopsgate housed many French-speaking immigrants, it was able to attract later arrivals from French-speaking areas, particularly the Huguenots in the seventeenth century. With the injection of a considerable amount of skills and capital by the Huguenots after 1685, the original 'Bishopsgate silk industry' expanded and became the 'Spitalfields silk industry'. The silk industry in Cripplegate and Southwark, on the other hand, does not seem to have survived.

Table 6.6 Residential distribution of alien silk workers in London, 1571

Wards	All alien HH No.	%	Silk workers No.	%	Silk workers as % of all alien HH %
Riverside Wards					
Billingsgate	113	6.0	3	2.0	3.0
Bridge Within	22	1.0	3	2.0	14.0
Castle Baynard	24	1.0	1	1.0	4.0
Dowgate	45	3.0	4	2.0	9.0
Queenhithe	10	1.0	1	1.0	10.0
Tower	158	9.0	6	3.0	4.0
Vintry	33	2.0	10	6.0	30.0
Sub-total	405	22.0	28	15.0	7.0
Eastern Wards					
Aldgate	128	7.0	7	4.0	6.0
Bishopsgate	127	7.0	41	22.0	32.0
Broad Street	73	4.0	9	5.0	12.0
Portsoken	53	3.0	9	5.0	17.0
Sub-total	381	21.0	66	36.0	17.0
Northern and Western Wards					
Aldersgate	126	7.0	9	5.0	7.0
Coleman Street	19	1.0	9	5.0	47.0
Cripplegate	82	5.0	19	10.0	23.0
Farringdon Without	105	6.0	9	5.0	9.0
Farringdon Within	83	5.0	4	2.0	5.0
Sub-total	415	23.0	50	27.0	12.0
Central Wards					
Bassishaw	7	0.4	1	0.5	14.0
Bread Street	16	1.0	2	1.0	13.0
Candlewick Street	35	2.0	1	0.5	3.0
Cheap	20	1.0	1	0.5	5.0
Cordwainer	5	0.3	—	—	0.0
Cornhill	21	1.0	—	—	0.0
Langbourn	109	6.0	4	2.0	4.0
Lime Street	12	1.0	—	—	0.0

Walbrook	23	1.0	1	0.5	4.0
Sub-total	248	14.0	10	6.0	4.0
Southwark					
Bridge Without	366	20.0	29	16.0	8.0
Total	1 815	100.0	183	100.0	10.0

Notes: HH = Head of household.
Source: Kirk and Kirk, *Returns of Aliens 1571*.

Silk Production in the Seventeenth Century

The expansion of the silk industry in London during the seventeenth century and its growing diversification were ensured by the continued influx of immigrants into the Capital, from the Continent and other parts of England. This was facilitated by the policy of the Weavers' Company, which by the seventeenth century had established a clear and systematic procedure for admission. To obtain admission, aliens were required to show proof of church membership (French and Dutch church), a proper qualification acquired there or abroad, and a fee (11*s.* 10*d.* for journeymen and £4 or £5 for masters).[89] Those with exceptional skills were admitted *gratis*. The Company also sought to encourage the production of new types of silk. In January 1684, two silk-weavers from Nimes, John Larquier and John Quet, requested admission, claiming they could weave and perfect lustrings, alamodes and other fine silks. The Company gave them six weeks to produce a sample piece and appointed a member to supervise the work to ensure that the weavers could do what they claimed. Eight months later, John Larguier produced a piece of alamode silk. The Company considered that the skill would be of great benefit to the nation, as no similar products had been made in England, and admitted him *gratis* upon the condition that he would employ some English persons in making alamode and lustring silks for one year.[90]

Between 1610 and 1694, the records of the Weavers' Company show that nearly 900 alien weavers were working in London (see Table 6.7). Of these, 252 were admitted as masters (216 of whom were new masters, while 36 were admitted as masters after a period working as journeymen in the capital), 33 foreign brothers, whose names indicate that they were descendants of strangers and had moved to London from other parts of England, 437 were admitted as foreign journeymen, a further 131 were ordered to fulfil the requirements needed for admission, and 38 were ordered to leave, having failed to meet these. A complaint by native weavers in the 1630s, however,

Table 6.7   Admissions of alien silk-weavers, 1610–1694

Year	M	M(2)	B	J	P	L	Total
1610–1642	10	0	1	13	6	2	32
1648–1654	2	1	6	2	2	0	13
1551–1664	21	0	19	27	6	0	73
1666–1677	140	18	7	300	113	3	581
1683–1685	15	8	0	47	4	26	100
1692–1694	28	9	0	48	0	7	92
Total	**216**	**36**	**33**	**437**	**131**	**38**	**891**

Notes: M = Masters. M(2) = Masters formerly journeymen. B = Brothers. J = journeymen. P = Numbers ordered to prove service and take admission. L = Number ordered to leave.

Sources: GL, Weavers' Court Minutes MS 4655 vols 1–9; an incomplete version is printed in W.C. Waller, *Extracts from the Court Books of the Weavers Company of London, 1610–1730* (Huguenot Society Publications, 1931, Vol. 33); transcriptions have been thoroughly checked against the originals before quoting them here.

claimed that as many as 1500 journeymen and apprentices between the age of 16 and 18 were employed and paid in wages by alien masters in London.[91]

Between 1610 and 1654, the number of admissions was low, but there was a dramatic increase after 1662. Many probably arrived a few years earlier, given the Company's policy of admitting only those who had been in England for ten years. The number of admissions increased after 1666, and peaked in the early 1670s. The number of masters peaked in 1668, steadily declined after 1671, and fell to a low point in 1676, when the Company declared that henceforth, it would not admit any alien or stranger born as master, except 'upon some weighty grounds and reasons'. This new ruling, however, encouraged aliens who had been working in London as journeymen to apply for admission as masters. In 1677, eight were admitted. On 25 June 1677, John le Noir was admitted as a master, paying a fee of £4 8s. 2d., because he had been living in London for six years and he was married to an Englishwoman. Claude Drolle was also admitted as a foreign master, paying the same fee, because he had been a member of the Company for seven years, and he was a widower with two children, as his English wife was now deceased.[92] The number of admissions of foreign journeymen rose steadily from 1666, and peaked in 1671, when 63 were admitted.

There are no surviving records for the period between 1619 and 1653, but by that time the influx of aliens was causing increasing concern. On 27 June

1653, the Company declared its intention not to admit any aliens who had recently come over, to prosecute those who were not members of a foreign congregation or admitted members of the Company, and to discuss with the French and Dutch churches 'some ways and means for preventing any further coming over of strangers into this nation'.[93] In 1662, two members of the French church came before the Court to ask for a respite of proceedings against a member who had been 'persecuted for his religion in Paris', and the request was conditionally granted. However, the Court declared that it was not to be made a precedent, but that, as ordered before, 'all such strangers that have been here ten years shall be admitted and no others'.[94]

The policy became more lenient after the Great Fire in London in 1666, and in 1668 the Company allowed the admission of aliens who had been in England for three years.[95] This policy still caused much concern among the French and Dutch churches, because it meant that those who had newly come over as a result of the growing troubles in France were particularly affected. In November 1669, representatives of both churches came and asked the Company to admit those who came because of 'persecution in France'.[96] From its reply to this request, it is clear that the Company was not satisfied that all refugees came on religious grounds, and believed that 'the foreign members have invited and do invite more strangers over, and they come under pretence of a Persecution'. It promised, however, to do whatever it could to satisfy the churches.

Centres of Immigration: Canterbury, Paris, Amsterdam and Tours

Stranger silk-weavers in London in the seventeenth century continued to come from Walloon-speaking areas of the southern Netherlands, but the majority originated from France, with a sizeable number from Holland and from Canterbury in England. Among those admitted between 1610 and 1694 with places of origins known, the largest groups of masters were those from Canterbury (24 masters), followed by Paris (9 masters), but among the journeymen, the largest groups were from Paris (41), Canterbury (28), Amsterdam (27) and Tours (25). London was thus drawing in skills from a variety of areas, and a brief survey of the specialization of these areas gives some indication of the influence on London.

Canterbury specialized in the production of mixed fabrics, striped silks as well as half silks, but did not manufacture any expensive materials such as tissues, velvets or brocaded silks in the seventeenth century.[97] In the late seventeenth century, many active silk-weaving families moved from Canterbury to London. All of the masters and journeymen from Canterbury were admitted after 1662, indicating that problems afflicting the trade at this date precipitated such a move. Rising indignation against alien weavers in the mid-seventeenth century by Canterbury weavers, who increasingly saw them as rivals in trade rather than as refugees for religion,[98] may have been an important factor, but so too were increasing opportunities in London after the Restoration. There were good economic reasons for moving to London. Canterbury weavers relied on London for the supply of raw materials and as an outlet for their finished goods. The Canterbury weavers sent their goods to factors with whom they had long-standing family connections. The latter found customers for them, and presumably suggested the types of material to be woven.[99] However, this system of marketing proved increasingly risky, as the roads were prone to robberies and not all carriers were trustworthy. In the middle of the seventeenth century, when prosecuted by English carriers for employing their own carrier to take the goods to London, Canterbury weavers claimed that they had previously entrusted the task to the accusers, but they were negligent. They had given the task to someone else, who had caused much damage to the silks by careless handling. The waggons had also been robbed several times at night, and silks to the value of £300 had been stolen. They therefore decided to employ their own carrier, who only travelled between sunrise and sunset and was able to act as their factor because he understood the trade.[100] The move to London was a sensible decision, not only giving the Canterbury weavers direct access to customers and access to merchants supplying raw silk, but also because they could be nearer to the centre of fashion, make more profit, and have a large labour force, or from the journeyman's viewpoint, a wider choice of employment.[101]

A significant number of journeymen came to London from Paris and Tours. These were also established centres of excellent silk manufacture in France, producing large quantities of high-quality silk, but they suffered decline partly as a result of the emigration of skilled workers precipitated by the continual religious and political conflict. At the end of the sixteenth century, all kinds of silk cloths and cloths of gold and silver were woven in Paris, and this eventually became the Parisian speciality. In 1601, and under royal patronage, Noel Parent and his brothers began making Bologna crepes, satins and damasks 'in the Italian fashion', while another member of the Parent family, Etienne, began making Bruges satins and 'damars caffards' at Tours in 1604. In 1603, the Milanese 'gold throwster' Turato obtained monopoly for the production of golden yarns in Paris, with the condition that he provide training for French craftsmen.[102]

Silk manufacture began in Tours in 1470, when Louis IX decided to transfer to Tours, the royal capital at the time, the Italian silk workers who had already been established in Lyons for a number of years. In the seventeenth century, its products were known throughout France, and probably overshadowed even the textiles of Lyons, 'since the consuls of that city had no qualms about wearing the famous gros de Tours' (plain taffetas). Tours also produced 'pannes of such beauty that they were sent to be sold in Spain and other foreign countries. Their red, violet and tannés velvets are more beautiful than those of Genoa: it is the only place producing silk serges.' Richelieu made many purchases for the Court in the workshops of Tours. In the 1630s, there were some 8000 looms working in Tours.[103] However, with the onset of the Dutch wars, and the closure of those markets at the end of the seventeenth century, Tours suffered an irreversible decline. By 1679, the number of looms had fallen to 1800, and by 1700 only some 1200 frames were in action, some 70 mills working, and only 3000 craftsmen at work.[104] The emigration of large numbers of Protestants in the late seventeenth century also affected silk manufacturing areas in France. Reims, Tours, Nimes and Rouen may have lost half of their workers, while 9000 out of 12 000 silk workers are believed to have left Lyons.[105]

Besides France, a significant number of journeymen also left Amsterdam to seek better opportunities in London. The silk industry in Holland, particularly Amsterdam, was recently established by the silk workers from Antwerp and other towns of the southern Netherlands after 1585. Between 1585 and 1606, more than 400 silk workers from these areas may have settled in Amsterdam. This, combined with the new sea-borne trade with Italy and the East Indies, the countries which produced raw silk, prompted leading merchants of the city to take steps to encourage the weaving of broad silks as well as the dyeing and processing of silk yarns. In 1605, five prominent merchants of the city concluded a contract with the East India Company by which the Company was to supply raw silk at a fixed price, and the merchants engaged to have the silk manufactured in Amsterdam. By the second half of the seventeenth century, the industry was well established in Amsterdam, and Amsterdam silks could compete in European markets with those of Lyons and Tours.[106] However, the departure of William of Orange for England after 1685 may have encouraged some silk-weavers to follow the Court.

Diffusion of Skills to Native Weavers

The skills in silk-weaving were spread rapidly to native weavers during the seventeenth century, most notably in silk throwing. In 1608 native silk workers, in an attempt to seek a ban on imports of wrought silk, claimed that in Queen Elizabeth's days, 'the Englishmen were not so skilful in trades ... But now is the people ... skilful of all kind and manner of trades as ... silk weaving of silk lace of silver and gold lace, and broad tufted taffities, all kinde of broad stuffs and fustians but especially the throwing of raw silks by silk throwsters'.[107] By 1620, native silk throwsters had successfully acquired the skills, and petitioned the City to allow them to form a Company. They claimed that silk throwing was introduced by a stranger towards the end of the 1570s, and diffused principally by 'some few persons who were skillful in the art' and who passed on their knowledge by training servants.[108] It is believed that Anthony Emerick and John James, two Netherlanders dwelling in St Martin-le-Grand, introduced silk throwing into London during the 1570s.[109] As late as the 1590s, the Dutch church claimed that silk throwing was still a 'trade not used by Englishmen'.[110] This suggests that the rapid growth of silk throwing did not take place until the late 1590s. By the early seventeenth century, the number of silk throwsters in London was believed to have increased from three or four to fifty, of which 'above three parts are English men, and of them most freemen and the rest strangers'. They provided work for several thousand people in winding and throwing silk,[111] and by 1631, these trades are believed to have provided employment to 7000 people, rising to 40 000 by 1662.[112]

The scale of apprenticeship training provided by aliens during the sixteenth and seventeenth centuries can be assessed using two types of source. The first is the 1593 Return with a detailed breakdown of the number of English and alien servants employed by silkworkers, and the second comprises the bindings of apprentices at the Weavers' Company in the seventeenth century. The Return of Aliens of 1593 shows that the majority of the servants employed by the stranger silk workers in 1593 were English. Out of 180 servants employed by the silk weavers, 66 per cent were English, and the proportion was higher among the velvet workers, where three-quarters of their servants were English, and among silk throwsters, 84 per cent. The total number of English servants employed, however, is not the most suitable measure of the degree of dissemination of skills. A more useful indicator is the ways in which English servants were employed. In the case of silk throwing, most of servants, employees or dependants on the craft were English, many of whom were pauper apprentices. Silk throwing demanded a lot of unskilled labour to attend to such tasks as putting on new bobbins and tying broken threads. Formal training was not offered, as the skill could be learnt on the job. Silk winding was one of the simplest and worst-paid jobs in the trade. In Spitalfields, by the mid-eighteenth century, much of it was casual labour performed by women, children and the poor, and it became a common occupation for the inmates of London workhouses.[113]

In weaving, the work varied from the simple weaving done by women, who quickly learnt this semi-skilled task, to the skilled work of those weaving figured fabrics on a draw-loom. The weavers of flowered silks, damasks, brocades and velvets were considered to be the elite, and Campbell in the eighteenth century thought they were 'very ingenious tradesmen'.[114] In silk-weaving, there was some formal training of English servants through apprenticeship, although many of these probably learned simple silk-weaving techniques. In 1593, for example, 27 per cent of the silk-weavers' English servants were apprentices. Like the silk throwsters, the silk-weavers also kept and set to work many English servants, who may have been involved in silk-weaving in some way. In comparison to the number of stranger journeymen, very few English journeymen found employment with stranger silk-weavers in 1593. It is unclear whether this was a reflection of the informal system of recruitment within the stranger community, or the preference of stranger silk-weavers to employ their own countrymen, or the continued lack of skills among the native craftsmen at this date. This apparent willingness of the silk-weavers to offer formal training to English servants may have been due to several factors. Silk was a highly differentiated product, and the level of skills required years of practice, or the *economies of practice*. This means that it would take a long period of time for the newcomers to catch up with the established practitioners of the craft. There was also a diversity of tasks in silk manufacture to which stranger silk-weavers could put English servants to work – reeling, warping, weaving or drawing looms. These factors meant that stranger silk-weavers probably had little fear of losing their monopoly of the craft by teaching the skills to the native population.

In the more specialized and high-quality weaving, such as velvet and taffeta, the majority of English workers were kept and set to work. There were no apprentices, which suggests that perhaps there was no formal training. The complexity of the skill in these types of weaving, or indeed the very recent establishment of these in London, might explain why no English apprentices were recorded at this date. The number of stranger journeymen employed again far surpassed the number of English journeymen. Although insignificant, the employment of one English journeyman suggests that by 1593, some native craftsmen had the skill in both general and more specialized silk-weaving.

Alien silk dyers did not employ any English servants, perhaps because untrained hands could spoil expensive materials. In June 1564, for example, Paul Testelet, a stranger, gave his journeyman 'two or three blows with a little stick, one of which fell on his head, and caused him to bleed a little' for having spoilt six ounces of silk.[115] Silk dyeing was highly skilled and required careful handling of the materials – the lustre of silk could easily be lost by using the wrong chemicals or too much heat, and the silk could also be damaged by allowing it to come into contact with certain metal surfaces.[116] Silk also needed boiling to remove the natural gum before dyeing, and this was carried out by a 'silk gommer'. This also involved considerable skill because 'it was dangerous to boil off too much of the gum sericin before dyeing since the silk would be too greatly weakened, but equally bad to boil it insufficiently since the dyes could not take on the gum'.[117]

The second method to assess the significance of aliens as providers of training is to use the evidence from bindings of English apprentices. In the seventeenth century, the employment of English servants was no longer optional, but was made compulsory by the Weavers' Company. Aliens were also required to employ a greater number of English servants among their workforce, a policy rigorously enforced. On 30 March 1685, after several members of the Weavers Company complained that many foreign members now employed more French than English, 'contrary to the Ordinances', the Company instructed them to give the names of offenders, who were ordered to appear before the Court. Henry Hess appeared and 'was very sorry for his offence and pretending his ignorance by his not understanding English'. He was fined 10 shillings, and promised to conform. Peter Marishall declared he employed seven journeymen, four of whom were English, but he claimed two of them went away 'of their own accord'.[118]

Table 6.8 shows that a total of 443 alien and English servants were trained between 1662 and 1694 (with gaps). Of the 238 alien apprentices recorded, the largest number (143, or 60 per cent), as expected, were bound to other alien masters, a fair proportion (14 per cent) received training from their own fathers, and a significant proportion with English masters (61 or nearly 26 per cent). Alien silk-weavers also provided training to some 205 English apprentices during this period. If these figures are added to the 891 alien masters and journeymen working in London, then the total number of aliens working or were under training in the seventeenth century was more than 1334 people.

Table 6.8   Number of alien and English apprentices trained by aliens, 1662–94

Year	A1	A2	A3	A4	A5	A6	E1	E2	E3
			Alien apprentices				English apprentices		
1662–7	3	6	1	0	4	0	6	0	0
1668–73	25	3	1	1	1	7	62	1	0
1674–7	18	4	1	1	3	8	52	2	4
1683–5	30	11	0	5	4	9	31	1	0
1692–4	47	10	1	9	2	23	38	6	2
Total	**123**	**34**	**4**	**16**	**14**	**47**	**189**	**10**	**6**

Notes: A1 = Alien apprentices bound to alien masters. A2 = Alien children bound to their fathers. A3 = Aliens now free masters but had previously been trained by aliens. A4 = Aliens being admitted as masters and had received training from aliens. A5 = Aliens now free and had received training from English masters. A6 = Alien apprentices bound to English masters. E1–3. English apprentices receiving training or had been trained by aliens

Sources: GL Weavers' Court Minutes MS4655, Vols 1–10.

Aliens, Native Weavers and the Weavers' Company

The spread of skills in silk manufacture to the wider native population had an undesirable effect on the strangers because it resulted in increased competition and the likelihood of conflict with the native weavers. Although alien silk-weavers had been working in London in large numbers since the 1560s, it appears that their presence did not arouse much native agitation until the 1590s. This suggests that native weavers may not have been involved in significant numbers in silk-weaving until this date, and therefore were not affected by the competition likely to have been posed by the strangers. The conflict between natives and strangers was exacerbated by two factors. The first was the heavy concentration of strangers in the trade – in fact, silk-weaving in London was a trade most heavily dominated by alien workers, with possibly two thousand individuals involved. Their introduction of the skills and their monopoly of these partly accounted for this domination. But modern studies have shown that the textile-related trades have been a pole of attraction for immigrants wherever they settle in the twentieth century.[119] One theory which has been put forward to explain this tendency is the 'congruence between the demand of the economic environment and informal resources of the ethnic population'.[120] The industry is organized in small production units, and requires a flexible organization of production and a large pool of cheap labour traditionally filled by women and children. The barriers to entry are low, making it particularly attractive to immigrants, as only a small amount of initial capital is required to start working. It is also one of the few industries where immigrants are not too handicapped by their limited knowledge of the native language and can increase competitiveness by exploiting the resources at their disposal – their labour – by working long, unsocial hours and all year long.[121] The second factor related to the nature of the trade itself. Weaving was a labour-intensive trade, and vulnerable to technological innovations. It was also afflicted with fluctuating and irregular demand as a result of changes in levels of income and in fashions.

The general deterioration in economic and social conditions in the 1590s appeared to have badly affected the textile related trades in London. In 1595, for example, the stranger weavers became a main target of a series of riots that rocked London. Some historians have often attributed these disturbances to xenophobia intensified by economic dislocation.[122] In 1595, the yeomen weavers sent a petition to the minister and elders of the French church in London, requesting them to exhort the French weavers to conform to local law and custom. In it, they outlined how their livelihoods were threatened by aliens in four ways: (1) aliens kept many apprentices and looms, twice or thrice as many as they ought, causing a great increase in the number of workmen; (2) aliens taught their countrymen newly come over the skills in silk-weaving, although before they tailors or cobblers, and these were able to work without having served 7–10 years' apprenticeship; (3) they set women and maids at work who, when married, passed on their skills to their husbands of different trades, and (4) they disclosed the manual processes of the weavers' craft to the clothiers, who were better able to drive hard bargains with the artisans. Aliens also undercut English weavers by accepting lower wages.[123]

While the French church could accept these grievances, the offensive and condescending way in which the petition was written caused much offence. The yeomen weavers, for example, described how the strangers were 'Christianly entertained', yet 'they live not like Strangers of another Country, nor like obedient subjects to the laws and customs of this land, nor like Christian brothers, nor like friends nor like goods neighbours'. The freemen weavers added that 'the poor Silk weavers and freedom of the city ... nourish Serpents in our bosoms, who sting us to the very heart'. The freemen then reminded the church elders that when English Protestants had fled to Geneva during Mary's reign, its magistrates had prohibited them and other aliens from entering the market until ten o'clock in the morning.[124] The City governors found the pamphlet unacceptable. The Lord Mayor ordered an immediate investigation to find the culprits. In his report to the Lord Treasurer on 27 June 1595, he stated that he had arrested 15 people for examination. From the interrogation, he was able to ascertain that only 3 were actually responsible for the printing of the pamphlet, because the other 12 people, after having read the pamphlet, objected 'the same proceed into print'. He had sent the 3 men to prison, and ordered the other 11 men to 'take bond jointly and severally'. He also reported that it was originally intended that 40 copies would be printed, of which 11 were to be delivered to the French church, and one copy each to the Dutch church, the Lord Mayor, and the Aldermen. In fact, only 22 copies were printed, and he had already managed to confiscate 19 copies, but had not found the other 3 copies. Finally, he reported that the freemen had substantially altered the form of the pamphlet.[125] This incident shows that there were acceptable channels of redress of grievances, and the City governors took a firm line on those who transgressed. This clear demarcation may explain why there were plenty of complaints and libels but little bloodshed on the streets of the capital.

In the early seventeenth century, in addition to the controversy over the admission of strangers, the debate over technological innovation also preoccupied members of the Weavers' Company. In 1635, English weavers, among whom were some 1400 freemen, again sent a petition to the elders of the French and Dutch churches, penning four main grievances: (1) the great number of strangers who daily flocked to the city, and none of them had served the trade but were taught by stranger weavers to weave, and in short time became weavers, journeymen, masters and householders; (2) aliens employed youths aged 15–18 years with no skills in the trade, and this had caused much discontent among English youths who were bound as apprentices until they were 24, and were not allowed to take wages until then, and (3) aliens lived far more cheaply, with several families in one house, and since they had work carried out by unqualified labour, they were able to charge less, and therefore managed to get all the work from freemen who had to contribute to all public charges and expenses. When the bailiffs and the warden of the company conducted searches, they 'shut their doors against them and so remain here amongst us seven, eight or nine years without government, and when they are touched with a warrant to come before a justice, they fly to the Church for refuge'.[126] But the most serious grievance at this date was the introduction of an engine loom, with 16, 20 or 24 shuttles, enabling one man to do as much as eight men working on single looms in a day.[127] English weavers claimed that the use of such looms had robbed an estimated 486 weavers of work, and deprived 2000 native children between the ages of 7 and 12 of employment, as well as 'divers old men'.[128] According to the complainants, the products of such looms were poorly made and therefore injured consumers and undermined trade. They also claimed that the engine loom had been invented in Holland, where the government had quickly prohibited it for reasons of employment.[129] Complaints also cast doubts on the character of the incoming aliens:

> divers aliens come from beyond the seas and work in London, few or none of them having served for the trade of weaving, Neither have they any Certificate of what religion they are or of their learning the said trade, or of their good behaviour, or of their honest departure out of their own Country.[130]

The failure of the Weavers' officers to suppress the engine looms may have contributed to the riots of 1675. The disturbances began on 9 August, when groups of between 30 and 200 people destroyed looms throughout the metropolis, and they continued through to 13 August, when royal guards finally restored order.[131]

Debates among members of the Weavers' Company show that there were serious divisions within the Company. Their members, for example, complained against their governors (the Bailiffs, Wardens and Assistants) because they 'agree and take five pounds of *any* and *every stranger* [my italics] to make them bretheren of the Company'.[132] During King Charles's reign, the Weavers' officers became the focus of complaints from the Company's members. They accused the officers of profiting from putting their personal interests ahead of the Company. Joe Ward argues that this accusation may be unfair, as the officers were highly responsive to calls for reform and took steps to protect the interests of their members by inspecting the looms of strangers, monitoring the activities of strangers, and co-operating with the City and Crown to minimize the threat immigrants posed to freemen's economic rights.[133] This perception illustrates that the attitudes of the weavers towards the strangers were ambivalent and were influenced by their economic position within the Company. Some weavers may have profited from developments that reduced production costs, such as growing numbers of artisan weavers and the introduction of engine looms, while others may have suffered economically as a result of such innovations.[134]

Conclusion

The diffusion of the silk industry from China to Europe spanned over ten centuries. The Europeanization of silk production itself took six centuries to complete as a result of considerable obstructions to its distribution outside its first port of call in Europe – Italy. Trade as well as involuntary migration accelerated its dispersion within and outside Italy from the fifteenth century.

The foundation of the English silk industry during the second half of the sixteenth century owed much to the arrival of refugees, particularly the Walloons. Some of these refugees may not have been conversant in silk manufacture, but had developed this skill in London, in response to available opportunities and constraints. Strong social networks, forged and strengthened by socialization at the Stranger Churches, as well as residential congregations, helped the rapid dissemination of skills among the immigrants, especially among the smaller group of French-speaking Walloons with cohesive business and familial ties. Inter-group diffusion combined with continuous large-scale Continental immigration and the provision of training to native workers, ensured the rooting of the embryonic silk industry in London during the seventeenth century.

Contrary to the popular perception of a binary process of transfer, there were in fact three stages involved: transfer of skills from the southern Netherlands to London, spread of skills among the French-speaking community, and diffusion from immigrants to the native population. In the end, the successful transfer of the silk industry in London depended as much on the indispensable supply of foreign workers and their skills as on the quintessential role of consumer demand.

Notes

1. D. Kuhn, *Textile Technology: Spinning and Reeling*, Vol. 5, Part IX (Cambridge, 1988), pp. 421–2.
2. See M.F. Mazzaoui, 'Artisan migration and technology in the Italian textile industry in the late Middle Ages (1100–1500)', in R. Comba, G. Piccinni and G. Pinto, eds, *Strutture familiari epidemie migrazioni nell'Italia medievale* (Edizioni Scientifiche Italiane, 1984), p. 519.
3. A. Latour, 'Ceremonial Velvets', *Ciba Review*, February 1953, Vol. 96, p. 3458; S. Ciriacono, 'Silk Manufacturing in France and Italy in the XVIIth Century: Two Models Compared', *Journal of European Economic History*, 1981, Vol. 10, p. 193.
4. The following articles deal with their broad origins: S.R. Warner, 'The silk industry: Historical notes on the origins of silk production and manufacture and on the English silk industry', CLRO Research Paper, Box 5.18, 1956; G.B. Hertz, 'The English silk industry in the Eighteenth Century', *English Historical Review*, 1909, Vol. 24, pp. 710–27.
5. R. Davis, *The Rise of the Atlantic Economies* (London, 1973), pp. 204–5.
6. C.G.A. Clay, *Economic Expansion and Social Change: England 1500–1700*, Vol. 2, (Cambridge, 1984), p. 39.
7. G. Unwin, *The Gilds and Companies of London* (London, 1938), p. 246; E. Kerridge, *Textile Manufactures in Early Modern England* (Manchester, 1985), p. 126.
8. Kuhn, *Textile Technology*, pp. 418–21; M. Postan and E.E. Rich, eds, *Trade and Industry in the Middle Ages,: The Cambridge Economic History of Europe*, Vol. 2 (Cambridge, 1952), pp. 308–9; see also H. van der Wee, 'Structural changes in European long-distance trade, and particularly in the re-export trade from south to north, 1350–1750', in J.D. Tracy, ed, *The Rise of Merchant Empires: Long-distance Trade in the Early Modern World, 1350–1750* (Cambridge, 1993), pp. 24–5.
9. Mazzaoui, 'Artisan migration and technology', p. 525.
10. See ibid., pp. 525–6. The article also discusses the means by which Italian cities sought to entice silk-workers, including financial subsidy, safeguards against repatriation, grant of fiscal and legal benefits such as exemption from taxes, citizenship status, and free entry into guilds: see pp. 522–3.
11. Postan and Rich, eds, *Trade and Industry in the Middle Ages*, pp. 351, 352, 329.
12. D. Sella, 'European Industries, 1500–1700', in *The Fontana Economic History of Europe: The Sixteenth and Seventeenth Centuries*, Vol. 2, C. Cipolla, ed., (Hassocks, 1977), p. 404.
13. H. van der Wee, *Urban Industrial Development in the Low Countries During the Late Middle Ages and Early Modern Times* (Working Papers in Economic History, No. 179, 1994), p. 2.
14. J. Vermault, 'Structural Transformation in a Textile Centre: Bruges from the sixteenth to the nineteenth century', in H. van der Wee, ed., *The Rise and Decline of Urban Industries in Italy and in the Low Countries* (Leuven, 1988), pp. 191–2.
15. H. Soly and A.K.L. Thijs, 'Nijverheid in de Zuidelijke Nederlanden', in *Nieuwe Algemene Geschiedenis der Nederlanden*, Vol. VI (Haarlem, 1981), p. 43.
16. L. Guicciardini, *Description de Tout le Pais Bas* (Antwerp, 1568), p. 295.
17. See A.K.L. Thijs, *Van 'Werkwinkel' tot 'Fabriek': De textielnijverheid te Antwerpen, einde 15de-begin 19 de eeuw* (Antwerp, 1987); *De zijdenijverheid te Antwerpen in de zeventiende eeuw* (Pro Civitate, Historische Uitgaven, Reeks in Vol. 8, No. 23, 1969); 'De zijdenverheid te Antwerpen in de zeventiende eeuw', *Tijdschrift voor Geschiedenis*, Vol. 79 (1966), pp. 386–406.
18. J.A. Goris, *Etude sur les colonies marchandes mérdionales (portugais, espaguols, italiens)à Anvers de 1488 à 1567* (Leuven, 1925), p. 441.
19. H. van der Wee, *The Growth of the Antwerp Market and the European Economy*, Vol. 2 (The Hague, 1963), p. 258. The silk industry was significant in Antwerp, employing

more than 4000 people in 1584. Assuming that on average three persons were required to work on each loom, there were 1333 looms at work in 1584. On average, 1 ell was woven per day per loom, and assuming 264 days a year, the total annual production of Antwerp silk-weaving may have come to 351 912 ells. See Thijs, *Van 'Werkwinkel' tot 'Fabriek'*, pp. 125–6.
20 A.K.L. Thijs, 'Les textiles au marche anversois au XVIe siècle', in E. Aerts and J.H. Munro, eds, *Textiles of the Low Countries in European Economic History: Proceedings of the Tenth International Economic History Congress, Leuven, August 1990* (Leuven, 1990), p. 80.
21 For further information on the silk industry in Amsterdam, see L. van Nierop, 'De zijdenijverheid van Amsterdam historisch geschetst', *Tijdschrift voor Geschiedenis*, Vol. 45, 1930, pp. 18–40, 151–72; Vol. 46, 1931, pp. 28–55, 113–143; 'De bruidegoms van Amsterdam', *Tijdschrift voor Geschiedenis*, Vol. 49, 1934, pp. 329–44; Vol. 52, 1937, pp. 144–62; J.H. Hofenk de Graaf, *Geschiedenis van de textieltechniek: lakennijverheid – Sitsen – Zijde-industrie* (Amsterdam, 1992), pp. 131–236.
22 N.B. Harte, 'State Control of Dress and Social Change in Pre-industrial England', in D.C. Coleman and A.H. Johns, eds, *Trade, Government and Economy in Pre-industrial England: Essays Presented to F.J. Fisher* (London, 1976), pp. 139–40; C. Breward, *The Culture of Fashion: A New History of Fashionable Dress* (Manchester, 1995).
23 Harte, 'State Control of Dress', p. 141.
24 BL, Lansdowne MS 94/37.
25 C. Wilson, 'Cloth Production and International Competition in the Seventeenth Century', *Economic History Review*, 1960–61, Vol. 13, p. 210; D.C. Coleman, 'An Innovation and its Diffusion: The "New Draperies"', *Economic History Review*, 1969, Vol. 22, p. 425.
26 Sella, 'European Industries, 1500–1700', p. 376.
27 P. Stubbes, *The Anatomie of Abuses* (London, 1583), p. 10.
28 The following discussion is based on V. Harding, 'Some Documentary Sources for the Import and Distribution of Foreign Textiles in Later Medieval England', *Textile History*, 1987, Vol. 18, pp. 213–14.
29 Ibid., pp. 214.
30 A provisional list of London merchants who had accounts with the Milanese bank Filippo Borremei and Company of London between 1436 and 1439 has been compiled by Mr J.L. Bolton of the Borromei Bank Research Project at Queen Mary, University of London. He has been given permission to use the bank's ledger, Archivio Borromei dell' Isola Bella Libro Mastro No. 7, by the famiglia Borromeo-Arese.
31 H.L. Bradley, 'Italian Merchants in London, 1350–1450' (University of London unpublished PhD thesis, 1992), pp. 244–6.
32 M.K. Dale, 'The London Silkwomen of the Fifteenth Century', *Economic History Review*, (1933), Vol. 4, pp. 324–35.
33 M. Howell, 'Women, the Family Economy, and the Structures of Market Production in Cities of Northern Europe during the late Middle Ages', in B.A. Hanawalt, ed., *Women and Work in Pre-industrial Europe* (Bloomington, IN, 1986), pp. 198–222.
34 K. Lacey, 'The Production of "Narrow Ware" by Silkwomen in Fourteenth and Fifteenth Century England', *Textile History*, 1987, Vol. 18, p. 193.
35 Harding, 'Some Documentary Sources for the Import and Distribution of Foreign Textiles', p. 213.
36 Statutes of the Realm, 33 Henry VI, Cap. V.
37 Dale, 'The London Silkwomen of the Fifteenth Century', p. 332.
38 J. Ashelford, *A Visual History of Costume: The Sixteenth century* (London, 1983), p. 12.
39 The main fabrics were cambrics, lawns, sarcenets, satins, taffetas, tuftaffetas and velvets.
40 BL, Harleian MS 1878/82v.
41 BL, Harleian MS 1878/78; SP12/284/9; SP12/200/25 (1587).

42 L. Stone, 'The anatomy of the Elizabethan aristocracy', *Economic History Review*, 1948, Vol. 18, pp. 5–6.
43 See *Hist. MSS Com. Hatfield*, XII, pp. 75–6; PRO SP12/275/142I.
44 BL, Harleian MS 1878/78.
45 CLRO JOR 20, ff. 140v–143 (June 1574).
46 *Hist. MSS Com., Salisbury*, IV, p. 91.
47 Quoted from J.P. Collier, ed., *The Egerton Papers: A Collection of Public and Private Documents, chiefly illustratve of the times of Elizabeth and James I from the original documents* (Camden Society, old series, Vol. 12, 1840), p. 247.
48 *Hist. MSS Com. Salisbury*, XIV, p. 190.
49 *State Papers Domestic 1591–4*, p. 523.
50 CLRO, Book of Fines, 1517–1628.
51 *Hist. MSS Com. Salisbury*, XIV, p. 190.
52 There are two figures for 1593: one Return recorded 192 masters and 330 servants, but this excluded those in the suburbs; the other Return recorded 376 masters, and this included those in the City and suburbs.
53 Wrightson calculated that the average household size was 4.85 in 1557 (Norfolk) and 4.75 in 1599 (Middlesex), see K. Wrightson, *Earthly Necessities: Economic Lives in Early Modern Britain, 1470–1750* (London, 2002), p. 31. Littleton found that the average household size of French church members was 4.8 persons, with most households consisting of a stranger couple with an average of 1.9 children and 1.2 servants. See Littleton, 'Social interaction of aliens in late Elizabethan London', p. 152.
55 Lustrings were broad silks woven double or treble in the weft, and given a high gloss by special rolling and finishing. Kerridge, *Textile Manufactures*, p. 129.
56 Ibid., pp. 126–7.
57 N.K.A. Rothstein, 'The Silk Industry in London, 1702–1766' (University of London unpublished MA thesis, 1961), pp. 250–51.
58 The Book of Fines recorded offences committed by aliens and the fines paid.
59 CLRO Book of Fines 1517–1628.
60 Kerridge, *Textile Manufactures*, pp. 126–9.
61 GL, MS4655/1/f. 4.
62 GL, MS4647, f. 355.
63 GL, Weavers' Company, Ordinance and Record Book 1577–1641, MS4647/f. 355.
64 Brussels: AGR, CT MS 155; MS 315A, MS 315 bis.
65 G.W. Clark, 'An Urban Study During the Revolt of the Netherlands: Valenciennes 1540–1570', (University of Columbia unpublished PhD thesis, 1972), pp. 29, 32.
66 Ibid., p. 20.
67 A.C. Duke, 'Building Heaven in Hell's Despite: The Early History of the Reformation in the Towns of the Low Countries', in A.C. Duke and C.A. Tamse, eds, *Britain and the Netherlands: Papers Delivered to the Seventh Anglo-Dutch Historical Conference*, Vol. VII (The Hague, 1981), pp. 68–71.
68 R.S. DuPlessis, 'The light woollens of Tournai in the sixteenth and seventeenth centuries', in E. Aerts and J.H. Munro, eds, *Textiles of the Low Countries in European Economic History: Proceedings of the Tenth International Economic History Congress, Leuven, August 1990* (Leuven, 1990), pp. 66–75.
70 Karel Degryse, *Pieter Seghers. Een koopmansleven in troebele tijden* (Antwerp, Baarn, 1990), pp. 110–11. I am grateful to Raymond Fagel for this reference.
71 Rothstein, 'The Silk Industry in London', p. 28. In a recent study of the Huguenot silk-weavers in Spitalfields, Mary Bayliss also shows that many changed their occupations, see 'The unsuccessful Andrew and other Ogiers: A study of failure in the Huguenot community', in R. Vigne and G. Gibbs, eds, *The Strangers' Progress: Integration and Disintegration of the Huguenot and Walloon Refugee Community, 1567–1889* (Proceedings of the Huguenot Society, Vol. 26, 1995), p. 231.

72 G. Marnef, 'Antwerpen in Reformatietijd: Ondergronds Protestantisme in een internationale handelsmetropool, 1550–1577' (University of Leuven unpublished PhD thesis, 1991), Vol. 2, p. 112.
73 Brussels: AGR, Conseil des Troubles, MS 19, ff. 113, 134; MS 21(2), ff. 302, 317, 317v, 400, 402; Antwerp Stadsarchief, *Certificateboeken* 28 (1568), 30 (1569); Satijn-, Caffa- en Boratwerkers A 4424, A4425. The names of silk-workers from Antwerp have also been checked in sources such as the summon lists in the Conseil des Troubles Archive, *Certificatieboeken* and records of the guild Satijn-, Caffa- en Boratwerkers in the Antwerp Stadsarchief, to establish their previous occupations in Antwerp. However, none of the names listed could be traced in these records.
74 AGR, Conseil des Troubles, MS 18, ff. 9v–11v; MS 20, ff. 153–4; MS 155, ff. 116-.
75 See Spicer, *The French-speaking Reformed Community*, pp. 2–4, 10–12, 29. They were present in Southampton in December 1567, but by 1568 were recorded as living in London.
76 See PRO E190/5/5 (1571), f. 12, 12v, 41.
77 PRO Prob 11/55 (1573).
78 Quoted in Spicer, *The French-speaking Reformed Community*, pp. 38, 114n.
79 Scouloudi, *Returns of Strangers in the Metropolis*, p. 82.
80 PRO SP12/82/ f. 118.
81 A. Pettegree, 'The French and Walloon Communities in London, 1550–1688', in O.L. Grell, J.I. Israel and N. Tyacke, eds, *From Persecution to Toleration: The Glorious Revolution and Religion in England* (Oxford, 1991), p. 83.
82 A.P. Spicer, 'The French-speaking Reformed Community and their Church in Southampton, 1567–c.1620' (University of Southampton unpublished PhD thesis, 1994), pp. 18–26; idem, 'The Sohiers of Valenciennes and Southampton: A Walloon family in the Diaspora', *Proceedings of the Huguenot Society*, 1990, Vol. 25, pp. 157–166; idem, 'A process of gradual assimilation: The exile community in Southampton, 1567–1635', in R. Vigne and G. Gibbs, eds, *The Strangers' Progress: Integration and Disintegration of the Huguenot and Walloon Refugee Community, 1567–1889: Essays in Memory of Irene Scouloudi* (Proceedings of the Huguenot Society, Vol. 26, 1995), pp. 186–98.
83 For an interesting discussion of these issues, see R. Waldinger, et al., 'Ethnic business and occupational mobility in advanced societies', *Sociology*, 1985, Vol. 19, p. 589.
84 F. Consitt, *The London Weavers' Company* (Oxford, 1933), p. 313.
85 French Protestant Church of London, Soho Square, MS 194, f. 10v, 11, 14, 22v, 45, 88, 123v, 125v.
86 GL, Comm. 1596, MS 9171/18, ff. 287–9. See also A. Pettegree, '"Thirty years on": Progress towards integration amongst the immigrant population of Elizabethan London', in J. Chartres and D. Hey, eds, *English Rural Society, 1500–1800: Essays in Honour of Joan Thirsk* (Cambridge, 1990), p. 307.
87 Kirk and Kirk, eds, *Returns of Aliens*, Vol. 1, p. 391, Vol. 3, p. 386.
88 This is in comparison to only 4 per cent of native Londoners. In St Giles Cripplegate, of 2477 occupations taken from Parish Burial Registers between 1561 and 1606, 97, or 4 per cent, were described as silk-weavers; in St Olave Southwark, of 2405 occupations taken from burial registers between 1583 and 1593, 97, or 4 per cent, were described as silk-weavers. See GL, MS 6419/1; GLRO, MS P71/OLA/9.
89 W.C. Waller, *Extracts from the Court Books of the Weavers Company of London, 1610–1730, made and edited for the Huguenot Society of London*, Huguenot Society Publications, Vol. 33, 1931, pp. xvii–xviii.
90 GL, MS4655/9/ f. 12, ff. 37-8.
91 GL, Weavers' Company, Ordinance and Record Book 1577–1641 MS4647/f. 248.
92 Waller, *Extracts from the Court Books of the Weavers Company*, pp. 47–8.
93 Ibid., p. 9.

94 Ibid., p. xii.
95 Ibid., p. xiii.
96 Ibid., p. xiii.
97 N. Rothstein, 'Canterbury and London: The Silk Industry in the Late Seventeenth Century', *Textile History*, 1989, Vol. 20, No. 1, pp. 36–7.
98 F.W. Cross, *History of the Walloon and Huguenot Church at Canterbury*, Huguenot Society Publications, Vol. 15, 1898, p. 200.
99 Rothstein, 'Canterbury and London', p. 42.
100 Cross, *History of the Walloon and Huguenot Church at Canterbury*, p. 201.
101 Rothstein, 'Canterbury and London', pp. 42–3.
102 S. Ciriacono, 'Silk Manufacturing in France and Italy in the XVIIth Century: Two Models Compared', *Journal of European Economic History*, 1981, Vol. 10, No. 1, p. 169.
103 Ciriacono, 'Silk manufacturing in France and Italy', pp. 169–70.
104 Ibid., pp. 191–2.
105 A. Plummer, *The London Weavers' Company, 1600–1970* (London, 1972), p. 156.
106 V. Barbour, *Capitalism in Amsterdam in the 17th century* (Baltimore, 1950), p. 62.
109 W. Page, ed., *Letters of Denization and Acts of Naturalization for Aliens in England, 1509–1603*, Huguenot Society Publications, Vol. 8, 1893, p. li.
110 J.H. Hessels, ed., *Ecclesiae Londino-Batavae Archivum, Epistulae et Tractatus* (Cambridge, 1889–97, 3 vols), Vol. 3, No. i, [1287], pp. 963–4.
111 CLRO, Letter Book TT, f. 35. In 1664, Thomas Mun claimed that silk winding and twisting provided employment for 'fourteen thousand souls'. See T. Mun, *England's Treasure by Forraign Trade* (Oxford, 1664), p. 11.
112 S.R. Walker, 'The Silk Industry. Historical Notes on the Origins of Silk Production and Manufacturers and the English Silk Industry', CLRO; Research Paper Box 5.18, p. 3.
113 D.C. Coleman, *Courtaulds, An Economic and Social History: The Nineteenth Century Silk and Crape* (Oxford, 1969), p. 13.
114 Quoted in W.M. Jordan, 'The Silk Industry in London, 1760–1830' (University of London MA thesis, 1931), pp. 8–9.
115 Cottret, *The Huguenots in England*, pp. 242–3.
116 See Rothstein, 'The Silk Industry in London', p. 241; Jordan, 'The Silk Industry in London, 1760–1830', pp. 8–9; A.L. Gutmann, 'Social Organization of Cloth-making', *Ciba Review*, Vol. 2, October 1938, pp. 478–9.
117 Rothstein, 'The Silk Industry in London', p. 241.
118 GL, MS 4655/9/, ff. 61–2.
119 See M. Morokvasic, R. Waldinger and A. Phizacklea, 'Business on the Ragged Edge: Immigrant and Minority Business in the Garment Industries of Paris, London, and New York', in R. Waldinger, H. Aldrich and R. Ward, eds, *Ethnic Entrepreneurs: Immigrant Business in Industrial Societies* (London, 1990), p. 157.
120 Quoted in C.K. Bun and O.J. Hui, 'The many faces of immigrant entrepreneurship', in R. Cohen, ed, *The Cambridge Survey of World Migration* (Cambridge, 1995), p. 524.
121 M. Morokvasic, 'Immigrants in the Parisian Garment Industry', *Work, Employment and Society*, (1987), Vol. 1, pp. 444, 451–2; Bun and Hui, 'The many faces of immigrant entrepreneurship', p.524.
122 J. Ward, *Metropolitan Communities: Trade Guilds, Identity, and Change in early Modern London* (Stanford, CT, 1997), p. 126.
123 Consitt, *The London Weavers' Company*, pp. 148–9; Waller, *The Weavers Company*, p. xv.
124 Printed in Consitt, *The London Weavers' Company*, pp. 312, 313–4; also discussed in Ward, *Metropolitan Communities*, pp. 126–7.
125 Printed in Consitt, *The London Weavers' Company*, pp. 317–18.
126 GL, MS4647, f. 298.
127 GL, MS 4647, ff. 144–9, ff. 228–9, ff. 257–8; ff. 296–8.
128 GL, MS4647, f. 359.

129 Ward, *Metropolitan Communities*, p. 128.
130 GL, MS 4647/f. 300.
131 Ward, *Metropolitan Communities*, pp. 136–8.
132 GL, MS4647/f. 251.
133 Ward, *Metropolitan Communities*, pp. 130–42.
134 Ibid., p. 142.

Table 6.9   Stages of silk manufacture in London, 1571 & 1593

Activities	1571 (City) (1) No. of HH[b]	%	No. Svnt[c]	1593 (City) (2) No. of HH	%	No. Svnt[d]	1593 (City)[a] (3) No. of HH	%	No. Svnt
Preparatory									
Silk dress	—	—	—	1		1	—		—
Silk spinners	2		—	1		6	—		—
Silk throwsters	1		—	7		61	—		—
Silk twisters	11		6	4		3	20		—
Silk winders	4		—	14		—	32		—
Spinsters of silk works	—		—	—		—	61		—
Sub-total	18	10	6	27	15	71	113	30	—
Weaving									
<u>Narrow</u>									
Silk fringe maker	1		—	—		—	—		—
Silk lace maker	2		—	1		—	1		—
Silk rash weaver	—		—	—		—	1		—
<u>Broad</u>									
Lustringmaker	1		—	—		—	—		—
Silk weavers	149		42	120		180	219		—
Taffeta weavers	—		—	22		29	13		—
Tuftaffeta weavers	—		—	4		10	6		—
Velvet weavers	—		—	7		27	1		—
Sub-total	153	83	42	154	79	246	241	64	—
Finishing									
Silk gummer	—		—	1		3	1		—
Silk dyers	5		5	7		6	11		—
Cutters of velvet	—		—	—		—	1		—
Sub-total	5	3	5	8	4	9	13	4	—
Miscellaneous									
Miscellaneous	—		—	2		4	—		—
Silk 'trussers'	—		—	—		—	7		—
Silk workers	7		1	1		—	—		—
Silk workers on frame	—		—	—		—	2		—
Sub-total	7	4	1	3	2	4	9	2	—

Silk Industry 215

| Total | | 183 | 100 | 54 | 192 | 100 | 330 | 376 | 100 | — |

Notes: a = City wards, Middlesex and Surrey; b = heads of stranger households; c = includes only stranger servants; d = includes both English and stranger servants. Processes of silk manufacture are shown in Appendix 5.
Sources: Column 1, Kirk & Kirk, *Returns of Aliens*; Column 2, Scouloudi, *Returns of Strangers*; Column 3, Ellesmere MS 2514.

Table 6.10 Regions of origin and period of arrival of alien silk workers in London, 1571

Regions	Period of Arrival					Total %	
	1501–40	1540–59	1560–65	1566–71	Unknown	Silkworkers	All HH
Dutch/Flemish/German							
N Netherlands	—	1	1	2	1	3.0	8.0
Brabant	1	—	2	6	—	5.0	11.0
Flanders	—	3	3	29	—	19.0	15.0
Dutch	—	5	8	20	4	20.0	13.0
Sub-total	1	9	14	57	5	47.0	47.0
French							
French	1	1	1	3	—	3.0	5.0
Walloon provinces	1	6	12	34	1	30.0	9.0
France	—	4	4	3	—	6.0	6.0
Sub-total	2	11	17	40	1	39.0	20.0
Iberian & Italian							
Italy	—	1	—	3	—	2.0	3.8
Spain	—	—	1	—	—	1.0	0.9
Sub-total	—	1	1	3	—	3.0	5.0
Others							
Scotland/Miscellaneous[1]	—	1	—	—	—	1.0	17.0
Unidentified places	—	1	1	1	—	2.0	1.0
Origin not given	—	—	—	14	3	9.0	10.0
Sub-total	—	2	1	15	3	11.0	28.0
Total	3	23	33	115	9	100.0	100.0

Notes: [1] Regions with no silk workers have been grouped under 'miscellaneous' (Germany, Rhineland, Portugal)
Sources: Kirk & Kirk, *Returns of Aliens*

Table 6.11 Regions of Origin and period of arrival of alien silk workers in London, 1593

Regions	1540–59	1560–71	1572–83	1584–93	Unknown	Total % Silkworkers	All HH
Dutch/Flemish/German							
N Netherlands	—	—	2	3	—	3.0	5.0
Brabant	—	2	3	11	2	9.0	15.0
Flanders	—	6	9	4	2	11.0	14.0
Dutch	1	—	2	1	1	3.0	11.0
Rhineland	—	—	2	1	—	1.0	9.0
Sub-total	1	8	18	20	5	27.0	54.0
French							
French	3	1	—	2	—	3.0	3.0
Walloon areas	2	16	33	33	15	52.0	18.0
France	—	5	8	7	2	11.0	13.0
Sub-total	5	22	41	42	17	66.0	34.0
Iberian & Italian							
Italy	—	1	—	2	—	2.0	3.0
Spain	—	—	—	—	—	—	0.3
Sub-total	—	1	—	2	—	2.0	3.0
Scotland/England	—	—	—	—	1	0.5	1.4
Switzerland/Miscellaneous[1]	—	—	—	1	—	0.5	1.8
Unidentified places	—	—	—	2	1	1.5	2.2
Not given	—	1	2	1	1	3.0	3.3
Sub-total	—	1	2	4	3	5.0	9.0
Total	6	32	61	68	25	100.0	100.0

Notes: [1] Regions with no silk workers have been grouped under 'miscellaneous' (Germany)
Sources: Scouloudi, *Returns of Strangers*

Table 6.12 Individual alien silk workers in London, 1594–5

Name	No. of looms	Place of origin	Arrival in London	Denizen	Place of Residence
Jacques CEMBRONC	7	French/Walloon	1584		
John CASHER	6	Lille	1572		
Adrian de CROOK	7				
Jacques DEHOOK	6				
Peter DEMEAR	7	Burgundy	1561		Broad Street Ward
Guillam DEWISE Apostle	6	Amiens	1573	no	St Thomas
Michaell FEVER	9	Hainaut	1560	yes	Vintry Ward
Anthony GANIO	6				
John & Son de HOOGRE	12				
Roame de HOOGRE	12				
Jacques HUFFAUM	7				
Adrian LECH	6				
Guillam de SAGE	5				
Daniell SALAMBY	6				
Haunce van SPEARE	7	Oudenaarde			
Chosen VANDERBECK	7	Maastricht	1581		Aldgate Ward
Dennis VIALL	12	Normandy	1561	yes	Broad Street Ward

Sources: GL, Weavers' Company, MS 4647 Book 3, ff.121–3 (Details relating to the number of looms), (also printed in Consitt, p. 312 but several names are inaccurately transcribed); Kirk & Kirk, *Returns of Aliens* (1571); Scouloudi, *Returns of Strangers* (1593).

Chapter 7

Silver Trade

Overview

The London silver trade experienced a profound transformation between the sixteenth and eighteenth centuries, changing from an importer to an exporter of precious metals. While in the sixteenth and seventeenth centuries a higher premium was placed on silver works made abroad (Cardinal Wolsey had to send to Bruges for candelabra, and James I paid far more for Nuremberg plate than that produced at home), or those manufactured by foreign craftsmen working in the capital, by the eighteenth century London goldsmiths had built up a sufficiently credible international reputation to elicit regular orders from the rulers of Russia and Portuguese noblemen.[1] Yet much 'English' silverware supplied to the Russian Imperial family in the eighteenth century was made in London by Huguenots,[2] suggesting a continued reliance on foreign goldsmiths.[3] But the fact that orders could be placed directly with immigrant silversmiths demonstrated the different environment in which foreigners worked in the Capital by this date. Although aliens had dominated the London silver trade since the Middle Ages, they had nevertheless formed a *hidden* labour force working within the framework of *wanderjahre travels*, a practice whereby journeymen travelled several years to broaden their horizons, to learn new techniques and designs, and to consolidate their skills and experience, before returning to their native city and opening their own shop. During their stay, many undertook work sub-contracted out by English masters, stamping these with their own marks. After a few years, some alien journeymen returned to the Continent, leaving very few visible traces of their presence. But by providing a skilled and flexible source of labour without posing competition to native craftsmen, this set-up may have encouraged continued reliance on foreigners rather than refinement of native skills. This peculiar pattern of circular migration was both a product of the quintessential character of the silver trade, marked by its constant demand for novelties and new fashions, and the relative lack of opportunities for upward mobility for aspiring and talented journeymen in London. This hidden presence, combined with the dearth of material evidence, helps partly to explain the lack of historical research on their activities. There are a few studies covering the early periods. Reddaway and Walker have examined the presence of alien goldsmiths in the fifteenth century, but from the perspective of the

Goldsmiths' Company, while Philippa Glanville has written about sixteenth-century alien silversmiths, though her work has focused on eminent aliens and their designs and styles.[4] Joan Evans's and Hugh Tait's work on Huguenots has also devoted some attention to earlier immigrants in the trade.[5] Little attention, however, has been dedicated to the typology of earlier migrations, the skills and training of aliens, their origins, patterns of movements, role within the trade, and relationship with native goldsmiths and the Company.

The Huguenots have received a far greater historiographical attention, partly due to the copious survival of their works,[6] enabling a detailed and careful analysis of their impact. Dominated by art and design historians, the silver trade has been approached from the perspectives of general surveys,[7] and 'collections',[8] and a strong emphasis on biographies, a consequence of the focus on authorship and makers' marks,[9] and on the 'oeuvre' of leading figures like Paul de Lamerie, Paul Crespin, David Willaume, Simon Pantin, Louis Mettayer and Pierre Platel. By concentrating on these 'names', as Christopher Hartop has pointed out, we ignore the trade's complex specialization and the influence of other groups of foreign craftsmen during this period.[10] This strong historiographical bias towards the study of Huguenots consequently contributes to the oversight of the influence of other groups of foreign craftsmen in the seventeenth century, from Germany and elsewhere.[11]

These historiographical biases have meant that there are very few general surveys of the intermittent immigration of alien goldsmiths from the early sixteenth through to the seventeenth century, with the exception of Tait's article on 'London Huguenot Silver'. Only through this bird's-eye perspective can we establish the changes in the nature and patterns of migration as well as the contribution of immigrants. This chapter seeks to substantiate the view that there was a shift in the character of the incoming alien goldsmiths, from *wanderjahre* journeymen towards the permanent settlement of some eminent masters, and with it the greater degree of training provision. It has been argued that the Huguenots left an enduring legacy on the craft by 'providing a skilled and willing body of workers, [and giving] a new life to silver manufacturing in England'.[12] In addition, this chapter argues that their master status and permanent settlement made them important providers of training to their own community and English apprentices. Unlike the earlier mobile aliens who came only for a short period time before returning to the Continent, many Huguenots settled in London, and formed a permanent workforce, adding to the pool of accumulated skills in the capital. In response to the insatiable demand for 'French things', many also took on English apprentices, spreading their skills, resulting in the subsequent convergence of styles of Huguenot and English-born masters from the middle of the eighteenth century. In addition to providing a broad survey of immigration into London between the fifteenth and seventeenth centuries, using

7.1 Goldsmiths workshop
Source: Goldsmiths' Hall, London

qualitative sources such as the Goldsmiths' Company Court Minutes Books, the various listings of alien craftsmen in London and guild and civic sources in Antwerp, the chapter also explores the changes in the ways alien goldsmiths worked in London.

Demand for Silver Works in London

The demand for silver in London in the sixteenth century was immense. The concentration of wealth in London; the continued trend since the fourteenth century among the wealthy to store their wealth in plate and jewellery rather than in coin; combined with the effects of the Reformation which led to the refashioning of Mass plate into Protestant communion cups; and the surge in spending on domestic plate from those who had benefited from the redistribution of ecclesiastical property in the 1530s; are all seen by historians as significant factors in fuelling the demand for goldsmiths' works in London in this period.[13] London also housed a large number of aristocratic customers who spent considerable sums in the shops of jewellers and gold- and silversmiths. For the nobleman, possession of a splendid display of silverware was vital to his status. As Norbert Elias has commented: 'in a society where every outward manifestation of a person has special significance, expenditure on prestige and display is for the upper classes a necessity which they cannot avoid'.[14] Silver was acquired for several purposes: for ostentatious display, for dining and drinking, for lighting, for the bedroom and writing table, and from the seventeenth century, for drinking coffee, tea and chocolate,[15] and for gifts. Plate in particular was bought, given, exchanged and accumulated in great quantities. In 1589, the Countess of Rutland's New Year gifts to her friends in plate and jewellery cost her no less than £174. 6s. 8d. On New Year's Day 1578, the Queen gave away 5882 ounces of gilt plate.[16] Plate and other silverware was also acquired in great quantities by civic corporations, university colleges, the Church and landed gentry. Individuals also needed silver wares such as spoons as gifts when they were admitted into livery companies. As silver was a form of conspicuous consumption, for enhancement of status as much as for practical uses, 'designer label' and 'name recognition' were very much part of the trade, with a high premium placed on 'novelties', works of 'curious quality', or goods made and designed by craftsmen with an international reputation.

Visiting London around 1500, a Venetian visitor was struck by the abundant quantity of silver available and the high standards of craftsmanship, recording that: 'The most remarkable thing in London is the wonderful quantity of wrought silver ... In one single street named [Cheapside] leading to St. Paul's there are fifty-two goldsmith's shops, so rich and full of silver vessels, great and small, that in all the shops in Milan, Rome, Venice and Florence put together, I do not think there would be found so many of the magnificence that are to be seen in London.'[17] Another Italian, writing at the same time, described the working in wrought silver as 'very expert here [London] and perhaps the finest I have ever seen'.[18] Was this great quantity of fine wrought silver on sale in the goldsmiths' shops in Cheapside imported or manufactured in the Capital? Philippa Glanville, in her recent catalogue of the Tudor and early Stuart plate, claims that: 'English goldsmiths and their customers came into contact with foreign made silver via imported plate which was highly fashioned, inventive in form and splendid in effect, and via work made in England by foreign craftsmen.'[19] These craftsmen were probably drawn to London because of its wealth and the buoyant demand for silver to be found there. Although the poor survival rates of pre-Reformation plate render it difficult to establish the standards of English craftsmanship in this period, historians generally agree that the levels of skill demonstrated by Continental goldsmiths were higher than those of their English counterparts.

Since the Middle Ages, the leaders in the fashioning of European precious metals lay in the great towns of Flanders, Italy and Germany, where the richer, larger and more competitive market promoted higher standards than those in England. Consequently, it was these more significant centres of production which set the styles and standards for imitation elsewhere. Italian influence was paramount, and Lodovico Guicciardini unduly boasted about Italy's pedagogic role within northern art, recording in his *Description of the Low Countries* in 1567 that:

> almost all the painters, architects and sculptors [of the Low Countries] have been in Italy; some in order to learn, others to see works of ancient art and to make the acquaintance of people who excel in their profession, others to seek adventure and make themselves known. After having satisfied their desires, they return in most cases to their native country with new experience, ability, and honour; and from there they spread, having become masters, to England, all over Germany, and particularly through Denmark, Sweden, Norway, Poland and other northern countries, including even Russia, not mentioning those who go to France, Spain and Portugal.[20]

The influence, however, was reciprocal, as Flemish and Burgundian art was much admired and valued in Italy in the fifteenth and sixteenth centuries.[21] In the sixteenth century, Antwerp in particular exerted a pervasive influence on European arts.[22] Its geographical situation as a seaport, mid-way between northern and southern Europe, and its extensive trade connections brought its merchants into regular contact with the Italian seaboard cities and with the Hanse towns of the north. It therefore became a meeting point of influence from both north and south, from Italy, France and Germany. Its artists often developed their own individual style, and this was soon emulated elsewhere. From the late 1540s, European silver, especially English, was heavily influenced by designs emanating from Antwerp, characterized by strapwork and fruit motifs, and known as the 'Antwerp mannerism'. These designs were disseminated through engravings, woodcuts and the migration of Antwerp-trained goldsmiths.[23] Two surviving pieces bear these influences: the Bowes Cup (in the Goldsmiths' Hall) given to the Company in 1561 by Sir Martin Bowes, a former Lord Mayor of London and Prime Warden of the Company, and the silver-gilt Wyndham Ewer of 1554.[24]

The practice of gift-exchange among the European aristocracy and nobility also enhanced demand for products deemed 'fashionable' and of the highest standards. The apparent inability of London native goldsmiths to satisfy this demand, and the superior skills of Continental goldsmiths, had long precipitated a migration of a substantial number of these to the capital. The London Goldsmiths' Company conceded in 1607 that 'aliens and strangers [are] in better reputation and request than that of our own nation'.[25] Historians also agree that stranger goldsmiths were generally more skilled than English goldsmiths, or as Philippa Glanville put it: 'the finest craftsmen were almost certainly aliens, familiar with the newest fashion and perhaps capable of higher quality work ... than their English counterparts'.[26] Their works were likely to display more elaborate ornament and skilful execution,[27] and their higher levels of skill may explain why the Court and other wealthy consumers often employed aliens, who had specialized skills to offer such as garnishing, engraving, setting stones and making spangles.[28] This also helps to explain why, when the Brewers' Company wanted to make a standing well in 1582, it approached a stranger goldsmith to make and engrave it.[29] Ellenor M. Alcorn recently reiterated that:

> although London had a large and prolific goldsmiths' trade, some of the most skilled and innovative craftsmen working for the court in the mid-sixteenth century were aliens. Often at odds with the Worshipful Company of Goldsmiths, which sought to protect its members' interests, the aliens offered specialized skills such as engraving or casting that were in high demand by the most fashionable clientele.[30]

What factors accounted for these differences in skills? The higher levels of skills among Continental goldsmiths were due largely to the rigorous system of training imposed. Central to this was the Continental practice of *wanderjahre*. Continental journeymen were usually required to travel to different cities for four to 5 years, and to have worked with several masters before they could submit their masterpieces.[31] The formative influence of such an experience can be seen in the case of a Zürich goldsmith, Dietrich Meyer, in the seventeenth century. His first stop was Basel. Here he copied into his sketchbook patterns new to him. He then moved to Augsburg, then to Amsterdam, and back to Basel four years later. During the time of his travels, Meyer adopted the latest developments in ornamentation, and put into practice the experience of his travels when he came back to his native homeland of Zürich four years later.[32] The nature of demand in the goldsmiths' trade for a differentiated product, for 'novelties' and for works of 'curious' quality perhaps necessitated this travelling. By travelling to different countries under the system of *wanderjahre*, Continental goldsmiths were able to pick up the latest fashions and developments in the craft, and build up a collection of sketches and ideas for ornament upon which they could base their later work. Equally important, the *wanderjahre* enabled Continental goldsmiths to create a complex, self-renewing network of connections, through which fresh versions of fashionable ornaments could be shared and disseminated.[33] In the long term, Hayward believes that 'the possibility of working in widely different parts of Europe must have contributed to the development of the international style that was so characteristic of sixteenth-century goldsmiths' work'.[34] The demand for an international style, for specific designs and techniques deemed fashionable, in turn necessitated goldsmiths to travel around to learn it. The *wanderjahre*, however, did not form an integral part of craft training in England. Andrew Boorde, for example, remarked in 1544 that: 'I have travelled round about Christendom, and out of Christendom, and I did never see nor know seven Englishmen dwelling in any region beyond the sea, except merchants, students and brokers, not there being permanent nor abiding but resorting thither for a space.'[35] Consequently, English goldsmiths depended on alien goldsmiths as 'the conduit through which awareness of new waves of ornament flowed across the Channel'.[36]

The presentation of the masterpiece as a proof of skills was another distinguishing mark of Continental craft training. The making of a masterpiece was a prerequisite before many Continental goldsmiths could start working as a master.[37] In theory, London goldsmiths were also required to make a masterpiece, but in practice it was not rigidly enforced.[38] In October 1574, the Goldsmiths' Company agreed that: 'No workman apprentice in this mistery either of gold or silver … shall be suffered to keep open shop to work in or to work for himself, till he has made such a piece of work commonly called master pieces as by the judgement of the four wardens and four other good workmen of this mistery shall declare him to be no bungler but a skilful workman.'[39] However, the regulation was ineffective, as the *Order for the Masterpiece* in 1607 complained that 'very few workmen are able to furnish and perfect a piece of plate singularly … without the help of many and several hands, which inconvenience is grown by reason that many of the idler sort betake themselves to the sole practice and exercise of one slight and easy part … some to be only hammermen … work nothing but bell salts, or only bells, or only casting bottles'.[40] In other words, native goldsmiths were perceived to possess very rudimentary and basic skills. This, however, could be an indication of large-scale production and the concomitant specialization at this date rather than an overall decline in standards.

The longer periods of continental training may also have contributed to higher standards. In Ausburg, the length of training in 1593 was 12 years (six years as an apprentice and six years as a journeyman), and 14 years for foreigners.[41] In Antwerp, the average period of training was 13 years.[42] In England, the Goldsmiths' ordinance of 1469 required that apprentices should serve seven years, and in 1563, ten years.[43] However, it appears that after seven years, an apprentice was qualified, as in 1572 yeomen were allowed to take a second apprentice when their first apprentice had served seven years, and the second apprentice was to be trained up under their elder apprentice.[44] The apparently shorter period of training and the absence of *wanderjahre* may have contributed to lower standards of craftsmanship in London, and this proved a serious handicap when competing with Continental goldsmiths in the same labour market.

Alien Goldsmiths in London in the Sixteenth and Seventeenth Centuries

Immigrant goldsmiths had been working in London in large numbers since the Middle Ages, drawn to the capital by the fame of the Goldsmiths' Row in Cheapside,[45] the opulent market, the existence of an established alien community, the relative ease of travel, and to a large extent by the relative peace at a time of political and religious upheavals on the Continent. Most important, perhaps, their influx was also due to the insatiable demand for their skills. According to Hartop, the most significant groups, because of their sheer numbers, were the Protestants who came in the second half of the sixteenth century from Flanders and those who fled France at the end of the seventeenth century.[46]

Quantifying the presence of aliens is difficult, as evidence is fragmented. In the sixteenth century, it is possible to calculate the number of alien goldsmiths working in London using the evidence of admissions into the Company.

In order to obtain a licence to work, alien goldsmiths were required to produce a testimonial letter from their previous master to testify to their skills, swear to obey the Company's rules and regulations, and pay an admission fee. By counting the number of goldsmiths who took the oath and paid a fee, it is possible to estimate the number of alien goldsmiths working in London in a specific period, although admittedly this is likely to underestimate the number as some aliens inevitably failed to follow this procedure. Between 1558 and 1598, more than 500 aliens were admitted into the Company, either as journeymen or masters. This evidence thus throws up the limitations of the Returns of Aliens, which recorded only 39 masters and 38 servants in 1571, and 39 masters and 72 servants in 1593.

To establish the proportion of strangers working in precious metals requires an estimate of both the number of stranger and English-born goldsmiths working in London at any particular time. Philippa Glanville recently suggested that strangers may have accounted for 10 per cent of the total number working in this sector. As Glanville does not specify the number of stranger and English-born goldsmiths, the basis of this calculation is unclear.

In all likelihood, the proportion was greater. In 1566, the Company recorded 108 English goldsmiths (77 with shops in Cheapside, and 31 in Lombard Street). If it is assumed that each of these master goldsmiths had at least two journeymen or apprentices, then a minimum of 216 English goldsmiths and their servants were active in London in 1566.[47] Even if we accept the low estimate of 77 alien masters and journeymen in 1571, alien goldsmiths may still have formed 36 per cent of English goldsmiths in London around the 1570s.[48]

Available evidence, then, suggests that the number of Continental goldsmiths working in London increased in the early sixteenth century, peaked during Elizabeth's reign, and thereafter declined in the early seventeenth century, as shown in Table 7.1. This table does not show the periods of peak immigration into London. Using admission records, it is possible to chart the fluctuation in the number of goldsmiths accurately, as shown in Table 7.2. The number of alien goldsmiths increased dramatically after the accession of Elizabeth to the throne in 1558, and reached its peak in the turbulent period on the Continent between 1562 and 1569, when 20 goldsmiths on average were licensed annually. The ravaging civil wars in France and religious and political disturbances in the Low Countries were undoubtedly responsible for this high level of admission. The number of alien goldsmiths fell steadily after 1570, and was brought to a halt after 1624, with only one alien goldsmith being admitted during the period between 1624 and 1668. This was Francis Offley, admitted in 1633.

Admission records underestimate the number of aliens in London. Those lucky enough to gain royal appointment, for example, were not obliged to seek guild admission. Thus, between 1636 and 1668, the admission records indicate that no new aliens were admitted, but there were in fact five prominent alien goldsmiths working at the Court – Christian van Vianen, and Jean-Gérard Cockus, George Bowers, Wolfgang Howzer and Jacob Bodendick. Admission records are also silent on the number of Huguenot goldsmiths arriving in London both before and after 1685. In contrast to the Weavers' records, the Goldsmiths' Company Minute Books record no admission of Huguenots. It is possible that acquisition of naturalization or the freedom of the City, and admission into another livery company may have rendered a licence from the Company unnecessary. Pierre Harache, one of the most gifted Huguenot goldsmiths, was admitted in July 1682.[49] Joan Evans, who has consulted various sources such as indentures, apprenticeships and those based on Royal Bounty lists, has estimated that in the years just before the Revocation to 1710, there were some 120 Huguenot goldsmiths (masters, journeymen and apprentices) working in London, and a further 40 in related trades such as watch-matching, jewellery and diamond-cutting. There were ten working in other parts of

Table 7.1 Recorded numbers of alien goldsmiths working in London, 1468–1780

Date	Alien goldsmiths	Total aliens	Population of London
1458	113	c.3 400 (1483)	45 000
1535–62	232 (A)	5–6 000 (1547)	75 000
1558–98	>500 (A)	10 000 (16th century)	120 000
1615	183[1] (C)	10 000 (1621)	200 000
1621	183[1] (C)		
1627–39	>200		
1641	140[1] (C)		
1664	150 (C)		
1684–1710	120		
1710–80	223		

Notes: GC = Goldsmiths' Company. CMB = Court Minutes Book. (A) = Based on admission records. (C) = Based on Company's own estimates. [1] = includes both foreigners and aliens.
Sources: 1468: GC, CMB A, Vol. 2, ff. 120–21; 1535–62: Glanville, *Silver in Tudor and Early Stuart England*; 1558–98: L.B. Luu, 'Skills and Innovations: A Study of the Working Stranger Community in London, c. 1550–1600' (University of London unpublished PhD thesis, 1997), Chapter 7; 1615: CMB P, Part I, ff. 115v–116; 1621: PRO SP14/127/12; 1627–39: Glanville, *Silver in Tudor and Early Stuart England*, p. 94; Prideaux, *Memorials*, Vol. 1, p. 196; 1664: Court Minutes Book 4, 1663–5, f. 68v; 1684–1790: J. Evans, *Huguenot Goldsmiths in England and Ireland* (London, 1933), pp. 17–19.

England, and a further 43 in Ireland. The number of Huguenot goldsmiths rapidly increased in the next few decades, and during 1710–1780, Evans found 223 Huguenots working in the goldsmith's and jeweller's trades in London, and 78 in Dublin.[50]

In the seventeenth century, admissions of alien goldsmiths into the Company appear to have fallen drastically, and fewer entries were recorded as a result. The only evidence available on the number of alien goldsmiths is afforded by the Company's own estimates, which tended to include both aliens and foreigners (those who came from other parts of England). As these figures were produced to show the degree of competition posed by alien goldsmiths, the Company's own estimates tended to exaggerate their number in London. In 1615, for example, the Company listed 183 aliens and foreigners in London. However, a careful examination of the names on the list shows that just over half of these were aliens; the others were probably foreigners, coming from other parts of England to work in London.[51] Other sources also suggest that the actual number of Continental goldsmiths

Table 7.2 Numbers of alien goldsmiths admitted to the Goldsmiths' Company of London, 1546–1668

Date	Recorded aliens taking oaths	Aliens recorded as employing aliens	average admission per annum
1546–9	31	8	5
1550–53	24	6	6
1554–7	4	1	—
1558–61	41	10	9
1562–5	66	17	7
1566–9	88	22	6
1570–73	35	9	2
1574–8	27	7	8
1592–5	22	6	2
1596–8	12	3	3
Sub-total	350	9	48
1600–1603	8	3	
1604–7	15	5	
1608–11	3	1	
1612–15	8	3	
1616–19	12	4	
1620–23	4	1	
1624–7	0	1	
1628–31	0	0	
1632–5	1	0	
1636–68	0	0	5
Sub-total	51	—	5
Total	**401**		**53**

Sources: Goldsmiths' Hall, Court Minutes Books H–Z, 1 (1654–7), 2 (1657–60), 3 (1660–63), 4 (1663–65), 5 (1665–69)

working in London in the seventeenth century was lower than the figure produced by the Company. The Minute Books of the Goldsmiths' Company, which recorded important matters dealt with by the Wardens, mention only 83 aliens working in London between 1600 and 1668.

The fall in the number of alien goldsmiths coming to London, especially in the seventeenth century, was due to both overseas and domestic factors. With the general onset of an economic depression in Europe in the 1620s, and particularly the outbreak of civil war in England in the early 1640s, the production of plate was brought to a halt.[52] Large quantities of plate were also destroyed as corporations, the clergy and the landed gentry gave up their holdings of plate to pay for heavy taxation levied upon them to finance the huge military expenditure.[53] Moreover, during the middle of the seventeenth century, the demand for goldsmiths' skills was low and the plate produced was relatively simple, due to the unwillingness of consumers to invest heavily in 'fashioning' – the price paid for the goldsmith's work as opposed to the investment in the material itself – when it was likely that the work would soon have to be melted down in response to new tax demands.[54] On 18 January 1643, the beadle of the Goldsmiths' Company complained to the Court of Assistants that he was unable to collect quarterage from the members of the company. He said the economic crisis had taken away the goldsmiths' trade, and as a result, many shops were shut. In the last quarter, he claimed, he had made up the payments out of his own pocket.[55] However, a recovery began in 1648, but was temporarily set back by the Plague in 1665 and the Great Fire in 1666. In 1664, the Goldsmiths' Company complained that for lack of orders, many London goldsmiths did not have even one-third of a day's work.[56] Under the reign of Charles II, substantial new quantities of plate were ordered, and by the 1670s, production of plate had returned to the 1630s level.[57] This recovery was due to several factors. Charles II, during his years spent in exile on the Continent, had cultivated a luxurious taste and lifestyle, and on his return to England was notable for his extravagant ostentation. Encouraged by Royal precedent, his immediate Court circle followed suit, and they in turn influenced the rising and increasingly prosperous merchant classes. The trade was also stimulated by the elimination of punitive taxes, the large-scale disbandment of the military, and the restoration of royal favour dispersed through gifts of plate.[58]

The issue of the Edict of Nantes in 1598 and the increasing attraction of other economic centres such as Amsterdam probably also lay behind the weakened immigration flow. Wages in Amsterdam were high, and foreign silversmiths enjoyed greater freedom. Those who could prove their skill were admitted without much difficulty to the guilds.[59] Research by Briels has shown that many goldsmiths from the southern Netherlands, in particular those from Antwerp, migrated to the northern Netherlands, and settled in large numbers in Amsterdam during the late sixteenth and early seventeenth centuries. The number migrating, particularly from Antwerp, increased substantially after 1585, but fell drastically after 1605.[60] This suggests that emigration of goldsmiths from Antwerp may have dried up by the seventeenth century, when increased opportunities may have persuaded many to stay in their home city. Indeed, as Alfons K.J. Thijs has demonstrated, despite the attraction of north Netherlands cities, the number of goldsmiths in Antwerp did not diminish appreciably (from 124 in 1566 to 110 in 1584 and 90 in 1605), because there was a great demand for church plate immediately after 1585. The success of the Counter-Reformation Church stimulated demand for works of art until 1648, after which date the number of gold and silversmiths declined. In 1687, although there were still some seventy master gold and silversmiths, several of them lived 'very soberly', and after 1700, their numbers declined sharply.[61]

Origins of Aliens

Judging by the origins of immigrants, it appears that the influence on English silver shifted from Antwerp-dominated styles in the sixteenth century to Germanic and French fashions in the late seventeenth century. In the mid-sixteenth century, many Continental goldsmiths came from Antwerp, as indicated by the places of origin mentioned in the testimonial letters. Of the 64 letters brought to the Wardens of the Goldsmiths' Company from the Continent between 1546 and 1598, 39 per cent of these had been sent from Antwerp, and a further 8 per cent from Bruges. The over-representation of Antwerp in the letters testimonial may reflect not only the good lines of communication between Antwerp and London, but also the particular demand for Antwerp-trained goldsmiths in the capital, as a result of the spread of designs emanating from Antwerp.

In the seventeenth century, however, the cultural influence of Antwerp appeared to have weakened. Many newly admitted Continental goldsmiths came from German and French towns, rather than Antwerp. Of those 51 goldsmiths admitted in the early seventeenth century, the places of origins of 11 were recorded in the Minutes Books. Besides one 'Dutchman' and one from Utrecht, there were three from Germany (Ausburg, Emden and Heidelberg), and six from France (one each from Lyons and from Chartiers, and four 'Frenchman'). Other records suggest that Flemish influence was still strong. In 1617, the Dutch Church Register recorded some 24 of its members as goldsmiths, jewellers and diamond cutters, and many were recorded as having originated from Bruges, Brussels, Kortrijk, Utrecht, Ghent, Middelburg and German towns such as Augsburg, Nuremberg, Bremen and Bohemia.[62] However, both the Court Minutes and the Dutch Church records indicate clearly that Antwerp was no longer an important source of immigration by the seventeenth century. In the early seventeenth century, then, Glanville concluded that while there was a strong demand for Flemish, and German craftsmanship, there was also an increasing recognition of the special qualities of French Court goldsmiths' work.⁶³ After the Restoration, the commercial and cultural ties between the Netherlands and England encouraged Dutch influences on decorative art and designs. Dutch sources were frequently drawn on and used in the production of elaborate display plate. Between 1658 and 1670, floral motifs derived from Dutch fruit and flower paintings proved particularly popular. The predominantly Dutch influence on English goldsmiths' work was increasingly challenged by the Huguenots who began to arrive in London after 1685.⁶⁴

Conditions of Work

Letter Testimonials

Immigrant goldsmiths practising their craft in London faced a number of restrictions on their activities. First, they had to submit themselves to the jurisdiction and authority of the Goldsmiths' Company. Although the testimonial letter was essential for Continental goldsmiths to acquire a permit to work, many did not possess such a letter. The Wardens of the Goldsmiths' Company were happy to grant them a licence to work, as long as they or their masters promised to procure such a letter as soon as possible. On 24 January 1566, Heyndrick de Coninck (or Henrie Cannynge), working with Arnold Roste, an alien goldsmith, brought in his letter testimonial from his former master in Antwerp, Willem van den Heuvel, confirming that he had served a six-year apprenticeship in silversmithing with him. However, he refused to be sworn for his 'true workmanship', and subsequently was ordered by the Company to stop practising the craft.⁶⁵ In January 1570, a month after he had begun work, Jacques de la Choutiere, working with a stranger, Garrett Vandebus, was able to bring in a letter from his former master in Antwerp, Jan van Meerten, to confirm his skill.⁶⁶

The Company attached great importance to the letter testimonials, and imposed harsh punitive measures on those who failed to satisfy the requirement. In the early 1560s, a time when the Company was concerned with the excessive number of goldsmiths, and alien goldsmiths who failed to produce a letter or who showed no intention of doing so, were expelled from London. On 14 August 1562, the Wardens ordered John Allaix, a Frenchman, presumably after several warnings, 'to depart out of the city within 14 days upon pain of imprisonment. And he that after the same 14 days shall set him on work to pay for a forfeiture' of £6 13s. 4d.⁶⁷ The levy of such a massive fine discouraged alien goldsmiths from taking risks by employing alien journeymen without a letter. On 30 August 1562, for example, Guillam Lurier refused to employ a Frenchman who had no letter of testimonial.⁶⁸ The

Company also employed informers to report on those strangers who worked in London without having met this requirement,[69] and in March 1565 issued a warning to its members that if they 'set on work strangers without a letter of testimonial, they would be fined £5 or be sent to prison'.[70] It is unclear how many alien goldsmiths who failed to bring in a letter were expelled from London and how many were deterred from coming.

Despite these stringent measures, only 18 per cent of the 350 alien goldsmiths licensed between 1546 and 1598 actually succeeded in procuring a letter of testimonial, therefore, by implication, only a small proportion could prove their skill and competence. The failure of others to obtain a letter can be explained by several factors.[71] Lines of communication between London and the Continent were severely disrupted by the disturbances. Some letters took years to arrive, while others may have been lost.[72] Cornelis van Aken waited seven-and-a-half years before his letter arrived from Antwerp in December 1574, and Dirick Maior over twelve years before his letter finally arrived from Strasburg in 1574.[73] The circumstances in which the alien goldsmith left his home town may have been another factor. Before setting off from their home town for their *wanderjahre* travels, journeymen goldsmiths usually had to register the reason for their absence.[74] If the alien goldsmiths had escaped for religious or political reasons, the possibility of procuring a letter to testify to their good character was remote. The Company recognized this problem, and became more willing to accept other methods of vouching. In February 1575, the Company admitted Peter Drouet after his master in London, Antonie Godmere, confirmed that Drouet had been his apprentice in Paris, and continued to work with him here, and that he was 'an honest, true man and of good behaviour'.[75] In December 1592, Robte Raynes, a stranger, was admitted after he obtained a testimonial from the Dutch church of London.[76] In some cases, the Company seemed to believe that the strangers did not make genuine efforts to procure a letter after they had been licensed to work, and therefore in 1574 changed its policy, refusing to admit them until they had produced a letter.[77] In 1602 the French Ambassador pleaded on behalf of a goldsmith from Lyons, Jean Designes, and the company agreed to give him three months to bring in 'his letters testimonial for his good demeanour and good workmanship from Lyons'.[78]

Levels of Skills and Experience

The levels of experience among alien goldsmiths varied, depending on whether they had come as masters or journeymen. A small proportion possessed considerable experience, as they had been working as master goldsmiths for a number of years before coming to London. Adrian Brickpott, for example, worked as a master goldsmith in Antwerp before coming to London. Denys Volckarts, likewise, started work as a foreign master in Antwerp in 1562, and in March of the following year became *poorter* (citizen) of Antwerp, where he had one apprentice. By 1567, he had arrived in London.[79] In Antwerp, the majority of apprentices started their four or more years of training at the age of 12, followed by several years of *wanderjahre* with one or more masters. Most were 25 years of age by the time they had completed their training.[80] Thus both Brickpott and Volckarts probably had about thirteen years of training, plus further experience as masters, before arriving in London.

The levels of experience among alien journeymen also varied considerably. In the case of Antwerp-trained goldsmiths, some came to London straight after they had completed their apprenticeship, others after they had travelled to other places. Hans Lambrechts, for example, in January 1568 declared his intention of travelling to Germany and other countries to practise his trade. It appears that he came straight to London, as he is known to have been in London in June 1568.[81] Guilliam van Swaersvelt, on the other hand, left Antwerp in September 1568, and does not appear to have arrived in London until 1574. He had stated his intention of going to practise his trade in Augsburg and other towns in Germany, where indeed he may have spent the years 1568–74.[82] Such movement meant that the place of birth was far less significant than experience in assessing a man's likely skills and knowledge.[83]

Status

Although more skilful and more experienced, alien goldsmiths faced a number of disadvantages inherent in their status as aliens, and as a result, had few opportunities for advancement. Many alien goldsmiths had served their apprenticeship and worked for some years as journeymen, but both phases had been completed overseas. The Goldsmiths' Company had no knowledge of them, and with its various obligations to maintain standards of workmanship, was invariably suspicious of the unknown and untried newcomers.[84] In foreign soils, the unknown reputation of the newcomers meant that their opportunities for advancement were limited because the goldsmiths' trade relied on an aristocratic and elite market, and a successful goldsmith had to be far more than a good craftsman. An essential but intangible aspect of being successful was a good address, a reputation as a man of integrity and discretion, the right family network and marital opportunity, and access to consumers.[85] Many of these qualities would take years to build. An alien goldsmith could improve his chances of success by bringing in a letter of recommendation from a Continental master who possessed an international reputation, or securing employment with a prominent alien master in London, or with an English goldsmith who had a prestigious address.

On top of these obstacles, there were sundry guild and civic regulations that severely curtailed the activities of alien goldsmiths. The inability of aliens to open shops was undoubtedly serious. In 1451, English-born goldsmiths urged the Company to ensure that alien goldsmiths sold their goods only to English goldsmiths, and not to 'strangers of other crafts which they [had] done hereafore'. In 1469, the Goldsmiths Company enacted an ordinance allowing alien goldsmiths to open a shop only after they had been working as a servant for five complete years.[86] In the sixteenth century, they could theoretically open a shop as soon as they arrived, providing they were in possession of a letter of denization. In practice, the privileges conferred by the letter of denization were reduced by restrictive civic laws introduced during the 1560s, in response to rising indignation against their perceived mass influx. Adrian Brickpott, a denizen goldsmith from Antwerp, was licensed in May 1571 by the Court of Aldermen to 'open his shops windows and to work therein, so long as he sets a lattice before his shop windows according to the old orders and laws of this City'.[87] This, according to Philippa Glanville, was partly to discourage any passers-by going in and placing an order,[88] and to prevent aliens from retailing.

With the exception of Nicaise Roussel, goldsmith and engraver from Bar-en-Lisle in northern France, who lived in Trinity Lane in the City from at least 1588 until the 1620s, and was apparently successful in obtaining Court orders,[89] it appears that none of the alien master goldsmiths of the Elizabethan period were of sufficient quality and stature to elicit aristocratic heed and patronage. None received the freedom of the City through redemption. This lack of freemen among alien goldsmiths meant that they could not train the second generation, nor could they assay and touch goods at the Goldsmiths' Hall.

Unmarked silver could not be sold anywhere in England. This had several implications. To gain a livelihood, an immigrant goldsmith had to work as a journeyman in the workshop of a native English goldsmith, or induce a freeman of the Company to take in their work with his own to the Hall for assay and touch, or sell their goods to English goldsmiths.[90] In November 1575, Jacob Lyste, an alien goldsmith, sold some salts to Robert Sharpe, the owner of the 'Baskett' in the Goldsmiths' Row, who in turn sold it to an English aristocratic client.[91] Strangers could not easily evade these restrictions by settling in exempted places such as Blackfriars and St Martin-le-Grand, or in areas outside the City's jurisdiction. Their membership of the Goldsmiths' Company meant that the latter could prosecute and punish offences committed anywhere, and the high intrinsic value of goldsmiths' products meant that customers preferred to buy their goods from an established retailer with a creditable reputation, rather than from a hawker selling in an unregulated market.

The sale of unmarked silver by foreigners continued to plague the Company, but it was unanimously agreed in February 1609 that 'every foreigner and such as are not free of this company shall be debarred of assay and touch'. Those with exceptional talents were granted such a privilege. In July 1608, Rowland de Freeze, a stranger, was allowed to have his mark and the right to assay and touch because 'he has presented a great cup with a cover made after the Nuremberg fashion well liked by the wardens for the clean & fashionable workmanship'.[92] In other cases, royal intervention was necessary, but the Goldsmiths' Company protested against such moves. The Goldsmiths' Company had complained to the King in 1664 when two aliens, Wolfgang Howzer, born in Zurich, and Jacob Bodendick, native of Limburg in Germany, presented letters from the King instructing the Wardens to assay and mark their wares. The King acknowledged the reasons for the Company's reluctant agreement, adding that both men would only employ native subjects, not strangers, in their manufacture. This royal assurance was designed to allay the fears of the Company that the workshops of prosperous alien goldsmiths would employ fellow countrymen.[93]

Preponderance of Journeymen

The inability of aliens to retail meant that they could not receive direct orders or commissions from customers, and helps explain the preponderance of journeymen among the aliens working in London. Between 1546 and 1598, 398 alien goldsmiths were recorded working in London: of these, 22 per cent operated as masters, but 55 per cent were employed as journeymen, with the status of the remainder unclear, suggesting that the proportion of journeymen could be as high as 78 per cent. As expected, the largest group of journeymen (31 per cent) worked with alien masters, but the proportion working with English-born masters (24 per cent) was also significant (see Table 7.3). In contrast to the period from 1479 to 1510, when nearly all the 319 aliens who swore to observe the Company's rules took service with aliens already established in England,[94] a considerable number of alien goldsmiths found employment with English masters during Elizabeth's reign. Due to the reputation of Antwerp, Antwerp-trained goldsmiths were probably in greatest demand in Elizabethan period. Of the 45 Antwerp goldsmiths known to have been working in London during Elizabeth's reign, nearly a quarter are known to have worked with English goldsmiths at some point of their stay in London.

What was the background of the alien journeymen and of the English masters who employed them? For alien goldsmiths, there were several possible reasons why working with an English master was an attractive option. The first possible advantage, especially for those who had a shop in the Goldsmiths' Row, was a good address and business and social connections.

Table 7.3 Employment categories of alien goldsmiths in London, 1546–98

Categories	Alien goldsmiths No.	%
Masters (with servants)		
Alien goldsmiths	74	19.0
Alien goldsmiths who began their career in London as journeymen working for:		
• alien masters	5	1.0
• English masters	8	2.0
Sub-total	87	22.0
Journeyman		
Alien goldsmiths working with alien masters	122	31.0
Alien goldsmiths working with English masters	97	24.0
Sub-total	219	55.0
Unknown		
Alien goldsmiths, status unknown	92	23.0
Total	398	100.0

Sources: Goldsmiths' Company, Court Minutes Books H, I, K, L, N–O; Kirk and Kirk, eds, *Returns of Aliens*, Vol. 10, Nos 1–4 (Returns of 1568 and November 1571); I. Scouloudi, ed., *Returns of Strangers in the Metropolis.*

Equally important was the ability of English goldsmiths to own shops, where they could display their goods, and customers could come freely and place orders. The advantages were immense, for through these prestigious shops, alien goldsmiths could possibly find patrons among the well-connected and aristocratic customers who visited. Indeed, of a total of 65 English goldsmiths who employed alien goldsmiths between 1546 and 1598, 17 per cent have been identified as owners of shops in the most prestigious district of the goldsmiths' trade: in the Goldsmiths' Row, in Lombard Street and St Mathews Alley. Prominent among these were Diricke Anthony, who occupied No. 5 in the Goldsmiths' Row, and who was chief engraver to the Mint from 1551 to 1599; Francis Heaton; Edward Gylberd of No. 52, who owned the 'Ship', and Richard Hanberrie, who owned the 'Maidenhead' (see Table 7.4).[95]

Table 7.4   Prominent English employers of aliens, 1549–73

Name	Name of shop	No. of aliens employed	Date
William Bereblock	The 'Logge' and the 'Grey Houd', Cheap	1	1549
Thomas Denham	St Mathews Alley	1	1573
Diricke Anthony	The 'Queens Arms', Cheap	1	1549
Edward Gylberd	The 'Ship', Cheap	3	1566–71
Richard Hanberrie	The 'Maidenhead', Cheap	2	1567
Thomas Harryson	The 'Swan', Cheap	1	1566
Francis Heaton	The 'Tonne', Cheap	3	1566
Mr Kettelwood	Lombard Street	1	1573
Thomas Pope	Lombard Street	1	1566
John Pynfold	St Mathews Alley	1	1566
Thomas Sympson	Lombard Street	1	1568

Sources: Goldsmiths' Company, Court Minutes Book L, Part 2, Vol. 10, f. 469 (A list of Goldsmiths in Cheap, St Mathews Alley and Lombard Street); T.F. Reddaway, 'Elizabethan London – Goldmsith's Row in Cheapside, 1558–1645', *Guildhall Miscellany*, 1963, Vol. 2, pp. 181–206.

Sub-contracting

The reverse question should also be asked: what benefits did English-born goldsmiths derive from employing aliens in their workshops? Some English employers employed alien goldsmiths because they had little skill in the trade. In 1567, James Vanderaste from Antwerp was employed by Thomas Southwark in Cornhill, who had 'some skill in the workmanship of goldsmithry, keeps open a goldsmiths shop under the widow his mother, and is not yet free himself, but intends to be made free of the Merchant tailors by his fathers' companie'.[96] It is possible that Southwark's father had been a merchant tailor and his mother had subsequently married a goldsmith, as whose widow she was entitled to keep the shop, thereby enabling her son to run it. Vanderaste was well qualified for the job. Following the completion of his apprenticeship in 1563, he came to London to broaden his training, and after spending several years here, returned to Antwerp by 1577, when, presumably on his application to become a free master of the City, his master had to confirm his legitimate birth.[97] In October 1569, Thomas Southwark was recorded as working as a servant to Dionyse Volkaert, a native from Bruges who had also worked in Antwerp, presumably to learn the skills after Vanderaste had returned to Antwerp.[98] The majority of alien journeymen were probably employed as sub-contractors. Those who had shops in the Goldsmiths' Row were likely to have a large and successful business, catering for a wide range of demands, and they possibly employed alien goldsmiths to produce goods of high quality to meet the demand of their most fashionable clientele. As John Styles has pointed out, the ability to provide customers with appropriate, fashionable designs was crucial to the successful marketing of fine goldsmiths' ware.[99] Alien master goldsmiths could probably offer their customers a wider range of choice, because they usually had a collection of sketches and ideas for ornament which they had acquired during their journeyman years.[100] One way for native goldsmiths to compete with alien masters was to employ alien journeymen. This enabled them to maintain their competitiveness by increasing the range of goods and designs, and keep up with the latest Continental designs and fashion in demand.

Through the system of sub-contracting the work to alien specialists, denoted by the term 'hiring to work on their own piece', English masters could maximize the extent of their services, and minimize the cost of permanently employing a specialized workforce.[101] The system of sub-contracting meant that most strangers were not working within the workshop of an English goldsmith. Rather, the work was sub-contracted to strangers who worked in secret, or in cheaper locations. In March 1574, a Frenchman told the Company that there were 'diverse strangers goldsmiths working some within shoemakers, some within tailors, some within saddlers and other within others'.[102] A search conducted in January 1593 found a stranger 'working in a garret in a linen draper's house in St Martins'.[103] The use of a large network of specialists is symptomatic of the increasing division between manufacturers and retailers, necessitated by the growing scale of production. Its use meant that large orders could be completed quickly.

Detailed studies for the seventeenth and eighteenth centuries provide a fuller insight into the business of London goldsmiths. David Mitchell's study of Thomas Fowle is particularly illuminating.[104] Fowle had a thriving business in Fleet Street, selling plate and jewellery and providing a range of financial services to an expanding West End gentry population. Some plate was made to specific orders, which normally indicated the general type and size of the piece required, as well as details of the engraving. However, the majority of sales probably came from stock. Fowle's shop sold large plate such as chased cups, cans and tankards, chafing dishes, candlesticks, teapots, but also small, relatively cheap items of jewellery or dress and personal accessories. There were rings of several sorts; locks, corals and clasps; buttons for cuffs and buckles for shoes, and a variety of boxes – for counters, money, snuff and tobacco. Many small drinking cups were sold, as well as a large quantity of spoons (500 were sold in a three-year period). The majority of the goods were made by sub-contractors, whom he provided with raw materials. In 1664,

Fowle's Day Book lists 50 subcontractors, who either made particular items or provided specialist services such as gilding, engraving, burnishing or the repair of watches. Two of them were famous alien plate workers – Wolfgang Howzer and Jacob Bodendick.[105] Specialist sub-contractors were also used for particular types of plate, including flatware, casters, chafing dishes and snuffers, and most sub-contractors worked concurrently for several goldsmiths.[106] Helen Clifford's study of Parker and Wakelin's business in the eighteenth century also illustrates the complexity of the organization of the trade. However, as Hartop has observed, this 'complex, hidden, web of specialist workers who made up the silver trade in the seventeenth and eighteenth centuries' was previously neglected in studies focusing on makers' marks ('sponsor's mark').[107]

Training of English Servants in the Sixteenth Century

In 1444, English-born goldsmiths complained that alien goldsmiths in Southwark and Westminster took as their servants 'aliens born and never of English nation'.[108] In the twenty years between 1449 and 1469, 15 alien goldsmiths took 32 apprentices, nearly all of them boys with Dutch names.[109] By the end of the sixteenth century, this pattern seems to have been reversed. A Return of Aliens shows that in 1593, alien goldsmiths employed more English than stranger servants, and of the apprentices bound to them, all were English (see Table 7.5).

The number and proportion of English servants employed by alien goldsmiths increased at the end of the sixteenth century, for several reasons. It is possible that as aliens became more assimilated, they tended to employ more English people. This was partly determined by the length of residence in England. Of the 12 alien master goldsmiths who employed English servants in 1593, two-thirds had been there between ten and thirty years, a quarter between five and ten years, and only 10 per cent less than five years. The greater demand for servants engendered by the increase in the scale of business and diversification may also have enhanced dependence on native servants. In 1571, only a quarter of the 39 alien master goldsmiths employed servants, yet by 1593, 64 per cent of 39 alien masters did so. The size of the workshop also expanded. In 1571, only one alien goldsmith had five servants, yet in 1593, three alien goldsmiths had more than five servants, and one as many as eleven servants. These larger concerns employed English servants, possibly to produce goods attuned to local tastes. In the eighteenth century, for example, some of the best Huguenot goldsmiths, while making the most elaborate pieces, also produced goods to meet the needs of those who preferred a simple design or those who could not afford goods of elaborate fashion.[110]

Table 7.5   Employment of servants by aliens in London, 1593

Categories	Servants No.	%
English		
Servants	7	9.6
Female servants	4	5.0
Journeymen	6	8.2
Apprentices	14	19.1
Kept	17	23.3
Set to work	7	9.6
Sub-total	55	75.0
Stranger		
Servants	9	12.3
Female servants	8	11.0
Journeymen	1	1.4
Apprentices	—	—
Sub-total	18	25.0
Total	73	100.0

Source: Scouloudi, *Returns of Strangers*.

The restrictions on the employment of stranger servants also raised the demand for native servants. Since 1451, native goldsmiths had been exhorting the Company to ensure that alien goldsmiths take only one skilled servant of their own nationality and thereafter only English servants, and also take only English apprentices.[111] To ensure that alien goldsmiths did not employ an excessive number of journeymen and only took English apprentices, the Company employed informers, and set up a council to advise the Company on the steps to take against strangers. On 26 August 1575, the Company agreed that 'the advice of learned council shall be used to understand what this company may do by virtue of our corporation for reducing of strangers occupying this mistery to conformable order in taking apprentices and journeymen'.[112] Aliens appear to have abided by this order. In 1593, of the 20 alien goldsmiths who employed more than two servants, only two violated the rule by employing more than one stranger servant each. Ellyard Hundera, a Dutch goldsmith living in St Martin-le-Grand employed three stranger servants; Jacup Vanvuier, a goldsmith from Ghent, took on four stranger servants and maids.

The procedures involved in binding English apprentices to alien goldsmiths were cumbersome. English apprentices were required by an ordinance in August 1565 to be bound first to freemen (English) goldsmiths before they could be turned over to strangers.[113] In April 1574, Manasses Stockton[114] transferred over his apprentice, Abraham Stockton, to John Moenen, stranger, 'within him to dwell and serve ... to the end of 3 years ...'.[115] Those who disobeyed the rule were punished with dismissal. In October 1562, Jaspar Frederick, a Dutchman, was ordered to discharge William Purfege, the son of Robert Purfege, merchant tailor, 'whom he kept and instructed in the science of goldsmith craft to the intent to be made free by his fathers' company'. Jaspar promised 'not to teach him in the said occupation, unless he for time hereafter to be bound apprentice to a goldsmith and by the same goldsmith to be put over to him to learn the said occupation'.[116] The intention behind this rule is unclear. It was perhaps designed to protect English goldsmiths by ensuring that English apprentices were bound to them rather than alien masters. If English apprentices spent a number of years with an English goldsmith, they could go to an alien goldsmith to complete their apprenticeship, and receive the additional skills they could offer as well. This may reflect the differences in the levels of skill between English and alien goldsmiths. It could, on the other hand, simply reflect a wish to retain cheap apprentice labour for Englishmen. How apprenticeship premiums were split, and whether these cumbersome procedures reduced the propensity to take on English apprentices, are questions worthy of further investigation.

Limited Upward Mobility and Circular Migration

Opportunities for upward mobility were not only limited for first-generation aliens, but also for second-generation ones, as their children could not serve apprenticeship. Denied the chance of acquiring the freedom of the City through the normal route of apprenticeship, aliens' children in effect had no hope of a better life than their parents. Both the Goldsmiths' Company and the City of London forbade alien children from serving apprenticeship. The ordinance of the Goldsmiths' Company in 1469 permitted its members to take only the sons of freemen as apprentices, and since most aliens were not freemen, this order in theory effectively prevented children of alien parents from being bound apprentice to English masters. This prohibition also prevented sons from learning the trade from their fathers, as demonstrated in 1562 when the Company ordered John Waterscott to 'bind to some other occupation Costerd his boy born in Antwerp or else to send him home into his native country or else to set him to other business in his house and not to instruct him in the goldsmith's occupation'.[117] In practice, this order was probably not strictly enforced or adhered to in times of economic prosperity. This may explain why the Common Council had to issue another Act in August 1575 reiterating the illegibility of the sons of non-Englishmen to be bound apprentices.[118]

The lack of opportunities for upward mobility may have rendered London an unattractive place of permanent residence, and many Continental goldsmiths returned to their place of origin. Of the 45 goldsmiths from Antwerp who are known to have worked in Elizabethan London, at least 17, or nearly 40 per cent, returned there. Many of these had come for their *wanderjahre* training, and stayed for a period of anything between a few months and twelve years. Peter van Doncke was recorded working in London in 1571. Later that year, he returned to Antwerp, but by 1587 was recorded as a master goldsmith in Frankfurt; presumably he emigrated there after the fall of Antwerp in 1585.[119] Peter Noblet, who came to London for religious reasons in 1568, returned to Antwerp by 1578.[120] In 1578, Noblet became a free master of Antwerp, and presumably due to the Sack of Antwerp in that year, he moved to Frankfurt, where he became a *poorter* in 1581.[121] Marten van de Sande, a jeweller from Bruges, is known to have been in London in 1568. Later, he went back to Antwerp, and after 1585 moved to the Dutch Republic.[122] Many alien goldsmiths, then, returned to their home town but then re-emigrated to the northern Netherlands and German towns when conditions in the south deteriorated. According to Glanville, such movements were normal. A goldsmith born, for example, in Bruges might spend some years as a journeyman in Antwerp, then London, and then return to Antwerp as a master, move to Frankfurt, perhaps marrying twice and running a workshop with local apprentices or journeymen in each town.[123] It is unclear, however, whether the movements of Antwerp-trained or born goldsmiths were indicative of the general pattern. As Antwerp enjoyed a high reputation as a centre of excellence, it is possible that Antwerp-trained goldsmiths were particularly mobile, as demand for their work and their ability to exact higher yields for their skills were probably greater. This mobility prevented the formation of a permanent body of skilled labour, or the possibility of training native workers, and required a continuous flow of new immigrants to sustain the level of skills.

Huguenots in the Seventeenth Century

In the seventeenth century, French influences on English silver were pervasive. French-style silver first appears in Court circles during the Restoration, and French objects were popular at the very top of the social scale.[124] This is partly because many new innovations introduced in this period originated from France,[125] and partly, as Tait has explained, because William of Orange, although a Protestant and a Dutchman, favoured the French style in the field of the arts. His own court architect and designer was the Parisian Huguenot Daniel Marot, who had fled to Holland.[126]

Tait has argued that comparatively few Protestant refugees crossed the Channel in the early part of King James II's reign because he was a Catholic and deeply committed to Catholicism, and that the main influx of refugees only began after 1687, when James II proclaimed his Declaration of Indulgence promising his subjects liberty of conscience and free exercise of religion.[127] Yet, despite the Revocation of Nantes in 1685, it is curious that there is no evidence in the Goldsmiths' Company to suggest a massive influx of Huguenots.[128] Unlike the silk-weavers who arrived largely during the period between 1666 and 1677, fragmentary evidence (grants of letters of denization, naturalization and freedom of the City) suggests that significant Huguenot immigration may not have occurred until after the Glorious Revolution when the accession of Orange to the English throne in 1688 encouraged Huguenot refugees to follow the Dutch Court to England.[129]

The evidence from the records of the distribution of the Royal Bounty funds (Parliament approved an annual grant of £15 000 from 1690 and 1702 to assist Huguenots in need) has made it possible to identify the towns in which French silversmiths originated.[130] The payments from this fund frequently give the town of origin of the recipient of relief. The payments were mostly made to elderly persons or widows, and the individuals whose names appear were not therefore goldsmiths, but their parents or elderly relatives. Nevertheless, the family names enable us to establish the origin of a great many of the leading Huguenot goldsmiths. In the 1687 lists, we find names of many of the best-known masters, including Archambo from the Isle d'Oléron, Mettayer from Poitou, Harache and Margas from Rouen, le Sage from Alençon, Liger from Saumur, Platel from Lorraine and Pilleau from Maine, while from other sources we know that David Willaume came from Metz.

Some Huguenot masters appear to have been of eminent status, as they were granted the freedom of the City soon after arrival. On 21 July 1682, for example, the Lord Mayor and the Council of Aldermen ordered the Goldsmiths' Company to admit to the Company Pierre Harache, 'lately come from France to avoid persecution'. The Company gave way, and Pierre Harache was made a freeman on payment of a fee of 10 pounds.[131] David Willaume, from Metz in Lorraine, arrived in England and was granted letters of denization in 1687, and in the following year his mark was registered with the Goldsmiths' Company. He received his freedom in 1693. Pierre Platel, perhaps possessing sufficient means to apply for naturalization, was naturalized in May 1697, and admitted to the Goldsmith's Company two years later.[132] At least four Huguenots received their freedom through redemption. The status of these Huguenot goldsmiths as freemen was highly significant for their success, as it allowed them to do four things in particular: (1) touch and assay silver works at the Goldsmiths' Hall, and therefore market their goods directly; (2) open a shop in a central location if desired; (3) take on apprentices thereby boosting their income by providing them with a cheap source of labour, and (4) train their own children in their trade.

The first-generation Huguenot goldsmiths played a vital role in training the second generation (see Table 7.6). Some Huguenots who later became prominent goldsmiths had come over to England as boys, and had never actually worked in France. Paul de Lamerie was born in Holland, was brought to England as a baby, 11 months old, in 1689,[133] and was apprenticed to Huguenot goldsmiths.

Pierre Harache was the master of Simon Pantin, who later became a distinguished goldsmith. David Willaume was the master of David Tanqueray in 1708 and later became his father-in-law in 1717,[134] and of Louis Mettayer, who was the son of the minister of the French church.[135] Pierre Platel was the master of Paul de Lamerie. Despite their training in London, Tait has found that 'this second generation remained steeped in the French Huguenot styles and techniques – quite distinct from the native English ones', and offers several reasons for retention of such a strong identity: the hostile attitude of the London goldsmiths, inter-marriage, close informal networks, and the practice of young Huguenot apprentices set under Huguenot masters, adding that 'rarely was an English apprentice to be found in a Huguenot workshop'.[136] Some of these second-generation Huguenots later played a formative role in the training of the third generation. Simon Pantin, for example, trained Augustine Courtauld, and Paul de Lamerie took on 13 apprentices during his career.[137]

Contrary to Tait's conclusion that Huguenot goldsmiths did not provide training to English apprentices, other evidence shows this was not true (see Table 7.7). Between 1693 and 1777, 23 Huguenot masters trained a total of 158 apprentices: 71 of these were English, 79 were sons of other Huguenots, 6 were their own sons, and 2 were their brothers. Although the more numerous second-generation masters were the main providers, first-generation masters also offered training to some English apprentices. Despite their 'clannishness', there are good reasons why many Huguenot masters took on English apprentices. Irrespective of their nationality, whether sons of Englishmen or other Huguenots, apprentices brought apprenticeship premiums, as well as providing a cheap source of labour for a few years. Premiums paid to Huguenot masters ranged between £5 and £45, with the overwhelming proportion at the upper end of the scale. Thus, the more

Table 7.6 Huguenot apprentices and masters

Name	Master	Date of apprenticeship	Date of freedom	Origins/ occupation of father
Henry Aubin	Edward Blagrave	1692	1699	Island of Jarsey, merchant
John Charteir			1698 (Redemption)	Blois, France
Augustin Courtauld	Simon Pantin	1701	1708	Ile of d'Oleron/ Wine cooper
Samuel Courtauld	Father	1734	1747	
Paul de Lamerie	Peter Plattel	1703	1712	's Hertogen-bosch, Holland
Anthony DuChesne	Wm Richards	1720	1729	
Edward Feline	Augustine Courtauld	1709	1721	Tailor
Peter Harache (Sen.)	Trained abroad		1682 (Redemption) paid £10)	Rouen
Peter Harache (Jun.)	Probably father		1698 (Redemption)	
John LeFebure (turned over to brother Daniel)	Peter Harache	1707	1714	Canterbury/ Weaver
Daniel LeFebure	Peter Harache (Jun.)	1701	1708	Canterbury/ Weaver
John Hugh Le Sage	Lewis Cuney	1708	1718	St Martin in Fields/Gent
Lewis Mettayer	David Williams	1693	1700	Clerk/ Ile de Re
Simon Pantin (I)	Peter Harache	1694	1701	Rouen/ Goldsmith
Peze Pilleau	John Charteir	1710	1724	Covent Garden/ Goldsmith
Peter Plattell			1699 (Redemption)	Lille

Philip Rainaud	Pater Plattell	1700	1707	Poitou/Gent
David Tanqueray	David Williams	1708	1722	Normandy/Weaver
David Williams I	Father of a Metz goldsmith		1693 1693	Metz/Goldsmith
David Williams II	Father	1706	1723	

Sources: Goldsmiths' Hall, Masters' Index; Apprenticeship Books 4–6; A. Heale, *The London Goldsmiths, 1200–1800: A Record of the Names and Addresses of the Craftsmen, their Shop-signs and Trade Cards* (London, 1972).

Table 7.7 Training of English and alien apprentices

Names	Dates	Huguenots	Sons	Brothers	English	Total
1st generation						
John Charteir	1698–1720	3	1	—	—	4
Peter Harache (Sen.)	1693–1701	2	—	—	1	3
Peter Plattell	1700–1708	2	—	—	2	4
David Williams I	1693–1724	10	1	—	8	19
2nd generation						
Henry Aubin	1703–26	4	—	—	1	5
Augustin Courtauld	1709–34	3	1	—	6	10
Paul de Lamerie	1715–49	5	—	—	8	13
Anthony DuChesne	1728–40	2	—	—	4	6
Edward Feline	1721–53	12	1	—	3	16
Peter Harache (Jun.)	1701–1708	6	—	—	5	11
John LeFebure	1718	—	—	2	—	2
Daniel LeFebure	1707–9	2	—	—	—	2
John Hugh Le Sage	1718–42	2	1	—	4	7
Lewis Mettayer	1709–25	2	—	—	5	7
Simon Pantin (I)	1701–32	6	1	—	1	8
Peze Pilleau	1726–39	2	—	—	2	4
Peter Plattell	1700–1708	2	—	—	2	4
Philip Rainaud	1707–22	5	—	—	2	7
John Ruffin	1719–51	2	—	—	5	7
David Tanqueray	1714–23	3	—	—	1	4
David Williams II	1726–39	2	—	—	5	7

3rd generation

Isaac Chartier	1748–77	3	—	—	4	7
Samuel Courtauld	1750–61	1	—	—	4	5
Total		23	79	6	2	71	158

Sources: Goldsmiths' Company, London, Masters' Index; Apprenticeship Books 4–9; Evans, *Huguenot Goldsmiths*.

apprentices a master had, the greater the level of apprenticeship premiums and income. If Huguenot masters experienced economic hardship, the need to take on apprentices among the first generation, to raise revenue for their business, was even greater. Given that many Huguenots arriving after 1687 were destitute and needing relief, many simply could not afford to pay for their sons' apprenticeship premiums, even if they wished to, and the main source of recruitment had to come from the native population.

Taking on English apprentices also conferred an added advantage: inroads into the wealthy local clientele market. English apprentices provided crucial connections with the gentry, as many were sons of local gentlemen from London and Middlesex, but also those further afield, such as Leicester and Winchester. Perhaps through these connections Huguenot masters could gain important commissions as well as spread their reputation and skills, upon which future commissions could rest. Of the 79 Huguenot apprentices, 13 (16 per cent) were sons of gentlemen, in comparison with 9 (nearly 13 per cent) of the English apprentices. Possibly through their Huguenot gentlemanly friends, English gentlemen were able to make arrangements for the apprenticeship of their sons with prominent Huguenot masters.

Impact of the Huguenots

Huguenots are believed to have engendered other changes in the London silver trade. First, their arrival is believed to have led to the introduction of fashions that were unknown or only beginning to become known in England. The Huguenots tended, therefore, to obtain important commissions from those rich patrons who attached great significance to keeping up with the latest fashions. Among the important commissions obtained by the Huguenots was the provision in 1734 of a large service, comprising 36 pieces of gilt plate and 329 of white, for the Empress Catherine of Russia.[138] Competition presented by the Huguenots is also regarded as crucial in speeding up the adoption of 'Huguenot' styles by London goldsmiths and raising standards. Indeed, less than forty years after the arrival of the Huguenots, it was impossible to distinguish Huguenots from non-Huguenots without looking at the makers' mark.[139] The ability of Huguenots to compete on equal terms with their English counterparts was a crucial difference distinguishing the contribution of the Huguenots from earlier migrants. Many Huguenots possessed the freedom of the City, and had the right to keep open shops and retail and to mark and assay their works, just like any other free English goldsmiths. Their possession of superior skills further rendered them serious competitors. In the sixteenth century immigrants had a more limited impact because, although many possessed superior skills, they could not compete on equal terms. Consequently, they were forced to work in hidden workshops, and their skills were harnessed as a source of a cheap, flexible and skilled labour, rather than of serious competition. Their presence, then, did not promote competition and the concomitant effect of raising standards in the silver trade.

The second impact may have been the enhancement of standards of workmanship without raising prices. It is believed that the destitute situation of Huguenots made them willing to work harder and for less money than their English counterparts. A petition of English goldsmiths in 1711 demonstrated how native craftsmen were affected: 'by the admittance of the necessitous strangers, whose desperate fortunes obliged them to work at miserable rates, the representing members have been forced to bestow much more time and labour in working up their plate than has been the practice of former times, when prices of workmanship were greater'.[140] There was also greater choice, as the range of English silver wares on sale was enlarged by the introduction of items such as the tall helmet-shaped ewer with shaped basin en suite, the pilgrim bottle, the soup tureen, and the écuelle, a flat covered bowl with two flat ear-like handles.[141] Lastly, the adaptation of French style and ornament by both Huguenot and English craftsmen onto traditional English forms led to the production of some unique objects as a result of cultural infusion – like the tankard (unknown in France, even in beer-drinking areas) and the two-handled cup.[142]

Native Attitudes

The increasingly hostile attitudes of members of the Goldsmiths' Company towards immigrants in the seventeenth century reflects the problems experienced by the trade as well as competition posed by aliens. In the sixteenth century, there were few complaints against immigrants. Indeed, in the period between 1546 and 1598, only two entries were recorded in the Minutes Books concerning actions against strangers: one in 1562 concerning a payment to an informer to report against strangers, and the other in 1593 concerning advice taken against strangers. In 1573, when asked by the City about aliens within their trade, the Goldsmiths' Company expressed its satisfaction: 'we certify that all such strangers being free denizens ... within our rule and government have hetherto behaved themselves from time to time as men tractable and conformable to the good rules of our mistery and willing to be ruled by us'.[143]

However, in the seventeenth century, the Company's attitudes appeared to have changed. Between 1600 and 1668, at least 22 court sessions were held to discuss the problem of aliens, and at least five petitions were presented against aliens between 1641 and 1717. In December 1653, the Wardens agreed to pay for the costs involved in employing certain 'persons to suppress the free working of aliens and strangers'. Tait has claimed that the Company's unrelenting and unwelcoming attitude towards alien craftsmen, especially if they were men of substance and quality, was apparent even in the early sixteenth century, with its refusal to admit the talented goldsmith Hans von Antwerpen in the 1530s.[144] To Tait, the pattern was clear: 'the more gifted and influential the alien goldsmith, the more unwelcoming his reception at Goldsmiths' Hall and the more frequently court patronage and royal intervention was needed to safeguard his freedom to prosper in London'.[145]

Complaints in the seventeenth century centred on two principal issues. The first related to the usual grievance about the 'great number' of aliens working in London. In 1621, when the City asked the Company to write a report on any inconveniences caused by the presence of aliens, it drew up a long list of grievances, including the loss of livelihood of free goldsmiths as a result of competition from aliens, and the difficulties of searching the premises of alien goldsmiths, as they lived in remote areas and secret places. It argued that the 183 aliens working in the capital 'do take away a great part of the lyving and maintenance of the free goldsmithes of this Citie who are thereby exceedinglie impoverished and disable in theire estates to bear publique charges', and proposed a drastic reduction in their number.[146] In January 1641, freemen claimed that they were greatly outnumbered by aliens: there were 140 strangers, as opposed to 50 freemen. In a petition of 1653, they described how they were 'almost ruined by the encroachment of aliens who work privately' and desired to expel them from the capital.

From the mid-seventeenth century, native goldsmiths became more concerned with the grant of the right to touch and assay silver by aliens at the Goldsmiths' Hall, a privilege which had been the preserve of native freemen. In 1664, for example, they sought to prevent two 'Dutch' plateworkers (Howzer and Bodendicke)[147] acquiring the right to touch and assay their work. Native plateworkers and goldsmiths complained to the Goldsmiths' Company that there 'are soe many aliens and strangers in and about this city ... and keep so many servants under them', resulting in the 'want of employment' among native workers who were 'unable to maintain themselves and their families'. Native workers warned that unless something was done to remedy the situation, the abuses committed by aliens would 'threaten the ruin of the most ancient, principal branch of the Goldsmiths' trade'. The Goldsmiths' Company then petitioned the Lord Mayor and the Aldermen to intervene. They replied, however, that they had been instructed by the King to grant the privileges to the Dutchmen. Failing to obtain support, the Goldsmiths' Company then petitioned the King directly, necessitated by the 'extreme sad condition of very many families of their members is so pressing'.[148] Their petition was unsuccessful because Howzer had powerful friends, including Edward Backwell and Thomas Vyner (both were Prime Wardens of the Goldsmiths' Company), whose support he obtained in his petition to the Privy Council for the right to mark and sell his goods.[149] In May 1664, the King wrote of:

> his gratious acceptance of the submissive decent compliance of the Wardens and Company of Goldsmiths, with his desire that Jacob Bodendick and Wolfgang Howzer ... might have the plate by them wrought, Assayed, touched, allowed of and permitted to be sold in the same manner as if it had bin wrought by Natives Freemen of this City.[150]

In 1678, the Goldsmiths' Company opposed a bill in Parliament proposing the grant of equal rights to aliens. In October 1703, members urged the Company to petition the Court of Aldermen to withhold the grant of freedom by redemption to aliens, and insisted in another petition of 1716–47 that only those who had served a seven-year apprenticeship should be allowed to have their works touched and assayed. Their persistent efforts were driven by the fear that free aliens would provide outlets for the non-free. In 1715, it was alleged that Paul de Lamerie 'covered Foreigners work and got the same touched at the Hall'.[151]

The repeated efforts by some members of the Goldsmiths' Company to suppress strangers and aliens suggest that their campaign was perhaps not very effective. According to David Mitchell, this is because the strangers possessed not only the support of powerful patrons at Court, but also those of the ruling elite of the Goldsmiths' Company. Stranger goldsmiths, for example, were helped by those who while expressing sympathy with English workmen when sitting on the Court of Assistants of the Company, continued to employ the likes of Van Vianen, Howzer and Bodendick. Doubtless they would have argued that if they could not provide their wealthy customers with fashionable wares, they would certainly have got them through personal contacts in Paris or London.[152] Edward Backwell, a goldsmith-banker, for example, used Howzer to fashion his finest and most expensive plate, and the French jewellers Isaac Maubert and Estienne Caillate to cut diamonds and rubies and then to set them into costly rings and jewels. In fact, he should not have employed the Frenchmen nor Howzer until they had been granted the right to touch and assay in May 1664.[153] This example shows the division of interests between the elite and the 'workmen' of the Goldsmiths' Company.

Conclusion

The vitality of the London goldsmiths' trade was ensured by its constant exposure to Continental tastes and fashions, through the intermittent flow of alien craftsmen from the Middle Ages to 1700. The backgrounds of these foreign craftsmen who worked and lived in the capital, however, changed fundamentally during this period. In the first place, there was a shift in their place of origins, from being predominantly Flemish, then Brabantine in the sixteenth century, to German and Dutch in the early seventeenth century, and to French by the end of the seventeenth century. Their contributions to the craft differed in nature. The foreign artisans in the sixteenth century were predominantly journeymen, whose principal motive for coming to London was to gain *Wanderjahre* experience, with perhaps no intention of permanent settlement. Deterred by discrimination and sundry restrictions, many returned to their city of origin to set up as master. There were a few skilled alien goldsmith masters working in the Elizabethan period, but they were probably not of any significant stature, as implied by the absence of aristocratic patronage and lack of requests for the grant of freedom on their behalf by leading figures in local or national government. Deterred, too, by restrictions, some alien masters re-emigrated.

The Huguenots differed from these earlier artisans in several ways. Pushed out from France by persecution and had few prospects of return, they had a greater propensity to permanent settlement. Some became highly prominent, and the key to that success was undoubtedly their possession of the freedom of the City. With their freedom, first-generation Huguenots were able to work within a fundamentally different framework. They could touch and assay their wares with their own marks at the Goldsmiths' Hall, set up shops in the most prized districts, and take on apprentices. While on the one hand their provision of training to second-generation Huguenots, who in turn trained the third-generation, allowed the perpetuation of Huguenot styles, their training of English, on the other hand, encouraged convergence of styles. This, combined with the popularity of French styles, led to the embracing of these foreign fashions by English masters.

Notes

1. P. Glanville, 'Introduction', in D. Mitchell, ed., *Goldsmiths, Silversmiths and Bankers: Innovation and the Transfer of Skill, 1550 to 1750* (London, 1995), p. 1.
2. J. Evans, *Huguenot Goldsmiths in England and Ireland* (London, 1933), pp. 26–7.
3. Although they mainly worked in silver, they are referred to as 'goldsmiths' because they belonged to the Company of the Goldsmiths: see H. Tait, 'London Huguenot Silver', in I. Scouloudi, ed., *Huguenots in Britain and their French Background, 1550–1800* (London, 1987), p. 89.
4. T.F. Reddaway and L.E.M. Walker, *The Early History of the Goldsmiths' Company, 1327–1509* (London, 1975); P. Glanville, *Silver in Tudor and Early Stuart England* (London, 1990).
5. Evans, *Huguenot Goldsmiths in England and Ireland*; Tait, 'London Huguenot Silver', pp. 89–112.
6. The Alan and Simone Hartman Collection comprises 111 items made in London between 1680 and 1760; some two-thirds of the objects bear the marks of Huguenot silversmiths: see C. Hartop, 'Art and industry in 18th-century London: English silver 1680–1760 from the Alan and Simone Hartman Collection', *Proceedings of the Huguenot Society*, 1998, Vol. 27, No. 1, pp. 50–63.
7. J.F. Hayward, *Huguenot Silver in England, 1688–1727* (London, 1959); Evans, *Huguenot Goldsmiths in England and Ireland*; Tait, 'London Huguenot Silver', pp. 89–112.
8. H. Tait, 'Huguenot Silver Made in London (c.1690–1723)', Part 1, *Connoisseur*, August 1972, Vol. 181, No. 726, pp. 267–76; Part 2, *Connoisseur*, September 1972, Vol. 181, No. 727, pp. 25–36; Hartop, 'Art and industry in 18th-century London', pp. 50–63.
9. S.M. Hare, *Paul de Lamerie: An Exhibition of the Work of England's Master Silversmith 1688–1751: Goldsmiths' Hall, Foster Lane 16th May to 22 June 1990* (London, 1990); S.M. Hare, 'Paul de Lamerie: a retrospective assessment', *Proceedings of the Huguenot Society*, 1991, Vol. 25, No. 3, pp. 219–29; C. Lever, *Goldsmiths and Silversmiths of England* (London, 1975); see Hartop, 'Art and industry in 18th-century London', pp. 51–2, 62, for a discussion of this historiographical bias.
10. Hartop, 'Art and industry', p. 52.
11. Ibid.
12. Ibid., pp. 54–5, 62–3.
13. R.H. Britnell, *The Commercialisation of English Society, 1000–1500* (Cambridge, 1993), p. 180; Glanville, *Silver in England*, p. 27.
14. Quoted in Hartrop, 'Art and industry', p. 51.
15. Ibid., pp. 51, 55.
16. Stone, 'The Anatomy of the Elizabethan Aristocracy', *Economic History Review*, 1948, Vol. 18, No. 1, p. 8.
17. C.A. Sneyd, ed., *A relation ... of the Island of England ... about the year 1500* (Camden Society, old series, Vol. 37, 1847), pp. 42–3.
18. Quoted in T.F. Reddaway, 'Elizabethan London – Goldsmith's Row in Cheapside, 1558–1645', *Guildhall Miscellany*, 1963, Vol 2, pp. 181–2.
19. Glanville, *Silver in Tudor and Early Stuart England*, quoted in H. Clifford, 'London Goldsmiths 1500–1750', a paper presented to the Skilled Workforce Conference, Museum of London, 26 November 1994.
20. Quoted in J. Hale, *The Civilization of Europe in the Renaissance* (London, 1993), pp. 305–6.
21. W. Prevenier and W. Blockmans, *The Burgundian Netherlands* (Cambridge, 1986), p. 282.
22. In 1566, there were 124 goldsmiths working in Antwerp, without counting a large number of lapidaries and other cutters and engravers of precious stones in the latter. See

M. van Gelderen, *The Political Thought of the Dutch Revolt, 1555–1590* (Cambridge, 1992), p. 14; G. Marnef, 'Antwerpen in Reformatietijd: Ondergronds Protestantisme in een internationale handelsmetropool, 1550–1577' (University of Leuven unpublished PhD thesis, 1991), Vol. 1, p. 34.
23 P. Glanville, 'The Crafts and Decorative Arts', in B. Ford, ed., *The Cambridge Cultural History: Sixteenth-century Britain*, Vol. 3 (Cambridge, 1989), p. 288.
24 Tait, 'London Huguenot Silver', p. 94.
25 GCCB O, Vol.14, (4/11/1607), ff. 551–2.
26 Glanville, 'The Crafts and Decorative Arts', p. 286.
27 Glanville, *Silver in England*, p. 226.
28 Ibid., p. 223; Glanville, *Silver in Tudor and Early Stuart England*, p. 92.
29 GL, BCCB MS 5445/6 (17/July 1582).
30 E.M. Alcorn, '"Some of the Kings of England Curiously Engraven": An Elizabethan Ewer and Basin in the Museum of Fine Arts, Boston', *Journal of the Museum of Fine Arts*, 1993, Vol. 5, p. 74.
31 In Augsburg, for example, a goldsmith had to serve four years as a journeyman before he was eligible to submit his masterpiece. If he was not a native of Augsburg, the period of service in 1555 was six years, which had to be spent with three different masters. See J.F. Hayward, *Virtuoso Goldsmiths and the Triumph of Mannerism, 1540–1620* (London, 1976), pp. 40–41.
32 P. Lanz, 'Training and workshop practice in Zürich in the seventeenth century', in Mitchell, ed., *Goldsmiths, Silversmiths and Bankers*, pp. 39–41.
33 Glanville, *Silver in Tudor and Early Stuart England*, p. 88.
34 Hayward, *Virtuoso Goldsmiths*, p. 41.
35 F.J. Furnivall ed., *Andrew Boorde's Introduction and Dyetary* (Early English Text Society, Extra Series, 1870), No. X, p. 144.
36 Glanville, *Silver in Tudor and Early Stuart England*, p. 86.
37 In Nuremberg, the applicant to mastership had to make a 'columbine-cup', a gold ring set with a precious stone, and a steel seal-die. The successful master was therefore equipped to be a goldsmith, jeweller or seal-die cutter. In other European cities such as Zurich, a masterpiece was not required: Hayward, *Virtuoso Goldsmiths*, pp. 36–7.
38 P. Glanville, 'Alien goldsmiths at the Court of Charles II', in R. Stockland, ed., *The Grosvenor House Antiques Fair: The Antique Dealers' fair, 9th–19th June 1993* (London, 1993), p. 20.
39 GCCB L, Part 2, Vol. 10, f. 211.
40 Quoted from Hayward, *Virtuoso Goldsmiths*, p. 37.
41 Ibid., pp. 40–41.
42 *Zilver uit de Gouden Eeuw van Antwerpen* (Antwerp, 1989), pp. 23–4.
43 Quoted from T.F. Reddaway and L.E.M. Walker, *The Early History of the Goldsmiths' Company 1327–1509, including The Book of Ordinances 1478–83* (London, 1975), Book of Ordinances, p. 228; GCCB K, Part I, Vol. 8, f. 233 'An Order for Taking Apprentices, 5th August 1563'. Some served longer. In 1571, for example, Robert Gybbyns started his fourteen-year apprenticeship with Henrie Watson; Goldsmiths' Company, Book L, Part 1, Vol. 9, f. 85.
44 GCCB L, Part 1, Vol. 9, f. 121.
45 Reddaway and Walker, *The Early History of the Goldsmiths' Company 1327–1509, including The Book of Ordinances 1478–83* (London, 1975), p. 181.
46 Hartrop, 'Art and industry', p. 53.
47 In 1579, only 88 English goldsmiths were recorded in Cheapside and Lombard Street' Goldsmiths' Company, Court Minutes Books, Book L, Part 2, f. 469. See Evans, *Huguenot Goldsmiths in England and Ireland*, p. 6; for the names of English goldsmiths working in London, see C.J. Jackson, *English Goldsmiths and their Marks: A History of the Goldsmiths and Plate Workers of England, Scotland, and Ireland* (Dover, 1921), pp. 239–42.

48 If the number of alien masters in London in 1571 (39) is expressed as a percentage of the recorded number of English-born goldsmiths (108 in 1566), the proportion also comes to 36 per cent.
49 E. Turner, *An Introduction to English Silver from 1660* (London, 1985), p. 14.
50 Evans, *Huguenot Goldsmiths*, pp. 17–19.
51 GCCB P, Part I, ff. 115v–116; this list of names was sent to the Privy Council in 1621: see SP14/127/12.
52 See D. Mitchell, 'Innovation and the transfer of skill in the goldsmiths' trade in Restoration London', in idem, ed., *Goldsmiths, Silversmiths and Bankers: Innovation and the Transfer of Skill, 1550 to 1750* (London, 1995), p. 11.
53 Turner, *An Introduction to English Silver from 1660*, pp. 5–6; see G.B. Rawlings, *The story of the British Coinage* (London, 1898) pp. 85–88 for an interesting discussion of siege pieces (money of necessity) to provide money for the payment of troops.
54 Ibid., p. 6.
55 W. Prideaux, ed., *Memorials of the Goldsmiths Company* (2 vols, London 1896), Vol. 1, p. 209.
56 Tait, 'London Huguenot Silver', p. 97.
57 Turner, *An Introduction to English Silver from 1660*, p. 6; Mitchell, 'Innovation and the transfer of skill in the goldsmiths' trade in Restoration London', p. 11.
58 Turner, *An Introduction to English Silver from 1660*, p. 6.
59 See J. de Vries, 'The labour market', in Davids and Noordegraaf, eds, *The Dutch Economy in the Golden Age* (Amsterdam, 1993), pp. 63–73 for a discussion of wages; A.L. den Blaauwen, *Dutch Silver 1580–1830* (Amsterdam, 1979), p. xxiv.
60 J. Briels, 'Zuidnederlandse goud- en zilversmeden in Noordnederland omstreeks 1576–1625' *Bijdragen tot de geschiedenis*, 1971, Vol. 54, pp. 89, 92.
61 A.K.L. Thijs, 'Antwerp's Luxury Industries: the Pursuit of Profit and Artistic Sensitivity', in J. van der Stock, *Antwerp: The Story of a Metropolis, 16th–17th Century* (Ghent, 1993), pp. 109, 111–13.
62 See A.S. Phillips, *Records of Some London Goldsmiths: Foreign Goldsmiths Settled in London and Some Accounts of London Goldsmiths* (Goldsmiths' Hall, 1932), p. 32, taken from Dutch Church Registers, Book 10, No. 40.
63 H. Tait, 'London Huguenot Silver', in J. Scouloudi, ed., *Huguenots in Britain and their French Background, 1550–1800* (London, 1987); Tait also concludes that foreign-looking silver-plate made in London during the Jacobean period shows Dutch or Germanic quality; 1987, p. 95.
64 Turner, *An Introduction to English Silver from 1660*, pp. 6, 9–10.
65 Mrs G. van Hemeldonck is currently preparing *De Antwerpse Goud- en Zilversmeden 1550–1600*, a two-volume study of Antwerp goldsmiths due to be published on CD Rom in Dec 2005. I am extremely grateful to her for giving me the necessary information relating to Antwerp goldsmiths in London; Antwerp Stadsarchief, Cert. b.25 f.510v; GCCB L, Part 1, Vol. 9, p. 339.
66 Antwerp Stadsarchief, Cert. b. 30, f. 244v.
67 GCCB K, Part 1, Vol. 8, f. 196.
68 Ibid., f. 198.
69 In March 1564, an informer notified the Wardens of two strangers working in St Martins without a letter testimonial; GCCB K, Part 1, Vol. 8, f. 277.
70 Ibid., f. 279.
71 In 1566, the Wardens considered the question of whether stranger free denizens should be compelled to produce a testimonial. It was decided that a letter of 'denizenship' was sufficient. GCCB L, Part 1, Vol. 9, f. 337.
72 After 1568, the Dutch church was sometimes forced to waive the requirement that young people should have written permission to marry from their parents when it was proved that a genuine effort to obtain such permission bore no fruit. Letters could reach the

Dutch church in three days from Antwerp, but might take up to ten weeks. See A. Pettegree, *Foreign Protestant Communities in Sixteenth-century London* (Oxford, 1986), p. 227.
73 See GCCB L, Part 1, Vol. 9, f.48; GCCB L, Part 2, Vol. 10, f. 216.
74 In Antwerp, this information is recorded in the Certificatieboeken. See H. van der Wee, *Growth of Antwerp*, Vol. 2, p. 178.
75 GCCB L, Part 2, Vol. 10, f. 223.
76 GCCB N-O, Part 1, Vol. 12, f. 10.
77 GCCB L, Part 2, Vol. 10, f. 213.
78 GCCB O, Part 2, f. 268.
79 Antwerp Stadsarchief, A 4487; see also J. Briels, 'Zuidnederlandse goud- en zilversmeden in Noordnederland omstreeks 1576–1625', *Bijdragen tot de Geschiedenis*, 1971, Vol. 54, pp. 87–141; 1972, Vol. 55, pp. 89–112; D. Schlugheit, 'Alphabetische Naamlijst op de Goud en Zilversmeden te Antwerpen voor 1600', *Bijdragen tot de Geschiedenis*, 1936, Vol. 27, pp. 6–69.
80 *Zilver uit de Gouden Eeuw*, pp. 23–24.
81 Antwerp Stadsarchief, Certificatieboeken 26, f. 264v; GCCB L, Part 1, Vol. 9, f. 406.
82 Antwerp Stadsarchief, SR 317 GA II f. 271v; GCCB L, Part 2, Vol. 10, f. 216
83 Glanville, *Silver in Tudor and Stuart England*, p. 92.
84 Reddaway and Walker, *The Early History of the Goldsmiths' Company*, pp. 120–21.
85 Glanville, 'Introduction', in Mitchell, ed, *Goldsmiths, Silversmiths and Bankers*, p. 3.
86 Reddaway and Walker, *The Early History of the Goldsmiths' Company*, pp. 127, 130.
87 CLRO Rep 17, f. 150.
88 Glanville, *Silver in Tudor and Early Stuart England*, p. 86.
89 Glanville, 'Contributions of the Aliens', p. 95.
90 Hayward, *Huguenot Silver in England*, pp. 19–20.
91 GCCB L, Part 2, Vol. 10, f. 247.
92 GCCB O, 3, f. 577.
93 Tait, 'London Huguenot Silver', p. 97.
94 Reddaway, and Walker, *The Early History of the Goldsmiths' Company*, p. 171.
95 See Reddaway, 'Elizabethan London – Goldsmith's Row in Cheapside, 1558–1645', pp. 181–206.
96 GCCB L, Part 1, Vol. 9, f. 368.
97 Antwerp GA 4487, f. 29, 37; Col. 12, f. 531.
98 GCCB L, Vol. 9, f. 14 (17/10/1569).
99 J. Styles, 'The goldsmiths and the London luxury trades', in Mitchell, ed., *Goldsmiths, Silversmiths and Bankers*, p. 116.
100 Glanville, *Silver in Tudor and Early Stuart England*, p. 174.
101 H. Clifford, 'London goldsmiths, 1500–1750', a paper presented to the Growth of a Skilled Workforce Conference, Museum of London, 26 November 1994.
102 GCCB L, Part 2, Vol. 10, f. 187.
103 GCCB N-O, Part 1, Vol. 12, f. 32.
104 See also his fascinating paper on 'To Alderman Backwells for the candlesticks for Mr Coventry: The manufacture and sale of plate at the Unicorn, Lombard Street, 1663–72', *The Silver Society Journal*, 2000, Vol. 12, pp. 111–24. This paper discusses the business of Edward Backwell.
105 D. Mitchell, 'Dressing Plate by the "Unknown" London Silversmith "WF"', *Burlington Magazine*, June 1993, Vol. CXXXV, No. 1083, pp. 386–400.
106 Mitchell, 'Innovation and the transfer of skill in the goldsmiths' trade in Restoration London', p. 16.
107 Hartrop, 'Art and industry', p. 51. See also D. Mitchell, 'Marks, Manwarings and Moore: the use of the "AM in monogram" mark, 1650–1700', *The Silver Society Journal*, 1999, Vol. 11, pp. 168–184, who discusses the problem of identification of marks.

108 GCCB A, Vol. 2, ff. 2–3.
109 Reddaway and Walker, *The Early History of the Goldsmiths' Company*, p. 128.
110 Hayward, Huguenot Silver in England, p. 7.
111 Reddaway and Walker, *The Early History of the Goldsmiths' Company*, p. 127.
112 GCCB L, Part 2, Vol. 10, f. 240.
113 GCCB K, Part 1, Vol. 8, f. 291.
114 Stockton had a shop in the Goldsmiths' Row in Cheap called the 'Key' in 1569: No. 5. See Goldsmiths' Company, Court Minutes Book, Vol. 10, f. 469; see also Reddaway, 'Goldsmith's Row in Cheapside', p. 186.
115 GCCB L, Part 2, Vol. 10, f. 189.
116 GCCB K, Part 1, Vol. 8, f. 204.
117 GCCB K, Part 1, Vol. 8, f. 194.
118 GCCB L, Part 2, Vol. 10, f. 237.
119 Kirk and Kirk, eds, *Returns of Aliens*, Vol. 2, p. 11; Briels, 'Zuidnederlandse goud- en zilversmeden in Noordnederland omstreeks 1576–1625', *Bijdragen tot de geschiedenis*, Vol. 54, 1971, p. 137.
120 See Antwerp Stadsarchief, A4487, f. 100v, 159; D. Schlugheit, 'Alphabetische Naamlijst op de Goud en Zilversmeden te Antwerpen voor 1600', *Bijdragen tot de Geschiedenis*, 1936, Vol. 27, p. 22.
121 Van Hemeldonck, *De Antwerpse Goud- en Zilversmeden, 1550–1600*, entry 1135.
122 Briels, 'Zuidnederlandse goud- en zilversmeden in Noordnederland omstreeks, 1576–1625', *Bijdragen tot de geschiedenis*, 1972, Vol. 55, p. 102.
123 Glanville, 'The Contributions of the Aliens', p. 88.
124 Hartop, 'Art and industry', p. 59.
125 See Mitchell, 'Innovation and the transfer of skill in the goldsmiths', p.13, for a discussion of innovations precipitated by the new practice among noblewomen to entertain formally in their private apartments, by the introduction of new beverages; for a discussion of changes in eating habits (new dishes like oille – a rich stew of game and meat – required new types of silverware, like covered tureens) and dining (the move towards more intimate dinner parties with less reliance on servants for serving require cruet stands and sauce boats), see Hartop, 'Art and industry', p. 62.
126 H. Tait, 'Huguenot silver made in London c.1690–1723', *Connoisseur*, Part 1, 1972, p. 274.
127 Tait, 'London Huguenot Silver', p. 107.
128 Ibid., p. 99.
129 H. Tait, 'Huguenot Silver made in London c.1690-1723', pp. 267–76.
130 Ibid., p. 274.
131 Ibid., p. 268.
132 Ibid., pp. 270, 274.
133 Tait, 'London Huguenot silver', p. 108.
134 Ibid., p. 104.
135 H. Tait, 'Huguenot silver made in London c.1690–1723', *Connoisseur*, Part 2, Vol. 55, 1972, p. 29.
136 Ibid., pp. 25–7.
137 Hayward, *Huguenot Silver in England, 1688–1727*, pp. 9–10; Tait, 'London Huguenot Silver', p. 108; Hartop, 'Art and industry', p. 61.
138 Hayward, *Huguenot Silver in England*, pp. 15, 11.
139 Ibid., p. 4.
140 Ibid., pp. 20–21.
141 Ibid., p. 8.
142 Hartop, 'Art and industry', p. 60.
143 GCCB L, Vol. 10, f. 186.
144 Tait, 'London Huguenot Silver', p. 90.

145 Ibid., p. 91.
146 PRO, SP14/127/12.
147 They were referred to as Dutch, but Howzer actually came from Zurich and Bodendicke from Lüneburg. See Mitchell, 'To Alderman Backwells', pp. 119–20, for more information on Howzer.
148 Goldsmiths' Company, J.V. (i), containing various petitions against alien goldsmiths in the seventeenth century.
149 Mitchell, 'To Alderman Backwells', p. 119.
150 Quoted in Ibid..
151 Hartop, 'Art and industry', p. 52.
152 Mitchell, 'To Alderman Backwells', p. 123.
153 Ibid.

Chapter 8

Beer Brewing

Overview

The art of beer brewing originated in northern Germany in the thirteenth century, and it spread rapidly to Holland and the southern Netherlands before reaching England in the early fifteenth century. Its introduction was a major landmark in the English economic landscape, spearheading not only a revolution in the brewing industry, but also the coal industry. Until this period, English brewers produced only ale, in which only malt, water and yeast were used. Lacking any preservative, ale deteriorated rapidly, and this meant that producers could not risk making large batches of drink. The short longevity of ale thus meant that production had to be carried out frequently on a small scale, and the end product was destined largely for local consumption rather than for distant markets. A large number of brewers was also necessary to supply domestic need, but these had few opportunities for amassing a great fortune. These bottlenecks in production were overcome with the introduction of beer which, brewed with the addition of hops, gave it unique qualities. To start with, beer could be stored for a much longer period, thanks to the natural preservatives contained in the hops. While ale went sour after two weeks, strong beer (such as March or October beers) could be stored for up to a year. Beer also transported better, with less chance of going off as a result of jostling, sloshing, unpredictable temperatures and other accidents of transport.[1] Brewers could now significantly expand production to take advantage of the economies of scale, widen their market by exporting their beers, and introduce mechanization in production. By the early seventeenth century, brewing in England had been transformed from a small-scale, humble, domestic and female-dominated craft into a large-scale, capital-intensive, commercialized, and highly lucrative business. Production, along with wealth, became concentrated in a few hands. In 1380, when the population of London was less than 30 000, there were 1000 brewhouses in the City, but by 1600, when the population had risen to some 200 000 people, there were only 83 ale and beer brewers.[2] By this date, brewers had become enormously wealthy and their Company had emerged as a leading city guild.

Yet this change was surprisingly slow to come about. This was partly due to the opposition of the English brewers, who sought to ban beer production in England. For nearly two centuries, hopped beer was regarded as an alien drink, or more precisely a Dutch drink, shunned by English drinkers, and its production was undertaken largely by aliens. It was not until Elizabeth's reign that Englishmen began to drink beer in large quantities and English producers engaged in beer production. But its popularity was uneven. By the late sixteenth century, beer was only drunk in major cities in the south-east and other smaller towns (Leicester, Coventry, Oxford, Chester, Winchester and elsewhere), and was still not popular in northern towns. Beer was slowly finding drinkers in rural villages, but this was confined largely to those with trade connections with the Continent. In many areas, no beer was sold until the late sixteenth century or later. In South Tawton (Devon), beer did not replace ale until 1649, while in Ottery St Mary (Devon), only ale was being sold as late as 1681.[3]

London was significant in setting the national trend for beer drinking. With a large foreign population and extensive trading links with the Continent, Londoners were among the first to drink beer. Beer had been imported into the City as early as the fourteenth century, and by Elizabeth's reign, most Londoners had switched to beer drinking. This change in consumers' preference accelerated the process of diffusion of skills in London, which occurred in five stages over a period of three centuries, as summarized in Table 8.1. From the beginning beer brewing was closely associated with the 'Dutch', who introduced the skills. Throughout the fifteenth and the early part of the sixteenth centuries, aliens owned the majority of beer brewhouses and monopolized production in London. However, their position was undermined during Elizabeth's reign, ironically by the increasing popularity of beer which, combined with London's explosive demographic expansion, set off an exponential growth in the brewing industry there, which presented enormous opportunities for investment. This encouraged English entrepreneurs to enter the industry in larger numbers, and subsequently to impose discriminatory measures against the alien brewers to mitigate the stiffening competition. Increased demand also quickened the introduction of large-scale production, consequently squeezing out small producers as a result of the higher fixed capital investment required. With the gradual separation between capital and labour, English entrepreneurs found it easier to enter the industry, and by the early seventeenth century, ownership of brewhouses was largely in the hands of English producers. The Dutch still maintained a significant but dimishing role, supplying the skilled labour necessary for the running of the brewhouses. After the 1650s, however, few Dutch names were recorded in the Company's records, marking the end of Dutch domination and the completion of the industry's Anglicization.

Although the Continental origins of beer are recognized in the historiography of brewing, little attention has been devoted to discussing the

Table 8.1 Stages in the diffusion of beer brewing technology to London

Stage 1	13th century	Hops were first used in brewing in German ports
Stage 2	14th century	Diffusion of hopped beer to Holland, Flanders and Brabant
Stage 3	c.1400	Diffusion of hopped beer from Holland to London
Stage 4	1400–1500	Aliens controlled the majority of brewhouses
Stage 5	c.1570s	Popularity of beer and acceleration of diffusion of skills to natives
Stage 6	c.1600	A majority of brewhouses were now in native hands. Few brewhouses were owned by aliens
Stage 5	1650	The industry became indigenous – aliens no longer mentioned in Brewers' Company records

process by which beer brewing was brought to England, the backgrounds of the alien brewers, and the ways in which beer became an intrinsic part of English culture. The focus of the older historiographical tradition is on the history of brewing in England, the Brewers' Company, and the growth of the industry from the seventeenth century; while recent works have taken a social stance, looking at the rise of alehouses and the pub culture, and a gender perspective. Judith Bennett, in her recent book, has compellingly argued that the shift from ale to beer production was instrumental in the marginalization of women in the brewing industry because they had less access to the skills brought by the male alien brewers. This implies that the elevation of brewing witnessed in this period, from a humble to a highly respectable trade, was connected both with structural (larger scale of production and the eclipse of ale) and gender changes (masculinization) within the industry. The focus of this chapter is on the diffusion of beer brewing to London, and the subsequent structural changes in the industry. It begins with an examination of the origins of beer, the mechanisms by which it was introduced into England, and the reactions of local brewers to its introduction, before moving on to investigate the factors which contributed to the massive growth of the industry in the late sixteenth and early seventeenth centuries, the backgrounds of alien brewers, and the ways in which they were affected by the commercial changes outlined above.

International Diffusion of Beer

Hopped beer was first brewed in the port towns of northern Germany, particularly Hamburg, during the thirteenth century. During the late thirteenth and fourteenth centuries, Hamburg not only possessed an important beer brewing industry, but also developed a thriving export trade to Holland. In 1376, more than 457 (43 per cent who stated their trade in a survey of the town) were beer brewers.[4] Of these, 126 exported their entire production to Amsterdam.[5] The popularity of hopped beer in Holland encouraged local producers to switch from *gruit* (where a mixture of herbs such as bog myrtle, rosemary and yarrow was used) to beer brewing. By the second half of the fourteenth century, they had successfully mastered the skills, probably through trial and error, and began to compete with German brewers in selling high-quality beers within Holland, and in markets in Flanders and Brabant. In the late fourteenth and early fifteenth centuries, Dutch producers began to experience difficulties in their export markets when a native beer brewing industry was set up in Flanders and Brabant.[6] Under these circumstances, some began to look to England for new opportunities.

Diffusion of the Brewing of Beer to England

Beer brewing was introduced into England by foreign brewers, rather than developed indigenously.[7] As Richard Unger has noted;

> In the case of England the import of the technology was embodied in the brewers who immigrated into the country. It is the only case, it appears, in northern Europe in the later Middle Ages where in the first instance it was not domestic brewers who imitated the new method but rather it was skilled and experienced practitioners from elsewhere who transferred the technology to new surroundings. Any beer brewer in England mentioned in the fifteenth century is said to have had a foreign name.[8]

In the early sixteenth century, most of the important names among alien brewers were German or Dutch, and Mathias has maintained that the aliens had as great an effect on changes in the brewing industry as they had in mining and textiles.[9] However, historians differ widely in their explanations of how these skills were brought to England. Some believe that they were introduced by soldiers or camp followers coming back after foreign service at the beginning of the fifteenth century,[10] some contend that it was German visitors who set up beer brewing in England to meet the needs of German mercenaries employed by the English army,[11] while others suggest that the Flemings arriving in the 1560s played an important role.[12]

A careful analysis of available evidence suggests that beer breweries were in fact first set up in London by migrants from Holland in the early fifteenth century, to satisfy the growing demand for beer from the Dutch immigrants in the city. Prior to this period, beer had been imported from the Continent to meet demand. From the 1370s, merchants in towns along the eastern and southern coasts of England began to import and sell beer, and from the 1380s, beer was carried in significant amounts from Holland through many English ports along the east coast. However, as a result of the burgeoning alien population in the fifteenth century, demand for beer in England had grown sufficiently large to necessitate the establishment of an industry here. In 1441, there were more than 3600 aliens in England, with the majority (2200 aliens) settled in London.[13] The vast majority of aliens (90 per cent) in London were *Doche* (a term used to include Dutch, Flemish and Germans[14]), clustering preponderantly in Southwark, which, according to the available evidence for 1436, housed 44 per cent of aliens living in London.[15] With such a dense concentration of alien customers and its proximity to the Thames allowing convenient access to water supply and transport, Southwark became the centre of beer brewing in London.

Beer was brewed in England after 1400, when a small number of alien beer brewers began to settle here. However, they were few in number: one alien beer brewer was recorded working in Shrewsbury in 1409 and one in York in 1416.[16] In London, there were seven alien brewers in 1436. Their presence in the Capital prompted considerable discontent. As early as 1424–5, there was a complaint from native brewers of 'aliens nigh to the city dwelling [who] brew beer and sell it to retail within the same city'.[17] A complaint by the Commons in 1437 concerning the number of taverns kept by Flemings in London, 'where aliens of all nations congregated',[18] suggests that alien brewers may have been supplying beer to these taverns.

The majority of alien beer brewers in England in the fifteenth century came from Holland. Of the seven brewers recorded in London in 1436, for example, five stated their place of origin as Holland, one as Antwerp, and one as Picardy in France. Migrants from Holland formed the largest group in London in the fifteenth century, and it is not surprising that they were also over-represented in the brewing trade. In addition to finding new opportunities after the loss of markets in Flanders, Brabant and Zealand, these brewers from Holland may have migrated to avoid political conflicts in their homeland. London was probably a favourable choice, as it offered some advantages to beer brewers: a potentially large market, and availability of essential elements of production such as good water, grain and fuel.

The number of alien beer brewers in London increased significantly between 1440 and 1483. In 1440, there were 11 alien beer brewers recorded in the subsidy rolls for Southwark, but by 1483 their number had increased to 119 aliens, including wives and servants. There were, however, only 8 brew masters, employing 54 male and 4 female servants.[19] Each brewhouse thus employed seven servants on average. Martha Carlin has also noted the establishment of eight brewhouses in Southwark between the 1450s and 1490s, most found near the river in Tooley Street and Horselydown Lane.[20] The dramatic increase in the number of aliens involved in brewing clearly reflected the rise in demand for beer. The rise in the import of hops also supports this argument. In the 1470s, substantial quantities of hops were unloaded in London, most of which were shipped by inhabitants of the Low Countries, which was the main area of hop cultivation.[21]

Demand for beer grew for two reasons. The first was the expansion of the alien population, from 2200 to 3400 persons, between 1440 and 1483.[22] The second was the growth of the export trade. By the 1480s exports from London were substantial, but this trade rested almost entirely in the hands of aliens. John Evynger, who was assessed in Tower Ward in 1483, although his brewery seems to have been in St Martin's-in-the-Fields, kept ten servants and brewed for export as well as for consumption in London.[23] By the late 1480s, there were two main centres of production in London: Southwark, perhaps for local consumption, and the eastern suburbs, both for export and local consumption.[24]

Reactions amongst the English to the Introduction of Beer

Beer was not popular among the English in the fifteenth century, even though it was sold at half the price of ale. Ale was considered to be more wholesome and nutritious. Even in the early sixteenth century, it was generally thought that, as one contemporary writer put it, ale was 'cherishing to poor labouring people, without which they cannot well subsist, their food being for the most part of such things as afford little or bad nourishment'.[25] Although it is possible that the bitter taste of beer may have contributed to its unpopularity among English drinkers accustomed to drinking sweet ale, there were other more forceful factors in explaining its relative unpopularity. The most important was probably suspicion about anything foreign. In the fifteenth century, beer was regarded as a Dutch cultural product, and there were frequent attacks on foreigners, especially the Dutch. In 1436, for example, anti-Dutch feelings ran high in London following the Duke of Burgundy's defection to the French. This political event provoked suspicion of the Dutch, and rumours were rife in the City that Dutch beer was poisonous, resulting in attacks on breweries belonging to Hollanders and Zeelanders. As a consequence, the King had to issue a writ urging:

All brewers of *biere* to continue to exercise their art as hitherto, notwithstanding the malevolent attempts that were being made to prevent natives of Holland and Zeeland and others who occupied themselves in brewing the drink called *biere* from continuing their trade, on the ground that such drink was poisonous and not fit to drink, and caused drunkenness, whereas it was a wholesome drink, especially in summer time. Such attacks had already caused many brewers to cease brewing, and would cause greater mischief unless stopped.[26]

It is possible that the ale brewers encouraged such anti-beer campaigns in London for several reasons. First, they strongly opposed the introduction of beer, partly due to concern about foreign competition, especially when the beer brewers proved that they were wealthier. In 1436, 223 ale brewers contributed a total of £13 3s. 6d. to the relief of Calais, and the seven beer brewers alone raised £3 5s.[27] But there was a significant reason for the ale brewers' opposition: fear of unemployment. Brewing had been carried out on a small scale, and provided an important source of employment for many. If brewers could now brew on a larger scale, many would be driven out of business. And even if they wished to take up beer production, they faced a formidable problem: lack of necessary skills. On the surface, ale and beer brewing were essentially the same, with beer requiring merely the additional stage of adding hops. In reality, beer brewing was much more complex, as one of the essential skills was knowing the exact combination of hops, grain, water and boiling time. Incorrect quantities of hops yielded a poor taste and did not enhance the preservation of the beer. The beneficial effect of the oils in the hops could be boiled away if the beer was heated for too long. On the other hand, if it was not boiled for long enough, bitters from the hops remained, giving the beer a harsh taste.[28] The exclusion of the ale brewers from the new skills and technologies helps explain their resistance. Beer initially met with similar resistance in Holland, and this has led Richard Yntema to conclude:

> When a technology with lower production costs is applied in an industry, those who do not, or cannot, apply the new technology will lose revenue and market share, thus reducing the return on their skills and capital investment. In an effort to avoid such losses, brewers who could not switch to the better production methods appealed to have them outlawed.[29]

The friendly attitude of the City and the King was essential to enable the alien brewers to establish themselves in London. The City of London welcomed alien brewers because it felt foreign competition would act as an effective means of preventing native craftsmen raising prices too high. In 1478, the City declared that 'inasmuch as brewers of the city enhance the price of beer against the common weal, foreign brewers should come into the city, and there freely sell their beer until further notice'.[30] The ale brewers' generally low status helps explain their inability to exert political influence over the City's policies. Brewers, predominantly women, did not have a very good reputation – they were associated with dishonesty and malpractices, and their product with drunkenness,[31] and their guild, lacking prestige and economic power, was not an important political force in the City.

The King's actions also facilitated the acceptance of beer. In 1441, five years after the campaign to stigmatize beer as poisonous, the King appointed two royal surveyors to control the quality of beer production in England in an effort to reassure the general public of its quality. However, neither of the men had practical knowledge of the trade or the brewing process, so they made enquiries abroad about how to make and judge good beer. They then reported that to brew good beer, both malt and hops must be perfect; the malt must be of good, sound corn, not too dry, rotten, or having any worms, and the hops must not be rotten or old. Good beer must be sufficiently boiled, contain enough hops, and not be sweet. Finally the beer must not leave the brewery for eight days after brewing.[32] By the 1460s, beer brewing in London had grown to such an extent that the two royal officials entrusted with the task of surveying all beer in England were no longer able to cope with the task. The beer brewers therefore applied to the city to elect two men to act as searchers in London, because 'the common people for lack of experience cannot know the perfectness of beer as well as of ale'.[33] By 1493, beer brewers had managed to form a guild, with their own wardens and ordinances. However, they remained separate from the ale brewers until 1550, when they were united as one guild. In retrospect, this union was fateful for the alien beer brewers who were now greatly outnumbered by English ale brewers in the new Brewers' Guild. As will be discussed below, English brewers were able to use their majority position to discriminate against alien members who increasingly faced stiff barriers of entry to the industry.

Increased Popularity of Beer in Sixteenth-century London

The union of beer and ale brewers into one company in the early sixteenth century ended the ale brewers' resistance to beer and marked the beginning of a period of spectacular growth of the brewing industry. This growth resulted in part from the increasing popularity of beer among English drinkers, both among the laity and the nobility. In 1504, when a banquet was held to celebrate the enthronement of William Wareham as Archbishop of Canterbury, 4 tuns of London ale and 20 tuns of English beer were ordered. Account books of noble households indicate that beer rather than ale was given to their workmen in this period. In 1512, for example, workmen at the Percy family of Northumberland were given between half a gallon to a gallon of beer for breakfast.[34] The growing popularity of beer, however, caused great concern among some Englishmen, as Andrew Boorde expressed it in 1542:

> Ale for an Englishman is a natural drink ... It makes a man strong. Beer is the natural drink for a Dutchman, and now of late days it is much used in England to the detriment of many English people; specially it kills those [who suffered from a colic] ... for the drink is a cold drink, yet it does make a man fat and does inflate the belly, as it does appear by the Dutch men's faces and bellies.[35]

This commentary suggests that by the 1540s, ale was still thought to be more nutritional than beer. However, thirty years later, much of the prejudice against beer had eroded, and beer had replaced ale as the main drink of Londoners. From the 1570s onwards, it was beer, not ale, which was consumed at prestigious City livery companies' banquets and meals, a clear indication of the acceptance of beer among the higher echelons of society. Other contemporary writings also reflected changing public attitudes. Reynold Scott, writing in 1574, described how 'most part of our countrymen do abhor and abandon ale as a loathsome drink'.[36] William Harrison, writing in 1577, spoke contemptuously of the old ale as thick and fulsome, and felt that it was 'an old and sick man's drink', no longer popular except with a few.[37] Beer – weaker, drier and less sweet – was finding a large number of converts, perhaps because it was now appreciated as a more refreshing beverage than strong, heavy and sweet ale.[38] Thus it took nearly two centuries before beer became popular in England. What factors facilitated the shift to beer drinking?

English soldiers returning from military service in Europe may have been an important medium in the changing taste for beer among Englishmen. Beer was adopted very early on as the primary drink of English soldiers and sailors, since it cost less than ale, carried better and kept better,[39] a large quantity could be produced in a short time, and it was more readily available on the Continent than ale. Thus in 1418, the City of London sent more beer than ale to the army of Henry V in France: 300 tuns of beer and 200 tuns of ale. The cheaper price of beer also made it attractive. While ale cost 30s. a tun, beer was sold at less than half the price, only 13s. 4d. In the sixteenth century, the number of English soldiers who drank beer increased as military campaigns in this period involved a substantial number of men. The invasion of France in 1513 involved 30 000 men (equivalent to the population of Norwich, at the time the second largest city in England), and campaigns in 1522 and 1523 in France, whilst smaller in scale, still involved 10 000 soldiers each time. In the 1542 invasion of Scotland, the English army had 20 000 men, and in the 1544 invasion of Boulogne, 40 000 men.[41] In September 1542, a month before the Duke of Norfolk led the invasion of Scotland, the Privy Council made a contract with two London brewers, Giles Harrison, an alien, and Duffelde, probably the John Duffelde in East Smithfield, for the provision of beer. They promised to deliver 1000 tuns of beer in eight days (approximately 250 000 gallons) at the price of 20*s.* per tun, and guaranteed that the beer should keep for five months.[42] Assuming an average consumption of a gallon to a gallon-and-a-half of beer per day, that would last between eight and twelve days. In total, the numbers conscripted into the armed services may have involved more than 2 per cent of the population between 1542 and 1546.[43] It is most likely that upon demobilization, these returning soldiers would continue to drink beer and spread their habits to other Englishmen in London and other parts of England.

The adoption of beer by the military in the fifteenth century may have encouraged Englishmen, perhaps those with Court connections, to invest in beer brewing. By 1483, there were several Englishmen involved in beer production, notably John Saunder, draper, Robert a More, Edmund and William Clerk, Richard Reynold, Thomas Asshford and Martin Blondell.[44] These people came from outside the industry and had no relevant skills, which is presumably why they employed alien servants. They probably assumed an entrepreneurial role, leaving the actual brewing to the aliens. By 1502, English interest in beer brewing had grown sufficiently noticeable to prompt the publication of a recipe by Richard Arnold in his *Chronicle (Customs of London)*. To brew beer, 10 quarters of malt, 2 quarters wheat, 2 quarters oats, and 40 lb hops were stated as necessary to make 60 barrels of single beer.[45] However, this recipe was of little use to inexperienced brewers, as it gave no detail of what was involved in each stage of beer brewing, and thus was probably aimed more at noble and wealthy households and monks in monasteries, who brewed beer for their own consumption and who could afford to experiment. It was not until 1577 that a detailed step-by-step guide to brewing was published by William Harrison.[46] The growing involvement of Englishmen in beer production, however, was instrumental in helping to make beer socially acceptable by sapping the cultural stigma against beer, and by making the drink more widely available as a result of wider distribution networks. By the 1570s, brewhouses were to be found all over London, in Cripplegate, Dowgate, Langbourn, Queenhithe, Westminster and St Katherine, but the largest concentrations were still in Southwark and East Smithfield.

Galloping inflation from the 1540s may have encouraged consumers with reduced spending power to find a cheaper substitute for ale. The composite price index in London rose steadily, from 116 in 1540 to a peak of 248 in 1563, thereafter remaining at 200 until the 1590s, when it jumped to more than 300.[47] During this period of steep price rises and falling living standards, many consumers may have found beer more attractive as in most localities throughout the sixteenth century, it was sold more cheaply than ale. The price differential between the two drinks began to narrow, and eventually disappeared. By the mid-sixteenth century, a barrel of ale and beer were equivalently priced in London: double ale and beer were sold at 4s. in 1576, and strong ale and beer at 8s.[48] Even so, beer still worked out cheaper, as a barrel of beer contained 36 gallons of drink, while one of ale contained only 32.

Inflation also decisively altered English producers' attitudes towards beer. In periods of rising prices, English brewers realized they could significantly reduce their production costs, especially for grains, by switching to beer. Grains formed a high proportion of total costs, because ale brewers had to brew their drink strong in order to improve the longevity of the product. They were thus able to draw only about 8–9 gallons of ale from a bushel of malt. Beer, on the other hand, could be brewed much milder because seething the wort in hops assisted both fermentation and preservation. Beer brewers, therefore, were able to draw 18–20 gallons of good beer from a bushel of malt.[49] These considerations may have persuaded a number of enterprising ale brewers to switch production. Among the 20 English beer brewers surveyed in 1574, 7 of these had been recorded as ale brewers when they were admitted into the Company during the late 1540s and 1560s. It is unclear when they switched production, but the majority probably did so during the 1560s, when prices began to rise steeply. What this also indicates is that the merger of ale and beer brewers in 1550 had made it possible for ale brewers to switch production, for now they could do it without having to transfer craft.

In switching production, English producers faced serious obstacles.[50] The lack of skills was a serious problem, but so too was the subtle, inseparable issue of cultural branding. For nearly two centuries beer had been regarded as a Dutch drink and a Dutch skill. Thus the beer brewed by Englishmen may not have been considered as authentic or as good. Englishmen wishing to open a beer brewhouse therefore had to employ Dutch workmen, both for their reputable skills and name. In the beginning, then, all ale brewers employed alien servants. However, as consumption increased, the exotic quality of beer diminished, reducing barriers of entry for English producers. In 1568, four of those previously recorded as ale brewers are known to have employed a total of 16 alien servants. Richard Platt, who switched production between 1549 and 1550 and whose production was one of the largest in 1574, employed the highest number of alien servants: seven in 1568.[51] But recruitment of skilled alien servants was by no means easy, partly due to the process of chain migration. This meant that new arrivals to London often had friends and relatives already active in the industry, or had work lined up. Even those with no friends or relatives were likely to be drawn to areas with a high foreign population, finding work with fellow countrymen who shared similar cultural and linguistic backgrounds. This made it difficult for English brewers to recruit foreign brewers with the necessary skills, and helps explain why alien brewers were able to dominate the industry for nearly two centuries.

However, restrictive employment laws steadily undermined the advantages enjoyed by alien brewers. During the 1530s, a period when there was a widespread labour shortage, the City of London rejected the request by stranger beer brewers to retain servants of their own nation,[52] hoping thereby to encourage new arrivals to find work with English employers. The Act of 1540 further laid down that no subject or denizen should keep more than four alien servants, yet in 1562 several alien brewers in Southwark were found to employ between 16 and 18 alien servants. Henry Leake and Peter van Duran were both accused of having 18 alien servants each, and Nicholas Gunporte 16. It has been argued that the failure of aliens to comply with these Acts proves that native brewers 'had not acquired sufficient knowledge of the principles of beer-brewing to permit the brewers … to take them into their service in place of workmen of their own nationality'.[53] The skill factor was obviously important in the choice of servants, because beer brewing involved risks and uncertainties in every stage of the production process. Key aspects of brewing such as fermentation could not be properly controlled due to a lack of understanding of the biological and chemical processes involved.[54] Servants with the 'economies of practice' were naturally preferred, to reduce the risks. Equally important as the skill factor was the need for trustworthy and reliable servants, to deliver goods and collect payments, as brewers sold their products both by wholesale and retail. The misfortunes of William Kellett, a Southwark brewer, in the 1530s reveal just how the wholesale side of the business was conducted. Kellett sent a petition to the Chancellor in which he explained how he had hired one John Robyinson to be his brewer for a year, to take charge both of the brewing and the delivery of the ale to his customers. But Robynson, after ten weeks of brewing and delivering the ale, disappeared with the money, leaving him with neither cash nor records of what had been paid and what was still owed him.[55] The importance of trust explains the preference of alien brewers to employ servants of similar cultural and ethnic backgrounds, who perhaps had been recommended or known to them. Wassell Webling from 'Cleves', for example, was recorded as employing six alien servants in November 1571, and of these, four were from 'Cleveland', one from Gelderland and one from Holland.[56] Recognizing the greater need for alien servants as brewing expanded, an Act of Parliament was passed in 1567 allowing beer brewers to employ up to a maximum of eight alien servants each, on the condition that they employed 'an Englishman born either as his first brewer, called the master brewer, or as his second brewer, called the under brewer'.[57] This was clearly intended to provide opportunities for English servants to learn secrets of the trade. These restrictions helped increase the availability of alien servants to work in English breweries, and over time reduced the advantages alien brewers enjoyed.

An enterprising ale brewer who switched production also faced higher risks and higher costs for equipment, supplies and overheads.[58] Although it was possible to brew beer with the same tools used to brew ale, beer brewing was much easier with additional equipment. As with ale brewing, a single copper and single heating source (either an open fire or a closed furnace) sufficed for beer brewing, and was used both for boiling the water initially and later seething the wort in hops. But additional coppers and heating sources, one set for the initial boiling of water and a second set for seething the wort in hops, made beer brewing much easier and quicker. Additional furnaces, gutters, troughs, pails and sieves also facilitated the process. Beer brewers also kept more barrels and kilderkins than ale brewers, because beer needed to be stored longer.[59] To brew beer instead of ale, a brewer had to buy hops and additional fuel. Neither of these commodities cost as much as malt, but they were not cheap, and not always readily available.[60] Beer brewing was also more labour-intensive, requiring the employment of more servants.[61] For these reasons, beer brewing was not only more risky, but also required a higher level of capital investment.

The growing importance of capital in brewing led increasingly to the separation between capital and labour, thereby reducing barriers of entry for English entrepreneurs. By 1574, of the 20 English beer brewers surveyed, 10 had been admitted to the Brewers' Company between 1561 and 1571 (suggesting the point of take-off of the industry), and had transferred from other companies. They were two drapers, two mercers, two tilers, one butcher, one girdler, one leatherseller and one stationer. Yet it is surprising that many transferred companies, because London's custom allowed a freeman to pursue any occupation, even if it was not related to the trade in which he was apprenticed. However, brewing was exempted from this rule. Partly to avoid public health risks, the Brewers' Company forbade non-members from practising their trade, and insisted upon transfer of company. This was the only way to ensure proper regulations of the craft (for example, making sure brewers use good hops and malt). Freemen from other companies who wished to pursue beer brewing had to transfer companies or risked facing a hefty fine. In 1583, the Brewers' Company imposed a hefty fine of £25 on a stranger brewer who 'disorderly and contrary to the laws and ordinances … entered beer brewing … and not being sworn to make good and holsom beer for man's body'.[62] While the separation of labour from capital reduced barriers of entry for English producers, it caused problems for alien brewers, not only by reducing the value of their skills, but also by increasing competition.

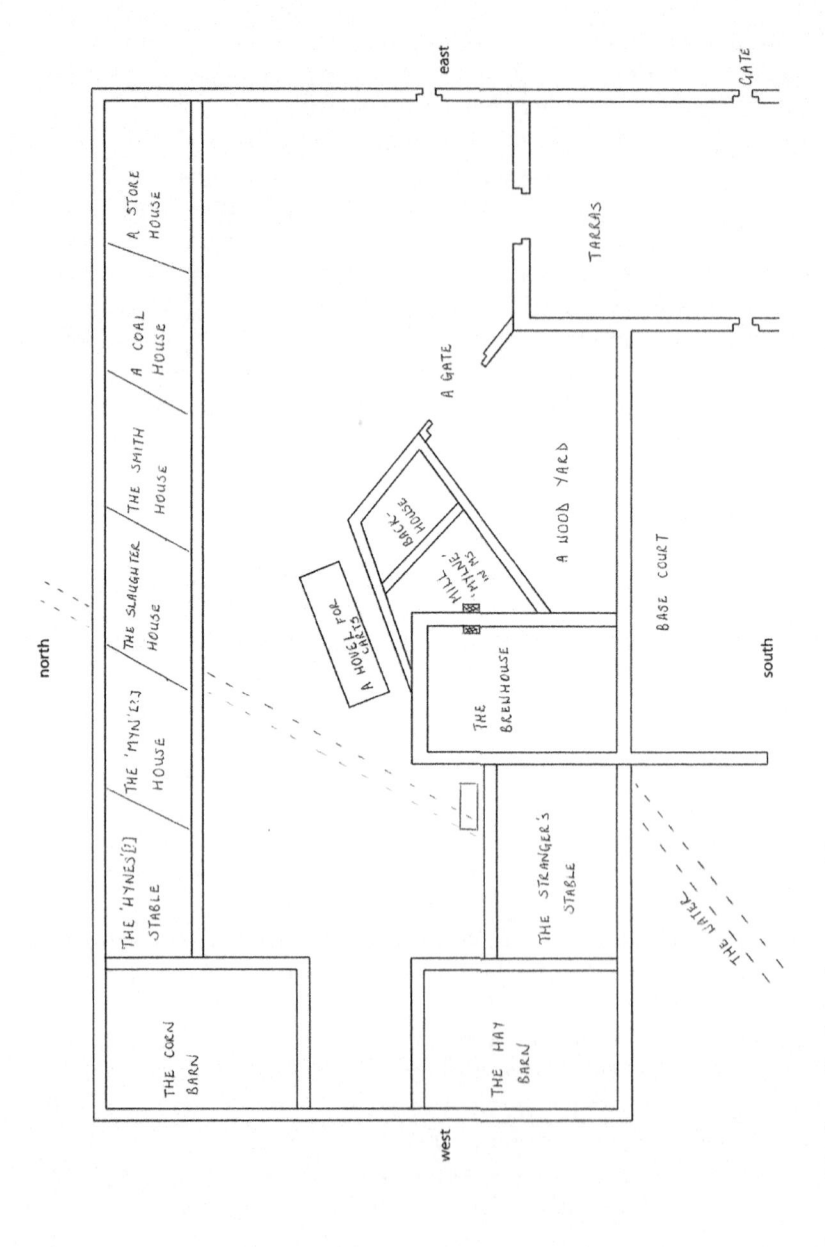

8.1 Ground plan of a brewhouse, 1561
Source: PRO SP12/20/8 I

Expansion of Beer Production

The brewing industry in London grew rapidly in the second half of the sixteenth century. The growing popularity of beer combined with the enormous demographic expansion of London were the main lubricants of this growth. The overall demand for drinks in London probably experienced a fourfold increase, as its population soared from 50 000 in 1500 to 200 000 by 1600. The alien population expanded at least threefold, from some 3400 to more than 10 000 persons by the 1570s. A thriving inland and overseas trade also boosted the growth of the industry. London beer was shipped throughout England during Elizabeth's reign. In 1564–5, £6408 13s. 4d. worth of beer was transported, and in 1572–3, 1728 tuns of beer.

A significant proportion of London beer was also exported to the Low Countries. In 1591, Stow noted that 26 400 barrels of sweet or strong beer were shipped annually to Emden, the Low Countries, Calais and Dieppe.[64] If this figure is added to a generous allowance of 42 000 barrels exported to serve English troops in the Low Countries, then annual exports may have amounted to 68 400 barrels, or nearly 11 per cent of total production.[65] Most of the beer exported was strong beer, which could be stored much longer than double beer. This suggests that although beer was a bulky product, containing a high percentage of water, it was still economical to export strong beer to distant markets. Furthermore, it also indicated the popularity of English beer abroad. In 1580, Stow claimed that: 'of the commodities which were of the growth or manufacture … I find that much Beer was transported, and became a great Commodity in Queen Elizabeth's Reign, and shows in what Request our English beer was then abroad.'[66] Beer from England was especially popular in Amsterdam, and from the middle of the sixteenth century, the authorities there repeatedly established the maximum price at which English beer could be sold.[67] When visiting London in the 1590s, the Swiss Thomas Platter recorded how its citizens 'drink beer which is as fine and clear in colour as an old Alsatian wine'.[68] London beer was qualitatively different, and contained a high percentage of barley, whereas Dutch beer had more oats. In 1613, Londoners spoke of Hollanders coming to buy beer in exchange for grain and other commodities.[69] However, evidence does not allow one to conclude with any certainty whether the export of beer was rising or falling. It is possible that as London's own consumption increased in the second half of the sixteenth century, exports may have become relatively less significant. Indeed, despite foreign markets in the Baltic, Ireland and elsewhere, Peter Mathias argues that as late as the eighteenth century the metropolitan market was the real determinant of the size and success of London breweries.[70] This argument can also be applied to the sixteenth century, and the enormous demographic expansion may have been the 'engine of growth' of beer breweries in the Capital.

Estimating total beer production and consumption is difficult, as there is little available evidence. However, the weekly quantity of malt used by brewers gives us a rough idea of the total level of production and consumption in London. This data is available for 1574 and 1595, when, prompted by concerns of grain shortage, the Brewers' Company was asked to report to the City authorities the amount of malt used weekly by its members, as shown below. Table 8.2 shows that the total production of ale and beer rose by 30 per cent between 1574 and 1595, a period when the population of London more than doubled. There are limitations to using these data to calculate production and consumption. In the first place, it is not possible to calculate the *actual* level of production and consumption, because these data do not tell us the amount of malt brewers devoted to brewing different types of beer, which would determine total output.

Brewers could produce a higher volume simply by increasing the amount of malt devoted to brewing cheaper and weaker types of beer such as small (single) beer, made by pouring fresh water over the wort in the vat after the strong beer had been drawn off.[71] In the second place, they do not indicate the amount devoted to export. In 1590, when the price of malt rose to more than 25*s.* per quarter, brewers were forbidden to brew types of drinks which used a lot of grain, such as strong beer, march beer and strong ale, and to export beers.[72] In the third place, the Brewers' Company may not have known the

Table 8.2   Ale and beer production in London, 1574–1595

	No. of Brewers 1574	1595	Total quantity of malt used weekly (quarters) 1574	1595	Total beer brewed weekly (000s of gallons)[1] 1574	1595	Quantity of malt per brewer (quarters) 1574	1595
Beer brewers Alien & English	32	27	1 539	2 160	167–277	233–389	48	80
Ale brewers English	58	56	700	672	42	40	12	12
Total	90	83	2239	2832	209–319	273–429	—	—

Notes: [1] Total quantity of drink brewed weekly is estimated based on the assumption that one quarter of malt produced 60 gallons of ale and 108 gallons of strong beer, or 180 gallons of double beer.

Sources: BL, Cotton Faustina CII, ff. 177–88; GL, MS 5445/9 (21/10/1595).

actual amount of malt used by its members. The Company allowed only six brewings per week, but many brewers brewed on Sundays as well. Thus the reported weekly quantity of malt used underestimated the actual level of output. Lastly, this figure represented output of commercial brewers, but did not include domestic output by women or by aristocratic households for their own consumption. Thus the data almost certainly underestimates total production and consumption.

Table 8.2 suggests that in 1574, between 167 000 and 277 000 gallons of beer, or approximately 759 000–1 259 000 litres were brewed, rising to 1 million 1.7 million litres by 1595. These figures grossly underestimate total consumption. Assuming a population of 120 000 in the 1580s and 200 000 by 1600 and a daily consumption of 2 litres of drink per head, total consumption was likely to be at least 87 million and 146 million litres, respectively. These approximate figures are comparable to Richard Unger's calculations for London of 51 million litres in 1574 and 106 million litres in 1585.[73]

Following the increase in demand, the brewing industry underwent significant changes in its organization. The most notable change was the relative shift in ale and beer production. Ale production fell by 5 per cent between 1574 and 1595, while beer production rose by nearly 40 per cent over the same period. The scale of production also expanded enormously, with the average weekly output of beer breweries rising by nearly 170 per cent between 1574 and 1595 (Table 8.2). In 1574, beer brewers used on average 48 quarters of malt per week, producing 5184 gallons, or 144 barrels, of strong beer each. By 1595, the average weekly consumption of malt had increased to 80 quarters per week, suggesting a production of 8640 gallons, or 240 barrels, of strong beer each. By the early seventeenth century, the weekly output of breweries in London had increased even further. In 1612, the Brewers' Company allowed beer brewers to brew only four times a week, with 80 quarters of malt per brewing, and ale brewers twice a week, using 20 quarters per brewing.[74] Larger-scale production drove out smaller brewers, and as a result the number of beer brewers dropped from 32 to 27 between 1574 and 1595, a 16 per cent fall. During this period, other towns also had a small number of core full-time brewers. In 1585, Leicester had five such men dominating town output. Coventry, which had 60 public brewers in 1520, had about 13 common brewers around this time, with an average production each of 4 tuns, or about 1000 gallons a week.[75] Larger scale of production, requiring higher capital investment and greater risks, may have necessitated concentration of production in fewer hands, as smaller or less enterprising brewers were forced out of business.

The increase in output was reflected in the number of servants employed. In the fifteenth century, a typical beer brewery employed eight servants. By

1574, breweries on average still employed some seven workers, including one clerk, one master brewer and five other servants.[76] By the 1590s, however, a dozen workers was quite common, although four alien breweries employed more than 30 servants each, and one 43 servants.[77] By the 1630s, an average staff of two dozen workers was quite normal. One estimate from 1636 suggests that on average, a beer brewer employed 22 workers, including three clerks, a master brewer, an under brewer, four tun men, a stoker, a miller, two coopers, six draymen, two stable workers and a hog man.[78] The demand for servants was so great that in 1612 the Brewers' Company, in an effort to reduce the enticing away of brewers' servants, ordered brewers not to take servants without the consent of their previous masters.[79] Significantly, by the seventeenth century, the highest paid employees in a brewery were the brewer's clerks, who filled orders and collected payments.[80]

Brewing became a highly profitable enterprise. In 1574, a government estimate of a typical brewery shows that the total cost of each brewing was £17 3s. 10d. From it, the brewer produced 13 tuns of beer, and the total income from the sale, together with the yeast and grains, was £18 14s. 2d., giving the brewer 30s. 4d. by the day. Another estimate in the 1630s shows that the profits had greatly increased (see Table 8.3). According to this, the total cost of each brewing was £30 18s. 4d. From this, the brewer produced 12 tuns of 8s. (strong) beer, and 6 tuns of 4s. (middle) beer. The brewer made a net profit of £7 13s. 5d. per brewing, and assuming 312 brewings per year (six to seven times a week) the total annual income was estimated at £2,393 19s.

The net profit margin was doubtless lower, because of the allowances to tipplers for returned beer.[82] In 1592, the Brewers' Company, presented their own estimate of the actual profits of brewing, claiming that the brewer made a profit of only 3d. on every quarter of corn used to make strong beer, and 9d. small beer.[83] As the brewers used on average 80 quarters of malt in this period, and assuming that 40 quarters was devoted to brewing strong beer and the other half small beer, the net profit was £2 every brewing, and with 312 brewings a year, their profit may have amounted to £624. Other evidence suggests that profits may have been lower. Wassell Webling, an alien brewer in Southwark, claimed in 1571 that the profit from his brewery was £160 per annum, rather than the expected level of £400.[84] Profit level was determined by the types of beer brewed and the market. With prices in the domestic market fixed by the City, brewers may indeed have found it hard to increase their profit margin.

Overall, Clark feels that larger breweries had a healthy turnover and income, and the prospects of the trade were sound. This was in distinct contrast to traditional urban industries such as clothing, which were often beset by trade disruption and decay before the Civil War.[85] The immense wealth of beer brewers enabled the Brewers' Company to emerge as a leading

Table 8.3 Estimates of costs of brewing a tun of beer in London, 1574–1636

Expenditure	1574 Cost	%	1592 Cost	%	1636 Cost	%
Grains	21s. 6d.	82	32s. 2d.	63	29s. 2d.	85
Hops	2s. 4d.	9	5s. 8d.	11	1s. 6d.	4
Fuel (coal)	0s. 8d.	3	1s. 7d.	3	0s. 9d.	2
Wages	0s. 7d.	2	11s. 7d.	23	1s. 3d.	4
Rent/other charges	0. 12d.	4	—	—	1s. 9d.	5
Total cost	26s. 4d.	100	51s. 2d.	100	34s. 4d.	100
Profit per tun	2s. 4d.		1s.		£0 8s. 6d.	
Profit per brewing	30s. 4d.		No data		£7 13s. 5d.	

Notes: One tun = 250 gallons.
Sources: PRO SP12/98/37 (October 1574); GL, MS 5445/9 (8 June 1592); PRO SP16/341/124 (1636).

City guild after 1600. By the mid-seventeenth century, they were said to be using 'their interests, parts and purses which are very considerable to stop the collection of the excise tax on beer'.[86] In 1665, the Brewers' Company had four members serving as Aldermen of London,[87] testifying to their considerable political influence by this date.

The expansion of the beer brewing industry in London stimulated other important changes in the English economy, particularly the expansion of the coal industry. Fuel costs were one of the largest expenses in beer brewing, and as production increased, it was imperative to find a cheaper source of fuel. Fuel costs formed a larger proportion of the total cost of beer brewing than ale, because it used more fuel due to its larger scale of production and lengthier boiling process (Harrison calculated that wood accounted for a quarter of the cost of brewing beer). While ale brewing may have taken two to three hours, beer brewing took between eight and thirty hours.[88] Brewers could substantially reduce their fuel costs by finding a cheaper substitute, such as coal, or developing methods to economize wood consumption. Although the substitution of coal would have been a much cheaper and viable option in the long term, the prevailing concerns about air pollution in London in the 1560s and the belief that the smell and the dirt of sea coal fire would affect the taste of beer prevented the adoption of coal in brewing.[89] Efforts were focused instead on economizing on fuel consumption by developing a more cost-effective furnace. In 1565, it was reported that the new furnaces introduced by aliens enabled beer brewers to reduce their wood consumption by one-third, and save two hours in heating the furnaces.[90]

As the demand for wood rocketed and the supplies of wood dwindled, the substitution of coal became the only practicable alternative for large industrial users such as brewers, especially when coal could be transported cheaply by water from Newcastle to London.[91] From the 1570s, brewers were switching to coal on a greater scale.[92] Coal was cheaper than wood, and it was now considered better by brewers because it provided more even and intense heat.[93] Ale brewers, however, continued to use wood, as they brewed smaller quantities, so wood was a more convenient source of fuel.[94] Pollution from coal caused great annoyance, and in January 1578 brewers were instructed not to burn any coal while the Queen was at Westminster because she was 'grieved and annoyed with the taste and smell of sea coals'.[95] A week later, nine beer brewers were sent to prison for disobeying this order. The plea by the Wardens and Masters of the Brewers' Company to the Lord Mayor to allow their members to use coal, as they did not have adequate provision of wood, was rejected. In February 1578, therefore, the Brewers' Company petitioned for the restriction of burning coal to apply only to 'some special days with warning'. In 1585, the dispute was finally settled when brewers proposed that breweries near Westminster would only use wood, while beer brewers elsewhere would use coal. This switch to coal was thus a crucial development, enabling not only individual brewers to increase their profit margins, but also the industry as a whole to sustain and fuel its expansion.

Alien Beer Brewers in London

Alien brewers controlled a significant proportion of beer production in London during the sixteenth century. The City's survey of weekly use of malt by brewers in 1574 shows that there were 12 alien brewers, responsible for more than a third of total beer production in London (see Table 8.4). The Return of Aliens, however, suggests that the number of alien brewers was much greater, listing 21 masters in 1571. It is likely that the 1574 survey only counted major brewers, and excluded some of the smaller producers.

The importance of aliens in beer production is magnified if we also include those aliens employed in English-owned breweries. Of the 22 English beer brewers recorded in 1574, it is certain that 8 of them had previously employed 22 alien servants between 1564 and 1571. In November 1571, ten alien servants were recorded as working with English masters. If we assume that these eight English beer brewers (who used 403 quarters of malt per week) still employed alien servants in 1574, aliens may have been involved in the

Table 8.4 Scale of production by alien and English brewers in London, 1574

	Brewers No.	%	Malt used weekely Quantity (quarters)	%	Quantity per brewer (quarters)
Beer brewers					
Aliens	12	37.5	542	35	45
English brewers known to employ alien servants	8	25.0	403	26	50
English brewers	12	37.5	594	39	49.5
Total	32	100.0	1 539	100.0	48 (average)

Sources: British Library, Cotton Faustina CII, ff. 177–88 (1574). See Table 8.8 for names and other details.

production of more than 60 per cent of beer brewed in London. While this evidence clearly confirms the importance of aliens in the late sixteenth century, at the same time it also indicates that by this date, English producers had made significant encroachments into the industry, now controlling a large part of beer production in London.

Who were the alien brewers? Alien brewers were generally referred to as 'Dutch', but this term is highly misleading. In the fifteenth century, the majority of 'Dutch' beer brewers came from Holland, but by the second half of the sixteenth century, by far the largest number of them originated from the Rhineland, Cologne, Cleves, Julich, and Liege in particular, an area which was also renowned for its brewing industry. The Returns of Aliens of 1568, 1571 and 1593 show that aliens from the Rhineland made up 41 per cent of the 137 stranger brewers and servants surveyed. The proportion from the Rhineland was likely to have been higher still, as many who simply indicated that they were 'Dutch' may have come from here. The proportion from Brabant and Flanders was 11 per cent, that from northern Netherlands (Holland and Gelderland) 5 per cent, but the number from Germany and Walloon provinces was negligible. There are two reasons for the changes in the origins of alien brewers. The Rhineland was experiencing great economic, political, religious and social upheavals, but the convenience of water transport and the existence of an established Dutch community in London may have also been responsible for encouraging many to leave their homeland. In addition, the decline in the number from Holland reflected better prevailing economic opportunities, which in turn reduced the need for brewers to migrate. Domestic demand for beer in Holland rose in the sixteenth century, partly due to demographic growth and rising per capita consumption. Production in Delft, one of the three principal brewing centres in Holland, for instance, expanded enormously in the sixteenth century.[96] Many alien beer brewers arrived before the mass migration of the 1560s, largely for economic reasons. More than half of 21 alien beer brewers recorded in the Return of 1571 arrived in London between 1541 and 1559. Ten of these gave reasons for migration: three for religion, one to join a family member, but six confessed to having come for work. Of the 44 alien servants listed in 1571, 29 gave their reasons for coming to London, of whom 27 stated their motive as to 'come to work' and 'labour in brewing', one for 'god's words', and one for the political reason of serving the Prince of Orange.[97]

Alien brewers settled predominantly in two main centres of brewing in London: the eastern suburbs and in Southwark, especially in the parish of St Olave, close to the river. In 1567, 12 Dutch brewers settled in Bridge Without Ward (Southwark), in comparison to 13 found living in East Smithfield, and 5 in St Katherines in 1568 (see Table 8.5).

Table 8.5 Residential distribution of master and servant brewers in London, 1568 and 1571

Areas	1568 M	%	1568 S	%	1571 M	%	1571 S	%
City								
Castle Baynard	—	—	—	—	—	—	1	3
Farringdon Without	—	—	—	—	—	—	1	3
Cripplegate	—	—	—	—	1	5	—	—
Dowgate	—	—	—	—	3	13	—	—
Langbourn	—	—	—	—	1	5	—	—
Queenhithe	—	—	—	—	1	5	8	23
St Olave, Bridge Without	—	—	—	—	10	45	13	38
St George, Bridge Without	—	—	—	—	4	18	6	18
Tower	—	—	—	—	1	9	5	15
Middlesex and Westminster								
East Smithfield	13	65	26	76	—	—	—	—
St Katherine	5	25	3	9	—	—	—	—
Westminster	2	10	5	15	—	—	—	—
Total	20	100	34	100	21	100	34	100

Notes: Information for the suburbs has been used here to supplement details for 1571 Return.
M = masters; S = servants
Sources: 1568 and 1571: Kirk and Kirk, eds, *Returns of Aliens.*

Most breweries in the eastern suburbs were small, suggesting that they were probably only brewing for local consumption, rather than for export: only 27 per cent employed any servants. However, two breweries were quite substantial. Henry Loberry and John Pegnets had ten servants each. The others were smaller, like that of Henry Went, who employed three servants, or John a Kent and Edward Winard, who employed one each, making a total of 25 servants in all. Of the 21 brewers in the City wards in 1571, 28.5 per cent employed servants: Hawnse Hulst in Queenhithe had 8 alien servants, Peter van Durant in St Olave Soutwark 9 servants, Wessell Weblyn in the same parish 6 servants, Peter Androwes 1 servant, William Jeymes in St Georges Parish (Southwark) 6 servants, and Roger James in Tower Ward 4 servants, making a total of 34 servants. The largest alien breweries in the eastern suburbs, then, were bigger than those in the City wards.

The spatial distribution of brewhouses was dictated by several factors. The first was the need for water, which, as far as we can tell, came from two main sources in the sixteenth century: drawn directly from rivers, and obtained from wells and conduits. In the sixteenth century, according to Harrison, Thames water was the best for brewing, and this was drinkable if taken far enough upstream from the built-up areas. By 1655, however, with expanding industrial activities and pollution, brewers were advised to use other river water, as 'the Thames water will never do well'.[98] Alternatively, brewers could use water from conduits. Stow listed 17 conduits within the City in 1598, but this water, free to domestic users, had to be paid for by commercial operators such as brewers.[99] Brewers also required access to water transport for the supply of raw materials such as grain and coal, as well as for shipping beer to export markets. Large brewhouses therefore came to cluster alongside the Thames.[100]

In comparison to other aliens, brewers were wealthy and, on the whole, settled, as indicated by their considerable length of residence in London. However, their careers and fortunes varied somewhat. It appears that many spent a considerable number of years working as journeymen before setting up their own brewery, but the length of time varied. Those who had no relatives already active in the industry spent longer periods working as journeymen, partly to accumulate sufficient capital to set up their brewery, and partly to acquire the necessary skills and experience. John Smithe from Cologne worked for over thirty years before he was able to set up his own brewery in 1571; Derick Gorth from Cleves worked in London for 36 years, and Godfrey Derickson from Cologne 47 years before he was able to set up his own brewery in 1568. However, those who had family members already active in the industry had a clear advantage, as they could quickly learn from them secrets of the trade accumulated over many years of experience, and perhaps could also borrow money to set up their own brewery. Wassell

Webling, for example, ran a brewery as a partner less than three years after his arrival in London. Arriving in London probably in 1565 at the age of 16 (the Return of Aliens of November 1571 gives his age as 22), Wassell worked as a servant to his brother, Nicholas Webling, a brewer. Unfortunately, Nicholas died in 1568.[101] After that, Wassell ran a brewery in partnership with Nicholas's widow, Elizabeth. However, this did not last, as soon there developed an acrimonious dispute over profits, resulting in a legal battle. Elizabeth and her new husband, Thomas Dolman, had apparently pressurized Wassell into promising to give £200 as profits for the first six months of the partnership. Wassell, 'a stranger born, inexperienced in the trade of beer-brewing, and having no friends or kinsfolk of whom to take counsel', had agreed to pay the requested amount. However, he was unable to meet this, as the actual profits only amounted to £80 for six months – so each partner would pocket only £40 each, instead of the expected £200.[102]

After the partnership broke up, Wassell went to work with William Coxe, an Englishman, who married the widow, Alice, of Henry Leeke, a prominent alien brewer in Southwark who, in 1564, had worked with his brother.[103] Two years later, in 1570, Wassell Webling found himself embroiled in another dispute, this time with the widow of his partner, Alice Coxe. After the death of her husband, Alice wanted to sell the brewhouse. However, the division of the estate, valued at £2400 net, was not straightforward, as most of the assets (£2000) were locked up in debts, and most of these debts, as the assessors pointed out, 'will be long time in gathering in and many of them can very hardly or never be had'[104] if the business was to terminate. So Alice Coxe was given a choice: either to pay Wassell £750 for his share of the business, or lease the brewhouse to him and receive approximately £900 and an annual rent of £130.[105] Running a successful brewery was not an easy matter for a woman,[106] and this realization may have persuaded Alice to lease the brewhouse to Wassell. By 1586, Wassell had moved from Southwark to the neighbourhood of the Steelyard on the other side of the river. By 1593, he was running a large brewery, employing more than 34 servants. Wassell died a wealthy man in 1610, with bequests totalling more than £1100 in cash. He had no heirs, and left lands and properties to his cousin, Nicholas Webling, who became a Brother of the Brewers' Company in 1591, and his son. His bequests showed he had developed extensive kinship and friendship networks in London. But unlike others, he also remembered the poor of his native home town, 'Groten Recken in Westphalia', leaving them a small bequest of 20s.[107]

The career of Roger James, another prominent alien brewer, shows that a good marriage was also important for an aspiring brewer. At the age of 17, Roger came to London around 1541 with his brother, Derick James, also a brewer, from the Duchy of Cleves. His early years in London are unknown, but presumably he and his brother worked as servants for other brewers. By

8.2 Roger James, alien brewer
Source: From G.H. Gater and W.H. Godfrey, eds, *Survey of London*, Vol. 15 (London, 1934), p. 62

8.3 Beer brewer, sixteenth century
Source: From L.F. Salzman, *English Industries of the Middle Ages* (London, 1970), p. 290

1562, he was running a brewery in partnership with a Dutch brewer, John Cornellis, which appears to have lasted until at least 1567. During this period, Roger James bought Clare's Quay in 1566. It is unclear when he got married and how much Sara, the daughter and sole heiress of Henry Morskin of London, brought to the marriage. By 1573, he was running a brewery sufficiently large to necessitate the employment of a master brewer. In April 1573, he was recorded giving the job to John Frenge, a Dutchman.[108] Later, he acquired the brewhouse known as 'The Ram's Head' some time between 1576 and 1579. By 1582, he had become quite wealthy, paying the highest rate of £300 in the subsidy of that year. By the time of his death in 1591–2 at the age of 67, he had amassed a great fortune, with bequests totalling more than £6000: his wife, Sara, alone received £1500. Upon his death, his second son, Arnold James, probably took over the business, and was still active in London in the early seventeenth century.[109] His will shows that Roger James was more than a successful brewer. He was also a shrewd entrepreneur, and had invested in other related activities. In addition to the possession of three brewhouses, he also bought a water mill, presumably for grinding grain and perhaps to drive pumps used in the mashing process, several quays for loading goods from water-transport, inns to provide outlets for his beers, and owned extensive properties in London, Essex and Kent. By the early seventeenth century, it was common for brewers to seek vertical integration of their business. Despite official efforts to stop them, many became prominent maltsters. They also used profits to acquire landed property to enhance their social standing and ensure supplies of corn for their brewhouses.[110]

By the 1590s, it appears that aliens with capital were entering brewing. One of the most successful examples of these was Jacob Wittewrongle, son of a Ghent merchant, whose trade connections and capital may have helped to give him a promising start. Wittewrongle does not appear to have run a brewery on his own, but always in partnership with other more established alien brewers, indicating either his lack of skills in brewing or the necessity of partnerships engendered by the growing capital requirements. In 1591, he ran a brewhouse in Grantham Lane (later Brewer's Lane) with two established Dutch brewers – Mathias Otten (a member of the Company since 1572 who had worked as a partner with Roger James)[111] and Peter Leonards the elder. But Otten and Leonards were more than just business partners: they were also members of his family. Otten was the father-in-law of his daughter, while Leonards was his brother-in-law. By the time of his death in 1621, Wittewrongle was extremely wealthy, with bequests totalling more than £8000. His second wife, Anne, alone received more than £3000. He also owned a brewhouse in Great Allhallows near Dowgate, and a third share in the brewhouse called the 'Katherine Wheele' in East Smithfield. He also bequeathed to his two sons-in-law, Mathias Otten and Peter Leonards the younger, also brewers, £2500 each to buy their own land and tenements.[112]

The examples of the careers of men like Roger James, Wassell Webling and Jaques Wittewrongle show that some alien brewers were able to accumulate vast fortunes. Others, however, left more modest sums. John Powell, Wassell Webling's father-in-law, left more than £2000 in bequests in 1599, Dericke James (Roger James's brother) owned two brewhouses at the time of his death in 1589, but his cash bequests amounted to only £300. Mathias Rutten the elder left only some £100 in 1599, while Jacob Janson, a brewer from Friesland, did not mention any sums of money or a brewhouse in his will of 1634.[113]

In comparison with other aliens, beer brewers were on the whole wealthier and more privileged. In the subsidy of 1582, for example, alien beer brewers, along with merchants, paid the highest tax rates. Of the 1840 aliens liable to pay tax, only 12 paid £10 or more, of which 3 were brewers (Roger James, taxed at £30, Tice Rutton at £15, and John van Holst alias Haunce at £10) and 7 were merchants (including Sir Horatio Pallavicino, taxed at £35, Martin de la Falia £30, Nicholas Fountayne at £20 and Philip and Bartholomew Curseyne at £15).[114] What also distinguished them from other aliens was their possession of citizenship, obtained in several stages. The first stage was the acquisition of a letter of denization giving them the legal right to work as a brewer and employ a certain number of alien servants. This was followed by the acquisition of the freedom of the City through redemption, conferring upon them extensive privileges such as the ability to purchase land, pass on wealth to children, and most important of all, giving their children the right to serve apprenticeship. This method was neither cheap nor easy, requiring both political influence and wealth. This explains why only a small proportion of first-generation aliens ever became freemen. In 1581, probably in recognition of their valuable service to the City, the Court of Aldermen granted nine alien brewers (Roger James, Matthew Rutton, John Powell, Wassell Weblinge, John Smith, Dirricke James, John Vanhulse, Dirricke Helden and Henry Hopdenaker) the freedom of the City, costing each £50.[115] This grant gave the parties involved mutual financial benefits: the City of London was £450 richer, while the alien brewers obtained considerable freedom and privileges. As freemen, for example, they could place their sons to be apprentices with other freemen. In 1584, Roger James placed his son, Arnolde James, to serve apprenticeship with Mathew Merten, a London brewer for the term of eight years but then 'set him over' to him. In August 1592, Arnolde James was admitted into the Brotherhood of the Company. Two days later, his father, Roger James, the youngest warden, gave 'one bazon and one ewar of silver' to the Company out of good will.[116] The freedom of the City and its concomitant opportunities for upward mobility were crucial to success because it made aliens feel settled in their new homeland, in the knowledge that they could accumulate and pass on wealth to their children. This in itself was an important incentive to work hard.

Declining Opportunities for Alien Brewers

Although aliens still controlled a large part of beer production in the 1570s, it is clear that their significance declined steadily after this date. Evidence shows that while in the fifteenth century most beer brewers are known to have been aliens, by the late sixteenth century they only made up one-third of beer brewers in London. By 1607, of the 50 brewers who contributed money to the Brewers' Company only 8 per cent can be identified as aliens.[117]

So what caused this significant shift in the beer brewing industry in London? The spectacular growth of the industry in the late sixteenth century may have been the key factor, as it precipitated three significant changes. The most important was the rise in capital investment, which in turn raised the barrier of entry, as brewers now needed more money to start up, to buy equipment and to invest in greater amounts of stock and raw materials.

It is unclear how much capital was needed to set up a brewhouse in the sixteenth century. In 1450, a brewhouse cost 320 marks (c.£213),[118] but brewers could lease this. However, money was required to buy equipment and raw materials. The inventory of Jacob Wittewrongle for 1621 shows that his equipment, including a great copper kettle, a mash tun with a loose bottom, a woort tun, a yield tun, coal barks, four hand kettles and one scouring fork, was valued at approximately £84 (see Table 8.6).[119]

More critical was the necessity of maintaining a large working capital to cover credit to customers. Debts constituted a large proportion of brewers' capital. Although all brewers provided credit to customers and had to absorb unpaid debts, these were an acute problem especially for beer brewers, perhaps because their larger operations produced more customers and bigger debts.[120] Throughout the sixteenth century, beer brewers constantly complained about bad debts. When Roger Mascall died in 1573, he left more than £1400 in 'desperate and doubtful debts' owed by more than 200 customers. He had more of his wealth in bad debts than in assets.[121] In other words, alien brewers wishing to set up needed at least a few hundred pounds. They also needed to pay approximately £20 admission fee into the Brotherhood of the Brewers' Company, which was essential for them to set up independently, and £50 to gain admission to the freedom of the City. This was a considerable sum considering that the average annual wage of a journeyman brewer was only £10.

Partnership was one way to raise the necessary capital (see Table 8.7). The

Table 8.6 Jacob Wittewrongle's inventory of a brewhouse, 1621

In the brewhouse

1. One greate kettle of copper, one old Combe & Seven plancks	£51
2. Item a mash tonne with a loose bottome, four ruddersone stickforde shed a stewke fourteen stickmans, three hop ouanndy?, A Tap and the Stilling round about the same Tonnne & the underback	£6 10s.
3. A woort tonne with an apron of lead	£6
4. A yeld tonne with an apron of leade, a float, two funnels with two pypes of Iron	£8
5. Four Coal backs standing upon their frames with all their Iron works to hang them on	£12
6. Four hand kettles of white copper or brasse with handles of iron	£0 6s.
7. Certaine old stelling	£0 6s.
8. One Skowring forke and an Iron rack	£0 8s.

In the malt loft

1. A myll sack, a Cradle, a Call, a hopper, one ronner, two ledges, a myll ring, one other Cradle & hopper and skreene	£0 51s.
2. One myll wheel with the furniture & one trundle wheele with the frame unto that and one olde wheel without a trundle	£5

Total	*c.* £84

Notes: Kettle: used to boil water. Mash tun: used boil or steep malt in hot water. Wort tun: used to boil wort (a sweet extract from malt) with hops.
Sources: Hertfordshire Archives and Local Studies, Jacob Wittewrongle Inventory DIEwB1.

survey of 1574 mentioned four partnerships among the stranger beer brewers, and none among the English brewers, reflecting perhaps the lower financial resources of aliens. Among the 35 strangers who were admitted as Brothers into the Brewers' Company between 1566 and 1597, at least a third had worked together as partners. Of the 13 partnerships formed, nearly half were cemented during the 1570s, indicating perhaps the increasing capital requirements necessitated by the growing scale of production. By the 1580s, partnerships were becoming so popular in the City that the Guild ordered that no brewer could be in more than one partnership at one time.[122]

But partnerships were short-term business liaisons, and could prove acrimonious, especially over profits when one of the partners died, as clearly demonstrated in the case of Wassell Webling. Possible complications inherent in partnerships persuaded brewers like Wittewrongle to draw up detailed

Table 8.7 Partnerships among alien brewers, 1568–97

Date	Alien brewer	Partner
1560–68	Roger James	John Cornellis
1568	Henry Loberry	Dirricke James
1568	John Pegnets	John Portman
1572	John Powell	James Heyth
1572–4	Mathew Rutton	Roger James
1575	Arnolde Ludbery	Unknown
1575	Harry Arnolde	Dirricke James
1575	John Picknett	Unknown
1575	Roger James	Mathew Rutton
1582	Roger James	Wassell Weblinge
1582 September	Henry Hopdemaker	John Jacourte
1587 May	John Du Buis	John Vanhulse
1597 January	Desmeitres James	Henrye Cruel

Sources: 1574: BL, Cotton Faustina CII, ff. 177–88 (1574). 1568 and 1571: Kirk and Kirk, eds, *Returns of Aliens*. GL, Brewers' Company, Court Minutes.

contracts, stipulating clearly who would take over the business if one of the partners died.[123]

Besides a higher fixed capital investment, larger scales of production also presented a greater managerial challenge. Running a large enterprise demanded a level of managerial competence and interpersonal skills that young and inexperienced aliens, especially those whose English was poor, would find difficult to learn. This was especially so because the workforce was made up largely of male English workers. As a result of restrictions on the employment of alien servants, brewhouses became more and more dependent on English servants as they increased in scale, for two reasons. They needed English servants to meet their labour needs. The Act of 1567 only allowed London brewers to employ up to eight alien servants, but this number was insufficient as the size of breweries increased in scale. Alien brewers coped with the restrictions by employing English servants to supplement their labour needs. In 1593, for example, the brewery run by Mary James (Roger James's sister-in-law) employed 33 servants, of whom 25 were English, and 8 aliens. Wassell Webling employed 36 servants in 1593, only 5 of whom were aliens, and 31 English.[124] In addition, aliens also needed English servants for their financial and accounting skills. They employed English clerks to keep records of their accounts, and perhaps also to facilitate relations with English customers. However, this was seen by other English brewers as a clever ploy to get English business.[125] There were also other practical problems with managing a large workforce, including theft by servants. In 1599, for example, a time when the price of malt increased steeply, John Vanhulse dismissed six servants after they were caught stealing malt and other goods from his cellar.[126]

But the most important reason for the difficulties facing aliens setting up after the 1570s was discrimination imposed by the Brewers' Company. As we have seen earlier, the high profitability of brewing persuaded many English producers to switch production from ale to beer, and others to move companies so that they could run a brewery. With an increased number of entrants to the trade, alien brewers faced growing competition from English brewers, who sought to undermine their perceived advantages. English producers, especially large ones, resented aliens' domination of the industry, the key to which, they believed, was aliens' control of the export trade, giving them a lucrative outlet for their beers and access to imported hops. In 1593, it was reported that the Flemings brought over fish and hops, and used the same ships to transport beer overseas.[127] Second, it was believed that alien brewers, as first-comers to the industry, enjoyed the best location. In the early seventeenth century, alien brewers were still perceived to possess unfair advantages, and English producers complained how they relied on alien ships and servants, and that aliens controlled foreign markets and had convenient wharves along the Thames.[128]

From the 1570s, English producers sought to reduce aliens' monopoly of the industry by imposing a ban on the admission of aliens into the Brewers' Company, and later by increasing entry fees. In 1573, native brewers encouraged the Brewers' Company to restrict the number of strangers admitted into the Brotherhood, an essential requirement to setting up independently. As strangers paid a large admission fee to the Brotherhood, native producers, in exchange for limiting the number of strangers, offered to compensate this financial loss. In July 1573, the Brewers' Company decided not to admit any strangers or foreigners to the Brotherhood for ten years. In enforcing this, the Company was aware that this order might 'be ... looked unto to keep out these Flemings and strangers'.[129] The aim, however, was not to *exclude*, but *reduce* competition from stranger master brewers, by preventing their admission into the Brotherhood. Since aliens could not run or own a brewery unless they were Brothers, this rule effectively limited them to journeyman status. The effect of the order in July 1573 was a fall in the number of alien brewers admitted to the Brotherhood. Between 1565 and 1572, ten alien brewers were admitted, but between 1573 and 1582, only three. Two of these were admitted following a request by Sir Francis Walsingham. After the ban expired in 1583, there was an increase in the number admitted. Between 1583 and 1597, approximately 21 alien brewers were admitted into the Brotherhood, on average of one per year. However, these measures were not sufficient to satisfy English producers, as is evident from the complaint lodged in 1607. Following this, the Brewers' Company decided to raise the admission fee for aliens from £20 to £50. This was regarded as necessary because the Company felt that the admission of foreigners at a small fee had greatly prejudiced and hindered freemen of the Company.[130]

Discrimination, along with the diminishing supply of Dutch immigrants in the seventeenth century, eventually ended alien domination of the brewing trade. This decline in immigration was largely a result of the prosperity of the Dutch Republic from the late sixteenth and early seventeenth centuries. This reduced the need of its inhabitants to migrate, and also probably rendered the Republic a magnet for migrants from neighbouring areas. In the seventeenth century, migrants to England came largely from French-speaking areas, but they had little association with the beer brewing trade.

Methods of Diffusion to Native Brewers

The demise of alien brewers in the seventeenth century is reflected in the records of the Brewers' Company, where no alien beer brewer is mentioned in the Court Minutes Books (which document admissions of new members, disputes, and activities of members) after the 1650s. The Anglicization of beer brewing had been completed by the mid-seventeenth century. The transition from a Dutch to an English industry raises an important question: how were the skills acquired by native brewers? The discussion above has suggested several ways in which English brewers acquired the necessary skills. The first was through marriage of widows of prominent alien brewers: Thomas Dolman, for example, married Elizabeth, the widow of Nicholas Webling; William Coxe married Alice, the widow of Henry Leeke, a prominent Southwark brewer. These Englishmen took over existing brewhouses and facilities, and assumed an entrepreneurial role, managing the brewhouse and organizing production, and leaving the actual brewing to experienced alien employees. They also employed English servants to work alongside alien brewer servants. The employment of alien servants in English-owned brewhouses presented a second medium by which skills may have been transferred. It is possible that aliens were hired as master brewers and at the same time were required to teach their skills to English servants working in the same brewery. It is unclear, however, how many alien servants worked in English brewhouses altogether. In 1567, a governmental Act allowed the 32 beer brewers in London to employ a maximum of eight alien servants each; assuming that beer brewers employed this number, some 256 alien servants were needed. Yet, only 44 alien servants were recorded in the Return of 1571, 34 of whom were employed by alien masters, and 10 by five English brewers (Thomas Westrame, John Bird, James Heath, Mackworthe and Mr Payne). Although this figure may underestimate the actual number of alien servants working in brewing, clearly there was a shortage of skilled alien servants, which explains why, as evident from disputes, there was such great competition for them.[131] The third possible method by which English brewers acquired the necessary skills was to gain employment with alien masters. In 1593, there were more than 147 English servants working in alien brewhouses, but it is not clear what tasks they performed. The Return of 1593 stated that many of them were 'set to work' and 'kept', indicating that perhaps they were set to carry out unskilled manual tasks, such as carrying water and fetching fuel, rather than being taught the secrets of brewing. So it remains a great mystery how breweries fulfilled their labour requirements. It has been suggested that this need may have been satisfied by brewer-monks. Monks, with their ample leisure time, had for centuries possessed a reputation for being the best brewers. They also had the advantage of being able to read those recipes that were published. Upon the dissolution of the monasteries, a considerable number of monks were left without a source of income. By November 1539, 560 monasteries had been suppressed, leaving some 7000 monks, nuns and friars dispossessed in England.[132] Many of them were not provided with any pensions, and this may have compelled them to find work in breweries to earn a living. The contribution of brewer-monks may throw much light on the brewing industry, and this aspect, which has been overlooked, merits further exploration.[133]

Conclusion

Dutch brewers brought the art of beer brewing to England in the early fifteenth century from Holland, but beer took a long time to gain popularity among English drinkers. Indeed, in the mid-sixteenth century, more than one-and-a-half centuries after its introduction in England, beer was still regarded as a Dutch drink. One important factor was the fierce resistance from the ale brewers, who sought to suppress the brewing of beer in England. Xenophobia partly hampered the process of diffusion. As beer was closely associated with the Dutch, the suppression of beer brewing was concomitant with the dislike of the Dutch. These factors led to a campaign in 1436 to stigmatize beer as poisonous and unhealthy, and to attacks on beer breweries. Only with the intervention of the City of London and the King were the alien beer brewers able to continue their trade.

But beer was slowly gaining popularity among Englishmen. By the 1570s, it had become the favoured drink of Londoners, thanks to its lower price and superior quality. As beer was much cheaper than ale, stored better and kept better, it was adopted very early on as the drink of soldiers, and upon their return from service, these may have played an important role in encouraging other Englishmen to embrace the beer drinking culture. Inflation, too, made beer much more attractive, both to consumers and producers. Consumers found it a cheaper substitute, and producers a more lucrative enterprise. This encouraged Englishmen to take a greater part in beer production, and their involvement may have boosted the popularity of beer through greater availability. The popularity of beer, combined with massive demographic expansion and the availability of coal as a cheaper source of fuel, enabled the beer industry to enjoy an unprecedented expansion in the late sixteenth century.

In retrospect, the expansion of the beer brewing industry in London in the sixteenth century undermined the dominant position of the Dutch brewers. First, expansion led to increased competition, resulting in turn in discrimination. Second, aliens were indirectly affected by the changes in the industry resulting from a massive expansion. The enormous growth of the industry, for example, led to a larger scale of production, necessitating a higher level of initial capital investment. Modern studies show that immigrants in general do not tend to concentrate in industries characterized by demand for standardized products, scale economies, high absolute costs, and mass production and distribution.[134] The changing structure of the brewing industry between the fifteenth and seventeenth centuries may hold the key to explaining the declining fortunes of the alien brewers.

Notes

1. P. Mathias, *The Brewing Industry in England, 1700–1830* (Cambridge, 1959), p. 4; J. Bennett, *Ale, Beer and Brewsters in England: Women's Work in a Changing World, c.1300–1600* (Oxford, 1996), p. 85.
2. M. Ball, *The History of the Worshipful Company of Brewers: A Short History*, (London, 1977), p. 23.
3. Bennett, *Ale, Beer and Brewsters*, p. 81; P. Clark, *The English Alehouse: A Social History, 1200–1830*, (London, 1983), pp. 96–7.
4. R.W. Unger, 'Technical Change in the Brewing Industry in Germany, the Low Countries, and England in the Late Middle Ages', *Journal of European Economic History*, 1992, Vol. 21, p. 286.
5. R. Yntema, 'The Brewing Industry in Holland, 1300–1800: A Study in Industrial Development' (University of Chicago, unpublished PhD thesis, 1992), p. 115.
6. Ibid., pp. 122–23.
7. N.J.M. Kerling, *Commercial Relations of Holland and Zealand with England from the Late 13th Century to the Close of the Middle Ages* (Leiden, 1954), p. 115; Unger, 'Technical change', p. 292.
8. Unger, 'Technical Change', p. 292.

Table 8.8 List of beer brewers in London in 1574

Name (1)	Weekly grain consumption in 1574 (quarters) (2)	Date of admission to Company (3)	Amount paid (4)	Previous Company recorded (5)	Number of alien servants employed (6)	Location in 1581 (7)
Aliens						
Harry Arnolde and Dirricke James his partner	43	1571/1566	20s. £20 6s. 8d.	'Shoemaker' 'Stranger'		St Katherine Thames St
Henry Campion Peter Durante	60 30	1549–50	40s.	'Mercer'		Thames St
Dyrricke Helden	50	1572	£14	'Dutchman'		Thames St
John Hulse	28	1571	£20	'Dutchman'		Thames St
Roger James and Rutton, his partner Arnolde Ludbery	60	1560 1572	£20/£16	Alien/'Dutchman'		Thames St
and his partner	51	1559–60	£3	'Stacioner'	8 (1568)	
John Picknett and Porton (John)	50	1566 1566	£6 13s. 4d. £23	'Alien/ 'Stranger'	10 (1568)	
John Powell	40	1572	£16	'Dutchman'		Southwark
John Reynoldes	30	1564	40s.			
John Smyth	30	1569	£13 6s. 8d.	'Stranger'		Bermondsey St, Southwark
Wassell Weblinge	70	1569	£22	'Stranger'		

English

Name					
William Beiston	50	1555–6	15s.	'Girdler'	
William Besswicke	60			'Ale brewer'	(1554)
John Bradberye	60	1564	30s.	'Bowchar'	
John Burde	52	1569	40s.	'Draper'	2 (1571) Southwark
John Draper	60	1564	£9 10s.	'Foreigner'	4 (1571) Thames St
Anthony Duffelde	90	1569	30s.	'Mercer'	St Katherine
Rycharde Grene	30	1571	29s.	'Leatherseller'	
Roberte Jackson	40	1565	6s. 8d.	'Ale brewer'	Thames St
William Longe	70	1558	£5	'Berebrewer'	10 (1564) Thames St
William Lovington	24	1571	£11	'Tyleman'	7 (1576)
John Mackworth	32	1560	50s.	'Skinner'	3 (1571) Thames St
James Maskall	39	1566	6s. 8d.	'Ale brewer'	3 (1568)
Richarde Palmer	30	1562	6s. 8d.	'Ale brewer'	5 (1568) Southwark
Richarde Platt	80	1549–50	6s. 8d.	'Ale brewer'	8 (1568) Thames St
Thomas Randall	40	1566	6s. 8d.	'Ale brewer'	1 (1568) Thames St
Edmonde Taylor	30	1563	21s.	'Draper'	St Katherine
John Taylor	60	1569	41s. 8d.	'Tiler'	Thames St
Thomas Westree	40				Unknown
William Wood	40	1561	20s.	'Mercer'	Southwark
John Wood	70	1548	6s. 8d.	'Ale brewer'	

Sources: Columns 1–2, 1574: BL, Cotton Faustina CII, ff. 177–88. Columns 3, 4, 5, 7, 1547–62: GL, Brewers, Company, Wardens' Accounts, MS 5442/2–4, MS 7885/1. Column 6, 1568, 1571: Kirk and Kirk, eds, *Returns of Aliens*, Vol. 1, pp. 293–315; 1576: Vol. 2, pp. 157–200.

9   Mathias, *The Brewing Industry in England*, pp. 3–4.
10 Ibid., p. 3.
11 F.A. King, *Beer Has a History* (London, 1947), p. 43.
12 R. Davis, *The Rise of the Atlantic Economies* (London, 1973), p. 205.
13 S. Thrupp, 'A survey of the alien population in England in 1440', *Speculum*, Vol. 32, 1957, pp. 270–73.
14 S. Thrupp, 'Aliens in and around London in the fifteenth century', in A.E.J. Hollaender and W. Kellaway, eds, *Studies in London History Presented to Philip Edmund Jones* (London, 1969), p. 259.
15 C. Barron, 'Introduction: England and the Low Countries, 1327–1477', in C. Barron and N. Saul, eds, *England and the Low Countries in the Late Middle Ages* (Stroud, 1995), pp. 1–28.
16 GL MS 5440, f. 267; Bennett, *Ale, Beer and Brewsters*, p. 80.
17 Quoted in Bennett, *Ale, Beer and Brewsters*, p. 80.
18 H.E. Malden, ed., *The Victoria History of the County of Surrey*, Vol. 2, (London, 1905), p. 381.
19 J.L. Bolton, *The Alien Communities of London in the Fifteenth Century: The Subsidy Rolls of 1440 and 1483–4* (Stanford, CT, 1998), p. 20.
20 M. Carlin, *Medieval Southwark* (London, 1996), pp. 53–4.
21 G. Asaert, 'Antwerp ships in English harbours in the fifteenth century', *The Low Countries History Yearbook*, 1979, Vol. XII, p. 37.
22 Bolton, *The Alien Communities*, p. 8.
23 Ibid., p. 21.
24 Carlin, *Medieval Southwark*, p. 53, referring also to a report by Derek Keene to the ESRC on Stage 2 (Aldgate Project) (typescript, *c*.1987) which describes the cluster of large beer brewhouses, first recorded about 1480, lying on the riverbank to the east of St Katherine's Hospital.
25 K.Wrightson, 'Alehouses, Order and Reformation in Rural England, 1590–1660', in E. Yeo and S. Yeo, eds, *Popular Culture and Class Conflict, 1590—1914: Explorations in the History of Labour and Leisure* (Brighton, 1981), p. 2.
26 Letter Book K, p. 205.
27 GL, MS 5440, f. 267.
28 Unger, 'Technical Change', p. 288.
29 Yntema, 'The brewing industry in Holland', p. 171.
30 Letter Book L, p. 157.
31 Ball, *History of the Worshipful Company of Brewers*, pp. 22–4.
32 King, *Beer Has a History*, p. 54.
33 Letter Book L, p. 52.
34 H. Monckton, *History of English Ale and Beer* (London, 1966), pp. 84–5.
35 Ibid., pp. 86–7.
36 H.S. Corran, *A History of Brewing* (London, 1975), p. 58.
37 L.F. Salzman, *English Industries of the Middle Ages* (London, 1970), p. 299.
38 Corran, *A History of Brewing*, p. 61.
39 Bennett, *Ale, Beer and Brewsters*, p. 93.
40 P.W. Hammond, *Food and Feast in Medieval England* (Stroud, 1993), p. 86.
41 C.S.L. Davies, 'Provisions for Armies, 1509–50: A Study in the Effectiveness of Early Tudor Government', *Economic History Review*, 1964–5, 2nd series, Vol. 17, pp. 243–4.
42 *Acts of the Privy Council*, Vol. 1, p. 25.
43 D.M. Palliser, *The Age of Elizabeth: England Under the Later Tudors, 1547–1603* (London, 1992), p. 140.
44 Bolton, *Alien Communities*, p. 21.
45 Corran, *A History of Brewing*, p. 53.
46 F.J. Furnivall, ed., *Harrison's Description of England in Shakespeare's Youth, AD 1577–1587* (London, 1877); see section on 'Of the Food and diet of the English'.

47 S. Rappaport, *Worlds Within Worlds: Structures of Life in Sixteenth-century London* (Cambridge, 1991), pp. 403–7.
48 GL, BCCB MS 5445/5 1576; Bennett, *Ale, Beer and Brewsters*, p.16.
49 Corran, A History of Brewing, p.57.
50 Clark discusses several obstacles: greater difficulty involved in beer brewing, less opportunity to substitute cheaper grains when barley prices soared, and reliance on imported hops: Clark, *The English Alehouse*, pp. 101–2.
51 *Kirk and Kirk*, eds, *Returns of Aliens*, Vol. 1, p. 376.
52 Rappaport, *Worlds Within Worlds*, p. 88; CLRO, Rep 10, f. 170v.
53 Malden, ed., *The Victoria History of the County of Surrey*, pp. 384–5.
54 Yntema, 'The brewing industry in Holland', p. 151.
55 Carlin, *Medieval Southwark*, p. 206.
56 Kirk and Kirk, *Returns of Aliens*, Vol. 10, No. 2, p. 98.
57 *Calendar of Patent Rolls, 1566–69* [85], p. 19.
58 This is based on discussion in Bennett, *Ale, Beer and Brewsters*, pp. 87–8.
59 Ibid., p. 87. The beer had to be kept for six weeks in winter, and three or four weeks in summer, see RS, Boyle Papers, Vol. 25, p. 176, p. 183 (1655–7).
60 Bennett, *Ale, Beer and Brewsters*, p. 87.
61 Ibid.
62 GL, BCCB MS5445/7 10 September 1583 and 12 September 1583.
63 BL Lansdowne MS 10/29 (1564–5), MS 14/49 (1572–3); Clark, *The English Alehouse*, p. 98.
64 J. Strype, *A Survey of the Cities of London and Westminster* (London, 1720), Book 5, p. 204.
65 It appears that 500 tons of beer were exported monthly to the Low Countries 'for the Queen's use'. Strype, *A Survey of the Cities of London and Westminster*, Book 5, p. 292.
66 Ibid.
67 Yntema, 'The brewing industry in Holland', pp. 119, 122.
68 Clark, *The English Alehouse*, p. 97.
69 Ibid., p. 106.
70 Mathias, *The Brewing Industry in England*, pp. xxii–xxiii.
71 Beer offered greater variety. Unhopped ale came in two basic types – strong (or good), and small (or common). Three grades of beer were sold: double, middle and small beer (small beer was the daily liquor of the lower classes and servants). See Clark, *The English Alehouse*, pp. 97–8.
72 GL, BCCB MS5445/9 2/10/1590.
73 R.W. Unger, 'Consumption of Beer in England and Holland, 1500–1700', Economic and Social History of Pre-industrial England Seminar, 24 May 2002, Institute of Historical Research. These figures (exact figures are 51 060 000 for 1574 and 106 158 000 for 1585) are given in a handout, but the basis for these calculations is unclear.
74 GL, BCCB MS 5445/13 1612.
75 Clark, *The English Alehouse*, p. 106.
76 PRO SP 12/98/37 October 1574.
77 The size of breweries in London may have been larger than continental breweries. In Antwerp, the average number of servants employed c.1580 was 10 (7–8 male servants, and 2–3 female servants), while in Holland larger breweries in the eighteenth century employed no more than 20 people. See Yntema, 'The brewing industry in Holland', p. 177.
78 PRO SP16/341/124 1636.
79 GL, MS5445/13.
80 PRO SP16/341/124.
81 PRO SP12/98/37 October 1574; SP16/341/124 1636.

82 Clark, *The English Alehouse*, p. 106.
83 GL, MS5445/9, 6 and 8 June 1592.
84 Malden, ed., *The Victoria History of the County of Surrey*, Vol. 2, p. 385.
85 Clark, *The English Alehouse*, p. 107.
86 Ibid.
87 GL, MS5445/19/ ff. 377–80.
88 Yntema, 'The brewing industry in Holland', p. 285.
89 J.U. Nef, *The Rise of the British Coal Industry*, Vol.1 (London, 1932), p. 213.
90 PRO SP12/36/40.
91 Clark, *The English Alehouse*, p. 101.
92 In 1577, when two strangers brought their cost-saving furnaces to the City, they were told by the Brewers' Company that these were no longer needed because 'the most part of our company had transported their furnaces to brew with sea coals and the rest would follow as soon as they are able ...'; GL, BCCB MS 5445/5 (5 September 1577); MS 5442/4 (1578).
93 See Yntema, 'The brewing industry in Holland', p. 165.
94 In 1580, two ale brewers – John Hill and John Taylor – bought 30 acres of wood at the cost of £4 per acre in Hornsey Park and Wicam in Essex from the Bishop of London, presumably for use in brewing: PRO SP12/137/10 & 12 (1580).
95 GL, MS 5445/7 17 February 1585.
96 In 1477, average annual production in Delft was 10 500 brews or 304 500 barrels. By 1571, this had risen to 17 700 brews or 637 200 barrels: see Yntema, 'The brewing industry in Holland', pp. 34–6.
97 London had the largest beer brewing industry in northern Europe in this period: in comparison to 51 million litres of beer produced in London in 1574, the figure for Gouda was 10 million litres, Haarlem 1.7 million, Leuven 7.4 million, Ghent 12 million, and Antwerp 29 million litres: Unger, handout given at Seminar at IHR London, 24 May 2002.
98 Furnivall, ed., *Harrison's Description of England*, p. 160; RS, Boyle Papers BP 25, f. 183 (1655).
99 See C. Spence, *London in the 1690s: A Social Atlas*, pp. 25–7, for a discussion of water supply.
100 Strype, *A Survey of the Cities of London and Westminster*, Book 5, p. 204.
101 See PRO Prob 11/116/ f. 328 (97 Wingfield 1610).
102 See Malden, ed., *Victoria History of the County of Surrey*, Vol. 2, pp. 385–6, for more details.
103 GL, BCCB MS 5445/3 10/01/1564.
104 CLRO Rep 17, ff. 102v–103 6 February 1570.
105 CLRO Rep 17, ff. 102v–103 6 February 1570.
106 see Bennett, *Ale, Beer and Brewsters*, pp. 90–92, for an interesting discussion on difficulties facing a woman in brewing trade.
107 PRO Prob 11/116/ f. 328 (97 Wingfield 1610)
108 GL, BCCB MS 5445/4 23/4/1573.
109 In 1602, he was ordered not to proceed with a building in Soper Lane, CLRO, Rep 26(1), f. 42. For Roger James's will, see PRO Prob 11/79 ff. 147–51 (20 Harrington 1591–2)
110 Clark, *The English Alehouse*, p. 108.
111 GL, BCCB MS5445/4 10/7/1572.
112 Hertfordshire Archives and Local Studies, D/ELW F6 Account of personal estate and original will.
113 PRO Prob 11/98 1599 (John Powell); Prob 11/75 1589 (Derick James), Prob 11/102, f. 38 1599 (Matthias Rutten), and GL, MS 9052/8/32v (Jacob Janson) 1634.
114 Scouloudi, *The Returns of Strangers*, p. 23.

115 GL, MS 5445/6 11 July 1581, 12 October 1581.
116 GL MS 5445/7 7 July 1584, MS 5445/9 15 August 1592, 17 August 1592.
117 GL, Brewers' Company, Old Warden's account books MS 5442/5 (1582–1616) (An assessment of money the 30th June 1607); PRO SP14/28/136 (1607 Brewers' certificate touching Strangers).
118 Carlin, *Medieval Southwark*, pp. 53–4.
119 Hertfordshire Archives and Local Studies, D/ELW F6 Account of personal estate and original will.
120 Bennett, *Ale, Beer and Brewsters*, p. 87.
121 Ibid.
122 Ibid., p. 89.
123 Hertfordshire Archives and Local Studies, D/ELW B1 Partnership deeds in brewing.
124 Scouloudi, *Returns of Strangers in the Metropolis*, names in alphabetical order.
125 PRO SP14/28/136.
126 GL, MS 5445/10, 17 January 1599.
127 GL, MS5445/9 10 April 1593.
128 PRO SP14/28/136 1607; also quoted in Bennett, *Ale, Beer and Brewsters*, p. 82.
129 GL, BCCB MS 5445/4 (30/7/1573).
130 GL, BCCB MS 5445/13 1 August 1620.
131 In September 1573, the dispute between William Tilman, a Dutch miller, working for John Mackworth, an English brewer, was brought before the Court of Assistants and Wardens of the Brewers' Company. Apparently, Tilman wished to leave the service of Mackworth, but was refused. The court therefore ordered Tilman to continue to work with Mackworth until the end of the month; in return he was to be paid 25s. After that, he was free to 'be at his choice wheare and with whom he will serve'. Mackworth also promised the court that he would allow Tilman to 'quietly depart with his good will'; GL, BCCB MS5445/5 3/9/1573 .
132 J. Guy, *Tudor England* (Oxford, 1988), p. 148; *Oxford History of Britain*, Vol. 3 on Tudors and Stuarts, ed. J. Guy and J. Morrill (Oxford, 1992), p. 31.
133 Monckton, *History of English Ale and Beer*, p. 96.
134 R. Waldinger, *Through the Eye of the Needle: Immigrants and Enterprise in New York's Garment Trades* (New York, 1986), p. 21. There are always some exceptions to this rule. See, for example, the influence of an Amsterdam immigrant, Louis De Geer, on the Swedish iron industry in the early seventeenth century, in an article by J. Thomas Lindblad, 'Louis de Geer (1587–1652): Dutch Entrepreneur and the Father of Swedish Industry', in C. Lesger and L. Noordegraaf, eds, *Entrepreneurs and Entrepreneurship in Early Modern Times: Merchants and Industrialists within the Orbit of the Dutch Staple Market* (The Hague, 1995), pp. 77–84.

Chapter 9

Conclusion: Immigration in a Historical Perspective

Recent fresh waves of foreigners arriving in Britain have again brought the issue of immigration to the forefront of public debate, with opinion deeply divided. On the one hand economists advance sound and logical explanations as to why Britain should welcome immigrants. They point first to the accepted link between economic growth and immigration, and to historical evidence which plainly demonstrates that countries with an open immigration policy, such as the United States, grow faster and create more jobs. Some economists further argue that as a result of demographic changes precipitated by a declining birthrate and ageing population, immigration of young workers from abroad is the only viable solution to resolve the acute skills and labour shortages in Britain. Workers are needed in both low-skilled jobs, such as construction firms and hotels, where there is a strong demand for temporary, low-skilled and cheap labour, and in skilled professions, especially those with medical, engineering and teaching skills. An additional reason for welcoming immigrants is that they make good workers because they tend to be self-selecting, more educated, more entrepreneurial and more skilled.[1] As such, they might set good examples for English workers to emulate. Their presence in the labour market is also believed to increase social competition and as a result might encourage native workers to work harder.

These beneficial effects are not always transparent in the face of deep-seated concerns that immigrants might impose a financial burden on the state. Although a recent Home Office report shows that migrants make an annual net contribution to the economy of £2.5 billion, and in fact pay more in taxes than their costs in benefits, it is unclear whether it has succeeded in changing public views.[2] Besides financial burdens, there is also the traditional fear that immigrants may take away jobs from natives. The government argues that as long as immigration is not seen as a cheap substitute for educating native workers, temporary flows of workers can create a more 'flexible labour force', and seeks to adopt a 'managed migration' policy. This policy might apply to economic migrants, but not to the case of asylum seekers and illegal immigrants, whose influx prompts much public concern. The solution may lie in the adoption of a clearer immigration policy with well-defined selection criteria, such as that which exists in Australia and Canada.

Many sceptics have also expressed concerns about increased pressures on certain areas such as London and the south-east of England, to where most immigrants move. It is argued that there is no space for mass immigration in these areas because the region is already suffering from overcowding, and that its facilities, such as hospitals, schools, housing, roads and transport, will not be able to cope.[3]

These immigration issues confronting policymakers today are by no means new or novel. In the face of the mass influx during the Elizabethan period, policymakers were beset with similar dilemmas, and the ensuing public debates centred on the same questions: Should immigrants be welcomed? Is immigration beneficial to the economy? What economic benefits do immigrants bring? Who should be allowed to stay? Do they take away jobs from native English workers? Should they be encouraged to assimilate?

What answers did they provide to these questions? What lessons can we learn from the early modern experience?

The early modern period experience of immigration shows that it was greatly beneficial to the development of the English economy. Contemporaries saw a clear connection between immigration, expansion of trade and growth of prosperity. In a parliamentary debate in 1592, Sir John Wolley urged a positive immigration policy because he believed that the 'riches and renown of London' stemmed from 'entertaining of strangers and giving liberty unto them'. Antwerp and Venice, he firmly declared, could never have been so rich and famous without the strangers, because these brought much trade and commerce.[4]

The most dynamic economies in the late sixteenth and early seventeenth centuries were those countries with high rates of immigration, principally cities in the United Provinces, and to a lesser extent London. Many Dutch cities contained a staggering proportion of immigrants from the southern Netherlands, which in 1622 ranged from 18 per cent in Delft, 33 per cent in Amsterdam, 51 per cent in Haarlem to 67 per cent in Leiden.[5] Immigrants brought with them not only industrial skills, capital and entrepreneurship, but also invaluable social contacts and external trading links. In an article on the diaspora of the Antwerp merchants in the late sixteenth century, Brulez showed how their geographical spread to England, Holland, north Germany and France helped disseminate new commercial techniques and reinforce trading links.[6] Why did Dutch cities attract so many immigrants? Although the adverse economic and political circumstances in the southern Netherlands were partially responsible for the high emigration to the north, growing opportunities as well as a positive immigration policy in the Dutch Republic also enabled it to draw in much of the floating human capital. In an age when many communities suppressed religious nonconformity and discriminated against aliens, Amsterdam welcomed people from all religions and nationalities. There was also no obstruction to upward mobility, as the status of *poorter* (citizen) could be acquired at a small cost (8 florins until 1622, and 14 florins thereafter). The city of Amsterdam also assisted newcomers, finding housing for them and offering inducements to masters deemed capable of starting new industries or improving techniques in those already established.[7]

Like the modern period, London was the principal magnet for overseas immigrants, thanks to its good transport links with European towns and cities, its relative air of cosmopolitanism conferred by the long tradition of immigration into the capital, its display of religious tolerance and freedom as embodied in the establishment of the Stranger Churches in the 1550s, its peace and stability (except the period of the Civil Wars), and its unrivalled economic opportunities offered by the large and opulent metropolitan market. But in comparison with Dutch towns, aliens in London formed a more modest proportion, fluctuating between 5 and 10 per cent in the late sixteenth century. Besides the larger absolute size of the capital, the Elizabethan government's policy of containment and dispersal constituted a major factor behind this inhibited growth, but so too was the relative difficulty of upward mobility in London society. Unlike the Dutch Republic, where there was a greater ease of obtaining citizenship, climbing the London social ladder was generally more difficult, with steeper barriers. The question of what rights, freedoms and liberties aliens should have was perennially debated and reviewed. Unlike the Dutch Republic, where positive discrimination was adopted to harness economic growth, the guiding principle in England was that natural-born subjects should receive preferential treatment. During the Elizabethan period, the restrictions on the economic activities of aliens increased, and ensured that London never became a 'Mecca' for immigrants. But this was a missed opportunity, and prevented it from fully tapping the outpouring of human capital from the southern Netherlands after 1585.

The need for skills to bolster the English economy was prominent in the immigration debate in early modern London. Many who advocated an open immigration policy did so on the basis of the desperate need of the Elizabethan economy for Continental skills to develop its industrial base and to 'catch up' with more advanced European cities. So how did London acquire the skills and build up its stock of human capital? Who were the aliens in the capital? Immigrants in early modern London were highly heterogeneous, and composed broadly of three groups. The first consisted of economic migrants, typified by the beer brewers and coopers, who arrived via chain migration at a young age, and who concentrated overwhelmingly in the eastern and southern parts of London. As the group was preponderantly male, intermarriage into the host community was not uncommon, and immigrants tended to be more settled and less mobile. The second group consisted of 'career builders', as exemplified by the goldsmiths, whose primary motive for migration was to broaden their craft training. Until the late seventeenth century, they tended to be more invisible, as many did not settle permanently in London. The absence of opportunities for upward mobility in London was a compelling reason for the return of many to their home town to pursue their careers. The religious refugees and exiles formed the third group, who played a signal role in the introduction of new and luxury trades such as silk-weaving, papermaking and glassmaking.

Chain, circular and mass migration provided three channels by which Continental skills arrived in London. While in the older literature the development of a particular industry or craft is often traced to the date of arrival of immigrants, this book has stressed the need to combine supply and demand factors in explaining 'take-off'. It has also reinforced Wrigley's argument that economic change was cumulative and progressive, rather than abrupt.[8] Factors affecting local market demand, such as population growth, tastes and fashions, price and wage levels, were potent forces in explaining industrial success and occupational patterns of immigrants. Demand emanated from two principal sources: the host population, and the immigrant population. In the case of silk-weaving, the impetus for development in the sixteenth century originated from the host population, where there was a broad demand base, and this explains why the industry took off at a prodigious speed. In the space of fifty years, Londoners claimed to be conversant in the skill, as demonstrated in their petition in 1608 to ban silk imports because, while during Elizabeth's reign 'Englishmen were not so skilful in trades, to make all kind of wares ... but now ... the people [had mightly] increased both in number ... and in all good skill, and [were] skilful of all kind and manner of trades'.[9] Beer brewing, on the other hand, was established in London in the fifteenth century in response to the cultural needs of the alien population. The initial market base was much narrower, and this may explain why beer took nearly 150 years to gain widespread popularity in London. Yet this different pace of development may also have been linked with the different types of migration experienced by these two groups. While the beer brewers arrived in trickles through chain migration, the large influx of the silk-weavers may have provided a critical mass for the take-off of the industry. Equally significant for the commercial success of the industry was the existence of a related trade and continuous immigration. Both silk-weaving and beer brewing were built upon existing foundations, and the successful planting of new branches of production was only ensured by the continual immigration of aliens over the period of three centuries.

There were essentially three ways in which skills could be acquired by an 'industrializing' country: (1) workers could travel to the originating country of the technology for training; (2) workers could learn by doing without formal training, and (3) workers with appropriate skills could travel from the originating to the host country.[10] Here the focus has been on the third element, but this was by no means exclusive.

Elizabethans were fond of travelling abroad, and these travellers may have introduced new ideas and techniques.[11] In 1570, Richard Dyer, a citizen of London, sought a patent to make pots in England, a skill which, he claimed, he had acquired in Portugal. He had originally gone there to recover his goods, but 'necessity [had] driven [him] to labour for his living and [he] became servant to a potter with whom he learned perfectly to make a kind of earthen pot to hold fire to seeth meat … the use of which pot … will greatly spare wood and coal a very little'.[12] Another Englishman, Richard Mathewe, learned to make 'Turkye haftes' for knives, which he had learned through living abroad.[13] Other Englishmen sometimes went abroad in search of new methods of production.[14]

This in some ways reflected the underlying cultural receptiveness of the English, which Cipolla believed was one of their distinctive cultural traits. He suggested that this was probably the result of their living in close proximity with far more economically advanced areas, therefore developing a strong spirit of emulation. Although recognizing that there was no shortage of conservatives, Cipolla maintained that many Englishmen looked 'beyond[their] parochial horizons with intense curiosity', with foreign travels, the 'Grand Tour' and the sending of young men to study at foreign universities (Padua, Paris, Leiden) highly popular among the upper class. While the craftsmen learned the techniques and trades practised by the immigrants, travellers imported new ideas.[15] If England was culturally receptive, it raises the question of why English artisans did not embrace the practice of *wanderjahre* to acquire foreign technologies and skills and enrich their experience by 'living and working' abroad. The answer was probably because those lower down the social scale did not share this intellectual curiosity exhibited by elite classes.

Other historians have also discussed 'stimulus diffusion'. The news that some technical process had been accomplished successfully in some far-away part of the world might encourage certain people to solve the problem in a new way. Thus reports brought by widely travelled merchants to local craftsmen could spark off innovations.[16] Stimulus diffusion could also occur as a result of artisans living as neighbours in close proximity, emulating each other.

The next stage of diffusion involved the spread of skills within the immigrant population. Often, a key skill was introduced by a core group of immigrants who then disseminated it within the community. The speed of dissemination depended upon intra-group ties and the availability of other economic opportunities. In early modern London, silk-weaving came to be closely identified with the Walloon/French-speaking community, which was successful in sharing the skill among its members. This was ensured by its smaller, more manageable size and its tight-knit networks, enhanced by the shared experiences of its members, their tendency to congregate in certain areas, and their common membership of the French church. These strong intra-group ties facilitated trade emulation and explain the phenomenon of 'ethnic' occupational clustering. But there was also an economic rationale for maintaining close networks. In early modern London, the prohibition of aliens and their sons from serving apprenticeship with English masters effectively forced them to look to their community, their parents or relatives to teach them a skill to earn a livelihood. It was in their best interests to maintain close ties with members of their community.

The process of skills development among immigrants was dynamic, with new products invented in response to new market conditions and demands. In the late seventeenth century, for example, the Huguenot silversmiths developed some unique objects as a result of cultural infusion, such as the tankard, which was unknown in France, and the two-handled cup. In contemporary Britain, the development of dishes such as sweet-and-sour and chow mein by Chinese restauranteurs to cater for the British market are good examples of cuisine innovations as a result of cultural infusion.

The transmission of relevant skills to the native population constituted the third stage in the process of diffusion. This could be achieved by English workers learning the skill on the job, or undergoing formal training. Both of these methods required the willingness of alien masters to employ English servants or teach them the skills. This willingness, in turn, was contingent upon a multiplicity of factors, including relations between immigrants and natives, the social and economic structure of the immigrant population, government policies, the degree of discrimination, as well as the existence of protection of 'intellectual property rights'. Without protection of their skill, a form of property, immigrants were disinclined to impart their trade secrets. As this book has shown, immigrants need not displace native workers. In fact, immigrants could play a vital role in *creating* local employment – directly by taking on English workers, or indirectly by encouraging trade emulation.

Immigration into early modern London often provoked strong public reactions. These responses were shaped by a host of factors, including supposed numbers of immigrants, perceptions of their plight, fears of pressures on resources, prevailing political, social and economic conditions, and demography. The perception of over-population in the sixteenth century produced popular pressure on the government to adopt a 'restraining immigration policy', whereas the fear of under-population in the seventeenth century resulted in a more welcoming immigration policy.[17] The most critical influence on the public reaction to immigrants, however, was probably their visibility – social, racial, or religious. Immigrants with more conspicuous identity and presence tended to arouse greater apprehension. The arrival of Protestant refugees around the 1560s, for example, was greeted with much apprehension, partly due to their *en masse* movement, their greater visibility, the wider political conflicts associated with their plight, and the worsening economic and social climate in London. But their plight was capable of generating a more intense public debate, with opinion oscillating between compassion and fear. Their friends stressed the shared Protestantism and their virtues as godly, hard-working and thrifty. It was felt that they would set good examples to the English, as their children were 'taught to serve God and to flee idleness'. Those who objected to their arrival portrayed them as 'bogus' refugees who would take away jobs from natives. In early modern London, the government sought to resolve this dilemma between compassion and fear by allowing only genuine religious refugees, defined as those with membership of the Stranger Churches, to settle in London, and by encouraging these to employ and provide craft training to English workers. The question of whether the government was successful or not in achieving these aims was perhaps less important than the need to be *seen* to be in control and to do something constructive.

The question of whether immigrants should be encouraged to assimilate into the native culture is another common theme. Schilling has argued that economic change was stimulated by differences and autonomy, rather than conformity. In other words, *segregation* of immigrants provided a positive force for economic change, furnishing them with freedom and autonomy to pursue new ideas.[18]

The contribution of aliens to early modern London society and economy was not only confined to the introduction of new skills and the provision of labour supply. Their arrival also had other impact. In the medieval period, Englishmen were ale drinkers, yet by the 1570s many Londoners had become beer drinkers, with important economic and social repercussions. This conclusion encourages us to modify Wrigley's original conception of the links between the growth of London and the Industrial Revolution. In fact, the growth of London was intricately connected with overseas immigration, which formed the principal vehicle for the inflow of a wide range of Continental skills. The process of absorption of these skills precipitated changes in consumption; enrichment of national diet; diversification in textiles e.g. from wool to silk; shifts in division of labour between the sexes, from female participation to male domination in brewing and silk weaving; and a fundamental shift in the fuel economy from wood to coal. In his recent book, Pomeranz has shown how the utilization of coal was essential to Britain's subsequent technological breakthrough, particularly in respect of iron and steel production, and the application of steam power to industrial applications and transportation, and how the extensive employment of coal exacerbated the 'great divergence' between the economies of Western Europe and Asia from the nineteenth century onwards.[19] But nor should the less tangible facets of immigration be ignored. Continual immigration into London conferred upon it considerable social assets, creating a diversity of cultures, encouraging the constant infusion of new blood and movements of people, and discouraging insularity and complacency.[20] These qualities constitute the hallmarks of the metropolitan *greatness* which, in both the historical and contemporary settings, lay in the sheer diversity of its people, cultures and skills.

Notes

1 The *Guardian*, 'Britain slips open fortress door', 21 May 2002, p. 22; The *Guardian*, 'The Pains of Cheap Labour', 22 May 2002, p. 25.
2 The *Guardian*, 'Britain slips open fortress door', 21 May 2002, p. 22; The *Guardian*, 'The Pains of Cheap Labour', 22 May 2002, p. 25.
3 *The Sunday Times*, 3 November 2002, 'It's easy: A few forms, a tired nod and you beat the asylum barrier', pp. 8–9.
4 S. D'Ewes, *The Journals of all the Parliaments during the Reign of Queen Elizabeth* (London, 1682), p. 505.
5 J. Briels, *Zuid- Nederlandse Immigratie, 1572–1630* (Haarlem, 1978), p. 21.
6 W. Brulez, 'De diaspora der Antwerpse kooplui op het einde van de 16e eeuw', *Bijdragen voor de geschiedenis der Nederlanden*, 1960, Vol. 15, pp. 279–306.
7 V. Barbour, *Capitalism in Amsterdam in the 17th Century* (Ann Arbor, MI, 1963), p. 16.
8 E.A. Wrigley, 'The divergence of England: The growth of the English economy in the seventeenth and eighteenth centuries', *Transactions of the Royal Historical Society*, 6th series, Vol. X, 2000, p. 120.
9 BL, Lansdowne MS 152/64/237.
10 K. Bruland, *British Technology and European Industrialization: The Norwegian Textile Industry in the Mid Nineteenth Century* (Cambridge, 1989), p. 110.
11 See C. Cipolla, *Before the Industrial Revolution: European Society and Economy, 1000–1700* (London, 1993), p. 267.
12 PRO C66/1077 m.16; see *Calendar of Patent Rolls 1569–72*, p. 268.
13 See E.W. Hulme, 'The history of the patent system under the prerogative and at common law', *Law Quarterly Review*, 1896, Vol. 12, pp. 141–54; 1900, Vol. 16, pp. 44–56.
14 L.A. Clarkson, *The Pre-industrial Economy in England, 1500–1750* (London, 1971), p. 113.
15 C.M. Cipolla, *Before the Industrial Revolution*, pp. 261–3.
16 J. Needham, *Science and Civilisation in China*, Vol.1 (Cambridge, 1961), p. 244.
17 D. Statt, *Foreigners and Englishmen: The Controversy over Immigration and Population, 1660–1760* (London, 1995), especially Chapter 3.
18 H. Schilling, 'Confessional Migration and Social Change: The Case of the Dutch refugees of the Sixteenth Century', in P. Klep and E. van Cauwenberghe, eds, *Entrepreneurship and the Transformation of the Economy (10th–20th centuries): Essays in Honour of Herman van der Wee* (Leuven, 1994), pp. 321–33.
19 K. Pomeranz, *The Great Divergence: China, Europe, and the Making of the Modern World Economy* (Oxford, 2000), pp. 32, 59, 61.
20 See D. Landes, *The Wealth and Poverty of Nations: Why Some are So Rich and Some So Poor* (London, 1998).

Appendix 1

Places of Origin Recorded in the Returns of Aliens, 1571 and 1593

The Returns of Aliens sometimes stated the province of origin, city, town, and sometimes simply recorded immigrants as 'Dutch', 'French', 'German', 'Flemish'. For the purposes of this study, I have used the following broad groupings and listed below the provinces/towns/cities included.

Notes

Inverted commas denote the spellings in original MS; square brackets indicate my own identification.

North Netherlands

Bentheim: Ootmarsum, Oldenzaal; Friesland: Friesland, Emden, Leer; Gelderland: Arnhem, Dieren, Gelderland, Lochem, Ninwegen, Tiel [Thile?], Zutphen; Holland: Holland, Amsterdam, Delft, Haarleem, Hague, Leyden, Purmerend [Pummerlande near Amsterdam?], Rotterdam, Schouwen; Overyssel: Deventer; Utrecht; Zealand: Borssele, Flushing, Middelburg, Veer, Zealand.

Brabant

Brabant, Antwerp, Bergen op Zoom, Breda, Brussels, Diest, Enghien, Grave, Herentals ('Harantall'), s'Hertogenbosch, Leuven/Louvain, Lier, Ligny ('Lugnes, Dutch'), Mechlin ('Malkine'), Nivelles ('Nievell'), Ottignies, Turnhout.

Flanders

'Flanders', Fleming, Adinkerke ('Arnicker, Flanders'), Bergues-Saint-Winox,

Breskens, Bruges, Cassel, Courtrai, Dendermonde, Dunkirk, Ghent, Halluin ('Halwynne'), Hondschoten, Mark, Menin ('Meenen'), Mesen, Flanders, Nevele ('Newell, Flanders'), Nieukerk, Nieuwpoort, Ostende, Oudenaarde, Poperinge, Roby, Roeselaar, Ronse, Sas Van ('Saxson, Flanders'), St Nicolas, Sluis ('Slowes'), Temse, Tourcoing ('Tungall, Dutch'), Wervik, Ypres, Desbright, Hembar, Marson, Newseld, Ruremounte.

Dutch

King Philip, 'Dutch', Under Emperor, Netherland, High Dutchland, Low Country, Burgundy, Dutchland.

Germany

Germany, Augsberg, Bielefeld, Bremen, Brunswick, Frankfurt, Hamburg, Lette (near Münster?), Low Germany, Lübeck, Nuremberg, Münster, Saarland, Westphalia.

Rhineland, Mosel and Meuse Valleys

Aachen, Beek [near Maastricht], Brunen [Brune, near Wesel], Cleves, Cologne, Dortmund, Duisburg, Dusseldorf, Emmerich, Essen, Eschweiler, Geldern, Goch ('Goughe'), Heinsberg ('Hensbrys, Cleveland'), Julich, Liege, Limburg, Luxemburg, Namur, Maastricht, Meerssen [near Maastricht], Solingen, Steinford [near Arlon], St Trond, Tongeren ('Tonger, Tongres'), Trier, Trewel, Valkenburg ('Falkenborowe' [near Maastricht]), Venlo, Weerte, Wesel, Xanten.

Walloon Provinces

Armentieres, Arras, Artois, Bailleul, Bethune, Blangy (Sur-Bres), Boulogne, Calais, Cambrai, Dour, Douai, Hainaut, Lille, Merville ('Mervine'), Mons, St Omer, Tournai ('Turnell'), Valenciennes, Walloon.

French, France

Abbeville, Alencon/Maine, Allier, Amiens, Anjou/Angers, Aumale, Bohain,

Bordeaux, Bourges, Brittany, Chartres, Cherbourg, Coutances, Dieppe, Doffyn, Dornes [near Nevers], Falaise, Fontoy ('Fontenoy' [near Metz]), Gascony, Honfleur, La Fere, Le Havre, Limons [near Vichy], Lusieres, Lyons, Maunter, Mezieres, Montdidier, Montherme, Moussey, Movuse, Nimes, Normandy, Noyan, Orbraunce, Orleanais/Orleans, Orsay, Paris, Peronne, Picardy, Poitiers, Pontoise, Rouen, St Denis, St Malo, Sedan, Senlis ('Shanye'), Tancarville ('Tankerfield'), Thiers [near Lyons], Toulouse, Tours, Valence.

Denmark

Denmark, Danzig.

Italy

Italy, Bergamo, Ferrara, Florence, Genoa, Milan, Naples, Piedmont, Tregosa, Venice.

Portugal

Portugal, Valbom ('Valbowne').

Spain

Spain, Bilbao, Sardinia, Seville, Teneriffe.

Switzerland

Switzerland, Geneva, Aarrau, Artemare ('Artmart' [near Geneve]), Basel, Bons ('Bonse' [near Geneve]), Dutchy of Savoy.

Turkey

Scotland/England

Scotland, English born, English.

Missing Data

Origin not given.

Unidentified

1571

Barbyne, Branworth, Canger, Gwillicar; Doriep, Edenor, Eldener, Grice, Isle, Kingbury, Loraband, Mesland, Murrey, Okehain, Otnar, Stegehera, Trocheampy, Weyne.

1593

Adenkrisen, Alle, Arentuter, Aske, Autelbas, Beteya, Bisler, Brokett, Brordients, Casteell, Cettwick, Clevenforde, De Malle, Ennesbarye, Grane, Hiluben, Hingen, Hoskett, Learminge, Maryn, Mchillard, Megar, Mountyem, Owantrdy, Petlam, Satredge, Sertheyey, Soliccy, St Thomas, St Tomons, Stedum, Teuke, Tewesell, Towane, Vanesall, Voleschan, Vorrosel, Warkell.

Appendix 2

Occupations Recorded in the Returns of Aliens, 1571 and 1593

The occupations recorded in the Returns of Aliens have been classified as follows.

Non-manufacturing

Professions

Accountant; advocate; chaplain; civil lawyer; clerk of Dutch Church; doctor; the Elder; keeper of school; minister; parson; physician; preacher; priest; reader in French Church; scholar; schoolmaster; student; teacher; surgeon.

Miscellaneous Services

Apothecary; barber; falconer; gardener; king's servant; midwife; musician; nurse; notary public; scrivener; soldier; washer/laundress; belong to Spanish Ambassador; receiver to King France; queen's Majesty man.

Officials

Gatherer of alms for the poor.

Mercantile

Broker; draper; factor; keeper of shop; linen draper; mercer; merchant; buyer and seller; seller of tapistry; trade of merchandise.

Transport

Boatman; drayman; mariner; post/postmaster; shipmaster/captain; sailor; waterman/waterbearer; live by Venetian ships.

Labouring

Labourer; servant/maid.

Manufacturing

Traditional Trades

Building Carpenter; freemason; glazier; joiner; marbeller; painter; sawyer; sawyer of stone; slatore.

Clothing Attiremaker; bobbin maker; botcher; button makers; capper/cap knitter/maker; cardmaker; cloth worker/thicker; collarmaker; comber of wool; dyer; embroiderers; feltmaker; girdler; hatband maker; hat makers; hat trimmer; hemp beater; hemp dresser/flax dresser; hosier; jacketmaker; jerken maker; kynner of wool; linen weaver; linen packer; maker of 'hear for hose'; male shirt maker; mending old apparell/old garments; milliner; mouldmaker for buttons; packthread maker; pointlace maker; ribbon weaver/lace maker; sackcloth weaver/ maker; sewing/sempster; sley maker; spinner wool/yarn; tailors; thread twister; thread dyer; thread maker; throwster; twisted yarn winder; twister; weaver; whitsters (washers/bleachers of linen); wool carding/combing; wool droster; worsted yarn maker; yarn twister/winder; work with fine sleues.

Decorating Chair maker; chandler; painter stainer; stationer; tallow chandler; turner.

Leather Cobler; cordwainer; currier; featherdresser; furrier; glover; leather dresser; leather dyer; leather seller; parchementer/parchementmaker; parchment lacemaker; pointmaker; pursemaker; shoemaker; skinner.

Metalwork Armourer; blacksmith; brazier; bugle maker/seller; crossbowmaker; cutler; coppersmith; engraver of copper; filebeater; finer; gunflask maker; gunpowder maker; gunstock maker; gunmaker; locksmith; morrispike maker; needle maker; pickmaker; pin maker; pinner; sealmaker; shear maker; sheath maker; smith; swordblade maker.

Miscellaneous Production

Ballmaker; basket maker; box girder; boxmaker; brushmaker; candle maker; combmaker; cordmaker/rope; dicemaker; flaskmaker; glassmaker; glasshouse keeper; graver; hermaker; instrument & string makers; maker of matches of hemp sticks; painter of pots; pen maker; picture makers; pot maker; quilt maker; stone cutters; stone engravers or carvers; tomb maker; virginal maker.

Victualling

Baker; bittern maker; brewer; brewer clerk; brewer's servant; cooper; cook; drawer of Rhenish wine; hosteler & serving man; keep table for strangers; miller; salter; stiller; suttel maker; tunman; victualler.

Luxury trades

Agate cutter; arras worker; bonelace worker; bookbinder; bookprinter; bookseller; buglelace maker; caulmaker; clockmaker; diamond cutter; goldbeater; goldsmith; jeweller; lace maker; lustringmaker; refiner of sugar; silk dresser; silk dyer; silkfringe maker; silk gummer; silklace worker; silk spinner; silk throwster; silk twister; silk weaver; silk winder; silk worker; silversmith; sugar baker; taffeta & tuftaffeta weaver; velvet weaver

New trades

Aqua-vitae maker; baymaker; confit maker; diaper weaver; engraver of copper; fustiannaples maker; fustian weavers; orris worker; painter of pots; perfumer of gloves; playingcard maker; pot maker; printer; racket maker; rash worker; say maker; shearer of rash; starcher; stiller; virginal maker; weaver of diaper, sackcloth, canvas; weaver of crewel & lace.

Appendix 3

Numbers of Strangers Engaged in Luxury and New Trades in London, 1571 and 1593

Luxury	No. of heads of household		New	No. of heads of household	
	1571	1593		1571	1593
Agate cutter	-	1	Aqua-vitae maker	1	-
Arras worker	9	9	Baymaker	4	3
Bonelace worker	-	2	Confit maker	2	-
Bookbinder	15	-	Diaper weaver	-	1
Bookprinter	2	-	Engraver of copper	-	2
Bookseller	-	2	Fustiannaples maker	1	-
Buglelace maker	-	1	Fustian weavers	2	-
Caulmaker/			Orris worker	1	-
Silkweaver	1	-	Painter of pots	1	-
Clockmaker	3	8	Perfumer (gloves)	1	4
Diamond cutter	-	8	Playingcard maker	-	1
Goldbeater	1	-	Pot maker	2	-
Goldsmith	39	39	Printer	5	1
Jeweller	1	5	Racket maker	1	1
Lace maker	1	-	Rash worker	-	4
Lustringmaker	1	-	Say maker	-	1
Refiner of sugar	-	3	Shearer of rash	-	1
Silk dresser	-	1	Starcher	-	2
Silk dyer	5	7	Stiller	-	1
Silkfringe maker	1	-	Virginal maker	1	-
Silk gummer	-	1	Weaver of diaper,		
Silklace worker	2	1	sackcloth, canvas	2	-
Silk spinner	2	1	Weaver of crewel &		
Silk throwster	1	7	lace	2	-
Silk twister	11	5	Sub-total	26	22
Silk weaver	148	120			
Silk winder	4	14	TRADITIONAL		
Silk worker	7	3	TRADES	791	447
Silversmith	-	2			
Sugar baker	-	2	TOTAL NO. IN	1,071	744
Taffeta &			MANUFACTURING		
tuftaffeta weaver	-	26			
Velvet weaver	-	7			
Sub-total	254	275			

Sources: 1571 Kirk and Kirk, *Returns of Aliens*, vol. 2, pp. 1–139; *1593* Scouloudi, *Returns of Strangers*, pp. 144–221.

Appendix 4

Processes of Silk Manufacture

Stage 1: Basic Tasks

- Cultivating mulberry plants and silkworms.

Stage 2: Preparatory Tasks

(1) **Silk reeling:** Threads from cocoons are wound on a reel. To reduce breaking, several threads are combined, usually by women who pass the finished reels on to the merchant.
(2) **Silk throwing:** Then the silk is thrown, that is, two or three threads are twisted together. At first, men operated the twisting mills, but later women took over.

Stage 3: Main Tasks I

(1) **Degumming:** After twisting, workers called 'boilers' cleanse the silk of gum by boiling it in built-in kettles, with sides of bricks and bottoms of copper. The skeins are boiled in soapy water, wrung, shaken, and hung out to dry.
(2) **Dyeing:** Silk is dyed, before or after weaving, in dyeing establishments located along the river or canal.
(3) **Warping**
   (a) Dyed silk is prepared for the warp (threads are cut into equal lengths, and divided into groups), a task usually performed by women.
   (b) Dyed hanks of silk are wound onto bobbins.
   (c) Spools of silk are taken to be warped, using a shear-like instrument consisting of two wooden poles with prongs. The strands of silk are unwound from several bobbins simultaneously.

Stage 4: Main Tasks II

- **Weaving:** Simple looms are used only for plain weaves such as taffeta, and draw looms are required for elaborate patterns. Most of the looms for patterned or figured cloth have beams for two separate warps. The cords of the drawloom, which controls the pattern, are pulled by a draw-boy.

Stage 5: Final Tasks

- **Finishing.**

Sources: Grete De Francesco, 'The Venetian Silk Industry', *Ciba Review*, Vol. 3, No. 29 (1940), pp. 1027–35; F. Edler de Roover, 'The Manufacturing Process', *Ciba Review*, Vol. 7, No. 80 (1950), pp. 2915–20; D. Kuhn, *Textile Technology: Spinning and Reeling*, Vol. 5, Part 9 (Cambridge, 1988).

Appendix 5

Processes of Beer Brewing

Stage 1: Malting

In malting, the grain is made to germinate, and this process is stopped by drying the grain to conserve the sugars or farinaceous matter necessary for fermentation.

Stage 2: Milling

The grain is then milled, to facilitate the extraction of the sugars and starches.

Stage 3: Mashing

The malt is steeped or boiled in hot water, in order to convert the starch in the grain into maltose (sugar). With other constituents of the malt, this dissolves, forming a sweet extract called *wort*, which is drawn off from the spent grains.

Stage 4: Adding Hops

Wort is boiled with hops (and other additives) to give flavour and for preserving qualities.

Stage 5: Fermentation

Yeast is added after the hopped wort has been separated from the spent hops and cooled. In fermentation, the yeast converts the maltose in the wort to alcohol, and after the yeast has been removed, the resultant liquor is beer.

Stage 6: Vatting

The beer is vatted and clarified prior to consumption.

Sources: P. Mathias, *The Brewing Industry in England, 1700–1830* (Cambridge, 1959), p. xviii; R. Yntema, 'The brewing industry in Holland, 1300–1800: A Study in industrial development', (University of Chicago unpublished PhD thesis, 1992), p. 151.

Appendix 6

Goldsmiths of Antwerp Origin in London, 1548–86

Name	Arrival in London	Return to Antwerp	Other Information
John Bearle	1572		
Adrian Brickpott	1566	Died in London	
Bernard van den Broecke	1567		
Henrie Cannynge	1566	1569	
James de la Choustiere	1569	Before 1579	
Jan de Cord	1562		
James Couman	1567	1580	To Bruges c.1580
Henrie Dewarte	1566		
Peter van Doncke	1571	c.1571	
Alexander Dormall	1566	1567	Poorter of Antwerp in 1567
Hans Franke	1548		
Xpofer Gerrell	Before 1570	Before 1571	Freemaster of Antwerp c.1571
Nicasius de Glasso	1568		Died in London c.1600
Marcus Haye	Before 1567	1569	
David Hellynck	1570		
Christopher Hicks	1566	Before 1580	
Anthony Horny	1571		
Powl Hubbart	1568		
Balthazar Laett	1569		
Hans Lambrechts	1568	c.1571	
Lucas de Lannoye	1566		
Christopher Lardenoys	1568		In London in 1618
Nicholas Lardenoys	1561	1574	Poorter of Antwerp in 1575; moved to Heidelberg in 1588
Cornelius van Leemputte	1566	1570	Freemaster of Antwerp in 1572
Maturine le Jude	1561		
Balthazar Lompe	1568		

Jan Mennock	1568		
Peter Noblet	1568	Before 1578	Freemaster of Antwerp in 1577/8; poorter of Frankfurt in 1581
Michael Nowin	1571		
Hans Peniable	1571		
Nichas Prouenchere	1563		French, but worked in Antwerp
Hans Raett	1566	Before 1571	Free master of Antwerp in 1571; worked for the King of Denmark
Peter Tamyer	1561		
Cornelius Vanaken	1567		Born in Leiden; died in London in 1583
Arte Vanbourne	1571		
Joose van Mynden	1567	1568	Freemaster of Antwerp in 1568
James Vanderaste	1567	Before 1577	
Martine vanden Sande	1561	Before 1584	Poorter of Antwerp in 1584; in Vlissingen 1604
Josep van Dueren	1574		
Peter Vvan Macheren	1566		
John Vantawyien	1586		
Guillem van Zwaervelt	1572		
Hans Verhagen	1567	1569	Freemaster of Antwerp in 1576
Dionyse Volkaert (Denys Volckarts)	1567		Died in London after 1576
Nicolas Whosons	1568		

Sources: Antwerp Stadsarchief, Gilden en Ambachten, A 4487 and 4488; Certificatieboeken; London, Goldsmiths' Company, Court Minutes, Books K–O; J. Briels, 'Zuidnederlandse goud- en zilversmeden in Noordnederland omstreeks 1576–1625', *Bijdragen tot de Geschiedenis*, Vol. 55 (1972), pp. 89–112; G. van Hemeldonck, *De Antwerpse Goud- en Zilversmeden 1550–1600*, 2 vols (forthcoming); Kirk and Kirk, eds, *Returns of Aliens*, Vols. 1–4; D. Schlugheit, 'Alphabetische Naamlijst op de Goud en Zilversmeden te Antwerpen voor 1600', *Bijdragen tot de Geschiedenis*, Vol. 27 (1936), pp. 6–69; *Zilver uit de Gouden Eeuw van Antwerpen* (Antwerp, 1989).

Note: Poorter = citizen

Bibliography

MANUSCRIPT SOURCES

LONDON
BRITISH LIBRARY
Lansdowne Manuscripts
Harleian Manuscripts
Cottonian Manuscripts
Additional Manuscripts

CORPORATION OF LONDON RECORDS OFFICE
Jour 15–26	Journals of the Court of Common Council, 1544–1604
Rep 11–25	Repertories of the Court of Aldermen, 1544–1604
Rep 26–30	Repertories of the Court of Aldermen, 1603–15
Rep 35, 54	Repertories of the Court of Aldermen, 1620–21, 1639–40
Rem I–II	Remembrancia, 1579–1609
Letter Books	T, V, X, Y, Z, & C, AB, AA, BB, 1560–1605

Courts of the Manors of Southwark AD, 1539–1564 [SCM 1]
Book of Fines, 1517–1628 [GLMS 87]

FRENCH PROTESTANT CHURCH, SOHO SQUARE
MS 194	Deacons' Account Book, 1572-3

GOLDSMITHS' HALL
B39.1520	Court Minutes Book A, Vol. 2, 1444–1516
B39.1524	Court Minutes Book G, H, I, Vol. 6, 1543–1556-7
B39.1525	Court Minutes Book, K, Part I, Vol. 8, 1557–66
B39.1526	Court Minutes Book K, Part II, and Book L, Part I, Vol. 9, 1566–73
B39.1527	Court Minutes Book L, part II, Vol. 10, 1573–9
B39.1528	Court Minutes Book N and O, Part I, Vol. 12, 1592–9
B39.1529	Court Minutes Book N and O, Part II, Vol. 13, 1599–1604
	Goldsmiths' Court Book, Vol. 7; 1682–1688, Vol. 9; 1688–1708, Vol. 10; 1709–1719, Vol. 11

Apprentice Books 4–6; Index of apprentices and masters

J.V. (i) [6] Petitions of the plateworkers and other goldsmiths to the Goldsmiths' Company and draft petitions by the Goldsmiths' Company to the King against the admittance to the freedom of the City of an alien plateworker named Bowers, with a council's opinion, c.1663

J.V. (i) [7] Draft petition to the King and Privy Council voicing their opposition to the application by two Dutchmen, Bodendike and Hawzer, to have their plate assayed at Goldsmiths' Hall, 1664

J.V. (i) [9] Abstract of the petition of certain working goldsmiths to the Lords of the Council concerning the increase of aliens, 1668

GREATER LONDON RECORD OFFICE
P71/OLA 9   St Olave Southwark, Parish Register, 1583–1627

GUILDHALL LIBRARY, MSS SECTION

PAROCHIAL RECORDS
MS 819/1   Allhallows the Great, Vestry Minutes, 1574–1684
MS 4384/1   St Bartholomew by the Exchange, Vestry Minutes, 1567–1643
MS 877/1   St Benet Paul's Wharf, Vestry Minutes, 1578–1674
MS 9236   St Botolph Aldgate, Vestry Minutes, 1583–1640
MS 943/1   St Botolph Billingsgate, Vestry Minutes, 1592–1673
MS 4424   St Christopher le Stocks, 'The Book of Records', 1559–91
MS 6419/1   St Giles without Cripplegate, Parish Registers, 1561–1606

LIVERY COMPANIES

Brewers' Company
MS 5445/2–21   1557–1676
MS 5442/3   Old Wardens' Account Books, 1547–62
MS 5442/4   Old Wardens' Account Books, 1563–81
MS 5442/5   Old Wardens' Account Books, 1582–1616
MS 7885/1   Yeomanry Account Books, 1556–86
MS 7885/2   Yeomanry Account Books, 1586–1618
MS 5496   Oath and Ordinance Book, containing ordinances 1579, 1580, 1593

Weavers' Company
MS 4629   Judgment in the Court of Exchequer against two foreigners for trespass, 28 June 1569
MS 4630   Ordinances, 1577
MS 4631   Miscellaneous papers
MS 4637   Rates paid by English and stranger weavers, 1638
MS 4645   Ordinance, oath and memorandum book, known as the 'Ancient Book', fourteenth–sixteenth centuries
MS 4646   Account and Memorandum Book, known as the 'Old Leidger Book', 1489–1741
MS 4647   Ordinance and Memorandum Book, chiefly containing bills of grievances, petitions, decrees and ordinances relating to the disputes between English and alien weavers, 1585–1641

A9.1 No 39   The case of the Commonality of the Corporation of Weavers of London truly stated: humbly presented to the consideration of the Honourable House of Commons, 1648 (printed pamphlet)
MS 4655/1–10, 1610–1694

PROBATE RECORDS
MS 9051/2–5   Archdeaconary Wills, 1549–1604
MS 9171/15–19   Commission Court Wills, 1559–1603

DUTCH CHURCH RECORDS
MS 7386/1   Attestation Papers, 1570–1626
MS 7402/4   Register of Members of Congregation, 1573–84
MS 7402/5   Register of Members of Congregation, 1584–1611
MS 7403   General Register of Members, 1550–1694
MS 9620   State of the Dutch Community in London, 1550–1605
MS 10,055   Chronicle of the community, 1547–1618

MERCHANT TAILORS' HALL, THREADNEEDLE STREET
MTC, Ancient MS Books, Vol. 54, T3, Miscellaneous papers from 1575, including original precepts, receipts, petitions, including a survey of unfree tailors, 1599

SOUTHWARK ARCHIVES
St Olave Southwark, Churchwardens' Accounts, 1546–92
St Olave Southwark, Vestry Minutes, 1552–1604

HERTFORDSHIRE ARCHIVES AND LOCAL STUDIES
D/ELW F1   Household Account of Jaques Wittewrongle, with record of birth and baptism of his children [in Dutch]
D/ELW F3   Letter of denization, 1582, Jacob Wittewrongle (1558–1662)
D/ELW F4   Licence to eat meat in Lent, 1619
D/ELW F6   Account of personal estate and original will of Jacob Wittewrongle, 1622
D/ ELW B1   Partnership deeds in brewing between Jacob Wittewrongle and Mathias Otten

OXFORD
BODLEIAN LIBRARY
MS 6429 (Barlow 19) 'Of the munsters of the straungers congregacion in London'
MS 21642 (Douce 68) Names of Dutch

ANTWERP (STADSARCHIEF)
CERTIFICATIEBOEKEN

GILDEN EN AMBACHTEN
GOUD EN ZILVERSMEDEN
A4485   Ordinances of gold and silversmiths in Antwerp, 1524–1730
A4487   Account book of the silversmiths gild in Antwerp, 1564–92
A4488   Papers relating to goldsmiths in Bruges, Brussels, 1440–1593

SATIJN-, CAFFA- EN BORATWERKERS
A4524   Ordinances, 1532–1710
A4525   Miscellaneous, 1571–1751, including a list of *zijdenlakenverkoopers* (silk merchants), 1570

BROUWERS
A4441–4   Ordinances, quantities and prices of beer, names of breweries, 1480–1653

BRUSSELS (ARCHIVES GENERALES DU ROYAUME)
CONSEIL DES TROUBLES
MS 6 Sentences 1567–75
MS 18–21 Summons lists
MS 103 Legal records (Valenciennes)
MS 155 Lists of those executed and banished (Valenciennes and Tournai)
MS 165, 166, 170, 171 Confiscation records
MS 315A, 315 bis Confiscation records (Valenciennes)
MS 328 Confiscation records (Tournai)

CHAMBRE DES COMPTES
CC 1203 Tournai
CC18.312 Antwerp
CC18.313 Antwerp
CC19.018-21 Antwerp

USA
FOLGER SHAKESPEARE LIBRARY, WASHINGTON
MS V.b. 142 f. 87, Members of Dutch Church in London, 1593

HENRY E. HUNTINGTON LIBRARY, SAN MARINO, CALIFORNIA

ELLESMERE MANUSCRIPTS
MS 2514–19, Extract of returns of the 7113 aliens living in and around London, 1593; record of the number of aliens in various trades and professions, 1593; undated complaints against merchant strangers living and trading in England (temp. Elizabeth or James I)

PRINTED SOURCES

A Discourse of the Common Weal of this Realm of England, ed. E. Lamond (Cambridge, 1929)
A Relation, or Rather a True Account, of the Island of England; with Sundry Particulars of the Customs of these People, and of the Royal Revenues under King Henry the Seventh, about the Year 1500, ed. C.A. Sneyd (Camden Society, old series, Vol. 37, 1847)
Actes du Consistoire de l'Eglise Française de Threadneedle Street, Londres, Vol. 1, 1560–65, ed. E. Johnson (Huguenot Society Publications 38, 1937)
Actes du Consistoire de l'Eglise Française de Threadneedle Street, Londres, Vol. 2, 1571–77, ed. A.M. Oakley (Huguenot Society Publications 48, 1969)
Acts of the Privy Council of England, ed. J.R. Dasent (32 vols, 1890–1907)
Andrew Boorde's Introduction and Dyetary, ed. F.J. Furnivall (Early English Text Society, extra series, No. X, 1870)
Antwerpse Poortersboeken 1533–1608, ed. Dr J. van Roey (3 vols, Antwerp, 1977)
Analytical Index to the Series of Records known as the Remembrancia Preserved Among the Archives of the City of London, 1579–1644, ed. W.H. and H.C. Overall (London, 1878)
Arnold, R., *The customs of London, otherwise called Arnold's Chronicle* (London, 1503)
Boorde, A., *Compendyous Regyment or Dyetary of Health* (London, 1542)
Calendar of the Patent Rolls, Edward IV, Philip and Mary, Elizabeth (1924–)
Calendar of State Papers, Domestic, Vols I–VIII, ed. R. Lemon and M.A.E. Green (1856–75)
Calendar of State Papers, Foreign, 1547–1553; May 1592–June 1593
Calendar of State Papers, Spanish, Vol. 10 Edward VI 1550–1552, ed. R. Tyler (1914)
Calendar of State Papers, Venetian, 1558–1603 (3 vols, 1890–97)
Calendar of Letter Books Preserved Among the Archives of the City of London at the Guildhall, ed. R.R. Sharpe (11 vols, London, 1899–1912)

Calendars of the Proceedings in Chancery, in the reign of Queen Elizabeth; to which are prefixed Examples of earlier Proceedings in that Court, namely from the reign of Richard the Second to that of Queen Elizabeth, inclusive, Vol. 1 (London, 1827)

Clapp, B.W., and Fisher, H.E.S. et al., eds, *Documents in English Economic History* (London, 1977)

Collier, J.P., ed, *The Egerton Papers: A collection of Public and Private Documents, chiefly illustrative of the times of Elizabeth and James I from the original documents* (Camden Society, old series, Vol. 12, 1840)

Cooper, W.D., *Lists of Foreign Protestants and Aliens, Resident in England 1618–1688* (Camden Society, old series, 82, 1862)

Cramer, J.A., ed, *The Second Book of the Travels of Nicander Nucius of Coreyra* (Camden Society, old series, Vol. 17, 1841)

de Coussemaker, E., ed, *Troubles religieux du XVIe siècle dans la Flandre maritime 1560–1570. Documents originaux* (Bruges, 1876)

D'Ewes, S., *The Journals of all the Parliaments during the Reign of Queen Elizabeth* (London, 1682)

Dietz, B., ed, *The Port and Trade of Early Elizabethan London Documents* (London Record Society, Vol. 8, 1972)

Furnivall, F.J., ed., *Harrison's Description of England in Shakespere's Youth, AD 1577–1587* (London, 1877)

Hessels, J.H., ed., *Ecclesiae Londino-Batavae Archivum, Epistulae et Tractatus* (3 vols, Cambridge, 1889–97)

Historical Manuscripts Commission, *Hatfield House* (24 vols, 1883–1976)

———, *Third Report* (1872)

Janssen, H.Q., 'De hervormde vlugtelingen van Ypren in Engeland', *Bijdragen tot de oudheidskunde en Geschiedenis, inzonderheid van Zeeuwsch-Vlaanderen*, Vol. 2 (1857), pp. 211–304

Jelsma, A.J. and Boersma, O., eds, *Acta van het consistorie van de Nederlandse gemeente te Londen 1569–1585* (RGP, Kleine serie 76, Instituut voor Nederlandse geschiedenis, 1993)

Journals of the House of Commons, Vol. I (1852)

Journals of the House of Lords, Vols. I–II (1846)

Kirk, R.E.G., and Kirk, E.F., eds, *Returns of Aliens Dwelling in the City and Suburbs of London* (Huguenot Society Publications, Vol. 10, 4 parts, 1900–1908)

Letters of Denization and Acts of Naturalization for Aliens in England, 1509–1603, ed. W. Page (Huguenot Society Publication 8, 1893)

London and Middlesex Chantry Certificate, 1548, ed. C.J. Kitching (London Record Society, Vol. 16, 1980)

Middlesex County Records, Vol. IV, ed. J.C. Jeaffreson (London, 1892)

Moens, W.J.C., *The Marriage, Baptismal, and Burial Registers of the Dutch Reformed Church Austin Friars, London, 1571 to 1874* (Lymington, 1884)

———, *The Walloons and their Church at Norwich* (1888)

Porder, R., *A Sermon of gods fearefull threatnings for Idolatrye ... with a Treatise against Usurie ... Preached in Paules Churche* (London, 1570)

Porter, G.R., *A Treatise on the Origin, Progressive Improvement, and Present State of the Silk Manufacture*, (Vol. xxii of Dr Dionysius Lardner's Cabinet Cyclopedia, 1831)

Proceedings in the Parliament of Elizabeth I, 1558–1581, ed. T.E. Hartley (Leicester, 1981)

Returns of Strangers in the Metropolis 1593, 1627, 1635, 1639, ed. I. Scouloudi (Huguenot Society Publications, Vol. 57, 1985)

Rye, W.B., *England as Seen by Foreigners in the Days of Elizabeth and James the First* (London, 1865)

Stow, J., *A Survey of London*, ed. C.L. Kingsford (2 vols, Oxford, 1908)

———, *The Annales, or Generall Chronicle of England ...*, continued and augmented by Edmond Howes (London, 1615)

Strype, J., *A Survey of the Cities of London and Westminster ... Now lastly ... brought down from the year 1633 ... to the present time* (5 vols, London, 1720)
——, *Annals of the Reformation* (4 vols., Oxford, 1824)
Stubbes, P., *The Anatomie of Abuses* (London, 1583)
The Statutes of the Realm, 1509–1624 (Vols 3–4, 1817–19)
Tudor Economic Documents, eds. R.H. Tawney and E. Power (3 vols, 1924)
Two Tudor Subsidy Assessment Rolls for the City of London: 1541 and 1582, ed. R.G. Lang (London Record Society, Vol. 29, 1993)
von Bulow, G. (ed.), 'A Journey through England and Scotland made by Lupold von Wedel in the Years 1584 and 1585', *Transactions of the Royal Historical Society* (new series, Vol. 9, 1895, pp. 223–70.
Waller, W.C., *Extracts from the Court Books of the Weavers Company of London, 1610–1730, made and edited for the Huguenot Society of London* (Huguenot Society Publications, Vol. 33, 1931)

SECONDARY SOURCES

Al, N., and Lesger, C.M., '"Twee volken ... besloten binnen Amstels wallen?" Antwerpse migraten in Amsterdam omstreeks 1590', *Tijdschrift voor sociale Geschiedenis*, 1995, Vol. 21, pp. 129–44
Aerts, E., and Munro, J.H., eds, *Textiles of the Low Countries in European Economic History: Proceedings of the Tenth International Economic History Congress*, Leuven, August 1990 (Leuven, 1990)
Aerts, E., and Unger, R., 'Brewing in the Low Countries', in E. Aerts, L.M. Cullen and R.G. Wilson, eds, *Production, Marketing, and Consumption of Alcoholic Beverages Since the Late Middle Ages* (Proceedings of Tenth International Economic History Congress, Leuven, 1990)
Alcorn, E.M., '"Some of the Kings of England Curiously Engraven": An Elizabethan Ewer and Basin in the Museum of Fine Arts, Boston', *Journal of the Museum of Fine Arts*, 1993, Vol. 5, pp. 66–103
Aldrich, H., Cater, J., Jones, T., et al., 'Ethnic Residential Concentration and the Protected Market Hypothesis', *Social Forces*, 1985, Vol. 63, pp. 996–1009
Alsop, J.D., 'An Immigrant Weaver's Inventory for 1573', *Textile History*, 1983, Vol. 14, pp. 78–9
Antwerpen in de XVI[de] Eeuw (Genootschap voor Antwerpse Geschiedenis, Antwerp, 1976)
Appleby, A.B., 'Diet in sixteenth-century England: Sources, problems, possibilities', in C. Webster, ed., *Health, medicine and mortality in the sixteenth century* (Cambridge, 1979), pp. 97–116
——, 'Nutrition and Disease: The Case of London, 1550–1750', *Journal of Interdisciplinary History*, 1975, Vol. 6, pp. 1–22
Archer, I.W., 'Material Londoners?', in L.C. Orlin, ed., *Material London, ca.1600* (Philadelphia, PA, 2000), pp. 174–192
——, 'Responses to Alien Immigrants in London, c.1400–1650', in *Le Migrazioni in Europa secc. XIII–XVIII*, Istituto Internazionale di Storia Economica 'F. Datini' Prato, Serie II – Atti delle 'Settimane di Studi' e altri Convegni 25, S. Cavaciocchi, 1994, pp. 755–74
——, 'The London Lobbies in the Later Sixteenth Century', *Historical Journal*, 1988, Vol. 31, pp. 17–44
——, *The Pursuit of Stability: Social Relations in Elizabethan London* (Cambridge, 1991)
Arnold, J., 'A Study of Three Jerkins', *Costume*, 1971, Vol. 5, pp. 36–43
Asaert, G., 'Antwerp ships in English harbours in the fifteenth century', *The Low Countries History Yearbook*, 1979, Vol. XII, pp. 29–47

Ashelford, J. *A Visual History of Costume: The Sixteenth Century* (London, 1983)
——, *Dress in the Age of Elizabeth I* (London, 1988)
Ashtor, E., 'The Factors of Technological and Industrial Progress in the Later Middle Ages', *Journal of European Economic History*, 1989, Vol. 18, pp. 7–36
Backhouse, M.F., *The Flemish and Walloon Communities at Sandwich during the Reign of Elizabeth I (1561–1603)* (Brussels, 1995)
——, 'The Flemish Refugees in Sandwich, 1561–1603', in *Revolt and Emigration* (Dikkebus, 1988), pp. 91–110.
——, 'The Strangers at Work in Sandwich: Native Envy of an Industrious Minority, 1561–1603', *Immigrants and Minorities*, 1991, Vol. 10, No. 3, pp. 70–99
Baelde, M., 'The Pacification of Ghent in 1576: Hope and Uncertainty in the Netherlands', *The Low Countries History Yearbook*, 1978, Vol. 11, pp. 1–17
Baldwin, F.E., *Sumptuary Legislation and Personal Regulation in England* (John Hopkins University Studies Series 44, No. 1, 1926)
Ball, M., *The History of the Worshipful Company of Brewers: A Short History* (London, 1977)
Barbour, V., *Capitalism in Amsterdam in the 17th Century* (Baltimore, MI, 1950)
Barker, T., 'London: A Unique Megalopolis?', in T. Barker and A. Sutcliffe, eds, *Megalopolis: The Giant City in History* (London, 1993), pp. 43–60
Beier, A.L., *Masterless Men: The Vagrancy Problem in England, 1560–1640* (London, 1985)
——, 'Poverty and Progress in early modern England', ed. A.L. Beier, D. Cannadine and J. Rosenheim, *The First Modern Society: Essays in English History in Honour of Lawrence Stone* (Cambridge, 1989)
——, and Finlay, R., eds, *London 1500–1700: The Making of the Metropolis* (London, 1986)
——, 'Social problems in Elizabethan London', *Journal of Interdisciplinary History*, 1978, Vol. 9, pp. 203–21
Benedict, P., 'Faith, Fortune and Social Structure in Seventeenth-century Montpellier', *Past and Present*, 1996, Vol. 152, pp. 46–78
——, 'French cities from the sixteenth century to the Revolution: An overview', in idem, ed., *Cities and Social Change in Early Modern France* (London, 1992)
——, *Rouen During the Wars of Religion* (Cambridge, 1981)
——, 'The Catholic Response to Protestantism: Church Activity and Popular Piety in Rouen, 1560–1600', in J. Obelkevich, ed., *Religion and the People, 800–1700* (Chapel Hill, NC, 1979), pp. 168–90
Bennett, J.M., *Ale, Beer and Brewsters in England: Women's Work in a Changing World, c.1300–1600* (Oxford, 1996)
——, 'The Village Ale-wife: Women and Brewing in Fourteenth-century England', in B.A. Hanawalt, ed., *Women and Work in Pre-industrial Europe* (Bloomington, IN, 1986), pp. 20–36
Beresford, M.W., 'The Common Informer, the Penal Statutes and Economic Regulation', *Economic History Review*, 2nd series, 1957, Vol. 10, pp. 221–38
Berg, M., ed., *Markets and Manufactures in Early Industrial Europe* (London, 1991)
——, and Bruland, K., 'Culture, Institutions and Technological Transitions', in M. Berg and K. Bruland, eds, *Technological Revolutions in Europe: Historical Perspectives* (Cheltenham, 1998), pp. 3–16.
——, Hudson, P. and Sonenscher, M., eds, *Manufacture in Town and Country Before the Factory* (Cambridge, 1983)
Berlin, M., 'Civic ceremony in early modern London', *Urban History Yearbook*, 1986, pp. 15–27
Beuzart, P., *La répression a Valenciennes après les troubles religieux de 1566* (Paris, 1930)
Bimbenet-Privat, M., 'Goldsmiths' apprenticeship during the first half of the seventeenth century: The situation in Paris', in D. Mitchell, ed., *Goldsmiths, Silversmiths and Bankers: Innovation and the Transfer of Skill, 1550–1750* (London, 1995), pp. 23–31
——, *Les Orfèvres Parisiens de la Renaissance 1506–1620* (Paris, 1992)

Blair, J., and Ramsay, N., eds, *English Medieval Industries: Craftsmen, Techniques, Products* (London, 1991)

Blanchard, I., 'Northern Wools and Netherlands Markets at the Close of the Middle Ages' (*Studies in Economic and Social History Discussion Paper* No. 92–3)

Blok, P.J., *History of the People of the Netherlands: From the Beginning of the Fifteenth Century to 1559* (London, 1907)

Boersma, O. and Jelsma, A.J., eds, *Unity in Multiformity: The Minutes of the Coetus of London, 1575 and the Consistory Minutes of the Italian Church of London, 1570–1591* (Huguenot Society Publications, Vol. 59, 1997)

Bolton, J.B. *The Alien Communities of London in the Fifteenth Century: The Subsidy Rolls of 1440 and 1485–4* (Stamford, 1998)

Boulton, J., 'London 1540–1700', in P. Clark, ed., *Cambridge Urban History of Britain, Volume II: 1540–1840*, pp. 315–46

——, *Neighbourhood and Society: A London Suburb in the Seventeenth Century* (Cambridge, 1987)

——, 'Neighbourhood migration in early modern London', in P. Clark and D. Souden eds, *Migration and Society in Early Modern England* (London, 1987)

——, 'Residential mobility in seventeenth-century Southwark', *Urban History Yearbook*, 1986, pp. 1–14

Bowden, P.J., 'Wool Supply and the Woollen Industry', *Economic History Review*, second series, 1956, Vol. 9, pp. 44–58

Bratchel, M.E., 'Alien merchant colonies in sixteenth-century England: Community organisation and social mores', *Journal of Medieval and Renaissance Studies*, 1984, Vol. 14, pp. 39–62

——, 'Regulation and Group-consciousness in the Later History of London's Italian Merchant Colonies', *Journal of European Economic History*, 1980, Vol. 9, No. 3, pp. 585–610

Bray, F., 'Textile production and Gender Roles in China, 1000–1700', *Chinese Science*, 1995, Vol. 12, pp. 115–37

Brenner, Y.S., 'The Inflation of Prices in Early Sixteenth Century England', *Economic History Review*, 1961, Vol. 14, pp. 225–39

——, 'The Inflation of Prices in England, 1551–1650', *Economic History Review*, 1962, Vol. 15, 266–84

Brett-James, N.G., *The Growth of Stuart London* (London, 1935)

Breward, C., *The Culture of Fashion: A New History of Fashionable Dress* (Manchester, 1995)

Brewer, J., and Porter, R., eds, *Consumption and the World of Goods* (London, 1994)

Bridgen, S., *London and the Reformation* (Oxford, 1989)

——, 'Religion and Social Obligation in Early Sixteenth-Century London', *Past and Present*, 1984, Vol. 103, pp. 67–112

——, 'Youth and the English Reformation', *Past and Present*, 1982, Vol. 95, pp. 37–67

Briels, J., 'De Zuidnederlandse immigratie 1572–1630', *Tijdschrift voor Geschiedenis*, 1987, Vol. 100, pp. 331–55

——, *De Zuid-Nederlandse immigratie, 1572–1630* (Haarlem, 1978)

——, 'Zuidnederlandse goud- en zilversmeden in Noordnederland omstreeks 1576–1625', in two parts: *Bijdragen tot de Geschiedenis*, 1971, Vol. 54, pp. 87–141; 1972, Vol. 55, pp. 89–112

Briggs, E.R., 'Reflexions upon the first Century of the Huguenot Churches in England', *Huguenot Society Proceedings*, 1978, Vol. 23, pp. 99–119

Britnell, R.H., *The Comercialization of English Society, 1000–1500* (Cambridge, 1995)

Bruland, K., *British Technology and European Industrialisation* (Cambridge, 1989)

——, ed., *Technology Transfer and Scandinavian Industrialisation* (Oxford, 1991)

Brulez, W., 'Bruges and Antwerp in the 15th and 16th centuries: An antithesis?', *Acta Historiae Neerlandicae*, 1973, Vol. 6, pp. 1–26

——, 'De diaspora der Antwerpse kooplui op het einde van de 16e Eeuw', *Bijdragen voor de geschiedenis der Nederlanden*, 1960, Vol. 15, pp. 279–306
——, 'De handelsbalans der Nederlanden in het midden van de 16e eeuw', *Bijdragen voor de geschiedenis der Nederlanden*, 1966–7, Vol. 21, pp. 278–309
Buckatzch, E.J., 'The Constancy of Local Populations and Migration in England before 1800', *Population Studies*, 1951–2, Vol. 5, pp. 62–9
Bun, C.K., and Hui, O.J., 'The many faces of immigrant entrepreneurship', in R. Cohen, ed., *The Cambridge Survey of World Migration* (Cambridge, 1995), pp. 523–31
Burch, B., 'The Parish of St. Anne's Blackfriars, London, to 1665', *The Guildhall Miscellany*, 1969, Vol. 3, pp. 1–54
Burn, J.S., *The History of the French, Walloon, Dutch and other Foreign Protestant Refugees settled in England, from the Reign of Henry VIII to the Revocation of the Edict of Nantes* (London, 1846)
Burt, R., 'The international diffusion of technology in the early modern period: The case of the British non-ferrous mining industry', *Economic History Review*, 1991, Vol. 44, pp. 249–71
Canny, N., ed., *Europeans on the Move: Studies on European Migration, 1500–1800* (Oxford, 1994)
Carlin, M., *Medieval Southwark* (London, 1996)
——, and Rosenthal, J.T., eds, *Food and Eating in Medieval Europe* (London, 1998)
Carus-Wilson, E.M., *Essays in Economic History* (3 vols, London, 1954–62)
Challis, C., 'Currency and the economy in mid-Tudor England', *Economic History Review*, 2nd series, 1972, Vol. 25, pp. 313–22
——, *Tudor Coinage* (Manchester, 1978)
Chitty, C.W., 'Aliens in England in the Seventeenth Century to 1660', *Race*, 1969–70, Vol. 11, pp. 189–201
Chitty, C.W., 'Aliens in England in the Sixteenth Century', *Race*, 1966–7, Vol. 8, pp. 129–45
Cipolla, C.M., *Before the Industrial Revolution: European Society and Economy, 1000–1700* (London, 1993)
——, 'The Diffusion of Innovations in Early Modern Europe', *Comparative Studies in Society and History*, 1972, Vol. 14, pp. 46–52
——, 'The Economic Decline of Italy', in B. Pullan, ed., *Crisis and Change in the Venetian Economy in the Sixteenth and Seventeenth Centuries* (London, 1968), pp. 127–45
Ciriacono, S., 'Silk Manufacturing in France and Italy in the XVIIth Century: Two Models Compared', *Journal of European Economic History*, 1981, Vol. 10, pp. 167–99
Clair, C., 'Refugee Printers and Publishers in Britain during the Tudor Period', *Huguenot Society Proceedings*, 1970–76, Vol. 22, pp. 115–26
Clark, P., 'A Crisis Contained? The Condition of English Towns in the 1590s', in idem, ed., *The European Crisis of the 1590s: Essays in Comparative History* (London, 1985), pp. 44–66
——, 'Migration in England during the late seventeenth and early eighteenth centuries', *Past and Present*, 1979, Vol. 83, pp. 57–90
——, *The English Alehouse: A Social History, 1200–1830* (London, 1983)
——, 'The migrant in Kentish towns, 1580–1640', in P. Clark and P. Slack, eds, *Crisis and Order in English Towns, 1500–1700* (London, 1972)
——, and Souden, D., eds, *Migration and Society in Early Modern England* (London, 1987)
Clarkson, L.A., 'The Organization of the English Leather Industry in the Late Sixteenth and Seventeenth Centuries', *Economic History Review*, 1960–61, Vol. 13, pp. 245–53
——, *The Pre-industrial Economy in England, 1500–1750* (London, 1971)
Clay, C.G.A., *Economic Expansion and Social Change: England 1500–1700* (2 vols Cambridge, 1984)
Clode, C.M., *The Early History of the Guild of Merchant Taylors* (London, 1888)
Coleman, D.C., 'An Innovation and its Diffusion: The "New Draperies"', *Economic History Review*, 1969, Vol. 22, pp. 417–29
——, *Courtaulds, An Economic and Social History: The Nineteenth Century Silk and Crape* (Oxford, 1969)

——, *Industry in Tudor and Stuart England* (London, 1975)
——, 'Labour in the English Economy of the Seventeenth Century', in E.M. Carus-Wilson, ed., *Essays in Economic History*, Vol. 2 (London, 1962), pp. 291–308
——, 'Technology and Economic History, 1500–1750', *Economic History Review*, 1959, Vol. 11, pp. 506–14
——, 'Textile Growth', in N.B. Harte and K.G. Ponting, eds, *Textile History and Economic History: Essays in Honour of Miss Julia de Lacy Mann* (Manchester, 1973), pp. 1–21
——, *The Economy of England, 1450–1750* (Oxford, 1977)
Collinson, P., 'Calvinism with a Human Face', in *Archbishop Grindal, 1519–1583: The Struggle of a Reformed Church* (London, 1979), pp. 125–52
——, 'England and International Calvinism, 1558–1640', in M. Prestwich, ed., *International Calvinism, 1541–1715* (Oxford, 1985)
——, 'Calvinism with an Anglican Face: The Stranger Churches in Early Elizabethan London and their Superintendent', in idem, *Godly People: Essays on English Protestantism and Puritanism* (London, 1983), pp.213–244
——, *Godly People: Essays on English Protestantism and Puritanism* (London, 1983)
Consitt, F., *The London Weavers' Company* (Oxford, 1933)
Cooper, J.P., 'Economic Regulation and the Cloth Industry in Seventeenth-century England', *Transactions of the Royal Historical Society*, 5th series, 1970, Vol. 20, pp. 73–99
Corfield, P.J., *The Impact of English Towns, 1700–1800* (Oxford, 1982)
——, 'Urban Development in England and Wales in the Sixteenth and Seventeenth Centuries', in D.C. Coleman and A.H. John, eds, *Trade, Government and Economy in Pre-industrial England: Essays Presented to F.J. Fisher* (London, 1976), pp. 214–47
——, and Keene, D., eds, *Work in Towns, 850–1850* (Leicester, 1990)
Cornwall, J., 'English Population in the Early Sixteenth Century', *Economic History Review*, 1970, Vol. 23, pp. 32–44
Corran, H.S., *A History of Brewing* (London, 1975)
Cottret, B., *The Huguenots in England: Immigration and Settlement c.1550–1700* (Cambridge, 1991)
Crafts, N.F.R., 'Industrial Revolution in England and France: Some Thoughts on the Question "Why was England First?"', in J. Mokyr, ed., *The Economics of the Industrial Revolution*, Totowa, NJ, (1985) pp. 119–31
Crawford, P., *Women and Religion in England, 1500–1720* (London, 1993)
Cressy, D., 'Describing the Social Order of Elizabethan and Stuart England', *Literature and History*, 1976, Vol. 3, pp. 29–44
——, 'Levels of illiteracy in England, 1530–1730', *Historical Journal*, 1977, Vol. 20, pp. 1–23
——, 'Occupations, Migration and Literacy in East London, 1580–1640', *Local Population Studies*, 1970, Vol. 5, pp. 53–61
Cross, F.W., *History of the Walloon and Huguenot Church at Canterbury* (Huguenot Society Publications, Vol. 15, 1898)
Crouzet, F., 'The sources of England's wealth: Some French views in the eighteenth century', in P.L. Cottrell and D.H. Aldcroft, eds, *Shipping, Trade and Commerce: Essays in Memory of Ralph Davis* (Leicester, 1981), pp. 61–79
Cummins, J., *Francis Drake* (London, 1995)
Cunningham, W., *Alien Immigrants in England* (London, 1897, reprint 1969)
——, 'The Formation and Decay of Craft Gilds', *Transactions of the Royal Historical Society*, 1886, Vol. 3, pp. 371–92
——, *The Growth of English Industry and Commerce in Modern Times*, Vol. 2. (Cambridge, 1907)
Dale, M.K., 'The London Silkwomen of the Fifteenth Century', *Economic History Review*, 1933, Vol. 4, pp. 324–35
Davids, K.A., 'Beginning Entrepreneurs and Municipal Governments in Holland at the Time of the Dutch Republic', in C. Lesger and L. Noordegraaf, eds, *Entrepreneurs and Entrepreneurship*

in Early Modern Times: Merchants and Industrialists within the Orbit of the Dutch Staple Market (Haarlem, Hollandse Historische Reeks, Vol. 24, 1995)

———, 'On the diffusion of nautical knowledge from the Netherlands to north-eastern Europe, 1550–1850', in W.G. Heeres and L.M.J.B. Hesp, eds, *From Dunkirk to Danzig: Shipping and Trade in the North Sea and the Baltic, 1350–1850* (Hilversum, 1988), pp. 217–36

———, 'Technological change and the economic expansion of the Dutch Republic, 1580–1680', in The Dutch Economy in the Golden Age (Amsterdam, 1993)

———, 'Openness or Secrecy? Industrial Espionage in the Dutch Republic', *Journal of European Economic History*, 1995, Vol. 24, No. 2, pp. 333–48

Davies, C.S.L., 'Provisions for Armies, 1509–50: A Study in the Effectiveness of Early Tudor Government', *Economic History Review*, 1964–5, 2nd series, Vol. 17, pp. 234–48

Davies, D.W., *Dutch Influences on English Culture, 1558–1625* (The Folger Shakespeare Library, 1979)

Davies, J., 'Persecution and Protestantism: Toulouse, 1562–1575', *Historical Journal*, 1979, Vol. 22, pp. 31–51

Davis, E.J., 'The Transformation of London', in R.W. Seton-Watson, ed., *Tudor Studies* (London, 1924), pp. 287–314

Davis, N.Z., *Society and Culture in Early Modern France* (London, 1975)

———, 'The sacred and the body social in sixteenth-century Lyon', *Past and Present*, 1981, Vol. 90, pp. 40–70

———, 'Women in the Crafts in Sixteenth-century Lyon', in B.A. Hanawalt, ed., *Women and Work in Pre-industrial Europe* (Bloomington, IN, 1986), pp. 167–97

Davis, R., *English Overseas Trade, 1500–1700* (London, 1973)

———, 'The Rise of Antwerp and its English Connection, 1406–1510', in D.C. Coleman and A.H. John, eds, *Trade, Government and Economy in Pre-industrial England: Essays presented to F.J. Fisher* (London, 1976), pp. 2–21

Deceulaer, H., 'Entrepreneurs in the Guilds: Ready-to-wear Clothing and Subcontracting in late Sixteenth- and early Seventeenth-century Antwerp', *Textile History*, 2000, Vol. 31, No. 2, pp. 133–49

de Francesco, G., 'The Venetian Silk Industry', *Ciba Review*, 1940, Vol. 3, pp. 1027–35

Dempsey, S., 'The Italian Community in London during the Reign of Edward II', *London Journal*, 1993, Vol. 18, pp. 14–22

de Peuter, R., 'Industrial Development and De-industrialization in pre-modern towns: Brussels from the sixteenth to the eighteenth century, a provisional survey', in H. van der Wee, ed., *The Rise and Decline of Urban Industries in Italy and in the Low Countries* (Leuven, 1988), pp. 213–40

den Blaauwen, A.L., *Dutch Silver 1580–1830* (1979)

de Roover, F. Edler, 'Andrea Banchi, Florentine Silk Manufacturer and merchant in the fifteenth century', *Studies in Medieval and Renaissance History*, 1966, Vol. 3, pp. 223–85

———, 'The Beginnings and the Commercial Aspects of the Lucchese Silk Industry', *Ciba Review*, 1950, Vol. 7, pp. 2907–13

———, 'The Manufacturing Process', *Ciba Review*, 1950, Vol. 7, pp. 2915–20

de Roover, R., 'Labour Conditions in Florence around 1400: Theory, Policy and Reality', in N. Rubinstein ed., *Florentine Studies: Politics and Society in Renaissance Florence* (London, 1968), pp. 277–313

Deruisseau, G.L., 'Velvet and Silk in the Italian Renaissance', *Ciba Review*, 1939, Vol. 2, pp. 595–99

de Vries, J., 'Between purchasing power and the world of goods: Understanding the household economy in early modern Europe', in J. Brewer, and R. Porter, eds, *Consumption and the World of Goods* (London, 1994), pp. 85–132

———, *European Urbanization 1500–1800* (London, 1984)

———, 'Patterns of urbanization in pre-industrial Europe, 1500–1800', in H. Schmal, ed., *Patterns of European Urbanization since 1500* (London, 1981), pp. 79–109

———, 'The labour market',in K. Davids and L. Noordegraaf, eds, *The Dutch Economy in the Golden Age*, Vol. 4, Amsterdam, 1993, pp. 55–79

———, 'The Population and Economy of the Pre-industrial Netherlands', *Journal of Interdisciplinary History*, 1985, Vol. 15, pp. 661–82

Deyon, P., and Guignet, P., 'Royal Manufactures and Economic and Technological Progress in France before the Industrial Revolution', *Journal of European Economic History*, 1980, Vol. 9, No. 3, pp. 611–32

Dickinson, H.T., 'The Poor Palatines and the parties', *English Historical Review*, 1967, Vol. 82, pp. 464–85

Diederiks, H., and Balkestein, M., eds, *Occupational Titles and Their Classification: The Case of the Textile Trade in Past Times* (Göttingen, 1995)

Dietz, B., 'Antwerp and London: The Structure and Balance of Trade in the 1560s', in E.W. Ives and J. Knecht, eds, *Wealth and Power in Tudor England: Essays presented to S.T. Bindoff* (London, 1978), pp. 186–203

———, 'Overseas trade and metropolitan growth', in A.L. Beier and R. Finlay eds, *London 1500–1700: The Making of the Metropolis* (London, 1986), pp. 115–40

Driessen, L.A., 'Linen Weaving and Linen Bleaching in Holland', *Ciba Review*, 1944, Vol. 4, pp. 1733–8

Duke, A.C., 'Building Heaven in Hell's Despite: The Early History of the Reformation in the Towns of the Low Countries', in A.C. Duke and C.A. Tamse, eds, *Britain and the Netherlands: Papers Delivered to the Seventh Anglo-Dutch Historical Conference*, Vol. VII (The Hague, 1981), pp. 45–75

———, 'The Ambivalent Face of Calvinism in the Netherlands, 1561–1618', in *International Calvinism, 1541–1715*, ed. M. Prestwich (Oxford, 1985), pp. 109–34

Dunn, R.M., 'The London Weavers' Riot of 1675', *Guildhall Studies in London History*, 1973, Vol. 1, pp. 13–23

DuPlessis, R.S., *Lille and the Dutch Revolt: Urban Stability in an Era of Revolution, 1500–1582* (Cambridge, 1991)

———, 'The light woollens of Tournai in the sixteenth and seventeenth centuries', in E. Aerts and J. Munro, eds, *Textiles of the Low Countries in European Economic History Session B-15: Proceedings of the Tenth International Economic History Congress, Leuven 1990* (Leuven, 1990), pp. 66–85

———, 'One Theory, Two Draperies, Three Provinces, and a Multitude of Fabrics: The New Drapery of French Flanders, Hainaut, and the Tournaisis, c.1550–c.1800', in N.B. Harte, ed., *The New Draperies in the Low Countries and England, 1300–1800* (Oxford, 1997), pp. 129–72

———, and Howell, M.C., 'Reconsidering the early modern urban economy: The cases of Leiden and Lille', *Past and Present*, 1982, Vol. 94, pp. 49–84

Duthie, R., 'Introduction of plants to Britain in the 16th and 17th centuries by strangers and refugees', *Proceedings of the Huguenot Society*, 1987, Vol. 24, pp. 403–20

Dyer, C., 'English Diet in the Later Middle Ages', in T.H. Ashton, P.R. Coss and C. Dyer, eds, *Social Relations and Ideas: Essays in Honour of R.H. Hilton* (Cambridge, 1983)

———, *Standards of Living in the Later Middle Ages: Social Change in England c.1200–1520* (Cambridge, 1989)

Earle, P., 'The economy of London, 1660–1730' in P. O'Brien, D. Keene, M. 't Hart, and H. van der Wee, eds, *Urban Achievement in Early Modern Europe: Golden Ages in Antwerp, Amsterdam and London* (Cambridge, 2001), pp. 81–96

———, 'The female labour market in London in the late seventeenth and early eighteenth centuries', *Economic History Review*, 1989, Vol. 42, pp. 328–53

———, *The Making of the English Middle Class: Family, Society and Family Life in London, 1660–1730* (London, 1989)

Eastman, L.E., *Family, Fields and Ancestors: Constancy and Change in China's Social and Economic History, 1550–1949* (Oxford, 1998)

Elias, N., *The Civilizing Process: The History of Manners* (Oxford, 1978)

Elton, G.R., England under the Tudors (London, 1974)
——, 'Informing for profit: A sidelight on Tudor methods of law-enforcement', *Cambridge Historical Journal*, 1954, Vol. 11, pp. 149–67
——, *The Parliament of England, 1559–1581* (Cambridge, 1986)
Endrei, W., 'Manufacturing a piece of woollen cloth in medieval Flanders: How many work hours?', in E. Aerts and J. Munro, eds, *Textiles of the Low Countries in European Economic History Session B-15: Proceedings Tenth International Economic History Congress, Leuven, 1990* (Leuven, 1990), pp. 14–31
——, 'The Productivity of Weaving in Late Medieval Flanders', in N.B. Harte and K.G. Ponting, eds, *Cloth and Clothing in Medieval Europe* (London, 1983), pp. 108–19
Epstein, S.R., 'Craft Guilds, Apprenticeship, and Technological Change in Preindustrial Europe,' *Journal of Economic History*, 1998, Vol. 58, No. 3, pp. 684–713
——, 'Regional fairs, institutional innovation, and economic growth in late medieval Europe', *Economic History Review*, 1994, Vol. 3, pp. 459–82
——, 'Town and country: economy and institutions in late medieval Italy', *Economic History Review*, 1993, Vol. 46, pp. 453–77
Escott, M.M., 'Profiles of Relief: Royal Bounty grants to Huguenot refugees, 1686–1709', *Proceedings of the Huguenot Society*, 1991, Vol. 25, No. 3, pp. 257–78
Esser, R., 'From the Hansa to the Present: Germans in Britain since the Middle Ages', in P. Panayi, ed., *Germans in Britain since 1500* (London, 1996)
——, 'Immigrant Cultures in Tudor and Stuart England', in N. Goose and L. Luu, eds, *Immigrants in Tudor and Early Stuart England* (Brighton, 2005), pp. 161–24
——, 'News Across the Channel – Contact and Communications between the Dutch and Walloon Refugees in Norwich and their families in Flanders, 1565–1640', *Immigrants and Minorities*, 1995, Vol. 14, pp. 139–52
——, 'The Norwich Strangers and the Sandwich Connection', WH info. X afl. 2, July 1994, pp. 66–81
Evans, N., *The East Anglian Linen Industry: Rural Industry and Local Economy, 1500–1850* (Aldershot, Hants., 1985)
Evans, J., *Huguenot Goldsmiths in England and Ireland* (London, 1933)
Evers, M., 'Religiones et Libertatis Ergo: Dutch refugees in England and English exiles in the Netherlands', in *Refugees and Emigrants in the Dutch Republic and England: Papers of the Annual Symposium Held on 22 November 1985* (Leiden, 1986), pp. 7–27
Eykens, M.J., 'De Brouwindustrie te Antwerpen 1585–1700', *Bijdragen tot de Geschiedenis*, 1973, pp. 80–101
Fagel, R., 'Immigrant roots: The geographical origin of newcomers from the Low Countries in Tudor England', in N. Goose and L. Luu, eds, *Immigrants in Tudor and Early Stuart England* (Brighton, 2005), pp. 41–56
——, 'The Netherlandish presence in England before the coming of the stranger churches, 1480–1560', in R. Vigne and C. Littleton, eds, *From Strangers to Citizens: The Integration of Immigrant Communities in Britain, Ireland and Colonial America, 1550–1750* (Brighton, 2001), pp. 7–16
Fairlie, S., 'Dyestuffs in the Eighteenth Century', *Economic History Review*, 1965, Vol. 17, pp. 488–509
Farr, J., 'Consumers, commerce, and the craftsmen of Dijon: The changing social and economic structure of a provincial capital, 1450–1750', in P. Benedict ed., *Cities and Social Change in early modern France* (London, 1989), pp. 134–73
——, *Hands of Honor: The World of the Artisans in Early Modern France Dijon, 1550–1650* (Ithaca, NY, 1988)
Fine, B., and Leopold, E., 'Clothing: Industrial or consumer revolution', in *The World of Consumption* (London, 1993), pp. 120–37
——, 'Consumerism and the Industrial Revolution', *Social History*, 1990, Vol. 15, No. 2, pp. 151–79

Finlay, R., *Population and Metropolis: The Demography of London, 1580-1650* (Cambridge, 1981)
——, and Shearer, B., 'Population growth and suburban expansion', in A.L. Beier and R. Finlay eds, *London 1500–1700: The Making of the Metropolis* (London, 1986), pp. 37–59
Finn, M., 'Women, Consumption and coverture in England, c.1760–1860', *Historical Journal*, 1996, Vol. 39, No. 3, pp. 703–22
Fisher, F.J., *London and the English Economy, 1500–1700*, ed. P.J. Corfield and N.B. Harte (London, 1990)
Fleney, R., 'London and Foreign Merchants in the Reign of Henry VI', *English Historical Review*, 1910, Vol. 25, pp. 644–55
Foster, F.F., *The Politics of Stability: A Portrait of the Rulers in Elizabethan London* (London, 1977)
Friedrichs, C.R., *The Early Modern City, 1450–1750* (London, 1995)
Furnivall, F.J., ed., *Ballads from Manuscripts*, Vol. 1 (Ballad Society, 1868–72)
Gadd, I.A. and P. Wallis, eds, *Guilds, Society and Economy in London 1450–1800* (Centre for Metropolitan History, University of London, 2002)
Galloway, J.A., and Murray, I., 'Scottish Migration to England, 1400–1560', *Scottish Geographical Magazine*, 1996, Vol. 112, pp. 29–38
Gater, G.H. and W.H. Godfrey eds, *Survey of London*, Vol. 15 (London, 1934)
Gascon, R., *Grand commerce et vie urbaine au xvie siècle: Lyons et ses marchands (environs de 1520–environs de 1580)* (Paris, 1971)
Gibbs, G., 'The Reception of the Huguenots in England and the Dutch Republic, 1680–1690', in O.L. Grell, J.I. Israel and N. Tyacke, eds, *From Persecution to Toleration: The Glorious Revolution and Religion in England* (Oxford, 1991), pp. 275–306
Girouard, M., 'Some Alien Craftsmen in Sixteenth- and Seventeenth-century England', *Proceedings of the Huguenot Society*, 1959, Vol. 20, pp. 26–35
Giuseppi, M.S., 'Alien Merchants in England in the Fifteenth Century', *Transactions of the Royal Historical Society*, 1895, 9, 75–98
Glanville, P., 'Alien Goldsmiths at the Court of Charles II', in R. Stockland, ed., *The Grosvenor House Antiques Fair: The Antique Dealers' Fair, 9th–19th June 1993* (London, 1993), pp. 18–23
——, *Silver in England* (London, 1987)
——, *Silver in Tudor and Early Stuart England: A Social History and Catalogue of the National Collection, 1480–1660* (London, 1990)
Glass, D.V., 'Socio-economic status and occupations in the City of London at the end of the seventeenth century', in P. Clark, ed., *The Early Modern Town* (London, 1976), pp. 216–32
Godfrey, E.S., *The Development of English Glassmaking 1560–1640* (Oxford, 1975)
Goose, N., 'English pre-industrial urban economies', in J. Barry, ed., *The Tudor and Stuart Town: A Reader in English Urban History, 1530–1688* (London, 1990), pp. 63–73
——, 'The "Dutch" in Colchester: The Economic Influence of an Immigrant Community in the Sixteenth and Seventeenth Centuries', *Immigrants and Minorities*, 1982, Vol. 1, No. 3, pp. 261–80
——, 'Xenophobia in Elizabethan & Early Stuart England: An Epithet Too Far?', in N. Goose and L. Luu, eds, *Immigrants in Tudor and Early Stuart England* (Brighton, 2005), pp. 110–135
——, 'Immigrants and English Economic Development in the Sixteenth and Early Seventeenth Centuries', in N. Goose and L. Luu, eds, *Immigrants in Tudor and Early Stuart England* (Brighton, 2005), pp. 136–60
Goring, J.J., 'Wealden Ironmasters in the Age of Elizabeth', in E.W. Ives, J.J. Scarisbrick and R.J. Knecht, eds, *Wealth and Power in Tudor England: Essays pPresented to S.T. Bindoff* (London, 1978), pp. 204–27
Goris, J.A., *Etude sur les colonies marchandes mérdionales (portugais, espagnols, italiens) à Anvers de 1488 à 1567. Contribution à l'histoire des débuts du capitalisme moderne* (Leuven, 1925)

Grassby, R., 'Social Mobility and Business Enterprise in Seventeenth-century England', in D. Pennington, and K. Thomas, eds, *Puritans and Revolutionaries: Essays in Seventeenth-century History Presented to Christopher Hill* (Oxford, 1978), pp. 355–81

——, 'The Personal Wealth of the Business Community in Seventeenth-century England', *Economic History Review*, 1970, Vol. 23, pp. 220–34

Greengrass, M., 'Protestant Exiles and their Assimilation in Early Modern England', *Immigrants and Minorities*, 1985, Vol. 4, pp. 68–81

Grell, O.L.P., *Calvinist Exiles in Tudor and Stuart England* (Aldershot, Hants., 1996)

——, *Dutch Calvinists in Tudor and Early Stuart London: The Dutch Church in Austin Friars, 1603–1612* (Leiden, 1989)

——, 'Plague in Elizabethan and Stuart London: The Dutch Response', *Medical History*, 1990, Vol. 34, pp. 424–39

——, 'The French and Dutch congregations in London in the Early 17th Century', *Proceedings of the Huguenot Society*, 1987, Vol. 5, pp. 362–77

Griffiths, T., Hunt, P.A., and O'Brien, P.K., 'Inventive Activity in the British Textile Industry, 1700–1800', *Journal of Economic History*, 1992, Vol. 52, pp. 881–906

Gross, L.F., 'Wool Carding: A Study of Skills and Technology', *History of Technology*, 1987, pp. 804–27

Guignet, P., 'The Lacemakers of Valenciennes in the Eighteenth Century: An Economic and Social Study of a Group of Female Workers under the Ancien Regime', *Textile History*, 1979, Vol. 10, pp. 96–113

Gutmann, A.L., 'The Distribution of the Flemish Textile Industry', *Ciba Review*, 1939, Vol. 2, pp. 481–83

——, 'Technical Peculiarities of Flemish Cloth-making and Dyeing', *Ciba Review*, 1939, Vol. 2, pp. 485–87

Guy, J., *Tudor England* (Oxford, 1988)

——, 'The distribution of Huguenot refugees in England', *Proceedings of the Huguenot Society*, 1965–70, Vol. 21, pp. 404–36

——, 'The Arrival of Huguenot Refugees in England, 1680–1705', *Proceedings of the Huguenot Society*, 1969, Vol. 21, No. 5, pp. 366–73

——, 'James II in the light of his treatment of Huguenot refugees in England, 1685–1686', *Proceedings of the Huguenot Society*, 1977–82, Vol. 23, pp. 212–24

——, 'The number of Huguenot immigrants in England in the late seventeenth century', *Journal of Historical Geography*, 1983, Vol. 9, pp. 384–95

Gwynn, R.D., *The Huguenot Heritage: The History and Contribution of the Huguenots in Britain* (London, 1985)

——, 'Patterns in the Study of Huguenot Refugees in Britain: Past, Present and Future', in I. Scouloudi, ed., *Huguenots in Britain and their French Background, 1550–1800* (London, 1987), pp. 217–35

——, *The Huguenots of London* (Brighton, 1998)

Hale, J., *The Civilization of Europe in the Renaissance* (London, 1993)

Hall, A.R., 'Early Modern Technology, to 1600', in M. Kranzberg and C.W. Pursell, eds, *Technology in Western Civilization: The Emergence of Modern Industrial Society, Earliest Times to 1900*, Vol. 1 (London, 1967), pp. 79–103

Hall, B., 'Lynn White's *Medieval Technology and Social Change* after Thirty Years', in R. Fox, ed., *Technological Change: Methods and Themes in the History of Technology* (Amsterdam, 1996), pp. 85–101

Hanawalt, B.A., 'Peasant Women's Contribution to the Home Economy in Late Medieval England', in B.A. Hanawalt ed., *Women and Work in Pre-industrial Europe* (Bloomington, IN, 1986), pp. 3–19

Harding, V., 'Cross-Channel Trade and Cultural Contacts: London and the Low Countries in the Later Fourteenth Century', in C. Barron and N. Saul, eds, *England and the Low Countries in the Late Middle Ages* (Stroud, 1995), pp. 153–68

——, 'Some Documentary Sources for the Import and Distribution of Foreign Textiles in Later Medieval England', *Textile History*, 1987, Vol. 18, pp. 205–18

——, 'The Population of London, 1550–1700: A review of the Published Evidence', *London Journal*, 1990, Vol. 15, pp. 111–28

Hare, S., 'Paul de Lamerie: a retrospective assessment', *Proceedings of the Huguenot Society*, 1991, Vol. 25, No. 3, pp. 219–29

——, 'Paul de Lamerie, 1688–1751', in *Paul de Lamerie: An Exhibition of the Work of England's Master Silversmith, 1688–1751* (London, 1990), pp. 8–29

Harris, J.R., 'Industrial Espionage in the Eighteenth Century', *Industrial Archaeology Review*, 1985, Vol. 7, pp. 127–38

Harris, T., *London Crowds in the Reign of Charles II: Propaganda and Politics from the Restoration Until the Exclusion Crisis* (Cambridge, 1987)

Hart, M., 'Freedom and restrictions: State and economy in the Dutch Republic, 1570–1670', in K. Davids and L. Noordegraaf, eds, *The Dutch Economy in the Golden Age*, Vol. 4 (Amsterdam, 1993), pp. 105–30

——, 'Intercity Rivalries and the Making of the Dutch State', in C. Tilly and W.P. Blockmans, eds, *Cities and the Rise of States in Europe, A.D. 1000 to 1800* (Oxford, 1994), pp. 196–218

Harte, N.B., 'State Control of Dress and Social Change in Pre-Industrial England', in D.C. Coleman and A.H. John, eds, *Trade, Government and Economy in Pre-Industrial England: Essays Presented to F.J. Fisher* (London, 1976), pp. 132–65

Hartop, C., 'Art and industry in 18th-century London: English silver 1680–1760 from the Alan and Simone Hartman Collection', *Proceedings of the Huguenot Society*, 1998, Vol. 27, No. 1, pp. 50–63

Hatcher, J., *The History of the British Coal Industry before 1700: Towards the Age of Coal*, Vol. 1 (Oxford, 1993)

Hayward, J.F., *Virtuoso Goldsmiths and the Triumph of Mannerism, 1540–1620* (London, 1976)

——, *Huguenot Silver in England, 1688–1727* (London, 1959)

Heal, F., 'The crown, the gentry and London: The enforcement of proclamation, 1596–1640', in C. Cross, D. Loades and J.J. Scarisbrick, eds, *Law and Government under the Tudors: Essays Presented to Sir Geoffrey Elton* (Cambridge, 1988), pp. 211–26

Henderson, W.O., *Britain and Industrial Europe, 1750–1870: Studies in British Influence on the Industrial Revolution in Western Europe* (Leicester University Press, 1965)

Herbert, W., *The History of the Twelve Great Livery Companies of London*, (2 vols, London, 1836)

Hermans, T., and Salverda, R., eds, *From Revolt to Riches: Culture and History of the Low Countries, 1500–1700* (London, 1993)

Hertz, G.B., 'The English Silk Industry in the Eighteenth Century', *English Historical Review*, 1909, Vol. 24, pp. 710–27

Hexter, J.H., 'The myth of the middle class in Tudor England', *Explorations in Entrepreneurial History*, 1949–50, Vol. 2, pp. 128–40

Hickman, D., 'Religious belief and pious practice among London's Elizabethan elite', *The Historical Journal*, 1999, Vol. 42, No. 4, pp. 941–60

Hill, C., *The Penguin Economic History of Britain: Reformation to Industrial Revolution, 1530–1780*, Vol. II (London, 1967)

Hilton, M., 'The Female Consumer and The politics of consumption in twentieth-century Britain', *Historical Journal*, 2002, Vol. 45, No. 1, pp. 103–4

Hinton, R.W.K., 'The decline of Parliamentary government under Elizabeth I and the early Stuarts', *Cambridge Historical Journal*, 1957, Vol. 13, pp. 116–32

Hocquet, A., *Tournai et le Tournaisis au XVIe siècle, au point de vue politique et social* (Brussels, 1906)

Hoenselaars, A.J., 'Foreigners in England, 1558–1603', *Images of Englishmen and Foreigners in the Drama of Shakespeare and His Contemporaries: A Study of Stage Characters and National Identity in English Renaissance, 1558–1642* (London, 1992)

Holderness, B.A., *Pre-industrial England: Economy and Society* (London, 1976)
——, 'The Reception and Distribution of the New Draperies in England' in N.B. Harte, ed., *The New Draperies in the Low Countries and England, 1300–1800* (Oxford, 1997), pp. 217–44
Hollaender, A.E.J., and Kellaway, W., eds, *Studies in London History* (London, 1969)
Holmes, M., 'Evil May Day, 1517: The Story of a Riot', *History Today*, 1965, Vol. 15, pp. 642–50
Holt, M.P., *The French Wars of Religion, 1562–1629* (Cambridge, 1995)
Hooper, W., 'The Tudor Sumptuary Laws', *English Historical Review*, 1915, Vol. 30, pp. 433–49
Howell, M., 'Woman's Work in the New and Light Draperies of the Low Countries', in N.B. Harte, ed., *The New Draperies in the Low Countries and England, 1300–1800* (Oxford, 1997), pp. 197–216
Hughes, M., *Early Modern Germany, 1477–1806* (London, 1992)
Hulme, E.W., 'The history of the patent system under the prerogative and at Common Law', in two parts: *Law Quarterly Review*, 1896, Vol. 12, pp. 141–54; 1900, Vol. 16, pp. 44–56
Hurstfield, J., and Smith, A.G.R., eds, *Elizabethan People: State and Society* (London, 1972)
Inkster, I., 'Mental Capital: Transfers of Knowledge and Technique in Eighteenth Century Europe', *Journal of European Economic History*, 1990, Vol. 19, pp. 403–41
——, 'Motivation and Achievement: Technological Change and Creative Response in Comparative Industrial History', *Journal of European Economic History*, 1998, Vol. 27, No. 1, pp.
Irsigler, F., '"Ind Machden alle lant beirs voll": Zur Diffusion des Hopfenbierkonsums im westlichen Hanseraum', in G. Wiegelmann and R.E. Mohrmann, eds, *Nahrung und Tischkultur im Hanseraum* (1996), pp. 377–97
Israel, J.I., *The Dutch Republic: Its Rise, Greatness, and Fall, 1477–1806* (Oxford, 1995)
——, *Dutch Primacy in World Trade, 1585–1740* (Oxford, 1989)
Jack, S.M., *Trade and Industry in Tudor and Stuart England* (London, 1977)
Jackson, C.J., *English Goldsmiths and their Marks: A History of the Goldsmiths and Plate Workers of England, Scotland, and Ireland* (Dover, 1921)
Jamees, A., *Inventaris van het archief van de Raad van Beroevten* (Brussels, 1980)
Jeremy, D.J., 'Damming the Flood: British Government Efforts to Check the Outflow of Technicians and Machinery, 1780–1843', *Business History Review*, Spring 1977, Vol. 51, No. 1, pp. 1–34
——, ed., *International Technology Transfer: Europe, Japan and the USA, 1700–1914* (Aldershot, 1991)
——, ed., *Technology Transfer and Business Enterprise* (1994)
Jervis, F.R.J., *The Evolution of Modern Industry* (London, 1960)
Johnson, D.J., *Southwark and the City* (London, 1969)
Jones, D.W., 'The "Hallage" Receipts of the London Cloth Markets, 1562–c.1720', *Economic History Review*, 1972, Vol. 25, pp. 567–87
Jones, E., 'London in the Early Seventeenth Century: An Ecological Approach', *London Journal*, 1980, Vol. 6, pp. 123–33
——, 'The Fashion Manipulators: Consumer Tastes and British Industries, 1660–1800', in L.P. Cain and P.J. Uselding, eds, *Business Enterprise and Economic Change: Essays in Honor of Harold F. Williamson* (Kent, OH, 1973), pp. 198–226
Jones, W.J., *British Nationality Law and Practice* (Oxford, 1947)
Kahl, W., *The Development of London Livery Companies: An Historical Essay and a Select Bibliography* (Boston, Massachusetts, 1960)
Kamen, H., *The Iron Century: Social Change in Europe, 1550–1660* (London, 1971)
Kaplan, S.L., 'The Character and Implications of Strife among the Masters inside the Guilds of Eighteenth-century Paris', *Journal of Social History*, 1986, Vol. 19, pp. 631–47

Keene, D., 'Continuity and development in urban trades: Problems of concepts and the evidence', in D. Keene and P.J. Corfield, eds, *Work in Towns, 850–1850* (Leicester, 1990), pp. 1–16

——, 'Growth, Modernisation and Control: The Transformation of London's Landscape, c. 1500–c. 1760', *Two Capitals: London and Dublin 1500–1840, Proceedings of the British Academy*, 2001, Vol. 107, pp. 7–37

——, 'Material London in Time and Space,' in L.C. Orlin, ed., *Material London, ca.1600* (Philadelphia, PA, 2000), pp. 55–74

——, 'Medieval London and Its Region', *London Journal*, 1989, Vol. 14, pp. 99–111

——, 'The environment of Hanseatic commerce in London, A.D. 1100–1600', paper presented at Istituto Universitario di Architettura, Venice, June 1996, published in J. Bottin and D. Calabi, eds, *Les étrangers dans la ville, xv–xviii siécles* (Paris, 1998) (published in French)

Kellett, J.R., 'The Breakdown of Gild and Corporation Control over the Handicraft and Retail Trade in London', *Economic History Review*, Series 2, 1957–8, Vol. 10, pp. 381–94

Kellenbenz, H., 'German Immigrants in Britain', in C. Holmes, ed., *Immigrants and Minorities in British Society* (London, 1978), pp. 63–80

Kent, D.A., 'Ubiquitous but Invisible: Female Domestic Servants in Mid-eighteenth Century London', *History Workshop Journal*, 1989, Vol. 28, pp. 111–28

Kenwood, A.G., and Lougheed, A.L., *Technological Diffusion and Industrialisation before 1914* (London, 1982)

Kerling, N.J.M., *Commercial Relations of Holland and Zealand with England from the Late 13th Century to the Close of the Middle Ages* (Leiden, 1954)

Kerridge, E., *Textile Manufactures in Early Modern England* (Manchester, 1985)

Kiernan, V.G., 'Britons Old and New', in C. Holmes, ed., *Immigrants and Minorities in British Society* (London, 1978), pp. 23–59

King, F.A., *Beer Has a History* (London, 1947)

Kitch, M.J., 'Capital and kingdom: Migration to later Stuart London', in A.L. Beier and R. Finlay eds, *London 1500–1700: The Making of the Metropolis* (London, 1986), pp. 224–51

Klep, P.M.M., 'Urban decline in Brabant: The traditionalization of investments and labour (1374–1806)', in H. van der Wee, ed., *The Rise and Decline of Urban Industries in Italy and in the Low Countries* (Leuven, 1988), pp. 261–86

Knecht, R.J., 'Francis I, "Defender of the Faith?"', in E.W. Ives, R.J. Knecht and J.J. Scarisbrick, eds, *Wealth and Power in Tudor England: Essays presented to S.T. Bindoff* (London, 1978), pp. 106–27

Knotter, A., and Luiten van Zanden, J., 'Immigratie en arbeidsmarkt te Amsterdam in de 17e eeuw', *Tijdschrift voor Sociale Geschiedenis*, 1987, Vol. 4, pp. 403–31

Knowles, J., 'The Spectacle of the Realm: Civic consciousness, rhetoric and ritual in early modern London', in J.R. Mulryne and M. Shewring eds, *Theatre and government under the Early Stuarts* (Cambridge, 1993), pp. 157–89

Koenigsberger, H.G., 'Decadence or shift? Changes in the civilization of Italy and Europe in the sixteenth and seventeenth centuries', *Transactions of the Royal Historical Society*, 5th series, 1960, Vol. 10, pp. 1–18

——, 'Orange, Granvelle and Philip II', *Bijdragen en Mededelingen betreffende de Geschiedenis der Nederlanden*, 1984, Vol. 99, pp. 573–95

——, *Politicians and Virtuosi: Essays in early modern history* (London, 1986)

——, 'Prince and States General: Charles V and the Netherlands (1506–1555)', *Transactions of the Royal Historical Society*, sixth series, 1994, Vol. 4, pp. 27–51

——, 'The organization of revolutionary parties in France and the Netherlands during the sixteenth century', *Journal of Modern History*, 1955, Vol. 27, pp. 335–51

——, 'Why did the States General of the Netherlands become revolutionary in the Sixteenth Century?', *Parliaments, Estates and Representation*, 1982, Vol. 2, pp. 103–11

——, 'The States-General of the Netherlands before the Revolt', in idem, *Estates and Revolutions: Essays in Early Modern European History* (London, 1970), pp. 125–43

Konvitz, J.W., 'Port Functions, Innovation and the Making of the Megalopolis', in T. Barker and A. Sutcliffe, eds, *Megalopolis: The Giant City in History* (London, 1993), pp. 61–72

Kossman, E.H., and Mellink, A.F., eds, *Texts Concerning the Revolt of the Netherlands* (Cambridge, 1974)

Kranzberg, M., and Pursell, C.W., eds, *Technology in Western Civilization: The Emergence of Modern Industrial Society Earliest Times to 1900*, Vol. 1 (London, 1967)

Kuhn, D., *Textile Technology: Spinning and Reeling*, Vol. 5, Part IX (Cambridge, 1988)

Kusamitsu, T., '"Novelty, give us Novelty": London Agents and Northern Manufacturers', in M. Berg, ed., *Markets and Manufacturers in Early Industrial Europe* (London, 1991), pp. 114–38

la Force Clayburn, J., 'Technological Diffusion in the 18th Century: The Spanish Textile Industry', *Technology and Culture*, 1964, Vol. 5, pp. 322–43

Lacey, K., 'The Production of "Narrow Ware" by Silkwomen in Fourteenth and Fifteenth Century England', *Textile History*, 1987, Vol. 18, pp. 187–204

Lake, P.G., 'Calvinism and the English Church 1570–1635', *Past and Present*, 1987, Vol. 114, pp. 32–76

Landes, D., 'Religion and Enterprise: The Case of the French Textile Industry', in E.C. Carter, R. Forster and J.N. Moody, eds, *Enterprise and Entrepreneurs in Nineteenth and Twentieth Century France* (London, 1976), pp. 41–86

——, *The Unbound Prometheus: Technological Change and Industrial Development in Western Europe from 1750 to the Present* (Cambridge, 1969)

——, *The Wealth and Poverty of Nations: Why Some are so Rich and Some so Poor* (London, 1998)

Lane, F.C., 'The Role of Governments in Economic Growth in Early Modern Times', *Journal of Economic History*, 1975, Vol. 35, pp. 8–17

Lang, R.G., 'London's Aldermen in Business: 1600–1625', *Guildhall Miscellany*, 1971, Vol. 3, pp. 242–64

——, 'Social Origins and Social Aspirations of Jacobean London Merchants', *Economic History Review*, 1974, Vol. 27, No. 1, pp. 28–47

Lanz, H., 'Training and workshop practice in Zürich in the seventeenth century', in D. Mitchell, ed., *Goldsmiths, Silversmiths and Bankers: Innovation and the transfer of Skill, 1550–1750* (London, 1995), pp. 32–42

Laver, J., *A Concise History of Costume* (London, 1969)

le Boucq, P.J., *Histoire des Troubles advenues a Valenciennes: A cause des Hérésie 1562–1579* (Brussels, 1864)

Lemire, B., 'Consumerism in Preindustrial and Early Industrial England: The Trade in Secondhand Clothes', *Journal of British Studies*, 1988, Vol. 27, pp. 1–24

——, *Fashion's Favourite: The Cotton Trade and the Consumer in Britain, 1660–1800* (Oxford, 1991)

Lesger, C.M., 'Amsterdam, Harlingen and Hoorn: Port functions in the Zuiderzee region during the middle of the seventeenth century', in W.G. Heeres, L.M.J.B. Hesp et al., eds, *From Dunkirk to Danzig: Shipping and Trade in the North Sea and the Baltic, 1350–1850* (Hilversum, 1988), pp. 331–61

——, C.M., 'Clusters of achievement: the economy of Amsterdam in its golden age', in P. O'Brien, D. Keene, M. 't Hart, and H. van der Wee, eds, *Urban Achievement in Early Modern Europe* (Cambridge, 2001), pp. 63–80

——, and L. Noordegraaf, eds, *Entrepreneurs and Entrepreneurship in Early Modern Times: Merchants and Industrialists within the Orbit of the Dutch Staple Market* (Haarlem, Hollandse Historische Reeks, Vol. 24, 1995)

Lever, C., *Goldsmiths and Silversmiths of England* (London, 1975)

Limberger, M., '"No town in the world provides more advantages": Economies of agglomeration and the golden age of Antwerp', in P. O'Brien, D. Keene, M. 't Hart and H. van der Wee, eds, *Urban Achievement in Early Modern Europe: Golden Ages in Antwerp, Amsterdam and London* (Cambridge, 2001), pp. 39–62

Lindeboom, J., *Austin Friars: History of the Dutch Reformed Church in London, 1550–1950* (The Hague, 1950)
Lindenbaum, S., 'Ceremony and Oligarchy: The London Midsummer Watch', in B.A. Hanawalt and K.L. Reyerson, eds, *City and Spectacle in Medieval Europe* (Minneapolis, MN, 1994), pp. 171–88
Lindley, K., 'Riot Prevention and Control in Early Stuart London', *Transactions of the Royal Historical Society*, fifth series, 1983, Vol. 33, pp. 109–26
Linthicum, M.C., *Costume in the Drama of Shakespeare and his Contemporaries* (Oxford, 1936)
Lipson, E., *The Economic History of England: The Age of Mercantilism*, Vol. 3 (London, 1934)
Littleton, C., 'Social interaction of aliens in late Elizabethan London: Evidence from the 1593 Return and the French Church consistory "actes"', in R.Vigne and G. Gibbs, eds, *The Strangers' Progress: Integration and Disintegration of the Huguenot and Walloon Refugee Community, 1567–1889: Essays in memory of Irene Scouloudi* (Proceedings of the Huguenot Society, Vol. 26, 1995), pp. 147–59
——, 'The Strangers, their Churches and the Continent: Continuing and changing connections', in N. Goose and L. Luu, eds, *Immigrants in Tudor and Early Stuart England* (Brighton, 2005), pp. 177–191
Loades, D., *The Tudor Court* (London, 1992)
Lopes Cordeiro, J.M., 'A Technology Transfer in Portugal's Late Eighteenth Century: The Royal Silk Twisting Mill of Chacim', *Textile History*, 1992, Vol. 23, pp. 177–88
Lopez, R.S., 'China silk in Europe in the Yuan period', *Journal of the American Oriental Society*, 1987, Vol. 72, pp. 72–6
Louw, H.J., 'Anglo-Netherlandish architectural interchange c.1600–c.1660', *Architectural History*, 1981, Vol. 24, pp. 1–23
Lucassen, J., *Dutch Long Distance Migration: A Concise History, 1600–1900* (IISG Research Papers 3, Amsterdam, 1992)
——, *Migrant labour in Europe, 1600–1900* (London, 1987)
——, 'The Netherlands, the Dutch, and Long-distance Migration in the Late Sixteenth to Early Nineteenth Centuries', in N. Canny, ed., *Europeans on the Move: Studies on European Migration, 1500–1800* (Oxford, 1994), pp. 153–92
Luiten van Zande, J., 'Economic growth in the Golden Age: The development of the economy of Holland, 1500–1650', *The Dutch Economy in the Golden Age*, Vol. 4, 1993, pp. 5–27
——, 'Aliens and their impact on the goldsmiths' craft in London in the sixteenth century', in D. Mitchell, ed., *Goldsmiths, Silversmiths and Bankers: Innovation and the Transfer of Skill, 1550–1750* (London, 1995), pp. 43–52
——, 'Assimilation or Segregation: Colonies of alien craftsmen in Elizabethan London', in R. Vigne and G. Gibbs, eds, *The Strangers' Progress* (Proceedings of the Huguenot Society, 1995, Vol. 26), pp. 160–72
——, 'Migration and change: Religious refugees and the London economy, 1550–1600', *Critical Survey*, 1996, Vol. 8, pp. 93–102
——, 'French-speaking refugees and the foundation of the London silk industry in the sixteenth century,' *Proceedings of Huguenot Society*, 1997, Vol. 26, No. 5, pp. 564–76.
——, 'Spatial segregation, occupational enclaves and the diffusion of skills: Stranger artisans and the economy of London, 1550–1600' in J. Bottin and D. Calabi, eds, *Les étrangers dans la ville, xv-xviii siècles* (Paris, 1998) (published in French)
——, 'Continental goldsmiths in London in the 16th and early 17th centuries, with special reference to Antwerp', *Silver for Sir Anthony* (Antwerp, 1999) (a publication to celebrate the life of Sir Anthony van Dyck) (in Dutch and English), pp. 49–69.
——, '"Taking the bread out of our mouths": Xenophobia in early modern London', *Immigrants and Minorities*, July 2000, Vol. 19, No. 2, pp. 1–22
——, 'Dutch and their beer brewing' in A. Kershen, ed., *Food in the Migrant's Experience* (Aldershot, 2002), pp. 101–33
——, 'Natural-Born versus Stranger-Born Subjects: Aliens and their status in Elizabethan

London', in N. Goose and L. Luu, eds, *Immigrants in Tudor and Early Stuart England* (Brighton, 2005), pp. 57–75

Luu, L.B., Alien communities in transition, 1570s–1640s', in N. Goose and L. Luu, eds, *Immigrants in Tudor and Early Stuart England* (Brighton, 2005), pp. 192–210

———, 'Alien Immigrants to England, One Hundred Years on' in Goose and Luu, eds, Immigrants in Tudor and Early Stuart England, pp. 223–228

MacCulloch, D., 'England', in A. Pettegree, ed., *The Early Reformation in Europe* (Cambridge, 1992), pp. 166–87

Mack, P., 'The Wanderyear: Reformed Preaching and Iconoclasm in the Netherlands', in J. Obelkevich, ed., *Religion and the People, 800–1700* (Chapel Hill, NC, 1979), pp. 191–220

MacLeod, C., *Inventing the Industrial Revolution: The English Patent System, 1660–1800* (Cambridge, 1988)

Magen, B., 'The administration within the Walloon settlement in Canterbury, 1576–1599', *Huguenot Society Proceedings*, 1970–76, Vol. 22, pp. 307–17

Maltby, W.S., *Alba: A Biography of Fernando Alvarez de Toledo, Third Duke of Alba, 1507–1582* (London, 1983)

Manning, R.B., *Village Revolts: Social Protest and Popular Disturbances in England, 1509–1640* (Oxford, 1988)

Mansfield, E., *The Economics of Technological Change* (London, 1969)

Marnef, G., *Antwerp in the Age of Reformation: Underground Protestantism in a Commercial Metropolis, 1550–1577* (London, 1996)

———, and de Schepper, H., 'Raad van Beroerten, 1567–1576', in E. Aerts and H. Soly et al. eds, *De centrale overheidsinstellingen van de Habsburgse Nederlanden (1482–1795)* (Brussels, Algemeen Rijksarchief, 1994, Band 1), pp. 469–77

Martin, L., 'The Rise of the New Draperies in Norwich, 1550–1622' in N.B. Harte, ed., *The New Draperies in the Low Countries and England, 1300–1800* (Oxford, 1997), pp. 245–74

Mason, P., and Gregory, M., *Of Gilding: An Essay on the Traditional techniques of Gilding, Silvering and Goldbeating* (London, 1989)

Matthias, P., *The Brewing Industry in England, 1700–1830* (Cambridge, 1959)

———, *The Transformation of England* (London, 1979)

———, and Davis, J.A., eds, *Innovation and Technology in Europe: From the Eighteenth Century to the Present Day* (Oxford, 1991)

Mazzaoui, M.F., 'Artisan migration and technology in the Italian textile industry in the late Middle Ages (1100–1500)', in R. Comba, G. Piccinni and G Pinto, eds, *Strutture familiari epidemie migrazioni nell'Italia medievale* (Edizione Scientifiche Italiane, 1984)

McClelland, D.C., *The Achieving Society* (Princeton, NJ, 1961)

McCray, W.P., 'Creating Networks of Skill: Technology Transfer and the Glass Industry of Venice', *Journal of European Economic History*, 1999, Vol. 28, No. 2, pp. 301–33

McIntosh, M.K., 'Servants and the Household Unit in an Elizabethan English Community', *Journal of Family History*, 1984, Vol. 9, pp. 3–23

McKendrick, N., Brewer, J., and Plumb, J.H., *The Birth of a Consumer Society: The Commercialisation of Eighteenth-century England* (London, 1982)

McKisack, M., *The Fourteenth Century, 1307–1399* (Oxford, 1959)

Meldrum, T., *Domestic Service and Gender, 1660–1750: Life and Work in the London Household* (Harlow, 2000)

Merriman, N., and Holmes, C., eds, *The Peopling of London* (London, 1993)

Miskimin, H.A., *Cash, Credit and Crisis in Europe, 1300–1600* (London, 1989)

———, *The Economy of Early Renaissance Europe, 1300–1460* (Cambridge, 1975)

Mitch, D., 'The Role of Human Capital in the First Industrial Revolution', in J. Mokyr, ed., *The British Industrial Revolution: An Economic Perspective* (Oxford, 1993), pp. 267–307

Mitchel, D.M., '"By Your Leave my Masters": British Taste in Table Linen in the Fifteenth and Sixteenth Centuries', *Textile History*, 1989, Vol. 20, pp. 49–77

——, 'Dressing plate by the "unknown" London silversmith "WF"', *Burlington Magazine*, June 1993, pp. 386–400

——, 'Good hot pressing is the life of all cloth': Dyeing, clothfinishing, and related textile trades in London, 1650–1700', in H. Diederiks and M. Balkestein, eds, *Occupational Titles and their Classification: The Case of the Textile Trade in Past Times* (St Katharinen, 1995), pp. 153–75

——, 'Innovation and the transfer of skill in the goldsmiths' trade in Restoration London', in D.M. Mitchell, ed., *Goldsmiths, Silversmiths and Bankers: Innovation and the Transfer of Skill, 1550–1750* (London, 1995), pp. 5–22

——, 'Levantine demand and the London textile trades, 1650–1730', in *CIETA Bulletin*, 2003, Vol. 80, pp. 49–59

——, The Linen damask trade in Haarlem. Its products and its markets', in A.J. de Graaf, L. Hanssen and J. de Roode, eds, *Textiel aan het Spaarne. Haarlem: van linen damas tot zijden linten* (Amsterdam, 1997), pp. 5–33

——, 'Marks, Manwarings and Moore: The use of the "AM in monogram" mark, 1650–1700', *The Silver Society Journal*, 1999, Vol. 11, pp. 168–84

——, 'Mr. Fowle Pray Pay the Washwoman's: The Trade of a London Goldsmith-banker, 1660–1692', *Business and Economic History*, 1994, Vol. 23, No. 1, pp. 27–38

——, 'To Alderman Backwells for the candlsticks for Mr Coventry': The manufacture and sale of plate at the Unicorn, Lombard Street', *The Silver Society Journal*, 2000, Vol. 12, pp. 111–24

——, Sonday, M., 'Printed Fustians: 1490–1600', *CIETA Bulletin*, 2000, Vol. 77, pp. 99–117

Mokyr, J., 'Demand vs. Supply in the Industrial Revolution', *Journal of Economic History*, 1977, Vol. 37, No. 4, pp. 981–1008

——, 'The Political Economy of Technological Change: Resistance and Innovation in Economic History', in M. Berg and K. Bruland, eds, *Technological Revolutions in Europe: Historical Perspectives* (Cheltenham, 1998), pp. 39–64.

Monckton, H., *History of English Ale and Beer* (London, 1966)

Monnas, L., 'Some Venetian Silk Weaving Statutes from the Thirteenth to the Sixteenth Century', *CIETA Bulletin*, 1991, Vol. 69, pp. 37–55

Morant, V., 'The Settlement of Protestant Refugees in Maidstone during the Sixteenth Century', *Economic History Review*, second series, 1951–2, Vol. 4, pp. 210–14

Morawska, E., 'The Sociology and Historiography of Immigration', in V.Yans-McLaughlin, ed., *Immigration Reconsidered: History, Sociology, and Politics* (Oxford, 1990), pp. 187–238

More, C., *Skill and the English Working Class, 1870–1914* (London, 1980)

Moreau, G., *Histoire du Protestantisme à Tournai jusqu à la veille de la Révolution des Pays-Bas* (Paris, 1962)

——, 'La corrélation entre le milieu social et professionnel et le choix de religion à Tournai', in *Bronnen voor de Geschiedenis van Belgie* (Louvain, 1968), pp. 286–300

Morokvasic, M., 'Immigrants in the Parisian garment industry', *Work, Employment and Society*, 1987, Vol. 1, pp. 441–62

——, Waldinger, R., and Phizacklea, A., 'Business on the Ragged Edge: Immigrant and Minority Business in the Garment Industries of Paris, London and New York', in R. Waldinger, H. Aldrich, and R. Ward, eds, *Ethnic Entrepreneurs: Immigrant Business in Industrial Societies* (London, 1990), pp. 157–76

Morris-Suzuki, T., *The Technological Transformation of Japan: From the Seventeenth to the Twenty-first Century* (Cambridge, 1994)

Munro, J.H., 'Industrial entrepreneurship in the late-medieval Low Countries: Urban draperies, fullers, and the art of survival', in P. Klep and E. van Cauwenberghe, eds, *Entrepreneurship and the Transformation of the Economy (10th–20th Centuries): Essays in Honour of Herman van der Wee* (Leuven, 1994), pp. 377–88

——, 'Urban regulation and monopolistic competition in the textile industries of the late-medieval Low Countries', in E. Aerts and J. Munro, eds, *Textiles of the Low Countries in*

European Economic History Session B-15: Proceedings Tenth International Economic History Congress, Leuven, August 1990 (Leuven, 1990), pp. 41–65
——, 'The Origin of the English "New Draperies": The Resurrection of an Old Flemish Industry, 1270–1570" in N.B. Harte, ed., *The New Draperies in the Low Countries and England, 1300–1800* (Oxford, 1997), pp. 35–127
——, 'Urban Wage Structures in Late-medieval England and the Low Countries: Work Time and Seasonable Wages', in I. Blanchard, ed., *Labour and Leisure in Historical Perspective, Thirteenth to Twentieth Centuries: Papers presented at Session B-3a of the Eleventh International Economic History Congress, Milan 12th–17th September 1994* (Stuttgart, 1994), pp. 65–78
Murdoch, T., *The Quiet Conquest: The Huguenots 1685 to 1985* (London, 1985)
Murray, J.J., 'The Cultural Impact of the Flemish Low Countries on Sixteenth- and Seventeenth-century England', *American Historical Review*, 1957, Vol. 62, pp. 837–54
Musson, A.E., *The Growth of British Industry* (London, 1978)
——, and Robinson, E., 'The Diffusion of Technology in Great Britain during the Industrial Revolution', in idem, *Science and Technology in the Industrial Revolution* (Manchester, 1969), pp. 60–86
Muthesius, A., 'From Seed to Samite: Aspects of Byzantine Silk Production', *Textile History*, 1989, Vol. 20, pp. 135–49
Naphy, W.G., *Calvin and the Consolidation of the Genevan Reformation* (Manchester, 1994)
——, 'Geneva: hospitality and xenophobia', in *Calvin and the Consolidation of the Genevan Reformation* (Manchester, 1994), pp. 121–43
Needham, J., *Science and Civilisation in China*, Vol. 1 (Cambridge, 1961)
Nef, J.U., *Industry and Government in France and England, 1540–1640* (Cornell University Press, Ithaca, NY, 1967)
——, *The Rise of the British Coal Industry*, Vol. 1 (London, 1932)
Nevinson, J., 'The Dress of the Citizens of London, 1540–1640', in J. Bird, H. Chapman and J. Clark, eds, *Collectanea Londiniensia: Studies in London Archaeology and History Presented to Ralph Merrifield* (London and Middlesex Archaeological Society, Special Paper 2, 1978), pp. 265–80
Nicholas, D.M., 'Town and countryside: Social and economic tensions in fourteenth-century Flanders', *Comparative Studies in Society and History*, 1967–8, Vol. 10, pp. 458–85
Nicoll, A., (ed.), *The Elizabethans* (Cambridge, 1957)
Nijenhuis, W., 'Variants within Dutch calvinism in the sixteenth century', *The Low Countries History Yearbook*, 1979, Vol. 12, pp. 48–64
Noordegraaf, L., 'Dearth, Famine and Social Policy in the Dutch Republic at the End of the Sixteenth Century', in P. Clark, ed., *The European Crisis of the 1590s: Essays in Comparative History* (London, 1985), pp. 67–83
——, 'Dutch industry in the Golden Age', *The Dutch Economy in the Golden Age*, 1993, Vol. 4, pp. 131–59
——, 'The New Draperies in the Northern Netherlands, 1500–1800', in N.B. Harte, ed., *The New Draperies in the Low Countries and England, 1300–1800* (Oxford, 1997), pp. 173–95
North, D.C., and Thomas, R.P., *The Rise of the Western World: A New Economic History* (Cambridge, 1973)
Norwood, F.A., 'The London Dutch Refugees in Search of a Home, 1553–1554', *American Historical Review*, 1952, Vol. 58, pp. 64–72
——, *The Reformation Refugees as an Economic Force* (Chicago, IL, 1942)
Oakley, A.M., 'The Canterbury Walloon Congregation from Elizabeth I to Laud', in I. Scouloudi, ed., *Huguenots in Britain and their French Background, 1550–1800* (London, 1987), pp. 56–71
O'Brien, P., 'Reflections and mediations on Antwerp, Amsterdam and London in their golden ages', in P. O'Brien, D. Keene, M. 't Hart and H. van der Wee, eds, *Urban Achievement in Early Modern Europe* (Cambridge, 2001), pp. 3–35

——, 'The Mainsprings of Technological Progress in Western Europe 1750–1850', in P. Mathias and J.A. Davis, eds, *Innovation and Technology in Europe: From the Eighteenth Century to the Present Day* (Oxford, 1991), pp. 6–17
Oman, C., *Caroline Silver, 1625–1688* (London, 1970)
——, *English Silversmiths' Work Civil and Domestic: An Introduction* (London, 1965)
Ormrod, D., *The Dutch in London: The Influence of an Immigrant Community, 1550–1800* (London, 1973)
Overton, M., 'The diffusion of agricultural innovations in early modern England: Turnips and clover in Norfolk and Suffolk, 1580–1740', *Transactions of the Institute of British Geographers*, new series, 1985, Vol. 10, pp. 205–21
Owen, H.G., 'A Nursery of Elizabethan Nonconformity, 1567–72', *Journal of Ecclesiastical History*, 1966, Vol. 17, pp. 65–76
——, 'The Liberty of the Minories: a study in Elizabethan religious radicalism', *East London Papers*, 1965, Vol. 8, No. 2, pp. 81–97
Page, W. ed., *Letters of Denization and Acts of Naturalization for Aliens in England, 1509–1603* (Huguenot Society Publications, Vol. 8, 1893)
Paillard, C., *Histoire des troubles religieux de Valenciennes, 1560–1567* (Paris, 1874–6)
Palliser, D.M., *The Age of Elizabeth: England Under the Later Tudors, 1547–1603* (London, 1992)
Parker, G., 'New Light on an Old Theme: Spain and the Netherlands 1550–1650', *European History Quarterly*, 1985, Vol. 15, pp. 219–236
——, 'Spain, her enemies and the revolt of the Netherlands, 1559–1648', *Past and Present*, 1970, Vol. 49, pp. 72–95
——, *The Dutch Revolt* (London, 1977)
——, 'Why did the Dutch Revolt last eighty years?', *Transactions of the Royal Historical Society*, 5th series, 1976, Vol. 26, pp. 53–72
Parry, D.L.L., 'The eccentricities of England', *European Review of History*, 1994, Vol. 1, pp. 59–65
Patten, J., 'Urban occupations in pre-industrial England', *Transactions of the Institute of British Geographers*, 1977, Vol. 2, pp. 296–313
Pearl, V., 'Change and Stability in Seventeenth-century London', *London Journal*, 1979, Vol. 5, pp. 3–34
——, *London and the Outbreak of the Puritan Revolution: City Government and National Politics, 1625–43* (Oxford, 1961)
——, 'Social Policy in Early Modern London', in H. Lloyd-Jones, V. Pearl and B. Worden, eds, *History and Imagination: Essays in Honour of H.R. Trevor-Roper* (London, 1981), pp. 115–31
Peeters, J.P., 'De-Industrialization in the small and medium-sized towns in Brabant at the end of the Middle Ages, a case-study: The cloth industry of Tienen', in H. van der Wee, ed., *The Rise and Decline of Urban Industries in Italy and in the Low Countries* (Leuven, 1988), pp. 165–86
Perkin, H.J., 'The social causes of the British Industrial Revolution', *Transactions of the Royal Historical Society*, 5th series, 1968, Vol. 18, pp. 123–43
Persson, K.G., *Pre-industrial Economic Growth: Social Organization and Technological Progress in Europe* (Oxford, 1988)
Peters, J., *A family from Flanders* (London, 1985)
Petersen, W., 'The demographic transition in the Netherlands', *American Sociological Review*, 1960, Vol. 25, pp. 334–47
Petrascheck-Heim, I., 'Tailors' Masterpiece-books', *Costume*, 1969, Vol. 3, pp. 6–9
Pettegree, A., *Emden and the Dutch Revolt: Exiles and the Development of Reformed Protestantism* (Oxford, 1992)
——, *Foreign Protestant Communities in Sixteenth Century London* (Oxford, 1986)
——, 'The exile churches during the *Wonderjaar*', in J. van den Berg and P.G. Hoftijzer, eds, *Church, Change and Revolution: Transactions of the Fourth Anglo-Dutch Church History Colloquium* (Leiden, 1991), pp. 80–99

———, 'The French and Walloon Communities in London, 1550–1688', in O.L.P. Grell, J.I. Israel and N. Tyacke, eds, *From Persecution to Toleration: The Glorious Revolution and Religion in England* (Oxford, 1991), pp. 77–96

———, '"Thirty years on": Progress towards integration amongst the immigrant population of Elizabethan London', in J. Chartres and D. Hey, eds, *English Rural Society, 1500–1800: Essays in Honour of Joan Thirsk* (Cambridge, 1990), pp. 297–312

Phelps-Brown, E.H., and Hopkins, S.V., 'Seven centuries of building wages', in E.M. Carus-Wilson, ed., *Essays in Economic History*, Vol. 2 (London, 1962), pp. 168–96

Phillips, P.A.S., *Huguenot Goldsmiths in England, 1687–1737* (London, 1933)

———, *Records of Some London Goldsmiths: Foreign Goldsmiths Settled in London and Some Accounts of London Goldsmiths* (London, 1932)

Pilgrim, J.E., 'The Rise of the "New Draperies" in Essex', *University of Birmingham Historical Journal*, 1959–60, Vol. 7, pp. 36–59

Piergiovanni, P.M., 'Technological Typologies and Economic Organisation of Silk Workers in Italy, from the XIVth to the XVIIIth Centuries', *Journal of European Economic History*, 1993, Vol. 22, No. 3, pp. 543–64

Plummer, A., *The London Weavers' Company, 1600–1970* (London, 1972)

Pollins, H., 'Immigrants and Minorities – The Outsiders in Business', *Immigrants and Minorities*, 1989, Vol. 8, pp. 252–70

Pollitt, R., '"Refuge of the Distressed Nations": Perceptions of Aliens in Elizabethan England', Journal of Modern History, 1980, Vol. 52, No. 1, pp. D1001–D1019

Pomeranz, K., *The Great Divergence: China, Europe, and the Making of the Modern World Economy* (Oxford, 2000)

Ponko, V., 'The Privy Council and the Spirit of Elizabethan Economic Management, 1558–1603', *Transactions of the American Philosophical Society*, new series, 1968, Vol. 58, pp. 5–63

Portes, A., ed., *The Economic Sociology of Immigration: Essays on Networks, Ethnicity, and Entrepreneurship* (New York, 1995)

———, and Rumbaut, R.G., *Immigrant America* (Oxford, 1990)

Postan, M.M., 'Italy and the Economic Development of England in the Middle Ages', *Journal of Economic History*, 1951, Vol. 11, No. 4, pp. 339–46

———, *Medieval Trade and Finance* (Cambridge, 1973)

Power, M.J., 'A "Crisis" Reconsidered: Social and Demographic Dislocation in London in the 1590s', *London Journal*, 1986, Vol. 12, pp. 134–45

———, 'East London housing in the seventeenth century', in P. Clark and P. Slack, eds, *Crisis and Order in English Towns, 1500–1700* (London, 1972), pp. 237–62

———, 'John Stow and his London', *Journal of Historical Geography*, 1985, Vol. 11, pp. 1–20

———, 'London and the Control of the "Crisis" of the 1590s', *History*, 1985, Vol. 70, pp. 371–85

———, 'Shadwell: The development of a London suburban community in the seventeenth century', *London Journal*, 1978, Vol. 4, pp. 29–49

———, 'The East London working community in the seventeenth century', in D. Keene and P.J. Corfield, eds, *Work in Towns, 850–1850* (Leicester, 1990), pp. 103–20

Prestwich, M., 'Calvinism in France, 1555–1629', in M. Prestwich, ed., *International Calvinism, 1541–1715* (Oxford, 1985), pp. 71–107

———, 'Victualling estimates for English garrisons in Scotland during the early fourteenth century', *Economic History Review*, 1967, pp. 536–43

Prevenier, W., and Blockmans, W., *The Burgundian Netherlands* (Cambridge, 1986)

Price, J.L., *Culture and Society in the Dutch Republic During the 17th Century* (London, 1974)

Prideaux, W., ed., *Memorials of the Goldsmiths Company* (2 vols, London, 1896)

Priestley, U., 'Norwich stuffs, 1600–1700' in N.B. Harte, ed., *The New Draperies in the Low Countries and England, 1300–1800* (Oxford, 1997), pp. 275–88

———, *The Fabric of Stuffs: The Norwich textile industry from 1565* (Centre of East Anglian Studies, University of East Anglia, 1990)

Pullan, B., ed., *Crisis and Change in the Venetian Economy in the 16th and 17th Centuries* (London, 1968)
Pulman, M.B., *The Elizabethan Privy Council in the Fifteen-seventies* (London, 1971)
Rahlenbeck, C., 'Les Chanteries de Valenciennes. Episode de l'histoire du seizième siècle', *Bulletin de la Commission pour l'Histoire des Eglises wallonnes*, 1st series, 1888, pp. 121–88
Ramsay, G.D., 'Industrial Discontent in Early Elizabethan London: Clothworkers and Merchant Adventurers in Conflict', *London Journal*, 1975, Vol. 1, pp. 227–39
——, 'The Antwerp Mart', in idem, *English Overseas Trade during the Centuries of Emergence* (London, 1957), pp. 1–33
——, *The City of London in International Politics at the Accession of Elizabeth Tudor* (Manchester, 1975)
——, 'The Recruitment and Fortunes of Some London Freemen in the Mid-sixteenth Century', *Economic History Review*, 2nd series, 1978, Vol. 31, pp. 526–40
——, 'The smugglers' trade: A neglected aspect of English commercial development', *Royal Historical Society Transactions*, 5th series, 1952, Vol. 2, pp. 131–57
——, 'The Undoing of the Italian Mercantile Colony in Sixteenth Century London', in N.B. Harte and K.G. Ponting, eds, *Textile History and Economic History: Essays in Honour of Miss Julia de Lacy Mann* (Manchester, 1973), pp. 22–49
Ramsey, P.H., *Tudor Economic Problems* (London, 1968)
Rappaport, S., 'Social Structure and Mobility: In Sixteenth-century London', *London Journal*, in two parts: 1983, Vol. 9, pp. 107–35; 1984, Vol. 10, pp. 107–34
——, *Worlds Within Worlds: Structures of Life in Sixteenth-century London* (Cambridge, 1989)
Read, C., *Lord Burghley and Queen Elizabeth* (London, 1960)
——, *Mr Secretary Cecil and Queen Elizabeth* (London, 1955)
——, *Mr Secretary Walsingham and the Policy of Queen Elizabeth, Vol. 1* (Cambridge, 1925)
Reddaway, T.F., 'Elizabethan London – Goldsmith's Row in Cheapside, 1558–1645', *Guildhall Miscellany*, 1963, Vol. 2, pp. 181–206
——, 'The Livery Companies of Tudor London', *History*, 1966, Vol. 51, pp. 287–99
——, 'The London Goldsmiths circa 1500', *Transactions of the Royal Historical Society*, 5th series, 1962, Vol. 12, pp. 49–62
——, Walker, L.E.M., *The Early History of the Goldsmith's Company, 1327–1509* (London, 1975)
Reynolds, V., and Vine, I., eds, *The Sociobiology of Ethnocentrism: Evolutionary Dimensions of Xenophobia, Discrimination, Racism and Nationalism* (London, 1987)
Richardson, H.W., *The Economies of Urban Size* (Farnborough, 1973)
Rickwood, D.L., 'The Norwich strangers, 1565–1643: A problem of control', *Proceedings of the Huguenot Society*, 1984, Vol. 24, pp. 119–28
Rogier, L.J., 'Over karakter en omvang van de Nederlandse emigratie in de zestiende eeuw', *Historisch Tijdschrift*, in two parts: 1937, Vol. 16, pp. 325–67; 1938, Vol. 17, pp. 5–27
Roker, L.F., 'The Flemish and Dutch Community in Colchester in the Sixteenth and Seventeenth Centuries', *Proceedings of the Huguenot Society*, 1965, Vol. 21, pp. 15–30
Rosenberg, N., 'Economic Development and the Transfer of Technology: Some Historical Perspectives', *Technology and Culture*, 1970, Vol. 11, pp. 550–75
——, *Perspectives on Technology* (Cambridge, 1976)
——, *Inside the Black Box: Technology and Economics* (Cambridge, 1982)
Rosser, G., *Medieval Westminster, 1200–1540* (Oxford, 1989)
Rothstein, N., 'Canterbury and London: The Silk Industry in the Late Seventeenth Century', *Textile History*, 1989, Vol. 20, No. 1, pp. 33–47
——, 'Huguenots in the English Silk Industry in the Eighteenth Century', in I. Scouloudi, ed., *The Huguenots in Britain and their French Background* (London, 1985), pp. 125–40
——, *Silk Designs of the Eighteenth Century: In the Collection of the Victoria & Albert Museum* (London, 1990)

———, *The Victoria & Albert Museum's Textile Collection: Woven Textile Design in Britain to 1750* (London, 1994)
Ruddock, A.A., *Italian Merchants and Shipping in Southampton, 1270–1600* (Southampton, 1951)
Rule, J., 'The property of skill in the period of manufacture', in P. Joyce, ed., *The Historical Meanings of Work* (Cambridge, 1989)
Sacks, D.H., 'London's Dominion: The Metropolis, the Market Economy, and the State', in L.C. Orlin, ed., *Material London, ca. 1600* (Philadelphia, PA, 2000), pp. 20–54
Salgados, G., *The Elizabethan Underworld* (London, 1977)
Salmon, J.H.M., *Society in Crisis: France in the Sixteenth Century* (London, 1975)
Salzman, L.F., *English Industries of the Middle Ages* (London, 1970)
Scheerder, J., 'Les condamnés du Conseil des Troubles', *Rue d'histoire Eccléslastique*, 1964, Vol. 59, pp. 90–100
Schilling, H., 'Confessional Migration and Social Change. The case of the Dutch Refugees of the Sixteenth Century', in P. Klep and E. van Cauwenberghe, eds, *Entrepreneurship and the Transformation of the Economy (10th–20th Centuries): Essays in Honour of Herman van der Wee* (Leuven, 1994), pp. 321–33
———, 'Innovation through Migration: The Settlements of Calvinistic Netherlanders in Sixteenth- and Seventeenth-century Central and Western Europe', *Histoire Sociale/Social History*, 1983, Vol. 16, pp. 7–33
Schlugheit, D., 'Alphabetische Naamlijst op de Goud en Zilversmeden te Antwerpen voor 1600', *Bijdragen tot de Geschiedenis*, 1936, Vol. 27, pp. 6–69
———, *De Antwerpse Goud- en Zilversmeden in het Corporatief Stelsel 1382–1798* (Wetteren, 1969)
Schneider, J., 'Fantastical Colors in Foggy London: The New Fashion Potential of the Late Sixteenth Century', in L.C. Orlin, ed., *Material London, ca. 1600* (Philadelphia, PA, 2000), pp. 109–27
Schofield, R., 'Taxation and the political limits of the Tudor state', in C. Cross, D. Loades and J.J. Scarisbrick, eds, *Law and Government under the Tudors: Essays Presented to Sir Geoffrey Elton* (Cambridge, 1988), pp. 227–55
———, 'The Geographical Distribution of Wealth in England, 1334–1649', *Economic History Review*, 1965, Vol. 18, pp. 483–510
Scholliers, E., 'De levensstandard der arbeiders op het einde der 16e eeuw te Antwerpen', *Tijdschrift voor Geschiedenis*, 1955, Vol. 68, pp. 81–103
———, 'Vrije en onvrije arbeiders voornamelijk te Antwerpen in de 16e Eeuw', *Bijdragen voor de geschiedenis der Nederlanden*, 1956, Vol. 11, pp. 285–22
Schroder, T., *The National Trust Book of English Domestic Silver, 1500–1900* (Middlesex, 1988)
Schwarz, L.D., 'Income Distribution and Social Structure in London in the Late Eighteenth Century', *Economic History Review*, 1979, Vol. 32, pp. 250–59
Scouloudi, I., 'Alien Immigration into and Alien Communities in London, 1558–1640', *Proceedings of the Huguenot Society*, 1938, Vol. 16, pp. 27–49
———, 'Notes on strangers in the Precinct of St Katherine-by-the-Tower', *Proceedings of the Huguenot Society*, 1989, Vol. 25, pp. 75–82
———, 'The Stranger Community in the Metropolis, 1558–1640', in I. Scouloudi, ed., *Huguenots in Britain and their French Background, 1550–1800* (London, 1987), pp. 42–55
———, 'The Stranger Community in the Metropolis, 1558–1640', *Proceedings of the Huguenot Society*, 1987, Vol. 24, pp. 434–41
Scoville, W.C., 'Minority Migrations and the Diffusion of Technology', *Journal of Economic History*, 1951, Vol. 11, pp. 347–60
———, 'The Huguenots and the Diffusion of Technology', *Journal of Political Economy*, 1952, Vol. 60, pp. 294–311, 392–411
———, *The Persecution of Huguenots and French Economic Development, 1680–1720* (Berkeley, CA, 1960)

Scribner, R., ed., *Germany: A New Social and Economic History, 1450–1630* (London, 1996)
——, 'Oral culture and the diffusion of Reformation ideas', *History of European Ideas*, 1984, Vol. 5, pp. 237–56
——, 'Why was there no Reformation in Cologne?', in idem, *Popular Culture and Popular Movements in Reformation Germany* (London, 1987) pp. 217–41
Seaver, P., 'Work, Discipline and the apprentice in early modern London', in P. Gouk, ed., *Wellsprings of Achievement: Cultural and Economic Dynamics in Early Modern England and Japan* (Aldershot, 1995), pp. 159–80
Sella, D., 'European Industries, 1500–1700', in C. M. Cipolla, ed., *The Fontana Economic History of Europe: The Sixteenth and Seventeenth Centuries*, Vol. 2 (Hassocks, 1977), pp. 354–421
Shammas, C., *The Pre-industrial Consumer in England and America* (Oxford, 1990)
Shaw, W.A., 'The English Government and the Relief of Protestant Refugees', *English Historical Review*, 1894, Vol. 9, pp. 662–83
Sheppard, F.H.W., 'The Huguenots in Spitalfields and Soho', *Proceedings of the Huguenots Society*, 1965–70, Vol. 21, pp. 355–65
Sherry, F., *Pacific Passions: The European Struggle for Power in the Great Ocean in the Age of Exploration* (New York, 1994)
Shoemaker, R., *Prosecution and Punishment: Petty Crime and the Law in London and Rural Middlesex, c.1660–1725* (Cambridge, 1991)
Simon, J.L., *The Economic Consequences of Immigration* (Oxford, 1989)
Simonton, D., 'Apprenticeship: Training and Gender in Eighteenth-century England', in M. Berg, ed., *Markets and Manufactures in Early Industrial Europe* (London, 1991) pp. 227–58
Slack, P.A., 'Vagrants and Vagrancy in England, 1598–1664', *Economic History Review*, 1974, Vol. 27, No. 3, pp. 360–79
Slicher van Bath, B.H., 'Historical Demography and the Social and Economic Development of the Netherlands', *Daedalus*, 1968, Vol. 97, pp. 604–21
Smiles, S., *The Huguenots: Their Settlements, Churches, and Industries, in England and Ireland* (London, 1880)
Smit, J.W., 'The Netherlands Revolution', in R. Forster and J.P. Greene eds, *Preconditions of Revolution in Early Modern Europe* (London, 1970), pp. 27–36
Smith, A.G.R., *The Government of Elizabethan England* (London, 1967)
Smith, C.T., *An Historical Geography of Western Europe before 1800* (London, 1978)
Smith, R., 'Financial Aid to French Protestant Refugees, 1681–1727: Briefs and the Royal Bounty', *Proceedings of the Huguenot Society*, 1970–76, Vol. 22, pp. 248–56
Smith, S.R., 'The Ideal and Reality: Apprentice–master Relationships in Seventeenth Century London', *History of Education Quarterly*, 1981, Vol. 21, pp. 449–59
Smith, W.D., 'The Function of Commercial Centers in the Modernization of European Capitalism: Amsterdam as an Information Exchange in the Seventeenth Century', *Journal of Economic History*, 1984, Vol. 44, pp. 985–1005
Smuts, R.M., 'The Court and its Neighborhood: Royal Policy and Urban Growth in the Early Stuart West End', *Journal of British Studies*, 1991, Vol. 30, No. 2, pp. 117–49
Soly, H., 'De Brouwerijenonderneming van Gilbert van Schoonbeke (1552–1562)', *Belgisch tijdschrift voor Filologie en Geschiedenis*, 1968, Vol. 46, pp. 337–92, 1166–204
——, 'Nijverheid en kapitalisme te Antwerpen inde 16ᵉ eeuw', *Studia Historica Gandensia*, 1975, pp. 190–99
——, 'Social Aspects of Structural Changes in the Urban Industries of Eighteenth-century Brabant and Flanders', in H. van der Wee, ed., *The Rise and Decline of Urban Industries in Italy and in the Low Countries* (Leuven, 1988) pp. 241–60
——, and Thijs, A.K.L., 'Nijverheid in de Zuidelijke Nederlanden', in *Nieuwe Algemene Geschiedenis der Nederlanden*, Vol. VI (Haarlem, 1981)
Sombart, W., *Luxury and Capitalism* (Ann Arbor, MI, 1967)
Sonenscher, M., 'Work and wages in Paris in the eighteenth century', in M. Berg, P. Hudson

and M. Sonenscher, eds, *Manufacture in Town and Country before the Factory* (Cambridge,1983), pp. 147–71
——, *Work and Wages: Natural Law, Politics and the Eighteenth-century French Trades* (Cambridge, 1989)
Spicer, A., 'A process of gradual assimilation: The exile community in Southampton, 1567–1635', in R. Vigne and G. Gibbs eds., *The Strangers' Progress* (Proceedings of the Huguenot Society, Vol. 26, 1995), pp. 186–98
——, *The French-speaking Reformed Community and their Church in Southampton, 1567–c.1620* (Huguenot Society, new series, No. 3, London, 1997)
——, 'The Sohiers of Valenciennes and Southampton: A Walloon family in the Diaspora', *Proceedings of the Huguenot Society*, 1990, Vol. 25, pp. 157–66
Spufford, P., 'Population Mobility in Pre-industrial England', *Geneologists' Magazine*, 1973, Vol. 17, pp. 420–29, 475–81, 537–43
Squire, S., *Dress Art and Society, 1560–1970* (London, 1974)
Statt, D., *Foreigners and Englishmen: The Controversy over Immigration and Population, 1660–1760* (London, 1995)
——, 'The birthright of an Englishman: The practice of naturalization and denization of immigrants under the later Stuarts and early Hanoverians', *Proceedings of the Huguenot Society*, 1989, Vol. 25, pp. 61–74
——, 'The City of London and the Controversy over Immigration, 1660–1722', *Historical Journal*, 1990, Vol. 33, pp. 45–61
Stern, W., 'The Trade, Art or Mistery of Silk Throwers of the City of London in the Seventeenth Century', *Guildhall Miscellany*, 1952–9, Vol. 1, pp. 25–30
Stone, L., 'Elizabethan Overseas Trade', *Economic History Review*, 2nd series, 1949, Vol. 2, pp. 30–58
——, 'State Control in Sixteenth-century England', *Economic History Review*, 1947, Vol. 17, pp. 93–120
——, 'Social Mobility in England, 1500–1700', *Past and Present*, 1966, Vol. 33, pp. 16–55
——, 'The Anatomy of the Elizabethan Aristocracy', *Economic History Review*, 1948, Vol. 18, pp. 1–53
——, 'The Nobility in Business, 1540–1640', in *The Entrepreneur: Papers Presented at the Annual Conference of the Economic History Society* (Cambridge, April 1957)
Styles, J., 'Product Innovation in Early Modern London', *Past and Present*, 2000, No 168, pp. 124–69
——, 'The goldsmiths and the London luxury trades, 1550 to 1750', in D. Mitchell, ed., *Goldsmiths, Silversmiths and Bankers: Innovation and the Transfer of Skill, 1550–1750* (London, 1995), pp. 112–20
Subacchi, P., 'Italians in Antwerp in the Second Half of the Sixteenth Century', in H. Soly and A.K.L. Thijs, eds, *Minorities in Western European Cities: Sixteenth–Twentieth Centuries* (Brussels, 1995), pp. 73–90
Sutton, A. 'George Lovekyn, Tailor to Three Kings of England, 1470–1504', *Costume*, 1981, Vol. 15, pp. 1–12
Swanson, H., 'The Illusion of Economic Structure: Craft Guilds in Late Medieval English Towns', *Past and Present*, 1988, Vol. 121, pp. 29–48
Tait, H., 'Huguenot silver made in London c.1690–1723: The Peter Wilding Bequest to the British Museum', Part I, *Connoisseur*, pp. 267–276, Part II, September 1972, Vol. 181, pp. 727, pp. 25–36
Tammel, J.W., *The Pilgrims and Other People from the British Isles in Leiden, 1576–1640* (Isle of Man, 1989)
Taube, E., 'German craftsmen in England during the Tudor period', *Economic History*, 1939, Vol. 3, pp. 167–78
Tawney, R.H., 'The Rise of the gentry, 1558–1640', *Economic History Review*, 1941, Vol. 11, pp. 1–38

——, and Power, E., eds, *Tudor Economic Documents* (London, 1924, 3 vols)
Taylor, G., *Continental Gold and Silver* (London, 1967)
——, *Silver Through the Ages* (London, 1964)
Te Brake, W.H., 'Air Pollution and Fuel Crises in Preindustrial London, 1250–1650', *Technology and Culture*, 1975, Vol. 16, pp. 337–59
The Cambridge Economic History of Europe: The Economic Organization of Early Modern Europe, Vol. 5, ed. E.E. Rich and C.H. Wilson (Cambridge, 1977)
The Cambridge Economic History of Europe: The Economy of Expanding Europe in the Sixteenth and Seventeenth Centuries, Vol. 4, ed. E.E. Rich and C.H. Wilson (Cambridge, 1967)
The Cambridge Economic History of Europe: Trade and Industry in the Middle Ages, Vol. 2, ed. M. Postan and E.E. Rich (Cambridge, 1952)
Thick, M., 'Root crops and the feeding of London's poor in the late sixteenth and early seventeenth centuries', in J. Chartres and D. Hey, eds, *English Rural Society 1500–1800: Essays in Honour of Joan Thirsk* (Cambridge, 1990)
Thijs, A.K.L., 'Antwerpse ververs uit Rijsel (16de EEUW)', *Vlaamse Stam*, 1969, Vol. 5, pp. 125–35
——, 'De Antwerpse lakenververs, 1563–1583', *Vlaamse Stam*, 1969, Vol. 5, pp. 37–46
——, 'De oprichters van het Antwerpse kamelotverversambacht', *Vlaamse Stam*, 1969, Vol. 5, pp. 389–97
——, 'De relatie woonplaats/werkplaats als een spiegel van de produktieverhoudingen. Het voorbeeld van de Antwerpse textielindustrie, (16de–18de eeuw)', *Bijdragen de Geschiedenis*, 1981, Vol. 64, pp. 193–235
——, *De zijdenijverheid te Antwerpen in de zeventiende eeuw* (Pro Civitate, Historische Uitgaven, Reeks, Vol. 80, No. 23, 1969).
——, 'De zijdenverheid te Antwerpen in de zeventiende eeuw', *Tijdschrift voor Geschiedenis*, 1966, Vol. 79, pp. 386–406
——, 'Een ondernemer uit de Antwerpse textielindustrie, Jan Nuyts, ca. 1512–1582', *Bijdragen de Geschiedenis*, 1981, Vol. 64, pp. 53–68
——, 'Structural Changes in the Antwerp industry from the fifteenth to eighteenth century', in H. van der Wee, ed., *The Rise and Decline of Urban Industries in Italy and in the Low Countries* (Leuven, 1988), pp. 207–12
——, *Van 'Werkwinkel' tot 'Fabriek': De textielnijverheid te Antwerpen, einde 15de-begin 19 de eeuw* (Antwerp, 1987)
Thirsk, J., *Economic Policy and Projects: The Development of a Consumer Society in Early Modern England* (Oxford, 1978)
——, 'England's Provinces: Did they Serve or Drive Material London?', in L.C. Orlin, ed., *Material London, ca. 1600* (Philadelphia, PA, 2000), pp. 97–108
——, 'Stamford in the Sixteenth and Seventeenth Centuries', in A. Rogers, ed., *The Making of Stamford* (Leicester, 1975), pp. 58–76
——, ed., *The Agrarian History of England and Wales, Volume 4: 1500–1640* (Cambridge, 1967)
——, 'The Fantastical Folly of Fashion: The English Stocking Knitting Industry, 1500–1700', in N. Harte and K.G. Ponting eds, *Textile History and Economic History: Essays in Honour of Miss Julia de Lacy Mann* (Manchester, 1973), pp. 50–73
Thorp, M.R., 'The Anti-Huguenot Undercurrent in Late-seventeenth-century England', *Proceedings of the Huguenot Society*, 1970–76, Vol. 22, pp. 569–80
Thrupp, S., 'A Survey of the Alien Population of England in 1440', *Speculum*, 1957, Vol. 32, pp. 262–73
——, 'Aliens in and around London in the fifteenth century', in A.E. Hollaender and W. Kellaway, eds, *Studies in London History: Essays Presented to P.E. Jones* (London, 1969), pp. 251–72
——, *The Merchant Class of Medieval London, 1300–1500* (London, 1962)
Tilly, C., 'Transplanted Networks', in V. Yans-McLaughlin ed., *Immigration Reconsidered: History, Sociology, and Politics* (Oxford, 1990), pp. 79–95

Trevor-Roper, H.R., *Religion, the Reformation and Social Change* (London, 1972)
——, 'The gentry, 1540–1640', *Economic History Review Supplements*, 1953, p. 1
Trim, D.J.B., 'Protestant refugees in Elizabethan England and confessional conflict in France and the Netherlands, 1562–*c*.1610', in R. Vigne and C. Littleton, eds, *From Strangers to Citizens: The Integration of Immigrant Communities in Britain, Ireland and Colonial America, 1550–1750* (Brighton, 2001), pp. 68–79.
——, 'Immigrants, the Indigenous Community and International Calvinism' in N. Goose and L. Luu, eds, Immigrants in Tudor and Early Stuart England, pp. 211–222.
Turnau, I., 'Consumption of Clothes in Europe between the XVIth and the XVIIIth Centuries (Research Problems)', *Journal of European Economic History*, 1976, Vol. 5, No. 2, pp. 451–68
Unger, R.W., 'Technical Change in the Brewing Industry in Germany, the Low Countries, and England in the Late Middle Ages', *Journal of European Economic History*, 1992, Vol. 21, pp. 281–313
——, 'Technology and industrial organization: Dutch shipbuilding to 1800', *Business History*, 1975, Vol. 17, pp. 56–72
Unwin, G., *Industrial Organization in the 16th and 17th Centuries* (London, 1963)
——, 'The economic policy of Edward III', in R.H. Tawney, ed., *Studies in Economic History: The collected Papers of George Unwin* (London, 1927), pp. 117–32
——, *The Gilds and Companies of London* (London, 3rd edition; 1st edition 1908, 1938)
van Cauwenberghs, C., 'L'industrie de la soie a Anvers depuis 1532 jusqu'à nos jours: suivi d'un relevé des fabricants et marchands de soieries reçu dans la bourgeoisie de cette ville au xvi siècle', *Bulletin de la Société Royale de Géographie D'Anvers*, Vol. XII (Antwerp, 1887), pp. 105–47
van der Stock, J., *Antwerp: Story of a Metropolis, 16th–17th century* (Ghent, 1993)
van Deursen, A.T., *Plain Lives in a Golden Age: Popular Culture, Religion and Society in Seventeenth-century Holland* (Cambridge, 1991)
van Dierickx, M., 'De lijst der veroordeelden door de Raad van Beroerten', *Belgisch Tijdschrift voor Filologie en Geschiedenis*, 1962, Vol. 40, pp. 415–22
van Dillen, J.G., *Bronnen tot de geschiedenis van het bedrijfsleven en het gildewezen van Amsterdam*, eerste deel, 1512–1611 (Rijks Geschiedkundige Publicatien, Vol. 69, 1929)
van Gelderen, M., *The Political Thought of the Dutch Revolt, 1555–1590* (Cambridge, 1992)
von Hammer, C.I., 'The Mobility of Skilled Labour in Late Medieval England: Some Oxford Evidence', *Vierteljahrschrift für Sozial und Wirtschaftsgeschichte*, Vol. 63, 1976, pp. 194–210
van Houtte, J.A., *An Economic History of the Low Countries, 800–1800* (London, 1977)
——, 'Bruges as a trading centre in the early modern period', in D.C. Coleman and P. Mathias, eds, *Enterprise and History: Essays in Honour of Charles Wilson* (Cambridge, 1984), pp. 71–88
——, 'The Rise and Decline of the Market of Bruges', *Economic History Review*, 2nd series, 1966, Vol. 19, pp. 29–47
van Nierop, L., 'De bruidegoms van Amsterdam van 1578 tot 1601', *Tijdschrift voor Geschiedenis*, in two parts: 1934, Vol. 49, pp. 329–44; 1937, Vol. 52, pp. 144–62
——, 'De zijdenijverheid van Amsterdam historisch geschetst', *Tijdschrift voor Geschiedenis*, in two parts: 1930, Vol. 145, pp. 8–40, 151–72; 1931, Vol. 46, pp. 28–55, 113–43
van Roey, J., 'Socio-economische Strukturen en Godsdienstkeuze. De correlatie tussen het sociale-beroepsmilieu en de godsdienstkeuze te Antwerpen op het einde der XVIe eeuw', *Bronnen voor de religieux geschiedenis van Belgie* (Leuven, 1968), pp. 239–99
van Strien, C.D., *British Travellers in Holland during the Stuart Period: Edward Browne and John Locke as Tourists in the United Provinces* (Leiden, 1993)
van Uytven, R., 'The Fulling Mill: Dynamic of the Revolution in Industrial Attitudes', *Acta Historiae Neerlandica*, 1971, Vol. 5, pp. 1–14
——, 'What is New Socially and Economically in the Sixteenth-century Netherlands', *Acta Historiae Neerlandicae*, 1974, Vol. 7, pp. 18–53
van Vloten, J., *Nederlands Opstand tegen Spanje*, 1567–1572, Volume 1: 1567–1572 (1856)

van Zanden, J.L., 'Economic growth in the Golden Age: The development of the economy of Holland, 1500–1650', *The Dutch Economy in the Golden Age*, Vol. 4, 1993, pp. 5–26
Vane, C.M., 'The Walloon community in Norwich: the first hundred years', *Proceedings of the Huguenot Society*, 1983–8, Vol. 24, pp. 129–40
Varron, A., 'Silk and Style', *Ciba Review*, 1938, Vol. 1, pp. 361–8
Veale, E.M., 'Craftsmen and the Economy of London in the Fourteenth Century', in A.E.J. Hollaender and W. Kellaway, eds, *Studies in London History: Essays presented to P.E. Jones* (London, 1969), pp. 133–51
Verheyden, A.L.E., *Anabaptism in Flanders, 1530–1650: A Century of Struggle* (1961)
———, *Le Conseil des Troubles* (Brussels, 1981)
———, *Le conseil des troubles: Liste des Condamnés, 1567–1573* (Brussels, 1961)
———, 'Une correspondance inédite adressée par des familes protestantes des Pays-Bas à leurs coreligionnaires d'Angleterre (11 novembre 1569–25 février 1570)', *Bulletin de la commission Royale D'historie*, Académie Royale de Belgique, 1955, Vol. 120, pp. 95–256.
Vermault, J., 'Structural transformation in a textile centre: Bruges from the sixteenth to the nineteenth century', in H. van der Wee, ed., *The Rise and Decline of Urban Industries in Italy and in the Low Countries* (Leuven, 1988), pp. 187–205
Voet, L., *Antwerp, the Golden Age: The Rise and Glory of the Metropolis in the Sixteenth Century* (Antwerp, 1973)
Waldinger, R., 'Immigrant Enterprise in the New York Garment Industry', *Social Problems*, 1984, Vol. 32, pp. 60–71
———, *Through the Eye of the Needle: Immigrants and Enterprise in New York's Garment Trades* (New York, 1986)
———, Aldrich, H. and Ward, R., eds, *Ethnic Entrepreneurs: Immigrant Business in Industrial Societies* (London, 1990)
———, Ward, R., and Aldrich, H., 'Ethnic business and occupational mobility in advanced societies', *Sociology*, 1985, Vol. 19, pp. 586–97
Walker, S.R., 'The Silk Industry: Historical notes on the origins of silk production and manufacture and on the English silk industry', (CLRO, GHA Paper 1956, Research Paper Box 5.18)
Walter, J. and K. Wrightson, 'Dearth and the Social order in early modern England', *Past and Present*, 1976, Vol. 71, pp. 22–42
Ward, J.P., 'Fictitious shoemakers, agitated weavers and the limits of popular xenophobia in Elizabethan London', in R. Vigne and C. Littleton, eds, *From Strangers to Citizens: The Integration of Immigrant Communities in Britain, Ireland and Colonial America, 1550–1750* (Brighton, 2001), pp. 80–87
———, '"Imployment for all handes that will worke": Immigrants, guilds, and the Labour Market in Early Seventeenth-century London', in N. Goose and L. Luu, eds, *Immigrants in Tudor and Early Stuart England* (Brighton, 2005), pp. 76–87
———, *Metropolitan Communities: Trade Guilds, Identity, and Change in Early Modern London* (Stanford, CT, 1997)
Ward, R. and Jenkins, R., eds, *Ethnic Communities in Business: Strategies for Economic Survival* (Cambridge, 1984)
Wareing, J., 'Changes in the geographical distribution of the recruitment of apprentices to the London companies, 1486–1750', *Journal of Historical Geography*, 1980, Vol. 6, pp. 241–9
———, 'Migration to London and transatlantic emigration of indentured servants, 1683–1775', *Journal of Historical Geography*, 1981, Vol. 7, pp. 356–78
Warner, F., *The Silk Industry of the United Kingdom: Its Origin and Development* (London, 1912)
———, *The Weavers' Company: A Short History* (London, 1925)
Warner, J., 'Shifting Categories of the Social Harms Associated with Alcohol: Examples from Late Medieval and Early Modern England', *American Journal of Public Health*, November 1997, Vol. 87, No. 11, pp. 1788–97
Watson, J.L., ed., *Between Two Cultures: Migrants and Minorities in Britain* (Oxford, 1984)

Watt, T., 'Aliens in England before the Huguenots', *Proceedings of the Huguenot Society*, 1953–9, Vol. 19, pp. 74–94

van der Wee, H., 'Structural Changes and Specialization in the Industry of the Southern Netherlands', *Economic History Review*, 1975, Vol. 28, pp. 203–21

———, 'Structural changes in European long-distance trade, and particularly in the re-export trade from south to north, 1350–1750', in J.D. Tracy, ed., *The Rise of Merchant Empires: Long-distance Trade in the Early Modern World, 1350–1750* (Cambridge, 1990), pp. 14–34

———, 'The economy as a factor in the start of the revolt in the Southern Netherlands', *Acta Historiae Neerlandicae*, 1971, Vol. 5, pp. 52–67

———, *The Growth of the Antwerp Market and the European Economy* (3 vols, The Hague, 1963)

———, *The Low Countries in the Early Modern World* (Aldershot, 1993)

———, *Urban Industrial Development in the Low Countries during the Late Middle Ages and Early Modern Times* (Working Papers in Economic History, No. 179, 1994)

Weekley, C.M., 'The Spitalfields Silkweavers', *Proceedings of the Huguenot Society*, 1950, Vol. 18, pp. 284–91

West, E., 'Anti-Dutch Feeling in Essex, 1570–1728', *Essex Journal*, 1988, Vol. 23, pp. 51–4

White, L., 'Technology in the Middle Ages', in M. Kranzberg and C.W. Pursell, eds, *Technology in Western Civilization: The Emergence of Modern Industrial Society Earliest Times to 1900*, Vol. 1 (London, 1967), pp. 66–79

White, P., and Woods, R., eds, *The Geographical Impact of Migration* (London, 1980)

Whyte, I.D., *Migration and Society in Britain, 1550–1830* (Basingstoke, Hants., 2000)

Williams, L., 'Alien Immigrants in Relation to Industry and Society in Tudor England', *Proceedings of the Huguenot Society*, 1953–59, Vol. 19, pp. 146–69

———, 'The Crown and the Provincial Immigrant Communities in Elizabethan England', in H. Hearder and H.R. Loyn, eds, *British Government and Administration: Studies Presented to S.B. Chrimes* (Cardiff, 1974), pp. 117–31

Williams, N., 'The London Port Books', *Transactions of the London and Middlesex Archaeological Society*, 1955, Vol. 18, pp. 13–26

Williams, P., *The Tudor Regime* (Oxford, 1979)

Willis, J.E., 'European consumption and Asian production in the seventeenth and eighteenth centuries', in J. Brewer and R. Porter, eds, *Consumption and the World of Goods* (London, 1994), pp. 133–47

Wilson, C., 'Cloth Production and International Competition in the Seventeenth Century', *Economic History Review*, 1960–61, Vol. 13, pp. 209–21

———, *Queen Elizabeth and the Revolt of the Netherlands* (London, 1970)

Wittlin, A., 'The Development of Silk Weaving in Spain', *Ciba Review*, 1939, Vol. 2, pp. 707–21

Woltjer, J.J., 'De vonnissen van de Raad van Beroerten', *Bijdragen voor de geschiedenis der Nederlanden*, 1963–4, Vol. 18, pp. 127–34

Woodward, D., 'Port Books', *History*, 1970, Vol. 55, pp. 207–10

———, 'The Background to the Statute of Artificers: The Genesis of Labour Policy, 1558–63', *Economic History Review*, 1980, Vol. 33, pp. 32–44

———, 'Wage rates and living standards in pre-industrial England', *Past and Present*, 1981, Vol. 91, pp. 28–45

Woolf, S., 'Order, class and the urban poor', in M.L. Bush, ed., *Social Orders and Social Classes in Europe Since 1500: Studies in Social Stratification* (Essex, 1992), pp. 185–98

Wrightson, K., *Earthly Necessities: Economic Lives in Early Modern Britain, 1470–1750* (London, 2002)

———, *English Society, 1580–1680* (London, 1982)

———, 'The Social Order of Early Modern England: Three Approaches', in L. Bonfield, R.M. Smith and K. Wrightson, eds, *The World We Have Gained: Histories of Population and Social Structure. Essays presented to Peter Laslett on this Seventieth Birthday* (Oxford, 1986), pp. 177–202

Wrigley, E.A., 'A simple model of London's importance in changing English society and economy, 1650–1750', *Past and Present*, 1967, Vol. 37, pp. 44–70
———, 'Parasite or Stimulus: The Town in a Pre-industrial Economy', in P. Abrams and E.A. Wrigley, eds, *Towns in Societies: Essays in Economic History and Historial Sociology* (Cambridge, 1979), pp. 295–309
———, *People, Cities and Wealth: The Transformation of Traditional Society* (Oxford, 1987)
———, 'The divergence of England: The growth of the English economy in the seventeenth and eighteenth centuries', *Transactions of the Royal Historical Society*, 6th series, Vol. X, 2000, pp. 117–41
Wrightson, K., 'Alehouses, Order and Reformation in Rural England, 1590–1660', in E. Yeo and S. Yeo, eds, *Popular Culture and Class Conflict, 1590–1914: Explorations in the History of Labour and Leisure* (Sussex, 1981), pp. 1–27
Wunderli, R.M., 'Evasion of the Office of Alderman in London, 1523–1672', *London Journal*, 1990, Vol. 15, pp. 3–18
Wuthnow, R., *Communities of Discourse: Ideology and Social Structure in the Reformation, the Enlightenment, and European Socialism* (London, 1989)
Wyntjes, S.M., 'Family Allegiance and Religious Persuasion: The Lesser Nobility and the Revolt of the Netherlands', *The Sixteenth Century Journal*, 1981, Vol. 12, pp. 43–60
Yntema, R., 'Entrepreneurship, and Technological Change in Holland's Brewing Industry, 1500–1580', in C. Lesger and L. Noordegraaf, eds, *Entrepreneurs and Entrepreneurship in Early Modern Times* (Haarlem, Hollandse Historische Reeks, Vol. 24, 1995), pp. 185–201.
Yungblut, L.H., *Strangers Settled Here Amongst Us: Policies, Perceptions and the Presence of Aliens in Elizabethan England* (London, 1996)
Zilver uit de Gouden Eeuw van Antwerpen (Antwerp, 1989)

UNPUBLISHED SOURCES

Adamson, N.L., 'Urban Families: The Social Context of the London Elite, 1500–1603' (University of Toronto PhD thesis, 1983)
Andrews, K.R., 'The Economic Aspects of Elizabethan Privateering' (University of London PhD thesis, 1951)
Archer, I.W., 'Governors and Governed in Late Sixteenth-century London, c.1560–1603: Studies in the achievement of stability' (University of Oxford DPhil thesis, 1988)
Archer, J., 'The Location and Organization of London Industry, 1603–1640' (University of London MA thesis, 1934)
Berlin, M., and Illiffe, R., '"Broken all in Pieces": Artisans and the Regulation of Workmanship in Early Modern London', paper presented to the International Urban History Conference, Strasbourg, 8–10 September 1994
Bradley, H.L., 'Italian Merchants in London, 1350–1450' (University of London PhD thesis, 1992)
Bratchel, M.E., 'Alien Merchant Communities in London, 1500–1550' (University of Cambridge PhD thesis, 1974)
Briels, J.G.C.A., 'De Zuidnederlandse Immigratie in Amsterdam en Haarlem omstreeks 1572–1630' (University of Utrecht PhD thesis, 1976)
Carlin, M., 'The Urban Development of Southwark' (University of Toronto PhD thesis, 1983)
Clark, G.W., 'An Urban Study During the Revolt of the Netherlands: Valenciennes 1540–1570' (University of Columbia PhD thesis, 1972)
Davies, M.P., 'The Tailors of London and their Guild, c.1300–1500' (University of Oxford DPhil. thesis, 1994)
Davids, K.A., 'Cities and Science in the Dutch Republic, c.1580–1750' (paper presented at the Achievement Project's conference on Clusters of Achievement, Amsterdam, 24–26 March 1994).
Dingle, A.M., 'The Role of the Householder in early Stuart London, c.1603–c.1630' (University of London MPhil. thesis, 1974)

Duncan, G.D., 'Monopolies Under Elizabeth I, 1558–1585' (University of Cambridge PhD thesis, 1976)
Esser, R., 'Niederländische Exulanten im England des späten 16. und frühen 17. Jahrhunderts: Die Norwicher Fremdengemeinden' (University of Cologne PhD thesis, 1994)
Fell, G., 'The Spatial Impact of the Immigration of the Strangers of Norwich in the Late 16th and early 17th Centuries' (University of Cambridge BA dissertation, 1975)
Goose, N., 'Economic and Social Aspects of Provincial Towns: A Comparative Study of Cambridge, Colchester and Reading, c.1500–1700' (University of Cambridge PhD thesis, 1984)
Hickman, D.J., 'The Religious Allegiance of London's Ruling Elite, c.1520–1603' (University of London PhD thesis, 1995)
Jordan, W.M., 'The Silk Industry in London, 1760–1830' (University of London MA thesis, 1931)
Lang, R.G., 'The Greater Merchants of London in the Seventeenth Century' (University of Oxford DPhil. thesis, 1963)
Littleton, C.G.D., 'Geneva on Threadneedle Street: The French Church of London and its Congregation, 1560–1625' (University of Michigan PhD thesis, 1996)
Lucassen, J., 'Amsterdam: A Golden Age, Based on Immigration' (paper presented at the Achievement Project's conference on Clusters of Achievement, Amsterdam, 24–26 March 1994)
Marnef, G., 'Antwerpen in Reformatietijd: Ondergronds Protestantisme in een internationale handelsmetropool, 1550–1577' (2 vols, University of Leuven PhD thesis, 1991)
Martin, L.N.D., 'Textile Manufactures in Norwich and Norfolk, 1550–1622' (University of Cambridge PhD thesis, 1992)
Merritt, J.F., 'Religion, Government and Society in Early Modern Westminster, c.1525–1625' (University of London PhD thesis, 1992)
Millard, A.M., 'The Import Trade of London, 1600–1640' (University of London PhD thesis, 1956, 3 vols)
Power, M.J., 'The Urban Development of East London, 1550 to 1700' (University of London PhD thesis, 1971)
Ramsay, G.D., 'The Wiltshire Woollen Industry in C16th and early C17th' (University of Oxford DPhil. thesis, 1940)
Rothstein, N.K.A., 'The Silk Industry in London, 1702–1766' (University of London MA thesis, 1961)
Scouloudi, I., 'Alien Immigration into and Alien Communities in London, 1558–1640' (University of London MSc. thesis, 1936)
Sleigh-Johnson, N.V., 'The Merchant Taylors Company of London, 1580–1645: With Special Reference to Politics and Government' (University of London PhD thesis, 1989)
Spicer, A.P., 'The French-speaking Reformed Community and their Church in Southampton, 1567–c.1620 (University of Southampton PhD thesis, 1994)
Sundstrom, R.A., 'Aid and Assimilation: A Study of the Economic Support Given French Protestants in England, 1680–1727' (Kent State University PhD thesis, 1972 – copy available in the Huguenot Library)
Thorp, M.R., 'The English Government and the Huguenot Settlement, 1680–1702' (University of Wisconsin PhD thesis 1972 – copy available in the Huguenot Library)
Wyatt, T., 'The Part Played by Aliens in the Social and Economic History of England During the reign of Henry VIII' (University of London MA thesis, 1951)
Yntema, R.J., 'The Brewing Industry in Holland, 1300–1800: A Study in Industrial Development' (University of Chicago PhD thesis, 1992)

Index

Acontius, Jamems, 66
Adraps, Lievin, 111
Aken, Cornelius van, 233
Alva, Duke, 3, 106
American colonies, 80
Amsterdam, 230
Androwes, Peter, 281
Antwerp, 69, 87, 107, 189, 231
  dyeing industry, 30, 60
  English mercantile community in, 30, 64
  fairs of Brabant, 27
  fall of Antwerp, 3
  finishing industry, 30, 60
  import substitution, 32,
  Italian merchants in, 31, 32,
  Antwerp-Italian connection, 32
  London-Antwerp trade axis, 29
  Portuguese merchants in, 31
  range of products on sale at, 32
  range of textile fabrics on sale at, 29
  rise of Antwerp entrepot, 28
  silk industry in, 32, 179
  south German merchants in, 31
Anthony, Diricke, 237, 238
Arnolde, Harry, 289
Aubin, Henry, 246

Backe, Peter, 66
Baet, Clement, 118
Becku, Anthony, 66
Beer brewing, 164
  ale brewing, 259,
  amount of capital investment required, 287
  areas of residence of brewers, 280–81
  Brewers' Company, 261, 277, 290–91
  chain migration of brewers, 269
  changes in brewing, 259, 275,
  consumption of beer, 266
  coal, 277–8,
  debts, 287
  diffusion of skills to native brewers, 291–2
  discrimination, 290
  differences between ale and beer, 259, 265, 266–7, 269, 271
  differences between London and Dutch beer, 273
  diffusion to England, 262–264
  Dutch origins of brewers, 260, 261–2, 263, 264, 279–80
  growth of industry, 273–5
  historiography, 261
  international diffusion of the industry, 259, 261, 262
  inventory of a brewhouse, 288
  investment in by English entrepreneurs, 268
  managerial difficulties, 289–90
  map of a brewhouse, 272
  marginalisation of alien brewers, 287–91
  military & consumption of beer, 268
  names of ale and beer brewers, 294–5
  native reactions to the introduction of beer, 264–6
  number of servants employed, 275, 289–90
  number of alien brewers, 278–79
  origins of alien brewers, 279–80
  partnerships, 287–89
  production, 274–75
  profits, 276
  reasons for increased popularity of beer in sixteenth century, 266–72
  recipes, 268
  restrictions on employment of aliens, 269–71
  scale of production, 274–6
  separation of labour and capital, 271
  switching of production by English brewers, 269, 271
  unpopularity of beer, 264–5, 267
  wealth of brewers, 281–287
Bereblock, William, 238
Berty, Francis, 66, 68
Beverloo, Janssz, 112
Bodendick, Jacob, 227, 236, 240

Bonange, Dennis, 189, 190
Bousin, Cornelis, 111
Bowers, George, 227
Brickpott, Adrian, 233
Bruges
  economic centre of Flanders, 28
  satin weaving in, 178–9, 187, 199
Buescom, Nychas van, 78 (pin making)
Byyott, Davy, 109

Calvinism, 91, 105, 107
Capel, Louis, 190
Capelle, Anthony, 190
Carden, Philip, 190
Carlishewe, Jean, 190
Carré, Jean, 12, 66, (glass making)
Casher, John, 217
Castelain, Pierre, 190
Cecil, William, Secretary of State, 56, 64, 67, 68, 70, 97
  economic planning, 61–3
  involvement in proposals to import foreign skills, 56
Cembronc, Jacques, 194, 217
Charteir, John, 246
Choutiere, Jacques de la, 232
Clothes, annual expenditure by nobility, 43
Coale, Peter, 162
Cockus, Jean-Gérard, 227
Collins, John, 66 (sailcloth)
Coninck, Heyndrick de, 232
Coppin, Guillaume, 113–14, 189, 190, 191–2, 193
Cornellis, John, 289
Council of Troubles
  sources in, 20
Courtauld, Augustine, 245, 246
Courtauld, Samuel, 246
Coxe, Alice, 282
Coxe, William, 282, 291
Cranick, Burchsard, 66 (engine for draining water)
Croce, Peter de la, 66 (dressing & dyeing of cloth)
Crook, Adrian de, 217
Cruel, Henry, 289

Dehook, Jacques, 217
Denham, Thomas, 238
Derickson, Godfrey, 281
Designes, Jean, 233
Demear, Peter, 217
Dewise, Guillam, 217

Diffusion of skills
  barriers to diffusion, 8
  channels of, 291–2, 304–305
  disincentive effects, 127
  factors determining successful diffusion, 8, 9
  receptivity, 10
  role of apprentices, 40
  role of migrants, 5, 6, 10,
  stages in, 304–6
  stimulus diffusion, 305
  teaching of natives, 126–131, 291–2
  travelling abroad and, 305
Domico, George, 56
Doncke, Peter van, 243
Dottegnie, Claude, 189, 190
Dottegnie, Ferninand, 190
Drolle, Claude, 197
Drouet, Peter, 233
DuBuis, John, brewer, 289
DuChesne, Anthony, 246
Durant, Peter van, brewer, 270
Dutch Revolt, 104–7
Dutch Republic
  migration to, 4
  policies to attract migrants, 302–33
  proportions of migrants, 302

Economic change, 1
  agents of, 2,
  cheapness of labour and effects on, 44
  London's demographic growth, 2
  social mobility, 2
  effects of urbanization, 37
Edward III, 53, 54, 55
Elizabeth I, 4, 53, 95, 98
Elste, Jan, 190
England
  balance of trade, 61
  cloth exports, 28, 55, 60
  cloth industry, 1
  cultural receptiveness, 305
  exports 1565, 1, 61
  imports 1565, 1, 61
  overseas trade, 1
  populations of selected cities, 36
  proportion with exposure to London's life, 37
  scale of immigration in early modern period, 3,
  value of cloth exports 1565, 29
  wool exports, 28
English workers, laziness of, 70

Entrepreneurs who sought to import foreign skills to England
  Cholmeley, William, 59–60
  Gentill, Edmond, 78
  Guidotti, Antony, 56
  Martin, Richard, 78–9
  Springham & Lok, 57

Faloize, Wolfgang de, 191
Feline, Edward, 246
Fever, Michael, 194, 217
Fitzwilliam, John, 64
Flanders, 54, 105, 106, 108, 171
Florence, 56
Fowle, Thomas, 239
France, 61, 108
French Wars of Religion, 107

Ganio, Anthony, 217
Gislinge, Danyell, 192
Godmere, Antonie, 233
Germany
  migration to, 4
Glastonbury, 71
Gorth, Derick, 281
Government
  agents of, 96
  development of cloth industry, 53, 54–5,
  dyeing and finishing industry, 59
  Edward III and Flemish weavers, 53, 54,
  fears of espionage and internal security, 95–6
  financial support for projects to bring over weavers, 57
  local government & industrial development, 76
  patents, 64–5
  planting of foreign immigrant communities in provincial towns, 70–76
  reasons for dispersing immigrants from London, 97–8
  role of William Cecil, 56, 58, 61, 63, 64, 183
  role in import of foreign skills, 53–80
Gresham, Thomas, 30, 33
Groyett, Stephen, 66, (white soap)
Gruel, Pierre, 191
Guicciardini, Lodovico, 64, 179, 223
Guidotti, Antony, 56
Gunporte, Nicholas, 270
Gylberd, Edward, 237, 238
Gylpin, George, 66, 68 (making ovens and furnaces)

Haemstede, Adriaen van, 110
Hanberrie, Richard, 237, 238
Harache, Pierre, 245, 246
Harderwijk, 162
Harryson, Thomas, 238
Heaton, Francis, 237, 238
Helden, Diricke, 286
Hendrixsz, Jan, 162
Heresy, 105
Hetreu, Roland de, 191
Heuvel, Willem van den, 232
Heuxtenbury, Roger, 66, 67, 68 (Spanish leather)
Heyth, James, 289
Historians
  Backhouse, M., 14, 15
  Beier, L., 80
  Bolton, J., 90
  Bratchel, 58, 87
  Bruland, K., 6
  Burn, J.S., 4
  Burt, R., 13
  Carlin, M., 163–64, 264
  Chartres, J., 27,
  Cipolla, Carlo, 8
  Clarkson, L.A., 2
  Coleman, D.C., 2, 9, 12,
  Cross, F.W., 5
  Cunningham, W., 5
  Davids, K., 13
  Davis, R., 175
  Elias, Norbert, 222
  Esser, R., 14
  Evans, J., 220, 227
  Fisher, F.J., 2
  Hill, Christopher, 2
  Glanville, Philippa, 220, 222
  Godfrey, E., 12
  Goose, N., 14, 55, 74
  Graves, M., 63
  Holt, M., 107
  Inkster, I., 6
  Jeremy, David, 6
  Keene, D., 87
  Littleton, C., 14
  Limberger, M., 60
  Manning, R., 147, 149
  Mathias, P., 262
  Mazzaoui, M.F., 177
  McKendrick, 27
  Mitchell, D., 239
  Morris-Suzuki, 11
  Munro, J., 55

Nef, John, 2
Norwood, F.A., 9
Perkin, Harold, 2
Pettegree, A., 14
Plummer, A., 148
Rothstein, N., 188
Schilling, H., 9
Scoville, Warren, 6
Smiles, S., 5
Stone, Lawrence, 29
Styles, J., 239
Tait, Hugh, 220
Thirsk, Joan, 45, 64
Thrupp, S., 90
Trevor-Roper, H., 9
Ward, J., 165
Williams, 63
Wrigley, E.A., 2
Höchstetter, Daniel, mining, 64, 66, 68, 69, 70
Hopdenaker, Henry, 286, 289
Honricke, Gerard, 69 (saltpetre)
Hoogre, John, 217
Huffaum, Jacques, 217
Howzer, Wolfgang, 227, 236, 240
Hulst, Hawnse, 281

Immigrants
  apprenticeships, 156–7
  areas of residence in London, 121–6, 194
  assimilation/ integration, 142, 163–5, 307
  attitudes to, 143–73
  broken families, 112–14,
  chain migration, 16, 269, 281–5
  changes in composition of community, 99
  communities in provincial towns, 71–6
  complaints against dual occupations, 14
  contemporary debates, 301–2
  definitions, 142–3
  denizens, 142–4
  Dutch, 5, 9, 72, 73, 100–101, 262, 263, 264
  economic contribution, 4, 5–6, 15, 308
  emigration of, 142, 162–3
  employment of alien servants, 152
  English born children, 99, 166–7
  Evil May Day, 58
  expulsion of, 94
  Flemish, 5, 9, 55, 61, 154, 263
  German, 67, 69, 262
  fluidity of occupations, 14
  freedom of City, 145
  goods and property confiscated,
  government policies towards, 165–7
  and growth of London, 15
  harassment of,160–62
  homesickness, 112–14
  Huguenots, 4, 9, 175, 243–9
  intermarriage with English, 152
  issues of conflict with English, 153–62
  Italians, 56, 57, 58, 99, 152
  legal rights and status of, 142–6
  length of residence, 165
  letters to, 112–14
  libels against, 147, 160, 205
  linguistic, difficulties, 18, 152,
  military involvement, 114
  minority status and high achievement of, 9
  mismatch of skills, 14, 72, 176, 188
  number of, 90, 91–4, 95, 96–8
  number of English servants employed by, 126–31, 152
  origins of, 100–104
  occupational determinism, 13
  occupational mobility, 189
  occupational profiles, 16
  occupations of, 114–18, 118–21
  patterns of church attendance, 151
  poverty, 20, 154, 190–92
  property, loss of, 20, 113
  Protestant religion and economic impact, 8
  public reactions, 306–7
  reasons for migration, 109–12
  reception of, 141–67
  regulations of, 143–5
  relations with native citizens, 146–62
  riots against, 141, 147
  reluctance to teach skills, 126–31
  retailing by, 184
  satisfaction of life, 142
  scapegoating, 148
  shops, 167
  social mixing, 152–3
  taxation, 143
  teaching native citizens, 126–31
  topographical distribution, 121–6
  trades, 73, 114–21
  travel to continent, 15, 31
  types of, 63, 141, 303–4
  Walloons, 5, 72
  wealth of, 281–7
  xenophobia, 147–9
Import of foreign skills
  difficulties involved, 58–9

Industrial Revolution
  cheapness of labour, 44
  origins, 1, 2
  industrial progress, 1
  industrious revolution, 45
  role of migrants, 3, 5
  role of women and children, 45
  social mobility, 2
Industries
  beer brewing, 16, 259–99
  cloth industry, 4, 54–5
  coal, 12
  dyeing, 11, 59, 60
  finishing industry, 59, 60
  fustian manufacture, 78
  glass-making, 12
  knives, 1
  mining, 13
  new, 1, 3
  New Draperies, 4, 9, 12, 73, 74
  pin making, 78
  salt making, 68
  saltpetre, 69
  shipping industry, 39
  silk industry, 3, 16, 56–9, 175–217
  silver trade, 16, 219–58
Italians who introduced skills to Antwerp
  Andrea, Guido, 33
  Franchi, Pietro, 33

Jacob, James, Merchant tailor, 60
James, Jan, 190
James, Roger, 164, 281, 282–3, 285, 286, 289
James, Mary, 289

Kellett, Willliam, 270
Kempe, John, 54, 55
Keswick,
  mining project, 69
Kettelwood, 238

Laloé, Robert, 127
Lambrechts, Hans, 234
Lamerie, Paul de, 245, 246
Larquier, John, 196
Leake, Henry, 270, 282, 291
LeFebure, Daniel, 246
Leonard, John, 146
Loberry, Henry, 281, 286
London
  ale houses in, 41
  and Antwerp, 29, 155
  apprentices, 40, 58
  attractions to immigrants, 39, 42–3
  Book of Fines, 184
  Bridewell, 39, 76, 77, 78–80,
  centre of consumption & trade, 27, 34, 43
  Christ's Hospital, 76
  city government involvement in promotion of industrial development, 76
  commercial links with Low Countries, 27
  consumption patterns, 27, 43
  demographic growth, 2
  division of labour & specialisation, 35
  dyeing and finishing, 60
  emulative spending, 40
  engine of English economy, 3
  engine of manufacture, 3
  fears of attacks in, 95–6
  guild's control, 124–6
  growth of, 15, 34
  importance, 27
  industrial development, 34, 35
  magnet for immigrants, 303
  mercers, 180
  merchants in, 43
  monopoly of the cloth trade, 30
  multi-functional roles, 27
  number of foreign immigrants in, 90–100
  number of merchants in, 43–4
  number of occupations in, 3, 35
  number of provincial immigrants, 38
  overcrowding and xenophobia, 35, 150–51
  places of settlement by immigrants, 121–6
  population levels, 34
  population structure, 27, 40, 42
  population turnover and xenophobia, 149
  provincial gentry, aristocracy, 42, 43
  provincial immigrants in, 39
  rate of immigration to, 38
  real wages, 44
  reasons for growth of, 38, 39
  role of absorption & dissemination new ideas, 27
  St. Bartholomew's Hospital, 76
  servants, 40
  social structure, 27, 42
  transportation of the poor to Virginia, 80
  unemployment, 155
  vagrants, 77
  wages, 39
  youthful structure, 41, 149

Lech, Adrian, 217
Leonards, Peter, 285, 286
LeSage, John Hugh, 246
Lyste, Jacob, 235

Maior, Dirick, 233
Malliard, Elizabeth, 190
Marquin, Francois, 189, 190
Martyn, Peter & Gielis, 190
Meerten, Jan van, 232
Merchant Adventurers, 60
Merchant communities in London
   Hansards, 87
   Italians, 87
Mettayer, Louis, 245, 246
Meyer, Dietrich, 224
Migration
   determinants of mobility of labour, 9
   process of, 111–12
   scale of migration in early modern period, 3–4
   selective nature of, 7, 9
   sources for study of, 15, 17, 19, 20, 21
   types of migration, 7, 16
Millehomme, Jan, 190
Morris, Peter, 66 (engine for raising water)
Mownttadewe, Jane, 190
Myeulx, Guillaume le, 113
Mynor, Abel, 190

Navegeer, Gilles, 118
Nenner, Jeremy, 66 (method of saving fuel)
Noblet, Peter, 243
Noir, John le, 197
Noot, Jan van der, 112

Otten, Matthias, 285

Palma, Marcus, 111
Pantin, Simon, 245, 246
Parent, Isabeau, 112
Parent, Noel, 199
Parma, Margaret of, 106
Patents
   conditions of grant, 67–8
   number granted to aliens, 64
   problems involved to attract skilled workers, 68–70
   use to attract skills, 64–5
   types of inventions granted, 65–7

Pegnets, John, 281
Peniable, Hans, 110

Petefryer, Mozes, 190
Plennart, Martin, 113
Philip II, 4, 22, 98
Pilleau, Peze, 246
Pitéot, Jean, 127
Plancius, Peter, 162
Plattell, Peter, 246
Ploiart, Justinne, 113
Pope, Thomas, 238
Portman, John, 289
Poullain, Valérand, 71
Powell, John, brewer, 286
Provincial foreign immigrant communities
   Canterbury, 71, 75, 175
   Colchester, 71, 73
   Maidstone, 71,
   Norwich, 71, 72, 161, 175
   Sandwich, 71, 72
   Southampton, 71, 74, 75
Pynfold, John, 238
Pynnotts, Martin, 78 (weaving)

Quet, John, 196

Rainaud, Philip, 247
Raleigh, Walter, Sir, 158
Raparlier, Bon, 189, 191, 193
Raw silk, 57
Remy, Nicholas, 193
Returns of Aliens, 17
   reliability, 18, 118,
   numbers of immigrants indicated by, 95
   total number ordered, 95
Rhineland, 101
Rodes, Henry, 146
Roste, Arnold, 232
Roussel, Nicaise, 235
Rotinge, Peter, 108
Rutton, Matthew, brewer, 286, 289

St Bartholomew Day Massacre, 96, 154
Sage, Guillam de, 217
Salamby, Daniell, 217
Sande, Martin van de, 243
Sandwich
   stranger community in, 4, 7, 15,109
Santere, Julian, 111
Saulyer, Jarmaine, 109
Scots, 100
Seelar, Gaspar, 67 (salt manufacture)
Silk industry
   demand for silk products, 179–84
   Dutch loom, 45

growth of manufacture, 184
imports, 58, 180, 182–4
increased consumption of silks, 181–3
international diffusion of, 175–9
manufacture of silks in fifteenth century London, 181
number of alien silk workers 1571–1593, 185–6
number of alien silk workers in seventeenth century, 196–8
occupational changes and experimentation, 188–93
origins of alien silk workers 1571–1593, 186–93
origins of alien silk workers in seventeenth century, 198–200
origins of the industry, 175–6
places of settlement of alien silk workers in London, 193–6
plans to establish the industry in England, 56–8
policies of Weavers' Company, 204–7
production of silks per day, 186
relations between native and alien weavers, 204–7
teaching of skills to native weavers, 200–203
types of silk goods made in London, 184–6
Walloon origins, 186–8, 191–2
Weavers' riots 1675, 206
Silver trade
 attitudes of native goldsmiths, 249–52
 Antwerp mannerism, 223
 circular migration, 242–3
 demand for silver, 221
 disadvantages faced by immigrant goldsmiths, 234–6, 242–3
 domination of journeymen, 236–8
 Goldsmiths' Company, 232, 234, 235, 249–52
 Goldsmiths' workshop, 221
 historiographical approaches, 220
 Huguenots, 220, 243–9
 lack of skills by natives, 224
 letter testimonials, 232–3
 nature of craft training of continental artisans, 224–6
 New Year gifts, 222
 number of immigrant goldsmiths in London, 226–31
 origins of continental goldsmiths, 231–2
 skills and experiences of continental goldsmiths, 233–4
 subcontracting, 238–40
 training of English servants, 240–2
 transformation in, 219
 Venetian visitor, 222,
 Wanderjahre travels, 219, 224–5
Skill
 economies of practice, 202, 270
 learning by doing, 7
 mismatch of, 14, 72, 176, 188
 unarticulated, 6
Skilled artisans
 Berty, Francis and salt making, 68
 Hochstetter, Daniel and mining, 68, 69–70
 Hondricke, Gerard and saltpetre, 69
Smith, Thomas, Sir, 76
Smith, Stephen, Fishmonger, 60
Smithe, John, brewer, 281, 286
Sohier, Peter, 190, 191
Southampton, 56, 71
Speare, Haunce van, 217
Spilman, John, 66 (making paper)
Spitalfields, 175
Stoughberken, Peter, 66, 68 (making ovens and furnaces)
Stow, John, 1, 72
Stranger Churches
 roles of, 15, 88, 91, 98, 151, 154, 156, 160, 164, 187, 205
Strype, John, 148
Stubbs, Philip, 180
Sumptuary legislation, 40, 181, 183
Swaersvelt, Guilliam van, 234
Sympson, Thomas, 238

Taberkind, Danyell, 109
Taffin, Jacques, Treasurer of Flushing, 4
Tanqueray, David, 245, 247
Technology transfer
 early modern period, 6,
 economies of practice, 12
 eighteenth & nineteenth centuries, 6
 endogenous technological change, 12
 formal & informal knowledge, 10
 migrants as sources of contacts & information, 11
 receptivity, 10,
 training of native workers, 11, 56, 67, 68, 79, 126–31, 200–203, 240–42
Thames, River, 59, 281
Thiefrize, Pierre, 191
Thurland, Thomas, 66, 68, 69, 70
Torr, Galetta, 190

Tours, 199
Trade, 1, 28–9
Types of migration
  betterment, 39
  chain, 16, 39
  circular, 16
  group, 7
  individual, 7
  mass, 13, 16
  minority, 7
  subsistence, 39

Utenhove, Jan, 72

Vagrancy, 39
Vandebus, Garrett, 232
Vanderaste, James, 238
Vanderbeck, Chosen, 217
Vanhulste, John, brewer, 286, 289, 290
Verberick, Bartholomew, 66, 67, 68 (Spanish leather)

Verselyn, James, 66 (drinking glasses)
Viall, Dennis, 217
Vianen, Christian van, 227
Virginia Company, 80
Voizin, Francois, 190, 191
Volckarts, Dennis, 234

Wages, 44, 45
Walsingham, Francis, 128
Weavers, 55, 56–7, 145, 159–60, 204–7
Webbe, William, Lord Mayor of London, 159
Webling, Nichas, brewer, 164, 282, 291
Webling, Wassell, brewer, 270, 281, 282, 286, 288, 289
Willaume, David, 245, 247
Wittenwrongle, Jacob, 285, 287
Wolley, John, Sir, 158
Wool, 55

Ypres, 55

Printed in Great Britain
by Amazon